375

DAVID FELLMAN
Vilas Professor of Political Science, University of Wisconsin
Advisory Editor to Dodd, Mead & Company

MODERN GOVERNMENT

A Survey of Political Science

Second Edition

MODERN GOVERNMENT

A Survey of Political Science

DELL GILLETTE HITCHNER

WILLIAM HENRY HARBOLD

Department of Political Science
The University of Washington

Second Edition

DODD, MEAD & COMPANY — 1965
New York — Toronto

JA66
H5
1965

Copyright © 1962, 1965 by Dodd, Mead & Company, Inc.
All rights reserved
No part of this book may be reproduced in any form
without permission in writing from the publisher
Library of Congress catalog card number: 65-14913
Third Printing
Printed in the United States of America

To O.K.H.

and to I.F.H.

In Libris Libertas.

OCT 23 1986

EDITOR'S INTRODUCTION TO THE SECOND EDITION

THE INSTANT SUCCESS of the first edition of this textbook is the best sort of objective evidence of its quality. It has been adopted by institutions of higher learning in forty of our fifty states and in the District of Columbia. Obviously, teachers of political science were prepared to take this opportunity to improve their introductory course. Furthermore, this book was written in the great tradition of western political thought, a tradition which began with the writings of Plato and Aristotle. Now, on the basis of concrete experience, the authors have revised the book; some parts of it have been completely rewritten, and all parts have been reviewed and brought up-to-date. Thus, full attention is given to the emerging new nations in the so-called underdeveloped parts of the world.

The purpose of this book is to spell out the political context of modern life. It seeks to describe the relationship of the state to society, and to explore the different textures of political activity and institutions in the perspective of both history and contemporary life. It describes the nature of the democratic state in the modern world, and deftly analyzes the contemporary challenges to democracy. It then inquires into the character of the main elements of modern states, their systems of public law, their politics, their institutions, their patterns of public administration, and their relations with one another.

In short, this book introduces the college student to the systematic study of modern government. It defines the important and persistent problems of political science. Its method is partly historical, partly philosophical, but mainly analytical, and always reasonable. Its coverage is impressively broad.

The authors, furthermore, recognize the importance of evaluating political phenomena in political science. They are not devotees of a narrow "cult of objectivity" which has all too often drained the serious moral quality from so much recent writing in political science. And it is clear that these two political scientists prefer some values to others, and make no secret of their preferences. They prefer democracy to dictatorship, they treasure the concept of human liberty, and they have confidence in the capacity of rational man to achieve self-control within a system of government which assures him an area of autonomous behavior. They believe in intellectual freedom and in the rule of law. They also believe in the possibility of extending the rule of law to relations among nations, and they put a high value on a just international order.

But I believe that above all else, the authors of this book have faith in the reason of man, and most assuredly they have faith in the reasoning and learning capacities of the college students for whom the book is written.

DAVID FELLMAN

PREFACE

THE KIND reception accorded this book has induced us to offer a second edition. In preparing it, we have been guided by the experience of many others as well as our own. While we have been encouraged to continue our original framework and coverage, we were also prompted to clarify and simplify the discussion wherever possible, and especially to sharpen the theoretical analyses and historical presentations.

Changes in this edition are therefore extensive. First, we have shortened and considerably rewritten Chapter 1 to make it a more effective statement of the scope and problems in the study of political science. Chapter 2, "Society and the State," has been entirely rewritten, simplified, and shortened to set out more clearly its themes and definitions. Comparison of the models of populistic and liberal democracy has been heightened by substantial revisions in Chapter 3. We have also rewritten the discussions of contemporary communist strategy and of totalitarianism in Chapter 4 to strengthen the analysis and reflect most recent developments. In Chapter 5, we have simplified and reduced the length of the presentation of constitutional government.

Second, in nearly every chapter we have extended our treatment of the developing states, giving new attention to their institutions and problems, so that their transitional position may be discussed in the appropriate context, and not as one isolated from the mainstream of contemporary politics. Among other additions here, we have included a discussion of "guided democracy."

Third, we have sought to reflect new topics and interpretations in political science; we have enlarged the range of example and illustration from modern politics; and we have considered many recent developments affecting various national governments, the United Nations, the East-West conflict, and world order generally.

Finally, we have taken the opportunity to correct errors, to register some new conclusions in our own thinking, and to bring all chapters and the Study Guide up-to-date with this writing. In short, our revisions run throughout; scarcely a page of the first edition has gone untouched.

The thrust of this book remains that of the first edition: to introduce the reader to the broad and complex subject of contemporary government and politics in a way that will prepare him for the critical responsibilities of citizenship and also serve as a foundation for more advanced and specialized studies in political science. We have sought not only to provide information about the political process but to furnish standards for its evaluation, and to foster an awareness of objectives and methods.

To provide a better understanding of political behavior and institutions, the text begins immediately with the analysis of theoretical concepts. These topics are more demanding of the student than the usual descriptive treatments, but we continue to believe their challenge is stimulating and yields an earlier sophistication in thinking about all political phenomena. Though we do not attempt a history of political thought, we call attention to many landmarks in ideas and writing; for those who wish to give it more emphasis, a short survey of that history is again presented in the discussion of political classics contained in the Study Guide.

Our debts for assistance in this work now go well beyond the possibility of adequate acknowledgment. Reviewers, teachers, and students have provided us useful comment and we continue to welcome it. In the present edition, we wish especially to mention the contributions of Professor David Fellman, University of Wisconsin; Professor Peter Campbell, University of Reading; our colleagues, Professors John S. Reshetar and Peter H. Rohn; and Messrs. John Redekop and Wolfgang Ulbricht. We are also most grateful to our editors at Dodd, Mead for assistance in bringing the manuscript to its final form. Our wives, Kathleen Hitchner and Mary Jo Harbold, gave us much help with the proofs. We must say again, of course, that we did not always accept advice tendered us, and none of those named is responsible for what appears in these pages.

D.G.H.
W.H.H.

Seattle, Washington
January, 1965

CONTENTS

ILLUSTRATIONS

PART ONE: INTRODUCTION

SPINOZA

I have made a ceaseless effort not to ridicule,
not to bewail, nor to scorn human actions,
but to understand them.

MONTAIGNE

We are born to inquire after truth; it belongs to a greater power to possess it. It is not, as Democritus said, hid in the bottom of the deeps, but rather elevated to an infinite height in the divine knowledge.

CHAPTER 1

The NATURE *of* POLITICAL SCIENCE

POLITICS is, along with love and religion, one of the vital subjects on which everyone has ideas and feelings. Few matters elicit such intensity of conviction and controversy. Furthermore, the world around us becomes increasingly political; little we do today escapes its restraints and rewards. Clearly, politics is important and exciting. Yet it is striking how little real communication there is in much political conversation. It sometimes seems as if people are not talking of the same thing. How, then, do we best begin a sensible discussion of our subject?

"If you wish to converse with me," said Voltaire, "define your terms!" This admonition of two centuries ago was most characteristic of the "age of enlightenment" in which he lived—a period so called because of its faith that all things could be made comprehensible through adherence to clear, consistent, and precise terminology. While our problem is hardly that simple—particularly in politics, which embraces not only the complex but even the paradoxical—it is evident that we cannot converse, or learn and teach, unless we share common meanings for the terms we use, and a common understanding of the nature and scope of the subject we are considering. Progress in this, as in any intellectual undertaking, must begin with agreement on what we are talking about and how it can be approached to attain an adequate understanding.

I. *The* STUDY *of* POLITICAL SCIENCE

What Is Politics? The subject to which this book is to serve as an introduction has traditionally been called "political science," in other words, "the systematic study of politics." Obviously, then, the meaning of the word "politics" is crucial. At first glance, "politics" is apparently a simple term. Most of us encounter it nearly every day, applied in common parlance to the affairs of political parties and politicians, of party conventions and electioneering, and of voting and maneuvering for partisan advantage. Certainly these are all familiar political activities, and they are a part of politics.

To political scientists, however, this only scratches the surface. While agreeing that these activities are political, they also agree that we must probe more deeply and extend our view to comprehend the whole subject. Yet when they try to do this, they begin to disagree. The discipline of political science, therefore, is not particularly unified, either in its scope or terms of analysis, despite its apparent simplicity. We should not be surprised or confused to find political scientists in violent and seemingly irreconcilable conflict; without being fully aware of it, they may not be talking about quite the same thing, or from the same perspective, or to the same purpose.

How, one may well ask, could this situation persist? It is not one that political scientists like, of course, nor one they have not sought to remedy. Many of the greatest thinkers of our culture have tried mightily to define politics, but the efforts of some twenty centuries have not won any agreement. We can only say that amid the host of attempts, we do find that three major perspectives from which to view politics stand out, with each one seeming to possess, as one might expect, its own grain of truth.

The first of these, not surprisingly, comes from the ancient Greeks. Our word "politics" was derived from the Greek name for their city-community, the *polis*. To the Greeks, political life was the distinctive way of life of the city-community, which they saw in sharp contrast with the less adequate, even less human, way of life in the more limited confines of family or tribe. They also distinguished it from the great orders of

Persia and Egypt, for these did not permit the active citizenship the Greeks deemed essential. The Greek view was powerfully expressed by Aristotle, who summed up this civilization even as it was being destroyed by Macedonia and Rome. Politics was to him all that concerned the "good life" in a well-organized, stable, and self-sufficient community. Political science had to study, therefore, the nature of the good life as it was revealed in the cities of Greek experience, and through analysis and criticism discern the laws and types of political order that would most effectively promote it. Aristotle claimed that the statesman exercised "the master art," and went so far as to describe the latter's proper knowledge as "the most sovereign of the sciences."

Aristotle's highly ethical conception of political science, devoted to the whole range of community affairs, has had great influence through succeeding centuries. Yet no single and integrated science of society and social interrelations has resulted from the classical Greek beginning. The Aristotelian approach was based upon the city, or comparatively small community, as the self-sufficient and ultimate organization and expression of human life. It assumed that the individual would find and realize himself most fully by citizenship therein. As these conditions no longer exist either as fact or ideal, Aristotle's idea of politics is much too broad for political science.

A second point of view has been offered in more recent times by many writers seeking a more limited perspective that would be practical and realistic. They have defined political science as the study of "the state." Those institutions and activities are political, therefore, which are related to "the state." Unfortunately it has proved most difficult to identify this entity. The term has been applied to so many different political, legal, and metaphysical concepts and phenomena in time and space that no one definition among hundreds offered satisfactorily covers it and can obtain general acceptance. Though political scientists frequently use the term in their discussions, it has not proved to be one sufficiently specific and fundamental to provide an adequate and agreed basis for a scientific discipline. Although any political community may for convenience be called a state—often requiring further qualification, as in city-state, nation-state, or modern-state—the name contributes little to our understanding of politics. For this, we need to look behind the state to see why it is a political phenomenon.

A third approach, still more modern, has its roots in the reflections of the early sixteenth-century Florentine diplomat, Machiavelli, and insists that politics is "power." To writers of this persuasion, the study of politics is the study of power "relationships" between men—the forms these take and the institutions they tend to create. Those rigorously taking this position eliminate from political science any moral content: politics, they say, is domination, and we must simply be observers and analyzers of the fact. Power, they insist, can equally serve good and evil; the political facts are not dependent on which is served, though the ethical ones may be.

Considerable force must be admitted to this claim, especially if "power" is broadly enough defined. Conceivably all human behavior is related in some way to the influencing of someone else. But it is precisely for this reason that the attempt to define politics as the study of "power" does not entirely succeed. The phenomenon of power is discernible throughout the entire area of social activities. Since the network of power relations in a community is, by and large, coextensive with the community itself, we have great difficulty in distinguishing political from nonpolitical relationships. Any attempt to equate politics with the exercise of coercive force is not satisfactory, either, because a relationship between them does not always exist. Most governments obtain compliance with many of their policies without resort to force; on the other hand, coercion may actually be present in contexts which we would never think of as being political. Few people obey their government solely, or even largely, out of fear of the policeman, but rather from interest, a sense of right, or loyalty; at the same time, a mob of gangsters holding a city in thrall is not an illustration of political action. Thus, a definition which offends our common sense is not likely to be correct, and we are probably justified in holding that the power concept does not adequately meet our needs.

What then? Obviously, such a very complex and age-old problem is not to be resolved simply—and, indeed, it is not even necessary that we resolve it here. Instead, let us adopt a practical expedient, which will serve to get our study under way. All of us, in our normal experiences, have come into direct or indirect contact with such people as tax collectors, license clerks, policemen, judges, and legislators. We are aware that the existence of these "offices" has a certain, quite concrete impact upon our lives at many points. We are also aware that these offices do not exist in isolation, but are interrelated within a structure of authority and influence we call "government." These officials do not ordinarily act in an entirely unpredictable way; their behavior, as officials, is to some extent controlled by a system of rules we call "law," relating that behavior to the larger structure of the community. It is this rather ordinary experience that political scientists attempt to understand in all its dimensions. However sophisticated political analysis may become, this commonsense perspective is always its base and starting point.

To summarize, government may be said to be the regulation of the activities of the people in a community by an organized body of officials, in accordance with the legal rules of that community. Government is not, however, a static entity or impersonal force. It is a process, an organized activity, through which people who are trying to meet the problems that inevitably arise in social life act through institutions, such as systems of law, legislative assemblies, or executive agencies, whose functions are closely related to those problems. This "process of government" always manifests broad patterns of order, but it is very complex because political behavior springs from diverse forms of thinking and feeling, both creative and conservative. However strange it may seem, we can say that *politics is art, science, and philosophy in the governmental process*—though, as the analysis develops, further refinements in this definition will be necessary. Understanding of politics will be advanced, therefore, if we consider it in each of these dimensions.

Politics as Art. The art of government among men, of ruling and being ruled, must surely be as old as society itself. If art is skill depending upon gift and practice, rather than knowledge of general principles, then one of the greatest accumulations of human artistry lies in the governmental process. Political skill certainly was at first, and to a large extent remains, an eminently practical art—"the art of the possible." Thus, some today still consider politics a form of human activity incapable of objective determination. Politics in this sense stresses the value of knowledge gained from common sense and insight, the importance of creative imagination and vision, and of achieving the chosen end successfully; hence, politics demands practical wisdom.

The exponents of politics as an art insist that its lessons may not be grasped by logic alone, but require the application of native talent and intuitive reasoning, and that such lessons most usefully impart, not so much information, as understanding and appreciation. It is true that the successful statesman or politician of any age, the skilled craftsman of politics, is more often than not self-taught in his art; he may even be spoken of as a "born politician"; his political lore has little to do with books, but is acquired as experience. Hence, we have the very extensive area of human behavior and relationships we call "practical politics" and "politicking."

To some degree, therefore, a share of the political scientist's attention must be devoted to the art of governing as such, not only because this aspect of the subject does not—or will not yet—lend itself to scientific inquiry, but because it seems capable of revelation by a kind of impressionistic treatment akin to artistic perception. The political scientist is obliged, much as is the art or literary critic endeavoring to appreciate a painting or a novel, to concern himself with matters of taste, balance, harmony, and inspiration. Science requires talent, it has been said, but art requires genius; some of the greatest contributions to the elucidation of the essence of politics have truly been made by stroke of genius. In the writings of statesmen, diplomats, administrators, and party bosses, for example, we may find useful reflections of the art of government, which are excellent, if unsystematized, sources of knowledge.

This situation may be more comprehensible if we recall that political science, as it views the works of mankind, stands between the humanistic studies and the physical sciences; it never entirely loses touch with the element of human sympathy provided by the former, even when it moves toward emphasis on the unemotional objectivity of the latter. Some of political science's most useful conclusions have been provided by those with the shrewdest perception of human nature. Thus, the study of politics is not likely ever to become solely a process of collecting facts about government; at its most rewarding, it must always have regard for and be alert to wisdom and imagination.

Politics as Science. The ideal has long existed that man could be governed in accordance with scientific knowledge, that is, by means superior to chance and guesswork, and without reliance upon intuition and personal skills, which are bound to be largely incommunicable. But from the time of its first expression in the teachings of Socrates, the possibility of realizing this ideal has been seriously questioned. Scientific knowledge is generally defined as organized and verifiable knowledge, based upon observation and experience. Within the terms of this definition, the knowledge of the process of government which has been collected since man began to organize his information about human association over two thousand years ago is clearly a science. Further, because the study of the political affairs of man treats an important aspect of social relationships, political science takes its place among the social sciences.

Yet these general definitions do not entirely clarify the position of the science of politics within the full array of the modern sciences, and may well be misleading if understood as suggesting that nothing more than differences in subject matter distinguish the scientific disciplines from one another. There are those, indeed, who cannot accept any divergence from the methods and results of the physical and mathematical sciences, and who assert that the term "science" should not be applied to the study of politics at all. We do not accept this conclusion, however, and feel that to view politics as a science is not entirely unjustified. What, therefore, do we mean in our use of the term "science of politics"?

We mean that scientifically founded knowledge is, and can be made, available to those participating in the process of government, so that politics may be more rational and its results more dependable. This implies, of course, that a "scientific method" of acquiring knowledge is applicable to political affairs—that is to say, that such a method is not restricted in its use to any one class of phenomena. The basic principle of scientific method is that inquiry must be guided by the subject matter as completely as possible, and not by the hopes, fears, and prejudices of the scientist, or by other extraneous factors. This is what is meant when it is said that scientific inquiry is "objective." The essential elements of the scientific method include, then, the definition of the problem to be solved; the acquisition of relevant data; the construction of hypotheses, or tentative theories, to explain the data in terms of the problem; and, finally, the verification, or attempted verification, of the hypotheses. This last procedure is the most notable characteristic of science: the basing of beliefs on the best available evidence.

We are further asserting that, through the application of such processes as description, comparison, and classification to political phenomena, we may obtain valid and useful conclusions about their nature and significance. That much has already been done along this line is evidenced by the intelligent conclusions of a vast array of existing political literature, based upon careful observation and historical scholarship. Of course, such results will probably lack the exactitude of those achieved by the physical sciences. We certainly do not wish to suggest that political science can possibly be a science that can confidently predict and control. The phenomena of politics hardly lend themselves completely, and perhaps not even significantly, to the establishment of quantitative terms of measurement, or the pure isolation of factors which appear unvarying and universal in their relationships. This is a situation, however, encountered in some degree by any science dealing with people rather than things—by medicine and psychology, as well as economics and politics.

Thus the conduct of government is not, and possibly never can be, based upon an exact science producing mathematically precise results. As a developing science, the study of politics is still concerned with improving its methods of acquiring and evaluating data, and has not yet been able to reach nearly enough of the kinds of generalizations and statements of probability it seeks. The obstacles to, as well as the possibilities for, its growth will be discussed at some length when we turn our attention to methods of study. For the moment we shall only note that the foundations of a science of politics are yet being laid. This conclusion may disappoint some students; others, however, may well be stimulated to realize that great opportunities still remain to develop the frontiers of political science.

Politics as Philosophy. When Plato observed that men would never be well governed until "philosophers are kings, or the kings and princes of this world have the spirit and power of philosophy," he stated as clearly as has any man since that politics cannot be understood apart from its philosophical foundations. Men have differed greatly, from his day to the present, on the exact nature of these foundations, but it cannot be rationally claimed that government either can or should exist independently of some philosophical commitment. If we are not to be content with an entirely unreflective attitude toward politics, therefore, we need to ask further: why men must be governed, how, and to what purpose? No amount of empirical study, description, and classification alone will give us the answers to these questions. Philosophical speculation must consider such questions as these, which get at the very roots of political life. Political philosophy, then, furnishes us with insight through which we can evaluate intelligently the institutions and policies of the concrete political world.

This is no esoteric matter, of little relevance to mundane affairs, but rather of immense practical importance. While we may *live* without an understanding of the "whither" and the "why," we shall not likely *live well.* Only those who have answers to these questions can avoid drifting aimlessly with the changing winds; only those whose answers are sound can escape joining Don Quixote in tilting with windmills. Democracy demands a great deal from its citizens in this respect; far more than a technical knowledge of the institutions of government do they need an understanding of the objectives being sought through them. Lacking this, they will be unable to fulfill their proper role, which is the intelligent criticism of the activity of their leaders and the functioning of political institutions.

This is not to say, of course, that the citizen can be provided by political philosophers or anyone else with a complete philosophy, neatly indexed for ready reference. Philosophy is really systematic thinking about basic matters, and its conclusions are much too complex to be handled like a table of weights and measures. Philosophers are "lovers of wisdom," and not necessarily possessors of it. To say, then, that governmental power in a healthy society must be founded in philosophy means that critical thought, seeking constantly to interrelate the various aspects of human experience and to discover the possibilities of harmony, must play a large role in political life. Because the essence of politics is the continual clarification of objectives, as well as the discovery of means for their realization, it follows that in the absence of philosophical thought politics degenerates rapidly into purposeless motions and transactions. In short, politics disappears as an activity, and the life of society becomes stagnant.

If we, as political observers, rulers, or citizens, are to contribute anything of value to government, based not upon accident but upon intelligence, it will be because we have succeeded in bringing our social life into perspective, and have achieved an understanding of the ends being sought through political action. Then and only then can we see in their full significance the institutions, procedures, and policies or courses of action that are found in the area of government. This, quite simply, is the meaning of "politics as philosophy," and its importance as well as its complexity should be obvious.

Politics in Perspective. We have discussed briefly the roles of art, science, and philosophy in the governing of men. We have thus attempted to suggest, also, that there is really room for each, and that we need not assume that the task is exclusively within the province of only one of these modes of thought and expression. Indeed, their functions should be viewed as complementary, we think, for none of them is so distinct from the others as, for the sake of analysis, our discussion might seem to indicate.

To philosophy, clearly, goes the job of suggesting the goals we seek through politics, and distinguishing, among the many courses of action which in the abstract are possible, those which we *ought* to follow. Yet even here the choice of means cannot be left to free invention; we do not discover the best means of attaining ends simply by contemplation or excogitation. Without reference to the controlled knowledge of the conditions of existence, which only science can render, philosophy is always in danger of losing contact with the possible and the real, and thus becoming a hindrance rather than a help to effective living. Many philosophers, from Aristotle to Dewey, Whitehead, and Russell, have been aware of this, and have shown a great and constant interest in the development of science.

The ideal, then, would seem to be a mutual relationship between these two: for philosophy to give science its direction, and science to prevent philosophy from becoming unrealistic, with the result being a harmonious and effective political life. But this ideal is to some extent a chimera. Neither the philosophy nor the science of politics has attained a level of development which yet enables either to perform its role fully; possibly they never will. Furthermore, in the past at least, each has been jealous of the other, tending to exaggerate its own role, so that they have more often been enemies than partners. There remains, therefore, always scope and need for the art of the politician to bring together science and philosophy, and, with his flair for the possible and the appropriate, to fill in the gaps that exist in our more systematic knowledge.

II. *The* DIMENSIONS *of* POLITICAL SCIENCE

At this point, let us examine the four major fields into which the study of political science is divided, particularly as it is taught and administered in American colleges. A description of these will not only indicate the very broad dimensions of political science, but will suggest how the outer bounds of this discipline touch many of those of the other social sciences. Consequently, we shall also want to see how political science is related to its allied disciplines.

THE FIELDS OF POLITICAL SCIENCE

The academic fields of political science are distinguished both by the focus of their attention, and by the varieties of approaches and materials they may employ. One need not be too concerned about fixing precise boundary lines and labels to set the fields apart, however, for necessarily they overlap. Such classifications are not intended to describe closed compartments, but are conveniences, rather, to provide rough groupings into which the data of political science may be gathered, to point out areas of specialization in instruction and research, and to permit some division of labor for scholars and students. We shall indicate how the principal fields are related to the commonly offered courses of study in political science, and also suggest some of the more important topics of research currently being followed to enlarge them.

American Government and Politics. For Americans, reasons for concern with their own institutions and processes are fairly obvious. These are entitled to, and do receive, considerable attention from abroad as well, given the current influence of the United States in the world, the importance of its contribution to the development and defense of representative and democratic government, and the extensive literature that has been produced on the subject.

This field deals with American affairs from the perspectives of public law, which is concerned with the relations of individuals and their government according to fixed rules; of political parties and public opinion, which treats the ways in which the contest for political power is conducted; and, of public administration, which centers on the application and enforcement of public policy.

Courses are commonly offered in American national, state, and local government; general courses on public, constitutional, and administrative law; courses dealing with American political parties, interest groups, political behavior and leadership, public opinion and propaganda; and, the principles of public administration as well as special phases of it, such as personnel administration, municipal government, public planning, and administrative management.

Research in American government and politics gives attention to such subjects as civil rights, the judicial control of administrative action, the philosophies of eminent jurists; voting behavior, the measurement of public opinion, the role of interest groups in the political process; and, to such problems as metropolitan government, civil-military relations, and governmental structure and intergovernmental relations.

Comparative Government. The field of comparative government is directed toward the study of the political experience, institutions, behavior, and processes in the major systems of modern government. The approach of this field is very broadly based, emphasizing the universal character of government, and seeking to determine what phenomena among political systems are variable and invariable, and which are unique or common. Its objective is not only to delineate the forms and patterns of the various political systems as they operate within their national settings, and to relate or distinguish them by comparative treatment, but to draw from them generalizations about the governmental process in practice. Thus, the field is a useful one in which to integrate many of the otherwise isolated findings of political science based upon the analysis of single national systems.

Although none of the diverse governmental systems appearing over the world has been entirely ignored by political scientists, they have tended to concentrate on those systems with the largest world influence, those representative of fundamental types, or those of unusual characteristics. Courses in this field are concerned with the political systems of western Europe, Great Britain and the Commonwealth, the Far East, and Latin America. In recent years, attention has also been extended to the Soviet Union and other communist countries, and the developing political systems in the newly emergent states of Africa, the Middle East, and Asia.

Some systems may be of special comparative interest because of their descent from common origins, as the Commonwealth states; as types of structurally similar systems, such as the parliamentary governments of western Europe; upon the basis of their geographical and cultural association, as with the Latin-American states; or because they demonstrate the problems that arise in new states when a colonial regime is liquidated and self-government replaces it. But comparative government courses range from intensive treatment of a single foreign government and its context to the analysis and comparison of universal institutions and processes.

Among the subjects which have received recent attention in comparative government research are the process of constitution-making, the sources and character of political leadership and elites, case studies of party systems and elections, problems of political change, variations in national ideologies, and experiments with western institutions by non-western states.

International Relations. The field of international relations treats the affairs of the world political community. The range of political phenomena in world affairs is so great that this field is further subdivided into three major areas: international law, dealing with the legal rules and practices of international relations; international politics, the study of the contest for power and influence between the states of the world; and international organization, the examination of the institutional structure and agencies of the world community. Here the political scientist seeks to analyze the character of state interrelationships, and evaluate the forces of conflict and co-operation determining them.

Courses offered in international relations include treatments of international law, politics, and organization; the practice of diplomacy; the foreign policies of states, separately or severally considered; and treatments of the international affairs of the world's principal regions. Others may deal with more specialized problems, such as war, imperialism, nationalism, colonialism, or the United Nations.

Developments in this field call for research proceeding along a number of lines. In international law, subjects of contemporary interest are the development of rules by international organizations, the status of such organizations and their officials, the definition of aggression, rules of international criminal law, jurisdiction over territorial waters and airspace, and theories of obligation affecting international law. Current matters of interest in international politics include the development of devices for handling tension situations, techniques in the conduct of propaganda and psychological warfare, diplomatic strategies, security systems and conflict resolution, the analysis of forces influencing foreign policies, and possible applications of the balance-of-power principle. Research in international organization is devoting attention to various aspects of international administration, its institutions and personnel; means of effecting peaceful change; sanctions and international enforcement actions; the development and character of supranational organization of states; the protection of individual rights by international action; and the work of the United Nations.

Political Theory. Finally, political theory is devoted to the philosophical and speculative consideration of politics. Its task is integrative; that is, through theoretical consideration of the area of politics as a whole and its relationship to the rest of social life, it seeks to give meaning and direction to more particular subjects of political investigation. For this reason it is the broadest of the political science fields, and provides the core of its discipline.

Within this field, political scientists undertake two tasks essential to the study of politics. The first is the process of definition, generalization, and classification necessary to establish the basic terms and concepts with which and about which we do much of our political thinking. The process of refining the signification of terms is manifestly a continuing one for the theorist. Secondly, we undertake to discover the underlying nature, functions, and purposes of the political community. Here are gathered the body of ideas, doctrines, and ideologies that provide the frame for the whole pattern of politics. It is through the theoretical approach that we come to grips with some of the most fundamental questions of political value: the source and basis of political authority; the scope of political activity; the determination of the individual's rights and duties; the nature of the obligation of obedience; the meaning of law; and the character of the ideal state, for example.

Courses of instruction in the field include those devoted to methods of research and the development of political knowledge; those devoted to analytical theory, or the analysis of principles, concepts, and institutions; and those concerned with political thought. The latter may survey the development of political thought either in terms of its historical evolution, or its characteristics in certain areas or periods. Still others may examine particular political theorists or types of political thought, like socialist or liberal.

Research in this field inevitably moves in many different directions. It seeks to elucidate, for example, the values and principles of political life; to sharpen the tools of political research and thinking; to study the history of political ideas and clarify the origins of those ideas and their relation to one another and to nonpolitical phenomena; to interpret the writings of political philosophers in changing circumstances; and, to bring out what conditions are necessary if particular ends—such as representative government or world peace—are to be realized. Obviously, all aspects of politics may be subjected to theoretical analysis, and theory should be a major concern of every political scientist, not only those calling themselves "theorists."

POLITICAL SCIENCE AND THE SOCIAL SCIENCES

The social sciences are devoted to the study of man in society—those disciplines dedicated to the principle that "the proper study of mankind is man." The affairs of civilized man are complex and many-sided, and invite contemplation from numerous points of view. Man has a physical heredity bequeathed by previous generations; his birth and every day of his life give him further human relationships; he becomes a member of many kinds of groups; with other men he draws on those physical resources of the earth available to him and gains a livelihood; he thinks and feels, and through communication with other men acquires knowledge and beliefs; he regulates his affairs and promotes his interests by action within political communities. His search for the good life, for comfort, pleasure, position, wealth, power, serenity, or whatever is his idea of it, always takes place in company with other men.

The meaning of all these facets of human society, viewed simultaneously, can be bewildering—even to human beings consciously engaged in them. To get a clearer and more detailed view of how and why humankind behave both similarly and variously in these activities, scholars attempt to isolate certain kinds of behavior. This means that they have relinquished the construction of a single science within which to explain the whole of social interaction for a number of such sciences. This has both good and bad results. It permits a higher degree of expertness and efficiency within each of several formally distinguished categories of learning, and better assures that no phase of social action will be overlooked. And given the vastness of the information man has or seeks to have collected about himself, and the limited possibility of finding single minds that can comprehend all of it, some kind of academic division of labor in this regard becomes a practical necessity.

However, the formal creation of several social sciences means that the divisions between them may be extremely arbitrary. Specialization can be pressed to such a degree that it succeeds in producing only the proverbial "everything about nothing." It has also sometimes produced the sorting out of human activity into such narrow categories that one is induced to presuppose an imaginary or hypothetical man—a social, historical, economic, or political man—who acts only with reference to one of these considerations. Needless to say, since there are no such men, this kind of thinking about them can be of only limited value. It is well to remember, too, that society itself is not broken into separate compartments resembling the academic disciplines that scholars organize. Ultimately, all social scientists must be concerned with the same problems. They may approach them from different directions, attempt to explain or solve them by different methods, and even place different degrees of emphasis on their importance; however, the differences lie in the viewers and not in what is viewed. Thus, although political science constitutes a large and independent area of study by itself, it is by no means completely detached in form, method, or interest from the other social sciences.

Political Science and History. The close relationship of history and political science is immediately apparent. The term "history" in its broadest sense denotes a systematic account of the past. All things may have a history, of course, and in this sense certainly not all of the historian's accounts are of interest to the political scientist. But the historian has always been especially concerned with the story of what man has done and, in developing this, in his political activities and experience. The result is that political science draws upon history for some of its data, as well as for the accompanying depth of perspective which history provides for the consideration of contemporary affairs. Historians and political scientists often deal with much the same incidents. The historian, however, is concerned with relating and explaining his data in terms of their chronological relationship; his work is valued for the expertise he applies in establishing the authenticity and historical relevance of data, although many historians seek broader meaning as well. The political scientist is enabled to extract useful generalizations, therefore, from the tremendous accumulation of historical lore.

Political Science and Economics. Economics and political science were once studied together in a discipline known as "political economy," on the assumption that the principal province of government was the supervision of financial and commercial affairs and the collection of public revenue. Though today we have separated the two studies, it should be clear that, if anything, the factors of economic and political life are ever more closely interrelated. Economics may be defined as the science of the production, distribution, and consumption of wealth—or, in somewhat more human terms, the study of man's efforts to satisfy his material wants. Such efforts are inevitably undertaken within the context, and subject to the rules, of a politically organized community; and it is a commonplace that economic ends and conditions always have political consequences. Thus, no hard-and-fast line can be drawn between political and economic activities; when one examines the question of the appropriate role for government in economic life—one of the most contentious of current problems—he finds that politics and economics tend to become confused. This has led to some attempts to explain all political life in terms of economic causation, but this is undoubtedly going too far. Nevertheless, the political scientist is always mindful of those findings of the economist which figure importantly in the determination and evaluation of public policy.

Political Science and Sociology. Another important branch of social science is sociology. Although this discipline has sometimes been defined so as to include all aspects of the study of society, like politics or economics it has become definitely specialized. Sociology is generally concerned with man as a product of group life. It examines social behavior and human interaction, customs and cultures, and the structures, functions, and values of social orders and groups. Both sociology and political science undertake a very comprehensive examination of social organization, and the result allows an interchange of findings produced by their varying methods and viewpoints.

Political Science and Geography. Geographers define their discipline as the study of human activities in their spatial context, involving patterns and relationships over the surface of the earth. Although geographers earlier emphasized the influence of physical environment on human activity, they have come to recognize how predominant is the role of modern man in shaping his world. Some of their attention is also directed to the territorial aspect of the state, its institutional framework, and its spatial relations. The field of political geography is therefore linked to that of political science; it is of particular interest to students of international relations, as well as of government generally.

Political Science and Other Studies. Political scientists have been placing increased emphasis on the usefulness of psychology in explaining the phenomena of political behavior. The examination of such topics as political leadership, public opinion, or international frictions requires reference to many matters where the insight of the psychologist can be useful. The study of political science may also parallel or draw upon the studies of anthropology, jurisprudence, philosophy, and ethics, at various points. In sum, the political scientist cannot be indifferent to the work of scholars in any discipline that is concerned with the character of human relations. The student's goal in relating the contributions of all these disciplines, or as many as he has opportunity to encounter, should always be to extend his interests and thereby achieve breadth as well as depth of understanding. Knowledge is never to be considered as the sole monopoly of any group of scholars nor of any single area of study.

III. *The* METHODS *of* POLITICAL SCIENCE

It is axiomatic that the type and value of the conclusions we reach in any study are dependent upon the methods of inquiry we use, and upon any limitations in method that the subject matter imposes. Some of the more vigorous disagreements among political scientists concern appropriate methods, since these often reflect different opinions about the nature of politics and about the knowledge political science should produce. Examination of some of the problems that arise in the investigation of political phenomena will therefore further clarify the nature and possibilities of political science.

HOW SCIENTIFIC CAN THE STUDY OF POLITICS BE?

We are inclined these days to be very much impressed by the term "science," and to feel strongly that if we could only be "scientific" about things—all things—we would be much better off. There is reason for this attitude, of course. It is obvious that we owe much to the accomplishments of those who have conducted the scientific investigations of natural phenomena. We have attained, as a result of their perseverance and intelligence, a degree of control over nature undreamed of a few generations ago. The great successes of the natural sciences have led many to believe that an extension of their methods into the area of human relations, wherein lie such a major proportion of the world's troubles, should be accompanied by equally beneficial results. It is most important, therefore, for us to know just how "scientific" we can be about politics.

Etymologically, the term "scientific" simply refers to what is *known,* as opposed to what is *believed,* and should be applicable in any discipline in which knowledge and not merely opinion is possible. As the term is most often used today, however, the reference is more specifically to knowledge based on controlled observations, or experiments, capable of repeated verifications, and precisely and systematically arrayed, ideally in mathematical formulations. The question, then, is whether political life lends itself to this sort of knowledge—whether an understanding of politics can be expressed in such scientific propositions, and whether crucially important political information is accessible to the observations and experiments of the scientist.

Human societies seem to be organized patterns of relationships, about which we should be able to acquire knowledge comparable to that which we have of the solar system or the metabolism of an animal body. And, indeed, historians and social scientists have over the ages arrived at a good deal of such knowledge, some of it as systematic and verified as any possessed by physicists or biologists. A good deal of it, however, is not of this character, lacking satisfactory systematization; and instead of being repeatedly verifiable appears extremely relative to changing and unpredictable circumstances. Or else it exists in the form of broad and not very helpful generalities, for example, that some sort of government exists everywhere. But what of the future—is a social and political science possible which would of itself yield full and precise understanding of human life? And what might its value be? These are very controversial questions among political scientists today, and brief consideration of them is thus necessary in an introduction to the discipline.

OBSTACLES TO A COMPLETE SCIENCE OF POLITICS

The Complexity of Politics. Aristotle long ago warned us not to expect greater precision in any science than its subject matter would admit. We will be well advised to take his wisdom to heart, and reflect upon what it is that political science studies—people in their relationship to government, or the political process. To what extent can this relationship be compared—to choose a simple illustration—with the reaction of iron filings to a magnet—a relationship which will be identical for each iron particle over and over again? The answer is immediately obvious: human reactions to government vary almost infinitely. It is clear that the human situation is enormously more complex, and contains elements of far more fundamental contingency than the physical one. To be sure, this circumstance does not make an exact social science impossible, but it makes it practically unlikely. It may no doubt be said that even physics has come to accept probability rather than certainty as its measure in recent years. But the modest level of probability to which social science can attain in its description of significant events is likely to be of limited utility.

Limitations are also imposed on the formulation of valid conclusions because the political scientist's data are often fragmentary. Whether he has much or little, he is always aware that there are aspects of the given situation with which he deals that may not and, indeed, cannot be revealed to him. It is quite possible, for instance, to make a detailed and illuminating study of the whole process whereby an idea about public policy comes to be enacted into law. But when such a study has been completed—and by the most exacting means—the political scientist knows that his analysis has some gaps. He cannot have accounted for all of the hundreds or thousands of persons who have exerted some influence on the legislative process; he cannot know of all of the decisions made in closed committee sessions or private conferences, in and out of government, which leave no records; he cannot explain precisely how the political climate in the United States, or even in Washington, D.C., affected the legislators at this particular time; and he cannot peer into the mind of even one of the men concerned with the legislation to fathom his deepest, perhaps even unconscious, motives. From the complexity and incompleteness of his evidence, the political scientist knows there is always a possibility that the key factor in a situation is not being taken into account at all.

The Difficulty of Experiment. Still other factors interfere with the development of political science. It is virtually impossible, for example, to establish anything resembling satisfactory experimental conditions. Social scientists are seldom permitted to manipulate people or events for their own purposes; and in the absence of such opportunities the chance to learn directly what causes have produced what consequences and to verify conclusions concerning them is greatly reduced. One finds on no college campus a political science laboratory wherein, under controlled conditions, the phenomena of politics may be reproduced for purposes of scientific inquiry. The political scientist, therefore, is largely restricted to the materials presented to him in the flow of events; he may dip into them with his questions, but, like the historian, the events he tries to explain are given to him, he does not create them.

It is sometimes suggested that in the multiplicity of political units which exist—states, counties, and cities—the political scientist has at least a field in which to see the results of experimentation. Thus, the fifty states of the American union are said to be that many "political laboratories"; one such state may "experiment" with a unicameral legislature, another with a unique scheme of primary elections, and a third with a new law to control political subversion. Or, two or more states may at the same time each establish a different highway patrol system, and thus offer an opportunity to see which is the most effective. Political scientists may well derive some valuable conclusions from this kind of "experimentation," but it lacks effective controls to ensure valid generalizations. For many different reasons a system effective in Texas will not work in New York; the circumstances which permit a device to be efficient in Illinois may make it extravagant in Idaho. Any two human situations may seem similar, but are never identical; each is always submerged in its own complex of conditioning factors, which vary endlessly. Under such conditions, a political scientist is much like a chemist who makes a variety of experiments without washing his test tubes—he may get all sorts of interesting results and reactions, but will be rather uncertain what elements produced them.

The Inadequacy of Quantitative Measurements. Of equal importance with experimentation in the natural sciences—and thus in any other science emulating them—is the subjection of data to quantitative measurement. The ability to count and measure, to express relationships and meanings with mathematical precision, is an essential concomitant of any exact science. The opportunity to use this kind of procedure is not entirely denied to the social scientist, of course. The economist, especially, derives great advantage from the situation of his discipline, which permits him, theoretically, to reduce a number of variables to economic values, and then to compare them in quantitative terms. The political scientist does not lack things to count—political units, laws, amendments, armies, courts, budget appropriations, opinions, party memberships, voters and votes, for example—but these sums and the relationships among them must usually be placed in a broader context to make them meaningful or useful, and that context is generally sufficiently unique to make quantitative treatment impossible.

It would be very misleading, for instance, to assume that one session of Congress which passed only ten laws was a "do-nothing" Congress because another session had adopted a thousand. Laws are not simply inscribed pieces of parchment, each of the same value, effect, or purpose. To mention two hypothetical extremes, the first session might have effected a thoroughgoing social revolution in the United States by a handful of drastic taxation and appropriation measures; the second might have done no more than make minor alterations in a thousand existing federal statutes. Or again, a public opinion poll may report that 53 per cent of the people favor a reduction in taxes; 40 per cent do not; and 7 per cent have no opinion. Even when gathered by the most exacting sampling techniques, these percentages do not show which opinions were held by informed persons, which were held by those most likely to be politically influential, or which were held most intensely and likely to produce political action. Thus, they really indicate neither what our public policy ought to be, nor what it is likely to become.

The Problem of Objectivity. More important, however, among the difficulties with which the social scientist is confronted, particularly in political affairs, is that he and his judgments are a part of the situation he is trying to describe and understand. Inevitably, his work is a product of his own heredity and environment; of his own temperament and emotions; and of his own values, preferences, and convictions. Especially when he is least conscious of them do these exercise their influence. And yet it is precisely of such "stuff" as these that political life is made. This cannot be said, for example, about astronomy, aerodynamics, or nuclear fission, and we are content, therefore, to have problems in those fields described "from the outside," so to speak. The physicist, after all, neither is nor need be personally involved with the atomic particles that his data and theories treat. Political affairs, however, must be discussed "from the inside," that is, by one sensitive to the background, hopes, and fears of the community involved. Indeed, one can wonder what a completely detached and objective view of political affairs might be, and we may doubt that one has ever been held.

A political scientist, because of his training and experience as an observer of, rather than as a participant in, the political arena may be more objective in his attitudes toward political phenomena than active politicians and their partisans. But he still faces a dilemma. The more he seeks detachment the less he is able to perceive relevant data. On the other hand, if he is too responsive to the values involved he becomes simply another political activist. Clearly, the biases of the political scientist are essential to his political analysis, but the line between too much and too little commitment is difficult to draw. Nonetheless, as no political scientist ever gets entirely free of his biases his conclusions will appear scientific and objective only to those who share these prejudices and tend to view political events as he does. Since the world contains many greatly differing political systems, and even within well-established states much basic controversy continues, objective analysis generally recognized as such remains rather limited.

There is also an obverse to this coin. Heisenberg's "uncertainty principle" has informed us that even in physics the event being observed is sometimes affected by the mere fact of observation, so that definite limits exist to what can be learned about the events themselves. If this is true for electrons, it is certainly also true for human beings, whose behavior is likely to be changed by the most subtle observation, and especially by any announced conclusions or predictions. Rather than being simply means of gaining objective knowledge, then, investigations in human affairs are, at least potentially, creative acts, in small or large ways shaping the future of the community. If this be the case, then, scholars can hardly disclaim responsibility for the consequences, whatever their initial intentions. But in any case, happen what may, the conclusions of social scientists are likely to remain untested, and their validity as scientific descriptions or explanation of reality uncertain.

The Absence of Clearly Defined Purpose. The foregoing points suggest that the development of a completely scientific study of politics faces some substantial difficulties. But there is a still greater obstacle in its path, and it provides one of the major reasons why the social sciences have thus far been unable to equal the physical sciences in distinctive and obvious contributions to knowledge. It is, simply, that social scientists have never been able to decide precisely what they are trying to do. The purpose of any science, of course, is knowledge of what is being studied. But what passes for knowledge depends on what is being studied and why. Those studying politics systematically have had diverse ideas of what politics is, of reasons for studying it, and of what sort of knowledge their work should produce.

Some, for example, have assumed that political systems are like a very intricate clockworks or solar system, their task being to identify all its parts and their interrelationships, so that they could state the "laws" governing such a mechanism. But this assumes that whatever happens is inevitable: that the patterns of behavior observed in social life are inherent and unchangeable, and that, further, there is no causal relation between the events and our knowledge of them. The conclusion follows, then, that men are no more capable of altering the course of political life than of stopping the rotation of the earth. Most of us would quickly deny any such rigid social and psychological determinism, and few political scientists would explicitly accept it, although it continues to dwell in the background of much political analysis.

More importantly today, social scientists have often conceived it their responsibility to develop models of social and political systems. The term "model" is used in quite different ways by various people, ranging from something like a physical model—as of a pyramid or chain, to characterize certain social or administrative relationships—to a rather broad theory—as "laissez faire liberalism." In any case, however, the model is used to state what are taken to be the particularly important elements of the social pattern and to characterize the system as a whole by deductions and inferences from these elements. It is thus intended as both a descriptive and explanatory device. A model enables one to understand any particular order by showing how it conforms to or deviates from the standard expressed in the model. Obviously it may also be used practically to facilitate criticism of existing and proposed policies and institutions among those who agree on the pertinence of the model. That models have been so used indicates what a fine line, if any, separates the attempted scientific explanation from the politically active opinion we call ideology. Many social scientists are therefore skeptical today of "model building," but others, while recognizing these difficulties, hold that it remains the only way of getting an over-all view of social life.

Finally, those social scientists who reject models as methodological devices but still feel they are called upon to be more than undiscriminating photographers of the whole scene, settle for the more modest task of answering the question: *What* happened *here, why,* and *how?* Thus, why did someone vote the way he did? Why did this official make this decision? What was the effect of that type of party organization on this election? Within these limits and guided by such specific questions much interesting and valuable work has been done. It is the conviction of many scholars, furthermore, that ultimately, out of a great body of such particular data and conclusions, a synthesis may be constructed that will give a general perspective on political and social life.

Yet none of these approaches contains intrinsically any answer to the question, "knowledge for what," and its derivative, "what sort of knowledge." It is far from clear whether the scientist is to use his knowledge to rule—benevolently, of course, as a modern substitute for Plato's omniscient "philosopher-king"; whether it is to be placed at the disposal of existing government officials, or political regimes, to strengthen their power in the community; whether private groups (vested interests or those seeking to become vested interests) will be able to use it, the better to make their own special needs prevail in public policy; or whether, somehow, it is going to enable the community as a whole to define its values more clearly and achieve them more effectively. Consequently, it is also not clear just what political science has, or should have, to say about the political order, and to what audience its conclusions are addressed.

It would be unfair to lay the blame for this situation altogether on political scientists, for it is rooted in the democratic and individualistic temper of the modern world. Today we are not inclined to believe that our objectives are static, unchanging in nature, and handed down to us from either the supernatural or the past. Nor do we generally believe that those objectives are, or ought to be, determined for us by any particular group of people with alleged "special qualifications." But we will listen, usually, to those who tell us what happened or is happening, and how we can do what we want to do. Sharing in this temper, as to some degree we all do, some political scientists have concluded that it is not their business to make "value judgments"—even though recognizing that values motivate and shape all political activity—but only to discover those that have been made and trace their consequences in public affairs.

Unfortunately, however, this position is not entirely tenable. Ends and means in political life are mixed and interdependent. A political institution is inseparable from the purposes it serves, and few human purposes do not imply appropriate political institutions and processes—even the purposes of "science." Furthermore, we know that these have varied according to time and place, and we can hardly assume that such changes and diversity will not continue. Political science, therefore, can hardly be as universal as physics or biology, since empirically speaking, what it studies is significantly dependent upon historical circumstances. Further, our interests in government—whether we are political scientists or simply citizens—are equally variable, and so, therefore, is the sort of knowledge we seek. The political scientist cannot avoid that the significance of his facts depends on the purposes entailing their collection and analysis, and that uncertainty as to those purposes introduces the possibility of irrelevance, if not error, into what he assumes to be political knowledge.

This may help to explain why people tend nowadays to greet the assertions of political scientists (indeed, of all social scientists) with somewhat mixed reaction. While sometimes impressed by erudition, the "man in the street" has not accorded to the propositions of the social scientists the same authority he freely grants to those of the natural scientists and engineers. He may well be right, in many instances. In the present state of development of the social sciences, at least, it is not at all certain that what they have to tell him about the effects of public borrowing, or the United Nations' ability to promote international cooperation, or the state of the nation's politics, is strictly comparable to the "scientific" truth about the state of his health, the safety of the airplane he flies in, or even the probable weather tomorrow. Unfortunately, the citizen may conclude that there is no truth at all in social affairs, and settle comfortably into hearing on social and political questions only what he wants to hear. The crank, the demagogue, and the self-interested can then more easily win a following and enforce political decisions based upon ignorance, prejudice, avarice, or passion.

Evidently, we must somehow resolve the conflict of purposes in social science, and thus render it more effective and useful—perhaps by recognizing that its object is less prediction than diagnosis. This implies, however, that political science is not independent of the political order it attempts to understand. It cannot be an isolated professional preserve, therefore, unless we are willing to accept the consequence that these professionals will either rule or be irrelevant. In democracy it is necessary for citizens as well as professional students of politics to distinguish between truth and error, knowledge and opinion, relevance and irrelevance, and good and bad in political life. In the end, we must insist, political science is the knowledge citizens possess—or should possess—about their political life, and if this is indeed the "scientific age" then we must all, to some extent, become political scientists or lose our citizenship and our freedom.

The Social Sciences Must Employ Their Own Methods. Our argument comes to this: if the social sciences are to develop, they must be envisaged as something quite different from the physical sciences, and not merely a pale copy of them. The objective investigation of observable reality for the sake of truth is a glorious pursuit, and one to which we should cling as we can; but we must recognize that reality in the human realm is not something inert, but that it interacts with the observer. Truth is not a characteristic of the external world; it is a product of the human personality in its adjustment to that world. This does not mean we must abandon the methods of science, but rather that we must learn to adapt them to the needs of our subject.

METHODS OF POLITICAL INQUIRY

How, then, can political scientists most fruitfully conduct their investigations? This subject is both complex and controversial. Because it is complex, what can be said here constitutes but the barest of introductions. Because it is controversial—which means simply that political scientists are far from agreement upon just how they work—the student should look upon what follows as no more than a suggested approach, and maintain an open mind.

One thing does seem clear. No single method is, in itself, scientific, or good, or capable of giving us a complete understanding of the universe. To judge at least from our present knowledge of it, the universe is too complicated for that to be true. And so we must limit our inquiries to parts of it, to single phenomena, or to determined classes of them, and adapt our methods to the requirements of the investigation. This means that how we work will be determined both by the characteristics of the phenomena being studied, and by the objectives of the study, or what we hope to accomplish.

All distinctively human activity is peculiarly marked by three characteristics: first, it is goal-oriented, that is, it seeks to realize some objective and does not simply happen; second, it is historical, which is to say that, while the present is never identical with the past, it has grown out of it and is founded upon it; and third, it is necessarily social behavior, and generally takes place within a complex institutional framework. Consequently, we shall not understand politics unless we consider it in each of these three characteristics. To do this, however—to see a political event as a relationship taking place within an institutional structure, possessing an historical background, and tending toward the realization of some objective—we cannot limit ourselves to a "monistic" methodology, or single-valued orientation. That this is true becomes still more evident when we recall that the objectives of our study, which largely determine the methods we must use, are seldom if ever simply "given," but must be set and clarified by the investigator.

Any adequate methodology for political science thus must be "pluralistic." This does not mean that we must investigate and explain different aspects of political life in terms of diverse, and perhaps unrelated, frames of reference (such as economic, social, geographic, or biological), but rather that for a full understanding of politics we must employ simultaneously several different techniques of study and thought, harnessing them for a common task. Such an approach is complex, to be sure, but it only mirrors the complexity of our subject, and it is difficult to see how such a procedure could be avoided.

What are these different techniques of study and thought? With some oversimplification, it may be said that, in political science as it is practiced, there are three: philosophical speculation and analysis, historical inquiry, and empirical research in contemporary relationships and events. Let us examine these in turn.

Philosophical Speculation and Analysis. Philosophy is reflection on the nature of reality, with particular emphasis upon what has been referred to as "the nature and destiny of man," and his relationship to the rest of the universe. As it proposes ideas on these fundamental matters and develops their implications, philosophy serves as both stimulus and starting point to the study of politics. Through it we acquire a sense of direction and means of organization, apart from which we are compelled either to accept passively that which simply is and has been, or to react sporadically and irrationally to momentary irritations. Without philosophy, in other words, we lack the necessary conditions for intelligent political inquiry—for political science.

Philosophy contributes directly in two ways to the intelligent consideration of politics. In the first place, that branch of philosophy called ethics undertakes a systematic examination of the values of a society, that is, the things, ways of behavior, and achievements which are considered desirable. It attempts to examine them critically, to test their validity, and to determine if there are contradictions within the system as a result of which the fulfillment of some values would render impossible the realization of others of equal importance. Many great philosophers of the past, however, have gone beyond the simple indication of conflicts to propose new formulations of social values, which they thought would eliminate the conflicts and thus make possible a better life. Such speculations are interesting, and often valuable in their own right, but they are vital to political science because they define and clarify the problems needing investigation, and suggest solutions. Without such aid from philosophy, the thoughts of the empirical researcher are likely to be random and his research largely irrelevant. He would not know what to look for, nor how to interpret what he saw.

The second way in which philosophy contributes to the study of politics, as it does to the study of any subject, is in its attempt to sharpen the tools of investigation. The importance of this should not be underestimated. Tools, or techniques of investigation and communication, must be properly adapted to the nature of the study, or the results of the study may be false. Furthermore, the limitations of any such tools must be kept clearly in mind, to avoid misleading conclusions. The reader should recall here previous references to the use of devices, such as techniques of measurement, and concepts of orientation—for instance, "political man"—in the study of politics. We need these tools of inquiry, but they are valuable only when intelligently used.

Several branches of philosophy—epistemology, semantics, and logic—are particularly related to this problem. Epistemology is concerned with the relative validity of various types of knowledge, and attempts to indicate what each can contribute to a true understanding of reality. It can, therefore, keep us from drawing unwarranted conclusions from "facts" that are not always as certain as they seem. Semantics endeavors to establish more definite meanings for the words that we must use, and thus seeks to avoid the misunderstandings that arise out of ambiguity. The proper relationship between statements or propositions is the subject matter of logic. By showing us ways in which valid conclusions can be drawn from premises, logic helps the political scientist test the correctness of his thinking, both in planning a new line of research and in evaluating the results of research already done.

Political theory is the mediating study between general philosophy and political science. One of its principal tasks is to translate into terms most relevant for political life the concepts of more general philosophy, such as ethics and metaphysics. It thus treats of such items as rights, duties, and responsibilities, whether of public authorities or citizens; the proper scope of governmental action; and the best organization of political life to accomplish the multifarious ends assigned it. Most important, it attempts to form a coherent system of thought from its conclusions on these matters, so as to bring all aspects of political life into perspective. Political theory deals also with methods of political inquiry, attempting to reconcile practical needs and limitations at any given time with more universal requirements, as in logic and ethics.

Such questions as are raised in these matters are never really answered; even new forms of logic are developed from time to time! We must particularly remember, then, that the study of politics will inevitably involve considerations of speculative and analytic philosophy. Those who deny this are only unaware of the bases of their own activity; a major premise is not less a major premise for being inarticulate, but it is certainly the worse for being unexamined. The serious student of government must, to some extent, be also a philosopher.

Historical Inquiry. History is a record of past experience, and as concerns us here, of man's political experience. No less eminent an historian than the author of the *Decline and Fall of the Roman Empire,* Edward Gibbon, has described it as "little more than the register of the crimes, follies, and misfortunes of mankind." Except that we might well know about the "follies" so that we could in the future avoid them, this opinion seems to allow little positive value to historical inquiry. However, this attitude was largely a peculiarity of the eighteenth century, and historical study has been resuscitated, and at times even glorified, by later generations. As a result, research into the past experiences of men has been conducted with ever-increasing scholarship, giving us constantly more complete and sound knowledge about that past and its relation to the present.

We have already mentioned the value to political scientists of such information. As has been noted, too, one of the major problems of the social scientist is that he lacks a "laboratory" in which he can observe processes working themselves out. Quite often he cannot find a sufficient number of current examples of the particular institution or event which he wants to study to enable him to generalize. But if his contemporary environment is thus limited, he can always turn to the past. Historical study, thus, by enlarging considerably the materials available to him, and giving him often, surprisingly enough, more complete information than he can obtain concerning his own time, is a great asset to the student of political phenomena.

The value of history, however, goes beyond this, and more needs to be said, even though we enter into a realm which has always been controversial. The eighteenth-century tendency to deprecate history resulted from the belief that history was not important: man lives in the present, it was said, and in accord with "reason," once he is freed from the trammels of superstition. A glorious dream, this, but hardly completely true. That which we assume to be "reason" is always, at least in part, received opinion, based upon past traditions and customs; a man who believes that he is "thinking for himself" is very likely at best to be doing no more than extending or developing his intellectual heritage. If this is true even of exceptional individuals, it is the more so for the so-called "masses" of a community. It follows that without knowledge of the past, we cannot understand the present, for that present can appear only as chaotic and meaningless unless we see it as it is—a continuation of past trends and the culmination of earlier developments.

Under the stimulus of such a view, men in the nineteenth century undertook the study of history, trying to trace the lines of development, and to discover the origins and the original forms of social institutions. They felt that in this way—often that *only* in this way—could the significance of contemporary events and institutions be portrayed, and guidance for the future be found. Of particular importance to political science was the work begun at this time on the background of law and legal institutions, of political philosophy and morals, of the functioning of various types of political and governmental forms, and occasionally, on the relationship of political struggles to other social developments.

Such historical research has continued to the present, and we have profited greatly from it, but in analysis of the results we have tended to become more and more critical. The past is not a collection of errors, nor is it sacrosanct, the repository of all wisdom; both of these positions of our recent ancestors are extreme. Neither does it seem that the present and the future are no more than a prolongation of the past. There is always the possibility that some significant changes may appear, not many, perhaps, but enough to disturb historical continuity and to undermine the certainty and utility of the knowledge acquired through historical study.

Thus, while history may give us many materials to think about, it cannot save us from the necessity of thinking. It can propose to us values and objectives more "realistic" than we might be able to conceive in our own heads, since they are part of our common heritage and therefore ingrained in our contemporary life to some extent, and it may suggest institutions and procedures that are likely to be more effective and useful in that they have worked before in reasonably similar circumstances; yet it cannot serve as a "grab bag" in which the solutions to all our problems will be found. We must go beyond the lessons of past experience, supplementing them with philosophy, which we have already discussed, and with empirical observation, to which we now turn.

Empirical Research. Empiricism is a point of view (in epistemology) which assumes that valid knowledge can be derived from direct experience. Empirical research, then, attempts to found our knowledge of social life upon such experience, but approached, for the most complete understanding, through intelligent and controlled observation and experiment. As is immediately apparent, this is the approach generally referred to as "science." However, as both history and philosophy can be quite scientific in their own ways, this usage is somewhat misleading. It should be kept in mind that the word "science" has both a narrow, popular meaning, and a broader, more comprehensive one, in which it signifies a method of study best adapted to its object and yielding the most fruitful results.

It is the ideal of empirical study to attain knowledge in the form of generalizations of high probability. When we observe the world about us the immediate result is only knowledge of this or that particular event, and as particular events do not repeat themselves, such knowledge cannot take us very far. What is necessary is to discover that which may be common to many events, and to arrive at a statement which will apply to a large number of individual cases. To the extent that such generalizations prove to be true, that is, that things do actually happen (or at least that there is a high probability that they will happen) as indicated, the generalizations are frequently referred to as "laws" of behavior. But even in the absence of such established generalizations, empirical study can test the correspondence of our opinions to "what is the case," and suggest alternative ideas more descriptive of political reality, thus promoting knowledge in any case.

While few of the many astute writers on politics since the days of Plato have completely ignored observed phenomena, or failed to attempt to formulate valid generalizations from the particular events or relationships observed, this approach to the study of politics has become increasingly important. It has manifested itself especially in the "behavioral analysis" that has become prominent in the last twenty years. Men of this orientation, while not necessarily denying the value of traditional philosophic, historical, or legalistic analysis, argue that political science most properly is concerned with observable patterns of political behavior, whether within governmental institutions or not, and that the task is to identify as precisely as possible their structures and their causes and effects. The result of this approach has been that the techniques of observation and of handling the data resulting from observation have steadily been improved. Especially has there been a growth and constant refinement of polls and surveys, of the use of psychological and sociological concepts to interpret political data, and of the use of mathematical devices to order that data. We have already referred to some difficulties in this sort of analysis in political studies. Yet, where relevant and accurate, it does enable us to have a great deal more information about some aspects of political life than we could otherwise possess, and relieves us to some extent from reliance upon guess and introspection.

Empirical research, however, extends also to the study of the operation of *all* our political institutions and practices, in an effort to understand what they do, how they do it, and how they are related to other institutions and practices. Legal analysis, for example, is concerned with systematizing the law of a community, eliminating, or at least suggesting the elimination of, its internal contradictions and inadequacies. It also attempts to discover how and why any particular law came into existence, by studying the governmental processes which led to its development, and by relating the law, or system of law, to general social conditions. At this point legal analysis merges with political analysis, which tries to indicate as clearly as possible how such things as the procedures of the legislative body, the party structure, organizations of interested citizens, administrative agencies, and so forth, as well as the attitudes of those involved in politics, have an impact on policy decisions. Furthermore, the governmental procedures of foreign societies are studied and compared with each other and to those of one's own country to give a broader basis for political understanding.

Even this cursory survey shows that the empirical study of contemporary events and relationships plays, and must play, an important role in political science. Dealing with the "given" materials of experience, the political scientist tries to select those relevant to his study—to describe them, to classify them in accordance with their similarities, to compare and contrast their differences, and to indicate the relationships which exist between them. As we have indicated, the limitations upon the knowledge that can be obtained in this way and its dependence upon philosophical and historical elements are not to be ignored; yet there is no doubt that some knowledge, vital to our study, can be obtained only in this way. There is likewise no doubt that even a little knowledge so acquired is better than none at all.

Political Inquiry a Joint Task. In sum, we may suggest that the limitations on the knowledge which empirical research can give us can be surmounted only through the use of philosophical and historical analysis. Much of the work done through empirical study has been criticized as being fragmentary and often irrelevant. The mere accumulation of facts neither constitutes "science," nor does it always give us useful information. The "facts" must be associated through theory; and theory, while it must remain in constant contact with observed experience, springs primarily out of the continuity which historical analysis indicates, and from the over-all view of human life, which it is the task of philosophic thought to develop. Actually, each supports the other, and no one approach can effectively exist and prosper in isolation.

IV. *The* VALUE *of the* STUDY *of* POLITICAL SCIENCE

In the politically minded world of the present, it should be unnecessary, perhaps, to dwell at any length upon the value of the study of political science. No one living today can avoid encountering the phenomena of politics continually in his daily life; and whether one thinks about them systematically or not, think about them one must. We can hope that the student who has begun this study brings with him at least a modest interest in some systematic thinking about the governmental process, and is already encouraged to go further. But for the benefit of those who are not yet assured that such effort will be justified, we may suggest several important reasons why the study of political science has value.

Political Science as a Liberal Art. Political science belongs, with the other social sciences and the humanities, to that group of studies commonly designated as the liberal arts. The term "liberal" so employed is intended to describe those studies that are appropriate or fitting for a broad and enlightened mind. The liberal arts are in effect the "liberating arts"—serving to free man's intellect from the bonds of ignorance and superstition. We study the liberal arts, then, not for their immediate and practical utility, nor necessarily for their accumulated technical information (though they may provide both), but because as thoughtful and intelligent beings we have a natural curiosity to know about the human society, institutions, and culture of which we are a part and in which we live. Cicero said, "Not to know what happened before one was born is always to remain a child." In pursuing a liberal education, therefore, we are broadening and maturing our understanding. We are, in short, simply joining the civilization of the centuries.

We have indicated that political science is the study of art, science, and philosophy in the process of government. In any advanced culture, government and its processes comprise a truly complex social institution, tending to create and maintain a political community, and manifesting several striking attributes. It is universally encountered; citizenship, or at least subjection, is virtually compulsory and practically inevitable; and, it affects nearly every aspect of modern life. Except at the cost of revolution or civil war, it has the power to command and enforce obedience, even to exacting from its people their property, their liberty, or their lives. How this power can be intelligently controlled by those subject to it, and be best employed to promote the general welfare, are great questions which modern man seeks to solve. Political science is thus brought to occupy a central position not only in the study of government and democracy, but in all of the vital problems that urgently concern our age.

Political Science as Training for Citizenship. A system of democratic government is based upon the essential premise that the people can and will participate intelligently in the process of selecting their leaders and determining public policies. Citizens of democracy, then, are particularly obligated to inform themselves on public matters if they are to make any real contribution to the governmental process, and to be fully effective in meeting this responsibility, they need a considerable understanding of the nature and objectives of their government. This is, of course, an unrealized and perhaps unrealizable ideal. Nevertheless, one of the important purposes of the study of political science is to gain some of the information and understanding upon which the successful performance of the duties of citizenship rest. Certainly, persons who receive the advantages of higher education have a greater-than-average responsibility for the assumption of civic obligations. And all of us would do well to measure ourselves against the standard described by Pericles, in his great oration on Athenian democracy, when he said: "An Athenian citizen does not neglect the state because he takes care of his own household; and even those of us who are engaged in business have a very fair idea of politics. We alone regard a man who takes no interest in public affairs not as a harmless, but as a useless, character; and if few of us are originators, we are all sound judges of a policy."

Political science as a study, of course, does not purport to give ready-made "right answers" to political questions, but it is able to assist in providing the bases of fact, experience, and judgment upon which intelligent decisions may be reached. Specific answers, we must note, can be offered only in terms of a whole broad system of values. It is not enough, of course, for the citizen merely to judge governmental programs and policies—he must act upon that judgment. Thus, the study of politics must be a guide to action. Oliver Wendell Holmes, Jr., once said, "As life is action and passion, it is required of a man that he should share the passion and action of his time, at the peril of being judged not to have lived."

Political Science as Career Preparation. In emphasizing the study of political science as an essential part of a liberal education and civic training, we need not overlook its importance in preparation for a variety of vocations. As is the case with many other disciplines, political science study generally becomes professional only at the graduate level of instruction, and advanced degrees in the subject are normally required of those intending to serve as professional political scientists in educational, governmental, or other employment. Undergraduate preparation in the subject, nevertheless, offers a number of possibilities for vocational application, as well as constituting the first step toward professional training.

One of the largest of such opportunities is provided by government employment. The federal, state, and local governments are together the largest single employer in the United States. To be sure, government agencies do not hire "employees," but use a great variety of persons with professional and technical training and specific skills; hence, like other employers, such services seek lawyers, doctors, teachers, accountants, statisticians, guards, engineers, clerks, and so forth. But in recent years the government services have encountered an increasingly greater need for persons whose formal education has been in the social sciences to fill administrative, staff, research, advisory, and planning positions. To recruit such young college graduates, who can also show promise of ability to rise to positions of high responsibility, the federal government offers appointments, for example, through federal service entrance examinations, to those who have specialized in political science, public or business administration, international relations, economics, and similar subjects, thus providing careers in administrative service of great variety. State and local governments also are attracting a larger number of persons trained in political science and public administration.

Political science can be useful as prelegal training. Because lawyers practice a profession involving large social responsibilities, they need a good general education as well as a knowledge of public affairs. Political science offers one possible field of specialization for the secondary-school teacher and the educational administrator. It may also be a frequently useful and sometimes necessary accompaniment to many other kinds of careers. Journalism, public relations, business and personnel management, librarianship, military science, and even home-making are only a few of the fields whose successful practice may require some augmentation from the content of political science. The increasingly large number of persons who go abroad in various professional, commercial, governmental, and private capacities also find that, whatever their specialization, they must inevitably be concerned with the political affairs of the foreign area in which they work, as well as of their own country. This proposition brings us again to the point where we began in discussing the utility of studying political science: whether we seek a liberal education, useful citizenship, or gainful employment, at home or abroad, politics concerns us all.

PART TWO:

POLITICAL COMMUNITY

PLATO

Surely, I began, we must admit that the same elements and characters that appear in the state must exist in every one of us; where else could they have come from?

ARISTOTLE

Every state is a community of some kind, and every community is established with a view to some good —for mankind always act in order to obtain that which they think good. But, if all communities aim at some good, the state or political community, which is the highest of all, and which embraces all the rest, aims at good in a greater degree than any other, and at the highest good.

CHAPTER 2

SOCIETY *and the* STATE

SOCIETY is always a blessing, while at its best, government is only a necessary evil: thus, in *Common Sense* (1776), Thomas Paine distinguished sharply between the social and political orders. They not only have different values, they have also different foundations. To Paine and many thinkers since, society is produced by our wants, while government is the result of our wickedness. Such distinctions are extremely important in political science; they shape both the character of what we study and the way we proceed. Because we can hardly investigate politics unless we know how it differs from other aspects of human life, the methods of political science will be set by those distinctions we think relevant. Treating that traditional distinction between "society" and "state" is a good way to begin.

This discussion involves very practical as well as academic concerns. Paine made his point, after all, in a revolutionary pamphlet; he assumed it reflected popular experience, and he expected people to act upon it in creating a new community. So even today, a judgment that the political order is or is not distinct, in a certain way, from other aspects of human life underlies all social organization and any decision of public policy. Indeed, the contemporary struggle between what we call the "free" and "unfree" ways of life involves sharply conflicting opinions about the "real" and "correct" relationship between the social and the political. We can understand modern government only if we see how it is related to, and yet distinct from, other realms of man's life.

It would be convenient if we could now neatly define our terms, "society" and "state," compare them, and point out their differences. Unfortunately, it is not that simple. Each term has numerous definitions, equally plausible, designed from a point of view to meet a particular need. Our problem, really, is to understand these diverse ideas about politics and social life and their implications for government today. Simply to choose one perspective would ignore the complexity and purpose of our subject. The terms "social," "political," and related expressions have acquired their meaning in our historical development, and must be studied in that context to avoid arbitrary definitions. This chapter, which lays the foundation for all subsequent discussion, must therefore treat several large topics. It will consider the history of the modern community, wherein politics became a distinctive activity; provide a more adequate definition of politics than that in Chapter 1; treat the relationships between social and political phenomena; and finally, examine how the patterns of western political regimes developed into the modern state.

I. *The* SOCIAL ORDER

Man, it has been said, is "social by nature." Not only do we normally live in intense and continuing association with others, but the sort of men we are is largely shaped in those relationships. Even when they are frustrating rather than enjoyable and supporting, we cannot seriously envisage their abandonment; they seem necessary to human existence. Nevertheless, when we attempt to specify how they are so, we run into difficulty. Though men have always lived in groups, their form and substance have changed considerably through ages past, along with their impact upon us. This change continues today, and we now live in a system of human relationships rich and complex. Since the "social order" is manifested in so many different ways, clear and useful generalizations about it are hard to make. By surveying our historical background, however, we can extract a sense of the term "social," which will be useful.

Early Social Life. We know very little about our remote ancestors. The findings of archaeology give us insight only into those communities advanced enough to leave significant artifacts. Nor can we look to contemporary primitive peoples for a reflection of very early human life, for this would require us to assume that any primitive community today simply remained on a lower rung of a ladder, beyond which others long ago climbed. Nevertheless, it is obvious that changes have taken place, and from anthropological and historical data we have drawn a few broad conclusions. While these will not thoroughly or profoundly describe the nature of man or of his social life, they will serve as a starting point for a survey of later developments and help us to understand them.

Briefly, human life originated in exclusive and for the most part undifferentiated family groupings. Primitive men lived in small and self-contained groups which monopolized meaningful activities, provided all legitimate regulation, and imposed all obligations. In effect, they were the exclusive source of benefits and duties; and no distinct sense either of individuality or of a transcendent humanity existed in possible opposition to the values of the particular community. At the same time, functional distinctions—those of responsibilities, offices, or roles—were extremely limited, largely to those necessitated by differences in sex and age. While such peoples were not always adept at generalizing, sometimes having a distinct name for every kind of tree without any word for "tree" itself, they tended, nonetheless, to see their own lives and social interrelations in a very general way. Obviously, this is not the world we know; western history, at least, has witnessed the gradual breakdown of undifferentiated order and the emergence of a diversified society.

THE GROWTH OF SOCIAL COMPLEXITY

Many events and ideas have contributed to the growth of diversity and differentiation in social life and to man's changed conception of the nature of social organization. Our discussion of this development must be limited to elements which illuminate our particular interest. After dealing briefly with the initial breakdown of the primitive community, as a result of its growth and changing membership, we shall proceed to later developments significant in western political history: the rise of Christianity, the organization of medieval Europe, the appearance of an individualistic perspective, and the emergence of modern economics.

From Kinship to Citizenship. So ingrained in human thought has been consanguinity, and so commonplace the community based upon blood relationships, that men have been able only gradually, at best, to emancipate themselves from such a homogeneous and exclusive social life. This radical transformation of the nature of the community—a transition from kindred to civic relationships—is most clearly exemplified in the history of ancient Rome. There, as a result of territorial expansion and conquest, peoples who were not original members of the city had nonetheless to be absorbed. The process of doing so extended from the earliest days of Rome until virtually the fall of its empire eight centuries later. The first group thus admitted was the plebs, an ancient class of common people within Rome. Unlike the patricians, or nobles, who by their family groupings comprised the city, the plebeians had no legally recognized families, and thus no initial share in that order. However, beginning with the creation of the plebeian tribunate in the early fifth century B.C., they were ultimately granted over several centuries a virtually unqualified citizenship. Similar steps taken to the benefit of other non-citizens, as Rome expanded, culminated late in the fourth century A.D. with the extension of citizenship to all free men in the far-flung empire.

This development has a simple explanation. The Roman community early became too large and complex to be organized on the narrow basis of kinship. First the plebs and then others became too important, economically and militarily, to the life of the city. Although patricians and plebeians originally had little or nothing in common, they were now so indispensable to one another that the plebeians could demand and the patricians concede rights of citizenship. The ultimate extension of citizenship came from the need to broaden the tax base of an empire in serious financial straits—thus continuing the pragmatic Roman response to changing conditions and practical problems.

The nature of the community was now radically altered. What plebeians and patricians acquired in common, for example, was not the kindred and religious ties that were the foundation of early Rome, but rather a more limited and mundane social intercourse. Although the Roman community and law were never entirely divested of religious associations, these became increasingly secondary. Instead, the law emerged as a framework of rights and duties tending to secure the harmonization of diverse and distinct interests, and the community comprising all those living within that law. An association defined in such broad and pragmatic terms is not only capable of indefinite expansion but is also totally different from the primitive community from which it sprang. Although persisting civic religions and nationalistic sentiments show that the transformation is not complete, the first important breach in the homogeneous and undifferentiated social order had been made, and events of succeeding centuries were to extend it.

The Rise of Christianity. In primitive culture religion pervaded every aspect of life. Later, the increasing diversity of the population in pagan Rome compelled some measure of religious differentiation and tolerance. The appearance of Christianity, however, introduced the principle: Render unto Caesar the things which are Caesar's; and unto God the things that are God's. Although there has always been considerable difficulty in determining what in the particular event belongs to God, and what to Caesar, western culture has generally accepted that at least two distinct, if interrelated, realms or dimensions in human life exist. Diversity has become, certainly in some measure, a cultural norm. This, in turn, has promoted respect for the individual person, because apart from God himself, the individual is the only link between the two realms. The principle also implies that religious obligation is distinct from other social obligations. Consequently, Christianity has both criticized and supported temporal orders and obligations. Civic or nationalistic religions, in which religious and secular obligations must support each other, could not do this.

Further, Christianity created an ecclesiastical institution parallel to that existing in the civic or imperial realm. It could not attempt to displace the latter—the realm of Caesar—which had its own special role in an imperfect world: the coercive maintenance of standards based in large part upon utility and expediency. But performing as spokesman and governor for the spiritual side of man's nature, and concerned with the ultimate freedom of voluntary obedience to divine law, the Church was to remain independent and inviolate. For the first time in history a division of social authority within a community existed both in fact and in principle. And since religious attitudes had been a central expression of the homogeneity of primitive culture, that unselfconscious and simple unity had now definitively been broken.

The Organization of Medieval Europe. During the approximately one thousand years between the fall of Rome and the rise of the modern world, western man became further accustomed to a community both unified and diversified. Despite the differentiation of religion in Rome's later days, its civic regime remained highly centralized. Although some leaders of the several Germanic tribes overrunning the empire were impressed by it and desired to preserve it, they were not able to do so. After a time, there emerged a highly complex system distributing power and responsibilities, rights and duties, among many organized territorial and functional groups. The basic unit of medieval society was the manor, a relatively complete local community. However, it did not exhaust social organization, as had earlier local communities, but existed within and alongside a broader community including the feudal nobility up to the emperor, the Church, and a great variety of corporate economic and cultural bodies—no part of which existed entirely at the sufferance of any other. As a result the associational life of the middle ages was extraordinarily rich in comparison with that of any previous period, establishing the idea that human life is fundamentally pluralistic.

The Rise of Individualism. In medieval pluralism, however, the individual was rarely considered independently of his place within established associations. However, after the fifteenth century primacy of the individual became emphasized. Increasingly, therefore, the groups to which men belong are no longer taken to be fundamental and given, but only as means to their activities and development. The ends to which they are means, and whether any group is an appropriate means, men must remain free to decide. With the assumption, now, that their needs are diverse and changing, men need no longer remain within existing groups, often those into which they were born, but rather they must be free to shift from one group to another, or to form new ones. Since this time, individuals have increasingly turned social organization into an instrument for the realization of their purposes, rather than being dominated by it. Despite the obvious fact that this freedom is always limited, the organization of human life in western civilization has become as a result ever more complex and changeable.

The Independent Economy. One of the ways individuals exercised their new freedom of activity and association has been in economic ventures. In the nineteenth century particularly, the theory and practice of laissez faire predominated, rejecting traditional, moral, religious, and political limitations on economic activity. This doctrine of "let alone" was firmly rooted in the scientific perspectives of the age. Newton had earlier projected a universe whose parts, once set in motion, continued harmoniously in their various ways in accord with their own law of nature. To analogous economic laws Adam Smith, in his renowned *The*

Wealth of Nations (1776), applied the term "the invisible hand," which presumably guided individual endeavors to the general advantage without additional regulation being either necessary or desirable.

Later economists—of the so-called Manchester School in England during the first half of the century and others who carried on their work—constructed on Smith's insights an imposing system of economic thought, comprising a considerable number of "laws" seen as both necessary and beneficial. In other words, the economic aspect of human life was taken to possess its own rules, derived not at all from politics or religion but inherent in its own nature. Economic activity should thus be left free, it was held, to follow those laws for the sake of efficiency and progress. Economics thus followed religion in asserting its autonomy.

The Modern Community. The modern western community, shaped by and extending the ideas and forces sketched above, has thus become intrinsically pluralistic. Only in the vaguest sense, if at all, can it be called the source and matrix of human life, as was the original primitive community. Much more realistically, it is a realm—rather difficult to define or describe—in which individuals pursuing diverse ends act through innumerable and more or less autonomous organizations according to rules appropriate to each. Of course, this description is only partially true, and to advocates of such a condition, an ideal not yet realized. Yet there can be no doubt that in modern western life the homogeneity, the common purposes, and the all-pervading authority of the ancient community are gone. Every community must have its basis in some sort of common good. We have today considerable difficulty in identifying such a common good, and can generally agree only on such things as protection against foreign enemies, the fulfillment of promises, and the preservation of freedom. To a very considerable degree, then, the community has been reduced to the form and not the substance of human life.

The Totalitarian Challenge. The fact that men continue trying to give a richer and less formal meaning to such phrases as "the American way of life," however, suggests that such a community does not altogether meet men's needs. A more extreme rejection of it is reflected in the appearance of various totalitarian movements and philosophies during the last century, and even in the conformism and uncertainty in the western world which numerous social critics have observed in recent years. Communism and extreme nationalism have not lacked supporters, even in established democracies, though their purpose is to integrate men into one unified community to which they owe an exclusive and total allegiance. We shall resume this topic in Chapter 4; here we may simply note the danger of failing to recognize that the highly integrated and pervasive community of earlier times provided a real, if narrow, cooperative life, minimizing anxiety and maximizing concrete, if limited, benefits. Thus meeting certain basic human needs, its contemporary counterparts can attract many persons for whom the somewhat abstract values of freedom and diversity have but limited meaning.

The Value of the Modern Ideal. Nevertheless, a realistic appraisal shows not only the strengths but also the weaknesses of the homogeneous and undifferentiated community—and of modern totalitarianism—as a response to human needs. In the past, as human life became more complex, such communities proved unable to contain the varied needs and activities emerging and could not survive. In the even greater complexity of modern life, therefore, totalitarianism is a fundamentally irrational response to the undeniably serious problems and emergencies of the twentieth century. Our difficulty today is much like that faced by the ancient Romans—basically one of harmonizing increasingly diverse activities and forces—and which they met by abandoning the primitive community. Following their lead, western culture has since been too much shaped by social and individualistic differentiation in all its activities and values to be able effectively to return to the ways of our remote ancestors. Totalitarianism may meet some contemporary problems, but often inefficiently and always at the cost of many of the leading values and achievements of western civilization—as the Germans painfully were taught, and as the Russians are beginning, perhaps, to learn. Therefore, far from being the "wave of the future," as its advocates claim, totalitarianism is today an atavism, an unrealistic attempt to escape the consequences of over two thousand years of history. We must have better and more appropriate solutions to the problems of modern life than it affords.

A CONCEPTION OF "THE SOCIAL"

Despite the rise of totalitarianism and related phenomena, however, it is clear that the modern community, unlike the primitive community, is not a homogeneous grouping that may be referred to, almost indifferently, as a family, or a church, or an economy, or a military association, or a polity or state. It includes all these and more, of course, but these activities have become differentiated and somewhat autonomous, and to understand the community as a whole we must see how they fit together. One approach, most characteristic of sociological study, views social life as simply those activities involving more than one person, and society as the complex of associations formed in those activities. However, the perspective lacks any inherent criteria in terms of which pattern or structure can be discerned, and "society" appears only as a congeries of human activities and associations, manifesting no necessary relationships or common elements.

We may doubt, indeed, that the primitive community has dissolved to this extent. No community is simply a collection of discrete elements, accidentally related. It does not resemble the moving balls on a billiard table, with neither a skilled player nor rules of the game. A community exists because the life of its members is pervaded by common standards of value and judgment. It also provides ways in which those standards are established and maintained, and this is a matter of especial importance for political science. In primitive life, these "ways" are very limited; the standards and patterns of conduct embodying them are largely dictated by custom, with little variety or choice. Also, one marries, works, worships, and fights within essentially the same frame of reference. By contrast, in the complex modern community each of these diverse activities has to a considerable extent its own standards. Furthermore, two different processes through which appropriate patterns of behavior are determined have emerged, and the differentiation is crucial to modern western life. These may be called the "social" and the "political" orders, and they are primarily distinguished by *how* things are done rather than by *what* is done.

Society as the Voluntaristic Order. In the modern community many activities and organizations exist only because some persons have chosen to participate, but are not obliged to do so. Normally, one may withdraw from economic life to subsistence farming, for example, if he is willing to accept the cost; in any event, no man is bound like a slave to a particular job, church, or social group. One important aspect of life in the modern community, despite some practical qualifications, is the reality of free, individual choice, and of standards and relationships created and maintained through voluntary acceptance of this obligation and of the discipline of that group. Some term to identify this aspect is essential, if only to distinguish it from the quite different political realm.

This voluntaristic realm, then, we shall call "society." It is an order, a network of associations, created through "social" relationships, i.e., those relationships and obligations voluntarily accepted. Here, the particular objectives sought are subordinated to the requirement of agreement. It is, therefore, most appropriately the sphere of small and intimate groups, shared purposes, and considerable informality in procedures, although this is a matter of degree.

Indeed, our definition is highly theoretical. It is less intended to identify any particular associations as social than to identify a quality which any association may possess, but which in some is clearly dominant and in others subordinate. Economic life and family life, for example, include elements not altogether voluntary, while in democratic political life consent to government is important. Such ambivalences do raise some problems, and we shall deal with them in the following pages. Nonetheless, this conception of society is taken for granted in the quotation from Paine with which this chapter opened, and in much thought and practice since. In keeping with a bias in favor of individual spontaneity and freedom, and recognizing that the modern community was in fact coming to give those attributes considerable scope, Paine and other liberals distinguished actions and groups in which those attributes are primary as properly "social." Our definition is rooted in this historical experience and thought.

II. *The* POLITICAL ORDER

Let us now turn to our principal concern, the clarification of modern politics, and in a brief historical résumé, note how the developments discussed above in relation to "society" also contributed to the emergence of a distinct and limited conception of politics. We can then identify a conception of political order comparable to that of the social order, indicate its extent in common experience, and finally, examine its relationship to the co-existing social order in the modern community.

Factors in the Differentiation of Politics. The foundations of a distinctive political order were laid fairly early in Greek and Roman times, when a division emerged between the city, or public realm, and the private sphere of life. The private realm was that of families in their internal affairs, and later of special religious sects, recognized as existing independently and having their rights—as we would put it today. The public realm was that of affairs common to all citizens in some way, having its own special institutions, procedures, and purposes. For our immediate concern, the distinction is important because it suggests that the term "political" is applicable only to certain aspects of human experience. For some two thousand years political science has tried to elucidate these aspects, and while the question has received diverse and conflicting answers, the basic issue has seldom been challenged: that a part only and not the whole of human experience is *directly* political.

The contribution of Christian doctrine to determining the nature and role of political order has been neither entirely clear nor consistent, because of the belief that even what is Caesar's belongs ultimately to God. Nevertheless, a distinct realm for government was generally recognized, with its role being that of a remedy for man's sins, limited in its purpose and domain. The full significance of this doctrine was concealed in the medieval period by the fact that the highly unified and organized Church not only collaborated with but often controlled secular authorities. In the religious controversies of the post-Reformation period, however, emphasis came to be laid on the element of private and personal conviction in religious faith; its consequence was a more clearly marked separation between religion and politics. This privileged privacy and freedom of religious conviction has also been extended increasingly to all moral convictions, and from distinctly spiritual to quite mundane matters. This breadth of respect for the felt needs, beliefs, and desires of individuals—as asserted in the American Declaration of Independence that every man has an "unalienable right" to the "pursuit of happiness" —is quite breathtaking, but it has shaped political developments over the last two centuries.

The political thought and practice thus influenced has granted universal and unqualified legitimacy to only one responsibility and function of government: the provision of order and security. Rarely in modern times —fascist regimes excepted—has government been seen as a creative force, or having any intrinsic moral value. It is rather an agent of people, who are not considered primarily as citizens but as private persons who need order and security for their private purposes. In this view, a political system performs two functions, then: it first enables people to identify their needs, and it then protects their rights and provides appropriate services and opportunities, so that they can effectively satisfy those needs. It is evident why many recent political scientists assume that their major task is to discover "who gets what, when, and how," since in modern life political systems are thought to differ primarily in regard to whose needs are taken into account and how they are satisfied. This is important but it is not the sole consideration.

A CONCEPTION OF POLITICS

A conception of political life appropriate to our needs—not only of political scientists but also of citizens—is implicit in the historical developments sketched above. Because these developments have shaped both the thought and practice of western culture, and reflect also its essential characteristics, such a conception of politics should effectively help us identify and understand the realities of actual political life. It should also be sufficiently persuasive that we intuitively recognize it to be meaningful. Our task is to bring it out as clearly as we can, and to deal with some of the problems that arise.

Politics as the Framework of Society. These historical developments may be summed up with three propositions. First, the modern political order is but one aspect of community life; the realm which is not directly political may be referred to as that of conscience, of voluntary association, or of private affairs. Second, the political order exists to help identify and safeguard the individual's rights and to aid him in the satisfaction of his needs. Third, government can best achieve these purposes without exceeding its limitations by maintaining a common framework of order, provided through both legal rules and basic services and opportunities.

Political order, then, is the framework within which other more particular aspects of human life may go on; it is the framework of society. Politics is activity concerned with the creation and maintenance of such an order. Politics has, therefore, its own distinctive responsibilities and characteristics; it is fundamentally temporal, and manifests values and procedures that are not necessarily those of private life. For this reason it is in important ways different from religious life, family life, and economic pursuits, and one canot assume that standards of conduct derived from these activities are always appropriate in the political realm. Nevertheless, politics does have an appropriate perspective of its own, from which standards can be derived. According to the historic values of western culture, wherein politics arose, the best political order supports freedom and diversity in social life.

Despite its obvious importance and value, however, a political order is extremely difficult to establish and maintain. This is so in good part because modern social life has been dynamic, resulting in a society more complex and fragmented than most others in history. Unless the fragments can be integrated and rendered coherent in terms of shared values and common standards, not only progress but even survival is unlikely. Yet the institutions and policies that will serve this purpose are never self-evident. They are related to the social forces they integrate, and reflect their tensions and changes. It is thus evident that in a dynamic community the search for an effectively integrating order never ends, and that different communities will have different political orders. Political processes and public policies, therefore, have no necessary stability or universality. We can discern when politics has failed, however, for the result is either chaos or totalitarianism, in neither of which can modern man live what he believes to be "the good life."

The Scope of Politics. We may well here anticipate objections to our definition of political order. Not all political scientists or practicing politicians would immediately recognize its relevance to their activities. This difficulty flows from continuing disagreement over the scope of political order—what is political, and how—and over what political institutions and policies are appropriate. The problem may be met by considering some generally admitted instances of political life today, endeavoring to relate them to our definition. Chosen because they also reflect the reasons for differences of opinion in and about politics, these are: first, that people are involved in politics in different ways and for different motives, and sometimes without being aware that they are; second, that politics is a matter of circumstance, and thus variable in its form and content; and third, that political power, inseparable from government, is not always clear in regard either to the functions it serves or to its sources and effects.

In the first place, few persons in any community are consciously and deliberately engaged in creating, maintaining, and perfecting political order. Most are rather endeavoring to obtain from government some special advantage, to manipulate others through existing power systems, to advance their self-interest, or to gain power and prestige through public office. Indeed, this is the behavior we tend to call "political" in popular parlance. We must, however, see these motives and behavior in context. That businessmen may pursue profit rather than the creation of an orderly and efficient system of production and distribution does not invalidate the science of economics; it simply gives economists the task of understanding profit-seeking in terms of the larger pattern of economic life. Political scientists must similarly attempt to understand a politician's campaign for election, an interest group's attempt to obtain a subsidy, and even a revolutionary conspiracy, as facets of a larger political life, because they have no *political* meaning in isolation. An interest group is a political phenomenon because of its efforts to secure recognition of its importance to the community as a whole in the form of protection, assistance, or honors, even though its methods of doing so may not appear the most rational way of establishing the fact. Politics is not always rational, and such groups truly participate in the creation of the framework of order government maintains, no matter how small their part, how they play it, or even what they may think they are doing. People may act politically by accident or design, out of self-interested or public-spirited purposes, and no political system has ever depended solely upon conscientious and public-spirited citizens for its existence. Consequently, of course, it is difficult to identify clearly the range of political phenomena.

Second, the character of any political order depends largely upon circumstances. The institutions, procedures, and policies that will serve to integrate the social order in the United States in the twentieth century would not have had that effect in the eighteenth, nor would they do so in twentieth-century Russia or China, or even in contemporary England or France. Political institutions and policies transplanted from a native to an alien soil yield rather surprising results, if they survive at all. Some Latin American countries in the last century modeled their new governments after the presidential system of the United States, but without remotely comparable results. It is obvious, then, that we cannot identify politics in terms of any particular institutions or policies, but only by examining what institutions enable a particular community to evolve policies sustaining a common life. In doing this, attention must be paid to such things as characteristic personality types, the level and nature of education, available communication facilities, and the structure of economic activities, for these will affect political needs and possibilities.

Also, one important circumstance that will greatly influence politics is public opinion; the political significance of an institution or policy is not determined solely by its intrinsic quality but also by what people think of it. A political scientist may advocate constitutional democracy in terms of its capacity for integrating a public. Yet if the people for any reason prefer dictatorship, political purposes may be served by the latter, whereas democracy would likely not work at all. Similarly, a laissez-faire public policy will not long survive among a people arrived at the opinion that government should actively foster economic development and full employment. Although "facts" undoubtedly exist in such matters, it is not always certain that we know them or how they are relevant to existing conditions; meanwhile political integration may be advanced through myth and misinformed opinion as well as through established truth. The viability of political orders is tested in political experience, not through a priori speculation or the application of non-political standards. In other words, it may be that the most applicable conception of truth in politics is the pragmatic one—that something works. This is what Machiavelli insisted, and though men have always been somewhat horrified by the idea, they have not succeeded in avoiding it in practice.

Finally, the centrality of government in politics, and of power in government, can easily lead to superficial perspectives in political thinking. Power is necessary if any order is to exist, and there are always men who like to exercise it and seek opportunities to do so. The basic importance of political order generally supports a concentration of the more potent forms of power—especially physical coercion—in the hands of government officials, whose activities therefore constitute especially striking instances of politics, as do struggles to gain those offices. Every analysis must have some starting point, and in political science governmental and immediately related phenomena are usually taken as the core of political life. It is dangerous, however, to isolate them from their context, and especially to give power-seeking an independent significance. This danger is especially acute in the study of democracy, in which it is extremely difficult to relate government and its power clearly to its context, showing its sources, flow, and limits, so vague and shifting are the boundaries in practice between political and non-political phenomena. Political science must consider many things not immediately or inherently political, therefore, in its effort to discern and understand the full scope and character of political life, but it must always consider them in their relationship to the political order.

THE INTERRELATIONSHIP OF SOCIETY AND STATE

Analytic distinctions are necessary for understanding, but they somewhat distort reality. We have distinguished two orders within the modern community: the social and the political. We know from experience, however, that in our communities few matters are exclusively political or social; there are elements of both. We must now endeavor to see how they are related if we are adequately to understand either in practice.

Neither the social nor the political order exists for its own sake. Men cannot live without co-operative association. Especially in western culture, they have to this end created two important and different ways of co-operating: one of voluntary and often evanescent relationship, and another of more or less permanent, generalized, and authoritative organization. Paine was thus right in the assertion with which this chapter began, insisting that society and state could be distinguished as to their sources, objectives, and methods. Yet he was wrong in his somewhat casual assumption that government can only be understood in terms of the needs and character of social life. The social order is as often shaped by the political, and distinctively political values do exist.

The Social and Political Orders Influence Each Other. Much private practice and opinion we now take for granted in social life, in which we assume government has no part, is really the product of past political activity. On the other hand, we can easily see the degree to which political standards and activities are affected by prevailing social practices and attitudes. The relationship between the two orders is clearly one of mutual influence. Democratic government itself, as will be more fully indicated in Chapter 3, is the result, at least in part, of applying to politics the idea of voluntary association already existing in the social realm, and insisting on a more literal interpretation of the old political idea of government by consent of the governed. However, democratic governments through their procedures and policies tend as well to break down restrictions on free association in the social order. No one can deny the profound effect public policies have on economic activity; in the United States these policies have often been intended to prevent monopolies and other concentrations of economic power. Finally, the contemporary problem of race relations can hardly be understood apart from such political background as the Declaration of Independence and party politics; it is surely not simply a matter of "private opinion."

Evidently, then, the consequences of political acts—both what is done and how—spread throughout a community, influencing the goals people pursue and the ways they do so, to an extent often difficult to trace. The role of politics has never been as negative as Paine suggested, and is certainly not likely to become so. Indeed, government seems destined to become ever more important and powerful. Communities are becoming more complex and their aspirations more demanding. In these circumstances realistic and compatible goals and appropriate techniques of co-operation are increasingly difficult to discover and maintain. It is therefore possible that politics as we have known it will vanish in an emerging totalitarianism—though this has not happened where politics was firmly established. Hence, the fear of those who oppose expanding government is comprehensible, although sometimes unreasonably violent. But whether we like it or not, as the means for identifying and implementing a framework of order for social life, government must continue to be the central and controlling force in modern life.

The Nature of Political Values. Certainly politics must express some central values in life. A few anarchists apart, no one has ever considered it a completely amoral power. Yet Paine's view hardly seems adequate; it is more than a remedy for wickedness, most especially for the human desire to get something for nothing. From a broader perspective another eighteenth-century writer, Jean-Jacques Rousseau, observed that the only way men could increase their individual powers was to co-operate, and that the political order is the greatest such co-operative association. To Rousseau, the terms and ends of political co-operation are stated in the "general will," or law, of the community. Thus, like any association, the state expresses human values and is a means to their realization. The values men pursue are many, diverse, and changing, and cannot be effectively monopolized by any one organization or order. However, some have particular characteristics, which may reasonably be said to make them political values, whatever their origin or final effect.

In the first place, the preservation of the political order itself is a political value of the highest rank, especially if taken to mean preventing degeneration into chaos or totalitarianism. Within this, then, we may distinguish two categories of political values. One comprises those values so essential to community life that they must be enforced, if necessary coercively. No one has ever suggested that uncontrolled killing of fellow citizens might be tolerated, and few that contractual obligations should not be enforced. The second category includes values whose realization requires widespread and highly organized co-operation beyond that available through any other association, and perhaps of a type not appropriate to any other. Foreign relations, military activities, and postal services are examples of long standing, to which have been added more recently programs of national economic development and organizations for regional development, such as the Tennessee Valley Authority. Differences over these programs, as well as disputes concerning to what extent racial equality should be a value of the first category, indicate the dynamic nature of political life and its values.

Rather than a necessary evil, then, government can be a positive good, an instrument for organized achievement when other means fail. Still, the classical liberal view that Paine expressed ought not be forgotten, for governments are scarcely perfect instruments even to the best ends. Even beyond the possibility of corruption, they cannot effectively serve all human purposes, and whatever they do inevitably runs counter at some point to such values as privacy and individual spontaneity. Even those values it does manifest and serve acquire their full meaning only in the context of other and larger values, primarily in the social realm. Therefore, the evaluation of political institutions and programs must always include their impact on diverse, non-political activities. Most immediately, politics sustains the conditions necessary for those activities, and through aid and regulation often furthers their capacity to contribute to the common good. Ultimately and ideally, political order is valuable because it promotes human freedom in an ever richer social life.

III. HISTORICAL PATTERNS *of* POLITICAL ORGANIZATION

A political order must have some sort of organizational form, and that of modern times is generally called the "state." Yet the modern state is not the only form of political order that has existed or is likely to appear. Furthermore, it has grown out of earlier and quite different regimes, and cannot be fully comprehended except when seen in an historical dimension. To broader our perspective, so that we do not confuse the familiar with the necessary, we should briefly survey these earlier systems before considering modern times.

GOVERNMENTS IN ANTIQUITY

The cradle of western civilization was the eastern Mediterranean area and the Middle East. Other civilizations existed elsewhere, but their significance for our study is uncertain or remote. Indeed, even that of the Middle East is far from clear; the later political life of Europe grew out of the Greek and Roman tradition, but these may have been influenced in their formative years by earlier Assyrian and Persian experience. In any case, similarities and differences between these ancient regimes and those of later times will be instructive.

We know relatively little about the governmental institutions of these very early civilizations. However, successive kings and emperors, from a legendary Sargon about 3750 B.C. to the Persian Cyrus, who captured Babylon in 539 B.C., succeeded in building great regimes, including systems of law and organizations of officials. The Code of Hammurabi, from somewhat before 2000 B.C., seems to have been a remarkably complete legal code, dealing with family relationships, property, trade and commerce, as well as individual rights and duties, and except for its sometimes rather primitive criminal conceptions was worthy of the most advanced civilization. Yet it was a codification of laws that had probably been followed for centuries. Each culture had temples that served as centers of religion and learning, and priests were especially powerful on the local level. Kings and emperors derived their power partly from military effectiveness and partly from priestly support; they often came to be accepted as gods. From their courts came a complex officialdom, comprising military aides, tax-gatherers, judges, provincial governors, as well as men charged with public works. The range of governmental activities was already wide: one of the leading titles a Mesopotamian king might possess was "irrigator"; the Code of Hammurabi even provided for a postal system. Thus, the great empires of Middle Eastern antiquity evidently performed, or attempted to perform, the major functions of government we take for granted today.

Yet as far as their power reached, these regimes were totally despotic. They rested entirely upon the activity of a few ambitious, energetic, and relatively enlightened men, and the vast mass of the community was more acted upon than led. For that mass, it would seem, life went on in accord with apparently timeless custom, interrupted only by occasional demands for military service and labor on public works, the objects of which were little understood. Such regimes could maintain a fairly high degree of internal order in a relatively static culture, but they were not effective organizations for a more truly common life or for more progressive purposes. They fell, then, before the attacks of less civilized but more aggressive and unified nomadic groups, or by their own degeneration into internal rivalries, leaving little but ruins to later ages.

THE CLASSICAL AGE: GREECE AND ROME

The communities of Greece and Rome developed after about 750 B.C. a much more dynamic political life and ideal than the ancient empires and undeniably influenced later western culture and politics. Each community had its own special characteristics, and consequently a different impact on later developments.

The Greek City-Community. Originally nomadic invaders of the eastern Mediterranean, the Greeks made a relatively rapid transition to a life as city dwellers; what had probably taken several thousand years in Mesopotamia was compressed for them into a few hundred. Perhaps for this reason, and because they were a people of unusual and quick intelligence not much inhibited by superstition, the Greeks soon came to show a considerable diversity among their city-communities and, in some instances, a rather dynamic, changeable character within. Their cities remained small, however; they did not create empires. In the face of Persian and Macedonian aggression, military alliances and hegemonies appeared with leadership for special purposes but no unified political system. The core of Greek life remained the city with its surrounding rural area. The largest of these, Athens, was at its greatest about one thousand square miles in extent and comprised less than 40,000 citizens, plus their families and a large number of resident foreigners and slaves. Most cities were much smaller; indeed, in their political commentaries Plato and Aristotle expressed a preference for cities of no more than six thousand citizens.

An explanation for this situation and attitude is to be found in the nature of the Greek city. To these citizens, their city was very different from those of earlier times and other places. Its "ethos," the spiritual atmosphere, was also different. It was not just a place where Greeks resided, but the framework and substance of their lives. It was a "way of life," clearly delineated and intensely shared. As such, it could not be divided into private associations and benefits, nor could it be submerged in a greater union. Each city had its own peculiar personality, expressed in its traditions, and in each the primary aim was that every citizen be raised to that city's standard of human excellence. Each city was both in ideal and substantially in fact a self-sufficient entity; citizens acknowledged no law, and resisted any power, transcending it. For the Greeks this was "political" life, and it represented freedom.

However different may be our experience, we can sense our Greek inheritance in attitudes we take toward government and its place in life, particularly when we maintain that government is the people's concern and that citizenship is morally significant. Clearly, the origin of this attitude is Greek; it was completely alien to any earlier civilization. Our political science is also a Greek inheritance. The interest and concern they felt for their political life eventually manifested itself in the study of laws and institutions, especially when they became aware of the diversity which their various cities had created. And when in crisis they became uncertain of their political values, the speculations that are the foundation of later political philosophy appeared. We shall treat some of these specific contributions further in later chapters, when they are relevant to the development of particular aspects of modern political life.

Roman Law and Institutions. The glory of Rome was its empire and its law. Both emerged within a republican constitution, further developing within an imperial constitution, and enduring as a whole close to nine hundred years. Rome's influence, both at that time and since, has been enormous. The explanation of their success—although perhaps for their ultimate failure as well—lies in the eminently practical approach the Romans took to their political problems. When confronted with the need to integrate the plebs into the political order they first created a new office, the plebeian tribunate, to give them protection and representation. Eventually plebeians were admitted to other offices of state, even to the consulate, the most exalted of all, but the plebeian tribunate remained. Similarly, assemblies were created in which they could share; these gradually became more important than earlier ones of more restricted membership, but did not eliminate them. The complex and often confusing pattern of institutions thus developed to meet immediate practical needs of the city, however, proved by the end of the second century B.C. no longer an effective government for Rome as an empire. After Julius Caesar, consequently, the office of emperor was superimposed on the institutions of the republic and generally dominated them.

Under both republic and empire, however, the particular Roman genius was manifested in the techniques devised to govern the far-flung dominions. Roman demands were generally quite limited—that peace and order be maintained, trade left free, and taxes paid. They could therefore permit local customs to stand and local leaders to continue in power to a considerable extent. To protect imperial interests, however, they developed and maintained a colonial administration of great effectiveness. Provincial governors, or proconsuls, of unusual competence and integrity, were dispatched throughout the empire. The justly renowned Roman armies were used not only to conquer new areas, but to maintain order. Their roads, designed to permit the mobility of their armies as well as to facilitate the flow of supplies to Rome, and their aqueducts and other public works, were incredible engineering achievements for the age.

One of the most cohesive forces of the empire, however, and one of its most enduring accomplishments, was the Roman law. As the city expanded into an empire the work of a special magistracy, the *praetor peregrinus* (law officer for aliens), in settling disputes involving noncitizens gave rise to a new body of law, the *jus gentium*. This systematization of standards common to many peoples throughout the empire came, through wide use, to create a measure of legal uniformity also among local customs. It maintained some measure of government under law even during the reign of the worst emperors, and after the barbarian conquests the Roman law was modified and partly discarded, but never destroyed. The traces of this law in local customs, and the rediscovery of its original rules in late medieval times, helped provide a foundation for whatever extensive political order was possible after the fall of the Roman empire. Meanwhile, the memory of that empire still inspires those who dream of a European or even a world order. Rome could bequeath this heritage because of the practical and thus potentially universal nature of its law, but it fell because it could not invent federal and representative political structures to match its creativeness in law and administration.

THE MEDIEVAL POLITICAL ORDER

The fall of the Roman empire was primarily the collapse of the great administrative system it had created. The idea of some sort of universal order did not vanish, however, nor was the legal order Rome had built up totally destroyed. Both were important elements in the feudal system, an extremely complex social and political order, which in time arose on the ruins of the empire. Furthermore, the medieval political order included an important role for the Roman Catholic Church, now freed from an earlier dependence upon the emperor and able to exercise a leading and unifying influence throughout the western part of the former empire.

The Feudal System. Despite the efforts of Charlemagne at the beginning of the ninth century, the leaders of the conquering tribes were able neither to preserve nor replace the unified governmental system of Rome. Thus, from roughly A.D. 500 to 1500 government in Europe was highly decentralized and divided. Community in the middle ages was for the most part, and for most people, extremely localized, and the manor—a village, in effect, dominated by its defensive walls and moat and by the living quarters of the "lord of the manor," and surrounded by agricultural and hunting lands—was the realm in which all but a few passed their entire lives. The lord was in practice the largely independent ruler of this domain; living upon the labor of his artisans and farmers, he in return maintained law and order among them—presumably according to the customs of the place—and protected them from external attack.

The manor was the basic unit of the feudal system, which comprised the relationships between diverse manorial lords in a hierarchical structure that came to include numerous kings and was capped by the "Roman" emperor. The relationships were of mutual service and protection, with the obligations consecrated in an oath of fealty. Although this feudal superstructure was of rather limited importance in medieval life as a whole, it did preserve some measure of broader social and political organization in an otherwise provincial age. Between the customary laws of the manor and the equally customary laws of feudal relationships the rights, duties, and authority of every person were identified. These were attached not to persons as such but to the positions they occupied in the hierarchy based on land ownership. Everyone had some position—even the serf, who had his customary rights within the manor and could not be expelled.

The Concept of Limited Government Emerges. Despite the evident limitations of this regime, which could provide only a minimal order even in fairly stable times, several aspects of it are notable. The feudal superstructure, in particular, was based to an unusual extent upon the supremacy of law, since in the absence of any overriding and unified governmental power, only law could define in any settled way the relationships among the various barons, counts, and kings. The system simply could not function without general acceptance of a common law. From this arises the most striking characteristic of medieval government —the stress placed in both thought and practice upon limited government, with its authority based upon law, and its power flowing from consent. This is the particular significance of the oath of fealty; in taking and in accepting it, both vassal and lord voluntarily entered into a relationship given in the law, and thus accepted both the rights and the duties of their respective positions. Ultimately, in feudalism's declining years, this same relationship was applied to the king and all his free subjects, and the idea that government flows from consent of the governed and is responsible under the law was passed on to the emerging modern community.

The Roman Church and Medieval Government. In the government and politics of medieval Europe, besides the manor and the feudal system, Christianity as organized in the Roman Catholic Church played an essential part. The Church, which had established considerable unity in doctrine and organization before the fall of the empire, survived and was for many years the sole power transcending tribe and village. Its hierarchy—from parish priests through bishops to the Pope in Rome—was more tightly organized than that of the feudal system at its best. Furthermore, few apart from its clergy were literate; the feudal lords were often dependent upon the Church for more than religion. Since this was a devout age, it is easy to understand how the Church was able to maintain and even extend its authority throughout the period. Evidence of this authority in political affairs is preserved in documents, including many admonitory letters from bishops to kings, which we have reason to believe were heeded. Also, such important aspects of life as marriage and inheritance were regulated primarily by the canon law of the Church, which maintained its own courts to enforce that law; the legal systems of central Europe still reflect this situation. In the medieval period, then, the Church was itself a central part of the governmental order, from the manor to the "Holy Roman Empire."

IV. *The* MODERN STATE

We have seen that the political order of medieval Europe was extremely complex, with governmental power decentralized and divided among various persons, groups, and orders, imperfectly organized among themselves. As an attempt to combine localism and universalism in both practice and ideal, the period is fruitful for political study. However, the tensions eventually proved too great, since governmental power largely depended upon agreements based on acceptance of customary arrangements for stability and effectiveness. Already in the twelfth century some of the more powerful feudal lords began to extend their dominions and to escape from the narrow feudal restrictions on their authority. By the seventeenth century the collapse of the medieval order was complete, at least in western Europe, and there had emerged the typical political organization of modern life, the "state." Consolidated where early established and extended continuously to new places over the centuries following, the dominance of the state form in political life is today unquestionable, although recently it has in turn been criticized as obsolete in modern circumstances.

THE NATURE OF THE STATE

Examples of the state are not hard to find; England and France have been thus organized for many hundreds of years, and the United States since 1789, at least. India, on the other hand, was not a state until recently. In contrast, the "states" of the American union, such as New York and Hawaii, are not states in the generic sense. Nevertheless, the term is somewhat ambiguous, and political orders are not easily classifiable. The reason for this is that the modern state is neither in theory nor in practice a logical concept, but a historical fact, and the complexities of historical development have produced in the state a political phenomenon that is extremely difficult to comprehend as a whole.

One can without difficulty, of course, identify some elementary and reasonably constant characteristics of the state. Political scientists have traditionally held as distinctive marks of the state the existence of an independent and unified government, effectively controlling a determinate population and territory. Thus, the modern state is distinguished from the overlapping jurisdictions and diverse legal rules of the middle ages by the unity and distinctness of its order, and from provinces, colonies, and dependent territories by its independence. In reality, though, boundary disputes, distinctions between citizens and noncitizen residents, and complications in governmental structure and power that seriously reduce unity, are so common that if these ideas were strictly applied, no states could be found. Furthermore, these ideas alone do not help us distinguish between the modern state and the city-state of ancient Greece, for example; failing to clarify the special ethos of the city-state, they cannot adequately describe it. To understand the complex phenomenon of the state we must consider its historical development.

Origins of the "State." Words describing types of political systems, such as kingdom, republic, and democracy, have been in use since antiquity, but the political order of which they are types has been known as the state, rather than the city, the commonwealth, or the empire, only for the last few centuries. The term appears in the writings of Machiavelli and his contemporaries around 1500, but even then the usage was not general. It is closely related to the words "status" and "estate," and was for many centuries used virtually synonymously with them, but it can also refer simply to any existing condition, as when we speak of the state of the weather or of one's health. These diverse usages are not unrelated and each contributes to the meaning of the political term. The modern order emerged out of the medieval, using its vocabulary and political relationships even while transforming them. Originally, a state, as a legal entity, was either an estate, a bundle of privileges and responsibilities, or the status of someone who possessed such an estate. In the feudal system, furthermore, many such estates in a hierarchical order distributed rights and duties in regard to valuable things among the population. Although the status of a king or emperor was superior in dignity to others it was not for that reason different in essence from that of commoner or baron; all were founded in customary law.

In the late middle ages, however, the more powerful lords succeeded in extending their dominions and increasing their power within them; in some areas the political order became more integrated. This development demanded greater unity and centralization of legal rights, responsibilities, and authority than the medieval order provided—a change in law and political thinking to accompany the changing power relationships. At first, quite naturally, the increasing power of the king gave to his status a significance all its own, becoming a majestic and special estate upon which that of all others seemed to depend. In this integration of the diffuse medieval political order the modern state was born, often identified with the person and position of the king. In seventeenth-century France Louis XIV is said to have exclaimed "L'état, c'est moi" (I am the state); the remark is fully characteristic of the early stage of the modern state's emergence.

Opposed to this appropriation of *the* state by the king, however, were those who insisted that the political order is founded not on mere power but on a common law, which is therefore superior to any estate or office, even that of the king. Actually, these were traditionalists seeking to preserve their customary privileges, but in attacking royal absolutism, they did give rise to the idea that the state is the community as a whole, manifested in its common law and in the agreement of all its ranks and orders. This perspective was largely dominant in England after the thirteenth century. In other developing states, such as France and Spain, it was advanced with less success; the state continued to be identified with the king alone until the popular revolutions of the eighteenth century and later.

These popular revolutions heralded still another pattern of the state, rejecting both the royalist conception and the traditionalist view of the state as law. It accepted the traditionalist idea of the political order as a community, but denied that a hereditary class structure is essential to that community. This view was held by those who were commoners in class and, often, individualists in philosophical perspective. Since individualism tends to deny any basic differences of interest or value among men in its assertion of freedom and equality, the community came to be seen not as a whole, or blending of different parts, but as a unity of like parts. This view of the state was expressed most radically in the French revolution, when the Abbé Sieyès insisted that the commons (third estate) is all. The state, then, is the organization of the commons to promote their common interests.

Different Concepts of the State. From this cursory historical discussion three quite different conceptions of the state emerge. Each presupposes a highly unified political order—although not necessarily or even generally the integration of the social order into it—but they differ as to who or what serves as the core of that unity. The state appears, in one view, as a legal order, within which the diverse parts of the community are politically related. From a second perspective, the state is the supreme power and authority of the king, or the government; by simple extension we may also see the state as the political means through which a dominant class or other group rules the rest of the community. Third, it is seen as an association through which common purposes are promoted among a community of equals. Each of these has been advanced as the "true" conception, with the others rejected as errors or historical anachronisms. This may be convenient for partisan purposes, but not for those of political science. Here, we must reject oversimplifications, and the historical phenomenon has in fact been too greatly affected by all three perspectives to be adequately described solely in terms of one. All three conceptions are reflected in the reality of the modern state.

If the state manifests all these different orders and powers, however, we face an apparent dilemma. It hardly appears possible that both law and supreme power could be the basis of the state, for example, or that the idea of the state as a co-operative association of equal men is reconcilable with the dominant power of a man or class. However, we must emphasize again that political associations are not logical but historical facts, and involve subtleties overriding logic. Created by men over very long periods of time, political institutions necessarily reflect the various objectives men have sought to realize through political life and the equally various conditions within which they have had to work. In our actual experience, power is usually supported by some legal and institutional base, but someone at some time had to create it; co-operation even among equals is generally impossible without some sort of authoritative leadership that may have its element of selfish domination. Political systems are consequently always complex, and tend in time to become more rather than less difficult to comprehend.

Any very concrete and specific definition of the state, then, will highlight some aspect of particular and immediate importance, but is not likely to catch all its facets. If we are concerned with international relations, for example, our definition would stress the state's independence and its capacity for relations with other states. If we are interested in effective policing, we would emphasize the superiority of the ruling man or men and assert the importance of adequate coercive power. If stable and harmonious relations seem of particular import, we would likely find in the rule of law the essential nature of the state. And if we feel that the activity of the state should reflect the needs and objectives of the citizenry we would stress, as did Aristotle, that politics is the common life of free men. Any particular state will manifest all these to some degree, but certain features will be predominant according to its particular historical circumstances.

The State as a Sovereign Legal Order. Despite its complexity, however, the modern state does possess some distinctive characteristics. Remember that the modern state arose in a revolutionary age, in which the complex and customary order of the middle ages was destroyed in the movements known as the Reformation, the Renaissance, the commercial revolution, and the "age of discovery" both in science and territorial exploration. Western culture was radically transformed—the means of power no less than the ends toward which they were employed. The severe reduction of customary and religious sanctions in political life, together with a great expansion of the sorts of values that men sought to realize—sometimes directly through politics but more often outside it, yet requiring some sort of political support—made necessary a fundamental transformation of the political order and of the organization and powers of government. The new character of political power may be summed up in the term "sovereignty"—basically the ultimate authority of some person or group to make law, unlimited either by customary law and rights or by any foreign lawmaking authority.

Early modern times, when the idea emerged, have with good reason been known as the "age of absolutism." Emphasis was placed on the absolute authority of rulers, tempered by appeals to their benevolence or enlightenment, as the only way anachronistic survivals of the feudal regime could be eliminated. However, no state since, whether monarchical, oligarchic, or democratic, has been able completely to escape at least a tinge of the absolutism—the potentially irresponsible power—inherent in its foundation. The reason, simply, is that change and innovation in the modern community limit the possibility of stable and precise standards to which any sort of government can be held responsible. Jefferson's assertion that "nothing is unchangeable but the inherent and inalienable rights of man" is illuminating, for no specific laws and public policies flow with universal and enduring necessity from rights thus considered. Not only as a founding but as a continuing aspect, therefore, the modern political order in some manner contains the power of sovereignty, whether in the person of a king or dictator or in the democratic but vaguer form of "popular sovereignty." It is as inextricably involved in modern political life as the idea of individual free will is in modern social life, though neither is easily defined.

The modern state, then, represents an attempt to maintain an effective, integrating order in a relatively large and dynamic community through the establishment of centralized control. In this process "Machiavellianism" plays its part, but other factors are equally essential. Such an order can never be created and maintained by despotic power alone; more fundamental support is provided by nationalism, and by constitutional and democratic practices and principles. Constitutional law, even though it be little more than a dynastic tradition, helps by furnishing a stable basis for the exercise of political power; even sovereignty presupposes some foundation so that the sovereign power can be recognized. In the modern community, moreover, with its extensive political objectives and disparate forces requiring co-ordination, an effective constitutional order must reflect the felt needs and opinions of many. Therefore, the modern state tends to be democratic, or at least popular, and to rest upon the unifying sentiment of nationalism.

THE STATE AND THE NATION

Nationalism has been, during the last two centuries, one of the most potent political forces the world has ever known. It has been so closely associated with political developments that we often speak of the modern state as the "nation-state," meaning that its citizens possess a common nationality, as though that were the only appropriate and true form. Although there is no necessary relationship between nations and states—nations have existed independently of any political embodiment and states have been formed with multinational populations—an empirical relationship in recent history can hardly be denied. From England and France in earlier days to the peoples of Asia, Africa, and the Middle East today, nationalistic sentiments have led men to destroy traditional orders, multinational states, and colonial regimes; to build new states on the ruins of these; and greatly to increase political power in the process.

Nationalism. If the power and effects of nationalism are self-evident, however, the precise nature of the "nation" is not. Only rarely are nations provided by nature, like trees and mountains. Broadly speaking, a nation is a body of people of common ethnic origin, language, and historical experience. But these factors create nationalistic sentiments only if men consider them important, which has not always been the case. Furthermore, men possessed by a nationalistic spirit have altered languages, customs, and their interpretations of history to suit their needs. Clearly, nationalism is primarily a sense of a common life and destiny, to which the facts of the past, and sometimes even the present, are subordinate. A nation, then, is the body of people who share that sense of common life—or those who nationalistic leaders think ought to share it, for nationalism is as often a nation-creating force, initially elitist, as it is simple recognition of an existing nation. It does seem, therefore, that nations are constructions of the human imagination, springing from and limited by the fact that men do always live in particular communities and manifest a natural ethnocentrism, or attachment to those communities and separateness from all that is alien.

Nationalism, as distinct from tribal or civic loyalties, is a fairly recent development. Its beginnings may be found in late medieval England and France, when the common people began to support kings against foreigners, including Emperor and Pope. But the predominant character of those centuries was their parochialism, tempered with a measure of cosmopolitanism; it was primarily in the French and American revolutions at the end of the eighteenth century, and in reactions to the threat they posed to established orders abroad, that nationalism as we know it emerged. Initially it was reflected in quite moderate form as love of a traditional way of life and desire for independence, as by Edmund Burke in England, von Herder in Germany, and George Washington in America. But nationalism soon acquired a different face, manifesting not a traditional way of life but a more abstract idea, as when Paine wrote in *Common Sense* that "a government of our own is our natural right."

Paine's view flowered in the French revolution. In seeking "liberty, equality, and fraternity" against traditions that denied this ideal, the revolution not only overthrew a government but transformed society. In the ensuing struggles the French were driven to a deeper sense of their national community. In the process, however, "liberty, equality, and fraternity" became less a universal philosophy than a symbol of France, a focus for French loyalty. In reaction, after French armies began to march in "defense" of the revolution, nationalistic sentiments emerged in central and southern Europe, and became more intense in England.

Sometimes these agreed with the revolutionary ideology and sometimes they did not, but they always expressed the increasing awareness of more and more people of their cultural differences, similarities, and potentialities. The effect of the Russian and Chinese communist revolutions in this century has been similar, stimulating nationalism in those countries and elsewhere, either in acceptance of Marxism as an answer to "imperialism" or in rejection of it as a new form of the same thing. Evidently the ideas of nationalist movements are largely reflections of circumstances. In all cases, however, they are popular movements, and nationalism will often be served by any idea or revolutionary activity that brings to political consciousness and action people who previously manifested little of either.

The Political Effects of Nationalism. Strictly speaking, the state is a political and legal association, membership in which entails subjection to its law, enjoyment of the rights that law provides, and sharing in its objectives. It creates bonds that may be completely independent of any physiological, sociological, or psychological characteristics of its population, as might describe a nation. Nevertheless, it is quite likely that the great political realms of the modern world could not have come into existence, or continue, without the particular form of communal loyalty called nationalism. The state alone could never arrogate the power men have freely granted to the nation-state. General military conscription appeared for the first time, for example, in the French revolution, and for the first time in American history in the civil war. Seeing in the nation-state "a government of our own" they have given it extensive functions and powers, which neither custom nor colder calculation might have supported, but which the intense and far-flung co-operation of modern life seems to demand. That the modern state must in practice be a regime based on common appeal and support has been recognized even by modern dictators who, since Napoleon III in mid-nineteenth-century France, have been of the people in dress, speech, and action. They have presented themselves as leaders of the masses, and have sought expressions of popular support—however contrived—through plebiscites and mass demonstrations, and their policies generally catered to popular prejudices.

Nationalism has not necessarily furthered political stability, however. Because of nationalistic sentiments, and regardless of other considerations, the number of independent states has multiplied enormously in recent years. Given the vagueness of the term "nation," it is difficult to know either where this development might end or to what nation any particular group of people might belong. Therefore, wherever national orders and their political organization can be a matter of dispute, as it is throughout most of the world even today, nationalism is revolutionary and promotes instability. In many instances, also, it introduces into political life the cultural animosities and pride that accentuate conflicts among states; the bitterness and frequency of warfare in this century may fairly be laid to nationalism. Furthermore, in seeking economic and military security nationalists have frequently fostered irrational economic policies and threatened the liberal individualistic values of our civilization. However one may evaluate its effects, nevertheless, nationalism has truly revolutionized political life by rooting it in a mass support it never before possessed; this support to the nation-state today shows few signs of waning.

THE FUTURE OF THE STATE

The nation-state is clearly the principal organization of political power and loyalty in the world today as for some time past, but this is no guarantee of its future. Like any historical phenomena, political orders appear, change, and disappear as they reflect prevailing needs. That some political order, or at least government, must exist implies nothing as to the exact form it will take. The seeds of change are already present in contemporary politics, the great achievements of the modern state having themselves produced new circumstances conducive to change. These are manifested in two quite different criticisms of the adequacy of the state form to provide for the political life and problems of the twentieth century. We must take these seriously, since however limited their present influence, they undoubtedly reflect a continuing and even accelerating trend in world politics. We may be reasonably sure that the dominant political structure of the next century will not be identical to that of today; to claim more than this would be to prophesy, however, and that is not the role of political science.

Challenges to the State. The state has been challenged in its domestic, or internal, jurisdiction. Jurists, ethical philosophers, and scientists investigating political practice have whittled away at the concept of sovereignty until it seems but a shadow of its former self. Many such scholars have declared that in both practice and ideal the role of government is merely one of mediation or arbitration, limited to the reconciliation of groups in conflict. The integrated and dominant authority of government basic to the state has been declared by some to be only a myth, despite the apparent reality of legal and political formulas; others have admitted its existence but denied its legitimacy. The argument, although often overdrawn, does seem to be valid in application to many of the more settled and mature western states, where the political order requires only limited government to maintain it. Whether this will continue to be so, and whether it will come to be so for new non-western states after a time, remains to be seen. Perhaps the state is but a transitional form of governmental organization; having served as the instrument for the reorganization of communities into the modern political order, it may then yield to a more diffuse and less coercive governmental system. Nevertheless, even in the United States, increasing dependence on government and the rise of strident nationalism suggest a trend that does not encourage either an easy optimism or facile judgment as to this possibility.

The state has also been challenged on the plane of world order and international relations. Change seems certain in face of ever-increasing economic and military interdependence and the threat of devastating warfare. As an alternative to potential anarchy, a "world-state" is often proposed, but the term seems scarcely appropriate. For the world as a whole there is at present little sign of the common law, centralized power, and developed sense of community sufficient to support the highly integrated political order called the state. Legal and ethical systems remain too diverse—in some instances even contrary—to permit more than a loose international political order. The existing power structure—involving the conflict between the communist and non-communist states as well as conflicts within those "blocs" and problems of relationships with the "non-aligned"—not only inhibits the development of a "world-state" but even interferes with the effective operation of loose international arrangements. And disparities in economic and social conditions in North America, Europe, Latin America, Africa, and Asia, are greater than have ever been found within an established or even nascent state.

Clearly, the difficulties in the way of creating an effective international order are great; the appearance of a "world-state" in the near future is highly unlikely. Yet despite understandable skepticism, we must not forget that the states we know arose out of somewhat similar conditions of diversity in the late medieval period. Furthermore, as the great feudal nobles struggled for leadership in the increasing chaos of that period, so do the greater nations of today endeavor to shape the course of history not only for themselves but for the entire world. Movements but dimly understood either by participants or observers are advancing in the world, and no one can foresee their denouement in the decades and centuries ahead. If no "world-state" is in the offing, regional and general international organizations are actually present and of constantly increasing significance. Some effective political order substantially different and broader than the states and international order of recent times will likely emerge.

The Nation-State Remains Dominant. The basic structure of political order remains the state, however, despite continual modifications in its activities, powers, and organization. Furthermore, tomorrow's order will evolve out of this order, as did the state out of its medieval and ancient predecessors; revolutionary change appears more abrupt and radical than it really is. We may well move to a new order in time through a gradual transition that is largely a shift in emphasis. The present reality of politics must be our principal concern, therefore, and our analysis must focus on the political life of the highly developed modern states.

CHAPTER 3

DEMOCRACY *in* *the* MODERN WORLD

GOVERNMENT of the people, by the people, for the people"—these words of Abraham Lincoln are undoubtedly the classic definition of democracy. As a symbol of democracy the phrase is unchallengeable, for in it the meaning and quality of this form of government are beautifully expressed. What it tells us about democracy, however, depends on how we read it. In the political context, what does "government" mean, who are "the people," and what can it mean to say that government is "of," "by," and "for" them? These questions must be considered if we are to understand democracy, the ways it can be realized, and its value.

These are not easy questions to answer today. Most political thinkers now recognize that democracy is neither as simple nor as inevitable as many thought but a few generations ago. Rather, it is extremely complex, and its realization depends both upon an understanding of it and a determination to establish and preserve it against its far-too-frequent enemies within and without. More often than democrats have liked to think, it is also contingent upon favorable circumstances that are, immediately anyway, largely matters of historical accident. Democracy is not always a practical possibility. In no way, then, can we afford these days to be complacent about democracy. In a world rapidly changing and torn by conflict, careful thought alone will enable us to distinguish what it is from what it is not.

I. *The* MEANING *of* DEMOCRACY

Throughout the world in the twentieth century the term "democracy" has become a strong and favorable symbol, an honorific or "hurrah" word. It has come to be so tied to the aspirations of most of the world's population that practically no political leader anywhere dares reject its label. A brilliant but politically irresponsible Bernard Shaw could quip that democracy is a form of government enabling the people to be as badly governed as they want to be, and H. L. Mencken could find democracy contemptible as government but good entertainment. This was several decades ago, however; today even an outright literary condemnation of democracy is hard to find.

Even Dictators Claim to Be Democrats. Political leaders, on the other hand, have been more circumspect for many years. The regimes of Mussolini and Hitler before World War II quite obviously had little in common with democracy, being based firmly upon the leadership of small, elite groups. Even so, both Hitler and Mussolini fostered demonstrations of mass support and produced any evidence they could that the German and Italian peoples consented to the Nazi and Fascist regimes. The Nazis organized "elections" in which virtually unanimous support of Hitler was manifested; of course, the voters had no choice. And Mussolini, criticizing the individualistic and "vulgar" democracy of the liberals, tried to save the term for his collectivist regime of discipline by writing that "if democracy means not to relegate the people to the periphery of the State, then Fascism could be defined as an 'organized, centralized, authoritarian democracy.' " The communists have appropriated the term even more energetically. Government by the party representing the working classes and in their interests, they have insisted, is the only "true" democracy, and since World War II "people's democracies" have been appearing in the wake of communist seizures of power. As these are as different from the regimes of the traditional democracies as the fascist systems, we may wonder if the French diplomat Talleyrand was not right when he said that language was given to man so that he could conceal his thoughts!

This almost universal attempt to appropriate the term "democracy" may well be rooted in the fact that all modern governments are popular in a sense. They overwhelmingly reflect the breakdown of narrow traditions, the rise of increasingly far-ranging interests among ever larger numbers of people, and the concomitant development of broader means of communication and of mass education. Modern governments are not dealing primarily with peasants, rooted in age-old ways, and where they do they must transform them, for the goals of modern governments cannot be realized without a fairly active co-operation of great numbers of people. Political leaders, therefore, cannot forego at least some of the "stage props" of democracy, and the policies they advocate must have some relation to the felt needs of peoples who have come to a political consciousness quite new in history.

Nevertheless, distinctions among governments must be made. There is no reason for assuming that all modern governments are democratic, even all those claiming to be so. Democracy is not a term that covers all modern virtues or vices; it has acquired some distinctive meaning through its use in western political history, and we should be as clear as we can about what that meaning is.

A Preliminary View of Democracy. The word "democracy," like many of our political terms, came to us from ancient Greece, where it meant the power or rule of the *demos,* or people, in the sense of the entire body of citizens. This group was quite limited and did not include women, children, resident aliens, and slaves (even in Athens, the model democracy, citizens comprised only about one-tenth of the population). However, in comparison with other types of regimes, democracy early acquired the connotation of a broad, popular participation in government. "The whole people, in parity of service, is our king," sang Euripides, the dramatist; and Pericles, the greatest of Athenian statesmen, declared that "We are called a democracy because the government is in the hands of the many, not the few." In the broadest sense, democracy still means popular self-government, but conditions have so changed that democracy is very different today from what it was for the Greeks.

The Greek *polis* was a small community, intensely united in the law and common affairs of the citizens. Rarely was anything else as important to the citizen, whether quite ordinary or highly distinguished, as the

ABOVE: "The Greek city . . . was not just a place where Greeks resided, but the framework and substance of their lives." (p. 63) The painting is an idealized portrayal of an Athenian civic assembly being addressed by Pericles, greatest of its statesmen, possibly about the decoration of the Acropolis in the background. (*The Bettman Archive.*) BELOW: "Community in the middle ages was . . . the manor —a village, in effect, dominated by its defensive walls and moat and by the living quarters of the 'lord of the manor.' " (p. 65) The Château of Saumur in the province of Anjou, at vintage time (*circa* 1400), painted for the September page of the "Très riches heures du duc de Berry." (*The New York Public Library.*)

ABOVE: "The problem of democracy is not ordinarily how to enable the majority of the people to govern or direct government, but rather how to develop governments that can and must win and retain the support of popular majorities. . . ." (p. 96) A traditional open-air political meeting at Yarra Bank, Melbourne, Australia. (*Australian News and Information Bureau.*) BELOW: "Totalitarianism may meet some contemporary problems, but often inefficiently and always at the cost of many of the leading values and achievements of western civilization. . . ." (p. 50) In a Red Chinese commune near Peking, peasants labor on the collectivized land. Rifles are issued, without ammunition, for intervals of military drill. (*Henri Cartier-Bresson—Magnum.*)

opportunities and responsibilities of public life. These opportunities, however, were not rights facilitating the pursuit of private objectives nor were the responsibilities extraordinary duties imposed by an unfortunate necessity. They constituted in themselves a "way of life" that to the Greeks was superior to any other; they found satisfaction and glory in public service and controversy in a way that we can hardly comprehend today. Citizens conducted their private activities, of course, but they also served in the army or navy, and in democracies debated and voted in the popular assembly, argued or sat in the courts, and served as magistrates and councilors. It has been estimated that on any particular day one out of every six Athenians was engaged in such service, and it is likely that the rest spent no small part of their time vigorously discussing the affairs of the city in the street, market, or gymnasium. If such opportunities are to comprise a satisfying way of life in themselves, however, and the rather demanding responsibilities adequately met, citizenship must not be diluted. Even in democracies, Greek citizens were an elite group, small in number and presumed to possess special qualifications.

Such a political life has little in common with our experience today. The political activities of the modern democratic citizen are rather modest in comparison with those of his Greek forebear and, on the whole, he would not desire such an intensely personal and demanding citizenship. To modern man politics is not a way of life, much less the supreme way; it is an important but specialized aspect of life in which we utilize many means to our ends. The relation of politics to the diversified values and acts that make life worth living today is much less direct than it was for the Greeks.

Naturally, then, democracy is no longer meaningful in the same way, or as likely to be practiced in the same way. Politics today is a specialized function in the community, and we are less inclined to "direct democracy," the immediate and constant participation of all citizens in government. Government by democratically elected representatives is more appropriate, not only because of the great size of modern states, but also because it is more compatible with the modern idea of government as a public servant—an idea which Greek democrats could hardly have comprehended. When we as citizens intervene in government, even through direct policy decision in initiatives and referendums, it is not usually for the sake of political action itself but essentially to compel "them" to do what "we" wish.

Since all political terms are somewhat ambiguous, however, the word "democracy" has been used as a symbol for all good things. It is frequently spoken of as a "way of life," although even to the Greeks it was citizenship that was a way of life and democratic citizenship only one, if perhaps the highest, form of it. Viewing democracy as a "way of life" has naturally led to psychological theories concerning the "democratic personality," which contrasts with the "authoritarian personality" in being open, adaptable, imaginative, and friendly. Likewise the term "economic democracy" has become current in recent decades, meaning, apparently, an economy favorable to the workers rather than one controlled by and for the benefit of the few.

Democracy Is a Political Term. These phrases introduce such variable factors into the discussion that it is impossible to attain any clear idea of what is being talked about. No one knows with any certainty, in today's complex communities, how personality types, economic and other social processes, and the forms and patterns of political life are related, or if any particular personality type or economic order is either required of or created by political democracy as such. Obviously some relationship exists; the actual working of any political system will both affect and be affected by the psychological and social conditions prevailing, but this fact should enter into a consideration of democracy only at the level of examining what its possibilities and implications might be in any given time and place. It is important to consider such practical and variable qualifications on democracy—much as friction must be considered in dealing practically with gravity in physics—but the qualifications should not be confused with the central phenomenon.

At the other extreme, democracy is not simply another word for equality, or freedom, or brotherhood. These more general terms can, after all, stand by themselves; democracy can reasonably be viewed as embodying their application in the realm of politics, but neither freedom, nor equality, nor brotherhood are likely to be quite the same thing in state, church, factory, or family. A broad philosophical discussion of these values would be useful but, at best, only the beginning of political science, which must deal explicitly with their meaning in the realm of politics, and how they may be furthered therein as well as limited. Apart from philosophical treatises, and often not even there, values do not exist in a vacuum. They are embedded in behavior, and our most cherished and established values are manifested in those stable and widely recognized patterns of behavior that we call institutions. They give meaning to those institutions, but also derive from them a concreteness and reality they could not otherwise possess.

Consequently it is to government, and its interrelated values and institutions, that the political scientist looks in order to develop his specialized definitions. The values underlying democracy, as the French put it long ago, are liberty, equality, and fraternity; a conception of democracy must include some indication of how these terms are meaningful in relation to how government is organized and operated, what it does and why, and the consequences of its policies. More immediately, however, government of, by, and for the people must be discussed in terms of institutions that enable a people subject to a government to control and influence it in a reasonably continuing and effective manner. Interpreted according to the ideals of freedom and equality, this gives us the only universal meaning of democracy compatible with consistent usage. Once one leaves this level of abstraction, however, any apparent simplicity quickly vanishes.

II. PATTERNS *of* MODERN DEMOCRACY

Democracy is government controlled by its citizens. Rather clearly, democratic government rests upon the consent of the governed, and the use of coercion, or its threat, is minimal. These characteristics, though generally present, are not limited to democracy, however. Many governments clearly not democratic, but also depending only in part on coercion and considered legitimate by their subjects, have existed in history. Furthermore, democracies have occasionally used coercion to maintain values with an effectiveness that many an absolute monarch could envy. The distinctive qualities of democracy lie rather in those special techniques used to organize government, which maximize consent and minimize coercion, and in a particular attitude toward men and their communities underlying and justifying these techniques. These may be indicated broadly, to start with, through comparing democratic and non-democratic ideas about the community and the place of government in it. In modern political life, however, these qualities have developed some originally unsuspected complexities, so that democracy itself may be best illustrated through presenting two versions of it.

DEMOCRATIC AND NONDEMOCRATIC POLITICS COMPARED

An early and poignant discussion of the issues dividing democrats from their opponents took place in seventeenth-century England, when the parliamentary army under Oliver Cromwell was deciding what to do with the power it had gained through the defeat of the royalists. In the Putney debates members of a movement known as the Levellers protested against continuing the tradition of reserving suffrage to those with a substantial landed estate. They also demanded regular and frequent elections, to prevent the parliament from assuming political authority independent of the people it represented. To them, the function of government was to make laws, and laws govern people, not property. That property rights were legitimate they did not deny, but they did not see why this must give property owners any special political privileges. They particularly rejected the idea that political privileges were themselves a form of property to which their holders had any legitimate title. As one of them, Colonel Thomas Rainboro, put it, "The poorest he that is in England hath a life to live as the greatest he," and ought to have a voice in choosing any government which would regulate that life.

As reasonable as this argument may seem to us today, to Cromwell and, indeed, to most men of that time the position taken by the Levellers was highly original and hardly comprehensible. The democrats, in advocating that political authority flowed from persons as such and should not deny their inherent rights, were dealing as far as these conservatives could see in hopeless abstractions, upon which no orderly community could be built. In any practically important sense, and certainly as far as government was concerned, they felt that "man as such" was far less relevant than whether the man was English, French, or Chinese. In political life, a man must be defined in terms of the community to which he belongs, for a community is not just a name but a tradition, a set of customs, and the values and rights established in them. No person can be said to have created his community, nor does it depend for its legitimacy upon his consent to it; rather, the customary interests, rights, and duties demand the loyalty of Englishmen if their whole way of life is not to dissolve into chaos.

Cromwell, in fact, had just led an army against a king who attempted to usurp privileges that were not in custom his, and was hardly about to accept an argument that would generally sweep away all customary distinctions, so that one could no longer know who had a right to do what, either in private or in public life. For both public and private rights derived from the same source, the customs of England, and expressed in fact the inherent qualities of human life in that place. Cromwell could not avoid the feeling that those who questioned the customary rights of Englishmen probably also lacked a firm attachment to the values of English society and could not be depended upon to defend them. He was right, of course, but the Levellers were not the only spokesmen for revolutionary forces that were radically transforming English life. Many were working through the very customary privileges Cromwell defended; as, for example, those who also insisted on the rights and privileges of property, but interpreted them in an individualistic and capitalistic rather than in a feudal manner. These were as opposed as the traditionalists to the radical political ideas of the Levellers, whose impact on British politics was consequently small.

The Traditional View of Community. We see, then, that there are at least two ways here of understanding the human community, its members, and the foundation and responsibilities of its government. The traditional view—at least before democracy became a tradition—and one that has appeared in various guises in criticism of democracy throughout the years stresses the order, structure, and hierarchy of interests that the community exhibits. It is not persons as such that count, but the role they play in social life and the rights inherent in or necessary to that role. No one has any rights except as they flow from his social position, and since persons necessarily occupy quite different positions, fulfill different functions, and possess different responsibilities, they cannot possess the same rights. The more highly developed a community is, in fact, the more diversified and specialized will these responsibilities and their attendant rights become.

The political order being part of the community, these ideas are naturally applied to government as well. Only some of these responsibilities require participation in or direct control over the government, and only those trained in the exercise of such responsibilities are capable of a proper and effective use of that political power. This may be so because the political order pursues highly esoteric and demanding ends, as in the Greek *polis*. Moral development through intense political activity could be immediately meaningful only to a small group of citizens; women, children, and slaves would find their improvement in private relationships with citizens. But, in a way more appropriate to modern political life, restricted citizenship may be justified by observing that government pursues quite specialized ends, regarding which not all persons have an equal and informed concern. Government does not regulate man as man, but man only in certain social activities. It promotes some, but not all, human values, and similarly enforces only some social responsibilities. Those interests with which government is not concerned have other media for their expression and promotion—the church, for example, and the family. Only properly political interests should have a voice in government.

Until recently the ownership of real property has been the principal evidence of political interest and capacity. But payment of taxes, nationality, sex, race, religion, education, social class, and family headship have also been presumed social characteristics sufficiently important to justify differences in a man's share of political life in various western countries during the last few centuries. The middle classes were generally excluded from full citizenship in Britain until 1832, and the working classes for yet another five decades. Similarly, women had only limited political rights anywhere until well into this century.

In Belgium between 1893 and 1921, and in Great Britain until as recently as 1948, universal suffrage was to a degree qualified by "plural voting." A Belgian elector who was head of a family, possessed savings, or had sufficient education, received additional votes, and in Britain university graduates and owners of property outside the constituency of their residence were similarly favored. Again, in Britain, the special power exercised by the aristocracy through a House of Lords, almost equal to the popularly elected House of Commons, was not curbed until 1911. Social class, with a reverse twist, was made the condition of citizenship by the communists. After the Russian revolution, members of the old "exploiting" classes were denied political rights, which were reserved for the working class and its sympathizers, as supporters of the revolution.

Quite often, too, special political privileges are acquired by those accepting certain doctrines and the discipline of a party advocating them. Thus, members of the party have exceptional power in communist regimes as did members of the Puritan churches in early New England. Advocates of "technocracy" have demanded such special position for scientists and managers. These arguments (and actual arrangements) have in common the assumption that the social characteristics, interests, and capacities of men which distinguish one from another are alone relevant in government, and the proper ground of political rights.

The Democratic View of Community. In the democratic view, on the other hand, a community is primarily one of persons and only incidentally one of such special characteristics. Men undeniably have interests and perform activities which must be harmonized, organized, controlled, and promoted, and in this process government plays an important part. Nevertheless, those interests and activities have no meaning or value in themselves, nor do any of the other distinctions of status, possessions, class, or skills on which nondemocratic regimes have been founded. If they have any value, it is in that they are good for people; and if they have any meaning, it is in how they are so. People alone count, therefore; men are first of all men, and only secondarily are they rich men or poor men, nobles or commoners, philosophers or fools. Their political concerns, as their lives more generally, transcend differences of wealth, education, family connections and the like. Their political concerns will be adequately met only if citizenship is independent of such distinctions, if political rights attach to persons in virtue of their humanity alone.

Unlike interests or social position, however, humanity is something we all have equally in common. There is, at this level at least, no adequate reason for discriminating between persons. If people are different, how does one decide which is the more perfectly human? In no community, therefore, are there any "natural" superiors and inferiors, either of race, class, or profession. With no person having either greater or lesser claim to political rights than any other, citizenship must be universal and equal. Each man to count for one, and no man for more than one, is the logical conclusion of this argument. This idea is clearly fundamental to the democratic outlook, but when we turn to practical applications, difficulties appear. Man as such is an abstraction, and actual politics is not simply a matter of common humanity. People are involved in political life according to specific interests, which are always diverse to some extent, and it is the nature of these interests and conflicts between them that shape the "how" and "what" of politics. In short, a useful conception of democracy must indicate how the ideal of the equality of persons is actually expressed in political processes. Unfortunately, there is no universal pattern in either democratic practice or thought, but some order can be introduced if we consider two basic versions, or models, of democracy.

Basic Models of Democracy. These two versions of democracy, one of which we shall call "populistic democracy" and the other "liberal democracy," are not descriptions of any actual democratic regimes, nor does any regime necessarily fall clearly into one category or the other. The "models" serve the same purpose as the conception of political order developed in the preceding chapter—to direct attention to what is relevant to the discussion and furnish standards for appraisals. They help us identify and understand the democratic elements in any regime. We never simply experience "democracy," but many particular events that must be organized and simplified. Symbols, stereotypes, and prejudices help us to do this, and are therefore a normal and essential aspect of human life. Our task is to clarify these through imaginative and disciplined reflection on our experience—vicarious and immediate—seeking conceptions adequate to both cognitive and practical needs.

Ideally, one universally valid model is our objective. Unfortunately, any single model either ignores some of the facts or fails for excessive vagueness; history provides too many ideas and practices that are compatible with the democratic view of community but not always with one another. For the moment, anyway, it would appear that we can "capture" democracy only ambivalently, through using two models. Both have traditionally had an important place in political thinking and at least some practical embodiment. Which model is better is less a matter of which is true or false than of which is more useful, enabling us to deal effectively with particular problems. Actually, it is not entirely a matter of choosing between them; they both illuminate the complex phenomenon of modern democracy, but from different perspectives. These rather crude approximations should be used with care and sophistication in any event. We think that "liberal democracy" is more appropriate to the realities and values of modern communities, and believe it to be the sounder model. Yet "populistic democracy," though oversimplified and generally unrealistic, still conveys in sharp relief the central ideas of democracy, and appeals strongly to those not caught up in, or in rebellion against, the complexities of technological and individualistic civilization.

POPULISTIC DEMOCRACY

The populistic model of democracy is a simple one; its complexities arise solely in practical application. Its principal characteristic is an unqualified insistence that the larger number of persons in a community should conclusively determine what government does. Such majoritarianism, or majority rule, is viewed as *the* political technique realizing universal and equal citizenship, and any restrictions on it are considered to be equally limitations on democracy. To understand why and how majority rule occupies this central and dominating position in populistic democratic thinking it is necessary, first, to examine more thoroughly the idea of political equality and the historical context in which it emerged. We can then examine the relevance and adequacy of such ideas of political equality and majority rule in contemporary conditions.

Equal Treatment for All. The idea of political equality is not only asserted unequivocally but is understood in its simplest, most obvious sense. It is based, first of all, on the conviction that all men ought to be treated equally. This idea has very deep roots in the western tradition, which early asserted the equality of all men before God, before the law, and before reason. Men gradually became accustomed, thus, to considering themselves as equals within any political system that was rational, lawful, and according to God's will. During most of our history emphasis was laid rather on the rational and ethical aspects of social order than on whether men were equal in any immediate sense. After the fourteenth century, however, existing inequalities gradually lost their age-old justification in prevailing and generally accepted customs and religious doctrines, so that men began increasingly to wonder, "when Adam delved and Eve span, who was then a gentleman?" Inequalities, especially those of status and special privilege, which common experience could no longer understand and justify, were seen not as rooted in human nature and the conditions of human life but as illegitimate impositions for the benefit of a few.

The claim to political equality also found support in the developing conviction that men not only ought to be treated equally but were in fact equal and alike, both as to their basic rights and in their capacities to contribute to the common good. Early modern social thinking increasingly found unjustifiable not only traditional discriminations but any substantial distinctions among men. Special privileges result from accepting social life as a diversified and hierarchical pattern of values, needs, and abilities. The ideal of modern society, however, was to be one of the common, or unprivileged man, and of the values, needs, and abilities he shared with his fellows. Equal rights rather than special privileges, consequently, must be its foundation. The common man was the sole ultimate judge of whether law and public policy promoted the common good, for the simple reason that it was his good, and that of others like him, and it was taken for granted that he knew his own interest.

In principle, of course, the common man does not have, and can live without, special privileges. Common men could be any and all men. In practice, however, the struggle for democracy has often taken the form of class conflicts, generating animosities quite at variance with the high ideals of equality and the common life. For, in reality, the common man has not been merely an unprivileged man, but has had a distinctive way of life. Where and when democracy appeared, this common life, usually simple and highly traditional, was shared by many in a way that the highly differentiated values and interests of privileged orders cannot be. The rise of the ideals of equality and democracy has been accompanied by the assumption that this popularly shared way of life should be shared by all, or at least be the dominant way of life in the community. Naturally, privileged groups have been loath to give up the special personal, family, and class identities sustained by their privileges in favor of a rather anonymous membership in "the people" at large. Conflict resulted, then, not entirely over equality as such, but also over the way of life which the establishment of equality would maintain. Democrats themselves fell out over whether equality was to be realized in individualistic diversity or collectivistic uniformity, and the resulting ambiguity and tensions are far from resolved in contemporary democratic regimes.

Political Equality and Majority Rule. Within the framework of populistic democratic thought, then, political equality is expected to lead to government from which any inequalities of influence or benefit have been removed. This is the ideal. A political system is no better, however, than the institutions in which it can be embodied, and this democratic ideal is particularly hard to implement. Only when decisions are made through unanimous agreement would none be discriminated against and the decision be truly a common one. Some conceptions of democracy have, indeed, envisioned this. Taking their cue from such groups as the Quakers, who make decisions following the "sense of the meeting," these populists have assumed that men can arrive at unanimity.

Unfortunately, history gives us few examples to support such optimism, except in small groups of like-minded men. Unanimity is not generally to be found in political life at the level of problems that need to be resolved through government. Any political system, democratic or not, rests upon some sort of profound agreement, but men are seldom conscious of its terms. Attempts to state the universally acceptable—and by implication, uncriticizable—"fundamentals" of any society are frequently little more than attempts to evade the issues in current political controversy. Whether we like it or not, politics is the realm of controversy and not only of consensus. Few issues would be settled if democracy were forced to operate through unanimous approval.

The technique through which political equality is translated into actual influence in government is majority rule. In the populistic model of democracy the majority, the larger number of persons in the community, rules without qualification. It is the sole method of making decisions recognized to be ultimately binding and legitimate, and any limitations upon it can only be those which the majority has imposed upon itself and may equally later reject.

It is easy to see how political equality, especially when expressed in an idealization of the "common life," can be equated with majority rule. If men are truly equal, then no one man can or ought coerce another, making decisions for him. But, clearly, the larger number can coerce the smaller, and the only question remaining is whether they ought to do so. The answer must be affirmative, in strict logic, for equality of capacity and merit renders all standards but number irrelevant. The larger number is not only more powerful than the smaller, but also more deserving and aware of common needs, and therefore ought always to be preferred in case of conflict. Furthermore, in the actual development of western democracy minority groups have most often quite obviously been possessors or claimants of special privileges, not spokesmen for general rights that could serve as the basis of a life common to all. Democratic principles not only permit, but often require, the suppression of such privileges. Democratic thinkers have often assumed, not always incorrectly, that this could be done only by granting to the majority an unqualified dominance, whether acting directly or through agents it has chosen.

Finally, as we have seen, democratic thinkers have usually been particularly sympathetic to the ordinary man—the family farmer, the small businessman, the artisan, the worker. They have found his virtues and values to be the real foundation of the community and, sometimes, its glory. Also, in the simpler days of the past, even the fairly recent past, such "common people" were quite distinctive as a class, and the most numerous in any community. Naturally this influenced the development of democratic thought. That such people should dominate political life, as with majority rule they could, seemed only appropriate to those whose standard of comparison was the arrogance of traditional aristocracies, the selfishness of plutocracies, and the corruption of virtually all minority groups long in positions of power. In democratic thinking, consequently, government by and for the people came to mean government by and for the majority.

Difficulties in Populistic Democracy. Although much in populistic democracy must appeal to all who favor democracy in any form, serious difficulties exist concerning its value both as a guide to action and as an aid in understanding actual democratic governments. These flow from its assumptions that in any community there is *a majority* which has distinctive interests, that it knows what they are and can act to promote them, and that these interests are the only legitimate ones. If these assumptions are not true, then the absolute majoritarianism of this model of democracy is not an adequate vehicle for government of, by, and for the people.

In the first place, modern democracy, in thought as well as practice, is a historical phenomenon. Its thought, at any given time, has been largely a protest against prevailing practices, and a protest is usually most effective if it is one of extreme contradiction. Consequently, against the hierarchical regime of feudal or autocratic times, democrats urged equality; against special privileges, common rights; and against minority rule, majority rule. Whether a modern society could actually be organized on the basis of equality, common rights, and majority rule they scarcely considered; furthermore, there was little experience to support an answer one way or the other. Finally, in communities already highly organized—as were all those in which democratic movements appeared during the last several centuries—there could be no doubt as to the identity of the majority who, at the same time, constituted "the people." No faceless crowd or sheer numbers of men, the people that democrats lauded they also knew to have fairly definite political objectives, flowing from common values and experience. The needs of controversy and the existing social conditions were thus largely responsible for the absolute majoritarianism of populistic democratic theory.

Now that we have had considerable experience with actual democratic governments, however, we may doubt that democracy can adequately be defined by simply contradicting hierarchy, privilege, and minority rule. The conditions within which contemporary governments must exist, the demands made upon them, and the ways in which they must operate are generally very different from those which encouraged populistic democratic thinking in the past. Western civilization has evolved highly complex communities, in which government has a role that is both limited and yet extremely important, as suggested in the last chapter. One of the principal characteristics of contemporary social life is the virtual elimination of rigid social classes, and particularly of a vast mass of unprivileged "common people." Modern communities are marked by a greater degree of individualism, and a corresponding pluralism in group life, than ever before existed in history. None of their numerous and diverse, if interdependent, groups is of continuously dominant importance to individuals, nor is any one regularly the recipient of the loyalties of a majority of the population. In contemporary life, therefore, the term "majority" cannot have the significance simple democratic thought attributes to it.

Of course, this sort of community does not exist in most of the new states of the Middle East, Africa, and Asia. Neither, however, do these countries possess the sort of class orders found in Britain, France, and the United States during the last several centuries, and which early democratic thought took for granted. Their mass movements seem to be entirely anticolonialist, manifesting little else that could serve as the basis of a popular, majority-rule government. One may reasonably doubt, indeed, whether democracy in any form is possible at present for many of them. Thus, this model of democracy is no more applicable in, say, Ghana, than in the United States. Political action strictly based upon it could result only in chaos. There is no existing class or group, a majority in the community possessing a way of life of its own, which can rule to promote that way of life in opposition to that of a minority.

Realistically, therefore, in the contemporary world political action cannot follow a strict populistic model. It may well, of course, justify itself according to the values of that model, and almost certainly will have to work through mass movements that will give the appearance of democracy. Although majorities may not be "naturally" present, astute leaders are not prevented from creating them, or semblances of them. Indeed, in any country today, whatever may have been the case in the past, majorities are always the product of effective leadership. Such leadership may be cynically self-interested, or genuinely benevolent, but the fact remains that a majority does not rule, nor are the leaders its agents.

Nor can a majority control the leadership that brought it into existence and maintains it, for in this model of democracy there is no recognized place for opposition; one is either for the people, which in practice means supporting "their" leaders, or one is not. Any serious criticism is easily and quickly equated with disloyalty and suppressed. The possibility of revolution, more or less remote, is the only control, except the good intentions, if any, of the leaders; but revolution is no more a normal institution of democracy than of any other form of government, and benevolent despotism is not democracy. Only those confused by the simplicities of populistic democratic thought, in the face of a more complicated reality, however, will fail to distinguish the popular acclaim accorded a Hitler or Nasser, a Khrushchev or Castro, in public meetings and "elections," and in the almost total absence of criticism, from the much more modest but stable and uncoerced support given political leaders in the United States, Britain, and Canada. The language of populistic democracy hardly describes the political power of any of these leaders, though it is often used to justify that of the dictators.

Finally, the populistic democratic model is not only unsatisfactory as an explanation of political realities but seems equally undesirable as a recommendation. Most people today look forward to a continued improvement in their lot; the world is increasingly permeated with, if not a revolutionary, at least an innovating spirit. Such progressive change is impossible, however, without great complexity and adaptability in public policy, requiring many informed judgments on technical matters. Yet in the highly diversified and technological way of life essential to progress, the benefits of any particular program are rarely universal, nor can the program, often quite experimental, be made fully comprehensible to the mass of any population. Many citizens are likely to react conservatively to proposed changes, therefore, rather than spontaneously agreeing on progressive programs in awareness of the needs, the methods, and the costs. The danger in promoting democracy according to the populistic image, then, is that the rational pursuit of progressive ideals in changing circumstances would be inhibited by popular majorities of the uninformed, fearful, and satisfied. The populistic model, never having envisaged such a possibility, offers no defense.

Populistic democracy has thus proved to be an inadequate model because it is not useful in realistic analysis of any government at the present time; because it does not in fact provide political equality, but rather justifies inordinate power for those who can either create or simulate broad popular support; and, because it ignores the need in modern communities for continuing progressive leadership. Yet we must recognize that its ideal of political equality—that government be of, by, and for all and not the few only—must be the foundation of any democratic government. Similarly, we must acknowledge that all democratic regimes do in fact rest ultimately on the active support of their people, and particular democratic governments on that of majorities among them. The populistic model is right thus far, but it fails in not providing more specific standards according to which political equality actually can be maintained in the sort of world we both know and want. To meet this challenge, therefore, an alternative model seems necessary.

LIBERAL DEMOCRACY

It should now be evident that we do not get democracy simply by substituting "the people," or a majority of them, for a dominant oligarchy. The many cannot exercise political influence effectively through the same procedures as the few; such procedures will establish oligarchy whether the name of the people is invoked or not. Radically different from any other sort of government, popular government must find procedures appropriate to it alone. Our alternative model, liberal democracy, suggests those procedures and related attitudes.

The term "liberal democracy" is well established historically, for democracy in the western world arose in close association with the liberal demand for individual freedom. The term "liberal" in the nineteenth century was primarily associated with the idea that the best government was the least government, and more recently with appeals for more government in the interest of social reform. There have always been different views of what may be necessary to promote freedom and well-being for the greatest possible number of persons. Yet according to these meanings of the term, although they are important for democracy, not all liberals have been democrats, nor all democrats, liberals. The word is retained here because it has also a broader sense, connoting an undogmatic quality, an open-minded, generous, and tolerant attitude, which expresses well the character of this model of democracy and how it differs from the populistic form.

Although our experience with democracy has shown that the populistic model is inadequate for our needs, we have not yet arrived at certain knowledge of the particular attitudes, procedures, and policies which will, without qualification, support popular government. We may never do so. This model of democracy must be more empirical, therefore, reflecting to a greater degree than the other the range of values and institutions found in the more highly developed democratic regimes. Not all, however, is democratic even in such regimes, and the student of democracy must constantly judge experience against principles, as well as principles against the possibilities and limitations that experience reveals. In doing so the model of liberal democracy can be a guide, but it does not provide all the answers; it is far too tentative and incomplete for that. It suggests how the basic democratic doctrine must be interpreted if it is to be meaningful in relation to actual possibilities and ever-changing human values, but even its suggestions must be viewed undogmatically, in a word, liberally.

Basic Aspects of Liberal Democracy. It is obvious that democracy cannot mean that the people become the government, nor are representatives simply agents of the majority. The populistic model, failing to recognize this, simply assumes an effectively governing majority, and pays little attention to the all-important matter of continuing popular control over those who actually rule. Consequently, the door is opened to a quite undemocratic tyranny. The problem of democracy is not ordinarily how to enable the majority of the people to govern or direct government, but rather how to develop governments that can and must win and retain the support of popular majorities on specific issues, and the general loyalty of most of the population as well.

The liberal democratic model, therefore, emphasizes the conditions within which political power is acquired and exercised, and the effect of such conditions upon those who exercise power and upon what they do with it. In non-democratic regimes political power flows explicitly from such things as inherited titles, wealth, social status, or superior force, and serves these interests. Such interests and influences play a part in political processes in any community, beyond doubt, but the role of a model of democracy is to indicate realistic means through which the "consent of the governed" can be continuously maximized as the basis of the acquisition of political power and as a directing force in its exercise. In liberal democratic thinking, majority rule remains crucial. Realistically, however, the meaning and possibilities of majority rule must be qualified to some extent. Therefore, the model also stresses the importance of additional values and procedures. These may sometimes appear to compete with majority rule—even to deny it—but in this democratic perspective it is assumed that they are actually essential if majority rule is to be and remain effective.*

Underlying all democratic values and techniques is the ideal of political equality, of course. Yet this is clearly no simple idea in the world we know. The liberal observes that men differ among themselves considerably in their personal values, pleasures, interests, and capacities; he is thus not quite sure what, in any practical sense, it means to claim that men are, or ought to be, equal. He is likely to be concerned, however, that all persons find ways of pursuing happiness according to their own ideals, of developing their own potentialities, and of participating in government according to their own capacities and interests. All persons can and should be equal by this standard; in liberal democracy equality refers primarily to freedom and opportunities. We shall consider the problems of "freedom" in a later chapter; it should be evident immediately, however, that with this concern for the equal freedom of men who are not in fact identical in their needs and capacities the ideal of equality loses its mass, or leveling, character—equal amounts of the same thing for all—and becomes a much more intangible quality pervading a diversified community.

Such an idea of equality is clearly not compatible with public policies that grant and preserve special privileges, even if they are those of a majority. Special privileges are not substantially more acceptable because

* This model could alternatively be named "constitutional democracy"; as will be shown in Chapter 5, these additional values and procedures either are or imply constitutional institutions, whose purpose is to prevent tyranny of any kind.

possessed by large numbers rather than by few. Only rights which all can at least potentially enjoy and benefit from, and which do not create any special advantages for their possessors or special disadvantages for others, are compatible with the ideal of free and equal men. This is easy to state as a principle; unfortunately, how such rights might in practice be identified and implemented is far less clear. However, certain further ideas have traditionally been emphasized in democratic thought. In brief, these are individualistic pluralism, and rationality. Although not appreciably less ambiguous than equality and freedom, they have played an important part in the development of democracy in history and will be discussed further shortly.

Majority Rule in Liberal Democracy. Democracy implies political equality, and political equality implies majority rule. There is no escaping this logic, since the term majority is, strictly speaking, purely a matter of numbers, more than half of all the members of any group. When any decision must be made within such a group, and opinions are divided, the majority must prevail. Otherwise, some persons would be preferred over others, thus violating the tenet of political equality. Logic must be tempered by experience, however, and in fact things are not that simple.

The complications begin when we leave the realm of abstract numbers, and ask what majorities actually are and in what way they can reasonably be said to rule. When democratic movements arose in the western world, as we have seen, the majority was the commons, a class with a distinctive way of life and interests. In established democracies today, however, majorities of this sort can rarely be found. The fact is that in the modern community activities, needs, interests, and capacities are so diverse that, in regard to most of the issues which need to be met through government, majorities are neither present to start with nor do they arise spontaneously. Majorities simply do not exist as groups which in any meaningful sense can rule. Democratic thought, with rare exceptions, has failed to consider this as a serious possibility; the populistic model has been dominant, with the consequences noted above. Therefore, whether we are considering majority rule as a fact of democratic political life to be noted, or as a value to be implemented, we must recognize that it is more complicated than much oversimplified democratic thinking has led us to suppose.

If majorities do not exist to start with and do not arise spontaneously, then what does exist, and in what way do majorities arise? What exists as far as political life is concerned is a considerable variety of persons and groups with diverse ideas as to what government ought to be like and do. On some matters, of course, there is widespread agreement—the "fundamental consensus" necessary to support any government not depending upon sheer force. For such government to be a democracy there must be agreement on "majority rule," at least, but what that is can be learned only from how it works in resolving controversial issues. On such issues there are at least two, and often many more, points of view among those immediately concerned; there is also a substantial amount of initial indifference among the many in the population not directly concerned with any particular issue. There is no majority that simply needs to be consulted to learn what is the "right" thing to do; there are a number of minorities with various ideas and a large number of people with no particular ideas at all. Out of this, for the majority to rule, a majority must be created.

The majorities of democracy, then, are like all political forces; they are created by leadership and inseparable from it. Ultimately, leaders are those men whom other men will follow, for whatever reason. We know little of why some men become leaders and why others follow them; the factors are undoubtedly numerous and varied. It seems clear, though, that not all patterns of leadership are compatible with democracy. Even if democracy is not adequately and realistically defined as majority rule alone, we must not set aside the idea that in democracy the exercise of governmental authority must continuously depend upon the support of popular majorities. *Democracy in practice, thus, is a continuous interdependence of leaders and the popular majorities supporting them. At its core are those procedures and values tending to preserve that interdependence from day to day and year to year.*

Leadership in democracy must, therefore, be strong enough to create popular support, which does not arise "naturally," but equally it must not be so strong that it leads to dependence rather than interdependence among the leaders and the led. What leadership qualities, political procedures, and values necessarily support democratic, rather than traditional or autocratic, leadership is not clear. It is unlikely that there are any general rules of absolute validity, given the tremendous diversity of personalities and circumstances in history. A mechanical approach to democracy will not serve its realization or preservation, for both rules and institutions may work to different ends at different times.

Nevertheless, a few general observations may be pertinent. Obviously, leadership based primarily upon coercion, or the threat of it, is not compatible with democracy. Nor is it likely that "hero worship" is an appropriate foundation for democratic leadership. Such leaders do not sufficiently depend upon the people, and therefore cannot be held accountable to them; rather than respecting the people they are likely to hold them in contempt. Domination—if perchance benevolent—is more likely than democratic leadership within the intense and one-sided relationships of fear and worship. In principle—for many factors are always present and it is the balance that counts—democratic leaders prevail through an ability to persuade people to grant their support on fairly specific issues and for not excessively emotional or mystical reasons. Democratic leaders do not ask for a general mandate to do God's will or implement historical necessity!

The existence of democracy depends equally, of course, upon the capacity of a people to be able in general to respond to this sort of leadership, rejecting the blandishments of the prophets of "heaven on earth." They must, for the most part, be able to give their support according to decisions on the issues raised, and not simply surrender themselves to a leader. They must be able to recognize a leader without idolizing him, and thus losing any ability to criticize him. These conditions may seem somewhat idealistic, yet wherever democracy is firmly established they are substantially realized. The characteristic American distrust of politicians is a sign of health in the American democracy, although an occasional tendency to consider some political leaders as "above politics" is cause for reflection. At the same time, however, politicians should not be denied a certain respect. Professionally engaged in the creation of popular majorities they are the political leaders of a democracy, and are at the heart of democratic political life. Democracy could probably not long survive without them.

Also essential to democracy, particularly in its modern representative form, are certain formal requirements regarding elections and the rights of opposition. Whether a majority has truly formed in support of a leader or a program can be known only through a free election, with universal suffrage. To what extent elections can ever be wholly free is a complicated matter, but it may be suggested here that an election is probably a free one if no severe restrictions exist upon the freedom of candidates to present themselves for election or upon the issues they might raise. A candidate not nominated or an issue withheld because unlikely to obtain much popular support is not such a restriction. In free elections the electorate, and not a self-appointed "censor," is the ultimate judge of the qualifications of candidates.

But one election, no matter how free, no more creates democracy than one swallow makes a summer. A majority of yesterday has no inherent authority today, nor will today's majority necessarily carry over to tomorrow. The consequences of this for democracy in practice are great. In the first place, democratic control of government not only requires elections to be free but also to be regularly recurrent and not too infrequent. In this way officials must be sensitive to changing public opinion, in anticipation of the support they may or may not receive the next time around. If democracy is to be a *continuing* interdependence of political leaders and the people, then the regular testing of popular support in recurrent, free elections is indispensable.

The fact that in contemporary political life there is no clearly defined majority continuously behind government and all that it does, but rather that majorities are formed from time to time as the issues change, points to another necessity of effective democracy: the channels through which issues are raised, decisions proposed, and popular majorities rallied must be kept open at all times. Both free elections from year to year and democratic policy decisions by representatives from day to day are impossible in the absence of opportunities for those disaffected with previous and proposed decisions to challenge them and to attempt to obtain the support of new majorities for their alternatives. The absence of opposition and alternative policies, as well as of alternative candidates in elections, casts doubt on the genuineness of majority support at the time, and renders unlikely any majority rule in the future.

Consequently, democratic representation appropriately places in government not only spokesmen for a majority but also spokesmen for opposing ideas and interests—minority representatives—so that the majority may be ever renewed. The usual instrument to this end is a system of two or more parties, competing for popular support, and to some degree sharing in governmental functions, although this does not appear indispensable and other methods are available—as will be discussed later. What is essential is that the procedures with which democratic governments transact their business provide means through which these minorities can express themselves, attempting both to influence the development of public policy and to persuade a broader public of the justice of their views. Indeed, the elaboration of public policy in democracy is most often a process of accommodating diverse minority interests, expressed by their leaders in government as well as out of it, so that a previously nonexistent majority may be created.

Finally, underlying all of this are the private rights of individuals and their associations, upon which the free, rather than coerced, development of majorities depends. These matters can only be mentioned here, but they will also be discussed in greater detail in chapters to follow. Nevertheless it cannot be too much emphasized that in modern representative government, particularly, these sometimes confusing conditions must be met if government continually based upon the support of popular majorities is to be possible.

Yet, government with the consent of the governed, through majority support of leaders and programs, is not the same thing as government *by* the governed. The people acquire influence in and control over government, but it is hardly absolute. It is often negative rather than positive. Popular majorities can reject what leaders propose, but can rarely compel acceptance of something no effective leader is willing to propose. Furthermore, the decisions which must be made in government today are numerous and often extremely technical, and can be controlled by popular majorities only in the most general way. Likewise, the composite nature of majorities created out of diverse minorities and of the many partially indifferent people leads to practical situations in which it is often quite uncertain just what the majority stands for, and in which there is no clear distinction between majority and minority interests and claims. As a result, political leaders necessarily possess considerable discretion in their management of public affairs. It is probably good that they do; however, one must recognize it as a considerable qualification to any simple interpretation of majority rule.

Majority rule, although thus qualified and limited, remains an essential aspect of democratic politics. Put simply, those who immediately rule are dependent on the more or less continuous support of popular majorities. This statement reasonably reflects how democracies actually function in the modern world. Furthermore, the consequences of such majority rule are not insignificant. It does produce responsible government, and not tyranny under the cloak of popular rule. Political leaders possess considerable discretion; yet in their efforts to retain their popular support against repeated challenges they cannot diverge greatly from what the population on the whole will accept and prefer. And as such support must come from a highly diversified society, in which majorities must be constantly reconstructed as the issues change from time to time, democratic political leaders must be sensitive to the interests and ideas of individuals and minorities whose support they may need, and also be moderately amenable to adaptable and progressive government. The distinct result of such majority rule is a type of political system more complex than earlier ages could have imagined, and for the sustenance of which certain values and perspectives seem particularly necessary.

Individualistic Pluralism and Democracy. Modern democracy rose in the eighteenth and nineteenth centuries in company with a heightened sense of individuality. That government derives its just powers from the consent of the governed was only one aspect of the political theory of the American and French revolutions; equally important was that the governed were seen not as a mass of people but as individuals, each of whom possessed "natural and inalienable rights" to "life, liberty, and the pursuit of happiness," and to property. No government, not even one based upon the consent of the governed, had the authority to deprive individuals of those rights. Men such as Thomas Jefferson saw popular government and the natural rights of all men as mutually supporting aspects of good government; they could not imagine one without the other.

Many have argued, in reaction, that no rights exist independently of society and government; rather, private rights, social relationships, and political authority are all interrelated. They have pointed out, furthermore, that rights, in any specific sense, are extremely variable throughout history and around the world; therefore, if we desire to know what human rights are, we cannot find out simply by contemplating "the individual." In any event, there must be a power capable of defining them for any given time and place, and since the individual can hardly create his own rights, such power is logically, as it has been historically, government.

Yet, if government is the sole source of rights, then democracy is impossible, and benevolent despotism is the best that men can hope for. Democracy is a subtle interdependence of political leaders and the people. The people cannot hold down their side of the scale unless, as private persons, they have some independent powers, and the legal and political foundation for such powers are the rights people are presumed to possess. The people cannot control the government if they must do so on the government's own terms; it would appear that Jefferson's insight was sound. The argument against natural rights only proves that democracy is not inevitable. If the climate favorable to the recognition of fundamental private rights is a matter largely of historical accident, so then must be any democratic government. Actually, however, in most communities throughout history private rights of at least equal standing with public authority have been recognized. We need not be pessimistic about the likelihood of democracy on this count.

Yet not all types of private rights are compatible with democracy. Special privileges—rights reserved to particular, favored groups—may enable those groups to control and influence government, but this is not democracy. If all are to share in this control, and with the ultimate equality that democracy presupposes, then the objective must be equal rights for all. Only then will all not only benefit equally from what government does, but also possess equally the foundation for an effective democratic control of government.

Nevertheless, it has often been a failing of democratic thought to assume that the equal rights essential to democracy need be no more than a universally equal entitlement to the same rights. However, rights are meaningful only as they are opportunities to maintain and promote one's ideals and interests, and it is rare that the same opportunities are equally useful to all persons. Consequently, the universality and equality of any particular right is often somewhat illusory. A formally equal right to free speech, for example, is clearly a more significant right to those who have access to effective forums than to those who are only free to address family and friends. And the right to vote may be extended to all without necessarily enabling them thereby to control the government, as modern dictatorships have demonstrated, through their more or less subtle methods of limiting choice. In recent years, it must be admitted, we have learned that some rights, in appearance universal and equal—such as the right to an uninhibited use of one's property—may in time turn into *de facto* privileges very dangerous to democracy. In the end, the idea of equal rights is more easily professed than realized; it is not the clear and distinct standard early democratic thinkers took it to be.

In recognition that particular legal rights are often not of equal value to all men, and therefore that we must go beyond the concept of rights in our search for the basic democratic standard, some writers recently have asserted that democratic procedures and policies embody a "belief in human dignity" and "respect for personal integrity." It is hardly likely that these phrases include any meaning that Jefferson did not have in mind, so broad was his conception of the natural rights of men. Even such phrases as these must be continuously re-interpreted in practice as the problems of social life emerge and change, and such interpretations, if made in controversial circumstances, will themselves be controversial. What policy, for example, would most respect the personal integrity of the "high school drop-out" or the discontented Negro in contemporary America? Furthermore, no relevant policy would affect them alone. Clearly, to give the idea of respect for personal integrity, no less than the idea of equal rights for all, meaning and applications adequate to the conditions and problems of the day is no easy task. In democracy this must be done through a broadly shared and developing opinion, expressed ultimately through majority rule. Like most political standards, terms like natural rights and human dignity serve well only when broadly construed by men sensitive to their underlying but not easily communicable significance.

An additional weakness in the Jeffersonian view, undoubtedly, is its extreme commitment to "individualism" both as fact and value. Jefferson himself preferred the United States to remain a nation of small farmers, for he thought that in a commercial civilization persons were so dependent upon one another that the good life would be destroyed in both society and politics. Unhappily for the Jeffersonian, we have long since passed the threshold into commercial, industrial, urban life; individuals today live their lives largely through organizations, are identified with the values and interests of organizations, and can act in politics only through organizations of one sort or another. The dependence that Jefferson feared is an obvious fact of our lives. Psychologists, too, have concluded that the individualism of early liberalism was somewhat unrealistic. Our social relationships fulfill an emotional as well as an instrumental function for us; men fear being alone, and not only because they then lack opportunities for exploiting others.

Contemporary emphasis upon such democratic values as human dignity and personal integrity are, in part, attempts to come to terms with a renewed perception of the social nature of man. They do not isolate man from his fellows as the individual-rights perspective tends to do. Nonetheless, if individualism must be thus qualified in any realistic view of modern democracy, it appears that a contemporary counterpart of Jeffersonian individualism may be seen in our social and political pluralism. The meaningful control of government by the governed depends upon the existence of nongovernmental power, preferably scattered among numerous parties. These parties today are not individuals, in general, but private groups and their leaders. More powerful than any individual could be, they are therefore more effective in controlling and influencing government, keeping it responsive to the claims of the governed.

Nevertheless, if such a community is not to settle into some sort of feudalism, the ultimate primacy of the individual and the "openness" of the order must be maintained. Thus, on the one hand, the contemporary model of liberal democracy recognizes that most rights of political and social life are exercised largely through associations, if not by them. Rejecting the idea of Thomas Hobbes that such groups are "worms in the entrails of the body politic," liberal democracy extends to them many of the social and civic rights of persons, because the practical meaning and effectiveness of those rights to individuals is rarely more than the strength of the associations through which they exercise them.

On the other hand, it maintains the important right of individuals in democracy to create, join, and quit private groups and political parties, seeking associations through which they can express their values and needs. Such opportunities must reasonably be both legally and practically available if democracy is to survive. Specific means of implementing this right are complex and variable in all democracies, and given constantly changing conditions probably never completely satisfactory; but it is at least clear that if the population, or any large part of it, is the captive of an organization, public or private, democracy does not exist. Instead a dictatorship of the leaders of the organization exists, for they will either control or be the government and can be overthrown only by revolution. Of this situation the Soviet Union is a prime example. In such democracies as the United States, Australia, and Switzerland, there is no comparable group dominating the government and the social life of the people, and we can meaningfully speak of the control of the government by the governed.*

Rationality and Democracy. In the western world the search for the "best" political system has most often been the search for the most "rational" one. Although ambiguous, the term seems to refer to man's sensitivity to orderly and harmonious relationships, or law, and to his ability to conduct his activities according to such insights. Rationality is also often seen as a characteristic of anything that manifests such relationships; the universe is a rational one, accordingly, and so is a human community when law prevails, though not when accident or caprice seems dominant. Through reason and rational laws, it has been assumed, men can associate harmoniously and to their mutual benefit.

Although many have criticized democracy as a government based upon popular emotions, whims, and fancies—rather than reason—advocates of democracy have generally disagreed and asserted that in it the ideal of rationality is best realized. Not only are all—not just a few—capable of rationality, but the rule of minorities, whether based on wealth, warfare, or religion, leads to the overwhelming of reason by narrow and often selfish interests. Their rule is arbitrary, exerted through coercion and inculcated superstition. Democrats like Thomas Jefferson took it largely for granted that through democracy and majority rule men would be freed from these irrational controls, that reason would prevail, and men be governed by law.

As it has turned out, however, men have not manifested any universal agreement on the nature of the good life; quite often they have come to radically conflicting ideas about their rights and welfare. Despite the optimism of early democrats, the debate continues over whether democracy is even compatible with rationality in political life, much less the necessary and sufficient condition for it. For, clearly, emotion plays a large role in all our lives, and if we throw off one superstition or unreflective custom we seldom avoid acquiring another in its place. The rationality of which any individual is capable seems, at

* Somewhat confusingly, numerous intermediate and transitional regimes exist in practice, which are not fully democratic because of the dominance of a single political party, but are also not entirely dictatorial because a fair degree of opposition and controversy exists within that party. Attention will be given to this phenomenon in Chapter 8. Realism requires recognition, furthermore, that no theory—whether of democracy or dictatorship—is ever perfectly manifested in practice.

best, limited to calculating how to get what he wants, and rarely serves to put him in harmony with the universe and his fellow men. We can hardly ignore these facts; yet, as Jefferson said, if men are not capable of governing themselves, have they found angels in the form of kings . . . ? Actually, democracy does serve the end of rational government, but not in the simple and direct way that early democrats thought. Rationality as well as democracy is more complex than they assumed.

It is absurd to assume that rational action is necessarily "right," that it accords with perfect knowledge, for such knowledge is not available to us even in the most advanced sciences. Our knowledge, even that of the apparently most wise and informed, is inevitably more limited. Reason demands only that we act consistently according to the best knowledge we possess, remaining aware of its limitations and seeking constantly to improve it. Obviously, impulsiveness and prejudice are opposed to rationality in this sense, for impulsiveness interferes with consistent action, and prejudice with the effort to improve knowledge. Turning the matter around, however, it can equally be said that prejudice, transforming "mere" knowledge into inclination to act, is necessary for consistent behavior, while a person who never acts impulsively will never have the new experience that alone can lead to new insights. These natural qualities of humanity are at the same time opposed and necessary to rationality; one can only conclude that the rational man balances tendencies to impulse and prejudice. The rational man is a self-critical man.

The core of rationality, then, is disciplined self-criticism. One thus becomes aware of the entire nature of the problems that emerge within a continuing and developing experience and seeks the most valid solutions to them. In principle, an individual could be fully rational in this sense; in practice, he can rarely, if ever, adequately see all the factors relevant to his problems. Therefore, rationality demands an extensive co-operation in suggesting significant problems, calling attention to relevant factors, and testing and approving proposed solutions. In each area of human interest some methods of disciplined co-operation have been developed to promote rationality. In the realm of political life, the methods of liberal democracy clearly serve this end.

The discussion of individualistic pluralism and majority rule in liberal democracy should have made evident that this form of government is rooted in diversity of experience and opinion, which it must in an orderly way and largely through persuasion transform into agreements regarding particular public policies. The process of building majorities within a free people and its associations assures that proposals and counter-proposals will emerge into public discussion, to be evaluated, criticized, and supported. Within this framework the permanent suppression of information relevant to rational consideration of any issue is difficult, if not impossible. Democracy is, in fact, institutionalized self-criticism in public affairs, and the most intense form of it ever to exist in history. It was no accident that Pericles observed, rather smugly, that Athenians unlike Spartans thought before they acted, and his reference was to public debates far more than to personal reflections of citizens or leaders.

The critical consideration of all relevant information must in rational procedure be concluded by decisions. It is not rational to debate for the sake of debating, although it is important to keep the wits sharp and the channels of criticism open. The end, however, is to prepare the way for a decision which can win the enlightened support of those concerned with the problems. The problems of political life, ultimately at least, concern everyone. Also, political questions are not very much like those scientists pose; they ask "what should be done here?" not "what is the universe like?" Consequently the support of the greatest possible number among the population at large, who have tested proposals against their own experience, is the final test available to us at any time of the rationality of public policies. For the nature of political reason is to reconcile the many competing and sometimes conflicting ideas, values, and interests of the community within a view of the general welfare in which all men, or at least as many as may be, can see their own good.

There is no expert in such political rationality; no philosopher, no scientist, no political leader, no class of men, has *the* rational answer to the problems of political life. Only all the people, working through their political institutions, can develop such an answer, to the extent it can ever be developed. Each person, whatever his status or expertise, may have something to contribute to rational discussion and decision, and on this assumption the liberal democratic model provides political processes through which those contributions may be elicited, criticized, and fitted into decisions that the majority of men may approve. And as today's majority has no inherent authority tomorrow, neither is the reason of today necessarily that of tomorrow; like reason itself, liberal democracy is a continuing process of seeking the most valid conclusions, the community's best insight into its objectives, and the means of attaining them.

No one in his right mind, of course, would maintain that any existing political system is perfectly in tune with reason. Neither do the methods scientists use guarantee "truth"; they merely improve the probability that assertions are true. In real life, far too many men lack the education, the security, and the effective freedom to examine their lives, identify their deeper needs, acquire insight into what would satisfy those needs, and then press their claims and ideas in political life. Prey to undisciplined impulses and prejudices, most men have a limited ability to contribute to organized rationality. Political processes, furthermore, which should enable diverse ideas and interests to be integrated in the most rational program, are often only partially effective, producing compromises and temporary expedients satisfactory to none. Neither people nor institutions are anywhere perfect examples of the rational and democratic ideals.

Liberal democracy, however, is not itself responsible for our failure to realize it fully, and the claim above that the theory is "realistic" did not mean that its realization is automatic but only that it is possible and, in some places, reasonably achieved. This discussion suggests that liberal democracy furnishes the best hope we have for rationality in public affairs; acceptable government by the rational superman or superclass has been clearly established by logic and experience as a utopian dream. If the individuals in a democratic community are incapable of rationality, then rationality in social life is itself utopian. The rationalist and the democrat, therefore, may make common cause in extending education and liberalizing politics, so that an increasingly enlightened people can express themselves with greater effectiveness in public life. We conclude that majority rule—when majorities are forged in the forum of free criticism and represent the accommodations of a free people—is the best standard of rationality that we can have.

"GUIDED DEMOCRACY"

Until recently, democracy has been called, simply, democracy. If it were qualified at all, and usually only in academic discourse, such terms as "liberal," "constitutional," or "populistic" appeared as they have in the preceding pages to distinguish variant forms of popular government and to permit analysis and comparison of their effectiveness. Such qualifying terms, though important, bear on secondary matters; they do not qualify democracy out of existence or pretend to identify theoretically essential qualities. We have not argued above, for example, that liberal democracy is the "real" democracy. Since the end of World War II, however, a number of additional qualifying adjectives have appeared—not matters of academic usage, now, but of practical politics, and intended to do more than simply aid understanding. For several years we have regularly encountered in the daily news democracies that are "guided" or "basic," to mention two of the more prominent names. What is one to make of these?

For the most part, these allegedly new kinds of democracy have appeared in Asia and Africa, in countries newly independent of colonial administrations. "Guided democracy" is the name given by President (for life) Sukarno to the regime he created in Indonesia, and "basic democracy" is the product of the military coup which installed General Ayub Khan as President of Pakistan in 1958. Dictatorial regimes somewhat similar to these also exist in such countries as Ghana and Guinea. Many of these countries began but did not long continue with liberal democratic constitutions. There will probably be further failures of this sort, even though the relative democratic successes thus far in such states as Nigeria, India, and the Philippines suggest that liberal democracy is not entirely out of context in Africa and Asia.

The argument justifying the abandonment of liberal democracy in Indonesia and Pakistan is simple: it did not work, being inappropriate to the character and conditions of their peoples. No doubt, considerable political confusion marked the years before 1958 in Pakistan, and in Indonesia no effectively national popular forces existed that were more than anti-colonialist and supportive of Sukarno personally. Neither the people nor their leaders had much experience with national government, democratic or otherwise, although their situation on the sudden arrival at independence clearly demanded effective government at that level. In effect, in neither case did "a people" exist as envisaged in populistic democracy, nor were popular majorities organizable as in liberal democracy, capable of controlling the government in any responsible fashion. Similarly, they appear to have lacked political leaders capable of acting as responsible democratic politicians. Finally, they had no political traditions that could support leaders and people in the democratic path, given normal human inclinations to fail in their responsibilities and misuse their powers. Evidently, democracy as normally understood is unlikely if not impossible in such circumstances. There is little foundation for implementing its standard of political equality, and civil and political freedoms are bound to be abused by at least some for personal and sectarian advantage. These touchstones of democracy, therefore, have largely been abandoned.

To what degree, then, are the "guided" and "basic" regimes democratic? We must conclude, very little. The best that can be said is that they are not traditional aristocracies or oligarchies, but are dominated by a new leadership derived from a revolution that is social as well as political. This leadership seeks popular support in the democratic fashion, but rejects popular control, since the people are not as totally or consistently revolutionary as their leaders—or, at least, not revolutionary in the same way. It is undeniable that the problems confronted by these new countries would be extremely trying for any government, and that even experienced leaders attracted to the democratic ideal would be hard pressed to observe its standards in practice—although others in a similar situation, we have seen, have generally managed to do so. In Indonesia, then, the people are largely reduced to cheering for a leader who is clearly the focus for such national unity as exists amidst conflicting ideas and forces. And in Pakistan, popular participation in government is substantial only at the local level; at regional and national levels it is both limited and indirect, and the president and his appointees dominate. In the most favorable light—accepting the professions of the Pakistani Constitution, for example—these regimes are endeavoring to create peoples capable eventually of self-government in the modern world. Their use of the language of democracy is best understood as a tribute to its moral power and influence and, perhaps, an expression of their intentions. At present, however, though they may be good, bad, or indifferent regimes, they are not democratic, nor are their justifying ideas new forms of democratic theory.

III. *The* VALUE *of* DEMOCRACY

The value of democracy has been a matter of controversy since men first, in ancient Greece, came to reflect on their political experience. Throughout most of western history the consensus of learned as well as of ordinary men has generally been an unfavorable one; only in the last

ABOVE: "Mass activity is in effect offered as a harmless substitute for democratic participation in the governing process, hence the continual marchings, wearing of uniforms, mass calisthenics, chanted slogans, and party rallies." (p. 341) A physical culture parade on Red Square at the May Day celebration in Moscow. Carrying banners reading "Glory to the Soviet People," the marchers pass before the V. I. Lenin Mausoleum (formerly the Lenin-Stalin Mausoleum) also used as a reviewing stand. (*Sovfoto.*) BELOW: "To the glorification of the *Volk* and the expansion of its *Lebensraum* . . . were devoted the most impressive mass demonstrations and terroristic brutality of all time." (p. 137) Adolf Hitler overlooking an assemblage of 100,000 Nazis massed on the Zeppelin Meadow at Nürnberg for his speech to the Nazi Party Congress, 1935. (*United Press International Photo.*)

ABOVE: "Democratic leaders prevail through an ability to persuade people to grant their support on fairly specific issues and for not excessively emotional or mystical reasons." (p. 100) Delegates and observers from the Commonwealth countries assembled in Marlborough House, London, for the opening session of a Commonwealth Prime Ministers' Conference. (*British Information Services.*) BELOW: "The steady expansion of government services and regulation of formerly private affairs may generally be an honest attempt to resolve some of the difficult problems of modern life within democratic procedures and values. . . ." (p. 148) In the State of Washington, the municipally-owned Seattle City Light's Ross Dam and Powerhouse; standing 540 feet high, the dam impounds a lake 24 miles long. (*Seattle City Light.*)

century or so has democracy acquired any particular prestige, and even today it is challenged and misinterpreted.

The appeal to men of democracy, then, is not absolute. If we hold it to be of universal value, we are hard pressed to explain why some reject it and others interpret it in such different ways. Liberal democracy, in any case, is clearly related to the values and conditions that have appeared in modern western culture. Many of us feel that these are basically sound and good, but there are also many in the world who disagree and who find our attempts to justify our position not entirely persuasive. It is not likely that there is any way of overcoming this difficulty with argument alone. The sort of democracy which has evolved in western civilization serves certain values; we can only indicate what these are, and let the argument appeal to whom it may. What can be said against democracy, from various perspectives relevant to contemporary government, will be treated in the following chapter.

Government Beneficial to Many. Undoubtedly the most general attraction of democracy has been its promise to ensure government beneficial to the greatest number. Its procedures reasonably guarantee that widely shared values will be respected and furthered. Although the people can in no immediate sense govern themselves, democracy gives them sufficient participation in political life, at crucial points, to permit them strongly to influence those who do govern. They exercise this influence continuously, furthermore, so that it is the values of today, not those of yesterday, that dominate in political life; nor can the values of today be sacrificed in favor of some the people have not yet come to share, for the electorate can reject radical as well as reactionary advocates. They can insist, in other words, upon receiving here and now what they most generally believe to be the good things of life. It has always been held by political thinkers that the most general interests should be served by government, and what the people at large think those interests to be is certainly worth consideration. They may be mistaken, of course, but dictators are not likely to do better. Only democracy compels rulers to give such consideration to the claims of citizens whose ideas are not the same as theirs.

Adaptable and Progressive Government. In the modern world, however, neither the wants and needs of men nor the conditions within which they must live are static; adaptability is not only a virtue, it is a necessity. The status quo is a powerful force in any community, and no government can escape being at least partially rooted in it. Whatever may be said about "ideal" dictatorships or oligarchies, ruling in perfect goodness and wisdom, actual ones either are, or soon come to be, entirely rooted in the status quo, hence defending existing privileges and values against all change. Democracy, too, defends the status quo when the privileges and values it represents are acceptable to the bulk of the population. Yet, in its modern liberal form at least, democracy also creates channels through which attacks upon the status quo, no matter what their justification, can be vented. No policies or vested rights are immune from criticism, and such criticism can always lead to change and reform, if those dissatisfied can persuade enough others to follow them in their objection.

Only democracy among all known forms of government thus formally combines respect for traditional community values and opportunities for changing those values. In practice, these rather antithetical characteristics lead to gradual or piecemeal reform, rather than radical and revolutionary change. In democratic politics diverse and changing ideas must be accommodated to one another, with new and old interests compromised. Radicals find this distasteful because there is not enough—or rapid enough—change, and extreme conservatives, because there is too much. But the net result, if the recent history of democratic communities is any indication, is a flexible and adaptable regime, and one of stable evolution in public policy. Democracies in the English-speaking and Scandinavian worlds, especially, have accomplished enormous reforms in this century, while retaining and even extending most of their traditional values.

Government Promoting Individuality. What most thoughtful persons in modern western culture would hold perhaps as the greatest achievement of democracy, however, is even more subtle. This is to value democracy because it promotes responsible individualism. Democratic citizenship does not necessarily, or even ordinarily, mean membership in a howling mob, nor can automatic majorities normally be "delivered" on candidates or issues by the leaders of any special ideological or interest groups. A majority decision is only a large number of individual decisions, brought to coincidence through discussions and leadership. At the root of democracy, therefore, is the individual—potentially, if not in fact, any and all individuals—with his personal values, experience, and problems. The values and procedures of democracy begin and end with the individual, no matter what groups and collective judgments intervene in the process. They give him an opportunity to expand. Through his part, however small, in public life his self-esteem is encouraged and his awareness of issues transcending his petty private affairs is developed. Through many public policies his private activities are assisted so that he may face the future with greater self-confidence and explore new opportunities for self-expression.

Nevertheless, men are both individuals and social creatures, torn between asserting their personal worth and independence and merging themselves in aggregations for safety and a sense of significance or purpose. An individualism that holds a man to be an isolated unit, related only in an external way to other persons and refusing any responsibility for them or for the effect of his conduct upon them, is absurd and self-defeating. He must, and usually desires to, live in association with others, according to common rules and pursuing common objectives.

In modern communities, however, it is rare that in any one association men can find their greatest satisfaction and value. A diversity of available associations is essential; yet these many groups must be compatible and must, in some way, co-operate if the purposes of the groups and the persons in them are to be realized. Likewise, if individualism means, at the least, the possibility of a free choice of one's associations, then the power of groups to hold individuals captive must obviously be limited. Individualism depends, in short, upon freedom being exercised in responsible recognition of the freedom and needs of others, for no man or group can stand alone.

While there is no certainty that men will always desire individuality, nor any guarantee that any political machinery will inevitably work to promote it, the procedures of liberal democracy so channel political activity that a people can work out the requirements of responsible individualism for their time and place and effectively enforce them in public policy. Through democracy alone, we think, can the conflict be reconciled between the individualistic and social aspects of human life, as well as between the idealistic and the practical, which have posed dilemmas to philosophers and fostered revolutions in political life down through the ages.

In the end, we must remember that democracy is a relatively recent and untested experiment. The United States is the oldest democracy on a large scale in the world; as a democracy it dates back less than a century and a half, and through most of that time has enjoyed unusually propitious circumstances. There is no certainty that it, or any other existent democracy, can survive the trials of contemporary life; even less is it certain that any new democracies will emerge in the present troubled and difficult years. Whether the people at large can find and maintain instruments of self-government, and can choose wisely the policies necessary for survival and welfare, will be answered only in the future which those devoted to democracy make.

Ultimately, therefore, the question of democracy is also that of western civilization, for if democracy be lost it will take with it most of the values of that civilization. If western civilization has erred in its understanding of human life democracy is meaningless. If we share its values we really have no choice; as Abraham Lincoln observed, the only alternatives to majority rule—held in restraint by constitutional checks and always changing easily with deliberate changes of public opinion and sentiments—are anarchy and despotism.

CHAPTER 4

The CHALLENGE *to* DEMOCRACY

DEMOCRACY has never appealed to all men. Some have dissented from its aspirations, and others from its procedures. Some have flatly rejected even the name. Far more have denied its spirit while still pretending to serve it, presenting the gravest threat to democracy today. The threat is particularly dangerous because it is two-pronged: democracy is being attacked from without and weakened from within. On the one hand, ideas systematically critical of democracy as we know it, both as fact and as ideal, have arisen in the modern world. The most significant of these proposed alternatives today are communism and fascism, and the governmental form of both is totalitarian dictatorship. On the other hand, any democracy under contemporary conditions confronts serious difficulties of its own quite apart from ideological differences. These important practical problems are no less a test of democracy's capacity for survival; their identification and consideration will complete this chapter.

The "old-fashioned" enemies of democracy clearly favored aristocracy or monarchy as the rule of the "best men" and were contemptuous of "popular government" in any sense of the term. There are few of these now and their political significance is virtually nil. The modern enemies of democracy, like democracy itself, are products of the modern world. They respond, as democracy does, to the complexities and difficulties of contemporary life. They profess, also, to speak for "the people" and their aspirations, and for "science" or some other principle of organized action to realize those aims. In other words, they appeal to much the same audience democracy does; they beguile less those who flatly reject democracy than those who fail to understand it or to accept its difficulties, requirements, and limitations. To understand not only democracy but also contemporary politics we must understand communism and fascism, the totalitarian alternatives.

I. COMMUNISM

Beyond doubt, the most dangerous of the ideological challenges to democracy today is communism, partly because such powerful and dynamic regimes as the Soviet Union and the People's Republic of China are communist and promote its spread by all available means. Nevertheless, the ideas and ideals professed by communist regimes require sober consideration. They play a considerable role in "subverting" men throughout the world from liberal democratic ideals, which were the leading progressive views not long ago, and bringing them to support thoroughly nondemocratic movements and policies.

These ideas are not easily understood, however. They are today the result of a century's developing revolutionary thought, and have been affected by diverse personalities and circumstances. Despite some consistency in perspective, therefore, communist ideas are extraordinarily ambiguous at important points. This has enabled their leading adherents to be disconcertingly flexible in forging an effective theory for their purposes, while still claiming to follow basic communist doctrine. The resulting complexity of communist ideas, and why they have nonetheless appealed to many as both an aid to understanding social life and as a guide to action, may be most clearly shown if we follow the historical development of communism from the writings of Marx to the policies of contemporary Russia and "Red China."

MARXIAN COMMUNISM

Marx: Social Critic and Prophet. The modern age has been not only a revolutionary one, affecting all aspects of human life, but generally an optimistic one. Men have tended to assume that the changes taking place and those yet to come constituted "progress" leading to a glorious future. A profound force has been the "industrial revolution," which got under way in England at the end of the eighteenth century, spread to the European continent and America in the nineteenth, and is not yet completed. When the earlier phases of this revolution produced appalling living and working conditions for large numbers of people, and recurrent business crises appeared to portend increasing rather than decreasing misery, radical protests against the new commercial and factory system ensued. The natural and immediate response of many workers was to destroy the machines they saw displacing and humiliating them. Such a reactionary response, however, was not characteristic of the period, with its optimistic faith in progress; most thinkers called for reform and reorganization. The nineteenth century thus produced an unusually large number of schemes for the betterment of society.

Among these, one of the most comprehensive in scope, penetrating in insights, and total in criticism of the existing social order was the "scientific socialism" of Karl Marx and Friedrich Engels, epitomized in the *Communist Manifesto* of 1848. They called this a "scientific" program, because it was rooted in a scientific understanding of history, of how the existing social order developed, of why and how it must eventually fall. They contrasted their views with the "utopian" socialism of such men as Robert Owen in England, and Charles Fourier in France who, according to Marx and Engels, lacked knowledge of the necessary conditions of social reform. Those programs, the communists insisted, were utopian and idealistic dreams.

History and the Class Struggle. Marx assumed that he knew how social reform would necessarily occur because he thought he had discovered the law of historical change, and had identified the characteristics of existing society relevant to that law. The alleged law of historical change he termed "dialectical materialism," and it was manifested throughout history in the form of the "class struggle."

Dialectical materialism is one of the more frustratingly ambiguous of the important concepts coined by man. Briefly, the dialectic has long been used as a method of analysis and argument; a "thesis" is stated, then contradicted by an "antithesis," and finally the conflict is resolved in a "synthesis," which is presumably closer to the truth than its predecessors. The German philosopher, Hegel, had concluded that such a dialectical process is manifested in history, giving it meaning and accounting for changes. Nations, in their ideas of themselves and the actions flowing therefrom, represent from time to time the theses of the dialectic, and are thus the actors in history. They express "the march of God" in the world.

Marx accepted the Hegelian dialectic in form but rejected its idealism, which asserted ideas to be primary, in favor of materialism. "Materialism" is a term which appears simple but can mean in fact many things. In Marxism, it seems principally to mean that ideas are not causes but effects, and what they are effects of is thought to be economic conditions. How men are organized to produce and distribute food, clothing, and shelter, and particularly who owns the means of their production, determine fundamentally, Marx claimed, the nature and importance of everything men are and do. Economic systems thus replace the Hegelian ideas in the dialectical process, comprising the "theses" and giving rise to the "antitheses" which, in their opposition, make history what it is. Marxists consequently view their environment and their own role in it from a rather special perspective. According to the dialectical analysis there is room at any time for only two significant forces in social life, and these are in irreconcilable conflict. Furthermore, given the optimism of this way of thinking, it is inevitable that a new and better society will emerge out of the struggle. Therefore, if any person or group of persons is to be meaningful in history, according to the Marxists he must be identified with one or the other of these contending forces. Most, if not all, persons are actually so identified, Marxists think, and this is the most important fact about them.

In the Marxist dialectic the contending forces are economic classes—groupings of persons distinct in their position in the organization of the economy and acquiring special patterns of ideas, values, and needs as a result. Thus, as all Marxists have insisted, the class struggle is the fundamental concept of Marxism, both theoretically and practically. In all except very primitive communities Marx claimed to find a propertyless laboring class and a propertied class, which directs labor and appropriates as much of the produce as it can. This appropriation the communists term "exploitation," regardless of its extent or justification. The survival of the laboring class depends upon its ability to limit that exploitation; its freedom, upon successful revolution against those who exploit it. Progress in history, according to Marx, has flowed from such revolutions, for each economic class rising through them to domination is "progressive for its time," introducing new and more effective ways of organizing economic life. Class revolutions, therefore, are of broad historical importance, laying the foundation for expanded production of material goods as well as for greater freedom and equality among men.

Capitalism and the Class Struggle. To Marxists, "capitalism" is the characteristic economy of modern times, the "bourgeoisie" and the "proletariat" are the economic classes in conflict, and "communism" is the new society to emerge out of revolution as the "synthesis." One must keep in mind, of course, that Marx's ideas about capitalism, economic classes, and the nature of the "good society" to come, were products of the mid-nineteenth century in which he lived; however appropriate they may have been then, they do not accurately describe these phenomena today. Even communists sometimes recognize this, although more usually insisting that Marx's analysis of capitalism is still relevant.

The nature of each of these social classes and the relations among them in Marxist theory is very complicated, and can only be sketched briefly here. Marx used the term "bourgeoisie" to describe the dominant exploiting class of the capitalist economy. Exploitation is particularly pronounced, he asserted, because capitalism's central characteristic is the uninhibited pursuit of private profit, to which all ethical considerations are subordinated. The partial truth of this can be denied only by idealizing human beings; Marx, however, refused to admit that *any* limits to the "profit motive" are or can be present within the capitalistic system. The bourgeoisie, then, are those who have organized the modern factory economy as a matter of private property, and thus gained absolute control over the instruments of production in the modern world.

In the modern factory economy, as Marx saw it, the laboring class is especially at the mercy of its exploiters, having lost control of its tools. As defined in Marxism, the proletariat includes those persons who have nothing to sell but their labor power, and must do so at a price profitable to the capitalists. Class lines, Marx assumed, were becoming particularly rigid and opposed in modern capitalism; industrialism, given private property and the pursuit of profit, would have the effect of concentrating control of the instruments of production, and thus dividing men more sharply than ever before into those who have and those who have not, while at the same time accentuating exploitation. Marx came to such conclusions partly by observations of how people in industrializing societies actually behaved in the early and mid-nineteenth century, and partly by the logical requirements of his own thought and values. The result was an economic theory of capitalism of an undeniable logical rigor, but of quite variable realism.

Marx took capitalism as a necessary stage in world evolution; from his perspective its task has been to develop the highly productive modern industrial system. Only the subordination of all else to the pursuit of profit, apparently, could have brought about such radical economic and social change, and only the most complete exploitation of labor could have made available the necessary resources. Marx both admired and hated what the bourgeoisie had done. But he also thought that it had about finished its historic task, and its economy would soon grind to a halt. The recurrent and ever worsening crises were signs, to him, of the intrinsic weakness of an economy based upon the pursuit of profit. Intense competition among capitalists, he thought, was driving increasing numbers of the bourgeoisie into the proletariat, at the same time that it rendered the latter more impoverished and miserable. Eventually production and opportunities for work would become so restricted that the infuriated proletariat would rise in revolution, and the bourgeoisie —what was left of it—would be too weak and demoralized to resist effectively. Thus, as the *Communist Manifesto* put it, the bourgeoisie would create its own "grave-diggers," and die of its own contradictions. Although this Marxist prediction is over a century old, capitalism has not yet perished for these reasons anywhere. To understand communism we must follow its argument further.

Politics as Superstructure. Marxist materialism, or economic determinism, yields very little explicit political analysis. According to Marx, ideas, ideals, and all apparently noneconomic institutions are grounded in the needs of economic classes and have no independent value or meaning. They are, in other words, the "superstructure" upon the "base" of economic life. Despite some occasional mild qualifications of this extreme position, Marx and his followers persisted in holding that the economically dominant class is necessarily the politically and socially ruling class. Its influence, tending to preserve the sort of economy it has created, permeates all of society, creating even religious doctrines and ideas of family life appropriate to its needs. Needless to say, government is then no more than an instrument of domination of the exploiting class.

"Political power," the *Communist Manifesto* announced, "is merely the organized power of one class for oppressing another."

No governments, therefore, exist to promote the "general welfare"; all are in reality dictatorships, according to communist analysis. This is true regardless of their form; that is to say, democracies are no less dictatorships than are monarchies. Various forms of government are simply different ways in which the dominant class can most effectively maintain its power and economic regime. Given this opinion, it should be evident why Marx did not devote much time or energy to analyzing the subtleties of political institutions or procedures. Political activity within the legislative, administrative, or judicial agencies of any state is significant only as a means to something else. Progress, in the form of perfected economic functioning and realization of the full and rightful claims of the workers, can be achieved only through the overthrow of the existing state. This is the core of Marxist "politics." In modern conditions, the "bourgeois dictatorship" must be replaced by a revolutionary "dictatorship of the proletariat."

Marx's attitude toward democracy was not clearly defined. Apart from a casual remark in 1872 to the effect that in Britain, the United States, and perhaps the Netherlands, the revolutionary transformation of society *might* be implemented peacefully through existing democratic processes, he ordinarily assumed that as long as so-called bourgeois society existed neither was the democratic ideal possible nor were democratic institutions meaningful. "Force," he wrote in *Capital* (1867), "is the midwife of every old society pregnant with a new one." Whether he thought the proletarian society to come would be in any reasonable sense democratic is uncertain. When he used the term with approval, it was obviously the populistic and not the liberal form he had in mind; yet that this is a primitive and unrealistic concept has been established in the preceding chapter. As a romantic vision, it is inapplicable and unrealizable in any complex modern community, whether the interests of capitalists or laborers are being promoted.

In addition, Marx was dominated by his economic interpretation. "Real, living individuals," apparently, come only in economic classes, and not as individual persons or in noneconomic groupings. Thus, to Marx, lost as he was in his abstract "scientific" thought, people were either "bourgeois" or "proletarian." Likewise, popular majorities must be either properly "proletarian" and revolutionary—at least when the economic conditions have sufficiently advanced—or merely the disguised instrument of the capitalists. Such an automatic assumption that popular majorities "really" and "naturally" manifest only proletarian characteristics, and therefore express themselves most effectively through a proletarian dictatorship, not only misses the whole point of democracy as a dynamic political order but is inherently destructive of it. We can only conclude that Marx was not a democrat, if only because he did not know what democracy is.

The Marxian Dream. Marx generally scorned the sketching of utopias. The community to come would emerge, he thought, as an original product of the proletarian revolution; it certainly could not be predicted in detail by those still enmeshed in bourgeois society. Nevertheless, he could not help giving some indication of what he thought it would be like, and those few phrases and their implications have been important aspects of Marxist thought. The determinism of dialectical materialism, of course, implies not only the inevitability of revolutionary change, but also that the characteristics of the future will develop not accidentally but dialectically out of the present. In short, whatever the proletariat negates in capitalism will be eliminated in communist society.

This is primarily, of course, private property; private ownership of the means of production will vanish in the communist society. The means of production, communists assert, will be owned by all and controlled by all for the benefit of all. Just how this is to be organized, beyond the initial step of depriving the capitalists of their capital through heavy, progressive taxation and confiscation by the proletarian dictatorship, was never made clear. In actual communist regimes "ownership" of the means of production has merely been transferred from private capitalists to communist leaders and put to the service of their power. However, following the Marxist assumptions for the moment, the abolition of private property is seen as having vast implications for all aspects of human life. Private property was to Marx the sole foundation of classes and means of exploitation; after its elimination neither classes nor exploitation would remain. Convinced that classes exist only to exploit other classes, Marx concluded that the proletariat itself would eventually be "abolished as a class," lacking anyone to exploit once it disposed of the bourgeoisie.

The classless society resulting, according to this Marxist dream, will allegedly have still further desirable characteristics. The pursuit of profit, accompanying capitalistic private property, had prevented the workers from enjoying the full fruits of their labor. It had also, while leading originally to the creation of industry, ultimately prevented that industrial capacity from functioning most productively. Socialization of the means of production will thus, in the Marxist scheme, furnish both work and abundance for all. In these circumstances, Marx assumed, selfishness would disappear. Men would work because work was a psychological imperative, not only to obtain the necessities of life, and the fruits of labor could be distributed according to need. Not only would this represent a profound transformation of economic life, it would quite evidently be a profound psychological transformation as well. Marx asserted, in effect, that only in communist society would the conditions be present for the realization of true individual freedom, which liberals had advanced as an ideal but could not fully implement.

In these circumstances, if Marx were right, the coercive institutions of prerevolutionary societies would obviously be unnecessary. In Engels' phrase, the state would "wither away," as the distinction between oppressed and oppressing classes became meaningless. So would such institutions as churches, which to Marxists exist to coerce through superstition. All that Marxists have assumed still necessary would be "the administration of things." This government, if such it is, would apparently be largely a matter of simple bookkeeping and completely noncoercive. For in the communist utopia, as Marx seems to have envisaged it, there would be no private interests in opposition, and science or objective knowledge would replace private subjective opinions and superstition. Here, at last, would all men form a harmoniously co-operating fellowship, in which each can nonetheless be completely himself. As Marx put it, "the free development of each is the condition for the free development of all." A more remarkable "heaven on earth," synthesizing both the liberal and democratic ideas and the humanitarian ideals and values of modern times, could hardly be imagined. Unfortunately, it is a mirage.

MODERN COMMUNISM

Lenin: The Theory and Practice of Revolution. To say that something is a mirage does not mean that men necessarily will abandon its pursuit, but only that their thirst is bound to remain unsatisfied. The utopia of Marx, no less than his understandable criticism of the eco-

nomic and social order of his day, has made its mark in the world—due in no small degree to Vladimir Ilyich Lenin, the ruthless leader of the Bolshevik revolutionaries in Russia, who created the original seat of contemporary communist power. This power, together with Lenin's action-oriented interpretations of Marxism, gave to that doctrine a relevance in the twentieth century which it otherwise might not have had, although probably not the relevance Marx anticipated. Contemporary communist ideas are quite rightly termed "Marxism-Leninism."

Marx, as we have seen, envisaged the communist revolution and its success as historically inevitable, and for the most part assumed that it would be a spontaneous uprising of the proletariat. His own role, and that of his followers, was largely limited to educating the workers to their proletarian mission of revolution and social reconstruction. The *Communist Manifesto* protested that the communists "do not form a separate party opposed to other working class parties," and that they had no "sectarian principles of their own, by which to shape and mould the proletarian movement." They were but "the most advanced and resolute section of the working class parties of every country," and fought "for the attainment of the immediate aims" and "momentary interests of the working class." Qualifying this last, characteristically, was the assertion that "in the movement of the present they also represent and take care of the future of that movement," but Marx assumed in any event a proletariat on the verge of birth and the revolution not far behind.

By the end of the last century, however, the various disciples of Marx were bitterly disputing the proper Marxist interpretation of events. In fact, nothing was developing quite the way Marx had predicted. If the capitalistic order were nearing its collapse it was hardly obvious, nor was competition driving increasing numbers of the bourgeoisie down into the proletariat. Governments, not only in relatively democratic England but even in clearly autocratic Germany, were acting as something more than the armed guards of capitalism. Even worse, the working class was showing less interest in radical transformation of society than in immediate improvements in its working and living conditions, and when it showed unity of purpose it was more often of nationalistic than proletarian inspiration.

Marxist theory was clearly open to revision, but the corrections split the socialist fellowship. At one extreme were the "revisionists," among them Eduard Bernstein, in Germany, and Jean Jaurès, in France. They largely abandoned any rigid adherence to the doctrine of inevitable and violent revolutions, and endeavored to realize the Marxist ideals in peaceful evolution through democratic politics and education. From them sprang the "social democratic" movements of this century.

Equally revisionist, although vigorously proclaiming itself orthodox, was the Russian Bolshevik movement, led by Lenin, which explicitly rejected the name "social democrat" after 1917. Lenin, undoubtedly influenced at least as much by the repressive autocracy of Czarist Russia and its native revolutionary movements as by Marxism, radically altered the emphasis of Marxism. Under his leadership the seizure and stabilization of power by the Bolsheviks became the central interest of communism, and although the terminology of communist discourse and propaganda remained Marxist, it was Marxism seen, in Lenin's words, as a guide to action, not as dogma. Exactly what Lenin meant by this is hard to say; certainly he interpreted Marx quite liberally when it suited his revolutionary purposes, taking full advantage of the ambiguities of dialectical materialism. Committed fanatically to revolution, and particularly to revolution in Russia, Lenin was not about to await the inevitable, or even merely to act a "midwife" to its coming. Consequently, he added to the rather speculative Marxist "science" of historical development a more immediately practical "science" of revolution, creating a powerful if not entirely consistent doctrine.

The Conspiratorial Organization. The Leninist science of revolution has two particularly important aspects. First, Lenin rejected the idea of a communist party as a broad, popular association of workers and sympathizers with Marxist ideals. Because no effectively revolutionary proletariat yet existed anywhere, the party had to be its "vanguard." Its task was to seize power and destroy bourgeois institutions, which, Lenin assumed, were suppressing the proletariat. As a revolutionary group, and not merely an educational institution, the communists had to form a highly centralized and disciplined conspiratorial organization, with membership restricted to those who would devote themselves unconditionally to the revolution.

Second, Lenin understood that conspiracy alone cannot make a successful revolution. The core of Marxist teaching was that the revolution depended less upon its leadership than upon appropriate economic conditions. Marx had specified these conditions rather narrowly. Lenin, adapting Marxist doctrine to the actual problems of his day, concluded that the conditions necessary for successful revolutionary action were a general popular discontent of some sort, and division and weakness among the defenders of the old order. The organization could then exploit these circumstances to create a communist revolution; that is to say, one dominated by the communists, taking their guiding principles from Marx and applying them expediently where the revolutionary potential was greatest.

The Revolutionary Dictatorship. The revolution only begins with the communist seizure of power; the expropriation of the property of the bourgeoisie requires, as Marx had argued, the dictatorship of the proletariat. But, although he was aware that some difficulties might arise throughout the transition to the communist society, Marx did not contemplate the necessity of a dictatorship of the party over the entire population, including the working classes, much less that of the party leaders over the party. Such a revolutionary dictatorship was established as a leading characteristic of communist regimes by Lenin and his successors under the convenient name of "democratic centralism." A euphemistic phrase, it means in communist jargon that once decisions are made—presumably by majority vote—they are not further to be contested by dissident minorities.

This dictatorship was required, if for no other reasons, because from a Marxian point of view communism achieved its first victory—and later ones as well—under the most inauspicious circumstances. In the first place, the Russian economy the communists inherited was backward in both industry and agriculture, and it further suffered severely in World War I, the anti-Czarist revolution, and the civil war the Bolsheviks provoked. Second, they did not have the support of most of the population; even among factory workers the Bolsheviks could not always command a majority. Third, although Lenin anticipated numerous successful communist revolutions throughout Europe following that in Russia, he, and later Stalin, found that hostility to the new regime was virtually universal abroad, with only scattered support among working class movements and intellectuals. Thus, they had no choice but to build—in Stalin's slogans—"socialism in one country" in the midst of a "capitalistic encirclement," which of course posed both economic and defense problems. And finally, among the revolutionaries, even those claiming Marx as mentor, considerable and continuing disagreement existed as to what should be done in the circumstances.

Consequently, the communist seizure of power was not the end of the revolution but, in a sense, only its beginning. On the one hand, therefore, communism remained associated with dictatorship as the means necessary for completing the revolution, and this "necessity" has not yet been abandoned. On the other hand, communist leaders have always argued that, however little the Soviet Union may resemble the Marxist dream, it represents a foothold for communism in an otherwise imperfect and capitalistic world. The future of communism depending upon its success, the regime must be preserved and promoted at all costs. With the same single-minded devotion Lenin manifested in engineering the communist seizure of power in Russia, therefore, he and his successors have attended to preserving and strengthening the Soviet regime at home and abroad. Lenin and his followers were no more willing to sit by and permit the new order to emerge "naturally" than they had been willing to await the spontaneous revolution of the proletariat. Marxism, as Lenin said, was only a "guide to action"; the communist leaders learned from experience how and to what extent they should use that guide.

For example, when Lenin tried immediately after the revolution to move directly toward a communist economy, the disastrous results in production and to the security of his regime convinced him promptly that conditions were not yet ripe. With characteristic flexibility and determination, he shifted to a "New Economic Policy," a tactical retreat permitting limited free enterprise; yet at the same time he began to organize both party and government for later and more decisive attacks. Most particularly, he concluded that the party would have to remain the highly disciplined and centralized organization of prerevolutionary days, through which alone the necessary control could be exercised over the entire community, as well as over communist supporters abroad. Those who disagreed with either rigorous party discipline or his pragmatic policies he termed doctrinaires or opportunists, that is, either fools or "enemies of the people," and purged them from the party and from power. Stalin, with heightened ruthlessness, continued Lenin's methods, both of seizing and exercising power. The result was a communist movement throughout the world, controlled with almost unbelievable effectiveness from Moscow, and a party in the Soviet Union, dominated by the dictator, which in turn thoroughly controlled virtually every aspect of life in that country.

Communism Consolidated. Experience thus taught Lenin and Stalin what Marx had apparently not fully understood: that an efficient and despotic dictatorship was the necessary condition for the sort of radical social reconstruction which communists envisaged. Only when the political means were firmly established—and no idealistic considerations were ever permitted to endanger them—was the Soviet regime able to resume its revolutionary program. Indeed, the elements of that program as instituted by Stalin—the "five-year plans," the increasingly tight governmental control over industry and commerce, the collectivization of agriculture, the increasingly coercive regimentation of the lives of Soviet citizens, the efforts to ensure loyalty to the regime through intense indoctrination in communist ideas associated with Russian chauvinism—can be understood only if seen as serving a dual purpose: the security of communist (party) power as well as the realization of communist (Marxist) values. And as the full Marxist utopia is unrealizable, at least in the foreseeable future, it is safe to conclude that the revolutionary dictatorship is an inherent aspect of any communist community.

Communist principles today have not changed, but the conditions to which they are applied have altered radically. In the Soviet Union the task of building "socialism in one country" has been completed; so, at least, Stalin declared in 1936. In reality, this meant primarily that the communist dictatorship was then firmly established. However, it also meant that the control of the economy had been wrested from private hands, and could henceforth be devoted to the building of the communist society, the allegedly ultimate goal. Of course, the party, which is to say largely its leaders, was still alone competent to determine what had to be done to accomplish that task, and this role of dominant leadership was clearly reserved to the party in the "Stalin Constitution" of 1936.

Consequently, after 1936 and particularly after World War II, communism acquired a much more aggressive orientation. While Lenin and Stalin had been engaged in consolidating their power at home, after hope for communist revolutions abroad had been disappointed, "socialism in one country" was realistically accepted as expedient, and their machinations abroad were essentially defensive. But Stalin and his successors have been as aware as anyone that neither the security of their power nor the ideal communist society could be realized in one country alone. The world-wide revolutionary struggle against the bourgeoisie had to be resumed and won if full communism were to exist anywhere. With the enormous increase in Soviet power, especially as a result of World War II, and the fall of China to communist forces as well, communism has become today the principles, organization, and strategy of one of the most powerful revolutionary forces the world has known.

The Communist Strategy Today. In their challenge to the old order and the noncommunist world, the communist leaders have adopted a twofold strategy. In the first place, they have devoted themselves to creating and strengthening the economic and political foundations of communist society at home, especially a highly industrialized, technologically advanced, and centrally controlled economy. This is not only at the core of the communist ideal, but also essential in the revolutionary struggle. Central control of livelihood and production, to the degree it is effective, enables leaders better to control the lives of their peoples, and also to direct production to serve their needs in economic and military warfare. The revolutionary purpose is also promoted when their exceptional economic advances—economic weaknesses are concealed or minimized—are taken as influential examples by leaders of underdeveloped countries aspiring to modern industry. Technological development and industrialization are often more important than what is produced, and consumers' goods are of limited variety and often shoddy quality.

Second, complementing the exemplification of communism at home, they have intensified the promotion of revolutionary movements and conspiracies abroad. No longer primarily defensive, these leaders now seek to hasten the "inevitable" collapse of bourgeois power through attempts to exploit its difficulties and intensify what communists assert to be its "contradictions."

In communist thinking these contradictions of the noncommunist world exist on three levels: first, the conflict between capital and labor within any one country; second, the conflict between the bourgeois states themselves; and third, the conflict between the "imperialist" powers and their colonial and other dependencies. These are called contradictions because, in communist theory, they are not simply conflicts of interests which can be reconciled within the framework of capitalism and liberal democracy; they will be irreconcilable until they are transcended in the victory of communism. Such an absolute and irreducible conflict can only produce a "struggle to the death," a total war, as originally stated by Lenin. Proletarian and colonial rebellions against "exploitation" are inevitable and desirable; communists must support them, while the non-communist world can be expected to oppose both them and the communist states assisting them. This conflict is not at all like "old-fashioned" national rivalries. To the communists, anyway, it is a total conflict, and the only question is one of strategy: how to extend communism throughout the world and yet avoid, today, their own destruction in a nuclear holocaust unleashed by the doomed and desperate "imperialists."

The communist leaders appear in essential agreement on their revolutionary purpose and method. A fair description of how they have approached their problem, and presumably will continue to do so, was stated bluntly in *Red Flag,* organ of the Chinese Communist Party, on November 16, 1960. "While socialist countries make necessary and possible compromises with capitalist countries diplomatically," it was declared, "such compromises do not require the people [*read,* local communists and their supporters] of the countries of the capitalist world to follow suit and make compromises at home." In other words, they will stir up all the trouble they can, short of nuclear war. In tactical applications of this strategy during recent years the Soviet rulers, with more to lose, appear less inclined to risky adventures than the Chinese, newer to power and with a still largely rural community, but the differences seem minor.

The unity of the communist bloc may have been somewhat weakened in the struggle for dominance among Soviet and Chinese leaders and what they consider to be the needs of their respective countries and of the movement. However, as the Chinese leaders wrote to Soviet Premier Khrushchev on the occasion of his seventieth birthday in 1964, "Although at present there are differences between you and us on a number of questions of principle concerning Marxism-Leninism and there is a lack of unity, we are deeply convinced that this is only temporary. In the event of a major world crisis, the two parties, our two countries, and our two peoples will undoubtedly stand together against our common enemy." In explanation they said, "When one looks at the essence of the matter, so long as we take the Marxist-Leninist stand, imperialists and reactionaries headed by the United States will never relax in their policies of opposing the Soviet Union, opposing China, opposing Communism, opposing revolution and opposing the people." Khrushchev did not dispute the thesis, but only the good faith of the Chinese leaders, who had been attacking his judgment about what a Leninist must do today. Khrushchev's successors, after his dismissal late that year, appear even less likely or capable than he of pursuing peace on other than communist terms.

We must conclude, consequently, that although the situation is now more subtle and difficult to deal with, communists will continue to exploit the three "contradictions" they have identified in the noncommunist world. The tactics generally employed within established communities are intended to undermine a united anticommunist front by intensifying any and all controversies, and to acquire "fellow travelers" through exploiting the sympathies of some idealists. To these ends, they organize or infiltrate associations of industrial and agricultural workers, to turn them from "reformism"—the search for immediate benefits—into instruments of class warfare. They also create communist parties, more to inhibit the effective functioning of representative politics than in the hope of winning control of governments through elections, and form "communist front" organizations, under disguised communist domination, ostensibly to promote various worthy causes.

However, contemporary communists are especially concerned with the conflicts among bourgeois states and between them and their present or former dependencies. In exploiting these for their own purposes communists have achieved their greatest recent successes. Except for the period immediately following World War II, when communist regimes were established in eastern Europe and China by local communist parties, strongly supported by Soviet power, their efforts have recently been devoted largely to breaking the unity of the anticommunist states, and to fomenting anticolonialist revolutions throughout Asia, Africa, and Latin America. With ruthless realism, their appeal has been largely to nationalistic sentiments, economic ambitions, and the widespread fear of war, which they have succeeded in turning to their advantage in these areas, benefiting from a fairly general prejudice against white, European, and American civilization and power. Of course, the communists have been equally ruthless, when they have the power and find it expedient, in subordinating peace and the national interests, differences, and economic development of their supporters to the allegedly internationalist revolutionary movement—in fact identified with the leading power of the Soviet Union and China. This is justified by the Marxist theory that nationalism is reactionary, and that peace and plenty can and will be obtained only through total communist victory. In sum, the communists endeavor to intensify all sources of discontent among peoples and to control when possible the expression of that discontent, firm in the conviction that such incendiary activities will in the long run enhance their power. One need not look for any other purpose in communist policies; there is none.

In a world seething with discontent and anxiety, a theory giving a simple explanation for that condition and promising an eventual peace and general well-being easily finds support among frustrated masses and their ambitious leaders, and justifies almost any actions. Furthermore, to the ideological criticisms and promises of communism must be added the facts of Soviet and Chinese Communist power. These regimes have, by their open and continued hostility to the long-dominant western countries, shown their independence of them. The Soviet Union, in particular, has also launched great programs of technological development with obvious success. To many throughout the world these communist achievements prove the truth of communist doctrines, and demonstrate that those struggling for release from "imperialist domination" and for national independence—both political and economic—should emulate communist Russia and China and accept their aid and direction. In seeking to conquer the whole world and to transform human nature, the communist movement does encounter many of the same difficulties it proclaims as peculiar to capitalism and democracy. Nevertheless, communism continues to spread and—incompatible with democracy in both theory and practice—challenges democracy on every front.

II. FASCISM

Fascism is the other significant challenge to democracy in the modern world. Strictly speaking, the name was one taken by the regime established in Italy after 1922 and not overthrown until late in World War II. In a broader sense, however, the term "fascism" connotes a general political phenomenon of the twentieth century, the sort of regime resulting when some central ideas of modern political life—particularly those of the nation-state—are carried to a logical extreme and pursued with a fanatical zeal. Fascism in this sense, then, occurred not only in Italy, but also in Spain and Japan during the 1930's, and in Argentina under Perón after 1943; its principal and most virulent manifestation arose in National

Socialist Germany between 1933 and 1945. It appeared also as an occasional and threatening tendency in many other countries, even France and the United States; and the Union of South Africa has been flirting with it for some years. Although no powerful fascist regime exists in the world today, fascist ideas are by no means dead, and challenge democracy no less than those of communism. Indeed, some believe that one or the other must everywhere ultimately prevail; such an attitude improperly depreciates democracy, but it is illustrative of the dangerous character of our times.

Fascism is in principle an authoritarian ideology and movement. Fascists, like communists, have been totally opportunistic in practice, denying or distorting any doctrine which threatened to interfere with the seizure and exercise of power by leaders of these movements. Yet, as communism speaks in Marxist terms and claims to be the revolutionary movement of the proletariat, so in fascism do nationality and race play comparable roles. Promoting the unity and power of a national or racial group is the customary objective of a fascist movement, and fascist ideology is built around vague but potent nationalistic or racist symbols to which unqualified allegiance is demanded. To fascists, however, the highest expression of the nation or race is found in a leader and his elite party. A fascist regime, consequently, is necessarily a dictatorship, glorifying the authority of the leader through which alone the community can find its unity and power.

Nationalism and Racism. National and racial differences have long been recognized by mankind, of course. In western civilization, however, men have endeavored only in recent centuries to found political orders upon them, and most often even then with a moderation recognizing more universal values. Increasingly, however, sentiments of nationality, and occasionally of racial distinction, have become dominant themes and perhaps the most powerful forces in modern political life. Nor has moderation always survived; what in the late eighteenth century appealed to the German romantic philosopher, von Herder, as the manifestation of a lovely diversity in human life—all aspects of which should be fostered—became a century or so later the vehicle of a highly emotional exclusiveness and sense of superiority, productive of fear and animosity. On such extreme nationalism and racism and their consequences, fascism is founded.

Fanatical and extreme nationalism, often called "integral nationalism," appeared about a half-century ago. It found its most powerful voices first in France, although England did not lack for its "jingoism," nor was the United States completely immune, as the "yellow journalism" of the Spanish-American war period indicates. French "integral nationalists," such as Charles Maurras and Maurice Barrès, wrote in violent rebellion against the liberal principles of the revolution of 1789 and against the democratic republic of their day, which they saw as corrupt and petty. Instead they worshiped an "eternal France," fair and powerful, and demanded in brilliant writings unity and sacrifice for the glory of the nation. Their cry found willing ears; leaders appeared throughout Europe, and eventually elsewhere as well, championing the special destinies of their particular peoples.

In countries where nationalism had become strong, but where that sentiment was outraged by the absence or weakness of a national political order, the advocates of fascism found the most fertile soil. Germany and Italy, for example, both possessing old and distinctive cultures, had come only recently—after 1870—to a national political unity. Both communities were emotionally affected by the "national humiliation" they suffered in World War I and the economic difficulties which followed it, and by the fact that substantial national populations were oustide their state borders. Both, likewise, after that war had weak governments which reflected divisions and tensions within the countries far greater than they could overcome. As the jealous gods of nationalism were frustrated in these states, the reaction was violent. The call for national unity and the promise of national glory expressed by Mussolini and Hitler brought to their standards millions of the discontented—albeit for many different reasons. The substantial popular support such regimes have had should not be underestimated, even though no fascist party has ever gained a popular majority in a free election.

Despite its emotional appeal, however, the nationalism of the fascists has had little specific content. It was enough in itself to lead automatically to the condemnation of liberalism for its individualism, of socialism and communist theory for their emphasis upon economic conditions, and of any sort of internationalism. Though fascists insisted everything should be subordinated to the nation, what they thought the nation was or what it should become remained vague. Mussolini, seeking power in 1921, promised only to rule so as to "insure the moral and material greatness of the Italian people." Fascism could not be committed to a program, for it "builds the structure of its will and passion from day to day." Regardless of this vagueness as to the good to be served, however, Mussolini still insisted that "the State stands for the immanent conscience of the nation," and that "everything [is] within the State, nothing outside the State, nothing against the State." In other words, individuals can find morality and worth only in obedience and service to the nation as organized by the fascists. To support these arguments great nationalistic celebrations were promoted, while black-shirted gangs terrorized those who objected. Despite all this, however, fascism in Italy was moderated in its thoroughness, if not its brutality, tempered undoubtedly by the stubborn individualism and sense of humor of the Italian people.

It was in Nazi Germany that nationalism rose to a brief peak of unbelievable fury, and fascism flowered. To Italian fascism Hitler added embellishments derived from his Germanic background. The romantic Wagnerian operas, with their mystically inspiring music and legends of godlike heroes, set the mood, to which the exotically challenging nineteenth-century German philosophy, from Hegel through Nietzsche, added diverse but always antiliberal messages. Alongside this existed a widespread anti-Semitism, and often anti-Slav and anti-Latin attitudes as well, which gave to German nationalism a racist character generally lacking in Italy. The Nazi god was the *Volk,* a tribal Germanic population, which Hitler proclaimed to be the "blood-conditioned entity," and the "God-willed building stone of human society." "The individual is transitory, the *Volk* is permanent," and to its preservation all the institutions and values of society were but means. To that end there is nothing which may not be sacrificed; to the glorification of the *Volk* and the expansion of its *Lebensraum* (living space and domination) were devoted the most impressive mass demonstrations and terroristic brutality of all time. Millions of Germans cheered these, apparently finding in the Nazi regime, and its dramatic if perverse achievements, the manifestation of German honor and blood. Yet this "revolution of nihilism" could achieve only the sadistic suppression and extermination of "inferior peoples," and the holocaust of World War II.

The Fascist Movement and Its Leader. Although fascism depends upon the existence of widespread nationalistic sentiments, from which it derives its popular support, a fascist regime can survive only through accentuating these sentiments, often to the point of hysteria. For the nation, the state, and the *Volk* as envisaged by fascists do not actually exist but are "ideals" to be realized through a revolutionary struggle. In the process all the conflicting traditions of western civilization must be destroyed. The "ideal" and what it is opposed to find full and clear expression in the words of one Nazi: "There has arisen blood against formal reason, race against purposeful rationality, honor against profit, unity against bourgeois security, the folk against the individual and the mass."

Carrying the revolutionary torch, expressing the blood and honor of the nation to come, is the fascist movement and its leader. "The community of the *Volk,*" Hitler said, "[is] organized in the National Socialist movement," which is engaged in "stamping the Nazi *Weltanschauung* [roughly, 'view of life'] on the German people." Quite naturally, any rival political organizations, not only active parties but even any groups independent of fascist control, are eliminated as soon as fascists gain power. Into this revolutionary struggle are thrown all the resources made available in modern techniques of coercion and propaganda. Although not possible without mass response to its leadership, fascism is nevertheless highly elitist in its actual operation. The mass of the population does cheer and otherwise support the regime, but this is its sole function. Dominant in a fascist community is the party, a militant and quasi-military elite; its function is to destroy opposition and to exemplify the fascist ideals.

If in broad terms the fascist movement is the elite, however, it in turn can find its unity only in absolute devotion to one man, presumed to be the perfect representative of all that is vital and valid for the community, if not the world. Thus, the key aspect of fascism is the "leadership principle." Throughout Italy in the days of fascism appeared the slogan, "Mussolini is always right." In Germany, more ominously still, Hermann Göring was acclaimed for announcing defiantly to the world: "If abroad it is believed that chaos threatens Germany, the German people responds with the single cry 'We all approve always of what our leader does.'" And from Nazi Germany's leading lawyer came the assertion that "our constitution is the will of *Der Führer* [leader]." Rarely if ever has such personal infallibility been thus glorified and all traditional, legal, and rational limitations on political power so totally set aside.

The Background of Fascist Elitism. The fanatical and elitist politics of fascism have deep roots. The belief that political leadership and the fulfillment of essential governmental responsibilities are compatible with democracy and the liberal view has been severely attacked during the last century, and effectively undermined in many quarters. Literary figures of considerable note, such as Nietzsche in Germany and Carlyle in England, found in the activity of unique and dominant personalities the reality of human history. "Supermen" and "heroes" are the true representatives of mankind, they argued, and others should recognize and serve them. Nor did the developing "social sciences" lend much support to democracy against this romantic challenge. Psychology appeared to establish that irrational and aggressive elements in human nature are far more fundamental and dominant than rationality and co-operativeness. Furthermore, newly invented "intelligence tests" indicated that inequalities in human capacities are pronounced. Evidence from family histories was also adduced to show that both moral and intellectual qualities are inherited, not the result of environment or education. Thus, it was asserted, the capacities for leadership and responsibility are inherently distributed unequally not only among individuals but even among families and classes. There is, it was claimed, a natural aristocracy. These conclusions were often extreme and inadequately supported generalizations, but this did not prevent critics of democracy from widely proclaiming that "science" proved democracy impossible and undesirable.

In the unsettled conditions of the twentieth century these critics attracted considerable support; when men are insecure the need for strong leadership is felt with particular intensity. Furthermore, as an eminent German sociologist, Max Weber, observed early in the century, authority falls into three types: traditional, rational, and charismatic. The traditional form supports the leadership of aristocratic classes, within the limits given by custom. It is characteristic of stable communities, and is largely irrelevant in those we have lately known. Rational authority presupposes a community which understands its purposes, and is willing to accept the discipline of rational organization and a legal assignment of powers and responsibilities. Leadership within these limits is compatible with democratic procedures and liberal ideals, but it does not meet the needs of those driven by personality or circumstance to worship heroes, prefer the rule of ill-defined elites, or glorify mystical goals. For them the only true authority is that of the "charismatic" leader. The term "charisma" refers to the exceptional and extraordinary qualities of a man's personality, which catch the imagination of others and make them want to follow him, if necessary against all tradition and rationality. Obviously, such leadership may be used for good or ill.

Charismatic leadership is undoubtedly a vital aspect of political life in periods of radical change, and the greatest leaders in history, political and religious, have possessed such qualities. Nonetheless, one important difference between fascist dictatorship and democracy lies in the degree to which the charismatic form is limited by coexisting rational or traditional forms of leadership. The charismatic form is the very essence of fascism; allegiance to the country becomes personal loyalty to the leader. Thus, the dictator is "always right," and his "will" is the constitution. Of course, neither tradition nor reason can possibly justify either of these assertions. Nevertheless, whenever people in large numbers have lost both their traditional faith and their confidence in reason as means of arranging their lives successfully, they are likely to offer themselves up to fanatic and unscrupulous demagogues who play upon their fears and furnish them with myths of superior racial or national destiny to fill their emptiness. When such manipulation is possible, fascism threatens, and both civilization and liberal government are challenged. Unfortunately these conditions exist in many states of the world today.

III. TOTALITARIAN DICTATORSHIP

However different communism and fascism may be in their arguments and justifications and in some of their manifestations, they produce the same result: totalitarian dictatorship. Franklin D. Roosevelt, commenting a generation ago on the claims of the fascists to represent a "new order," proclaimed that it was neither new nor was it order. This profound insight into contemporary totalitarianism erred, however, in not recognizing the novelty of regimes based upon the glorification and near institutionalization of chaos, at war with every principle of law and morality. In contrast, authoritarian regimes, even dictatorships, have long filled the pages of history, but with few exceptions they have acknowledged objectives and standards distinct, limited, and realistic enough that they were to a considerable extent governed by them. They were governments responsible to something, if not to the people, and they have sometimes produced conditions in which democracy could arise. While not themselves democratic, they have not been—nor are they today—challenges to democracy. For the most part, they have been traditionalist regimes, deriving their authority from the laws and customs they profess to uphold, and limited thereby.

The present age, however, is one in which traditions and traditionalist governments are falling throughout the world. Furthermore, increasing millions aspire to the benefits of modern life. Governments that can provide these benefits and function effectively in the dynamic conditions of today must be both extremely flexible, even pragmatic, and capable of securing the active support and participation of large numbers of their people. Generally speaking, there are only two forms of government inherently pragmatic and founded on mass support: liberal democracy and totalitarian dictatorship. Basically, this is why they are in such conflict throughout the world; they are the ultimate alternatives in modern life. Of course, there will be transitional regimes, variations on the themes of each, and even regimes that in practice are not clearly either. Nonetheless, since we have already discussed the essential nature of democracy, we must do the same for totalitarianism. Democrats had best know the roots as well as the branches and fruit of this challenge to democracy.

The Struggle for Power. Communists and fascists alike see as the central reality of human history a brutal, if to them ennobling, struggle for power in which might equals right. Their justification for acting on this reading of history is that, in the end, a perfect community will emerge out of the ashes. Whether nationalist, racist, or proletarian, this community will be totally collectivist, resembling the undifferentiated community of primitive life but having escaped from the limitations of its rigid customs and small size. The persistent urge to return to this cultural womb is rooted in the fact that men are gregarious, tending to find pleasure and security in a close communion of values and emotional experiences which a pluralistic liberal order often fails to provide. But men are also individualistic, and have in fact created a social life highly diversified in the organization of its power and the nature of its values. As we suggested in Chapter 2, this flatly precludes any natural and stable return to an undifferentiated collectivism in social life, and liberal democracy represents the modern method of reconciling these two conflicting tendencies in mankind. Such efforts are imperfectly effective, however, and the collectivist urge erupts from time to time, particularly in mass movements of social protest which appear markedly susceptible to primitivism in periods of radical and disorienting social change.

Communism and fascism are the extreme forms of the eruption of collectivistic idealism in this century. Responding to the enormous social, economic, and political changes of recent times they envisage great national, racial, or proletarian communities, within which all divisive elements have been eliminated, and which exercise an absolute and imperialistic power over all they cannot absorb. So extraordinary an objective cannot function as a rational goal. It can and has, however, functioned as a myth—a vision whose truth or falsity is unprovable and irrelevant, and whose sole function is its emotional impact, leading people to march unquestioningly and without stint in search of power. To the drive for power, stimulated by the myth of the great family of tribe or working class, any of the values of civilization may be sacrificed, together with any persons who persist in defending them. The sole virtues recognized by totalitarians are unity and power; anything else would sooner or later be either destructive of their myth or inhibiting in their revolutionary struggle against a refractory world.

Total Revolution. The only adequate symbol of the totalitarian myth and expression of its virtues, furthermore, is the "leader." Only in him can even the party elite find its unity. One of the highest Nazi leaders, Göring, frankly admitted his fear of contradicting Hitler in any way; the virtual worship of Lenin and Stalin dominated Soviet life for three decades. Since Stalin's death and the rise of Chinese communism, the principal embarrassment of the communist movement has been an increasing lack of unity in voice and action, proving that communist doctrine alone cannot eliminate disagreement. Communist leaders have made every effort to remedy this failing, recognizing that the survival of their power both nationally and internationally depends on doing so, but the bitterness of the Sino-Soviet conflict, accentuated in early 1964, shows that the only method available to them is "power politics" at its worst, even among those calling themselves "comrades." Khrushchev's abrupt downfall in an interparty coup is further evidence that personal and conspiratorial leadership is at the heart of such regimes.

The natural political form of totalitarianism, therefore, is dictatorship; fascists deliberately recognize this and exult in it, while communist jargon, such as "proletarian democracy" and—most recently—"the state of the entire people," only disguises the brutal reality. Of course, no regime is ever perfectly totalitarian, if only because there are always some limits to human power and, even, madness. In principle and as far as possible in practice, however, the dictatorship must be absolute and unqualified. Such support can only be an act of will and not of reason. Totalitarian regimes rest fundamentally, therefore, on the means used to attract, sway, and coerce the wills of men. Intensive propaganda, overwhelming mass demonstrations, continuing repressions of "counter-revolutionary" challenges, and widespread violence against any convenient objects, have been those most generally employed, evidencing a remarkable if perverse psychological insight into human weakness. These methods of "government" have played on the aspirations, fears, and hatreds of men, isolating and terrorizing opposition, and hypnotizing supporters. Far from accidental developments or transitory expedients, they are inherent and inevitable characteristics of totalitarian dictatorships. Totalitarianism is primarily a "total revolution," aiming at a collectivism and at the same time atomization so unnatural that it must be pursued and maintained through systematic corruption of the human mind and will. It is probably doomed to failure in the long run, but in our time none of us can escape the consequences of the attempt.

IV. PROBLEMS *of* CONTEMPORARY DEMOCRACY

Virtue is sometimes said by stern but realistic moralists to be its own reward. The democratic ideal may be similarly transcendent, along with justice, and be pursued for its own sake though the world perish. One cannot deny that there is much of this sentiment in the literature of democracy. Nonetheless, the democratic governments of history arose as practical responses to practical problems, and the question to be confronted here is whether they are so today. The rise and spread of totalitarianism and its power in our world has not been a mere accident, nor do such regimes arise without considerable popular support. Unlike earlier enthusiasts for democracy, those of today know that people can and do reject the ends it is supposed to serve, or the responsibilities it entails, and sometimes both. They know, in other words, that democracy appears and survives only when it represents a widespread choice, and that the choice of democracy, in turn, depends upon a sustained conviction among men that they can best conduct their political affairs through that form of government.

Recognizing that such a conviction is far from universal, an analysis of democracy and the challenge to it must consider whether the conviction is actually justified in prevailing circumstances. Do the values democracy is alleged to serve sufficiently reflect the aspirations and meet the needs of twentieth-century man? Even more, do the procedures and institutions of democracy actually serve those values, so that the choice of democracy is a realistic one, given that social conditions of the present time are radically different from those prevailing when democracy first emerged? The mere existence of totalitarian regimes indicates that these questions cannot be definitively answered; democracy is everywhere under attack and is nowhere secure. At this point we can only consider some of the major problems democracies must solve if they are to survive. Later chapters will further elaborate selected aspects of them, and suggest how they are being met within the democratic framework, as well as apart from it. In the Epilogue we shall endeavor to evaluate the success of these efforts to preserve democracy.

THE ATROPHY OF DEMOCRATIC PUBLIC SPIRIT

Although modern democracy recognizes and is designed to protect a considerable diversity of values and interests among its citizens, it equally presupposes a community underlying that diversity. Advocates of democracy have always understood that diversity is enjoyed and can be tolerated by men only when it exists within a framework of agreement on basic values. Where democracy arose, such an agreement was at the time present and adequate to existing needs. The values shared defined a community of persons, in general terms, and a public, in more specifically political terms. Political responsibility was clear; it was to this public and for the values this public held. More recently, however, signs have appeared suggesting that this public has disintegrated. These may be simply the products of a transitional period in our history, but since democracy very much depends upon public-spirited political activity, they nonetheless signal a real danger.

The Weakened Sense of Community. One of the striking characteristics of political life today, especially in established democratic regimes, is widespread apathy among the people; except when some particularly spectacular election is being held, as for a president of the United States, large numbers of persons seem either little concerned with political issues or little confident that their interest is significant. Another characteristic is the tendency of people, when they do take an interest in politics, to do so from the point of view of "what's in it for me." A third characteristic is a pervasive lack of information and awareness among the population on the background and nature of the issues which, in a democracy, the citizens are asked—directly or indirectly—to settle.

None of these characteristics bodes well for democracy. They are not, however, as some have claimed, proof that most people are necessarily ignorant, apathetic, and lacking in public spirit, so that democracy is inherently absurd. They are, rather, signs of a weakened sense of community, apart from which public-spirited, intelligent, and self-confident political participation in democracy is impossible. For democracy is not primarily a matter of sheer numbers; the power of majorities springs from their organization and morale, and from a general recognition of a common good which majority rule may serve. Majority rule is not separable from a broad sense of community, which alone can make majority decisions legitimate and effective, and apart from which they are just as tyrannical—the exploitation of some by others—as those of any oligarchy. So, at least, thought every one of the American founding fathers, and more radical democrats of the time did not deny that a broad public interest alone should be promoted, even though they criticized undemocratic limitations on the suffrage and other processes through which it is identified and implemented.

There is little agreement today, however, over what the public interest might be or what democratic citizenship implies. The individual values of liberalism and the exceptional specialization of functions and outlooks inherent in modern technological society tend to encourage men to take if not a private at least a circumscribed view of what goes on around them. That our lives are organized in great and impersonal aggregations—such as urban metropolises, nation-states, and supranational and international bodies and agencies—has a similar effect. In such circumstances the average citizen is well aware that problems exist, for he immediately suffers their consequences in such things as threats to the peace, crowded schools, polluted rivers, and corruption in government. But he is often unable to determine clearly the nature and sources of these difficulties, or to come to agreement with others on how they may best be met. Education, in which democrats have always placed great stock, has come to be largely aimed at private occupational or recreational benefit, while its role of fitting people to be active citizens of a democratic community has been neglected, or conceived in the most banal terms, in sharp contrast to the ideas and practices of earlier days. One must recognize, however, that those earlier ideas were adapted to a simpler agrarian way of life. The future of democracy depends upon our ability to develop ideas that are relevant to present conditions.

The Sole Pursuit of Private Interest. In the absence of public-spirited citizenship, democratic politics loses coherence and legitimacy. The principal end of public policy comes to be less the advancement of a recognized common good—or even the promotion of particular interests clearly related to such a good—than the satisfaction of purely private individual and group interests, limited only by the necessities of bargaining. In such a process, general but unorganized interests often suffer. Most disadvantaged are the values and interests of groups both small and poorly organized; they may well experience a "tyranny of the majority." Among these are racial minorities, when the majority is not concerned about discrimination against them; cultural minorities, when popular taste is dominant and will not support either commercial or public ventures into diversity in education or entertainment; and those in "pockets" of poverty and economic insecurity in the midst of general prosperity.

The pursuit solely of private interest, permeated with the idea that "the devil take the hindmost," is not a principle upon which free democratic government can be founded; it gives rise to no standards in terms of which responsible solutions to social problems can be developed by political leaders and judged by citizens. Democracy will not long survive its dominance and the rejection of public responsibility which it implies. The selfishness of some, the resentments of others, and the increasing conviction of still others that a genuine moral community is incompatible with democracy—however perverse, unjust, or erroneous the sentiments—will eventually combine in their effects to destroy both freedom and democracy. Only the yet unproved capacity of democratic populations to create and sustain a sense of community sufficient to support public-spirited government through majority rule can prevent such a conclusion to their great experiment.

DEMOCRACY AND EXPERTS IN THE WELFARE STATE

Democracy has always taken for granted the independence and competence of its citizens. It is today being challenged in this basic assumption. Our forebears viewed democracy from the perspective of a way of life in which persons were not drastically affected by what others did, required relatively little co-operation from others in the achievement of any of their purposes, and generally possessed the knowledge required by their activities. Citizens of contemporary communities, however, no matter what ends they choose to pursue in the highly urbanized and technological societies of today, cannot accomplish them apart from intense co-operation and exceptionally knowledgeable decisions. For these, they are very much dependent upon a high degree of organization, often governmental, and upon the guidance and assistance of experts. Neither sort of dependence is readily reconcilable with democracy.

Increasing Dependence on Experts. First, the categories of professions and of highly skilled occupations have in recent years multiplied enormously, both as to new skills and in subtle differentiations within old ones, and have often advanced in level of technical development to the point where only the specialist can understand what he is doing and why. The common man, whatever he may have been in the past, is today the nonspecialist, and everyone is that in regard to most of the activities upon which his life depends. No "key" comparable to medieval theology has yet been discovered, despite efforts to create a "unified science"; even the relationship of diverse forms of expertise to each other remains unclear. Although the promise of the technological age is great, and its achievements already substantial, men as individuals have rather obviously lost control of their own lives.

Naturally, in modern government, technical experts have come to play an increasingly prominent role. There they combine the authority of their special skills with that of official position. It could hardly be otherwise, if we wish governments effectively to meet the sorts of problems created by contemporary life. Even more in public affairs than in private, experts are required to manage the complicated network of social and economic relationships so as to ensure any sort of public good whatever. The old adage, that the wearer of the shoe, the "common man," can alone and adequately tell whether and where the shoe pinches, remains true enough, but he is scarcely able these days to know why it pinches or what can be done about it. Because of this, government now relies heavily on those whose ability and training often make them insensitive to political needs and values, however professionally competent they may be otherwise.

The place of experts in government has long been recognized, but the democratic response was that they were to be "on tap but not on top." Despite occasional fears of a "managerial revolution," the danger is not that experts will create a dictatorship of their own, for they are not normally so inclined nor do they form a distinctive group which could do so. Rather, the danger is that government will move so far from the experience, knowledge, and values of the citizens at large that effective democratic control of government will be lost. Even their representatives—who are politicians, often expert in obtaining the support of the electorate in ways having little relation to policy issues—are frequently unable to control the agronomists, economists, lawyers, statisticians, and zoologists scattered throughout government without risking the benefits of their services through rejecting their judgments. Yet, in the absence of continuing and effective political control, public policy is likely to be governed by the disparate technical ideas of the experts, and to lose both unity and democratic responsibility. This will become an even greater problem as modern technology continues to develop.

Increasing Dependence on Government. Secondly, an urbanized, technological society is necessarily one in which the role of government and other great organizations is crucial. The necessity of this was for some time concealed from liberal democrats by their faith in a "natural harmony" of human interests and activities, and a belief that even selfish actions ultimately promote the best possible interests of all. This view has generally been abandoned or limited in recent decades, due to experiences in wars and depressions. The rise of "socialistic" governments and "welfare states" has not been brought about by some devious conspiracy, but is simply the consequence of present-day social and economic organization—big government along with big business and big labor—coupled with the democratic idea of a generalized distribution of benefits. It is only the political aspect of a society in which the control of very few things by private parties is of so little importance to others that it can be left unregulated in those hands.

Yet, many struggle against "socialism," sometimes because of genuine democratic convictions. The steady expansion of government services and regulation of formerly private affairs may generally be an honest attempt to resolve some of the difficult problems of modern life within democratic procedures and values—rather than destroying them outright, as do communism and fascism—but it also steadily reduces the realm in which private individuals may act spontaneously according to their own inclinations and ideas. If increased government control of social activities is one way of avoiding anarchy in those activities, and sometimes also of remedying private tyrannies, it also tends to deprive citizens of their independence of government—in ideas and values as well as powers of action—apart from which the democratic aim of popular control of government has little meaning or likelihood of success.

The problem is clear and formidable. The complex social activities of today cannot be harmonized and made productive of a general welfare except by experts and with much government action; yet how can we insure that these be the servants rather than the master of the community? Recent improvements in the old art of demagoguery, of swaying the opinions of men, make the problem particularly critical. Through use of the findings of psychology and sociology, and the means of mass communication, some men are becoming experts in the "engineering of consent," and have applied their talents not only to the merchandising of consumers' goods but also to political campaigns and the promotion of public policies. Very extensive and effective use of such procedures in political life would, quite obviously, render democracy meaningless.

DEMOCRATIC FREEDOMS AND THE TOTALITARIAN CONSPIRACY

Democracies are especially challenged today by the totalitarian threat to the peace and to their survival. The challenge is not merely one of an adequate external defense, but also one of maintaining democratic procedures and values in the face of this implacable attack. Tensions and conflicts between political regimes in the world have always existed, and domestic politics have always been affected by the requirements of foreign policy. But the problem today is whether the tension is not so great and pervasive that democracy will die in any event—either struck down from outside, or committing suicide in an effort to defend itself.

Early in American history Thomas Jefferson protested against the idea that democracy could be preserved by abandoning it. He insisted in his first inaugural address that a free country, in which error of opinion could be tolerated because reason was free to combat it, was the strongest on earth. "Every man," he said, "at the call of the law would fly to the standard of the law, and would meet invasions of the public order as his own personal concern." Clearly, Jefferson did not think that democratic communities needed dictators or censors to tell them what they stood for or what they needed to do, even in critical times. This has been the traditional democratic view, but many have come to wonder if it is still adequate.

The Intensification of Totalitarian Attack. In fact, the totalitarian conspiracy is more extensive and its techniques more insidious than anything Jefferson could have envisaged. He did not contemplate democracy under attack by a nihilistic revolutionary force capable of securing mass support. Nor did he realize that the defense of democracy would require vigorous action throughout the world, in realms far removed from the experience and values of the ordinary citizen. He trusted the people because he took for granted that they would be clearly aware of what the enemy was and where the struggle was being waged, and could and would make the rational choices which would protect democracy.

But the contemporary world is very complex and interdependent. Isolation is not a good survival policy; democracy can no more endure today in a world "half slave and half free" than it can in a country thus divided. The result is both foreign and domestic policy complicated beyond the comprehension of most people, demanding difficult insights and sacrifices. At the same time, the totalitarians are convinced that their victory will emerge inevitably out of chaos. They deliberately foment confusion, exploiting social discontent flowing from the radical changes through which the world is now passing. As tactics in their revolutionary drive they adopt any expedient guise. The communists generally pose as the more vigorous among liberal, humanitarian social reformers, and the fascists as defenders of conservative institutions and convictions. They soon discover their error who take the totalitarians at their word, but then it is generally too late. Yet it often remains difficult to identify the enemy in advance, such diverse masks does he wear and so many causes fully worthy of democratic support does he use for his ulterior purposes. In desperate reaction supporters of democracy are likely to strike out blindly, trapping dogs along with wolves, and democracy suffers.

The Problem of Democratic Defenses. Jefferson's faith that democracy is "the strongest government on earth" was based upon his assumption that most men are rational, moral, and public-spirited, capable of recognizing the friends and enemies of the liberal democratic communities they naturally create when given a chance. Our experience in this century, particularly, casts doubt upon the universal validity of this assumption, and even leads many to wonder if the peoples of long-established democratic communities are capable of living up to it. We have seen that force plays an important role in democratic governments as well as in others, despite the emphasis placed upon persuasion, and that the line between the two is not clearly marked. We have learned also that violence and terror have a far greater appeal and effectiveness as means of political integration than the democratic faith ever dreamed was possible or finds comfortable to admit. A much more sophisticated psychology than that of a century ago, finally, informs us of how tender are the emotional foundations of liberal democracy, and how much they depend upon a favorable environment for their development and survival.

In a world full of violence and frustration, and of widely disparate aspirations, needs, and conditions—in which democratic peoples are necessarily heavily engaged but can only imperfectly understand—what chance is there that the emotions and rational powers democracy requires can flourish? Clearly, much depends upon a resolute but democratic political leadership; yet the people must be able to recognize and support such leaders, for in a democracy the ultimate responsibility is theirs. Too often have they fluctuated between a denial of the danger—signaled in an attitude of "live and let live," or in one of "communism (or fascism) does a lot of good" despite its excesses—and a violent and unthinking antipathy which blindly fails to distinguish between subversive and responsible critics. This is not encouraging, for in that sort of game the totalitarians hold all the high cards, and will win through playing the extremes against each other. Democrats cannot beat totalitarians at their own game; democracy will survive only if it can work out means appropriate both to the character of democracy and the nature of the totalitarian attack. This is the third, and perhaps the most acute, problem democrats face in the world today.

The three broad problems indicated are, of course, interrelated, and the survival of democracy depends upon the concurrent resolution of them all. The difficulties are somewhat overwhelming, to be sure, but they probably will not prove insuperable if democratic populations become fully aware of the nature of the problems and devote themselves to meeting them. While success must flow basically from the resources of the people themselves, the institutions, procedures, and policies of government are important conditions of the adequate organization of those resources. The western tradition of "constitutional government," in which both strength and flexibility are combined, is an important asset in this effort. To this we may now turn, resuming in the Epilogue our reflections on the future of democracy.

PART THREE:

ORDER *and* FREEDOM

"JUNIUS"

We owe it to our ancestors to preserve entire those rights which they have delivered to our care; we owe it to our posterity not to suffer their dearest inheritance to be destroyed.

CICERO

Since, then, law is the bond that holds political society together, and since equality of rights is a part of law, by what principle of right can an association of citizens be held together, when the status of these citizens is not equal?

CHAPTER 5

CONSTITUTIONS *and* CONSTITUTIONAL GOVERNMENT

"ONE COUNTRY, one constitution, one destiny." Daniel Webster's oratory expresses forcefully the close relationship between a constitution and the political spirit of the nation-state. The term "constitution" and its derivatives are among our most important political concepts. The sort of order they identify has been since ancient times at the core of western political life. More recently, the term has been most frequently used, and its importance most especially felt, by those who value liberal democracy, since they have come to recognize that it is largely through constitutional government that democracy is secured. Like so many aspects of politics, however, the theory and practice of constitutions and constitutionalism involve more than is immediately evident, and we must probe rather deeply if we are to understand the significance of this topic.

CONSTITUTION AS THE FRAMEWORK OF POLITICS

A constitution is usually defined as the basic law of a political system. A synonym helps little here, however; in political analysis it is often difficult to determine exactly what that law is and how it operates. It is rarely simply a matter of looking at a document called "the Constitution," though this may be important evidence that a constitution exists and of what it is like. Actually, constitutions of government are the product of long experience; their existence as well as their specific provisions reflect the diverse and changing circumstances and purposes of political life. To understand them we must see how they emerged, what meaning they came ultimately to have, and what institutions and procedures of government are manifestations of them.

In a sense the concept of a constitution is coterminous with any sort of thought about politics and political life. We reflect about politics when we become aware of differences among actual governments, or that those governments are not what we would like them to be. Our reflections will be limited, however, unless we can delineate some clear types of governmental forms and procedures enabling us to compare and analyze the diverse regimes and ideals more effectively. Thus political analysis, seeking significant criteria for the study and evaluation of political institutions, also seeks to identify the fundamental, or constitutional, aspects of political order.

Despite much honest and careful study, however, students and practitioners of government have not always agreed on what these are. Some writers have included only specific powers of principal officials, especially if authorized in a constitutional document, while others have insisted that the spiritual force dominant in a society is fundamental. To Aristotle, reflecting ancient Greek life, the constitution was not only the arrangement of offices but also the underlying "way of life." Consequently he felt it necessary to probe behind the old classification of governments by the one, the few, or the many, to identify the virtues and vices of each form, in whose interests it ruled and how, and the sort of community it represented. Out of this came his influential classification of monarchy, aristocracy, and polity (moderate democracy) as forms of rule according to law and in the interest of the city; while tyranny, oligarchy, and ochlocracy (extreme democracy) were lawless forms, ruling in the interests of the tyrant, the wealthy few, or the mob—giving us, thus, six types of constitutions. Modern political science has concluded, however, that government is always immediately by "the few," and that constitutions are distinguished most importantly according to how those few exercise political power.

Obviously, then, to understand the constitutions of modern governments, and to appreciate the full meaning of the term in political analysis, we must examine those governments from many points of view. We must see them in their historical development and in the context of their present activities, taking into account both the values men pursue and the conditions within which they must act at any given time, if we are to distinguish the stable relationships underlying political life and see how these crystallize as constitutions. One of the most important characteristics of these constitutional relationships is that they susbtantially and persistently shape the distribution and exercise of political power; indeed, they are fundamental in the power structure that is government. However, the factors affecting political power are not always the same, and constitutions change and vary.

At the same time constitutions embody ideals to some extent. Undeniably facts of political life, they are nonetheless created by men, who likewise analyze and attempt to understand them. In these activities men seek fulfillment of their needs and security of their values. A constitution, then, channels the exercise of political power—limiting its scope or distributing its exercise—in such a way as to stabilize it and render it compatible with the needs and values of the community. This theoretical proposition will help us identify constitutional institutions as they emerge in history, and later serve as the foundation for a discussion of constitutional principles.

I. *The* ROOTS *of* MODERN CONSTITUTIONS

Although the importance of the constitution as a political concept has been fully recognized only in recent times, contemporary institutions that we call constitutional have a substantial historical development. They are the result of several thousand years of human thought and action, into which has gradually been built a pattern of political beliefs and practices. The constitutions of today would not be the "facts" they are were this not so, and we shall understand them better if we look first to their roots.

CONTRIBUTIONS OF THE ANCIENT WORLD

Although the conditions of contemporary political life are vastly different from those of classical Greece and Rome, our debt to that time is incalculable. All succeeding stages in the development of western civilization were strongly influenced by classical political thought and practice, which endeavored to cast political life in a mold of reason and law.

Greece: Political Philosophy and the Ideal of Justice. Most spectacularly expressed in the teachings of Socrates, Plato, and Aristotle, Greek political life introduced into our culture the spirit of rational criticism that is the foundation for constitutional politics. In the absence of this spirit, the basic elements of a political system tend to be arbitrary or mystical, but its presence encourages developing them into patterns of functions and responsibilities, methods of control, standards against which particular acts of officials can be evaluated, and powers necessary to accomplish some rather clearly defined goals. What follows in our discussion of the history of constitutional institutions is largely a statement of the ways in which the inherent logic of Greek political thought has been applied in practice throughout changing circumstances.

A specific contribution to constitutional development, however, was the Greek conception of, and attachment to, justice and law. Very broadly speaking, justice is the standard for the appropriate ends to be served in politics, while law is the standard for the means to be used; however, the two are really inseparable. Both express the well-being of the entire community, not the interest of any part of it, and a government that does not rule according to the law, promoting justice, is a tyranny.

In Greek political practice, also, institutions enforced these convictions, but the tendency to a rather monolithic view of political life that we have already noted limited their effectiveness. Justice and law were most often political, the preferences and interests of a ruling group; neither could be a stable and effective control over the exercise of political power. Their contribution to constitutional history, therefore, was primarily one of declaring aspirations and providing the intellectual instruments.

Rome: Government, Law, and Rights. The Romans developed institutions that were to be a solid foundation for those of modern political life. The core was a massive and systematic body of law. Within Roman society and by its law, private affairs were defined in terms of rights, and public affairs in terms of power and responsibilities; furthermore, this law became increasingly technical and its administration highly professionalized. The result was that it came to serve as a very real control over the exercise of political power, and further established as one of the functions of government the protection of private rights. In accord with Greek ideals, although not necessarily following them as such, Rome succeeded in practice where Greece had failed. Quite explicitly in Rome did all authority flow from the law, which conferred powers as it limited power.

The fact that Roman law was of this nature, expressing itself in terms of rights and responsibilities, ultimately gave rise to a new and different conception of citizenship, or membership in the body politic. The Greek view of citizenship had made it akin to membership in a family or church, intense and inherently exclusive, and in Rome this was also for some time true. But in time, largely in response to the demands of a growing empire, the essence of Roman citizenship came to be enjoyment of the rights that the law defined and public officials would protect. Our modern conception of citizenship is predominantly Roman; it could hardly be otherwise. Citizenship as "equal protection of the laws" is possible even in the enormous communities of the present, but citizenship according to the Greek view, as active participation in the affairs of state, can be but imperfectly maintained under the most ideal circumstances. The Roman practice is thus essential if citizenship is to be meaningful in our day. It, together with their creation in the realm of law, is central in modern constitutions.

CONTRIBUTIONS OF THE MIDDLE AGES

The thousand years or so following the fall of the Roman empire was a complex period of transition between the ancient and the modern worlds. The general character of political life during those centuries was treated briefly in previous chapters. The reader should recall that it was one of a remarkable multiplication of social organizations and dispersion of power. Lacking any clear center around which it could effectively be integrated, not only in practice but even in theory, the medieval social order was fundamentally pluralistic. In it were laid the foundations of modern political life, and most particularly of the institutions of modern constitutions, elaborated as ideas and practices concerning law and rights, political obligation and consent, representation, and public power as a trust.

Social Order, Rights, and Law. The medieval social order and thought were organic and functional. The various corporations and classes were considered natural parts of the whole community; each performed an appropriate and necessary function in the life of the whole from which flowed the rights of individuals and groups. Rights were attached to whoever performed such functions and possessed as much objective validity as did the functions served. Seldom was this viewed as a matter of conscious deliberation and choice; it was thought to be given in custom and scripture, which reason but interpreted. Consequently, individuals would come and go, but the positions in society, with attendant rights and duties, were thought of as "natural," as intrinsic characteristics of the community, and thus beyond the power of any man to alter.

These rights and duties, and the social order they expressed, were considered as rooted in law. Law, it was assumed, defined the position, the privileges and responsibilities, of every member of the community. None was outside that law and none above it. Although no one would likely maintain that practice always lived up to this ideal—and the exercise of government was often in fact inefficiently dispersed—the medieval idea was clear: the purpose of government was to maintain law and order, to preserve the peace and administer justice, by methods the law itself provided.

No better technique of controlling and channeling the exercise of political power has been devised than its subordination to law, provided that we are able to distinguish what law is applicable. To the Germanic tribes it was their custom; this view pervades the middle ages, even though the custom became steadily more complex through infusions of vulgarized Roman law and Christian moral concepts. But legal problems arise when a rule is not clear; custom itself cannot speak, and if it could it would not necessarily and always be with one voice. Who can declare law, and what criteria must be considered, therefore, became important problems. During the later middle ages much thought was given to both of these matters, and a pattern of legal thinking was created that has been influential to the present day.

Clarification of the appropriate source of law was particularly indispensable due to the extreme decentralization of power in the feudal system. For various reasons, monarchical government seemed the most natural to the medieval mind, although the frequent qualifications in the direction of representative participation must not be overlooked, and with this prestige, backed by his power as a great lord, the king was the most likely source of legal norms, through his ordinance or judicial decision. But neither a general preference for monarchy, nor the effective power of any man, necessarily made any particular man king. Legitimate title was acquired through laws of succession and conquest, renewal of oaths of fealty by the nobility, acclaim by the population, and sanctification by the Church.

The king, then, was subordinate to the laws governing how a man became king. But to medieval thinking these laws were not separable from other norms to which the king was also subject, derived from revelation and from reason, and called divine or natural law. Against these even the ordinance of a legitimate ruler had no authority; rather was he to follow reason and revelation, ruling in justice and preserving the peace. The king, then, was always under the law even if, in the most extreme view, he alone had authority to define it. While our ideas about the substance of this "higher law" have changed considerably through the intervening centuries, the belief that it exists and that conformity to it alone justifies government and positive law was firmly rooted in political life in the middle ages and has been a basic fact in our constitutional systems ever since.

Consent and Representation. One of the most interesting aspects of the medieval order was its confusion of private and public rights and responsibilities. The personal interest of a king or baron was totally merged with his public position; he could not resign either while retaining the other. Since public authority is thus a matter of personal status, voluntary acceptance of the position, its advantages and its disadvantages as given in law, was deemed necessary. In other words, consent was considered essential to any political obligation. Among the Germanic invaders of Rome, leaders were simply pre-eminent warriors under whom other men voluntarily accepted service, and who accepted them. This practice was reflected in the medieval oaths of fealty. A man became a vassal of a lord by explicitly placing himself under that lord's protection and pledging in return the customary services.

The grounding of political obligation in consent was not as marked outside the feudal structure because for a long time it could not play much of a role there. As the middle ages advanced, however, the free populations of the cities became increasingly important in the life of the communities, and also to the kings who were attempting to consolidate their power. They were then brought within the political order through royal charters, granting them special privileges as well as obligations, analogous to oaths of fealty. Manifesting not only an extension of the idea of consent to government but also the appearance of a written document expressing fundamental law, such charters are obviously prototypes of modern constitutions.

But to the modern mind consent to government demands continuing consent through representatives, if not more directly. In the middle ages, too, as we have seen in the discussion of the rise of democracy, participation in government by the governed, or by some of them, was firmly institutionalized from the manor to the Church. As early as the end of the eighth century edicts promulgated by Charlemagne always indicated that the leaders of the various tribes and populations affected had given their advice. Ultimately this practice became formalized in the great feudal councils of the emperor and kings, and any decisions that would affect private rights, particularly, could not be made apart from the consent of these councils. Ultimately, too, as in England in the thirteenth century, such participation was extended to commoners of town and country, whose advice and consent were necessary to success in an expanding policy. Here was laid the foundation upon which modern representative government was to be built.

Public Power as a Trust. Although political authority derives from the "higher law" we also require a body of positive law, because neither reason nor revelation can give us rules appropriate to the contingencies of our actual existence. The middle ages were well aware of this; as St. Thomas Aquinas put it, human law is an ordinance of *practical* reason providing for the common good and promulgated by him who has the care of the community. Political power must exist, then, to make and enforce those contingent and somewhat subjective decisions that alone can provide for the needs of practical life.

To meet this need and yet avoid arbitrariness the middle ages developed the idea of power as a trust. This was explicit in all late medieval political thought, and institutionalized in coronation oaths. In these oaths the king promised to rule the people justly and to provide them with peace and order; in return the people promised to obey.

Through trusteeship it was possible to hold the king responsible in terms of the broad objectives of government, but at the same time to give him the freedom necessary to pursue those objectives effectively through varying circumstances. Power thus held can be abused, and often has been, but trusteeship is probably the political perspective most suited to the complexity in values, needs, and conditions of a dynamic civilization. What we have done since the medieval period has essentially been to develop new institutions of control in an attempt to promote its realization.

II. *The* FEATURES *of* MODERN CONSTITUTIONALISM

The middle ages shade but gradually into the modern period; yet in the seventeenth century political life had obviously changed radically. New political ideas and needs were pressing for recognition and, during this and the two succeeding centuries, ultimately found institutional embodiment. The late eighteenth and early nineteenth centuries were, in fact, a spectacular age of constitutional development. There emerged new conceptions of the nature of political order and its foundation, of its proper organization, and of the relation between it and private persons. Expressed in patterns of procedure and policy they directly underlie the constitutions of the twentieth century.

Sovereignty and the State. Sovereignty as the core of political order is essentially a modern innovation, created in response to the need of a rapidly expanding European culture and economy for an effective law-making power. Though the term had existed in medieval usage, where it had meant little more than "superior," in the writings of Jean Bodin (1576) and after, it came to have a much more radical significance. Sovereignty became the concentration in a determinate person or group —the sovereign power—of the authority to create law. Rights and obligations acquired legal existence only as expressions of that sovereign's will. A legal term, sovereignty merely expresses the necessary conditions for the existence of law, primarily a unity of will, and implies nothing as to the content of what may be so willed, or even that there must be any sovereign or law at all.

The state, however, as the principal modern form of political order, has been forged through the doctrine of sovereignty and cannot be understood apart from it. The state is a legal phenomenon, not a broad sociological one. It is manifested not in laws of nature, which are discovered, and which describe unalterable phenomena such as gravity, but in positive laws, willed by men as conditions and forms for their social activities. Natural necessity obviously limits positive law, but the limitation is not a legal one. Consequently, the state, as the realm in which one common positive law is recognized, depends on the unified will, or sovereign power, which creates that law. And common citizenship in the modern state came to mean subjection to a common sovereign power, regardless of any other similarities or differences among the people. Neither common kinship, race, religion, nor customs are necessary characteristics of membership in the modern state. Quite often, instead, they pose limitations to be overcome in the movement toward greater political orders.

Of evident practical significance in such a political order is the location of the sovereign power. Initially, it was claimed in behalf of a king or prince by those who were especially disadvantaged by the confused legal situation that attended the decline of the middle ages. Only his unchallenged authority could create an effective and acceptable legal order. In this form, at least, sovereignty is indisputably clear, if not indisputably acceptable. Eventually, though, the inadequacy of having the entire political order rest on the shoulders of one man, albeit those of a king, became evident, and a more fundamental location for the sovereign power was sought.

Some, following Frederick the Great's assertion that he was only "the first servant of the state," found it in the state itself. Others, of a democratic persuasion, transferred sovereignty from the king to the people; hence the term "popular sovereignty." The inadequacy of these formulations, however, arises out of the separation of the state or people from the government of the day, since it is not clear how either can independently act as sovereign. In fact, in neither of these more complex expressions is the doctrine of sovereignty fully intelligible. The ideas, or ideals, of a unified legal order and a freedom from tradition and alien authority remain, but the determinate person or body capable of acting freely to promote that order has disappeared. Sovereignty, once a very concrete concept, has become quite abstract.

Underlying all modern politics, nevertheless, is the idea that behind the visible agency of government there is a power that usually acts through that government and according to existing law, but cannot be limited to those means of realizing its will. It seems largely a matter of convenience or ideological orientation whether one refers to that sovereign as the "people" or the more legalistic "state." Sovereignty persists, despite our manifest uneasiness with some of its implications, because we have not yet disavowed the revolutionary perspective which gave rise to it. Only the continuing concentration and liberation of authority expressed in sovereignty will enable us to live with the tensions inherent in the dynamic pluralism of modern life, with its rejection of custom in favor of continuing innovation. In short, sovereignty is the will to ordered change. Although often in conflict with the liberal ideal of individual freedom, sovereignty is really its societal counterpart.

The concept of sovereignty, however, does not alone sufficiently describe modern political life. Sovereignty, expressing its most general characteristics, is in itself too abstract; we need to know how it is manifested, through what channels it flows, and what may be the practical limitations surrounding its exercise. Let us now consider some of the more important of these conditioning factors in the evolution of modern constitutions.

Constitution: an Explicit Grant of Authority. To modern thinking, quite evidently, the foundation of political systems is no longer a matter of myth, or dim memory, nor is it a natural event. It is of human doing. As such, it must suit man's needs, values, interests, and capabilities. Consequently a constitution came to be seen somewhat as a blueprint, a standard which both authorizes the work of governors and permits that work to be evaluated.

A constitution even in this sense is not necessarily democratic, nor, in the institutions it provides, need it be completely innovating. Many constitutions in the early nineteenth century were promulgated by kings as allegedly free concessions, and most constitutions have been in their actual provisions firmly rooted in traditional practices, even though modifying them. But the modern idea of a constitution is most perfectly manifested in the "We the people . . . do ordain and establish," of the Constitution of the United States. Thomas Paine put it well, more than a century and a half ago: "A constitution is not the act of a government, but of a people constituting a government, and a government without a constitution is power without right."

Fundamentally, then, a constitution is an enactment of, or at least one accepted by, the people who are to be governed under it, creating political authority and defining its proper methods and competence. To Paine, and late eighteenth-century opinion generally, it had to be a document, drafted by a convention selected for the purpose, and approved by the public in special elections before being put into effect. The first constitution so established for an independent government was that of Massachusetts in 1780, and the American federal Constitution was similarly adopted a few years later. The practice has been dominant since throughout the world. Only Great Britain among the major powers, because of the unusual continuity of its regime, lacks an explicit constitutional document, although France from 1875 to 1940, and Israel more recently, were unable to agree on a complete constitution and proceeded under a number of "organic laws." Many of their fundamental laws and practices have been so well established, however, that the difference is essentially nominal. What is important is that law, recognized as such by rulers and ruled alike, should effectively condition the exercise of political power in the interests of stability and the realization of communal political values.

Constitutional Change. Modern constitutions characteristically provide explicit means for their own amendment. Thus, the idea of a constitution is related to that of sovereignty, for sovereignty implies freedom to create new powers and limit old ones, to adapt the constitution to changing circumstances and to the realization of newly recognized values. Deliberate provision of amending procedures expresses awareness of this, even though formal amendment is not the only or the most important means of constitutional change. Most alterations in constitutions take place through reinterpretation of the law by the courts and other key public officials, especially where constitutional provisions are broadly cast but the amending process is restrictive, as in the United States.

Yet it remains always possible that neither this informal method, nor the formal process of amendment, may be adequate to the need for change, in which case the traditional method of revolution remains even today the ultimate recourse. It was the hope, not the certainty, of the framers of modern constitutions to avoid the necessity of such recourse through providing the opportunity of peaceful amendment. The American experience for the most part justifies that hope, but the Civil War was necessary to secure the abolition of slavery and the preservation of the Union. The existence of amending processes is but a general recognition that constitutions must change in time, not a guarantee that they will be altered adequately. But if constitutions must change it is only because any particular constitution must embody more specific political objectives and procedures than those heretofore discussed. A number of these have emerged as particularly characteristic of modern constitutionalism.

Individual Rights against Government. One of the most striking aspects of most modern constitutions has been the protection they have aimed to furnish to individual rights, appertaining equally to all men, as distinct from special class or functional privileges. The constitutions adopted in France and the United States at the end of the eighteenth century, and the one then gradually being evolved in English policy as well, attempted to provide barriers against governmental interference with what were deemed essential realms of individual freedom, and to curtail such arbitrariness in the exercise of governmental powers as could not be eliminated.

One of the explicitly constitutional documents in English history is the Bill of Rights, set by Parliament in 1689 as a condition to the accession of William and Mary to the throne, which James II had been forced to vacate. Principally designed to guarantee the place of Parliament in the government of Great Britain, the Bill of Rights did, nevertheless, specify certain liberties of British subjects, which the government was to respect. Among these were the right to petition the government, to trial by jury, to reasonable bail and punishment, to the possession of arms for self-defense, and to a Parliament independent of the king.

The best illustration of this constitutional development, however, is found in the American constitutions adopted following the outbreak of the Revolution. The prevailing attitude was well expressed by Thomas Jefferson, protesting against the omission from the federal Constitution as proposed in 1787 of a bill of rights, which, he said, "is what the people are entitled to against every government on earth, general or particular, and what no government should refuse, or rest on inference." Alexander Hamilton, in *The Federalist* (number 84), argued in rebuttal that the Constitution, being established by the people, was in itself a bill of rights, that the proposed document already provided guarantees of jury trial and habeas corpus and prohibitions of ex post facto laws and bills of attainder,* and that the new national government would furthermore be one of explicitly limited powers, none of which gave it any authority to deprive individuals of the rights claimed. Nonetheless, ten

* Habeas corpus is a common law writ (order) whose effect is normally to prevent a person from being held indefinitely without trial, in violation of his rights. An ex post facto law is one that has effect retroactively, making punishable an act which was legal when committed. Bills of attainder are legislative enactments that, like judicial decisions, subject a particular person or group to penalties.

amendments to the Constitution were adopted in the first session of Congress, and in 1791 became part of that Constitution.

In this "Bill of Rights" we find the most striking example of the reservation of private rights in modern constitutionalism. Not only were provided such legal rights in the English tradition as jury trial, security against unreasonable search and seizure, and the requirement of reasonable bail and punishment, but in the First and Fifth Amendments the people were guaranteed there would be no government interference with freedom of religion, speech, press, and assembly, and they were not to be "deprived of life, liberty, or property, without due process of law." "Congress shall make no law," begins the First Amendment, "respecting an establishment of religion, or prohibiting the free exercise thereof." Not all provisions are as strong as this, and all have proved open to astonishing variation through interpretation, but the impression is undeniable that the American government was dedicated in its Constitution to the primacy of private rights.

Generally comparable was the French *Declaration of the Rights of Man and the Citizen,* adopted in 1789. It recognized that "the end of every political association is the conservation of the natural and imprescriptable rights of man," these being "liberty, property, security, and resistance to oppression." It asserted the equality of all men in their rights, and to public office according to capacity. It provided for freedom of religion, speech, and press, but also that abuses of these against public order should be controlled by law. It did not assert any freedom of association or assembly, except for the nation as a whole. Because of its form, more philosophical than legal, it has been a universally appealing expression of the liberal attitude toward government. Although more recent constitutions have carried on this tradition, they have also modified it in various ways, as will be shown in our discussion of contemporary constitutional developments.

Representative Government. Quite obviously, bills of rights do not enforce themselves, however useful they are as explicit statements of the rights to be secured. They must be supported by operating institutions that effectively control the exercise of political power and force officials to respect them. Lacking these, bills of rights have remained dead letters in political history. One of the most important methods of assuring that the rights recognized in law and cherished among the people are effective in practice has been representative government. Having discussed its history and operation previously we need not elaborate on it here except to observe that, when effectively functioning, representative government shifts ultimate political responsibility and power from officials to private citizens acting as an electorate, and thus ensures at least some correspondence between the acts of government and the values of the population.

Political Parties. For the community to exercise this political power some sort of organization is necessary; private persons, dispersed both in space and in their interests, cannot even support effectively, much less control, their government. Consequently political parties emerged rapidly as central constitutional institutions within all modern political systems, even though not usually provided for in constitutional documents. They were from the first a practical response to the needs of representative government, especially when democratic. In the complex politics of today they have become a practical necessity, and even dictators must organize some form of them.

Through political parties alone can governors and governed be related sufficiently for the existence of effective modern government. Over the last several centuries political leaders have had to devote an increasing proportion of their effort to the task of organizing support for themselves and their policies throughout the community, while, at the same time, private citizens increasingly interested in what governments were doing had to organize themselves to exert maximum influence. The modern political party was the result.

In contemporary western history generally, both the political leaders competing for power and the interests of citizens have been numerous and diversified, and two or more parties have developed without any deliberate attempt to create such systems. Occasionally, however, an unusual unity of interest accompanied by exceptional effectiveness of leadership, or dictatorial repression, has limited the parties to one. As will be discussed more fully in Chapter 8, one-party systems are not always totalitarian, but in any case such party structures are likely to be less significant as controls over the exercise of power, and therefore as constitutional institutions in our use of the term. Beyond these generalities, however, parties differ radically in their constitutional role, reflecting very substantially the peculiarities of their particular political environment.

Checks and Balances. A political system embodies "checks and balances" if the performance of any function is not entrusted exclusively to any one person or agency, but a share in it or control over it, however small, is possessed by other relatively independent agencies. Very few of the American founding fathers or their contemporaries believed that representative government alone would furnish good and just rule. The key to what was additionally necessary came to them out of their own English and colonial experience, supplemented by the philosophic and legal thought of their age, and also by practical ingenuity in dealing with conflicting ideas and interests throughout the former colonies.

The American Constitution, consequently, embodies a particularly complex pattern of checks and balances, expressed in, but also as modifications of, the separation of powers and federalism. Some checks and balances are characteristic of every developed constitution, but with great variations in numbers and subtlety. Those developed in the British constitution, in parliamentary government, for example, are effective but much less obvious. To treat the idea of checks and balances further we must discuss these more particular constitutional techniques of organizing government.

The Separation of Powers. The separation of powers was considered so important in the late eighteenth century that James Madison and Thomas Jefferson both wrote that its absence was the "very definition of tyranny," while the French *Declaration of the Rights of Man* asserted that a regime without the separation of powers has no constitution. To some degree a matter of common practical experience, especially for the American colonists, the doctrine received a classic and persuasive statement in the interpretation of English government in the *Spirit of the Laws* (1748) of the French philosopher, Montesquieu. In sum, Montesquieu found the secret of political liberty in a constitutional organization dividing the distinct political functions of legislation, administration, and adjudication, among different persons or groups. The legislator makes the rules for the community, the judge settles controversies according to those rules, while the executive maintains peace and order. Only if these powers are kept distinct, thought Montesquieu, can the rule of law be maintained; otherwise special interests will prevail over the law, and that is tyranny.

Neither in Montesquieu's statement of the doctrine, nor in its application in the state and federal constitutions in America, was the separation of powers rigorously applied. It was modified, both out of practical necessities and in the spirit of multiplying checks and balances. The American Constitution, for example, assigns the legislative power to Congress, but the House of Representatives and the Senate share in it and may not always agree. Furthermore, the authority of the President to veto congressional enactments and to recommend legislation gives him substantial participation in the legislative process. The President's primacy in the executive function, on the other hand, is limited by Congress' control over revenues and expenditures, and the requirement that the Senate approve ratification of treaties and many appointments, to mention only a few of the more formal methods available to Congress.

Of course, Montesquieu and other advocates of the separation of powers recognized that the co-operation of the three powers is essential for effective government, but they were far more concerned with avoiding a concentration of power that could not be controlled short of revolution. They had no faith in despotism of one or of many, enlightened or otherwise; that the necessary co-operation could not be commanded was to them the best guarantee of justice and the rule of law, for only in justice could the legislative, executive, and judicial powers work in harmony. Such an agreement on justice has not always been forthcoming, with resultant stalemate or with agreement on much less laudable aims, undoubtedly accounting for the fact that the separation of powers has not been universally adopted in modern constitutions, and often has been under severe attack even in its principal home, the United States.

Federalism. Another important innovation of the late eighteenth century is federal government. Confederations and alliances, limited associations for limited purposes, and comprising organizations of independent political units rather than distinct constitutions themselves, had been known since antiquity, but the federal system established in the United States in 1789 was a remarkable and original variation on the older theme.

Federalism is similar to the separation of powers, since it creates a division of powers and responsibilities, but the division is essentially territorial, based upon a distinction between general and local interests and powers. By a federal constitution two spheres of government are established. On the one hand, there is a general government for the whole community; on the other, several regional governments, with authority only over their more limited areas. Both derive their legitimacy from the same source, the constitution, and neither is the creature or the agent of the other.

The range of responsibilities, or competences, of each of the levels of government is determined with some distinctness in constitutional law, and is not subject to change at will by either set of authorities. However, within its proper competence both the central and the state or provincial governments possess all powers of government not specifically denied them in the constitution, as by the provisions of a bill of rights. This distinguishes a federal system from a confederation, in which the "central government" acts in domestic affairs only through the member states, not directly on the population. But similarly to a confederation, on the other hand, in federal regimes the member states are specifically represented in one or more aspects of the central government. In other words, federalism is a hybrid of confederal association and unitary government, in which one supreme government exists for the entire community.

The precise patterns of federal regimes, however, vary considerably. In the United States, for example, the Constitution assigns "delegated" powers to the central government; all others, or "residual" powers, are reserved to the states. A complex constitutional law has developed to regulate relationships between these, especially to specify when the states are precluded from action affecting the delegated powers of the national government and when they are not. In the Canadian federal system, on the other hand, delegated powers are assigned to the provinces, with the central government possessing the (extensive) residue. In the Canadian and other more recent federal constitutions, also, areas of "concurrent" powers have been specified in which both levels of government may act, although in case of conflict the acts of the central regime are superior.

Substantial diversity exists also regarding the other principal characteristic of federal systems, that of representation of local units in the central government. In Canada, federalism affects the distribution of seats in both houses of Parliament, and also of offices in the cabinet, but in no case so much as to effect an equal representation of all provinces. In the United States, membership in the House of Representatives is based on state population, but in the Senate each state has two representatives. Before 1913 these were chosen by the state legislatures; thereafter by the electorate within each state. Much more strictly federal in this respect has been Germany, both under the Empire after 1871 and in the Federal Republic since World War II. At present, alongside the *Bundestag,* representing the entire population, is the *Bundesrat,* in which each state (*Land*) has at least three representatives and the largest have but five. Furthermore, these are actually delegates of the state governments, replaceable at will, and those from any one *Land* must vote as a unit. The state governments are thus represented far more clearly than in the American Senate.

Federalism, as Professor Carl Friedrich has observed, is a method of combining a measure of unity with a measure of diversity; or, as Professor K. C. Wheare has put it, it is appropriate for those peoples who want unity but not uniformity. It is an important constitutional institution in that it limits political power by relieving a community of complete dependence upon any one government to accomplish its needs and preserve it from chaos. It has not always been viewed in this favorable light. Patrick Henry, in the Virginia convention to ratify the proposed Constitution in 1788, complained that the federal scheme was "unprecedented in history, the visionary project of modern politicians." He doubted that it could work, and in any event denounced it as creating "two co-ordinate, interfering, unlimited powers of harassing the community." But then, Patrick Henry did not think too highly of any government!

Judicial Review. One of the more striking of the checks and balances of the American Constitution, though but little emulated abroad, is judicial review. In this practice, not explicitly provided in the Constitution itself but written into American constitutional law by Chief Justice Marshall in 1803, the courts have become the central and ultimate interpreter of the Constitution, and their decisions may be overridden only through amendments. Marshall argued in *Marbury* v. *Madison* that judges must follow the law in their decisions, that the Constitution is the fundamental law and that any statute or administrative act incompatible with the Constitution is not lawful, and that the courts must hold it so, refusing to recognize and enforce it.

To the extent that constitutional law is clear, and the particular statute or act equally clearly in violation of it, Marshall's reasoning is hard to disagree with. To do so would be to abandon the idea of a constitution as an explicit grant of power. Furthermore, federalism evidently depends upon some impartial tribunal to settle controversies over the competences of central and regional governments; to permit legislatures or executives to have this power would obviously make someone a judge in his own cause, although in practice this problem is not entirely eliminated by giving the responsibility to the courts, which may well have nationalistic or local biases also. But on balance, in instances of these kinds a resort to the judiciary of the central regime is undoubtedly the best choice.

Controversy over judicial review, however, has been inevitable and frequently bitter because the constitutional law is often not clear on important and emotionally charged issues. Marshall himself insisted that the Constitution, unlike a statute, should be construed broadly. But, in fact, he did so only to enlarge the powers of the central government, and to restrict those of the states. Those, like Jefferson, who would have preferred the reverse, protested violently and have continued to do so, as have those who disliked the particular national policy the courts were maintaining. In short, we see that interpretation of constitutional law is not solely a judicial function but also a political one; it is undoubtedly dislike of vesting judges with such political power that prevented any other country but Norway from utilizing judicial review in its explicit form until very recently. It should be noted, however, that courts cannot in any case be prevented from interpreting the law they apply according to the basic legal and constitutional ideas of the judges, and also that many states practice judicial review of administrative action, either in the regular courts or through special administrative tribunals, as will be discussed further below.

Yet, judicial review of the constitutionality even of legislation cannot be disposed of so easily. Constitutions cannot enforce themselves, and therefore must be enforced by some agency if they are to be effectively superior to the political demands of the moment. Special constitutional courts that are immediately subject to the same political forces dominant in the executive or legislature, as recommended by the Abbé Sieyès early in the French revolution and often employed since, are of but limited adequacy in this respect. A judiciary that is not so controlled can perform this responsibility, and if the power is exercised with restraint constitutional government is generally strengthened. American judges have usually been aware of the necessity of such restraint, and furthermore, ultimate means of enforcing it are present in such checks and balances of the American Constitution as the possibility of constitutional amendment, the appointment and removal of judges by the President and Congress, and even the control over the agenda of the courts, which Congress legally possesses. The move in the Senate in 1964 to withdraw from the federal courts jurisdiction in cases concerning the representativeness of state legislatures was an attempt, legally sound but politically ineffective, to exercise this last power. In sum, judicial review may be a valuable constitutional institution, though it rarely produces "government by judges" as is sometimes argued. However, given the politics of constitutional interpretation, it alone is not adequate to save constitutional government.

Parliamentary Government. One of the most important and widely distributed forms of government in the modern world, however, is not fully in accord with the doctrine of the separation of powers, but has its own special methods of ensuring the responsible exercise of political power; hence, it must properly receive special mention here. This type is parliamentary government, and its distinguishing characteristic is that the executive officials, or ministers, are not independently elected, but represent the majority in one or more representative assemblies. This form of government began to emerge in early eighteenth-century Britain, became stabilized there in the nineteenth century, and also spread to the continent of Europe and to the British colonies, as they acquired relatively independent governments. In the present century it has been characteristic of most of the new constitutions adopted, although the presidential system, with its independent chief executive, has recently become popular once again.

In parliamentary government the legislative and executive functions are closely related because they are, in fact, exercised largely by the same men. However, this constitutional arrangement has manifested itself in two practically and significantly different ways. In Great Britain, the leaders of the majority in the House of Commons became ministers, and were generally able to command the confidence of that assembly for substantial periods of time; there was thus strong "cabinet government" within the limits of what a fairly coherent majority would accept. In France after 1875, however, majorities in the representative assemblies were usually extremely unstable and became more so as time went on. Ministries, therefore, were rarely able to maintain for long the confidence of the assemblies, without which they had to resign, and were thus rarely able to govern effectively. This particular pattern came to be called "assembly government" as distinguished from "cabinet government," in which the leadership of ministers is stressed.

In this discussion of governmental forms, we should point out that it is possible to combine various features of the separation of powers, the federal, and the parliamentary systems into effective constitutional government. Switzerland has produced a type that virtually defies classification. The Swiss Federal Council, or executive, is elected by the representative assembly, but is maintained on an essentially nonpolitical basis with extraordinary stability. Even though councilors recommend legislation, they do not resign if their proposals are defeated, but adapt themselves to the decision of the legislature and continue their administrative tasks. This arrangement is probably suited only to such a relatively small country, without serious internal or foreign problems, and capable of substantial self-discipline. Other democratic regimes as they emerged in this and the last century are, however, largely variations on the parliamentary system.

Parliamentary government appeals to those with democratic sympathies because it founds the government upon a majority in the representative assembly, which in turn is founded upon a majority in the electorate. It also appeals to those concerned with efficient government because it appears to weld into an operating unity the electorate, representative assembly, and executive. It undoubtedly does all of these things, provided that the political environment is such that it can function properly, as it usually has been in England but not in France. But it also is compatible with democracy only when joined with two other constitutional institutions: a solid dedication to the rule of law and the rights of citizens; and the existence in the assembly of one or more opposition parties, with a recognized right to criticize the majority and its government, no matter how embarrassing it may be to them, and thereby attempting to displace that majority at the next, and not too distant, election. These, too, are aspects of parliamentary government as a modern constitutional development which Great Britain, in particular, bequeathed to the contemporary world.

III. CONTEMPORARY CONSTITUTIONS

Most of the constitutions existing in the world today are products of the last decade or two. Only the United States has a written constitution that goes back over a century and a half to its adoption. Yet both the Constitution of the United States and the ancient but largely "unwritten" constitution of Britain have been substantially modified in recent years. Both the new constitutions and the altered old ones reflect the special political circumstances of the mid-twentieth century. To illustrate contemporary constitutions we shall first discuss briefly those of four important regimes, and then indicate some of the principal trends in constitutional development today.

FOUR MAJOR CONSTITUTIONS

In the creation of constitutions throughout the world in this century, as well as in political life more generally, four states have been particularly influential: Great Britain, the United States, France, and the Soviet Union. Well-established regimes, compared with most countries at the present, their constitutions warrant special note.

The British Constitution. Great Britain offers the only example of a major country with a constitution that is not written, which is to say that there is no single document, or set of them, undertaking to order the basic organization and proceedings of British government. There is, indeed, no difference between constitutional and ordinary law, as respects the legal methods of their enactment or alteration. Yet there are fundamental laws and practices according to which British government operates; they but appear in diverse guises.

The law of the constitution—those rules the courts will enforce—is supplied from several sources. First, there are the great charters and other historic agreements, such as Magna Carta of 1215, the Petition of Right of 1628, and the Bill of Rights of 1689. These constitutional landmarks were the products of major political crises, and manifest the terms of their settlement. Second, there are certain statutes of Parliament, such as the Act of Settlement of 1701, regulating succession to the throne and the tenure of judges; the Great Reform Act of 1832, which reorganized representation in the House of Commons; and the Parliament Acts of 1911 and 1949, limiting the powers of the House of Lords. Third, there are certain principles of the common law, derived from court decisions, which have defined the royal prerogative and many of the basic civil liberties, such as freedom of speech, press, and public meeting. Of course, an act of Parliament enjoys supremacy over any other

constitutional rule, and provides the formal method for altering the British constitution.

In addition, the British have developed a substantial body of constitutional customs, called "conventions." They include such practices as the annual meeting of Parliament, the sovereign's selection of the leader of the majority party in the House of Commons as Prime Minister, the Prime Minister's resignation when he loses the support of that majority, the collective responsibility of the ministers to the House, the exercise in practice by ministers of the royal prerogative, and so on. Obviously, these principles are very much at the heart of the parliamentary system; yet though they are regularly observed, they are nevertheless not rules which the courts will enforce. The conventions of the constitution derive their authority from the fact that parliamentary government would not function apart from them; they are closely interwoven with the law, with each element assuming the existence of the other; and they are strongly supported by the forces of tradition and public opinion. This latter is of greatest importance; with such support the slenderest customary rule can be maintained, but without it, even the law may fall into disregard.

The Constitution of the United States. The United States possesses the oldest documentary constitution now in effect. It may appear paradoxical that England, without a written constitution, should give rise to the country first to have one, but the explanation is to be found in differences of national experience. That of America began in royal charters and the compacts of the colonists, thus familiarizing the Americans with documents setting forth authoritative rights and powers. The colonial period ended in a revolutionary break with the homeland, requiring the explicit establishment of new, independent governments both for the former colonies and for their union. This experience, plus the rationalistic temper of the period, led to the general drafting of constitutional documents.

Unlike most later written constitutions, that of the United States is a relatively brief document, almost deceptively simple in its provisions. The American founding fathers never lost sight of the fact that they were framing an instrument to endure, and to fill it with minute specifications would soon render it obsolete. For this reason, and also because they had many diverse ideas and interests to compromise, the Constitution deals in quite general language. That there have been great controversies over the interpretation of its provisions is not the consequence of faulty draftsmanship, but of the close relationship of any constitution to a changing social life.

The Constitution provides for its formal amendment, although the process is somewhat complex and difficult. Amendments are proposed either by Congress, through a two-thirds vote in each House, or by a national convention called by Congress at the request of two-thirds of the states. Amendments must be ratified by three-fourths of the states, either through their legislatures or in special conventions, as Congress may direct. Twenty-four such textual alterations have been made. Most earlier amendments limited the central government's power in regard to the rights of private persons and the states; others have merely altered particular procedures, as in the election of the President and Senators, or the establishment of woman suffrage. Only a few—such as the Fourteenth, protecting basic national rights against state action; the Sixteenth, permitting a national income tax; and the eventually repealed Eighteenth, or prohibition, Amendment—have worked at all to enlarge the powers of the national government. Were this the only means of constitutional change the national government would today have less power than was inherent in the original document of 1789!

In extension of the original provisions, however, much more in the way of laws and practices has developed to round out the whole constitutional system. There are certain acts of Congress, such as those establishing the major executive departments and agencies, organizing the federal courts, ordering presidential succession, and the provision of the civil service and social security systems. Further, there are legal principles developed through judicial interpretation that have given broad meaning to various provisions of the Constitution, such as the commerce clause, tax powers, and the concept of due process of law. Finally, there are also customary practices which have grown up around the Constitution. Here, outside the legal rules, are important and relatively stable procedures respecting the political parties, selection of the President and Vice-President, congressional elections, the role of the President's cabinet, and other such governmental arrangements. Understanding the American Constitution in practice requires considering all these later developments.

The French Constitution. France has the distinction—a rather dubious one, all things considered—of having undergone more frequent and drastic constitutional changes than any other state. This fact reflects not a constant improvement in document writing, but rather the inability of the French people, after overturning the old regime in 1789, to reach agreement for any extended period on the fundamental character of their political institutions. More than a dozen constitutions, some republican and some monarchical, were adopted between 1789 and 1946, but none provided France with adequate and stable political institutions. In view of this history, and the continuing existence of the domestic tensions and difficulties that underlay it, uncertainty is justified as to the permanence of the most recent, adopted in 1958.

The most durable settlement in modern France followed the Franco-Prussian War and lasted from 1875 until 1940. Due to a continuing controversy between monarchists and republicans, but even more to disagreements among the monarchists as to who should be king, no comprehensive constitutional system could be adopted. Several "organic laws" established an intentionally temporary republic with an elective president, a bicameral legislature, and ministers whose responsibility to the assemblies was clarified only when President MacMahon failed in 1879 in his attempt to make them responsible to him. This "constitution" was all that the Third Republic was to have, "a scaffold of chance," as Hanotaux described it; but out of it grew an assembly-dominated parliamentary system that succumbed only to the invading German armies early in World War II. Most Frenchmen held it responsible for that defeat, however, as well as for failure to meet adequately several decades of economic crisis, and after liberation voted overwhelmingly in favor of drafting a new constitution. Despite their intentions, nonetheless, the Constitution of the Fourth Republic diverged remarkably little from the lines of its predecessor. Perhaps for that reason it was greeted with enormous indifference and lasted but twelve years.

The apparently interminable Algerian rebellion, which broke out in 1954 and which aroused animosities and posed problems that the government in Paris was unable to cope with, brought an end to the Fourth Republic in 1958. Insurrections among the army and police that threatened to spread led to the appointment of General Charles de Gaulle as Premier with emergency powers, including that to prepare a new constitution. Its final draft was submitted to a popular referendum in September of that year and received the approval of more than four-fifths of those voting, with few abstentions. This unusual display of agreement among the French seems to have been less a verdict on the Constitution than a demonstration that General de Gaulle offered the only leadership under which the nation might unite.

The Constitution of the Fifth Republic retains many features of preceding regimes, such as universal suffrage, representation through a bicameral parliament, and a ministry that must have the confidence of the National Assembly. The traditional individual rights of the *Declaration* of 1789 and the complementary "economic and social principles" of the 1946 Constitution were reaffirmed. However, it was designed throughout to provide a vehicle for General de Gaulle's leadership through the presidential office: ministers are appointed by the President and can no longer remain members of the Parliament; the National Assembly can defeat legislation proposed as a matter of confidence by the Council of Ministers only with absolute majorities, but then it runs the risk of being dissolved; and substantial authority to rule by decree has been vested in the President and the ministers. Proposed amendments to the Constitution must be adopted in identical terms by majorities in both National Assembly and Senate. They must then be submitted to popular referendum, unless the President decides to submit them instead to a joint meeting of the two assemblies, in which case approval by three-fifths of those voting is final.

In effect, the Fifth Republic under De Gaulle has been very much a limited monarchy, even if the "king" is called President and popularly elected. The objective, of course, is to give France a new political stability. Whether this regime can put down roots and provide a governmental system operable by a successor to the General is a matter for the future to reveal. President de Gaulle insisted in 1964 that after five years' experience his Constitution could be pronounced a success, but admitted that there were still critics—"who find the bride perhaps too beautiful and who suggest changes which, in fact, would upset the system from top to bottom." Since these changes range from a return to assembly government to the establishment of an American-type presidential regime, and reflect diverse political concerns and interests, it is evident that the French tradition of writing a new constitution to suit varying political moods and exigencies will not be easily discarded.

The Soviet Constitution. The Soviet Union has had three documentary constitutions. The first, proclaimed in 1918 for the Russian Soviet Federated Socialist Republic, announced the objectives of the socialist revolution and described the gross structure of the government. A second was issued in 1924, marking the new federation of the Union of Soviet Socialist Republics, and the improved stabilization of affairs following the civil war. The third, or Stalin Constitution, was promulgated in 1936, after a campaign of "popular discussion." One might well wonder why the well-entrenched dictatorship required a basic charter at all, much less a new one. The answer appears to lie in the ambition of the regime at that time to acquire a new liberal respectability, both at home and abroad. The Soviet Union, so it was claimed, had achieved "socialism," the first step to communism, and the Constitution was officially hailed as the "most democratic in the world."

In form, the 1936 Constitution contains much of the content usual in such documents. It provides a federal system, an elaborate arrangement of organs of government along "parliamentary" lines with definition of powers and accountability, and popular elections—all of which would appear to support a regular system of democratic and representative government. It also includes an extensive list of individual rights, not only the classic substantive rights of British, American, and French tradition, but an additional number of social and economic ones, far beyond those guaranteed at the time in the liberal democracies.

Yet the Soviet Constitution has an air of unreality. It made no change in the source or control of political power; Stalin emphasized that the Constitution preserved unchanged "the dictatorship of the working class" and "the present leading position of the Communist party." Equally, the "rights" described in the Constitution are without any means for their implementation; they do not create claims that are upheld by the courts and enforced against the government, nor is representative government available to those who do not choose the Communist party. In short, the Constitution established few if any limits on the power of the Soviet rulers, the leaders of the Communist party; rather it was dictated by expediency as an instrument of their policy. The document may be something more than a "scrap of paper," if viewed as a political document and a social and economic manifesto of communist aims expressed in a strange combination of communist and liberal terminology. But since it is neither controlling law nor convention, it is only formally a constitution. One may learn something about Soviet government by reading the Constitution, but the realities are on a different plane. We may reasonably doubt that a new constitutional document, allegedly being prepared, will alter this situation significantly.

This brief treatment of four major contemporary constitutions should make evident the limited significance of constitutional documents. Obvious similarities in crucial concerns are to be found in British and American political life, yet the latter alone has one great historic document. The former, having a much smaller and less complete body of constitutional law, has developed its constitution largely through practice and convention, although this method has played a substantial role in the political life of the United States as well. Existing in both systems, however, is a universal disposition to maintain the continuity of a set of effective fundamental rules. This spirit has been weak in France and completely lacking in the Soviet Union; consequently constitutional law—impressive documents notwithstanding—has been either unstable or ineffective. The Soviet Constitution coexists with a complete dictatorship that one could barely suspect from a reading of the document. Clearly, the distinctions among governments that constitutions express are far more profoundly rooted than in sheets of parchment!

MAJOR CONSTITUTIONAL TRENDS

The constitutions of the present are largely built upon those of the earlier modern period. This is true even of newly independent states, which have, at least in the letter, closely followed traditional constitutional ideas derived from the experience of the major European powers and the United States. Formally, this has not been a period of great innovation. Yet within the framework of those older ideas important developments have occurred in the realms both of fundamental political objectives and of governmental procedures, so that the effective constitutions of today are not the same as those of even a few decades ago.

Contemporary Political Objectives. The constitutions of the last century, whose basic institutions we discussed above, reflected the relatively limited political objectives of the period. Security of person and property, as defined in lists of civil liberties, was the principal end. In this century, however, governments are everywhere charged with at least a supervisory role in the development and effective functioning of the economy. Education, once largely a concern of church and family, has become predominantly a public responsibility that is ever growing. Much current scientific research would be impossible without public support, and public works are no longer primarily public buildings and monuments but highways, airports, dams, and slum clearance projects. More challenging yet is the leading part governments are often expected to play in fostering radical transformations in mores and developing a sense of community.

Those constitutions adopted in recent years have provided explicitly for these new responsibilities, as well as for the traditional rights that were at the core of earlier systems. The Indian Constitution of 1949 provides in article 17 that "untouchability" is abolished and its practice forbidden; and in article 38, under the general heading of "Directive Principles of State Policy," we learn that "The State shall strive to promote the welfare of the people by securing and protecting as effectively as it may a social order in which justice, social, economic, and political, shall inform all the institutions of the national life." The Japanese Constitution of 1947 includes among the "rights and duties of the people," to which almost one-third of its articles are devoted, the right to "maintain the minimum standards of wholesome and cultural life," and the right and obligation to work. Similar phrases are to be found in all the constitutions adopted in Europe after World War II.

Equally clearly, however, the older constitutions of the United States and Great Britain have not escaped this trend. The general lines of the "welfare state" seem as firmly established as any constitutional convention in Britain, and in the United States reinterpretations of constitutional provisions have given legitimacy to substantial governmental interventions in the economy, and to the use of public powers for such moral purposes as to reduce discrimination against Negroes, such as the framers—even the radical Alexander Hamilton—could hardly have foreseen. The American Constitution is now a much broader grant of power than most legal analysts thought a few years ago.

No government, however, can be devoted to such broad and positive purposes and yet remain dedicated to the absolute primacy of the private rights of individuals. Consequently, these rights have become increasingly qualified, especially those respecting property. The Italian, French, and West German constitutions, attempting to balance on this issue, "recognize and guarantee" private property, but observe immediately that law "determines the methods of its acquisition and enjoyment and the limitations designed to assure its social functioning and render it accessible to all," in the words of article 42 of the Constitution of Italy. The right to strike is similarly recognized and then qualified. In contemporary constitutions, private rights against government tend to be subordinate, in case of conflict, to more general public purposes and the instruments of effective government they demand. Serving so many purposes, constitutions today are inevitably more complex than those of even the recent past. One reflection of this is the increasing length of new documents, India's winning the prize with its 318 pages, including table of contents and index.

Executive Leadership. At the center of government in traditional constitutional thinking was the legislature, or, for some, the judiciary. The demands of contemporary government, however, have led to the elevation of the executive far above his earlier status in both prestige and power. The contemporary president or prime minister resembles the kings of several hundred years ago more than he does his more immediate predecessors. The Prime Minister in the British parliamentary system, and the President within the separation of powers of the American Constitution, have become the central figures in their governments. They have used and augmented the traditional powers of their offices, but the reason for their dominance lies in the need for unified leadership in the face of extensive and complex public responsibilities today. In other circumstances this same need gave rise to fascist and communist dictatorships, manifesting the absolute predominance of such leaders as Hitler and Stalin. It has been suggested that dictatorships appeared in these and other instances in good part because those countries were unable to develop effective executive leadership within the framework of their traditional constitutions.

This lesson has not been lost on the framers of the new constitutions of recent years. The Constitution of the German Federal Republic attempted to provide for the stable executive that had been lacking in the Weimar Republic twenty years earlier through limiting the control of the executive (the Chancellor) by the representative assemblies. The *Bundestag* is not constitutionally authorized to overthrow a Chancellor through a vote of censure or no-confidence unless at the same time it also votes its approval of a replacement for him; and the Chancellor is further given substantial powers to rule independently of a nonco-operative *Bundestag* if he obtains the consent of the Federal Council, the *Bundesrat*.

The Constitution of the French Fourth Republic in 1946 tried to strengthen the executive without curtailing the prerogatives of the National Assembly, but these half-steps proved insufficient in existing circumstances, and the Constitution of 1958 established a regime of executive dominance surpassing that of West Germany. Similarly, the Constitution of India, which Nehru observed is patterned "largely after the British model, with necessary variations," provides strong presidential powers, which are in practice exercised by the prime minister and his associates. The dependence of the developing political systems of most new states throughout the world upon effective executive leadership is most evident. It is in fact quite possible that only through a period of dictatorship can enough of a community be created in such places as Ghana, Indonesia, and Pakistan, for government according to a constitution to be practicable, since agreement is often lacking not only on governmental forms but even on basic political objectives.

One expression of the rise of executive leadership, as well as its principal support, has been the appearance of great popular political parties that find their unity largely in their support of a leader, be he a Tito, Khrushchev, or Mao, or a De Gaulle, Eisenhower, or Johnson. For many people, even most, such a leader is the incarnation of the regime, and to him they look for both policy and inspiration. No matter what his public office may be, neither the democratic leader nor the dictator can function effectively without that support, and its creation and preservation must be their principal concern, however diverse may be their ways of doing so. The more critical the times and the more demanding public responsibilities, the more sharply is this characteristic evident in all contemporary governments—a few anachronistic military despotisms apart.

At the same time, however, as the executive has become more intensely than before the personal leader of the country, he has also become more impersonally institutionalized within a complex machinery composed of secretaries, councils, committees, and bureaus. Through this machinery, created most often by executive orders or statutes, but sometimes by explicit constitutional provision, policy making is shared with experts, subordinate political leaders, and representatives of diverse interest groups. This institutionalization, which in all developed modern governments seems as much a part of actual constitutional government as the courts, chief executives, and representative assemblies, both limits and adds to the power of the executive. It limits him quite obviously in that he must carry all this machinery with him, and usually will have to adapt himself to it, at least as much as he directs it. But it also strengthens him in adding enormously to his resources of expert knowledge and of political intelligence, in assuring that policy decisions are reasonably appropriate and politically feasible, and in multiplying the army of those who will support him and check on the effective enforcement of "his" policy. And in this, as can easily be seen, the executive bureaucracy and the party can work hand in hand.

Limitations on Executive Dominance. The rise of the executive to leadership is probably necessary, and in any event undeniable, but it has not always meant dictatorship and the downfall of constitutions. Limits on political power have been maintained through modifications and extensions of basic and traditional constitutional devices. Checks and balances have been maintained in the interaction of the executive with representative assemblies, in some sort of judicial control, and in new patterns of federalism.

Representative assemblies are no longer the core of modern government, even democratic government, for it is the excutive who takes the lead in bringing popular support of government to a focus. But such  assemblies are now more clearly than ever before the forum for criticism of the government's policies on behalf of diverse interests and ideas that the executive has not adequately accommodated. Their role is no longer legislation, but, through their necessary approval of legislation and budgets, the exercise of a continuing control over the executive and his subordinates. This development is least marked in the United States, where Congress possesses a strong tradition of political independence. Nonetheless, Congress is rarely able to generate an independent public policy in any realm, and differs from the British Parliament, for example, largely in its greater ability to modify administrative proposals. For this reason it is a more effective constitutional control, but one more extreme than most countries apparently feel they can afford today. More widely imitated is the British system, in which criticism is primarily aimed at influencing the course of the next election, and will usually lead the ministers to modify their proposals only to avoid just such an outcome.

Judicial methods of controlling government have also enjoyed a renewed favor in recent years, not only as a control of administration but even of legislation. In India, Japan, and Nigeria, judicial review has specifically been established as a power of the ordinary courts. In Italy, West Germany, and France, special constitutional tribunals that are judicial and not merely political in nature have been created to guarantee the constitutional exercise of all powers. In Italy, for example, private parties may protest unconstitutional acts and laws before the Constitutional Court, which in its first year abrogated as contrary to the rights protected by the Constitution some police powers remaining from the Fascist regime and still being employed. The future of judicial review in these instances is still unsettled, but one should recall that even in the United States its constitutional significance has varied considerably in time and that the ability of judicial review to preserve the Constitution depends upon a general determination that the Constitution be preserved.

Furthermore in many countries a special system of administrative law, and sometimes also a special system of courts to develop and enforce it, serve to a degree the same function. In France, for example, over the last century a very impressive body of such law was created by the Council of State, under which the government was able to carry out its functions effectively, yet enabling the rights of citizens to be protected substantially. Even during the Vichy regime, under Nazi domination, the Council of State continued to uphold the standard of the rule of law; it could not deal with exceptional police activities, but judicial review by ordinary courts in the United States has also failed in emergency periods to remedy such obvious wrongs as the evacuation of Americans of Japanese origin from the West Coast in 1942. Such systems of administrative law and courts, found in most continental European countries, have become very important constitutional institutions.

Finally, federalism remains a significant method of controlling the exercise of political power, and although its use has spread in recent years it has also, like other basic constitutional devices, altered at the same time. It has spread because its utility as a method of organizing increasingly larger and more heterogeneous populations has been recognized as appropriate to the needs of India, Africa, and the supranational unions in Europe, from Benelux to the more recent European Economic Community.

However, the simplicity of earlier federalism, with its apparent assumption that the government of a community could somehow be neatly split across the middle, has largely vanished. In most recently created federal systems, and in older ones as they have evolved, the predominance of the central government is quite marked. Either the "residual" powers are assigned to it, or the powers constitutionally allocated to it, as in the United States, are most generously interpreted. Furthermore, in Indian federalism the unique authority of the central government is recognized for emergency conditions that include financial difficulties as well as military invasion. In the German Federal Republic the only power that is exclusively in the hands of the states is education.

Most interesting, however, in the evolution of federalism has been the development of co-operative action by the central and local governments. Recent federal constitutions specifically provide broad realms of concurrent legislation, in which both levels of government may act, although that of the central regime is superior. Furthermore, in German federalism most national legislation is administered, under supervision, by state officials, which demands some harmonization of central and local policies. Although American federalism did not originally provide for this, it has in fact developed in the form of conditional grants-in-aid from the national government to the states, for example, or in such assistance as is given by the Federal Bureau of Investigation to state and local police. Grants-in-aid, conditional on observance of national standards, have been used in such realms as education, public assistance, low-cost housing projects, and many others, where the central government has no direct regulatory authority. They have greatly extended actual national power, but it is at least disputable whether this has weakened the local governments, insofar as they might well have collapsed in the face of problems which they could not independently handle.

Contemporary federalism is, in fact, a "new federalism." We no longer have national and local problems that may be adequately handled by two distinct and independent governments, acting separately. Most of our important problems are instead divisible, if at all, only into national and local aspects, and they can be met only through co-operation—concurrent action that is mutually supporting—so that the diverse resources of the community as a whole can be "geared together" to identify and resolve them. Federalism, serving as a control over both national and local leaders, thus makes possible public policy that is adequate because it is not dominated entirely by either a national or a local perspective. Even in such traditionally unitary regimes as France efforts are being made today to decentralize public power and gain at least some of the advantages that federalism offers.

Constitutions in New Nonwestern States. The drafting of a constitution comparable to those of the older western states was virtually a prerequisite to independence for the formerly colonial dependencies in Asia and Africa. This was not an imposition; the new leaders of those countries wanted such constitutions, taking them and their principal provisions to be the symbol and substance of a political "coming of age." In most cases, it appears that they expected to be able to govern, effectively and responsibly, under and through them. Most of them adopted constitutional systems resembling those of their former masters, showing only limited inventiveness and retaining little of their indigenous cultural and political characteristics. They incorporated the traditional western ideas of civilian rule, through elected representative institutions, within a framework of public liberties. To these they added the more recent western assertions of social and economic rights of citizens and responsibilities of government, which have not yet been altogether absorbed even in the mature constitutional democracies.

In all but a few of them, however, it soon became evident that they lacked the basic social, cultural, economic, administrative, and political foundations that made those constitutions function as they have in their original homes. Some, particularly in southeast Asia, had an established cultural, and even political community, differing greatly from the western regime superficially imposed on it. Others, especially in Africa, had little or no cultural or political community corresponding to the artificial territorial boundaries they inherited. In all of them, a full political regime had to be built, appropriate not only to their new circumstances at independence but also to their special problems, inherited institutions, and traditional ways of thinking. Thus the need for effective leadership and executive power became paramount, and with the striking exception of a few countries like India, the Philippines, and Nigeria, their adopted western-style constitutions broke down, whether formally abandoned or not, to be replaced by dictatorial and oligarchic regimes.

If we insist, as we must to preserve the integrity of our terms of analysis, that a constitution is present only if it controls the exercise of political power, we must conclude that the so-called constitutions of most new states in Africa and Asia are, if anything, largely "promissory notes on the future," in Professor Robert C. Bone's expressive phrase. The good intentions and sense of responsibility of leaders are not in themselves a constitution, nor are the inevitable purely *de facto* limitations on their power. Remembering that constitutional institutions emerged in the west over many centuries in circumstances that no longer exist even there, we simply cannot predict what sort of constitutions, if any, the new nonwestern states will create and maintain in the future. This depends on whether they prove to be viable political communities, and on how they combine their traditional ways and special circumstances with the adopted elements of western life as they enter more fully into the modern world.

IV. PRINCIPLES *of* CONSTITUTIONAL GOVERNMENT

The preceding pages may have appeared to the reader as a "short course" in political history, and with good reason. Constitutional institutions are fundamental political facts, and consideration of their appearance and development must necessarily summarize the political life of the civilization. But we must now try to clarify further the term "constitution" and its derivative, "constitutional government."

CONSTITUTION AS A STANDARD FOR EVALUATION

In the early pages of this chapter it was observed that a constitution serves as the framework of politics, stabilizing the exercise of political power and adapting it to the realization of communal values. Our survey of the historical institutions of western constitutional government should enable us to understand this preliminary characterization better, and we may now develop its implications, indicating more specifically the purposes constitutions serve and how they function. At the conclusion of this analysis we should be able to see that constitutions are not only important political facts, but are also basic standards for evaluation for political science, and that whether or not a constitution is present is one of the most important judgments about any regime that a student of government can make.

Constitutional Objectives. The most immediate and obvious objective of any constitution is the limitation of arbitrariness, since constitutions attempt to define and control the proper scope of official behavior. However, this is not as easy as it may seem. Those who have created and developed constitutions have usually attempted to embody more positive commitments: they have sought to provide rational government, founded in common consent, serving the general welfare, and protecting diverse interests. More recently they have also sought through constitutional forms to make governments effective instruments for progress in a changing world. Thus, the purposes constitutions are intended to serve embrace most of our political ideals, and are correspondingly difficult to realize.

It is dangerous to underestimate the immediate goal of constitutions in politics—simply to limit arbitrariness in official acts. The personal security of citizens depends largely on whether their rights and responsibilities are determinate, known to them, and effectively maintained. Nevertheless, what those rights and responsibilities are is no less important; we have seen that in constitutional government they have traditionally been defined as well as implemented through the "rule of law," which includes among its standards not only determinateness but also reasonableness, with its implications of practicality and general benefit. Some thinkers have even insisted that only rational rules and acts are ultimately capable of giving us the determinacy in government that we seek, and most have asserted that rationality as well as determinacy in the political order are basic objectives of constitutional government.

In modern times, however, we have not been willing to found politics on reason alone. Instead, we have emphasized consent of the governed, assuming that it will ensure rational, good, and effective government. A constitution has thus come to be thought of as expressing this consent, and as being the means through which the public constitutes a government and orders its continuing activity. In western history, however, pluralistic social conditions have most often prevailed; consequently, constitutions truly expressing popular consent to government have had to accept diversity and limit the government's role to reconciling that diversity with the unity essential to the community's existence. Respect for individual and group differences, together with rational government for the general welfare based upon popular consent, are inherent in the constitutional experience of western civilization.

Differences may be respected within a static order as well as in a changing one, however, and many constitutions have tended to protect only existing customary interests. The dynamic character of western culture, especially in modern times, has nevertheless forced us to adapt to constitutional as well as social change. Also, we have gradually come to recognize that change can be progress—orderly change that maximizes realization of values. Increasingly, therefore, we have appraised constitutional institutions for their ability not only to protect diverse existing interests, but also to promote diversity and progressive change. In this century we have seen many constitutional systems challenged, and some overthrown, because they were too reactionary to progress with popular expectations. No constitution today can retain the loyalty of its people and express their continuing consent to government unless it is an effective instrument for progress.

Constitutional Mechanics. Given the objectives that constitutions serve, we must now consider how they work. In this discussion the special nature of constitutions and constitutional government will become evident and a final definition of the terms can be given. What is said must be sufficiently theoretical to be relevant to the great diversity of constitutional institutions we have noted, and yet sufficiently practical to enable us to understand and use the terms meaningfully in concrete instances.

A constitution is a system of devices through which political power is divided within a community. It is clearly distinct from absolutism, which signifies a concentration of political power. It is also distinct from anarchy, which seeks not merely to limit political power but to destroy it. In constitutional government, officials act under rules and through machinery that effectively control what they do, no one being the sole judge of the legitimacy of his acts, or unlimited in the exercise of power. The devices through which such government is established and maintained are of two general types: those tending to divide power between government and the governed, and those dividing power among officials.

It should not be difficult to recall the various constitutional institutions noted in the historical survey above and to see how this definition applies to them—or, historically speaking, how their emergence gave rise to the political order this definition reasonably describes. Representative government; establishment of constitutional documents or conventions, which officials cannot alter alone, as the fundamental and constitutive law of government; and recognition of civil liberties for private individuals and groups—all tend directly or indirectly to divide political power between government officials and private citizens. They ensure that what government does, and how it is done, will be an expression of a broader public opinion than that of the rulers themselves, giving to the community a variable but important participation in the process of government.

If the governed were simply confronted with a monolithic government, however, the effectiveness of these constitutional devices would be limited, as is evidenced by the difficulty of maintaining the rule of law in the middle ages or under the pseudo-constitutionalism of the Soviet dictatorship. An effective constitution includes also methods of dividing power within the government itself—such as systems of checks and balances. However diversely, they all distinguish responsibilities and powers, so that no one official or body dominates. Therefore, the citizens are not confronted with an integrated government against which they are defenseless, but one in which many centers of power exist, as officials control and limit one another. Because of this, furthermore, the citizens have opportunities to exert influence in government, promoting their diverse interests and ideas within the framework of generally accepted public policy.

To determine, then, whether a constitution is present, and not merely when one appears to be, the observer must consider: first, if the terms of public authority are set with some precision in a system of constitutional law or conventions, which receives general public support; and second, if through those rules and their authorized machinery the exercise of political power is divided, within and without the government. Obviously not all political systems are of this type, nor does any perfectly manifest these characteristics. Consequently, the idea of constitutional government provides a very important standard for political evaluation, and enables the political scientist to draw some basic distinctions among the governments of the world.

CONSTITUTIONS AND CONTEMPORARY LIFE

The relevance of a standard concerns both its value and its practicability. We must consider whether constitutionalism is relevant today, for it is not obviously so and is often questioned. No amount of analysis of constitutional machinery alone will help us here; we must contemplate the significance of that machinery in relation to the needs and possibilities of contemporary life.

Constitutional Dynamics. In the changing, even revolutionary, world of today neither the objectives nor the methods and organization of any political regime can any longer be interpreted in static terms. The distinctive feature of modern political life is the advocacy and pursuit of progress. The consequences have been great. Institutions that would inhibit orderly change—like law narrowly conceived to be specific and eternally valid rules—have been continually eliminated from political life in favor of broad popular rights and pragmatic procedures. The essence of the modern state, as proclaimed in the doctrine of sovereignty by the archdemocrat Rousseau two centuries ago, lies in its legislative power and not in its laws. Constitutions today must reconcile this view with the older ideals of good government; they must provide security in the midst of change—in which, furthermore, the government is more intimately involved than in earlier constitutional regimes. This is an unprecedented demand, and there is no guarantee of success; many claim it to be an impossible one, and abandon either constitutionalism or the modern way of life.

Clearly, constitutions must be flexible if they are to be successful. Yet we need not be pessimistic. Constitutional government emerged in diversified and progressive communities as the governmental form especially adapted to their needs, and despite the reaction of totalitarianism, modern life is marked primarily by an accentuation of those qualities. Consequently, rejection of constitutional government is often accompanied by continuing civil strife, dictatorial domination, or both, and the needs and potentialities of the community suffer. Though actual constitutions are often compromises—the product of exhaustion among contending forces, or an accidental equilibrium—they may nonetheless be durable, surviving great political and social transformations, as have those of the United States and Great Britain. Much depends on whether adequate flexibility is built into the settlement by its originators and later interpreters.

Men are capable of attaining sufficient rationality to create and preserve constitutional government, though they may often lack the will. If they consider the alternatives it is clearly to their interest. Furthermore, experience shows the appropriateness of constitutional government in periods dominated, like ours, by the formation into communities of ever larger and more heterogeneous populations, and by the scientific and technological revolutions, which continue to render obsolete much of yesterday's beliefs. It is unlikely that either a desire for absolute security and stable order or a utopian revolutionary zeal are rational reactions to this condition, but they underlie the challenges to constitutionalism today. Dictatorship, or government by arbitrary commands and purges, can be an efficient instrument only for limited purposes. Constitutional government alone can serve the broad objectives and utilize the diverse capacities through which the people's future can be built in freedom. Its power rests in its discipline; it is government according to rules, based on discussion and co-operation. As in science and technology, this discipline is ultimately more fruitful and powerful than one of commands and purges. Constitutionalism seems unusually relevant in a world which science and technology continue to shape.

To say that constitutional government is harmonious with modern needs and capacities, however, does not mean that institutions dividing power in familiar ways will necessarily prevail. No particular institutions are necessary to constitutionalism any more than any particular methods are necessary to science; institutions must reflect the problems and conditions present in the tradition and life of a people. Such factors as religious beliefs and organization, the consequences of geography, economic procedures and objectives, family life, and characteristic relations with neighboring states influence the development of political institutions. Knowing that these change, we may therefore expect constitutional systems to vary and change with them; it is important only that the essential principles of constitutional government be maintained.

Constitutions and Constitutionalism. To be realistic, however, we must recognize in conclusion that the constitutions of many countries today have relatively little to do with constitutional government. They serve instead as symbols of national unity, for in the contemporary world to possess a constitutional document has come to be the mark of political independence and maturity. At best, they are declarations of independence and statements of intentions; at worst, they are façades behind which leaders conduct an absolute rule. Nationalistic sentiment, and in some cases communist doctrine as well, aim at a highly unified political and social system and at revolutionary transformations that are incompatible with any division of power. Consequently these "constitutions" do not control the rulers but are really instruments of their power.

Were the generally accepted vocabulary of political life more precise, this usage could probably be termed a corruption of the term "constitution"; yet the matter is not that simple. Even in the United States the Constitution has become a symbol of national unity, endowed with considerable majesty, rather than the pragmatic political arrangement the framers intended. The resulting tendency is that loyalty to certain traditional interpretations replaces loyal use of the decision-making process provided in the Constitution, thus weakening the flexibility and disturbing the division of powers present in the constitutional system. It is always difficult, however, to avoid confusing particular constitutional institutions with constitutionalism, since we act in and through particular institutions, while constitutional principles are abstractions. The consequence of such confusion is that constitutional institutions, even constitutional documents, can be abused and cease to serve constitutional purposes. Therefore, we can understand when the leaders of new states, who confront overwhelming governmental problems, fail to observe constitutional procedures that are not perfectly realized even in advanced regimes. Constitutional government, though a political reality, is also an ideal.

CHAPTER 6

LIBERTY *and the* STATE

I KNOW NOT what course others may take, but as for me, give me liberty or give me death!" These words of the patriot Patrick Henry are familiar to every American schoolchild; comparable declarations have become part of the political heritage of every modern western community, spreading in this century throughout the world. Indeed, our most interesting and provocative political literature has asserted, claimed, or explained freedom.* Despite this, however, Abraham Lincoln's observation of a century ago that America was much in need of a good definition of liberty is today as true—and as unfulfilled. Lincoln also noted that the wolf and the sheep would not likely share the same idea of freedom and what promotes it—for the sheep call for protection from the wolves—a good example of why it is so difficult to arrive at a clear and general conception of freedom.

It is no less difficult to say what political order and government have to do with liberty. Some political theorists identify government with the wolves—that is, assert that government is an instrument through which

* "Freedom" and "liberty" are virtually synonymous, the only clear difference between them being that the former is derived from the Germanic and the latter from the Latin foundations of the English language. Usage, however, frequently distinguishes between freedom as a broad, philosophic concept, and liberty as something more specific, so that we speak more easily of liberties than of freedoms.

some men dominate and exploit others; to other political thinkers, government exists to protect the weak and to promote a common welfare. Even worse, dictatorial government is associated with some views of freedom; democracy, with others; and with still others, no government at all. The student of government who tries to keep an open mind can hardly avoid being quite confused. We cannot clarify the matter completely here, but perhaps we may set a few points straight, and also show what liberties are promoted in modern governments, and how this is done.

I. *The* MEANING *of* FREEDOM

One reason, at least, why we often have such difficulty understanding freedom is that its meaning varies with the context. We speak, for example, of free-falling objects as well as free men, and clearly do not mean the same thing in both cases. When we say that a man is free because he has escaped from jail we do not mean the same thing as when we speak of liberty in political concerns. To help clarify the matter, we may observe that human freedom, in its complexity, has both negative and positive aspects. Presumably these are related, but the negative aspects are by far the most obviously felt and easily identified. Consequently, in both political thought and practice, we tend to center our attention on the negative face of liberty. Although this may enable us to deal fairly adequately with immediate problems, only some sense of freedom's positive facets will enable us to meet the challenge, as stated in the preamble of the American Constitution, to "secure the Blessings of Liberty to ourselves and our Posterity."

The Negative Side of Freedom. It is much easier to say when a man is not free than when he is. We think it quite obvious that a slave is not free, for he is subject to the dominating power of his master. We would say much the same of a man in prison and a nation subject to alien rule. In each instance distinct external restraints are imposed on the lives of persons or groups. In significant ways their activities are determined by others, and so we say they are not free. That they may have chosen or accept their condition is generally held irrelevant; the willing slave is not a free man.

Is it only domination by men, however, which denies freedom? Ordinarily, throughout history, men have thought so. Slaves have claimed freedom from their masters; subjects have sought to gain liberty by restricting or overthrowing the authority and power of autocratic governments; and communities, by revolting against alien political rule. Throughout most of history, however, men have lived largely according to custom, and the only attack on their liberty which they recognized as such was in the acts of men who refused to follow their traditions. If such men became rulers they were called tyrants, and private persons of that ilk were easily disposed of as criminals or lunatics; no one assumed that the term "freedom" applied to them. The tyrant was clearly the enemy of liberty, but whether traditions themselves, or any other of the apparently natural conditions of life, might be tyrannical or inhibit freedom was rarely contemplated, except by a few philosophers.

Even slavery, or some comparable condition, was taken for granted as inherent in human life until about three centuries ago, and was hotly debated and fought over in the United States only a century ago. As recently as the beginning of the nineteenth century, Thomas Malthus proclaimed as a "law of nature" that the population would increase more rapidly than the food supply, so that most people would have to exist on the verge of starvation. This view was widely accepted. In other words, many of the more significant limits to the activities of men were viewed as somewhat analogous to the fact that all men must eventually die; the term "freedom" was not relevant as there was no point in talking of such limits as restraints.

Clearly, this outlook is not widely shared today. The limited purposes pursued by men in simpler societies have expanded greatly, and we have become much more ambitious for the goods and powers of this world. At the same time, modern science and industry have led increasing numbers of men throughout the world to view as remediable many limitations in life previously assumed to be natural and inevitable. We have consequently come to discern many new "restraints," some only vaguely associated with domination by men and others not at all. The idea of liberty has become much larger in its scope and application.

Correspondingly, however, freedom has become much more difficult to understand in any practical sense. For we tend to see its promotion not only as the release of men from the domination of other men, but also as their release from interference with the fulfillment of their desires by all sorts of conditions, including even ignorance, illness, fear, and insecurity. Moralists have long insisted that a man can be the "slave of his passions"; many persons, accepting recent psychological views, now hold that a man dominated by his obsessions is not free. In its negative aspect, then, liberty is the absence of avoidable impediments to choice and action, but this apparently simple formulation is complicated by the range and diversity of impediments which we tend to think today can and should be avoided. The difficult and very practical question now is not only what liberties people may have a right to against others, but what liberties they can actually possess and enjoy.

The Positive Side of Freedom. There can be no doubt that the pursuit of liberty, as the elimination of what are felt to be avoidable restrictions on doing and being as we wish, has released large numbers of people, particularly in recent years, from many of the inhibitions and frustrations of our ancestors. Yet have we become truly free as a result, or even more free than they? Clearly, viewing liberty merely as the absence of restraints will not enable us to answer that question. Many critics have observed that we seem to escape one restraint only by subjecting ourselves to others, sometimes worse, and that a life devoted solely to escaping restraints is aimless. We need, obviously, a view of freedom which suggests what the free man is like as well as what he has escaped from. The task is frankly beyond what can be attempted here, though some light may be thrown upon it.

Doubtless many men in history have demanded and won freedom from some particular burden or restriction, with little thought as to what that freedom might in turn demand of them. Despite this, to be free is, in fact, the greatest challenge in human life. Men have won liberty only through great sacrifices, and its preservation often demands no less. Those who are "born free," as frequently those who are born rich, are not always aware of the precariousness of their condition, and so sometimes lose it. The absence of restraints is only the beginning of freedom, as the possession of much money is only the beginning of wealth. The miser is not a wealthy man, nor will a monied fool long be so. Freedom is more than a minimum of undesirable and arbitrarily imposed limitations; the free man is one who is largely responsible for himself and to such authorities and standards as he himself accepts as valid. Liberty is self-rule, not no-rule.

Evidently, then, those incapable of self-rule are equally incapable of freedom; if set free they will soon drift from chaos into tyranny, for some sort of rule will always prevail. Unfortunately, this insight only points the direction a full consideration of liberty must take, for there is little more agreement on a precise meaning for "self-rule" than for "freedom." Nevertheless, it is reasonable to observe that freedom is meaningful only to a purposeful man who is determined to organize his choices, his acts, and the potentialities he discovers in his environment, to the fulfillment of that purpose. A bottle drifting in the ocean is neither free nor unfree; whether a man in similar circumstances will be free or not depends largely upon himself, although his opportunities are admittedly rather limited. Liberty, however, is only partly a matter of what or how many opportunities are available, and more of what one does with those which are. We never have available to us all the opportunities we might desire, and to define freedom as unlimited opportunity would be sheer utopianism. Freedom cannot, consequently, be realistically viewed as the ability to do anything one might wish.

Recognition of this finite quality of freedom has led virtually all philosophers to hold that only a rational man can be free. Reason, essentially a matter of logically relating ideas derived from imagination and from experience, enables one to harmonize purposes and actions—often to limit but sometimes also to expand—so that he can understand most fully what in any given time and place he can do and become. But a man's freedom is also proportionate to his competencies, his more or less mechanical skills, which alone enable him to exploit the opportunities reason points out.

Purpose, rationality, and skills, then, are the positive components of freedom; they are disciplines or restraints, of course, but they are those through which a free life can be built. Only arbitrary restraints—incompatible with the purposes of a man, with what reason at any time indicates as meaningful or feasible, and with use of skills a man possesses or may acquire—are denials of liberty. To conclude, we can only observe that the free life is the rational life, hinged at one side by the purposes which our moral ideals and scientific insights continually open up to us, and on the other by the physical and technological skills and capacities through which we effectively act. Freedom is never really possessed; it is a never-ending conquest of new liberties and the stabilization and modification of those which yesterday were new. It is unusually dependent, therefore, on the existence of appropriate conditions.

The Social Conditions of Liberty. Man does not live unto himself. The purposes he pursues and his capacity to realize them are largely determined by his community, which has shaped his character and provides him with means of action. In a very simple and isolated community no consideration of freedom is likely to arise; among all the native tongues in central Africa, for example, only one has had a word for freedom, and with the changing order there that word has begun to possess a general currency. The idea of freedom, it appears, is the product only of fairly complex civilizations, with their diversity of values and techniques and of social orders and authorities. It is relevant only when alternatives exist, when they arrive at conflicting ideas as to why they ought to choose one rather than another, and when they rebel against what they now see as arbitrary restrictions upon their choosing as they see fit. Perhaps a man in isolation is free, but we learn little about freedom by examining his situation. The condition of freedom, as well as limitations upon it, is inseparable from social life.

It is somewhat paradoxical that liberty becomes possible only in the same conditions which give rise to likely restrictions upon it. But then, it is equally paradoxical, as has long been recognized, that man is both the most noble and the most brutal among the animals of the world, and the two paradoxes are probably not unrelated. For freedom increases —and so does man's capacity to be noble or brutal—in direct proportion to his power to decide and to act in diverse ways. Primitive man is not free—nor is he particularly noble or brutal—because his social conditions rarely give him the power to be free. Both his imagination and his possibilities of action are severely limited. As culture becomes more complex, freedom inevitably appears, although usually in a limited form—for some rather than for all.

Modern western culture, after a long evolution with many sidetracks, has embraced the ideal of freedom for all more thoroughly than any other culture in history. Both in upholding the ideal and in creating conditions within which liberty can flourish, western societies have moved steadily forward over the last several centuries. Yet, the pursuit of "equal freedom" is always subject to peculiar difficulties, which have made that progress somewhat erratic and uncertain. In the first place, in the words of Daniel Defoe, "Nature hath put this tincture in our blood, that each would be a tyrant if he could." Men usually want freedom for themselves, but not always for others. Second, we are not always able to know what liberties comprise a meaningful liberty to others—

and even ourselves—or what requirements must be met if a general freedom is to be possible, and we may therefore err in our search for it.

Many people assumed not long ago—and some assume yet today—that liberty is best secured if people are just left alone, to pursue their own purposes in their own way. Undeniably there is truth in this view which is relevant to any age; liberty itself is not promoted by restraints. However, the conditions necessary for freedom may be so promoted. As a general rule it is clear that restraints necessary to social order are at the same time indispensable for liberty, for only as active members of an orderly community can men count upon one another sufficiently to develop worthwhile purposes and co-operate to promote them. Outside such an order all restraints are arbitrary from the point of view of human purposes, and in a "state of nature" men would be able neither to envisage nor to do very much. They would possess but a caricature of liberty.

Not all sorts of social orders, however, are alike in their support of freedom. All promote freedom for some, but some degree of equality must be secured if freedom is to be general; probably, indeed, if it is to persist for any. How much equality, and in what conditions or rights, has long been controversial, and the argument remains indeterminate. An absolute equality of conditions, pursued dogmatically, is most likely incompatible with liberty, given the diversity of human needs and talents. To secure and maintain it would probably require a drastic narrowing of opportunities, and would in effect be a sort of return to primitive life, wherein no meaningful freedom exists. This is why the communist ideal is utopian, and communist practice inevitably contradicts it. On the other hand, substantial inequalities breed domination, and tend to create a static class or caste order in which freedom is limited even for the upper classes, despite their advantages. Lincoln's sense of liberty was sure when he observed that he wanted to be neither slave nor master. Liberty, then, is found in social orders making available with reasonable equality to all men diverse opportunities of choice and achievement. Even thus qualified it is no easy objective or simple condition; it is but imperfectly realized anywhere.

Liberty in Theory and Practice. It is difficult to generalize about freedom—to develop an adequate over-all conception of it and how it may be maximized. Particular men in particular circumstances find their freedom in particular liberties; while these liberties might be compatible they are clearly not always so. As abstractly true as any general view of liberty may be, men are rarely fully rational or moral in their insights, and their ambitions are frequently enough extreme and self-centered; consequently, they are less interested in liberty as such than in certain liberties that they think would serve their present concrete ambitions. At times these liberties have been positive governmental grants of powers or other aid, and at others, merely the absence of governmental controls; but they have had only the most accidental coherence, if any, so that one man's liberty is often another's slavery. As a practical matter, therefore, in social and political analysis a discussion of freedom must be largely one of particular liberties possessed or claimed, of conflicts among them, and of the limitations and restraints which their recognition and guarantee would require or lead to.

If liberties and restraints are thus related, it is evident that some restraints upon the choices and actions of human beings are inevitable, but from this it does not follow that any particular one is, or that we are always able to know or to agree on which are arbitrary and which are not. The appropriateness of a restraint, even as to its effect in promoting or protecting a recognized liberty, is too much relative to time, place, and person. Nor does the idea that only persons capable of self-discipline can be free necessarily imply that restraints must be imposed upon men until they have proved their capacity to live without them. There are obvious instances in which this is true—with infants, for example—but more often such capacity can only be developed and "merit" proved through living in freedom rather than in slavery. Advocates of freedom have rightly maintained an optimistic outlook, insisting with Walt Whitman that there must be continual experiments in how much liberty society can bear.

Society, the preservation of orderly relationships among men, is a prerequisite of freedom. Yet, the free man is one governed by his own sense of what he should and wants to do, and, since this cannot be determined in advance without denying liberty, what he will come to demand is often unpredictable and may be explosive in relation to any existing social order. There seems to be no way of organizing "freedom" into a neat and tidy set of ideas or practices; it is not always comfortable to live with, but its denial is ultimately equally frustrating.

The values of liberty are manifold. In a free community alone is possible a continuing progress in thought and achievement, although the exact nature of that progress will depend not upon freedom itself but upon other values accepted. In freedom alone can any genuine individuality develop, with persons becoming aware of themselves as persons and not simply as manifestations of social classes or other impersonal powers, and having both the opportunity and encouragement to express their idiosyncracies. Finally, only in liberty is there any genuinely moral behavior, for a person who does the right thing only because he is forced to is, at best, being "educated" to moral conduct.

Yet a "perfect freedom" is not the lot of mankind; indeed, they can rarely even envisage it, much less achieve it, in the world as it is—full of incompatible ideas, interests, and conditions. Particular liberties rather than liberty in general is what men are most likely to enjoy, and they hold themselves free if they are more impressed by those liberties they have than by those they lack. And in a world which is not as moral or rational as one might wish, every liberty is realized at some cost, and generally the cost is some other liberty, whether one's own or someone else's. We must turn, then, to the liberties which modern political systems have made central in constitutional provisions and in public policy, and which make concrete the abstract ideal of freedom, to the extent it may be done.

II. POLITICAL LIBERTY

The relation between freedom and authority has posed some of the most perplexing questions in the history of political thought. Interminable arguments have ensued over whether the terms and the conditions they refer to are incompatible; or whether freedom is actually voluntary obedience to "true" authority; or whether authority, though not to be identified with freedom, may nonetheless be employed to promote it. Clearly, authority is a restraint upon men, making them do things they would not otherwise do; this is particularly true of the political authority of governments in large and complex modern communities, which regulate and direct our lives so pervasively.

Yet, most of us, upon reflection, can see that without that authority we would be not free but lost, in a world confused in purposes and unpredictable in events. The relation, then, between authority and liberty is ambiguous. Authority of some sort is necessary to maintain order, apart from which liberty is meaningless. But order apart from liberty is likewise meaningless. Since men differ in their purposes, and the conditions in which they must act change, "order for order's sake" is hardly a libertarian demand, or even a very comprehensible one. The balance of this chapter will be devoted to discussing those facets of political order which have generally been considered as especially furthering of freedom.

Freedom and Law. The "rule of law" has traditionally been held to be a form of political authority particularly compatible with liberty. Unfortunately, neither law nor liberty are simple concepts or realities; consequently, the ways men have combined them are many, diverse, and often bewildering. Nevertheless, the point does seem fundamentally sound: men find freedom only in communities in which law controls the exercise of political power, and in which the order government maintains is a legal order.

Although, in a narrow sense, a law is merely an authoritative rule governing the conduct of those subject to it—and thus appears a flat denial of their freedom—this perspective is not adequate. On the one hand, what men have called law is not just any rule or set of them, but rules in which arbitrariness is either absent or substantially minimized. Arbitrariness is a somewhat relative term; what we today accept with equanimity might well have been rejected with horror by our grandfathers, and vice versa, but it nonetheless implies that the rule must be in keeping with some standard if it is to be accepted as law. Apart from the fact that a legal rule must emanate from someone recognized as having proper authority, men have usually insisted also that a rule which is law is inherently right and reasonable—that it is an appropriate means to an acceptable end. Consequently, men can recognize it as law, and most will equally recognize their obligation to obey it, doing so voluntarily. To the extent this is true, the rule is not seen as a limitation on their freedom.

This view has been widely accepted in western political thought and practice. It led one of the principal philosophers of modern liberal government, John Locke, to insist almost three centuries ago that law directs a man to his own good, and that freedom exists within the law, not in independence of it. Difficulties arise, of course, when we try to pin this down to specific cases, especially in the rapidly changing and complex conditions of today. In a simple and stable community, where it is essentially custom, law is likely indeed to be largely complementary, if not identical, to the values, ideas, and usual behavior of the people.

But such a condition is not very relevant to our experience or to any useful analysis of liberty. If law is to secure liberty in contemporary social life it must harmonize a great diversity of changing purposes and facilitate their realization in constantly varying circumstances—which is to ask of it more, probably, than it can accomplish. That is, though law be as "right and reasonable" as it may be, and though individuals be likewise as rational and moral in their claims as they can, still irreconcilable conflicts seem certain, and some persons and some liberties will suffer whatever the decision.

Nevertheless, few people are unmitigated egoists in defining the good they wish to be free to pursue, and law which seems right and reasonable, because it reflects the customs, values, ways of thinking, technology, and circumstances of the community in which it develops, is certainly no enemy of whatever liberty we may be capable of. Law, which Aristotle so long ago nicely defined as "reason, unaffected by desire," is not immune to arbitrariness and bias, as Aristotle was himself aware. Yet when it reflects—as most law does—the continuing and responsible thought of a people and its leaders, and when it is oriented to the regulation of activities and the protection of general rights, partiality and arbitrariness are at least minimized. Through law at its best men are aided in knowing and pursuing their ends, finding their liberty within a common rule.

More concretely, however, law contributes significantly to human freedom even when, as in any modern society, it does not clearly embody any general identity of purpose. Equally important is that law is a determinate standard, known in advance, controlling the acts of public officials, and clearly identifying the responsibilities of private persons. It is almost as important that the rights and duties of persons be determinate as that they be "right." Many would hold that it is even more important that they be so, for our knowledge of the "right and reasonable" is so uncertain that our lives would be chaotic did we not have what Plato called "the golden cord of the law" to cling to in the absence of perfect wisdom. Be that as it may, quite obviously the freedom of a man is greatly extended if he knows how others will react to his ventures, and whether they will support him or attack him, and in what ways they may do so. This is most effectively realized in a liberal environment, where the rule of law authorizes a man to do whatever the law does not prohibit, and no effort is made to regulate the whole of life. In contrast,

ABOVE: "Political order, then, is the framework within which other more particular aspects of human life may go on; it is the framework of society." (p. 54) A member of the Republican Guard on sentry duty at the Élysée Palace, official residence of the President of the French Republic. (*French Embassy Press and Information Division.*) BELOW: "Judges, by virtue of their conservatism, training, and relative independence of position, are sometimes able to protect an individual's civil rights, when these are clear in law, and to support by their stands and arguments an environment in which civil liberties remain respectable." (p. 221) Members of the British High Court of Justice, led by the Lord Chancellor, in procession from Westminster Abbey to the House of Lords. (*British Information Services.*)

ABOVE: "Liberty, then, is found in social orders making available with reasonable equality to all men diverse opportunities of choice and achievement." (p. 204) An orphanage at Rome maintained by the Italian National Maternity and Infant Service as part of the government's social welfare program. (*Italian Cultural Institute, New York.*) BELOW: "The most controversial and difficult problems in civil liberties in recent times have concerned at what point and in what way governments may move to protect peace and their own authority." (p. 225) Students in Munich, West Germany, line up for a demonstration in a freedom of the press controversy. (*German Information Center.*)

in classical authoritarian regimes, a man is free to do only what is explicitly permitted, all else being potentially punishable. Yet there is law here also, and determinateness, so a man knows where he stands and can build a life somewhat to his purposes. Very little is this so when, in totalitarian regimes of modern times, the rule of law is flatly denied, and whatever is not forbidden is compulsory—words in jest, to be sure, but far too true nonetheless. In communist regimes most men can act freely only where they can preserve their privacy, which realm the government and party seek constantly to destroy.

Arbitrariness on the part of officials has always been a great enemy of liberty, and it remains so today, even though we now recognize that private power is dangerous as well and look to government for protection against it. Our age is one extraordinarily productive of power, both public and private; only through the discipline of law can that power be made to support freedom rather than to destroy it. Leaders today—and particularly those in government, because of our great dependence upon them—who were to evade the restraints and direction of the law, would be far more able than any before in history to attack the liberties of the people. More striking now than it was when he wrote it just before the American revolution is the truth of John Dickinson's phrase, "eternal vigilance is the price of liberty," and he meant vigilance that public officials do not depart from the authority granted them by law. We need only add, given a new demand for effective government, that freedom also depends upon the full exercise of the authority so granted.

Freedom and Democracy. Throughout the last few centuries the demand for liberty has generally also been a demand for democracy in government. There have been occasional exceptions; some have thought liberty could best be realized through the absolute rule of a rational despot or elite, while some have seemed to find their freedom in service to the cause of a totalitarian dictator and party. Far more often, however, men have seen democracy as the only government for a free community. Other forms of government ensure only the freedom of the ruling class, if that, and any liberty others possess is, as the phrase goes, purely coincidental. The liberties of subjects are largely dependent upon their acceptability to their rulers; a slave could be similarly free if his ambitions were not very great and if his master happened to be kind and easygoing. This is hardly a very significant sort of liberty, and those of yesterday and today who have demanded freedom and democracy cannot be gainsaid in thus linking the two. How and why liberty is promoted by democracy, however, requires some elaboration.

A democracy is a self-governing community, and would thus appear to be by definition a free one. In a sense, of course, any community is free and self-governing if it is not dominated by an external power. Many people—especially those with a recent history of colonial rule—are able to think only in these terms, and accept dictatorship as a necessary means to securing and preserving their independence. In our transitional world the limited view of freedom manifested in nationalist and communist dictatorships is rather widespread, and may in some circumstances be the only one feasible. It is not, however, universally appropriate. Few established modern political regimes accept it. Independence obtained through dictatorial leadership is, at best, but the first step of a community on its way to freedom. Ultimately, democracy alone can perfect and stabilize that liberty, not only for individuals but for the self-governing community as a whole. Throughout the free world "developed" nations are generally committed to this proposition. The history of the states of the western world supports it; they originated in absolutism but moved continuously, if with setbacks, toward democracy. Although the resulting belief a half-century ago in the inevitable triumph of democracy everywhere was excessively optimistic, we may reasonably continue to affirm that democracy is indispensable to any fully developed liberty in the modern world.

A free community is not just one which has thrown off or never known the restraints of "foreign exploitation," but rather one which is effectively able to work out its own purposes and promote them through its laws and public policies. Obviously, the former is a necessary condition for the latter, but is not alone enough to ensure it. If the "community" lacks any clear purposes of its own, some discipline will surely be imposed upon it, whether by internal despots, outside power, or both in combination. Of this, the story of the former Belgian Congo is an extraordinarily apt illustration, although that of Cuba under Castro runs the Congo a close second. The "independence" of a country with little or no capacity for freedom is extremely fragile. In the end, the liberty of a people depends upon the strength of that people, and this is much less a matter of armaments than of their unity of purpose and capacity for effective co-operation. This strength they will have only if their government and its policies are firmly established in their affections, being rooted in their traditions, values, and ambitions. Only to a limited degree will fear and hatred of foreigners, or of a dispossessed ruling class, long furnish this "cement."

Generally accepted traditions did in the past furnish both cohesiveness and a sense of freedom to communities, even under monarchies and aristocracies. But the world of today is not particularly favorable to traditionalism—witness the frustration of conservatives everywhere, who, when they obtain power, usually have to do what they earlier had roundly condemned. The need today is for great popular involvement in nontraditional policies. Perhaps the totalitarian dictatorships of the present can meet this need for a time through their techniques of propaganda, demagoguery, and terror, leading their populations "freely" and effectively to support their governments. However, similar regimes, such as that of Fascist Italy, collapsed with remarkable speed and completeness when seriously challenged; we really have no way of knowing the strength and durability of popular support of such regimes as Communist China and the Soviet Union. Even though popular consent is always imperfect in any actual democracy, its characteristic institutions and values are the only ones which function explicitly to found public policy upon the opinions and purposes currently prevalent among the people. Democracy is, in a word, a regime of responsible government, conservative and progressive according to changing popular demand; as such, it supports not only the sense but also the reality of being truly self-governed, of being free.

Democracy, however, is not a regime solely of collective liberty; as the analysis of democracy in Chapter 3 clearly suggests, it requires a substantial amount of personal freedom as well. Accidental agreements of interest or astute manipulation may endow a dictator with much popular allegiance, but this is at best the shadow of democracy. While dictators can survive only through the suppression of controversy, democracy flourishes in its presence and deteriorates if it is suppressed. Controversy may be said, indeed, to be the fuel of democratic government. But, as James Madison remarked in *The Federalist,* "Liberty is to faction what air is to fire, an aliment without which it instantly expires." Democratic institutions, being no more than channels through which controversies are processed, must include a wide range of personal liberties.

The particular liberties democracies have tended to promote and protect will be discussed below; here we need only note that they give to private persons opportunities to identify their needs and potentialities; to act privately to further them as best they can, as long as the equal rights of others are respected; and to criticize governments and public policies, actively promoting such changes as they believe right and reasonable. From one point of view, this serves the ultimate freedom of the community in its independence and self-government, but at the same time it is the core of personal liberty as well. Freedom is of a piece —free men *and* a free community, or no freedom at all. Democracy alone serves the whole of freedom, and thus alone can for long preserve any of it.

III. CIVIL LIBERTIES

The full meaning of political liberty is not to be brought out through a discussion of the rule of law and of democracy, no matter how essential these may be both to freedom itself and to its preservation. Ever since the American and French revolutions, at least, men have generally assumed that only those governments served freedom which respected and protected certain fundamental rights or liberties. To complete our treatment of political freedom, then, we must indicate what these rights are, how they are defined and protected, and what problems have arisen in the process.

Types of Civil Liberties. Discussion of civil liberties may become somewhat confusing, due to variations in terminology and perspective. Subtle distinctions may be drawn between "civil rights" and "civil liberties," because, strictly speaking, a liberty may mean simply that one is not prevented from doing something, while a right is a liberty authorized and protected. However, civil liberties are nowhere possessed as a matter of accident—that no one has bothered to abolish them. Everywhere they are observed they are assumed to be possessed in some way as a matter of right; the term "civil rights," then, is fully appropriate, and in what follows we shall use the two phrases as essentially synonymous. Somewhat inconveniently for purposes of general discussion, nevertheless, the term "civil rights" has in the United States become rather strongly associated with the campaign against racial discrimination and the securing of equal enjoyment of rights for all men, as was evidenced in the adoption of the far-reaching Civil Rights Act of 1964. Equal treatment under the laws is, to be sure, a fundamental civil right, but it is not the only one; in the following discussion we shall not intend this restricted use of the term unless so indicated.

Broadly speaking, civil liberties in modern government refer to a variety of particular rights or opportunities which, if a person choose to avail himself of them, his government may protect and must not deny. Civil rights are the concrete result of significant historical experience; they are not abstractions, although it is sometimes tempting to treat them as though they were. One may expect, then, that they will differ somewhat from one time and place to another, for the relevant historical experiences have varied and continue to vary. What we call civil rights emerged in the western political tradition, and most of them are not recognized except in that tradition. In the most general terms, they characteristically include a right to life, personal liberty, and security; to freedom of conscience and religious practice; to freedom of speech and expression, including press and assembly; to freedom of association; and to the possession and use of private property. But these broad terms must be considerably qualified in arriving at the reality of them as civil rights in any given place. Such rights as these are often termed "substantive," in that they specify a condition of freedom or advantage the people are to enjoy; they are desired for their own sake and not primarily as means to ulterior ends, although they may be that as well.

In addition, as part of the array of civil rights, wherever these are effectively maintained, diverse "procedural" rights are also to be found. These rights, which are basically political and legal devices through which government officials are controlled and the people protected against arbitrary action, are not always of great importance intrinsically but without them no liberties are likely long to survive. Some of these are political rights, through which citizens exercise influence upon officials, and being associated nowadays largely with democracy, the central such right is voting. Others pertain to the judicial order, and tend to maintain the rule of law in the exercise of power by officials; of particular importance here are rights to habeas corpus and other procedures guaranteeing a fair trial. The details of procedural rights vary considerably from state to state, but it is usually quite evident when they are absent or inadequate to their task. The distinction between substantive and procedural rights, however, is not an absolute one; free speech is "procedurally" important in the political process, for example, while

voting may be considered important to freedom as a means of self-expression as well as a device for controlling officials.

Civil Rights and Government. In general, civil liberties are rights in regard to governmental policies and official acts; they are limitations upon those policies and acts. This, at least, is the traditional and least ambiguous view of them. Freedom of speech as a civil right means primarily that officials must not interfere with a person's speech. It does not give him any additional rights against his neighbors, whose possible assaults on him for what he says would be normally punished as being against peace and order, not as violations of his civil rights. Nor does it normally give him any particular claim to public assistance in finding audiences to address or to their attentive listening. It means only that officials must not obstruct his collection of an audience in appropriate times and places, or prohibit him from saying what he will, or punish him for saying what he did, apart from certain exceptions and qualifications to be discussed hereafter. Government does not really promote substantive civil rights, but simply recognizes that with some sorts of conduct it must not interfere. On the other hand, it does positively guarantee procedural rights for these are parts of its immediate constitutional order and express the forms of legitimate official behavior.

This traditional view is sometimes challenged today, however. Some, believing that civil rights are not just a defense of the citizen against government but represent the basic values of modern civilization, argue that government should actively promote these liberties, rather than simply refrain from direct violations of them, and should especially secure equal enjoyment of them for all persons. This challenge is particularly strong in the United States in reaction to the widespread discrimination against racial minorities, and many laws, judicial decisions, and executive acts have attempted to reduce this discrimination in regard to employment and educational opportunities, rental and sale of housing, and service in public conveyances, hotels, restaurants, and recreational facilities. But the argument has also run more broadly against unequal opportunities to enjoy these liberties, no matter what the reason—differences in wealth or family connections, for example. Such problems may be taken, however, as related to any government's concern with order, and to a liberal government's concern with justice—with equal enjoyment of civil rights and other benefits of a democratic order—rather than with the definition of civil rights themselves.

Yet, it cannot be denied that governments are increasingly involved in the ordinary lives of citizens, regulating and supporting the things they do in the exercise of their liberties. In the implementation of modern public policies, governments must be particularly careful that they do not violate civil rights indirectly—through making it possible for acts of some private persons, supported by or using government power, to deprive others of their civil rights. For example, for years the courts in the United States enforced restrictive covenants in real property, preventing a person from selling his house to a member of a racial minority if a private agreement renouncing that right previously existed. Only in 1948 did the Supreme Court, in *Shelley* v. *Kraemer,* finally conclude that this was an improper use of public power, through which the civil rights of those racial minorities were effectively violated.

Similar problems arise in the course of awarding public contracts, making available grants-in-aid or guarantees of loans, and in the exercise of regulatory, licensing, and even taxing powers, for these may give private persons the benefit of public power. Through discriminatory use of them, then, public action may indirectly attack or support the civil liberties of the people. No doubt, in democracy the choice should be made of the policy which supports civil liberties in such cases, but conflicting interests are likely to make any decision in these matters highly controversial and their effects upon liberties highly ambiguous. The discussion here would become impossibly complicated, however, did we not restrict our consideration of civil rights to the basic and limited perspective stated previously. There is a difference, anyway, between not being able to live, work, and speak as one will because of fear of the police, and because of private discrimination or lack of means.

The Definition and Protection of Civil Rights. The rights of men are claimed by some to be natural and inalienable, while others see them only as concessions of governments. To still others, they are policies relative to particular social and economic conditions—necessary as for any one order, but varying as such conditions change. As a practical matter, however, arguments concerning the source and foundation of civil rights are largely reflections of disputes over what rights should be protected, and if in any way limited, and thus involve the most fundamental political and philosophical perspectives underlying any regime. These matters having been discussed earlier, it is sufficient here to observe that where civil rights prevail, they are stated, clarified as to their meaning and scope, and protected, in a limited number of fairly definite ways.

Increasingly, since the French and American revolutions the initial definition of civil liberties has taken the form of declarations or bills of rights. These declarations have been central aspects of the written constitutions which create and are the fundamental law of new governments, ranging from those of the American states in 1776 and later, to that of Nigeria, say, which attained independence in 1960. There are few states in the world today without constitutions embodying such declarations of rights. Yet the British, who enjoy the oldest and strongest tradition of civil liberty in the world, do not have any such declaration. The civil rights of British subjects are not set forth in any one document, and some of the most important of their liberties are not set forth explicitly anywhere, but are simply the consequences of political attitudes widely shared, together with an effective subordination of official conduct to the rule of law. On the other hand, stirring declarations of rights have been and are today flouted with impunity by many governments, reducing them, at best, to statements of good intentions. Obviously, the definition of civil liberties is not just a matter of spectacular declarations thereof.

We shall better understand the significance of bills of rights, therefore, if we consider the conditions in which they can be useful and effective in preserving civil liberties. A declaration of rights, to begin with, may represent a firm commitment of a community to be governed according to such standards, and if so, then it will have considerable political force, unifying public sentiment against any violations of it. It joins other national symbols in crystallizing a constitutional tradition. The British, long accustomed to operating in a more casual fashion, may not need a distinct and overarching statement of their liberties—although they do have numerous distinct statements of their procedural rights. Canadians, however, must have come to feel the lack of one, for in 1960 they broke with the British tradition and adopted an "Act for the Recognition and Protection of Human Rights and Fundamental Freedoms," which includes a bill of rights. And in the constitutions of former British dependencies, as they acquired self-governing Commonwealth status in recent decades, declarations of civil liberties were included. Even the British appear recently to have become aware that where liberal political traditions are not firmly established, clear statements of civil rights may be particularly valuable.

Constitutional declarations of rights are not always the security for civil liberties, however, which they promise to be. Even if they represent a general commitment to civil liberties, there always remains the difficulty of making the declaration effective in particular instances, when violations prove far too tempting both to officials and their citizen supporters—no less in democracy than in other forms of government. Nor is their violation entirely a matter of deliberate tyrannical intent. Experience seems to show that to every liberty—especially every general liberty—some exceptions are requisite, springing either from conflicts between various liberties or between the exercise of a liberty and government action seen as necessary to public order, welfare, and security. The occasionally limited effectiveness of declarations of rights flows from two problems: that of defining rights which can actually be maintained, and that of providing means for their enforcement. These are difficult problems, and never perfectly solved.

Even more, however, they have not always been clearly recognized. Reflecting a considerable optimism, constitutions antedating the present century tended to ignore them, declaring rights in such unqualified terms that they could not always be maintained as written, and usually providing no means of enforcing them short of revolution. The First Amendment to the Constitution of the United States, for example, in prohibiting Congress from passing any law abridging freedom of religion, speech, or peaceable assembly, enunciates no distinction among various kinds of associations; yet, as criminal and seditious conspiracies, some sorts of conduct are commonly considered abuses rather than exercises of these freedoms. Consequently, such declarations had to be qualified by later political and legal interpretations, and in many instances could be ignored entirely under the guise of security needs, or whenever popular prejudices ran against them. Statements of principles tend to be most powerful when cast in absolutistic terms, but for that reason precisely are usually not entirely effective as legal standards.

Not all the clauses of the American Bill of Rights are cast in such terms, however. The Fifth Amendment provides, *inter alia,* that no person shall "be deprived of life, liberty, or property, without due process of law." It would not appear that the rights to life, liberty, and property, were considered to be unqualified when thus broadly stated, although in the aspects of them protected by the First Amendment they were so. This peculiarity has not promoted a consistent interpretation of constitutional rights in American law, yielding a continuing conflict between the views of rights as absolute and as qualified. Outside the United States, however, twentieth-century constitutions generally tend throughout their declarations of rights more to resemble the Fifth than the First Amendment, that is, to express them distinctly as qualified.

The Constitution of the German Federal Republic, for example, permits limitation of any civil right, even though its authors were unquestionably devoted to liberal government. They provided, however, that this may be done only by law, and that the law must be general and not specific in its applicability, to avoid discrimination against persons, races, or classes. Furthermore, the basic nature of the right must not be changed—whatever that might mean. The Constitution itself additionally pronounces that civil rights are not guaranteed to those who use them to attack the basic democratic order—a consequence of Germany's experience with both fascists and communists. The French Constitution distinguishes between the right—as that of workers to organize and strike—and the exercise of it, with the latter being appropriately regulated by law. There is danger here, of course, that what is given on the one hand may be taken away on the other. The Nigerian Constitution attempts to guard against this by limiting permitted qualifications of guaranteed rights to those "reasonably justified in a democratic society." It also spells out many such qualifications, distinctly excluding from the normal right to personal liberty, for example, criminals, minors, prohibited immigrants, lunatics, alcoholics, drug addicts, vagrants, and persons suffering from infectious diseases, all of whom are thus constitutionally subject to special regulation. Thus recent constitutions have attempted to cope with the problem of declaring civil rights in such a way that they will be meaningful and yet can be maintained.

Nevertheless, it is unlikely that any declaration of civil rights, no matter how detailed and "realistic," can in itself guarantee what liberties will be effectively maintained. While declarations of principle can be important and influential, they cannot serve to define the precise nature and limits of civil liberties. And more specific constitutional provisions are equally likely to fail in this, due to lack of flexibility throughout changing circumstances and needs, for while "freedom" is eternally desirable, particular "freedoms" are much more relative both as to desirability and possibility in time and place. Consequently, the civil liberties which people will actually desire and governments actually recognize are and must be continuingly redefined. This function is normally carried on through the institutions of government, through its legislative, executive, and judicial processes, acting under the influence of public opinion and within the broad standards given in bills of rights or similar constitutional laws and traditions. And, in fact, in those states whose citizens have long enjoyed civil liberties, we learn a great deal more about those liberties through examining decisions of courts of law, administrative practices, and the behavior and enactments of legislative assemblies, than by reflecting on the phrases of their declarations of rights, if any.

Political and Judicial Protection of Civil Rights. Thus, the definition of civil rights cannot be separated from the means through which they are maintained, enforced, and protected; if no such means exist, no civil liberties exist, and those which do exist are those which are effectively preserved through the political and legal machinery of government. The 1936 Constitution of the Soviet Union includes a declaration of civil rights, including virtually all of those to be found in liberal regimes, but no one would argue that most Soviet citizens have effectively enjoyed many of them in the years since. Examination of the practices of Soviet officials suggests that these rights are largely ignored—as they must be, for they are incompatible with communist dictatorship.

British civil liberties, on the other hand, rest firmly on the effective constitutional tradition that private persons may do anything not forbidden by law, but that any official act must be specifically authorized by law. The courts of law have regularly provided protection, therefore, for persons whose rights have been violated by illegal administrative action. Within this regime, individual Britons enjoy civil liberty because of the reluctance of Parliament—and the electorate behind it—to enact laws limiting civil liberties. These liberties are from time to time limited, of course, but only when justification is sufficient to stand the test of public scrutiny and criticism and the ultimate electoral accountability of representatives. French civil liberties are sustained in a way roughly similar, for the declarations of rights generally included in the modern constitutions of that country have not been considered as binding upon the legislative power. However, both administrative and ordinary courts, when they have discretion, have tended to interpret legislation and control administrative acts according to the terms of those declarations. Somewhat as in France, in Canada the "bill of rights" noted above is only a statute and not binding on Parliament. The courts are to control administrative action and interpret laws according to its provisions, unless Parliament specifically legislates otherwise.

In the United States, in contrast, the Bill of Rights has been considered an integral part of the Constitution, controlling all processes of government. This, together with the institution of judicial review of legislation as well as of administration, has given to the definition and protection of civil liberties a markedly legalistic cast. Parliament is quite obviously the principal guardian of British civil liberties; in the United States, the Supreme Court is often said to have this role. Although legislative authorities initiate new interpretations of civil rights as they seek to regulate subversive activities, public meetings, and so on, it is the Court which ultimately must decide if these regulations are compatible with the Constitution. Since 1925, furthermore, the Supreme Court has become the defender of civil rights, not only against the national government, but against state and local authorities as well, for in *Gitlow* v. *New York* it was decided that the provisions of the Fourteenth Amendment, prohibiting the states from depriving persons of liberty without due process of law, implied enforcing the more important provisions of the federal Bill of Rights against the states as well as Congress.

In the United States, then, the courts have acquired the function and responsibility of redefining the civil liberties of Americans through limiting or extending from case to case the authority of officials. The impact of this activity upon the definition of rights should not be underestimated. Who would suspect from a simple reading of the First Amendment that the religious liberty of the American people was violated if they were compelled to salute the flag against their religious scruples, or if voluntary classes in religious instruction were held in schools, though not if pupils were released during school hours to attend them in private buildings? One is reminded here, as in many other matters in American government, of the dictum of a former Chief Justice, Charles Evans Hughes, to the effect that the Constitution is what the Court says it is. Nevertheless, though the Court may sometimes lag behind, it is not unresponsive to currents of political opinion; only in the short run are American civil liberties judicially defined and protected. In the long run, public opinion shapes and sustains them, as much in the United States as in England.

Yet, if in the long run all processes which effectively preserve civil rights are political processes, and depend upon the devotion of the people and their leaders to their liberties, in the day-to-day activities of government judicial protection of them has played an important part and remains valuable. When, in times of stress, government officials are most likely to attack the civil liberties of the people, the devotion of political leaders and the people generally to civil rights may falter in the face of an apparently conflicting need or passion. Judges, by virtue of their conservatism, training, and relative independence of position, are sometimes able to protect an individual's civil rights, when these are clear in law, and to support by their stands and arguments an environment in which civil liberties remain respectable. Although the effectiveness of this remedy should not be overrated—even in the United States with its uniquely long tradition of judicial protection—its value has become increasingly recognized of late. Since World War II, for example, such countries as India, the German Federal Republic, Italy, Japan, and Nigeria have authorized individuals to seek defense against governmental violations of their civil rights in courts of law.

Finally, as an aspect of the organization of the Council of Europe, ratification of a Convention for the Protection of Human Rights and Fundamental Freedoms (1950) has created for many west European states—France and Switzerland being the notable exceptions—obligations in international law to respect the rights there defined. An administrative agency, the European Commission of Human Rights, was created to investigate complaints from individuals or governments, and to undertake conciliation. The Committee of Ministers of the Council of Europe may direct remedial action by the violating state. And, in 1959, a European Court of Human Rights was constituted to which the Commission or the government concerned may appeal cases involving violations of the recognized rights. Through 1964 eight states have accepted the jurisdiction of this Court, but only two cases have come before it, and only one of these issued in a decision, not in itself favorable to civil liberties since it held that an emergency justified deprivation of citizenship without trial. Clearly, this experience and the practical ineffectiveness thus far of the United Nations' efforts to establish an international bill of rights suggest that protection of human rights and freedoms is still largely in the realm of national politics and law.

The Crucial Civil Liberties. Personal liberty, in the sense of security of life and limb and freedom of thought and movement, is certainly the most priceless possession in human existence. Nor is the security and free use of private property significantly less important, since we now know how totalitarian regimes, through denying private property, have been able to control the means of subsistence and self-expression and thus dominate the personal lives of their subjects. Men have struggled over the ages for such personal freedom and have never altogether won it; millions have been deprived of it in the totalitarian dictatorships of this century more completely than ever had been their ancestors. Where this freedom exists, it is in part secured by the ordinary criminal law, which when justly enforced prevents not only theft and murder but also the enslavement and terrorizing of the weak and conscientious by the strong and uninhibited. Thus, political order is indispensable to freedom. But governments may also endanger liberty—the more so for the great power they must possess.

Rarely, however, are governments directly interested in, or effectively capable of, limiting a purely personal and private liberty—unless, as in modern totalitarianism, they seek to destroy it entirely, making all things public and subject to control. Ordinarily a person "minding his own business" is not troubled by officials. Only behavior involving numbers of people, of broad or potentially broad impact upon society, and which tends to affect government and its interests, is of sufficient concern to officials that they seek to control it. Thus the crucial civil liberties are those of public speech and press, of assembly and association, of religious practice, and of the use of property and skills in economic and professional endeavors, for it is in the exercise of these that individuals are most likely to encounter the repressive powers of government. Of course, the basic procedural rights are also crucial to the protection of these, but no more need be said of them here.

No such liberties have ever been without qualification, however. Freedom of speech and press have always been limited by laws governing slander and libel, giving defamed persons opportunity for protection and redress. Traditionally, also, states have punished obscenity, blasphemy, and seditious expression as well as activity; and even where religious freedom has been allowed, the forms of worship and related social behavior have been subject to control in the interests of public order and morality. The Mormons in the United States were not permitted legally to continue polygamous marriages, for example, and the use of loudspeakers may be regulated to prevent a nuisance, even though they are used for religious purposes. Similarly, nowhere does a civil right of assembly prevent the police from breaking up a riot, or one of association authorize criminal conspiracy. Finally, the ownership of property and the possession of skills has never constituted a right to use them in anti-social ways, or—with rare exception—to be exempt from taxation and regulation for public purposes. If government could not do these things, it would not be government.

Serious controversies arise, however, in the process of defining what associations are conspiracies, of controlling disturbances at mass meetings, of balancing the prevention of nuisances and immorality against the claims of freedom, of deciding when a reputation has in fact been slandered, of finding that expressions and actions are truly seditious in that they undermine the authority of government, and of concluding whether private property has been abolished rather than limited, or a valid public purpose served. All these terms are obviously relative to variable circumstances; they are also relative to variable human attitudes and temperaments, which lead men to evaluate circumstances quite diversely. The consequence is that the limitations on liberty—which in practical terms define the boundaries of liberty itself—vary considerably in time and place. The topic is virtually inexhaustible; we can only sketch some of its characteristics. Various specialized works—particularly numerous in the case of the United States—deal with the subject in detail.

Methods and Standards of Limitation. Those most favorable to civil liberties have shown a marked distaste for censorship or any other form of "previous restraint" upon speech or other activities. They have favored, rather, subsequent punishment for abuse of rights, since the power to censor is far too often exercised in a petty and bigoted fashion and in an exaggerated fear of evil consequences. Censorship of publications and public meetings—requiring for the latter a permit which will be issued only when the purpose of the meeting is approved—usually guarantees that little new and nothing challenging is likely to be introduced. On the other hand, reliance upon subsequent punishment invokes public authority only when law and order have been broken in a specific way, and when it can reasonably be ascertained who is responsible. Appropriate individuals can then be held responsible to the extent of their offense. Assuming that the standards to which a person will be held responsible are clear and known to him, there can be no doubt that previous restraint is far more restrictive of liberty than subsequent punishment. However, although there is probably less censorship today than in the past, the distribution of moving pictures and popular literature is undeniably affected by censorship and control, and news is often limited by governmental secrecy or "management of the news," and by "voluntary" self-censorship by the news media. Because people are often reluctant to accept the difficult responsibility of predicting the consequences of releasing news or comment, it may well be that previous restraint of one sort or another is inevitable in these complex and critical times.

Similarly, those most favorable to civil liberties have sought to maintain the narrowest of interpretations upon even acceptable limitations. Standards governing slander and libel have not become especially controversial, since they do not normally bear on political affairs. However, these standards are extremely strict in Britain, foreclosing the attacks on personal reputation that are a common aspect of politics in the United States and France. To the contrary, the Supreme Court of the United States, reversing in 1964 a judgment for damages against *The New York Times* won by an Alabama official, ruled that the protection of political controversy justified privilege against libel suits for untruthful assertions in criticism of public officials, and a minority argued for an absolute privilege even if malice were proved.

Standards governing obscenity, on the other hand, have been extremely controversial in this century, and they furthermore involve public prosecution, or deprivation of such advantages as use of the postal service in the United States. Libertarians have always insisted that obscenity be narrowly construed if subject to proscription, and have protested that confusion of "realism" with obscenity, and of obscenity with pornography, is destructive of art and literature. The Obscene Publications Act (1959) in Britain, and various judicial decisions from *U.S.* v. *One Book Entitled Ulysses* (1934) to *Roth* v. *U.S.* (1957) in the United States, largely reflect this view. According to the latter decision, the test of obscenity is "whether to the average person, applying contemporary community standards, the dominant theme of the material taken as a whole appeals to prurient interest." And the British statute allows as a defense that the publication is in "the interests of science, literature, art or learning, or other objects of general concern," on which expert testimony is now admissible. Counter to such trends, paradoxically, after a century and a half of libertarian policy the French government has since 1958 been proscribing any publicity or even availability in book stores for publications found by a commission in the Ministry of the Interior to "present a danger to youth because of their licentious or pornographic character." Many books and magazines have been thus effectively banned, even though not intended for children or normally accessible to them; some of these have freely circulated in Britain and the United States.

Far more significant for political science has been the limitation of civil liberty on the grounds of disturbance of the peace or sedition. Riots and revolutions, of course, challenge governments in their most immediate responsibilities and interests, and rarely has anyone denied the authority of government to quell them. Quite comprehensibly, however, governments are not often willing to wait until the fire is raging before turning on the water. The most controversial and difficult problems in civil liberties in recent times have concerned at what point and in what way governments may move to protect the peace and their own authority. Few have denied officials the right to prevent irreparable damage in such matters by forestalling a riot or breaking up a seditious conspiracy. But as such action, unless carefully controlled, is likely to restrict freedom of expression, assembly, and association, those most concerned with these liberties have been highly at odds with those more sensitive to the danger to public order and security.

In American jurisprudence since World War I, two doctrines have competed as criteria governing when officials may intervene. One of these, held by those especially impressed by the threat to social order, provides that government may repress any ideas or actions manifesting a "dangerous tendency." The other, first stated by Mr. Justice Holmes in 1919, countered that officials could act only when a "clear and present danger" existed that a substantive evil would occur which they had authority to prevent—in other words, only in an emergency in which the constitutional order itself was manifestly endangered. Or, as it has been put more recently by some members of the Supreme Court, the "First Amendment freedoms" have a "preferred status" in regard to the rest of the Constitution and its grants of power to government, to be protected at almost any cost.

The ideal of minimal interference with individual liberty is a worthy one, with which most Americans agree—at least in the abstract. These "tests" of official competence were originally stated, however, in a day when the threats to the existing order and values were almost entirely those of indigenous movements of social protest, and which were for the most part highly idealistic and spontaneous, rather than a well-organized revolutionary conspiracy directed and controlled from a foreign state. The appearance of the latter, primarily in communism, has thoroughly confused the significance of the tests, for to many communism is a "clear and present danger" as soon as it appears on the scene as a tendency. The experiences of the last few decades furnish much justification for this attitude.

Consequently, the American government has sought to isolate the communists and to repress them. A number of top communist leaders were jailed in 1951 for conspiring to advocate the overthrow of government by force and violence, which the Smith Act of 1940 had proscribed, and "loyalty oaths" were widely employed in the rather vain hope that they would separate the sheep from the goats. The Communist party and all organizations found communist-dominated by the Subversive Activities Control Board—provided by the Internal Security, or McCarran, Act of 1950—were required to register as such, and to make public their membership and activities. And in the Communist Control Act of 1954, Congress accepted the idea of outlawing the party itself, barring it from any legal rights and from participating in elections, although the precise effect of the statute is not yet clear. Later in the decade, however, the Supreme Court moderated the impact of all this on civil liberties by requiring that "advocacy" of revolution be accompanied by some "effort to instigate action" if it is to be punishable, and similarly insisted that mere membership in a communist organization should not have disadvantageous legal consequences unless the person knew at the time of its seditious nature. It has since continued this policy, ruling in 1964 that citizens could not be denied passports only because they were Communists, and overturning on the ground of "vagueness" state laws imposing loyalty oaths on state employees.

Many of the provisions of these various statutes have never been used; on the other hand, for a few years congressional committees ruthlessly publicized the names, ideas, and associations of a few communists and many alleged "fellow travelers," in a modern form of punishment by pillory, upon accusation and without anything worthy of being called a trial. It remains yet uncertain how significant these activities have been and are in the struggle against communism; probably their greatest effect has been to alert the people to danger. However, as rather blunt instruments when more delicate ones were called for, they have not always hit the issues squarely on the head and the exact nature of the danger has become more than a little confused as a result. More important for the purposes of this chapter, their use has undoubtedly injured in reputation and profession some noncommunist idealists, and frightened many others, so that even the responsible exercise of civil rights has consequently suffered.

Attitudes Toward Civil Liberties Compared. Civil liberties are rarely considered abroad in quite the same terms as in the United States; most particularly, they do not receive the same legalistic and often highly moralistic analysis. Although they are generally as secure in England and France as in the United States, for example, thinking about civil liberties in those countries seems to be considerably more pragmatic. John Stuart Mill, an Englishman whose essay *On Liberty* (1859) is a classic of libertarian philosophy, considered freedom of thought to be absolute, but he did not think even of freedom of speech in the same light. Only in the United States—undoubtedly stimulated by the unique phrasing of the First Amendment to the Constitution—has the tendency appeared to assume that individuals have something approaching an absolute right to speak and act, providing they are in good faith, so that it is up to the government to protect them against the consequences of their behavior. Abroad, civil liberties are almost automatically considered in the context of their exercise, so that we find little tendency as in the United States to affirm them absolutely for some or most people, while denying them with equal absoluteness to others. This is appropriately illustrated in the characteristic British and French treatment of communists and other extremist groups, which is quite different from that in America.

Virtually all Britons and most French are as aware of communist purposes as Americans, and find them as distasteful, yet few are inclined to identify communist ideas and associations automatically with subversion, seeking to outlaw them. There are, actually, virtually no legal obstacles to doing so in either country. A very broadly stated criminal offense of seditious libel has in fact long existed in Britain, making possible punishment for using words arousing hatred or contempt of any of the institutions of government, or raising discontent or ill-will among the population, among other things. Truly, a communist could not avoid violating this law. But, in fact, it would be extremely difficult for *any* political opposition to avoid doing so either, with the result that it is virtually a dead letter, except in cases of incitements to immediate violence and efforts to subvert the armed forces and police.

As a practical matter, therefore, any person may say or write anything he wishes—subject to possible suits for slander or libel—and public meetings are subject only to minor inconveniences in regulation. If, however, activities threaten to give rise to a riot or other disturbance of the peace the police have great discretionary power to intervene and may jail any who do not follow their instructions. In reality, there have been in recent years few significant conflicts between this authority of the police and the civil liberties of private citizens, due undoubtedly to restraint both in the exercise of that authority and of those liberties. British public opinion, it is often said, is established in a tradition of responsible freedom. The activities of fascists and supporters of "unilateral nuclear disarmament," accusations of police brutality, and some police "scandals" in recent years indicate, nonetheless, that even the solid British fabric is subject to strain.

French officials have quite similar powers, and the result is much the same. However, organizations and movements on the continent are very fond of mass meetings, which in the case of extremist movements tend frequently to become unruly. This seems to be part of the French political game, as is also the toughness of the police in breaking them up. Neither communist nor any other political groups have in recent times been repressed, or even seriously harried, however. Their publications and activities continue unabated. A further illustration of French reluctance to subject persons to disadvantages for their political opinions, no matter how adverse to the existing regime, was a 1954 decision of the Council of State, the highest administrative court. Here, an effort of the executive to exclude young communists from the state school which prepares persons for the highest civil service positions was declared an abuse of power, for no legislation authorized it and the minister did not prove that the persons concerned were incompetent.

On the other hand, informal political arrangements have effectively excluded communists from critical positions in the government since 1947—even though they possessed for some time one of the largest representations in the National Assembly, a situation which greatly troubled the operation of the regime. Finally, in regard to the highly controversial Algerian war, to prevent what it considered attempts to interfere with the conduct of the war and undermine the morale of the army, the government regularly but selectively seized newspapers and books, and subjected occasional persons—many, in Algeria itself—to various forms of harassment and detention. This it did in the face of vigorous protest, most of which, nonetheless, circulated freely. It may be said that, considering the extreme emotions brought into conflict by the frustrations of that war, the inroads into civil liberties which resulted were remarkably limited.

Liberty, Responsibility, and the State. The idea of civil rights—of individual liberties limited only by the minimal necessities of peace and order, and the preservation of the similar rights of others—is one of the great achievements of modern liberal political thought. In numerous countries it is substantially realized in practice. Totalitarian communities do not honor the idea either in theory or practice, for they deny the value of individuality, upon which it is based, and also the constitutional methods of restraint upon official power, which are necessary to its preservation. Nowhere, however, can civil liberties be anything but contingent in particular instances, even if in ideal they should be clear, certain, and untouchable. The exercise of liberties breeds at least occasional conflicts, due to the very nature of man and the world he lives in. These conflicts can be resolved compatibly with freedom only if men can discover and maintain in their lives a balance—especially delicate and difficult to preserve in our day—of liberties and responsibilities. Government in a free society must be the defender of liberties and the enforcer of responsibilities, which are but two sides of the same coin—a fact which men are far too inclined to ignore. In each nation the history of civil liberties manifests the balance which has there been struck; it is the history of how much freedom men have actually learned to live with. Nowhere has the final chapter yet been written.

PART FOUR:

PEOPLE *and* POLITICS

TERENCE

That is a true proverb which is wont to be commonly quoted, that "all had rather it were well for themselves than for another."

JOHN GALSWORTHY

There's just one rule for politicians all over the world: Don't say in Power what you say in Opposition; if you do, you only have to carry out what the other fellows have found impossible.

CHAPTER 7

INTERESTS *and* OPINION

A MAN'S SKIN sits closer to him than his shirt." And so men think more carefully, as a rule, about their immediate concerns than about the general welfare; they are more likely to perceive their own interests in politics than the larger framework. Thus our discussions have sought to provide the reader with a vantage point from which he can now observe the political process at closer range and more narrowly conceived—that is, the interaction of men in the day-to-day activities of achieving political goals.

We should be reminded, first of all, that in the modern world men's beliefs and interests are marked far more by heterogeneity than homogeneity. Yet the creation of public policy demands a measure of agreement and unity. Agreement may be imposed and enforced at all costs in a dictatorial fashion, or it may be developed by reconciliation of interests through democratic processes. Of course, no regime uses one or the other means exclusively, but the differences in emphasis are enormous. We may recall from *A Thousand and One Nights* how Harun-al-Rashid, the caliph of Baghdad, disguised himself to go about the city and to inquire what people really thought of his rule; even under despotic government the ruler must find some means to act from time to time as a politician with his "ear to the ground."

We know rather little about how the variety of interests within authoritarian societies are weighed or assessed and may influence public policy. In democracies, where politics is largely conducted in the open, men are free to hold differing opinions and to act upon them; the expression and reconciliation of these differences generally provide the "stuff" of democratic politics, and this discussion will be conducted within that context. Yet even this qualification does not much simplify our task. So great is the range and so varied are the forms of human activities within the political process that to account for them all is incredibly difficult. Here we have, simultaneously interacting in extraordinarily complex ways, individual persons, interest groups, political parties, the election process and other political techniques, opinion and communications media, domestic organs of government, and foreign and international bodies of many kinds. Here in truth is a "seamless web" that defies any perfect and systematic unraveling.

Nevertheless, we must begin, and although we cannot offer a complete analysis, we can introduce some of its salients. Perhaps the most useful approach is through a twofold perspective toward popular political activity. On the one hand, in traditional democratic thought man is seen acting formally as a citizen and voter, motivated by a sense of civic duty and by appeals to his rational judgment of the public interest; he associates with others through a political party; and his political opinions are registered by votes in elections and plebiscites. He is, in a sense, acting thus as a "public person."

On the other hand, modern political science has come to consider of great importance that man may also be seen acting informally as an individual and as a member of diverse groups and classes, manifesting interests and a variety of psychological and social idiosyncrasies. His political opinions are thus partly assessable through polls and interviews, furnishing data for sociological and psychological analysis. This is man acting as a kind of "private person" in his relation to government. In this chapter we shall discuss this view and return in the following chapter to the "public person." Of course, this is not to suggest that the two approaches can be consistently separated without distortion. "Private persons" and "citizens" are, after all, the same people. Yet the political processes involved are different, though coexisting and even mutually supporting in some respects; political science must analyze them separately, and then try to fit them together, for a full understanding of political life.

I. INTERESTS *and* THEIR ORGANIZATION

Man, being a gregarious creature, is always found in groups of some sort. The kinds of groupings that can be made because of man's differential characteristics—that he falls into distinctive classes or categories according to whether he is left-handed, long-headed, or leaf-eating—are not relevant to our purposes, for men do not ordinarily associate on the basis of such characteristics alone. Of greater concern to social science are those which reflect the fact that men have values, ideas, and interests; that they are ambitious, yet weak except when co-operating with others; and that they seek through combining with others to promote their purposes. Though all such groups, whether familial, religious, social, vocational, economic, or other, may have some significance to the governmental process, political science is especially concerned with what are called "interest groups."

Interest Group Defined. For present purposes we prefer to simplify rather than complicate the attempts to define this variously used term. We shall employ it to describe any collection of persons with common objectives who seek their realization through political action to influence public policy. Still more simply, an interest group is any that wants something from government. Other terms inevitably come to mind. "Pressure group" is employed by some writers in an invidious sense to label political groups whose methods or objectives they deem questionable or reprehensible; other writers use it merely as a synonym for "interest group." Yet it is not so neutral a term, and suggests methods which are not always employed; groups may persuade as well as pressure. Our preference is for the term "interest group," and for separate judgments on tactics and ends. "Lobby" is also a well-worn political term, employed in some instances to denote interest groups or their agents. It seems preferable, however, to employ it in its original sense as an attempt directly and immediately to influence the decisions of legislative and executive officials. Individuals, corporations, and other bodies, as well as organized interest groups, may undertake lobbying.

Interest Politics and Their Importance. The realm of "interest politics"—the various ways in which individuals add their informal influence to their formal impact upon government—is a broad one. This very breadth has produced disagreement about the relative importance of the group. The representation of interests is unquestionably an important and central phenomenon in modern politics. In our previous discussions we have generally assumed that private interests are the foundation of the state, which exists entirely to promote them. And if the state is to be effective in this purpose, it is clear that those interests must possess ways of expressing themselves and influencing the development of public policy. Otherwise, they will be ignored, as is often the case in communist regimes, where, despite the claims of theory, only those interests acceptable to the party and its leaders are promoted. In the ebb and flow of political activity in the liberal democratic regimes, on the other hand, representatives of diverse private interests exercise influence, contend for dominance on issues involving them, and participate actively in the formulation and execution of public policy.

Yet in the recognition of the place of interests in modern politics some extremely important considerations are often overlooked. We are inclined to accept too simple a view of what these interests are, who has them, and how and under what conditions they are manifested. The whole picture is more than an enlarged version of those parts which we can bring into clear focus. Consequently, students of political life have assumed throughout history, with some oversimplification, that the active forces in politics are *either* the community as a whole (or its leaders), *or* the various social groupings comprising it, *or* the many individual persons who, as citizens, make up the commonwealth. The great political theories which have informed the western imagination have endeavored to combine all of these perspectives, yet always to accord one of them particular dominance.

In recent decades, the dominant theme in political analysis has been the second of the above perspectives. Philosophers and political scientists alike have tended to doubt both the real existence of "the community as a whole," and of individuals with interests taking action independent of group association. They have seen politics as the manifestation of conflicting group interests and the controversy or bargaining which such conflicting interests produce. The individual, insofar as he is politically important, is relegated to acting as a member of such groups and the community as a whole is manifested only in "the rules of the game" upon which the various groups have generally agreed.

This is not the place for extensive discussion of such theoretical matters, but two points seem clear. On the one hand, in many, and particularly the most highly developed, regimes the relevance of the "interest group approach" to politics cannot be denied. To do so would be to ignore significant factors in the making of public policies, and many of the most important values and characteristics of modern political communities. Private interests have a quite exceptional importance in modern life, but that life is also highly organized—a fact which alters both the nature of those interests and the way they express themselves in politics from the earlier, individualistic view. To say that the persons of contemporary states are its business associations, trade unions, professional societies, and so forth, rather than its individual citizens, is not as great a mistake as it would be to ignore them entirely. Contemporary political science has very largely accepted this view, which is reflected throughout this book.

On the other hand, it is equally clear that political life is not exclusively definable in terms of conflicts and compromises among private interest groups. Such groups come and go, or change in character over time; they interact with one another in quite different ways in different communities, and in any one at different times; they share some values and not others, and their conflicts and agreements vary in time and place. "The community as a whole," however difficult it may be to identify clearly, is important in all this as the basic, and at least partially independent, framework of accepted values and recognized forms of action. It is at least as reasonable to assert that a community produces appropriate groups to realize its values, as that diverse groups produce a community which their experience proves expedient.

The individual, likewise, whether acting as private person, citizen, political leader, or official, cannot be divided among his various group memberships without leaving a remainder. Not all members of labor unions, or even union officials, see all things alike in politics, for example, and it makes a great deal of difference which individual member is taken as representing the union interest. Nor can government officials be neglected in politics, after all; whatever they may be, their role in the political process is clearly not the same as that of any private interest group. We can thus conclude that the interest group approach is an important advance in political analysis, but that "interest" should be interpreted in the broadest way, and that the student should neglect no factors relevant to the political process. Those which appear remote are sometimes of the greatest impact in the long run.

The Formation and Organization of Interest Groups. Sociologists give a great deal of attention to the nature and structure of groups generally, and have demonstrated how complex and multiformed they are. We need not survey that ground here, however. Even so, we shall be obliged to adopt a fairly abstract view of groups for the purposes of analysis and make them appear artificial in ways they are not. Interest groups arise under many different circumstances, as when a number of people share common concerns or problems, whether in bird-watching or the conservation of natural resources; when they seek common objectives or support common causes, as prohibition or international peace; when they engage in common activities, as coal miners or stamp collectors; when they are gathered in a common location, as downtown merchants or suburban homeowners; when they are producers or consumers of common products or services, as naval stores or ferryboat commuters; and so on. The point is that interest groups come into existence because such experiences produce shared attitudes and a conscious mutuality of purpose; they induce reciprocal relationships; and they may encourage concerted action to make some political demand.

Although we have ample demonstration that men necessarily compete for the attainment of their ends, it is equally important that they also co-operate. Within any given group, the extent to which they do can vary enormously. Many interest groups are entirely unorganized; a collection of taxpayers, or consumers, or people who share a common skill, language, or religion may have only a vague sense of common interest, and the most limited sort of interaction. Yet they are not necessarily politically unimportant. They may have some self-chosen leaders and spokesmen; and even if they do not, political leaders, government officials, legislative representatives, or others may make decisions or take action with the specific group very much in mind.

Economists are aware of the phenomenon of "consumer sovereignty"—the power of entirely unorganized consumers to refuse to purchase everything offered in the market, whether ahead of or behind current tastes, and thus pronounce against their producers punishing economic judgments. There are full political analogies to this behavior; politicians, too, must compete for "consumer" support. Public policy is distinctly affected when groups of people behave—even if most spontaneously—in a certain political way; while this is true in any political system, it is especially so in a democracy. Many significant groups, then, particularly in the simpler societies, may not be organized. And important groups in advanced societies may choose to remain unorganized and to refrain from conscious concerted action, because their members may feel that their influence is greater if their attitudes are not already "committed," too readily expressed, too easily predictable—or, no less important, precisely because they are getting what they want from government! Similarly, groups that have achieved their goals may disband their formal association.

Clearly, a number of factors do encourage the members of a group—or some of them—to organize and thus form themselves into an association. Most important, perhaps, as government extends its regulatory activity, raises its levels of taxing and spending, and penetrates ever more deeply into the realm of private interests, the group may feel obliged to organize in order to defend its position. Second, as men become more specialized in their functions and activities, and develop refinements in their interests beyond the concern of political parties, they seek to promote their objectives through separate organizations. Thus, they may conclude that, in a society of many highly organized groups, the unorganized are not receiving their share of attention and government is not responding to their wants; they hope to intensify their influence by organizing, designating leaders, disciplining members, and conducting sustained and persistent programs. Third, the complexity of government and society has made the representation of group interests—the conduct of public relations, propaganda, and lobbying, for example—a highly specialized process requiring expert leadership and management available only to the organized group.

The formation of an association within an interest group—the formalization of membership, agreement upon objectives, selection of officers, and so forth—may have various consequences, not all of which are necessarily intended. Organization attracts the attention of other associations, and of some individuals outside the group; their opposition to and competition with the newly organized group's aims may be intensified. The fact that an association is formed does not automatically increase its strength; members may then expect the organization to exert all necessary efforts and may discontinue their own. On the other hand, some associations have a wider support than the size of their formal membership would indicate; they may have numerous adherents or "fellow travelers." In a formal organization, leadership and control tend to fall into the hands of a minority, in an oligarchic pattern common to such bodies. At the same time, leadership is often more moderate or more extremist than the membership, and, because it is not truly representative, may not best serve group interests. It also appears that organization generally promotes greater similarity of attitude among members and increases their loyalty to group interest. Pronouncements by officers, meetings, conventions, official journals, and the use of propaganda, symbols, and slogans—all work to standardize thinking to some degree and emphasize the need for co-operation, discipline, and concerted action.

The Classification of Interest Groups. Various proposals have been made for the classification of interest groups, yet no single system appears adequate to reveal every significant feature. Professor Gabriel A. Almond, however, has developed one that provides a broad view of interest groups. He distinguishes, accordingly, four kinds of structures. First, *institutional* interest groups, or organizations commonly existing to perform functions within government itself, which by their nature accumulate important vested interests to promote. Examples include government departments, such as the treasury or ministry of agriculture, armed services, central banks, or other bureaucratic groups. Second, *non-associational* interest groups, or those based on class, kinship, religion, or other traditional characteristics, and whose basis of communication is often informal and intermittent. Third, *anomic* interest groups, or those largely spontaneous in character, such as demonstrators, protest marchers, street mobs, or rioters. Such groups tend to break into the political arena suddenly, and may aim at a show of force or violence. Of course, such groups may be deliberately organized or abetted, and their spontaneity entirely a pretense. Fourth, *associational* interest groups, or those formally organized to represent the interests of particular persons and to enjoy the advantages that such association provides in dealing with other political structures.

Associational interest groups, which are most highly developed in the advanced societies of the western world, have been variously distinguished in other ways. They have been classified as self-interested, for example, the National Association of Manufacturers, or disinterested, for example, the Council for the Preservation of Rural England, with the

ABOVE: ". . . A one-party system in Mexico has succeeded in recent years in establishing political stability and moderation. Politics are monopolized by the *Partido Revolucionario Institucional*. . . ." (p. 282) Mexican voters crowd around a ballot box in a federal election. (*United Nations*.) BELOW: "Undoubtedly the most efficacious method of campaigning is through direct contact with the voters and organizing to insure that supporters turn out at the polls." (p. 290) A candidate for Parliament in England, standing by the loud speaker, canvasses for votes outside a London factory. (*British Information Services*.)

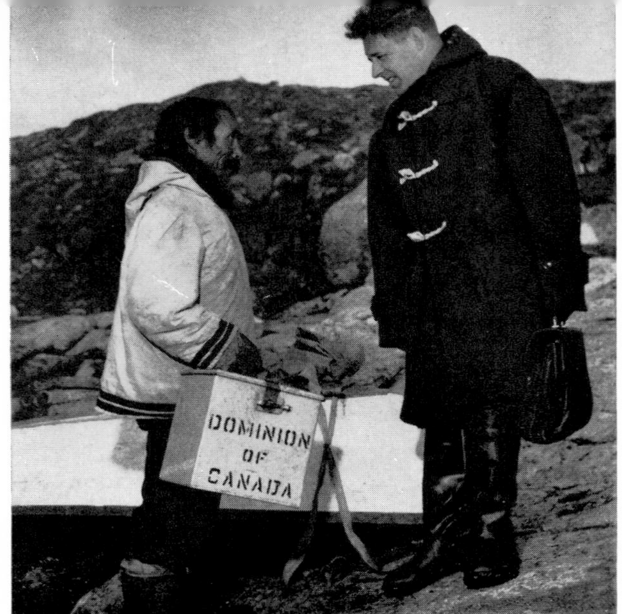

ABOVE: "An election offers the voters an opportunity to choose who are to take office and conduct government." (p. 289) A ballot box for use in a general election has been transported by plane and boat to the far north of Canada. (*National Film Board of Canada.*) BELOW: "In the development of woman suffrage, we have striking testimony to the speed with which social attitudes have changed during the present century." (p. 272) A woman validates her ballot with a thumbprint at a polling station in New Delhi, India. (*Press Information Bureau, Government of India.*)

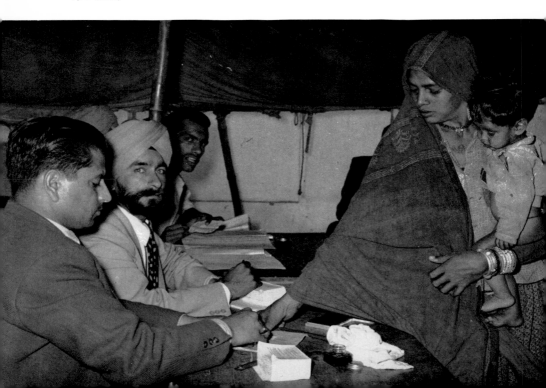

difference, of course, based upon whether they promote particular and private or universal and public interests. A difficulty immediately arises with this classification, however. Can we say that the Navy League, for instance, which seeks a strong navy and a high level of naval preparedness on behalf of national defense—certainly a public interest—is not also promoting the private interests of naval officers and shipbuilders? Many groups are at the same time self- and public-interested. Again, interest groups have been classified as to those interested exclusively in public policy, such as the League of Women Voters of the United States, and distinguished from those concerned with a variety of functions, for example, the Brotherhood of Sleeping Car Porters. Still other classifications have distinguished groups as offensive and defensive, economic and noneconomic, elite and mass, unitary and federated, and so on. Finally, it is common to classify groups according to the kinds of interests with which they are concerned, such as business, labor, agriculture, professional, veteran, civic, or religious. Within any such class, it should be noted, groups may compete among themselves; the interests of small business may be in conflict with those of large, cattle ranchers may oppose sheepherders, and one taxpayers' group may be in controversy with another.

What of the distinctions between interest groups and political parties? In the broadest terms, a party is also an interest group; yet there is justification for seeing that they have fundamentally separate as well as certain similar roles in the political process. It is traditionally asserted that the basic difference arises over whether a political association offers candidates for office and is thus willing in some sense to assume responsibility for its influence on public policy; a political party meets such a test and an interest group does not. The distinction is undoubtedly clearer within a state having a biparty system, where the two major parties not only offer candidates for office but take positions on most of the main issues of public policy. Where a multiparty system exists, or a number of minor parties operate, the difference between party and interest group is narrowed; a political group may well give rise to a new party, and small parties may revert to interest group status.

The American Prohibition party emerged largely from various prohibitionist groups, and has generally remained a "one-issue" party. The British Labour party was an outgrowth in the main, after the beginning of this century, of the trade union movement; this has been the case, indeed, with many socialist parties. More recently, after World War II associations such as the German *Bund der Heimatvertriebenen und Entrechteten* (Union of the Homeless and Disfranchised) and the French *Poujadistes* moved from interest group to party status and back again within a few years. In Israel, as another example, which has a political system including more than two dozen parties, many of the smaller ones are in fact little more than interest groups. Nevertheless, there is always a main difference: a political party submits its claims periodically to the stern and objective test of an election, whereas an interest group does not, and unlike a party, never assumes responsibility for the operation of the government.

The Variety of Associational Interest Groups. Interest groups are by no means a contemporary phenomenon alone. Even in medieval times, interests were represented by estates, by guilds of professional men and artisans, by cities, and by large property owners. Yet these were hardly voluntary associations; due to social and religious circumstances, individuals did not choose the groups of which they were members—indeed, they were the virtual prisoners of them. It is difficult to say precisely when or where nonparty political associations first appeared. They are clearly a concomitant of industrial societies and in their modern form could only become significant in liberal democracies, necessarily accompanied by representative government, a party system, freedom of organization, and a general recognition that there may be diverse ideas as to what government should do. In Britain, their origins are marked in the foundation of such bodies as the Society for Supporting the Bill of Rights (1769), National Union of Working Classes (1831), Howard League for Penal Reform (1866), Trades Union Congress (1869), and National Anti-Vivisection Society (1875). Comparable entities were also organized in the United States, including the American Temperance Society (1826), National Anti-Slavery League (1833), American Medical Association (1846), National Grange (1867), and the American Federation of Labor (1886). Each name of these organizations illustrates something of the character of interests and causes which then were concerns of public policy.

In the twentieth century, associational interest groups have emerged more widely, wherever democratic and representative government extends. Though now quite universally encountered, their nature, diversity, and role in any particular country are related to political circumstances.

In the United States, notorious as a "nation of joiners," they number in the thousands, in bodies as varied as the National Education Association and the National Institute of Diaper Services. In Great Britain, their number and variety are no less, reflecting again the Anglo-Saxon proclivity to embrace causes and organize, demonstrated in associations ranging from the Licensed Victuallers Defence League to the Lord's Day Observance Society. In Latin countries, such as France and Italy, where the sense of public-spiritedness is less developed, interest groups tend for the most part to be self-interested; yet thoughtful people in these countries behold with some wonderment civic-minded societies in which human behavior nonetheless apparently makes it necessary to organize a National Society for the Prevention of Cruelty to Children, as in Britain, or a Society to Maintain Public Decency, as in the United States. Interest groups in France are much more likely to aim at protecting "acquired rights," styling themselves "Society for the Defense of the Rights of ——" (taxpayers, banks, peasants, or whatever they may be). In states with strong authoritarian and bureaucratic traditions, such as Germany and Japan, interest groups have heretofore been inhibited, though they have begun to flourish under current regimes. The attitude toward such groups generally in the autocratic governments of the nineteenth and early twentieth centuries was repressive, denying them the opportunity to operate openly. Eventually, they were either stifled outright or converted into underground and revolutionary conspiracies, ultimately forming many of the extremist groups of the political world. In general, too, the presence of a multiparty system, in which the several parties reflect many narrow economic and ideological interests, also discourages interest group organization.

Any general survey of political associations quickly demonstrates how preponderantly they do reflect economic interests. This is probably an indication not so much that man's objectives are primarily and mainly economic—important as those are—but that economic affairs are widely regulated by government and that economic means are as well the most obvious and immediate to man's goals. The realm of business is characterized by a variety of organizations, and these are found, much alike, in all industrially developed states. We encounter, for instance, the Federation of British Industries, the Federation of German Industry, the Swedish Export Association, and the National Council of French Employers. Agricultural interests produce such bodies as the American

Farm Bureau Federation, the National Association of Swedish Farmers, the (Finnish) Union of Agricultural Producers, and the Dairy Farmers of Canada. Labor is invariably represented in such national organizations as the Confederation of Mexican Workers, the (French) General Confederation of Labor, and the German Workers' Union.

Professional groups are illustrated by associations such as the (British) National Union of Teachers, the Australian Dental Association, and the American Bar Association. Veterans' groups are equally ubiquitous—the American Legion, the Canadian Legion, the French Union of Associations of Combatants and Victims of War, and the (Australian) Returned Servicemen's League. Consumers undertake to protect their interests through such bodies as the (French) National Federation of Consumer Cooperatives, the (Japanese) Federation of Housewives, the (Swedish) Cooperative Union, the (Australian) Housewives Association, and the (American) Consumers Union. In the category of civic associations, we have the examples of the (American) National Congress of Parents and Teachers, the (British) Hansard Society for Parliamentary Government, and the (French) League for the Rights of Man. Many other countries of the West have their counterparts to these bodies; they only illustrate the ways in which individuals, through many different kinds of groups, enlarge their participation in public affairs and promote the various civic, economic, and vocational interests they share with others.

II. INTEREST GROUPS *in the* POLITICAL PROCESS

The range of techniques which interest groups may employ to promote their ends is extensive; we can examine them here only in summary fashion. In general, organized groups have two principal alternative strategies: to influence government, with its organs and officials, directly; or to influence the public—through individuals, political parties, and opinion media—and so exert an impact on government indirectly. Many groups, of course, undertake to do both, hoping thus to insure their optimum effectiveness.

The selection of strategies and techniques for any group is by no means arbitrary; it is distinctly conditioned by group nature, membership, means, and aims. The kind of government within which operations are undertaken is also important—devices usefully employed in a presidential system may not be effective in a parliamentary one. The nature of the party system and the whole national political climate are also decisive. Group activities are welcomed in some countries or accepted as a matter of fact; in the totalitarian states they are rigorously controlled or suppressed. As we examine some of these factors, note that these points will be much clearer when the reader has first read the discussion of government institutions.

Interest Groups and Government. First of all, in representative government, groups are much attracted to the legislative institution. Here important decisions of public policy are made and the opportunity is broadly presented to obtain or oppose not only legislation generally but the all-important tax and appropriation measures as well. The legislative process offers many different stages when any particular bill may be critically affected, and hence the importance of lobbying—persuasively communicating with individual legislators, committee chairmen, and other parliamentary officers.

Lobbying may well involve attempts to apply pressure on such persons, but this is by no means the only or even the most effective technique. Providing legislators with information, statistics, and research studies is common, and there may be opportunity to testify in committee hearings. Nor should it be supposed that all lobbying is unwelcome. Legislators not infrequently depend on it to assist their decisions; without the contact provided by group agents they could well lose touch with important group needs. Other methods utilized by groups in this realm include seeking the election of some of their own members to the legislature, supporting or opposing the election—or reelection—of others, organizing pressure from the constituencies, and so on. Some legislators are amenable to the influence of favors and gifts, and a few even to blackmail or bribery, though corrupt practices, if not unknown, are nearly everywhere illegal.

Executive and administrative officers are also the subject of organized group attention. The executive is ordinarily an important source of legislative proposals and also has the power to reject enacted bills. The administrative organs of government are active in enforcing laws and determining important aspects of public policy, as well as with spending, regulating, purchasing, and similar matters. Obviously, interest groups will seek access to administrators to make their views known, to furnish information, and to assist in policy making—sometimes even to make it. Other methods applied in this sector include influencing the selection of administrators, participating in advisory committees, publicizing administrative actions to call attention to grievances or abuses, and encouraging legislators to do the same. Administrative officials are also sometimes offered valuable inducements for their favor by "influence peddlers." The extent of their success largely turns on the prevailing business mores as well as on the rectitude of officialdom.

Judicial institutions may also be the target of interest group activity, though where judicial independence is secure, judges are usually protected from it. Nevertheless, groups as such are not denied the ordinary opportunities to secure their ends, where appropriate, through judicial procedures and claims for justice. Judicial rulings can be highly important, obviously, in the interpretation and enforcement of law, most especially so where courts have the power of judicial review. Political groups may also promote their objectives by assisting plaintiffs or defendants in particular cases of litigation or, if occasion affords, by acting as *amici curiae* (friends of the court) to provide additional legal arguments and briefs. They may exert some influence on judicial selection, whether appointive or elective; they may also publicize judicial decisions and praise or criticize them. Two well-known American interest groups, the American Civil Liberties Union and the National Association for the Advancement of Colored People, have had considerable success in advancing their objectives by litigation.

Interest Groups and the Public. Interest groups focus their attention on individuals to affect their attitudes, opinions, and behavior. We have already noted that they are concerned with influencing their own members, and have suggested the common means so employed; this must be a continuing process if the cohesion of the association is to be maintained. They are likely also to attempt to reach potential members and sympathizers—all persons with similar self-interest who might be induced to accept membership or to act in concert with the organization. They may even seek co-operative action with other organized groups, either because they share some related interests or are able to provide each other mutual support. Inevitably, too, organized groups seek to influence "the influential"—those whose role or function as civic, social, or business leaders, professional men, authors, journalists, or celebrities puts them especially in a position to influence others.

We have already referred to certain similarities between political parties and interest groups. It might be expected that they are mutually dependent to some degree. Influence with political parties offers avenues of access to the organs of government, and party support of particular interests can be highly effective in securing them. In consequence interest groups often collaborate with parties, sometimes merging themselves into the larger group for purposes of influencing its program, endorsing its candidates, participating in election campaigns, and obtaining office for the association's members. Such groups may provide campaign contributions and other financial assistance, as well as attempt to deliver the votes of its members.

Finally, organized interest groups not uncommonly seek to obtain support for their objectives by informing and winning over public opinion. Since this is a subject we shall be examining later in the chapter, we need only mention here some principal devices utilized. Groups may advertise their views, disseminate them by programs of public relations and publications, and conduct propaganda. Some groups, indeed, attempt to impress their views or wants upon the public by demonstrations, picketing, strikes, and even mob violence. To be sure, violence is hardly compatible with democratic processes.

National Variations in Interest Group Roles. Associations, it has been observed, are found operating in all free societies, but they do not everywhere customarily employ to equal extent or with equal effectiveness all of these techniques. In the United States, they have long had a significant role in the political process, for the American machinery of government as well as certain other national characteristics seem definitely to encourage them. The federal system, allocating many important functions to the fifty states, centers much political power in the state party systems, and allows groups great effectiveness at this level. The separation of powers also decentralizes the election process, with comparable effect. The vast number of elective offices, giving a very "popular" quality to American government, and the high cost of elections create official sensitivity to group demands; so does the decentralization of executive authority at national and state levels, where there are many independent establishments and regulatory boards. The operation of a biparty system in a country of America's continental proportions, heterogeneous in its interests, ethnic origins, and regional characteristics, leaves large room in its politics for additional political associations. No less important as a consequence of the foregoing factors, is the impossibility of exerting tight party discipline over legislators and elected officeholders.

Different circumstances prevail in other countries, though we can only touch briefly upon these. In Great Britain there are quite as many groups as effective as in the United States; differences in the two political systems, however, accord British groups a somewhat altered role. To mention a few of the differences, the executive originates all important legislation; hence the cabinet and ministers generally constitute the sensitive points at which groups seeking or resisting particular legislation may aim. At the same time, the ministries have long considered it routine to consult with interested groups when preparing legislation, making policy, and drafting regulations. British political parties, as well as governmental administration, are also more highly centralized than American; their leaders are among the most influential to which groups seek access. The party system keeps M.P.'s under distinctly close discipline, and thus free of many pressures of the lobby; at the same time, it is common practice for M.P.'s to be agents of organized groups, especially business associations, trade unions, and civic societies, and to speak for them inside the House of Commons, offer amendments they may desire to bills, and ask parliamentary questions of ministers in their behalf. The extent alone of group organization in Britain, even though less attention is given to the mass electorate and public opinion, is ample evidence of the effectiveness with which special groups work within the parliamentary system, either as component elements within the major parties or as bargaining and consulting units outside them.

To take a further illustration, France is another country in which interest groups flourish. Under the Third and Fourth Republics, indeed, given the tentative character of government majorities, the weakness of coalition cabinets, and the ever-splintering and undisciplined party system—not to mention a persistent venality in certain sectors of political life—all combined to make government, and politicians generally, inordinately vulnerable to powerful interest groups. Indeed, one may well ascribe much of France's continuing political instability to the ineffectiveness of its government machinery to contain, reconcile, or resist the importunate claims and clamor of many narrowly organized and uncompromising but powerful groups. Popular dissatisfaction with the Fourth Republic and support of the new Fifth were in no small measure a reaction to weak governments, strangled by interests.

By sharp contrast, in Sweden, also a country with a multiparty system and highly organized interest groups, conflicting group interests are conciliated largely by open negotiation and a "politics of compromise." Sweden is, of course, a relatively small state with a highly homogeneous population; and, with the "pluralistic" character of its society generally accepted, groups habitually make mutual concessions and aim at something like an equilibrium among themselves. The result is that parliamentary and administrative organs have well-established means for official or informal consultations with group agents. Indeed, in this atmosphere of moderation certain organized groups are even delegated authority to perform some administrative functions for the state.

As a further contrast, in the underdeveloped countries, interest groups tend as yet to operate quite differently from those in the industrialized western states. Their cultures are partly western and partly indigenous, and still in the process of change; their politics are commonly monopolized by traditional ruling families, a ruling class, or a single national party. Illiteracy and other factors impede communication between government leaders and the masses of the people. The most important classes are likely to include the wealthy landowners, religious leaders, bureaucrats, and army officers, who exert their influence through institutional and non-associational interest groups. The conduct of politics is thus dominated by these cliques, and the masses—mostly poorer peasants—have no significant representation. Hence, their interests may be expressed largely through anomic groups, and their political activity limited in the main to participation in sporadic demonstrations, riots, revolutionary uprisings, or other violence. Government reliance on the army to repel such disorders enhances the role of the military, which may thus come to be the principal center of politics and power itself. While this is not a precise pattern for interest politics in all of the new nonwestern states, it can be seen with individual variations in many countries of Latin America, Africa, and Asia where associational interest groups have not yet achieved importance.

Interest Group Effectiveness. A number of factors determine the relative success of particular organized groups. Size is an important criterion; larger groups will ordinarily enjoy advantages over smaller ones. The American Legion could be expected to exert more pressure than the American Association of University Professors. Yet size can be deceptive. The National Congress of Parents and Teachers is one of the largest associations in the United States, but not the most powerful by any means; its members are associated only on the most tenuous basis. Hence, cohesiveness counts; a group whose members accept discipline, whose votes can be delivered, or who otherwise act in close concert can be very effective even though small. Funds are also important—not that groups can usually buy what they want from government, but they thus enlarge enormously the variety of techniques which they may employ.

Qualities of leadership deserve consideration in gauging group success: efficiency, ingenuity, skill, and persistence. Group objectives also make a difference. It is generally less difficult to promote "public causes" (or what appear to be such) than limited private interests. It is usually easier for groups to operate defensively than offensively; given the character of government machinery, as a rule it is easier to obstruct than achieve. Finally, tactics and techniques determine success. They must be appropriate to the ends sought. "Enemies" are loudly attacked, but friends must be whispered to. Excessive pressure, display of funds, or strident propaganda can easily boomerang. In some societies, such as France, demonstrations of violence are not uncommon and may even be effective; in the contemporary world, indeed, political tempers seem to have shortened, and political disorder is no longer unusual anywhere. It should not be overlooked that the effectiveness of particular groups may depend upon what political party controls the government; fluctuations in public sympathies and in the temper of the times may also affect the success of competing groups.

Interest Groups in Totalitarian States. So far, we have discussed the group in free societies, but a few words are in order concerning totalitarian regimes. No matter what the monolithic unity claimed for their people by the modern one-party dictatorships, it should be obvious that they do have heterogeneous and conflicting interests. No modern industrial society can be turned into a one-class, one-interest, one-people state without repressive force. We have traced in Chapter 2, it may be recalled, the ways in which western social and political development made the undifferentiated community an impossibility for modern times. Yet the establishment of completely integrated and unified societies is precisely what dictatorial leaders seek. What, then, of interest groups and their role? This is a complex subject and we can offer only the outline of an answer here.

Basically, the totalitarian formula is to create a comprehensive system of government and party monopoly designed to encompass all possible bases of group interests, subordinating all possible activities to political control. Thus, organized groups are taken over and potential groups are given official organization; voluntary societies outside this rigid structure are forbidden. The party supervises associations and provides their leadership. Even religious groups, if tolerated, are thereby sanctioned. Any form of group expression is highly limited; all media of communication—publication, broadcasting, even public meetings—are officially controlled to insure conformity and prevent dissent. At the same time, all of these media are employed by the regime to instruct groups and individuals in what, presumptively, their interests are. Of course, the party must maintain an awareness of the more important group interests that are self-generating, and to some degree placate them. Those who cannot be "educated," appeased, or repressed, finally, are commonly liquidated outright.

Some illustration of this pattern may be seen in the Soviet Union. Certain obvious potential interest groups exist: party and government officials, military officers, the managerial elites, the police, and professional men, artists, and intellectuals. Being special beneficiaries of it, however, they have a distinct interest in the perpetuation of the regime, and fall into groups that have long been "co-ordinated" or created by it. Other elements in Soviet society, such as workers, peasants, and students, with less stake in the regime are gathered into various overlapping associations; these dispense certain benefits and services, thus forcing some level of attachment to them, and also serve as important institutions of control. Newspapers, periodicals, and books, whether general or of the group, are produced under license and censorship, so that the expression of dissent is virtually impossible. "Self-criticism" only is allowed, which is to say that complaints in performance or administration may be aired if they do not constitute opposition to or obstruction of the regime or its policies. The communist leadership is nevertheless always alert to mass restlessness, for the expression of even small discontents may reflect major disaffection. It can also be ruthless in dealing with recalcitrance. When substantial peasant groups stubbornly sought to resist the collectivization of agriculture in the 1930's and did not respond to "re-education," they were liquidated with bloodshed and starvation. Similar treatment was meted out to various minorities in the U.S.S.R. at the end of World War II.

Despite government efforts to prevent or conceal them, anomic groups do make their appearance in the Soviet Union and other totalitarian states. Isolated outbursts of restlessness, discontent, and resistance occur at intervals in the U.S.S.R.; substantial rebellions have flared in East Germany and Poland; and violent revolution broke out in Hungary in 1956. Even though these were all repressed, they were clearly enough expressions—by the only means available—of political interest and feelings to which the communist leadership was hostile.

Criticism and Control of Interest Groups. Even in democracies, groups are often an object of suspicion and concern. Rousseau, whose *Social Contract* (1762) helped inspire the French revolution, devoted much of his argument to emphasizing the danger of particular interests to the public interest—"the general will." Men should be dependent, he asserted, not upon narrow groups but upon the whole, united in a total solidarity of the free and equal. James Madison, too, in the tenth essay of *The Federalist,* expressed a concern over the dangers resulting from the expression of group or factional interests. He saw their effects as "adverse to the rights of other citizens, or to the permanent and aggregate interests of the community."

What, in sum, are the principal grounds for fearing evil consequences from groups in the political process? First of all perhaps is the feeling that they permit the "part" to prevail over the "whole," and in so doing distort the democratic process. To see, or appear to see, "group interests" triumph over "the general interest" results in the conclusion that organized groups enjoy inordinate power. Then too, their methods often make them appear sinister. So many of the terms applied to discussion of them—"lobby," "pressure boys," "influence peddlers," and even their exposure by "muckraking"—have an odious sound. In this realm of "anonymous government" the plutocrats, the unprincipled, and the corruptors seem to enjoy special advantage. Again, interest groups are not always democratic in their organization, and unscrupulous leaders may exploit the funds and the power of the organization in selfish and irresponsible ways. Unlike political parties, interest groups generally cannot be held to account for their policies; their leaders cannot be turned out of public office and punished at elections. Finally, it appears that, though selfish and narrow interests effectively organize, important and socially significant ones go unrepresented. The battle between producers and consumers, for example, is notably uneven.

Nonetheless, interest groups hardly ever succeed in having their will of the public; controls of various kinds impose limits to their operations and effectiveness. No group ever commands the total loyalty of individuals, except in rare instances. All persons have common cause with many groups, and most support several. Whatever the basis of their organization, whether economic interest, social class, or religious, ethnic, or occupational lines, no association gets very large before its members begin to divide again on one or more lines. Groups also compete with each other, a situation which encourages discretion and compromise. Those with extremist ends ordinarily engender their own opposition, and these sometimes cancel each other out entirely.

There are institutional controls upon group power. Though without complete efficiency, most political party systems ameliorate group influence if only because parties must offer broad programs and organize majorities. By their aggregate efforts they moderate many demands. The machinery of government itself does the same; if it is at all broadly based and supported, it offers concessions but not surrender. The weighing up and mediating of group interests is indeed at the heart of the governmental process.

There is the possibility, finally, of formal control. This generally takes the form of publicizing and limiting campaign contributions and prohibiting undue influence, inducements, and threats. Any further attempts at formal control have been mainly American, where Congress and some state legislatures have required the registration of group agents and declaration of the amounts collected and spent to obtain passage or defeat of legislation. Such efforts have nowhere been especially effective. They relate narrowly to the legislative process, and even there the exertion of influence takes forms far too delicate to be captured within a statutory clause. Such restrictiveness can quickly begin to restrain freedom of speech, press, petition, and association. It should not be overlooked that the only really efficient controls are those applied by the totalitarian states; these patently destroy the representative and democratic process.

Group Functions Are Important to the Democratic Process. As Professor David B. Truman observes in his study of interest groups, *The Governmental Process,* "The persistence and the dispersion of such organizations indicate that we are dealing with a characteristic aspect of our society." His work well demonstrates the importance of a behavioral approach to group theory—examining what in fact groups do—as well as the importance of the group itself. As we have earlier emphasized, it is therefore unrealistic to attempt to eliminate the group from our analysis of political life, or to conclude that interest groups, their conflicts, or their methods are bad in themselves. Rather, such associations perform demonstrably important functions compatible with and necessary to democratic government.

First of all, they help overcome the individual's insignificance, politically speaking, in a mass society. Few men at best can have more than a limited participation in the political process, and most, if only because of their lethargy and apathy, have almost none at all; the group serves to enlarge men, and frequently to represent them in areas where political parties cannot. Second, the political interest group may perform a valuable informing and advising function. In complex technological societies, governments continually require more and more expert and technical advice to assist their processes. Often group organizations alone are able to supply this. Third, there is the important "checking" function which they perform. If groups are in fact a fixture of our society, we had best accept their inherent contributions to their own control—their mutual restraining influence. Fourth, particular interests are always to some extent segments of the general interest. However difficult to decide what the general interest really is, it must somehow be compounded of the parts, high and low, broad and narrow. The most characteristic activity of the group is in fact nothing other than its effort to identify its needs with those of all.

The conclusion seems unavoidable that groups have the essential task of insuring that private interests receive public attention. It is important that this be done as openly as possible and in the presence of strong and effective government. Because there is never complete agreement on what is the general interest, the government of the day must be able at intervals to effect a reconciliation of narrower interests into broad policies and enforce them to the public benefit. Thus we may see the value of group moderation and reasonableness, and the need for resolving interest conflicts regularly, before they become extreme. "A democratic society is able to survive," Professor E. E. Schattschneider has observed, "because it manages conflict, usually at the point of origin. . . ." If this management fails, the political process is either reduced to a kind of continual "cold" civil war—eventually bursting into a real one—or so weakens political society that dictatorship is produced and one group forces its solution on all others. We cannot eliminate self-interest, of course. "Who is to be for me if not myself?" But when interest groups are reasonable in their aims and moderate in their methods, their responsible political activity will also contribute much to the realization of the common good.

III. PUBLIC OPINION

Even brief inquiry into the meaning of this very familiar term demonstrates immediately how ambiguous it is. Writers as eminent as Bentham, Bryce, Lowell, and Lippmann have not been able to establish agreement on a definition of public opinion. The subject has continued to attract the attention of historians, political scientists, sociologists, and psychologists, but in their attempts to define and study it, the concept has acquired even more disparate connotations. After a group of social scientists several years ago endeavored to agree on the meaning of public opinion, some concluded that there was no such thing, others that it was an imprecise term, and still others that an effort should be made to measure it even if definition were impossible.

The problem is obviously an important one. David Hume observed two centuries ago, and few have since disagreed, that all government is founded on opinion. Today, however, trouble arises in connection with efforts to determine what such opinion is—who holds it and what it concerns—and how it is related to government and political life so that it may carry the adjective "public." The problem is especially intriguing and important in democracies, which are often said to conduct "government by public opinion," and this in a fairly immediate and direct way.

The Nature of Public Opinion. When men began to reflect upon the importance of public opinion in political life, conditions then prevailing greatly simplified their ideas about that opinion and their attempts to identify it. The important political communities of the last century possessed traditional political values far more than those of today. These were well understood, and were shared by most of those private citizens who were politically active. Public opinion was very largely the opinion of this group—actually the informed middle classes—concerning the relatively few and simple problems which arose in the day-to-day conduct of government. In other words, public opinion referred both to a fairly distinct and homogeneous group of people and to the relatively limited number of issues and of standards which they recognized—largely as a matter of tradition—as affairs of public interest, not just of private concern. Furthermore, the members of this public shared much the same media of communication, enabling them to express and inform themselves, and thereby to maintain something approximating a widely held opinion reasonably related to the actual political problems of the day. Government controlled by this public opinion was not difficult to maintain, and was generally beneficial in its consequences.

More recently, however, this traditional sort of public has broken down, and its public opinion along with it. What we now have, it would appear, is either a great variety of publics, or no public at all! Expanding democracy has tried at least to make influential citizens of all persons, at the same time that many of the traditional political values and opinions which gave coherence to earlier public opinion have either disappeared or have been drastically modified, being "undemocratic" or out of step with changing social and economic conditions. Communications media, which once effectively served the public of old, have proved incapable of serving with equal effectiveness the more extensive citizenry of today. Regardless of the apparent potentialities of contemporary media of mass communication, "the democratic public" is not as well provided with means of informing itself and, through exchange of ideas, of developing a public opinion which can be communicated to the organs of government and to political leaders as was the more limited public of several generations ago. And to make matters worse, the problems of contemporary politics are far more difficult and diverse than those confronted by that earlier public. The modern democratic community is hard pressed to function as a public, identifying its common problems and reasonable approaches to them, and thus creating a public opinion which can effectively control government. The great public of modern democracy sometimes seems to exist only in a babble of unrelated demands and protests, and the meaning of the term "public opinion" is thereby reduced to a frustrating ambiguity.

Actually, however, neither our traditions nor our communications processes, nor patterns of leadership and social organization in the private realm, have collapsed completely. Public opinion is much more difficult to identify than in the past, both as to who expresses it and as to what it concerns, and thus the relation between it and government is much more complex. For a working definition of public opinion, therefore, we consider useful that of Professor V. O. Key, Jr., who employed the term to mean "those opinions held by private persons which governments find it prudent to heed." It is not necessary that the "public" in this sense be all of the people or even a majority; and governments may or may not be concerned to act upon, ignore, or even alter that opinion. But politicians know they must reckon with "public opinion"; it sets some bounds to what they can do and to some degree they are even positively directed by it. For some time social scientists have endeavored to understand better what public opinion is in the confusing conditions of contemporary social life; they have traced the processes through which opinions appear and change, and how communications media affect them. They have surveyed the population to discover what opinions are held on various issues, and how they are related to one another. A brief indication of the results and their political implications will conclude this chapter.

The Foundations of Opinion. To discuss the elemental foundations of opinion is to raise far more questions than can be answered. Nevertheless, the possession of any particular opinion, we may observe first of all, depends upon the nature and character of its possessor; those who seek to influence opinion never write upon blank slates. We must begin with the thinking process, the study of which falls largely within the area of psychology. Briefly, we must realize the complexity of the mental process even in its simplest forms. The way one thinks is bound to be important for the conclusions reached. Individuals, as a consequence of heredity, environment, and experience, acquire predispositions of many sorts: to be liberal or conservative, optimistic or pessimistic, imaginative or inhibited, and so on. The ways in which a person may confront any particular situation can range from rigorously logical thought to completely emotional response. Some persons find thinking, other than of the simplest sort, a painful process; others indulge in it as a pleasure. Differences of opinions, at all events, are bound to result.

Also of importance are the terms with which one thinks; these are made up, of course, of words, symbols, and images. Walter Lippmann emphasized that these take the form of "stereotypes" or "pictures in our heads," and though they are the currency of our mental transactions, they may well be counterfeit in reality. That is to say, they are highly subjective, impressionistic, oversimplified, and inaccurate; they tend to give much that is false and distorted to our thinking—we are obviously not thinking very precisely if we are using in the main such tokens, for example, as "communists," "Madison Avenue," "good books," "soft jobs," "Africans," "imperialistic war," or "eggheads." The kinds of stereotypes with which we are individually equipped is determined in many ways: by family influence, religious faith, peer groups, formal education, ideological beliefs, national traditions, and the entire culture which we share.

What one thinks about also significantly conditions opinion. Generally people do not think much beyond whatever is familiar and comprehensible to them. To some this may be immediate objects, persons, and events. Others are capable of abstraction; education, of course, greatly enlarges one's view of the external world. Self-interest, whether actual or supposed, also directs mental activity. Associations are obviously important; ideas, attitudes, and emotions have a high contagion among those interacting within a group. Even the character of the group, whether it is a deliberative assembly or a mob, is important. The ancient Goths, so runs the apocryphal story, debated every matter twice —once drunk and once sober—to insure that their discussions had both vigor and discretion!

The Formulation of Opinion. We may now examine something of the techniques available purposely to influence or change the opinions of others. By generalizing broadly, we may distinguish three approaches: propaganda, appeal, and education. The term "propaganda" acquired currency with the establishment by Pope Gregory XV, in 1622, of a Congregation for Propagating the Faith, a body devoted to the foreign mission work of the Church. Economic and political propaganda developed in importance in the nineteenth century; the twentieth has seen it become a major instrument in the struggle for men's minds.

The term has long since outrun any commonly accepted definition. To describe propaganda as any attempt to influence the thinking and behavior of others, is usage so broad as to be almost meaningless; to limit it to the dissemination only of lies and untruths is unduly restrictive. The term is better used, we think, to describe attempts to manipulate opinion, largely by emotional appeal, through concealment of origin and purpose or of falsity in content. In essence, the propagandist is concerned only with achieving an effect or end; he chooses to implant opinion through emotion, prejudice, and irrationality; he fabricates, distorts, and selects only those truths which support his cause. Propaganda may be undertaken by an individual, and is resorted to by some groups; its present advanced development arose out of government use in modern warfare. It has now become a disturbingly effective weapon and an instrument of control in the hands of the totalitarian states. Conceivably, propaganda can be for good ends as well as bad, but good ends risk being tainted by the propagandist's lack of scruples and his inevitable disrespect for his chosen audience.

A second device, the appeal, may be defined as an attempt to influence opinion by a call for aid, sympathy, or support, through reference to advantage or interest, and without concealment of source or intent, or claim to whole truth. Appeals seek to direct interest, win attention, and induce self-identification with their particular purpose; they may well constitute special pleading, but they allow their audience an opportunity to consider the source. The appeal is widely used in public relations, publicity, and advertising by commercial enterprises and interest groups; electric power, oil, steel, and other large companies frequently advertise in support of "free enterprise," "private ownership," or "government economy." Political parties, public officials, and governments make extensive use of the device in its simplest form: "Vote Labour," "Post Early for Christmas," "Keep Washington Green," "Buy U.S. Savings Bonds."

A third principal means for influencing opinion is through education—the imparting of knowledge through discipline and learning. It involves the entire process of pursuing the truth wherever it leads and disseminating or receiving its results with full freedom. Of course, not all that transpires in the schools is necessarily education. At the elementary level, for instance, in the interests of patriotism, children may be subjected to some traditional propaganda about the American revolution or foreign nations; in the interest of nutrition, to appeals to drink milk; and as first steps in the learning process, to memorize "the facts" in geography and arithmetic. At the same time, the process of education is not confined to schools; governments, groups, and enterprises may seek to educate particular audiences.

The techniques described may well be intermingled in practice, but they are still distinguishable in motive. Propaganda thrives best when accompanied by censorship as reinforcement to prevent contradiction with fuller information or truth. Education flourishes least in the presence of propaganda and censorship. It will not do to say there can be no distinction between education and propaganda because the whole truth may never be known or cannot actually be presented on any one issue. The difference remains in their object; the latter aims away from objectivity, and the former toward it. The effectiveness of propaganda is thus heightened by giving it the appearance of appeal or education. Election campaigns, for example, are commonly conducted by a combination of all three methods, though the proportion of education is ordinarily much too modest.

The Media of Mass Communication. The means of communication are various and extensive: conversations; letters; school, church, and other gatherings; and public meetings. These are all important, of course, involving personal and reciprocal communication. During the present century, however, four media of mass communication have been developed—the large-circulation newspaper and magazine, radio, television, and motion pictures. The technology of their production makes possible the communication of information with unprecedented uniformity and intensity. But it is almost entirely a one-way communication; virtually the only notable response audiences can make is to cease to read, listen, or watch. Precisely what impact these media exert on the masses of people is much debated. Undoubtedly they influence public thinking, but they are also equally influenced by it—they are as much product as producer of mass opinion.

The daily press is the most ubiquitous and politically significant source of news and opinion for the average individual, though some of the popular magazines are devoted in part to news stories. Newspapers, though performing a quasi-public function, are privately owned in the democracies; their freedom from governmental control is always a hallmark of full civil rights. Because there is no theoretical limit to the number of newspapers that can be published, a free press ought apparently to offer the widest range of political expression. But for several reasons it does not. Financial considerations have steadily shrunk the number of papers and now practically limit them one to a community, except in the largest of cities. Newspapers are subjected to "censorship" by community taste and the attitudes of their publishers and—to some degree—their advertisers. Their selection of the news to be presented—its coloration, emphasis, and extent—conditions the impression it makes. Even what is "news" is measured in terms of reader interest rather more than importance. Much of the press is partisan, without necessarily being the mouthpiece of particular political groups; in the United States, for instance, the press is overwhelmingly Republican, and in Great Britain, Conservative.

There are several counterweights to these factors. Much newspaper partisanship is confined to editorial opinion; purely one-sided news accounts tend to lose readers, circulation, and advertising. In recent presidential campaigns, many papers have editorially opposed a candidate, yet have given him valuable publicity, which still may have aided his election. There are also limits to the influence of advertisers; they are primarily buyers of circulation rather than content. True enough, very little of the mass press serves at or near the level upon which public opinion might ideally be informed and educated, yet a free press cannot publish much above the demands of its average readers and survive. And Oscar Wilde's wicked observation is hardly consoling: "Newspapers have degenerated," he said. "They may now be absolutely relied upon."

After World War I, radio broadcasting became a major medium of communication. Because it has devoted itself in the main to what is generally—if not always literally—described as entertainment, it has had far less political significance than the press. Whether it is privately owned as in the United States, publicly owned as in Great Britain, or with both types in competition as in many countries, has not made much difference in its effect on political opinion. Radio is generally regulated, and thus "censored" in ways the press is not; in consequence it has tended to avoid controversy. Studies show that political subjects rarely occupy more than 1 per cent of broadcasting time, and the issuance of short news bulletins does not encourage reflection. Radio is most effective in the immediacy with which it can transmit news. Probably its greatest contribution in the political sphere is its ability to give political leaders, national as well as local, direct access to mass audiences.

No medium of communication developed with such rapidity and exciting possibilities as television. An ability to combine transmission of sight and sound gives it easily the most striking potentialities as a communication medium yet devised or imagined. Recent surveys show that television viewing now occurs, for example, in upwards of 90% of American homes, 88% Japanese, 86% British, 77% Italian, 61% West German, and 53% of the French. But television's promise so far has gone disappointingly unfulfilled, and despite the contributions of "educational television," there are no signs of large future improvement. Its programs have come to be largely sponsor-controlled, and subject to so many internal and external censorships that what remains receives the sort of inattention it deserves. Television has tended to combine many of the less admired features of noncontroversial radio broadcasting, assembly-line motion picture production, and the medicine show. In the United States, it has been primarily devoted, not to the dissemination of information and opinion, nor even to entertainment—in a meaningful sense—but to merchandising. And it is not to disparage the importance of distributing consumers' goods to believe that this is not the highest human value the medium might serve.

In Great Britain, television sponsored by the British Broadcasting Corporation competes with independent television, but the latter, following American commercial patterns and the standard of "give the public what it wants," attracts the larger portion of the viewers. Surveys indicate that no more than 2 per cent of television time in either country is devoted to public affairs and political matters. Additional time is purchased, of course, for political advertising during American election campaigns. Television has made some significant contributions in its coverage of party conventions, news conferences, political debates, legislative hearings, and "news-in-depth" programs, but these are rare enough to constitute events. Only on such an occasion as that surrounding the assassination of President Kennedy does the medium demonstrate what it is capable of achieving. It has become so easy to criticize television's failure to meet its public responsibilities, indeed, that professional television critics have little employment. Perhaps we should say no more than that the medium only reflects the malaise of our times in the level of popular culture and concern.

Motion pictures have undoubtedly exerted the least impact upon public affairs. While they might well be used to inform public opinion, relatively few films have any political significance. Produced mainly in appeal to the emotions, they have at their best constituted a new art form, portraying dramatic slices of life, and at their worst formula-bound banalties of a fictional world. Films have been subjected to extensive censorship because of their frequent preoccupation with crime, immorality, and violence. Motion pictures generally have traded in illusion and vicarious experience, rather than social and political problems. In recent years, the cinema has been patronized mainly by the young, and those seeking sociability, personal escape, or transport into worlds otherwise foreign to them. Its films, in consequence, have concentrated on the box-office demand for spectacle and entertainment. As one Hollywood cynic concluded, "If you want to send a message, call Western Union."

Our conclusions must be brief. Except for newspapers, the major communications media do not figure much in political affairs; even the press, becoming largely commercialized, has reduced its partisanship. Yet certainly all these media are too important to the public needs to be devoted almost solely to commercial exploitation, as is the situation in the United States. While they partly distract mass attention from politics, they also demonstrate popular apathy toward it. Rather than sharpening the perception of real and current problems, they often tend to "wash out" the issues. They do convey a large amount of factual information about what goes on in the world, which can help those interested to form some reasonable opinion. And, at least, democratic audiences are free to choose; they are far better off than the "captive audiences" of the dictatorships, who get only what the government and party want them to have. But where media are free, we cannot expect much raising of their taste and content levels beyond that of their consumers. The impact of this condition is mitigated by the fact that political and opinion leaders, and other elites generally, are able to achieve a considerable face-to-face communication, and have recourse as well to other specialized media, of smaller but more influential circulation, such as journals of opinion and serious books. Indeed, virtually every significant group has its own media—farm journals, trade magazines, labor union papers, consumer reviews, and such materials—which are highly influential within their orbit. Yet, as Britain's *Guardian* observed editorially, "What people read and hear and see helps to make them the people that they are, whether we think of the cultures of nations or the characters of individuals. Dictators know it. Free people may take it too lightly."

The Measurement of Opinion. Executive and legislative officials, and politicians generally, have long been concerned with gauging opinion to determine public needs and to anticipate political behavior. A number of traditional methods are all employed today; they include talks with people, comments of the press and other media, legislative debates, reports of field agents, letters and petitions, representations from interest groups, exchanges in election campaigns, and votes cast in elections. Except for the latter—which do tell which candidate the voters wanted to elect, or in the case of referendum measures, for example, whether the voters support, say, new bonded debt—none of these methods is an accurate opinion indicator and can in fact be entirely misleading. Not surprisingly, political leaders, social scientists, and even interested citizens have long been concerned to obtain more precise information about popular thinking in public affairs.

From the beginning of the century, a number of American newspapers and magazines conducted "straw votes" in an effort to forecast for their readers the outcome of elections. These operated from a chance sample of voter preference provided in unofficial ballots returned to the publisher or by interviews with the "man-in-the-street." For some years *The Literary Digest* attracted much attention to its straw votes on presidential elections; it sent return postal cards to persons on mailing, telephone-directory, and automobile-registration lists, and successfully predicted a number of times which candidate would win. In 1936 over ten million "ballots" were mailed out, and on the basis of more than two million returned, a victory of Landon over Roosevelt was indicated. Landon subsequently received the electoral votes of only two states, and the magazine did not long survive this disaster, a result of its unrepresentative sampling. Meanwhile, considerable success in market research, employing the principles of statistical analysis, proved its commercial utility in measuring various kinds of consumer demand and buyer preference. The polling organizations of Gallup, Roper, and Crossley, later joined by others in the United States and abroad, began to apply these techniques to forecasting the outcome of elections, and reporting popular views on various issues. Though with varying margins of error, they enjoyed success for a number of years. Then in 1948 the polls confidently predicted a victory for Dewey over Truman, a polling debacle which widely shook confidence in their scientific character.

Although the statistical procedures involved in opinion surveys are too complex to be discussed here, the methodology of polling—the sampling process—rests on the simple proposition that an accurate sample demonstrates the character of the whole. The public opinion polls are conducted by obtaining individual opinions from a cross section of the universe being examined; according to mathematical probability, these will reflect the views of the entire population. Census and election statistics are used to determine what constitutes a correct sample, according to age, sex, residence, economic status, education, party affiliation, and the like, of the group being surveyed. The sample may be small; ordinarily less than five thousand people are consulted in a national poll.

Of course, polling involves human activity as well as mathematical operations and in the process small defects may be magnified into large distortions. The statistical procedures are subject to errors in sampling and subjectivity in question-framing. Interviewers may bias responses or misinterpret them. Respondents may not always do as they say, and sometimes change their minds. Where polling is conducted on a pro and con basis, it tends to conceal gradations in opinion, the intensity with which opinions are held, and their stability—and thus their likelihood of being subject to change. Someone must decide, finally, upon the meaning of the data collected. In view of these circumstances—and we have not exhausted the list—scientific polling encounters a variety of difficulties in its practice. When a high percentage of those polled respond as "undecided," as in the presidential election of 1948, or when the contest is an extremely close one, as in 1960, the pollers may fail to predict the outcome, or do so with such hedging and indecision that the prediction is little more valuable than a shrewd guess.

An Evaluation of Polling. We hardly need point out that public opinion polling is not regarded with entire enthusiasm in some quarters. It has been decried by politicians, investigated by Congress, and criticized by academicians. Its exponents insist that the polls help to preserve democracy by extending means to ascertain the will of the people. They thus serve to explore areas of ignorance and misinformation that require attention. Polls are used by, and are most useful to, political parties and their leaders, it is claimed, in revealing minority as well as majority opinion. The results may also serve as a check on exaggerated claims by interest groups. It has even been argued that the polls may be a better reflection of opinion than elections themselves! There is certainly recognition of the utility of polling as one of the tools of the social scientist in his study of human beings, entirely apart from its more sensational employment at election time.

The views of critics are aimed, to be sure, at much of the journalistic use of the polls rather than that of furthering knowledge of human behavior. Leaving aside criticisms of methodological inadequacies, these critics are much concerned whether, in any real sense, public opinion is being measured at all. As Professor C. H. Cooley put the matter many years ago, "Public opinion is no mere aggregate of separate individual judgments, but an organization, a co-operative product of communication and reciprocal influence." It is not at all clear that in view of extensive popular ignorance about many public matters, the sampling of such opinion in oversimplified terms, out of context, without consideration of alternatives, and in the absence of any deliberation, is especially meaningful. To be sure, we cannot have too much information about popular thinking, but if it is to be taken as eliminating the need for the decision-making process, private as well as governmental, it is also dangerous. Opinion must be created, of course, for it does not arise spontaneously, and there is further concern that polling may discourage courageous and independent leaders from contributing to this creative function. There should be no doubt, certainly, that constant preoccupation with the dead center of opinion, emphasizing what may well be the uninformed and the mediocre, must offer a threat to an enlightened society. Finally, it might be argued that polls devoted to predicting elections may undesirably condition their actual outcome; and even if they do not, they are only predicting what will soon be known for certain anyway.

Public Opinion and Democracy. The formation of effective public opinion in the theory of democratic society requires, as Professor Bernard Berelson has cogently stated, "that the electorate possess appropriate personality structures, that it be interested and participate in public affairs, that it be informed, that it be principled, that it correctly perceive political realities, that it engage in discussion, that it judge rationally, and that it consider the community interest." It ought to be apparent, as he also points out, that this is a very high ideal, and often unlikely of attainment by the mass of the people. We have ample indication that a very great many people, confused and frustrated in their attempts at understanding or influencing the many complex issues of public policy, have simply abdicated this function. Crucial to the whole process of creating adequate opinion is its leadership, and we may ponder whether today's democratic societies receive enough of the positive direction they require from either their political leadership or the popular communications media.

We have observed that the foundations for opinion are complex and its formulation subject to much manipulation. The individual is assaulted with so many strident appeals for his attention, often for trivial purposes, that he tends to acquire immunity to all—even those deserving his consideration. Despite the technological excellence of our media of mass communication, they function more as indices to the common level of popular interest than as significant contributors to opinion. The wide extension of literacy in the past century has not produced a corresponding elevation in popular taste.

Thinking about public opinion today is thus very much in a state of flux. Whether there is anything in contemporary societies worthy of being called "public opinion," and if so what it might be; what is, and what should be, the role of the various opinions held throughout populations in the political process—these are questions not easily answered. Relatively few assume, or have assumed, that the sort of opinions collected by polls ought to be directly and immediately translated into public policies, and the inevitable "don't knows" in large numbers would in itself preclude this. This is not to say that government is better conducted in ignorance of mass opinion than with knowledge of it. But we must continue to emphasize the quality of opinion; and we may wonder whether we have properly allocated values in a society, such as that of the United States, where we spend as much on tobacco and advertising as on the public schools. The central problem of liberal democracy is the creation of popular majorities upon which the exercise of government authority must depend. We need to hear the voice of the people, but it is not always a finished expression of the general interest; it must be filtered through and weighed by a number of agencies and institutions. To the discussion of these, we shall devote the next several chapters.

CHAPTER 8

VOTERS *and* PARTIES

GOVERNMENTS, like clocks, go from the motion men give them," wrote William Penn, and men put governments in motion many different ways. In the previous chapter we considered how individuals exert informal influence and pressure upon government and its policies. We shall now adopt the traditional perspective toward popular political activity and examine the role of individuals more formally organized for participation in political affairs. Once again it must be emphasized that we are not thus revealing distinct or disparate processes; on the contrary, they are interwoven and involve the very same people.

It may be seen, too, that the previous chapter is in part preliminary as well as prior to this one. We have shown that men have numerous and conflicting interests in society, and these give rise to groups and their organization. The emergence of political groups is a normal occurrence in the democratic context and, if moderate and responsible, they can contribute much to the reconciliation and satisfaction of interests. Interest groups also help to shape and express opinion and relate the individual to society at large. All of this is equally true of political parties, which are another kind of group—too well known to require much formal introduction, but not always so well understood. About few entities, perhaps, are there so many erroneous "stereotypes." Before examining the subject of parties, we shall first consider briefly the matter of the electorate.

I. *The* ELECTORATE

In the conduct of elections, universal suffrage is today so commonplace, at least among states making any pretense at democracy, that it is hard to believe how recently it has been realized. Yet democratic practice has always run—and still does—somewhat behind its professed ideals. To be sure, in many a newly created nation-state today, the vote has been given overnight to an entire electorate which had never cast a ballot before. This is not the way, of course, in which the suffrage developed in the older democratic states; there the opportunity to vote, originally possessed by the few, was only gradually extended. Poor and nonpropertied men fought for it in many countries of the western world. Thus, there has been struggle, but even so, a bestowal of the right has been as common as the conquest of it.

The Development of the Suffrage. Even after the adoption of the Constitution of 1789, perhaps one man in fifteen in the United States qualified to vote; that white manhood suffrage was established by the middle of the nineteenth century was one of the unique achievements of this country, demonstrating the practicability of popular government for the first time. Notwithstanding the Civil War and the Fifteenth Amendment, Negroes were effectively disfranchised in the southern states during the following decades as one of several forms of discrimination against them. In Great Britain, after the Great Reform Act of 1832, only one man in twenty-five voted, and, by the beginning of this century, one-third of the adult males were still ineligible. The revolution proclaimed the ideal of manhood suffrage for France in 1789, but only restricted electorates were allowed there until the establishment of the Second Republic in 1848. Even so, these privileges were extended only to the metropolitan territories; the position of the British and French imperial territories was another thing. In most of the states of western Europe, manhood suffrage was not established until near or after the turn of the present century. Woman suffrage was granted in only a few American states before 1900, and not achieved nationally until 1920. Britain extended the vote with some qualifications to women over the age of thirty in 1918—though ten years later they won equality with men. France did not enfranchise women until 1945, Italy until 1946, and Greece until 1952.

Theories of the Suffrage. From our earlier discussion of liberal democracy it may be recalled that there is no practicable way in which the people can "govern"; rather, it is through the conduct of free elections that they can choose governments that are popularly representative. In effect, the people are drawn upon to constitute an electorate, which becomes something like an organ of government itself. Who is entitled to participate in the electorate? To answer that question, there are two general theories: the vote is either a right or a privilege.

In ancient Greece and Rome, and among the Germanic tribes, the vote was considered to be an attribute of membership in the community. Though citizenship then had greater exclusiveness than it does today, the suffrage was considered the inherent right of the citizen. Later, in the middle ages, when systems of representation began to develop, the vote was seen as the privilege of status and ordinarily attached to the ownership of land—an idea persisting until quite recently.

The democratic movement revived a form of the older theory, and as an accompaniment to the ideas of the social contract and popular sovereignty, the vote was now claimed to be a natural right. First advanced by the Levellers in seventeenth-century England, this view was entertained by some leaders of the American revolution, for instance, Paine and Jefferson, and by Rousseau and Condorcet in France. Yet throughout the nineteenth century, a substantial body of opinion continued to oppose placing any governmental power in the hands of the "poor and ignorant masses"; the suffrage was a privilege appropriate only for those with education and property, who alone could properly speak for the whole community. Nor were these ideas immediately and everywhere abandoned in the present century. And, reversing the concept of who should be privileged, prior to 1936 the Soviet Union confined the electoral privilege to workers, peasants, and soldiers; other persons, for example, those who employed labor, and private businessmen, clergymen, and members of the former Czarist police were all excluded.

Probably no single conclusion embraces the various democratic views today. The wide extent of modern suffrage has been mainly the result of political expediency: the hope of political parties and their leaders to secure greater support from a larger electorate. Some view the suffrage as an office or function conferred by the state upon all persons capable of exercising it. To others it is a political right, if not a natural one, and like other such rights to be withheld only for most exceptional reasons. It is now generally recognized, however, that the vote must be widely extended on an equal and universal basis as the only practical means of ascertaining the wishes of the majority and of insuring that government will respond to the will of those being governed. Universal suffrage, then, is essential to the effectiveness of representative government and to the self-respect of the democratic citizen; if restricted on some differential basis, the result is to create a group of citizens denied the means of full political expression. Universal suffrage promotes not only an atmosphere of equality but, exercised through free elections, one of liberty as well. Important also, it promotes legitimacy in government—a sense of responsibility and obligation among both rulers and citizens—by providing the essential ingredient of consent.

Defining the Electorate. The widespread establishment of universal suffrage has worked to standardize the qualifications for voting among contemporary democracies, though individual national variations remain. As might be expected in this nationalistic world, citizenship is everywhere required, as evidencing a minimum degree of attachment by the voter to the political community. In the nineteenth century, some American states allowed aliens to vote on the ground that it was desirable to draw the then large immigrant population into the political community without delay; but this practice generally ended with World War I. Because Great Britain recognizes citizens of the Commonwealth states as "British subjects," those who reside in Britain are allowed to vote there if otherwise qualified; this seems to be a uniquely British practice, however. All states set minimum age requirements as well; these vary from eighteen to twenty-five, with the common-law standard, full legal age at twenty-one years, the most common. A residence requirement is also normally imposed; this is especially important in the United States, where one must be a citizen of some state or of the District of Columbia to vote. In many countries, required residence is not more than the lapse of time necessary to be entered in the periodically revised electoral register, which establishes what persons are legally qualified to vote in each locality. In an increasingly mobile population, however, residence requirements of even a few months will permanently disfranchise many migratory workers, and for occasional elections, those who move from time to time, with some distortion to the representativeness of elected officials.

Sex is rarely a basis for qualification today, though Switzerland, Paraguay, Libya, and a few other states exclude women from the electorate. In the development of woman suffrage, we have striking testimony to the speed with which social attitudes have changed during the present century. No more than fifty years ago, most men—and most women, apparently—were opposed to women voting. The arguments of opponents of female suffrage appear today as museum pieces of Victorian—and sometimes medieval—attitudes. Woman, they said, was simply not a political animal! To give woman the vote would unsex her and distract her from her proper functions of keeping the home and bearing children. The votes of women at best would only duplicate those of men and increase election costs needlessly; at worst, they would be dictated by their husbands, controlled by their church, or cast in ignorance. As a clinching argument, it was often asserted that women ought not to vote because they did not perform military service, and at all events should not risk threats to their virtue that might attend appearance at political meetings or polling places. It is surely unnecessary, as was still the case only a few decades ago, to answer such arguments and undertake a defense of woman suffrage. Indeed, in the face of such masculine casuistry as we have outlined, it is small wonder that women leading the suffragist movement occasionally felt provoked to violence.

Disqualifications in Voting. All states disqualify certain persons from voting—most commonly, those convicted of serious crimes and the mentally incompetent. Many disqualify illiterates and, if literacy tests are fairly administered, do so reasonably as long as all persons may have had access to free elementary education. Although some new states in Africa and Asia face difficulties in this regard, in the long run literacy is certainly an essential to modern democratic citizenship. Few countries still continue to disqualify persons who own no property or pay no property taxes. It would be a rare person today who does not pay taxes in some form or another or who, because he owns no significant amount of property, goes unaffected by government and public policy. In a few states of the American South, literacy and poll tax requirements are employed to discourage or obstruct Negro voting—practices which, whatever the historical origins of racial discrimination there, are not defensible today. Though the United States once led the way in extension of the suffrage to humble people, it has on this count fallen behind other democratic countries and suffers in conscience at home and in esteem abroad as a result. That an increasing proportion of Negro citizens votes in the southern states demonstrates gradual improvement in this situation, though it is one not yet fully solved.

II. POLITICAL PARTIES

Political parties are essentially modern contrivances, and like many recent phenomena, our knowledge and understanding of them are limited. Most parties operating today are less than a hundred years old, many are creations of the last few decades, and all tend to alter in character with time. They are also difficult to compare. Each party system has its own national setting and differing governmental form, history, and tradition, which uniquely shape its features. The term "political party" is also used to describe political organizations with substantially disparate forms and purposes. Not surprisingly, the French scholar Maurice Duverger, who produced one of the major comparative studies of parties, believes it may be another fifty years before we can describe their real workings. In order to conclude what parties are, we had best first examine how they developed.

An Outline of Party Development. The modern political party has its origins in seventeenth-century England and the quarrels of Royalists and Parliamentarians. With the establishment of parliamentary supremacy after 1689, members of Parliament divided into Tories and Whigs, in disagreement less on fundamentals than in degree over matters of royal prerogative, support of the established church, and economic policies. For the next century and a half these groups, joined by traditional and personal loyalties to certain leaders, were more nearly political factions than parties in the modern sense. The extension of the suffrage after 1832 required members of Parliament to broaden their appeal to larger electorates and get out the vote. To win a body of supporters, therefore, and ensure that they were registered, candidates organized local political associations. Thus in the course of the nineteenth century, the name "Whig" gave way to "Liberal" and "Tory" to "Conservative," and both parties became instruments for joining mass support to political leaders in Parliament. At the turn of the century, the Labour party appeared on the scene, and by 1922 had replaced the Liberals as the second major party.

Within American colonial government, Whigs also opposed Tories.

The American founding fathers, after separation from Great Britain, hoped to avoid faction and party; they are not mentioned in the Constitution, many of whose features aimed at preventing their rise. Yet the contest over constitutional ratification divided Anti-Federalist and Federalist. With some realignments, a continuing basis of division produced ultimately the Democratic party in Jackson's time and the Republican party in Lincoln's. Like their English counterparts, they were obliged, as the nineteenth century proceeded, to seek mass support; given the many different levels of American elections, they acquired an even more elaborate organization.

On the European continent, the slower development of representative government and the restriction of the suffrage largely limited political association to parliamentary factions. In 1848, however, popular discontent exploded into widespread European revolutions. Liberal constitutions, extended suffrage, and more popular parties were the result. In many countries, labor unions, workingmen's clubs, and student societies began the formation of socialist organizations. These emerged as socialist parties once working-class suffrage was granted, and though utopian ambitions for remodeling society were in some cases abandoned reluctantly, most such parties sought their goals by parliamentary means. Where parties and political activity were repressed, however, underground revolutionary conspiracies often formed. These were widespread in central and eastern Europe. In Russia, for example, no political parties were legalized until 1905; yet the Bolshevik faction of the Social Democratic movement had already committed itself to revolution.

World War I toppled the old citadels of privilege and repression in the eastern half of Europe, but its chaotic aftermath furnished no solid ground upon which to establish normal systems of parliamentary government and parties. The Bolsheviks in Russia rode to power on waves of popular discontent and political confusion; they monopolized rule for the Communist party and eliminated all others. In Italy, Germany, and other countries reacting to communism, the democratic parties quarreled bitterly among themselves, and in their division were swept away by the fascist movements. These, like the communist parties today, originally combined parliamentary with revolutionary means in their quest for power; but once they gained power the fascists also abolished party competition, free elections, and parliamentary government.

Other states attempted a still different path. Lacking the political experience to develop a workable system of competing parties on the one hand, but seeking to avoid totalitarian dictatorship on the other, various countries in Europe, Asia, and Latin America sought political order and national integration by means of "single national" parties. These commonly arose as nationalist movements which, after a period of revolution, provided politically inexperienced people with a sustained and unified government leadership. Thus another kind of party was created. With the retreat of colonialism after World War II, many such dominant parties, which began as independence movements, have taken over political life in the new states. It appears that these will be an important fixture on the political stage for decades to come.

The Nature of Party. The preceding sketch of party development should at least serve to demonstrate how diversified is the term "political party." It has been applied equally to eighteenth-century factions, caucuses, and political clubs; to informally organized groups of parliamentary leaders and supporters; to formally organized popular movements and their leaders; to confederations of militant labor unionists and socialists; to revolutionary conspiratorial movements; to political elites in totalitarian states; and, to nationalistic movements integrating government and popular masses into political community.

What all these disparate entities have in common, of course, is that they are groups trying to gain or hold political power. There is nothing necessarily wrong in applying the term "party" to all of them. We may also apply to term "cat" to kittens, cougars, and saber-toothed tigers; yet we might not be prepared with the same equanimity to meet each of these on a dark night. And, the term "party," used with no more discrimination, is equally not very useful. Perhaps we can restore our perspective, then, by restricting our connotation. Political party was originally associated with representative government and developed in its conventional sense along with the idea of democracy. It described a voluntary association, concerned with government office and public policy, and providing means to organize majorities necessary to free government. As party stood for only a "part"—one side in a political contest—it necessarily recognized the existence of other parties.

Thus, the term's longest usage was limited to describe a fairly specific pattern of political behavior—a group of people organized to gain office for their leaders and to exercise political power in competition with other similar groups. This seems to us the most useful definition of the term. Unfortunately, it has not been left undisturbed. Like many another word in the vocabulary of representative government—election, plebiscite, legislature—it has been borrowed for use in nondemocratic and antidemocratic contexts. We can only offer the *caveat,* therefore, that when it is employed with the qualifying adjectives "revolutionary," "single national," or "totalitarian" it is describing political bodies with quite different purposes and methods from those of conventional democratic parties. In the discussion which follows we shall use the term in its "normal" sense except when the context indicates otherwise.

The Bases of Party. Much literature has been devoted to accounting for the bases of party division. And how simple the matter would be could we but accept assurance from Gilbert and Sullivan's *Iolanthe:*

> How nature always does contrive
> That every boy and every gal,
> That's born into the world alive,
> Is either a little Liberal,
> Or else a little Conservative!

Yet these lines undoubtedly do touch upon a psychological aspect of the matter. People are divided by temperament and inclination, and any significant degree of commitment to party involves a measure of emotional response. As we noted earlier, charismatic leadership is always a reflection of it. Studies have also shown that party preference commonly accords with family tradition and social status; relatively early in life one acquires unconsciously stereotyped ideas about parties which thereafter condition the "image" that they project. Habit and custom, and the individual desire to appear generally consistent, all reinforce a continuance of party ties.

Yet socioeconomic factors, interrelated with the psychological, are probably of equal importance. We refer to our earlier discussion of interests: men have—or think they have, and it makes little difference—certain values and ends which they seek to promote and protect. These may be class, economic, vocational, religious, sectional, ethnic, or still other. We have seen that support of these gives rise to interest groups of many kinds for the influencing of public policy. But the supreme method to this end is manifestly through outright control of government; by organization on bases broader than those of interest groups this becomes possible, and party provides the principal vehicle for that purpose. People commit themselves to party, then, because they see it as a direct means for promoting self-interest, or the general interest as it appears to them, however variable or irrational their conception of these may be. Party may subsume some special interests but it overrides certain others. Aside from the additional objective of putting candidates in office, it is generally obliged by its greater size to promote a larger common denominator of interests, leaving to interest groups the task of filling in the interstices that remain.

These factors are roughly reflected in the kinds of parties which may be encountered, and account generally for three main types which are to be found in a competitive and democratic context. First of all there are the *pragmatic* parties; these may well promote interests, but they are largely unconcerned with doctrine and ideology. Their policies and programs alter considerably with changing times and circumstances; they tend to emphasize the personalities of their leaders rather than distinct principles. The American Democratic and Republican parties, the British and Canadian Conservative parties, and the Australian Liberal party—indeed, most contemporary liberal parties—are all bodies with these characteristics.

There are, second, the *doctrinal* parties; these are value-oriented, pursuing some particular principles or viewpoint. Parties based upon socialist ideologies, such as the Netherlands' Labor party and the Norwegian and Belgian Socialist parties, are common. Religious doctrine accounts to a large extent for the Austrian Christian Democratic party, the French Popular Republican Movement, and Israel's *Mizrachi* (Spiritual Center) party. Other examples of doctrinal parties are India's *Swatantra* (Freedom) party and South Africa's Nationalist party.

Third, there are *interest* parties; these are most commonly encountered in multiparty systems, though they also appear as minor parties in biparty systems, and reflect the determination of a large interest group to undertake formal political action. Interests may be ideal or material, or a mixture. The American Prohibition party is an example. Agricultural and rural interests have produced the Australian Country party, the Canadian Social Credit party, and the Swiss Farmers' party. Ethnic or sectional interests, often interrelated, are reflected in the organization of the Irish Nationalist party in the United Kingdom, the *Volkspartei* in Italy's Tyrol, and the Swedish People's party in Finland.

The Biparty System. The three major types of party systems found within popular government—biparty, multiparty, and one-party—

produce quite different results. They not only point to significant differences in the way political power is organized in various societies, but provide one important basis for the classification of contemporary political regimes. In a biparty system, two major parties vie in the political contest, attracting between them the overwhelming measure of electoral support. One or more minor parties may exist along with a biparty system, but they receive only marginal support. The two major parties alternate at intervals in the roles of government party and opposition.

Dualism in party division has often been considered—by American and British writers at least—to constitute the natural and normal form of political cleavage, with other arrangements as deviations from it. Yet the two-party system is anything but common beyond the United States and Great Britain. It appears now to have been established in the German Federal Republic if the pattern of recent elections is sustained, as well as in Austria, but these can be only tentative conclusions. It may also be seen in the *Colorado* and *Blanco* division of Uruguay, and the Liberal and Nationalist division in the Philippines. Two parties, Labour and National, have also alternated in control of New Zealand's government.

The classic biparty structure is the British. Here, according to the customary view, a party of stability and order opposes one of movement and reform. Both Conservative and Labour parties are unified in their organization, closely controlled from their centers, and disciplined at the parliamentary party level. Both are truly national parties, and have come close to excluding minor parties and independent candidates from Parliament. In recent years, however, the tightness of the political contest has closed much of the difference between them, so that despite their traditions, their fundamental disagreements are modest, and both have become essentially pragmatic.

In the United States, the Democratic and Republican parties are also pragmatic rather than doctrinal; they are parties of broad program rather than sharp principle. They are not national parties in the British sense, and have considerably less national organization and centralized control; rather, they are loose associations of state parties which cooperate, more or less, every four years in presidential elections. Elections are conducted entirely by the states, and the electoral system produces results on occasion where one party controls the presidency while the other controls Congress. There is, indeed, some truth in the observation that these two political labels but barely conceal what is really an American multiparty system. Certainly, Republican parties are rather different things in the Carolinas, Colorado, Connecticut, and California, just as are the Democratic parties in Massachusetts, Missouri, Minnesota, and Mississippi.

We pointed to development toward a biparty system in West Germany. This has been unexpected, of course, because under the imperial regime and the Weimar republic, Germany had a multiparty structure, reflecting class, religious, and ideological distinctions, until it was suppressed by the Nazi dictatorship in 1933. In the first postwar *Bundestag* election of 1949, some ten parties sought representation, following the earlier German pattern. But in the fourth election of 1961, the Christian Democratic Union acquired 45.4 per cent of the votes and 241 seats, the Social Democratic party 36.2 per cent of the votes and 190 seats, leaving only 66 seats won by the Free Democratic party. It seems likely the two major parties will continue to monopolize the political contest.

The biparty system has several consequences. It requires both parties to propose a national program and undertake organization on a national scale. It encourages pragmatic rather than doctrinal parties; since winning the election allows control of the government, both emphasize ability to govern. The system discourages extremism as both parties move toward the middle to attract a majority of the electorate. It has the final effect of offering the voter a clear-cut choice between alternative governments, if not always distinctly differing programs.

The Multiparty System. Where there are three or more major political parties in the electoral contest—and more than three is quite likely where pluralist division occurs—a multiparty system exists. There is no alternation in control of government; one party may be dominant and so situated that it participates in most coalitions organized in the parliamentary body. Or, electoral support is so dispersed that fragmented groups move in and out of ever-changing coalitions, as various parties form different combinations from one issue to another.

It is not possible to say precisely what produces a multiparty system, or to conclude that it constitutes some kind of deviation. The theory that a multiparty pattern is produced by the election system is, we think, unsupported by the evidence—a matter to be discussed further in the chapter dealing with the legislature. It seems to arise in states with deeply ingrained and complex conflicts in interests and ideas, whose differentiation is too great to be resolved into only two opposing sides. Yet even multiparty systems not infrequently display one major fault line; in France, for instance, with half a dozen party groups normally in competition, the major cleavage between Right and Left is the most substantial and long-standing.

The cleavages in multiparty systems vary with national circumstances. Australia displays a three-way Labour-Liberal-Country party division. In Canada, a basic twofold division between Liberals and Conservatives has been breaking down in recent years with the emergence of the New Democratic party—socialist and laborite—and the Social Credit party—rightist and nationalistic—with strength in British Columbia, Alberta, and Quebec. The Scandinavian countries have developed quite stable four-party systems composed of Socialists, Liberals, Conservatives, and Agrarians, with some minor, including Communist, parties. Israel demonstrates the extreme division of two dozen parties; here *Mapai* (Labor party), a dominant "national" party historically, leads every government coalition and is supported by a third of the voters. The wide incidence of multiparty systems is demonstrated by their presence, in addition to those countries already mentioned, in Argentina, Belgium, Brazil, Finland, Ireland, the Netherlands, and Switzerland, among others.

The dispersal of partisan support and organization has several consequences. Some groups may organize only in certain sections of the country; some parties may not offer national programs. Where governments are formed by coalition of several parties, they are weakened by the fact that the withdrawal of any member of the coalition may destroy it from within. It is certainly more difficult to assess party responsibility in these circumstances. Where one party is substantially stronger than the others, and controls or dominates the coalition over a long period, the excluded parties may be inclined to irresponsibility and extremism. Indeed, some parties, especially the totalitarian communists, may choose to occupy a position of permanent opposition. Finally, while the multitude of partisan views which arise from a multiparty system will certainly not oversimplify public opinion on political questions, they may well overcomplicate it.

The One-Party System. The one-party system is often equated with totalitarian government, but to do so misrepresents the political arrangements of a number of states. We have already pointed out that the communist and fascist states have totalitarian political regimes, but the single totalitarian "party" is a very different sort of thing from what we are now talking about, and we shall say something of it later. However, there are states which are not totalitarian, nor necessarily on the road to becoming so, where we may observe the phenomenon of the "dominant" or "single-national" party, which largely monopolizes political activity and government control. These states are emerging from absolutism, dictatorship, or colonial rule, and their leaders are aiming at least at something like what we earlier described as populistic democracy. Where such "national" parties are directed to democratic purposes, they deserve consideration within the context of democratic party systems.

The political leaders of these states face prodigious tasks. They are seeking simultaneously to create a new state, a new nation, and a new society among a people generally divided, poor, and illiterate. They must quickly improvise elaborate domestic and foreign policies. The operation of a delicately balanced biparty system is clearly beyond the immediate ability of such people; the operation of a multiparty system portends disintegration and chaos. Inevitably, the nationalist movement, which was organized to overthrow absolutist or colonial rule, and which is enthusiastically hailed for the achievement of liberation, offers the only auspices under which the masses may be united and governed with some measure of popular consent.

Most regimes of this sort are quite contemporary, but there are some older examples. Dr. Sun Yat-sen devoted great effort to establish a united and democratic China under the tutelage of the *Kuomintang* or Nationalist party. But the quarrels of the "war lords" and Japanese invasion led his successor, General Chiang Kai-shek, to adopt increasingly dictatorial methods; and, after further civil warfare, mainland China finally succumbed in 1950 to communist military conquest. Turkey took a different direction; on the ruins of the old empire, Kemal Atatürk sought to reconstruct and westernize his state through his Republican People's party. His successor, General Ismet Inönü, continued the program and ordered the organization of an opposition Democratic party in 1945, which five years later was elected to office. Nevertheless, the increasingly repressive character of the resulting Menderes government raised widespread resistance. In 1960, the Turkish army deposed the government, but under a new Constitution, popular elections were held in 1961 and four political parties emerged.

Despite the long traditions in Mexico of revolution and violence, a one-party system has succeeded in recent years in establishing political stability and moderation. Politics are monopolized by the *Partido Revolucionario Institucional* which, claiming inheritance of the 1910 revolution, has supplied Mexico with its presidents and congressional majorities from Plutarco Calles in 1924 to Díaz Ordaz in 1964. Opposition candidates and opposition party labels appear in elections, and though force and fraud are not unknown, the PRI has won the overwhelming support of the people.

Among the contemporary single-party systems of importance is India's. The Indian National Congress, created in 1885, operated originally as an interest group. Under Gandhi's leadership, it began agitation for national liberation, which won Hindu mass support and resulted in Indian independence in 1947. Overnight the Congress became a political party, continuing to supply the government and political leadership of the country. Under Nehru and his successors it has won three-fourths of the seats in parliament, beginning with the first election in 1952. The remainder are divided among numerous small political groups which have broken off from the dominant Congress party; in the long run a formal opposition and alternative governments could be developed in this fashion. Similar one-party systems, though without as yet any comparable stability, may also be observed in Algeria, Guinea, Thailand, and Indonesia. Such systems will probably be common among the newer Asian and African states.

The one-party system, given its particular national circumstances, is largely born of necessity. Even the most charismatic political leader must have some organization through which to conduct and co-ordinate his regime. It does offer means to infuse some popular quality into government, and to begin political training of the politically inexperienced masses. If stable and moderate government can be maintained, if leaders are steadfast in their loyalty to democratic ideals, and if the people can acquire some degree of political sophistication, a political opposition and alternative government may in time emerge. The danger of the single-national party is that its democratic forms can conceal authoritarian government. The absence of an opposition confronts the dominant leaders with neither rivals nor checks; all too easily they suffer the delusions of indispensability and omniscience and drift into unqualified dictatorship.

III. PARTY ORGANIZATION *and* FUNCTION

We have shown that both parties and party systems vary substantially among different countries. Our discussion in short compass of several remaining aspects of party must therefore be quite generalized to avoid what could become an almost endless task, the narrow description of individual parties.

Followers and Leaders. Membership is of obvious significance to the party: from it come voters, workers, contributors, lieutenants, and leaders. The dismal imbalance of "too few Indians and too many Chiefs" is fatal for party success. Each party has its own concept of membership, but two general patterns prevail, informal or formal. Among the pragmatic and conventional parties, membership is largely informal; they may encourage official membership and payment of dues, but do not require it. Thus the members of the party are those who decide they are and vote for it. In many American states, one must register as a party member to participate in its primary elections, but no further commitment is involved.

The highly doctrinal parties, however, and some of the "interest" type, especially labor, socialist, and communist, commonly establish formal admission to membership, attested by enrollment on the membership lists, acknowledgment of party doctrine and rules, and payment of regular dues. These differences reflect real distinctions between the parties themselves. The conservative or pragmatic parties appeal with program rather than doctrine, their financial support comes mainly from a limited number of donations, and they aspire to votes from the independent and the unorganized. The doctrinal parties attempt to furnish ideological training to their members, are more dependent on financial support from the rank-and-file, and aim at success through the disciplined solidarity of a specific membership. Whatever the conception of membership, there are also differences in the extent or intensity of participation within a party. Most persons are no more than sympathizers, fellow travelers, or adherents of a party, more or less consistently voting for its candidates. Others may be supporters or members, declaring their allegiance to it and encouraging others to a similar commitment. A still smaller number will be "militants," actively engaged in party work, publicity, canvassing, and meetings.

Political parties are agencies for the recruitment of leaders, of course, as well as followers. The leaders of successful parties hold office and exercise governmental power—the essential purposes for which parties operate—so that the means by which they establish their superior position within the party is of interest and importance. Various formal procedures are employed, but broadly speaking there are three possibilities. Party leaders may be appointed: the chairman of the Democratic and Republican national committees are named, practically speaking, by the presidential candidate; the leader of the British Conservative party designates its national chairman. Leaders are also commonly chosen by co-option within a party caucus; this is the case in both the British Parliament and the American Congress. Thirdly, leaders may be elected by delegate convention or popularly, though the latter method is practicable only at the precinct, branch, or local association level. Party conventions, for example, elect the leaders of the Canadian Conservative and Liberal parties and the national executive of the British Labour party. The more democratically inclined a party is, the more emphasis it ordinarily places on democratic selection of leaders. Yet such methods are not always as democratic in fact as they may appear in form. The very nature of party introduces a measure of autocratic or oligarchic control, and the higher the level the more likely is co-option of leaders by an inner circle to be found.

Great attention is always focused on those at the top. What circumstances or qualities bring men to the ultimate positions of authority? The historical "great man" theory sees certain men displaying "heroic" attributes and exercising special influence; others view the "great man" as only the expression of his times and challenges, and the tool of forces beyond his control. A psychological perspective suggests that leadership is a form of compensation; men seek power and position to make up for deprivations of affection, wealth, or status. A sociological approach has marked leadership as a function of the group, arising out of individual instincts toward dominance and submission. The conventional political view has emphasized leadership in terms of personal ability; thus, effective leaders have initiative and courage, self-confidence and persistence, facility in association and expression, and so on. We offer no final answers here to a problem we can only lightly touch upon. Perhaps Shakespeare's observation must do: "Some are born great, some achieve greatness, and some have greatness thrust upon them."

Party Organization. As may be expected, there is great variance in the structure of parties, not only from state to state but among those in any one country. Party organization is shaped in part by the form of government and the levels at which elections are held, but also by the kind of membership and degree of centralization which a party seeks. Organization begins locally, as at the precinct, ward, or municipality in the United States, the local association in Great Britain, or the commune in France, with party caucuses, committees, or branches. These will be gathered into constituency organizations within whatever area officials are elected to office; this may be at the county or provincial and national legislative district level. Party organs at this stage have quite important functions: to nominate candidates, see to the registration of their adherents, collect funds, and conduct campaigns for the election of their candidates. In federal governments, at least one more stage of party organization exists for the state, province, or canton, and in countries such as the United States and Canada these may well constitute the significant centers of party power.

At the national level, generalizing broadly again, the party normally has several other organs of importance. Most convene an annual or biennial congress or delegate convention representing the lesser units (though this is quadrennial in the United States) for the purpose of choosing national officers, discussing and adopting resolutions and programs, and proclaiming election manifestoes or platforms. Less formally, these convenings are intended to attract popular attention and publicity, to inform and invigorate the party workers, and to permit the leaders and workers to meet and "talk shop." The party congress may choose a national committee to act when it is not in session, and provide funds and staff for a national headquarters, central office, or secretariat. The amount of power actually exercised by such an agency depends on the party, of course, and its degree of centralization; commonly, it collects and distributes party funds, conducts studies and publishes literature, assists candidates in their election campaigns, and in some cases, gives official approval to party candidacies.

Another party organization of significance at the national level is the parliamentary party organization, which is the caucus of party members in the national legislature. This body, though it may not appear so in form, is likely to be the most powerful and important of the national organs. Its members have legislative seats and votes; it contains much of the national party leadership; it determines what the party will actually do in support of or opposition to various public policies; and, in the parliamentary form of government, its members may become ministers of the government. Then, too, parliamentary party members have not merely some mandate from the party; they are the elected representatives of their constituencies. For this reason, there is always something of a hiatus between the national party congresses and party executives on the one hand, and the parliamentary party organization on the other. Though the former may be given status as the highest party authority, real power is exercised by the parliamentary body.

Party Functions. It should be evident by now from the attention we have given to what parties are and how they organize that they perform functions vital to the governmental process. As Professor C. W. Cassinelli has written, "A representative government depends to an unusual extent upon the confidence of its citizenry, and by their very existence the parties contribute to this confidence." The selection and support of candidates for office, as we have seen, is the unique and exclusive function of party and all of its activities follow. It is certainly not difficult to imagine how chaotic would be the process of conducting representative government if millions of voters arrived at the polls with no candidates nominated among which they might choose. The party has the parallel task of formulating programs and policies. In general, the acceptance of an agreed program is what all the candidates of one party have in common and offers the basis upon which they seek the voters' support. In this way, the party offers its interpretation of what a majority of the voters want.

The two general functions just enumerated point next to the party's immediate aims: it undertakes, if successful, to operate the government and effect its policies, or in a multiparty system at least to join with other parties to this end. Alternatively, a party which is unsuccessful criticizes the party in control by opposing its programs and proposing alternatives, thus keeping public acts and policies subject to scrutiny. In this manner, elected government officials can be held to some account, for parties can be obliged to accept political responsibility for what they do; success and satisfaction result in return to office, failure and dissatisfaction in denial of it. It may be seen, then, that party provides the bond of loyalty and discipline which leads government officials to co-operate within and between organs of government, or means by which differences between them may be given orderly mediation and adjustment. This is important both for the executive and the legislative institutions.

For the electorate, the party also performs additional important functions. It informs the voter of the issues in public policy and their alternatives. Election campaigns, especially, induce the voter to weigh the issues and cast his ballot. In some states, such as India and Turkey, parties may undertake an even greater tutelary role: to reshape the country along modern and western lines. In still others, parties may seek to hold their adherents by performing services not really political at all; in Israel, parties operate insurance companies, housing developments, and welfare institutions. Finally, the party raises a standard to which majorities are invited to rally, and calls for the uniting of individuals who are otherwise divided to make common cause. In this way parties may make an important contribution, if not too narrow in their appeal, to the transcendence of sectional interests, and thus promote national unification.

An Appraisal of Parties. Political parties are made up of people and —from their nature as mass organizations—mostly of ordinary people. Not surprisingly, they often display certain human fallibilities. They are also voluntary associations, and obtain both their followers and leaders largely through appeal to self-interest. Parties belong, then, not to the kingdom of heaven; they are of this world. They are rather easily denigrated, of course; such criticism is aimed, in the main, at defects in their efficiency, responsibility, and attachment to the national interest. True enough, they are often short of ideal in these respects, but let us consider why and to what extent.

First of all, their efficiency is criticized on the grounds that they do not perform their chosen functions with full effectiveness. They do not always choose the best candidates, it is said, nor clearly define and differentiate the really important issues; they subject the voter to propaganda rather than education, and appeal to his prejudices and fears. Parties are mercenary organizations, it is also objected, collecting and distributing large sums of money in secretive and suspicious ways. As a rejoinder, it may be said first that these criticisms are as much—perhaps more—a reflection upon the electorate as upon the parties. Parties nominate for office men they believe can be elected, who are willing to do the hard work of campaigning for and serving in political office, and who have demonstrated their allegiance to the party and its program. These may not always be the "best," but it is difficult to see how they could otherwise be selected. It is further the case that parties choose the issues which they believe are of popular concern, and conduct their campaigns at that level to which ordinary voters will respond. Indeed, the very art of political polemics, as *The Economist* points out, "is first to over-simplify the issues, for true clarity's sake, and then to exaggerate them, for the sake of effect." Voters certainly can raise the level of political discussion by choosing to ignore irrelevant issues and refusing support to those who engage in emotionalism, personal malice, and appeals to bigotry. The mere mention of money in politics causes apprehension, implying that place and favor are being bought and sold. But it is obvious that political campaigns are exceedingly expensive affairs. Even so, in the United States, more money is spent in selling soap than on presidential election campaigns.

In the matter of party responsibility, much criticism arises out of a misapprehension as to what parties ought and can do. There are those who imagine an ideal party as something of a political army, under discipline, centralized in control, whose leaders and members obey all commands unquestioningly, and who subscribe to a precise and comprehensive program ideologically distinguished from that of all other parties. Yet it is not at all clear how such organizations could be at the same time democratic instrumentalities, responsible to the public, adapted to the configurations of local and sectional government, sensitive to changing circumstances and varying group needs, and amenable to compromise and adjustment with opposing parties. Most advocates of "responsibility" seem to have in mind that parties should have entirely distinguishable programs, and in office should perform according to a definite electoral mandate, doing exactly and only what they said they would. Some see as ideal the British parliamentary party organization, whose leaders, within the particular machinery there operating, are generally able to discipline their backbenchers in voting. But even those parties are not so "responsible" as they may appear on superficial examination, and exact their discipline at a price in other disadvantages—a matter we shall discuss in the chapter on the legislature. Democratic government is not government by plebiscite. Parties cannot itemize complex issues of public policy in the electoral programs; nor can voters decide them—their function is to choose between groups of men who will conduct government, and to assess the over-all results.

With respect to the attachment of parties to the national interest, people tend instinctively to fear that the "part" may dominate the "whole." Somehow, the ideal persists that what is wanted is not "government by party," but "government in the national interest," behind which all good men could unite. Yet it is an illusion to believe, with Macaulay, in some golden age when "none was for a party; then all were for the state." Parties exist because of differences of opinion over what programs and policies will best serve the national interest; parties arise because men inevitably disagree about them. Parties are not, after all, by nature selfish and sinful, though men may of course introduce any human weaknesses into the conduct of politics. The contest for power is inseparable from politics, and party interest is an interpretation of national interest. Professor William Goodman has thoughtfully pointed out that "parties do not create the power struggle nor do they either intensify it or make it more immoral. They simply mark out certain confines in the political sphere and direct the power struggle into distinctive channels." It is entirely proper to be critical of politicians and political parties as they may individually perform, but one cannot rightly be cynical about the need for them. Parties are the only effective means yet devised to permit popular participation in the decision-making process of government. Parties are truly the connecting link between government and people.

IV. ELECTIONS

An election offers the voters an opportunity to choose who are to take office and conduct government. Because most countries with representative government have parliamentary systems, their elections are confined to the choice of members of parliament, or additionally in some instances of a provincial or local government representative. Countries with presidential systems of government also elect the chief executive. In the United States alone a large number of administrative and judicial officers are also popularly elected at state, county, and local levels as well. As a result, American elections have a special complexity, frequency, and elaborateness unknown elsewhere; this method of choosing public officials has consequences beyond the realm of the election process, and we shall discuss them in later chapters.

Nominations. Voters are normally limited in an election to choosing between candidates who have been formally nominated, and thus the nomination process is a significant part of the entire electoral procedure.

We have already observed that this is commonly a function performed by party. Yet inevitably, party and public interest here conjoin, and some state regulation of the process may result. There must be some formal determination of whether a candidate meets the legal qualifications for office; and, the date for making nominations, the payment of filing fee or election deposit, the submission of nominating petitions, and so on, are also matters commonly established.

Generally, parties are free to select their nominees by whatever methods seem appropriate to them; most commonly, selection is by special committee or caucus of the party organization within the constituency. In some of the American states, and in those of the German Federal Republic, party conventions are employed. Rarely is nomination considered a popular prerogative; the Swedish Social Democratic party, however, permits a decision of a district nominating convention to be appealed by mail ballot to the party members. The United States is unique in the use by most of its states of the direct primary method of selecting nominees. Here, in effect, the nominal members of the party choose its candidates through an officially conducted election. In some states an open primary prevails, which permits any voter to participate in the selection of any party's candidates. Such procedures may give a more popular quality to the nomination process, but at the cost of making elections more confusing and campaigns more expensive, weakening party responsibility, and encouraging divisive contests within the party's ranks.

Election Campaigns. From country to country, election campaigns vary in their length, elaborateness, and expense, but all involve variations on certain well-established techniques. Undoubtedly the most efficacious method of campaigning is through direct contact with the voters and organizing to insure that supporters turn out at the polls. It is also most advantageous for a candidate, well in advance of the election, to establish a wide acquaintance in his area, join organizations, deliver speeches, and otherwise make himself and his views well known—a practice the British describe as "nursing a constituency." During the formal campaign, the candidate holds as many meetings and rallies as possible; even if attended only by the party faithful—and sometimes not many of these—they may produce some publicity. When campaigning, it is far less painful to be attacked than ignored! Candidates usually distribute party literature and posters, and buy what advertising space they can. In a number of European elections, the candidate is authorized to mail post-free a copy of his "election address" or manifesto to each registered voter.

The local candidate for national office expects some assistance, of course, from the national party organization as well as the local association. This may take the form of literature, funds, and sometimes campaign speeches delivered by national party leaders on the candidate's behalf. The major parties will also conduct some nationwide publicity and perhaps make use of radio and television facilities where the latter exist. If these media are state-owned, it is the practice to allot a limited amount of broadcasting time equally among the parties, or in some ratio related to the number of their candidates, for use by the national leaders. In the United States, commercial radio and television time can be purchased locally as well as nationally, of course, and has come to be one of the most important means of electioneering, although a very costly one.

Money in Elections. We have remarked before the popular suspicion which generally surrounds the subject of money in politics. Money is a form of power in the political realm no less than in others. While parties make extensive use of the volunteered services of their leaders and workers, they also require funds, especially for election campaigns. Most people do not realize how expensive these operations are; yet a well-organized campaign requires money for salaries, office equipment, travel, printing, postage and telephone, rental of halls, purchase of advertising space and, where available, expenditures for radio and television time. American presidential and congressional campaigns alone have lately involved outlays in the neighborhood of $100,000,000. A recent German election campaign cost more than $17,000,000. In Britain, the relatively short seventeen-day campaign for parliamentary elections has involved expenditures of something like $10,000,000.

Parties are obliged to tailor their campaign to fit their treasury; but they are driven to expend sufficient funds to reach the mass of the electorate, and the costs of doing so are not purely a matter of choice. In the countries just mentioned, this means appealing to an electorate of some thirty-five million in Britain and Germany, and perhaps one hundred million in the United States. To conduct an advertising program of any kind on this scale must be expensive. Furthermore, parties campaign competitively, and are thus also driven to attempt to spend as much as their principal competitors. These necessary funds must come from somewhere. The most common sources are party dues; levies on candidates or officeholders; money-raising events, such as banquets and social affairs; in some countries, from party newspapers, cooperatives, and other business enterprises; and from contributions. It is the latter resource which raises the particular problem of undue influence and corruption. Large contributors, interest groups, business firms, labor unions, and others, may well expect favors and privilege in return.

These concerns can scarcely be waved aside, of course, but there are mitigations. By their nature, parties cannot concede endlessly to narrow interests. Some contributors see their party's success as quite sufficient compensation for supporting it. To relieve parties of any obligations, however, it has been suggested that campaign expenses should be met from public funds; yet it has not proved easy to devise a practical means of doing so. More important, taxpayers have not warmed to the idea, critical though they may be of other fund-raising methods. To equalize the role of money in elections, Britain imposes a limit to expenditure by or on behalf of individual parliamentary candidates, but subjects national party organizations to no restrictions. In the United States, federal and state legislation have made various approaches to regulation: some limiting total campaign expenditures, some limiting the amount of individual contributions, and some requiring a post-election account of what has been spent. Most countries have no restrictions at all. In any case, the central problem of political finance goes unresolved.

The Administration of Elections. In unitary states, the administration of the electoral system is in the hands of a central government official, such as the Minister of the Interior in France and the Home Secretary in Britain. In the United States and most federal systems, control rests with state or provincial authorities. Immediate administration of elections is conducted by local officials: a county board or city clerk in the United States, a "returning officer" in British counties and boroughs, and the departmental prefects and subprefects in France. Usually local government employees preside at the individual polling places, though in the United States this function is commonly entrusted to bipartisan precinct boards, on the assumption—not always warranted—that corruption will thus be prevented.

An electoral register is essential to the conduct of efficient polling. Its preparation is a task for local government officials in most countries, and they revise it annually on the basis of local records and canvasses. With a permanent system of registration, the individual need make no effort to get his name on the voters' lists, and thus is qualified whenever elections occur. The American states, on the other hand, usually require individual personal registration, and this sometimes repeated at intervals; thus only those may vote who have taken the initiative to qualify. For the election day, polling places are set up in town halls, schools, and other accessible buildings. Except in English-speaking countries, elections are commonly held on Sundays, when all school buildings are available, and teachers can assist in clerking and tallying.

There are several principal methods of voting. Where the "Australian" ballot is used, the voter marks an official ballot paper containing the names of all candidates and deposits it in the ballot box. Voting machines, so widely used in the United States, are not employed elsewhere; indeed, with the short ballot they are scarcely necessary. In many countries, the parties supply ballots which name their candidate or candidates; the voter encloses the ballot of his choice in an official envelope and places it in the ballot box. Where much of the electorate is illiterate, as in some Asian and African countries, a ballot box displaying an identifying sign or symbol is provided for each party; the voter need only recognize the party box of his choice and deposit his ballot paper in it. Each country has, finally, in its particular electoral laws, provisions which make certain practices illegal; these commonly forbid treating, intimidation, personation, and bribery. In sum, the essentials of effective election administration must insure that only the legally qualified participate, that their vote is secret, that the ballots are honestly counted, and that voting is free of corruption.

Nonvoting. Nonvoting is a phenomenon which necessarily attracts attention when elections are discussed. Considering the efforts that went into the achievement of universal suffrage, "won by a whole century of heroism," and considering the efforts as well which political parties expend to turn out the vote, it may seem a matter for proper concern when many citizens fail to exercise the voting privilege. In recent national elections, the turnout of voters was on the order of 78 per cent in Great Britain, 87 per cent in West Germany, and 92 per cent in Italy. At recent presidential elections in the United States, by contrast, the proportion of potential voters participating was 63 per cent in 1952, 60 per cent in 1956, 64 per cent in 1960, and 61 per cent in 1964. The presidential elections are high-water marks in American voting; in others, especially local elections, participation sometimes drops to as low as 10 per cent.

What causes nonvoting? The greatest factor is always indifference, and most likely to be apathetic are those with the least education, those in the lowest income levels, young persons, and women. Inability of various kinds also prevents voting; conflicting hours of work, absence from the polling area, recent change of residence, illness, and family responsibilities are obvious causes. Also, some people profess to see no real choice between the parties, or live in a district where the election result is a foregone conclusion. All these circumstances prevail generally. however; hence other reasons must account for the lower level of American voting. For instance, personal and periodic registration requirements and weekday elections reduce participation. The unwieldy American "long ballot" and the frequency of primary and regular elections also do the same. Particularly, the situation in the southern states substantially reduces the national average; indeed, in half of the American states, 70 per cent or more of the potential voters have participated in recent presidential elections. The low rate of Negro voting, however—a product of disqualification, discouragement, and habit—as well as the absence of two-party contests, heavily reduce participation in southern elections.

Remedies for nonvoting need to be related to its causes. To be sure, nothing much can be done for those who through mischance are unable to reach the polls on election day; however, nonvoting in the United States would be considerably reduced by simplifying registration and absentee balloting procedures, and by respecting the voting rights of all citizens. But what of the indifferent—are they sorely missed on election day? A number of countries have laws which make voting compulsory—Austria, Brazil, Italy, and Peru, for example—but impose no penalties for failure to do so. Others, such as Australia, Belgium, and the Netherlands, however, seriously undertake their enforcement and regularly fine offenders. Obviously, such laws transform a right or privilege into a legal duty. But voting is scarcely an end in itself; it ought to involve a considered choice, and the value of the vote of the least interested and least informed is most questionable. Some may well have no choice to express in the political order, and this is not necessarily damaging to it. The conscripted voter is likely to be an incompetent one; still worse, he may feel as coerced as the citizens in a totalitarian state, where sometimes 99 per cent of the eligible voters voice confidence in their leaders!

A high level of election participation is not necessarily a measure of democratic health, for it can reflect declining cohesion and political disarray. In a stable democracy, many may feel the outcome of an election will not make much difference. In any event, the level of popular voting is not an index of popular influence on government.

V. *The* TOTALITARIAN PARTY

We introduced the concept of "party" as an instrument of totalitarian dictatorship earlier in our discussions; we shall make further references to it in later chapters as it relates to the organs of government. Our treatment here will only undertake to emphasize that the term "party" associated with totalitarianism is really a misnomer; though such usage is so common we are obliged to employ it, it is certainly misleading. Let us be clear: true parties are instruments of democratic government which institutionalize the contest over office and policy. The totalitarian party, on the contrary, refuses to be a "part" of the "whole"; it must either stand outside the democratic context, whose political order it seeks to destroy, or monopolize political power entirely.

The Totalitarian Party as Revolutionary Force. The purpose of the totalitarian party, whether a movement of communism or fascism, is to effect revolution. It may work underground to destroy a political order by intrigue, infiltration, violence, and coup d'état, or it may operate in part on the surface among the parliamentary parties, but with its object always to disrupt their functioning. The choice of methods is determined by circumstance and strategy, but in any case parliamentary operations are always a temporary expedient.

As a revolutionary conspiracy, the totalitarian party need not be large. Its leaders can function more effectively with a relatively small band of disciplined militants serving as the conspirators in their struggle for power. The Bolsheviks, for example, numbered less than 30,000 at the time of the collapse of the Russian monarchy in 1917, and only later did the party acquire numbers. If the leaders undertake to compete in the popular political contest, a mass following becomes necessary. The totalitarian party then takes the form of a private army, with at least some of its members drilled and armed to wage political warfare. The choice of such tactics led Mussolini to expand his original fascist militia, and Hitler his storm troop units, into parties of the millions. In France and

Italy as well, the Communist parties are mass movements, whose followers can be summoned into the streets by the party leadership for demonstrations, strikes, and riots.

The Totalitarian Party as Standard-Bearer. Once the totalitarian party seizes power, its very success obliges alteration in its role and methods. The attackers must become defenders, though of a beachhead which must continually be extended. The party is now the standard-bearer of permanent revolution, the rallying point for those who join its "marching column," and the perpetuator of the new ideology. With other political groups outlawed or destroyed, membership in the party becomes a privilege and the principal means of advancement; its militants become a political elite. The character of the membership also undergoes some change. With the consolidation of the dictatorial regime, many radical and zealous members, too well practiced in the destructive arts, are rendered superfluous, if not downright dangerous, and have to be purged. In the ranks, the virtues of dependability, discipline, and conformity prevail. As a matter of expediency, some further additions to party membership may be made of those whose abilities are of special value, but generally, recruitment thereafter is through the youth organizations, where political reliability is better established by previous innocence, youthful ambition, and thorough training.

Once in power, the party must devote itself to establishing a new totalitarian order; whether as the "vanguard of the working people" for the communists or as the "supermen" of the Nazis, its members acquire the task of indoctrinating and controlling the masses, inspiring loyalty by precept and example, and promoting a spirit of self-sacrifice. As Professor John S. Reshetar observes in his study of the Soviet Communist party, "admission to its ranks has involved oppressive obligations, unexpected personal compromises, and untold risks." It also carries rewards, of course, though of varying duration; through party membership lies almost sole access to preferment and prestige, to career opportunities, and ultimately, to the levels of real power.

The Totalitarian Party as Superbureaucracy. The totalitarian party in power has a second major function: to organize and direct government. To do so, the party becomes a superbureaucracy, co-ordinating and energizing the administrative process. As dictatorship destroys institutionalized power, and the legislature, courts, and the law cease to provide restraints upon the administrative machinery of government, power can be controlled only through the party and its centralized command. Dictatorship, too, in order to encompass total control of society vastly enlarges the government's administrative structure, as well as paralleling it with the elaborate machinery of the totalitarian party; these structures must be knitted together at various points, and every instrument from internal espionage to terror must be employed to keep the bureaucracy functioning. As we have seen, elections or plebiscites are also continued by the dictatorship, and these must be managed by the party. Their purpose, of course, is no longer one of inviting popular electoral choices, but the staging of a mass "educational" campaign, promoting a sense of popular solidarity and political identification with the regime.

Even within the government of a dictatorship, "politics" of a sort occurs: choices must be made at various levels between alternative policies, the measures for their administrative implementation, and the men to be given office and authority. And dictatorship destroys neither ambition, competition, nor opportunity for rewards. The quest for these, however, must take place entirely within the totalitarian party, which frequently seethes with subterranean intrigues, particularly among the ranks of the secondary leadership. On occasion, the violence of these contests erupts into the open. Since there are few ways to withdraw gracefully from the totalitarian political contest in any event, and none at all for those who win the enmity of the more powerful leaders, there are displayed at intervals the self-denunciations, "cleansings," "treason trials," and "blood purges" by which the politically inept, the inefficient, the unreliable, and the inconvenient—in a totalitarian state it can be as dangerous to know too much as too little—are retired from politics and sometimes from life.

PART FIVE:

INSTITUTIONS OF GOVERNMENT

ABRAHAM LINCOLN

No man is good enough to govern another man without that other's consent.

SAMUEL JOHNSON

How small of all that human hearts endure,
That part which laws or Kings can cause or cure!
Still to ourselves in every place consigned,
Our own felicity we make or find.

CHAPTER 9

The EXECUTIVE

TRADITIONALLY, the major branches for the conduct of government have been distinguished as the executive, the legislative, and the judicial. Montesquieu in particular popularized the idea, not entirely original with him, and wrote in his *Spirit of the Laws* (1748) of "those three powers, that of enacting laws, that of executing the public resolutions, and of trying the causes of individuals." He concluded, too, that such a separation of powers within a threefold governmental structure was essential to maintain liberty and avoid tyranny.

Certainly Montesquieu was stating a fundamental truth when he insisted that a single concentration of all political power inevitably produces despotic and arbitrary government. Since then, the principle of the separation of powers has pervaded to some extent all democratic thinking about the arrangement of governmental institutions. It also provides a useful approach to their study. Of course, to look at government, even in gross structure, only as a three-way grouping of institutions into executive, legislative, and judicial branches is in many ways unsatisfactory. It may tend to obscure such matters as the involved process by which public policy is really made; the relative influence of popular and expert opinion in the conduct of public affairs; or the role performed by institutions whose powers may be quasi executive, legislative, and judicial all at the same time. From one perspective, indeed, the functions of government may be broadly distinguished as rule making, rule enforcement, and rule adjudication; yet by no means do these correspond identically to the actual functions of the legislative, executive, and judicial organs.

Nonetheless, a comparative introduction to governmental institutions, with an awareness of such problems, can be usefully undertaken by examining in turn the three traditionally distinguished branches of government. Attention will be directed to the principal segments of state machinery, the methods by which their offices are filled, the general roles and functions which each performs, and the problems that surround their operations.

We may thus begin with the executive. In the simplest sense, an executive is concerned with enforcing the law and administering public policy. At the highest levels of government the executive functions are complex and varied. So, too, are the ways in which this branch may be constituted. It may include a ceremonial executive, who serves as a titular head of state. It must contain a chief political, or working, executive. In some instances, one office may combine both functions, as in the United States. Associated with the political executive are department heads and ministers who also partake of the executive function, and with him constitute the "government of the day," or "the administration." Also in the executive branch are the lesser officials, officers, and employees who constitute the bureaucracy. Their functions will receive attention, however, in the later treatment of the administrative process.

I. *The* DEVELOPMENT *of the* EXECUTIVE

In a broad sense the history of the executive is the history of the development of political authority, for the executive is above all the very essence of government. From the early patriarchal family emerged the warrior-ruler-judge, and as political societies increased in size and complexity, political headship and leadership were asserted and recognized as significant forms of social control. To be sure, it was many centuries—after the middle ages—before any rulers comparable to the modern executives emerged. Yet how this came about deserves attention.

Early Kingship. The institution of kingship was widespread in ancient societies. It was already well established in the city-states of what now is known as the Middle East over 4,000 years ago, when the ancient Sumerians began to write. A clay tablet of this era, on which are inscribed some of the earliest laws that have been found, indicates that the king, among other things, dismissed corrupt officials, standardized weights and measures, and looked after the needy. Tax collectors were then, as now, necessary and also unpopular.

Although the character of kingship in these ancient lands—Israel, Mesopotamia, Egypt, Crete, and elsewhere—differed in details, there were many similarities. Royal succession was commonly hereditary, but dynastic lines were frequently broken by court intrigue, palace revolution, assassination, foreign conquest, and other circumstances.

Such early kings came to administer empire over wide areas, and their responsibilities were likely to be broad. To them were usually attributed divine powers, and their priestly functions were important. They served also as chief lawgiver and judge. There were temples and public properties to administer; armies had to be raised, disciplined, and led into battle. The ancient world also knew civil servants, postal systems, public water supply and irrigation systems, and market regulations. Indeed, it was the Assyrian king Sennacherib who in ancient Ninevah put up the first "no parking" sign. Despotic as these rulers tended to be, they were not absolute in their authority. Popular resistance did now and again assert itself effectively, and despotism was partially tempered by practical difficulties of communication and control. Even this early the germ of the idea of modern constitutional government was emerging: that the law applies alike to the ruler and the ruled.

Greece. The early Greek tribes were ruled by hereditary kings who claimed religious sanction for their exercise of authority, and combined the functions of general, priest, and judge. As the influence of the rising class of nobility increased, however, government by a landed aristocracy succeeded that of the Homeric monarchs. In turn, these aristocracies gave way widely in the seventh and sixth centuries B.C. to rule by tyrants, who often justified their seizure of power as a means of providing security in times of stress. Such tyrannies might last for decades before their excesses brought about the tyrant's expulsion, and his replacement by some form of oligarchy or democracy. By classical times, each city-state had evolved its own particular system of government. Though not entirely representative of all of Greece in this era, two of these, Athens and Sparta, are of principal interest.

The outstanding example of Greek democracy, Athens, had no executive branch of government in the modern sense. General political powers were vested in a popular assembly, the *Ekklesia,* composed of the entire citizenry, and assisted by a Council of several hundred, chosen by lot from all the citizens. While the Assembly exercised control over all magistrates and determined general policy, the Council acted somewhat as an executive committee, concerning itself with the detailed supervision of civic affairs.

Administrative functions were also delegated to ten elected generals chosen for their qualities of political as well as military leadership, who administered the army and navy, supervised the food supply, and assumed extraordinary powers in time of war. In the Athenian view, the authority of officials was exercised in the name of the community on behalf of its general interests. They were, in most cases, chosen by lot, performed their duties according to the law, and were accountable for such responsibility.

The government of Sparta differed from that of Athens in many ways, reflecting important differences in the philosophies of the two communities. Sparta was organized to achieve maximum military efficiency, and though there was no separation of powers, the executive position stands out more distinctly. Spartan government was monarchical in form and oligarchical in fact. Two hereditary kings performed religious, judicial, and military duties, but the main executive authority rested in the five *Ephors,* or overseers, who were elected annually and actually governed. Their selection was democratic in form only, however, and a limited oligarchy kept the city-community under the discipline of an armed camp.

If the experience of ancient Greece made no practical contribution to the evolution of the executive institution, it definitely influenced political thinking. The word "tyrant" came to acquire strong moral implications: tyrants ruled irresponsibly, without accountability to their subjects; they disregarded the customary laws and monopolized and abused power. The ideal ruler, so Plato taught, was one who perfected the art of statesmanship, and was wise and just. Aristotle, as well, contrasted the rule of king and tyrant, with the distinction between them based essentially on their moral character.

Rome. Rome began its history as a city-state and, though ruled by kings in the early period, established a republic in the sixth century B.C. Full executive authority, formerly possessed by the king, was vested in two consuls elected for one-year terms, who exercised military and judicial powers. Acting in an advisory capacity was a Senate, composed of several hundred elder statesmen appointed for life and representing the wealthy patrician families. An assembly of citizens exercised legislative powers. In the early history of the republic this was an aristocratic body, but gradually it was obliged to share its lawmaking powers and was ultimately replaced by an assembly including the common people. The elaboration of government functions under the republic required the creation of additional executive offices in the form of magistracies. Originally these were reserved exclusively for the patrician class, but ultimately were opened to the plebeians.

The expansion of Rome, first over the Italian peninsula and then to more distant Mediterranean lands, placed great strains on the republican government. To be sure, an elaborate system of provincial administration had been created, but provincial governors tended to become increasingly independent, and generals commanding far-flung armies were difficult to control. In the first century B.C. changes were instituted, after a period of civil war and military dictatorship, centering military, legislative, and administrative powers in an emperor. The Senate was relegated to a consultative role, and the assembly to insignificance; the entire empire was brought directly under the emperor's control. It was only a further step to encourage emperor worship as a state religion. Theoretically, political power continued to remain with the Roman people, and republican forms were preserved, but surface appearances were practically obscured by the deification of the emperor. Thus his absolute power came to constitute a model of splendor and centralized authority to which innumerable subsequent rulers would aspire for centuries.

During the period of the Roman republic, numerous dictatorships were established through the concentration of power in the hands of one man. Unlike the Greek tyrannies, however, the dictator was appointed by the Senate for a limited period of time to deal with a particular crisis; he was obliged to respect the basic law and answer for his exercise of office at its conclusion. The decline of the republic and the burden of imperial responsibilities introduced experience of the dictatorial tyrant to Rome, however, and an inevitable revulsion at the wickedness of tyranny. Roman rule, extended ultimately to wider areas than any before, achieved substantial accomplishments in the development of administration as well. Important, however, is the fact that the law steadfastly recognized the existence of basic rights enjoyed by all Roman citizens. Despite the interludes of dictatorship and tyranny, the idea remained that "the laws govern the magistrate."

Feudal Rulers. In the mingling of Roman and Teutonic political experience which followed the collapse of the Roman empire in the fifth century, the institution of monarchy continued in western Europe, though on a somewhat different basis. Whereas the Roman owed allegiance to his emperor as the embodiment of the authority of the state, the Teuton, bound by kinship to his fellows in a tribal organization, recognized the authority of his king on a personal basis as a leader or military chieftain. From the combination of Germanic and Roman attitudes—and which was the more influential is arguable—there thus grew up the intricate relations of personal allegiance that constituted the feudal system. An attempt was made, indeed, to revive the Roman concept of emperorship by conferring the title on Germanic rulers after A.D. 962 under the Holy Roman Empire, but western Europe was actually ruled thereafter by many kings rather than a single emperor.

The nature of feudalism, more a kind of civilization than a system of government, prevented the development of any idea of exclusive authority over a particular area. In the confusion following the fall of Rome, political authority was largely atomized, and was exercised initially on a quite local basis. In time, an arrangement of grants and subgrants of land created relations between lords and vassals on a combined basis of personal loyalty and contract. In the absence of any strong central government, then, the king was only an overlord, sitting at the apex of an intricate hierarchical organization. Feudal kings were not despots, ruling by their own fiat, but only a part of a whole system. Their authority was shared with their underlords, the free cities, the medieval estates and, not unimportantly, the Church. They had certainly to reckon with the power and influence of bishops and popes.

An increasingly significant restraint on kingly power was the law. Law rested largely on a customary basis, rather than on statute, and the king was himself expected to observe it. Medieval arrangements originally encouraged the king to look upon his kingdom as his personal property, the public treasury as identical with his private purse, and the exercise of royal authority only the assertion of his personal rights. Nevertheless, there was increasing insistence upon the idea that kingship was an office, not a right. Again the belief continued that the ruler had a priestly character: the king was God's vicar on earth, and set over men to punish their sins. Kings were expected to dispense justice and to maintain order. Thus, the idea was not abandoned that the king ruled for common interests and advantages, not solely his own; against the royal authority must be balanced the rights of individuals.

Absolute Monarchy. The fifteenth and sixteenth centuries witnessed the rise of national monarchies in western Europe to a position substantially effacing that of the feudal kings. Several factors account for this new situation. For one thing, the pretensions of the emperors of the Holy Roman Empire to overlordship of all Europe were never successfully asserted in practice. The Reformation shattered the claims of central religious and secular authorities—popes and emperors—to rule a unified Christian world. With the decline of feudalism, many circumstances permitted and encouraged strong national leadership under a single ruler. Absolute monarchy came to be esteemed as a means of drawing together larger areas under centralized control to provide order and security against both internal dissension and external attack. Inevitably, many of the medieval restraints imposed upon kingly authority were put aside.

Spain, the country of first rank during the early part of this period, was united under Ferdinand and Isabella after a long period of warfare with the Moslems. After successfully stripping power from the feudal nobles and the *Cortes,* or assembly, and reforming the Spanish Church, its rulers centralized authority in a strong royal government. In France the process of national unification was already under way, and was largely completed by Louis XI, who came to the throne in 1461. Again political authority was successfully taken from the nobles, the Estates General was practically denied any further influence, and the territorial consolidation of France centralized power in royal hands. Similar developments occurred in Scotland, the Netherlands, and Denmark. In central and eastern Europe, however, the process of centralizing authority in national monarchs was subjected to greater obstacles and developed more slowly. Here feudalism was much more difficult to dislodge, because society was almost completely agrarian and manorial, the aristocracy more powerful, and a well-to-do middle class either small or nonexistent. Even so, while unable to consolidate all territory on a national basis, powerful monarchies were forged in Prussia, Austria, and Russia in the seventeenth century.

By the sixteenth century, then, absolute monarchy was becoming the prevailing form of government in Europe. Only in England, among the important European states, was there to be a substantial variance in this pattern. The idea of absolutism, which was to continue dominant in the next two centuries, arose from the practical necessity of releasing the authority of the ruler from feudally imposed limitations by emperor, church, and nobility. It asserted that the monarch could not be bound by legal limitations of any sort. Reinforcement of this assertion was sought in the theory of the divine right of kings—the doctrine that kings hold office by direct appointment from God, to whom alone they are answerable, and that resistance to their authority is a sin. Necessarily, such philosophical justification of the king's right to govern not only refuted any claim that his authority rested on a popular basis, but also resisted any other concentrations of political power. The success of absolute rulers, too, was aided by the practice of Machiavellian tactics, through the creation of national armies and the development of efficient bureaucracies. Thus, the administrative arm of government expanded considerably.

Constitutional Monarchy. The successful assertion of monarchical absolutism had the obvious effect of bringing kings into sharper conflict with the middle classes, who had originally been willing to support the doctrine to escape the clutches of the nobility. The excesses of the absolute monarchs and their courts—their propensity to dynastic-interest war, secret diplomacy, financial extravagance, and other unpopular practices—invariably encouraged demands for their restraint or even overthrow. Of course, some kings exercised their power with benevolence, but others, disregarding the political and commercial interests of the growing middle classes, turned support to enmity. Inevitably, some rulers now sought to ally themselves with the aristocracy against the commoners in self-defense, and did so successfully.

The achievement of effective limitations upon royal authority and the establishment of constitutional monarchy came first in England. We have already noted that the pattern of constitutional development in this country was unlike that generally prevailing on the continent. In the fifteenth century, the conflict between contending factions of nobles in the Wars of the Roses substantially reduced the ranks of the barons, dealt a deathblow to English feudalism, and in 1485 brought Henry VII to the throne. The resulting line of rulers governed with a firm hand, allying to their cause not only Parliament, but a new class of loyal nobility, and ultimately broke with Rome to establish an independent Anglican Church. But if the monarchy was strengthened during this era of "Tudor absolutism," so were the gentry in local government, the common-law courts, and Parliament—and as well, their independence of the Crown.

The harmony among these elements was shattered, however, by the accession of the Stuart kings of the seventeenth century, and a struggle commenced between King and Commons over conflicts of interest and principle. Against attempts of the Stuarts to assert their absolutism and sanctify their rule by divine right were opposed the rights of Parliament and the supremacy of the common law. After a long series of quarrels, civil war broke out, and in 1649 Charles I was beheaded. The restoration of the monarchy eleven years later only led to renewing the duel between Crown and Parliament over constitutional issues. As a result, James II was forced to vacate the throne in 1688, and a new line of monarchs was installed.

King James, asserted Parliament, had "endeavoured to subvert the constitution of his kingdom by breaking the original contract between the king and people; and . . . violated the fundamental laws. . . ." To insure that kings would not henceforward overreach themselves, Parliament in 1689 enacted the Bill of Rights, which served as a constitutional document defining the monarch's position—now king only by act of Parliament—and asserting the rights of English subjects. Theories of absolutism and divine right were definitely rejected; the supremacy of the law and the sovereignty of the nation over the will of the king were assured.

The French revolution, coming a hundred years later, struck another telling blow at monarchical absolutism. Following the political vicissitudes of the Napoleonic period, France finally installed a constitutional monarch in 1815. Even then, French kings failed to learn the lessons of English constitutional history. In consequence, further displays of absolutist tendencies led to the final abandonment of monarchy and the establishment of a republic in 1871. Though the United States had substituted an elected president for a crowned head of state nearly a century earlier, such an office was still a novelty. But not for long, however. In the years after World War I, republics became commonplace.

Meanwhile, British and French constitutional practices influenced all of Europe in varying degrees. By the middle of the nineteenth century, the institution of constitutional monarchy was established in Sweden, the Netherlands, Belgium, Sardinia-Piedmont (extended later to all Italy), and Denmark. In states to the east, however, such as Prussia, Austria, and Russia, attempts to reduce royal absolutism enjoyed only limited success. Here rulers made some concessions, but hedged them with qualifications. Even so, there were no permanent victories for monarchical absolutism; none of these monarchies survived World War I. World War II took further toll of thrones and crowned heads.

The essence of constitutional or limited monarchy—all that remains of hereditary rule—is that the king's power is distinctly restricted by fundamental law or constitution. He serves as titular head of state, but without political power. The king (or in some countries, a queen) reigns but does not govern; instead, he is used as a convenient symbol of the continuity of authority and the unity of the state. "The king," as Edward VII stated, "never expresses any opinion on political matters except on the advice of his responsible ministers." In the classic phrase of Bagehot, the constitutional monarch enjoys three rights: to be consulted, to encourage, and to warn; but his acts must be those of responsible ministers, not his own. The king may exercise some personal influence, but it must avoid partisanship, and be exerted with tact and discretion.

II. MODERN EXECUTIVES

The working executives in the principal modern states may be broadly classified into three major types: parliamentary, presidential, and dictatorial. To reduce thus the forms taken by the chief executive over the world is to classify broadly indeed. Yet it does help us to distinguish significant types of executive office and their principal features. For example, methods of selection, tenure of office, means of enforcing political responsibility, relations with subordinate ministers, and processes of political succession vary distinctly among the three types. Within each category, there are extensive variations in detail, so that the possibility for political generalization is limited. Consequently, our discussion of executive forms will treat actual examples.

One word of caution. Our purpose in classifying is to get at significant realities. In politics things are not always what they seem, nor what they are labeled. Form and fact may well be at variance. Thus, a parliamentary type of government may operate with the head of state, the titular executive, designated "president." A state may also have a parliamentary or presidential type of executive in form, and yet be governed by a dictatorial executive in fact. Indeed, a king may even be a dictator.

THE PARLIAMENTARY EXECUTIVE

The parliamentary executive—sometimes described also as the "cabinet" type—is the most widely adopted form in systems of representative and constitutional government. It developed first in England by a process of historical evolution, was adopted on the European continent, and spread extensively. Its wide incidence may be explained by several factors: the transplantation of English institutions throughout the British Commonwealth, the wide extent of European political influence, and the fact that the parliamentary executive is compatible with either monarchical or republican forms of government.

Essential Features of the Parliamentary Executive. The essential features of the parliamentary executive include, first, a titular head of state, who may be a "constitutional" and hereditary monarch, as in Great Britain, Sweden, Belgium, the Netherlands, or Japan, or who may be a president, commonly some elder statesman chosen by an electoral body for a fixed term of years, as in Finland, Germany, Ireland, Italy, and Austria. In either case, his position in government is essentially as we have described it in the preceding section of this chapter—one primarily without political power. His principal function, beyond ceremonial duties, is to designate the political executive and to see, in short, that there is a government. The political executive—variously called prime minister, premier, or chancellor—is the leader of the major party in the parliament, or someone able to organize a coalition of several party groups, and he continues in office with his cabinet so long as he enjoys the support of a parliamentary majority. General elections, for the lower and popularly representative house of parliament, are held at intervals and provide a popular mandate to continue or replace the existing government. These features may now be examined in the British parliamentary executive.

The Executive in Great Britain: The Crown. Because the British constitution is not a documentary one, no fundamental single law describes the English executive. Its character cannot be accounted for as conscious choice; it can be explained rather as the result of English history, chance, and practical experience. Though its essentials may be duplicated in other countries, it may be seen nowhere else—even within states of the Commonwealth—with exactly the same details. Some of its aspects are, indeed, far too subtle to be captured in constitutional clauses. A description of it requires attention to the several institutions that comprise the executive: the Crown, the Monarch, the Prime Minister, and the Cabinet and Ministry.

We have seen that, until the seventeenth century, the principal executive in England was the king. For the most part, he performed the executive functions personally, or saw them performed under his immediate direction. Gradually, however, the royal functions were institutionalized and in the process their actual exercise was increasingly transferred into other hands. This did not mean that the executive powers were diminished, but rather that the king enjoyed steadily less personal discretion in their application; indeed, once the exercise of Crown powers was securely in the hands of responsible ministers, Parliament was quite willing to see the Crown's authority extended.

Thus the Crown today has come to represent the sum total of executive authority in British government, as well as the office of monarchy. Although Crown powers are related primarily to the executive and administrative processes, they have legislative and judicial character as well. Laws are enacted by the "Crown in Parliament"; the authority of the courts is also drawn from the Crown. These Crown powers are derived from two sources: the royal prerogative and acts of Parliament, with the former defined by common law and the latter, of course, by statute. The Crown is thus an abstraction, to be sure, "a convenient working hypothesis" to explain the changed constitutional situation whereby the executive powers are now exercised by the king's ministers.

The Monarch. The king (or queen, in the present reign) is a person, and by nature mortal; a monarch may abdicate, become incapacitated, or die. Yet there is never an interregnum in Great Britain, for Crown authority is never suspended; the Crown, like a corporation, enjoys a legal immortality. Then, why not dispense with the king entirely and employ only the symbol? As a matter of fact, kingship is not essential to the operation of a parliamentary executive. Royal functions are, indeed, performed by a regency when the monarch is underage or incapacitated. But if there is no king, someone must be found to take his place in a somewhat similar office of government. A republic with a parliamentary government, such as Italy or Germany, does just that; it substitutes the office of a president for that of a king.

A king or president is therefore necessary to the operation of parliamentary government—and the British prefer a hereditary monarch for the job. Kingship is the most ancient institution in British government, its continuity broken only once in a thousand years. The present sovereign, Elizabeth II, is descended from the Saxon King Egbert, who ruled in the ninth century. Coming to her office as queen regnant by inheritance, she has not been obliged to enter any political competitions, and has not been a member of any political party. She enjoys, in consequence, a position of political neutrality, free of partisan strife, and is uniquely able to claim to represent the entire nation in a way an elected politician scarcely ever can.

Queen Elizabeth's main political function as a twentieth-century monarch is to appoint a Prime Minister, and while this responsibility ordinarily offers little opportunity for the exercise of discretion so long as there is a strong biparty system, sometimes she may have some choice, as when no party enjoys a majority, or when the majority party in the House of Commons has designated no leader. In 1923, for example, the results of the election were such that neither the Conservative, Labour, nor Liberal parties commanded a majority of the seats in the House of Commons. King George V chose the leader of the Labour party, Ramsay MacDonald, to be Prime Minister. Again, in 1963, Harold Macmillan suddenly resigned the prime ministership because of illness. After hurried consultations among Conservative party leaders to determine which of some four or five candidates would be most acceptable as a successor, Mr. Macmillan recommended Sir Alec Douglas-Home. The Queen's selection of the latter was impartial, and on the best available advice, of course, but no one could choose for her.

Constitutionally, the Queen as reigning sovereign has many other duties. She appoints all important officials of the government: ministers, ambassadors, military commanders, and judges; she is head of the established Church of England and appoints its bishops; she issues administrative rules in the form of Orders in Council; she summons and dissolves Parliament, assents to legislation, makes treaties, and declares war; she is head of the Commonwealth and appoints governors-general in its members. All of these acts are performed as Crown powers on the "advice," to be sure, of ministers, who are responsible for them. Even so, Queen Elizabeth is here not merely a figurehead. All major policy decisions and appointments are discussed with her, she sees all important state papers, and receives firsthand reports of all significant developments respecting the work of the Cabinet, proceedings in Parliament, and the affairs of empire and Commonwealth governments. She is entitled to be fully informed of the nature and implications of all actions taken in her name. In a reign of some length, therefore, a British monarch sees a number of governments come and go, and acquires a unique overview, both of public affairs and those who engage in them.

The Prime Minister. The office of Prime Minister evolved slowly. The title was initially one of reproach, used to describe that minister of the king first in royal favor. It began to achieve real importance only in the eighteenth century, after George I ceased to attend cabinet meetings. Sir Robert Walpole is often described as the first Prime Minister. But it took another century, to the time of Sir Robert Peel, before that office acquired essentially its present-day form. For decades thereafter, although the term "Prime Minister" had come into general use, there was still no such "office" in the government, strictly speaking; the Prime Minister obtained official status and salary by taking the post of First Lord of the Treasury. In 1905, a royal warrant gave him precedence as the fourth non-royal person of the realm, but not until 1937 was he given by statute a salary to go with the office of Prime Minister alone. Long before this, however, the Prime Minister had become the real head of the government. Even today, there is still no constitutional document or basic statute prescribing and defining his powers; they rest largely on constitutional convention—that is, custom and usage—developed out of the workings of the whole parliamentary system.

We have noted that the reigning king or queen designates the Prime Minister. The latter comes to this office ordinarily because the voters have elected the members of the party which he leads to a majority of the seats in the House of Commons. Only in unusual circumstances will the monarch be able to exercise discretion in the matter. On being invited to form a government, the Prime Minister organizes a Ministry of some seventy or more members chosen from his party in the two houses of Parliament, and from these a smaller group of twenty or so, who constitute the Cabinet. The monarch then issues their formal appointments, and the government continues in office until it is no longer supported by a majority in the Commons, or the Prime Minister chooses to resign.

The Prime Minister thus has no fixed term of office. He may be dismissed only by the Sovereign, but the latter would not take such a step unless the Prime Minister had lost his majority, and another party leader was able to command one. Today, it is virtually impossible for this to occur—given the rigid division of the Commons membership between two parties, and the strict political discipline maintained over each of them—until a general election has intervened and the voters have altered the party balance in the House. Clearly, a Prime Minister is in a powerful political position. Not only is he the acknowledged leader of his party, and thus the leading member of Parliament, he is also head of the government and selects and removes all members of the Cabinet and Ministry.

The Prime Minister has a broad range of duties, falling into three classes, arising out of his relationships with the Queen, the administration, and the Parliament. First of all, he advises the Queen in the performance of the powers of the Crown, and keeps her informed of the state of affairs in the government generally. Second, as the "keystone of the Cabinet arch," he presides over that body, and supervises the work of the Ministry and the various departments of government, so that the activities of the executive branch are co-ordinated. Third, as a member of Parliament—since 1902 always in the House of Commons—he is the principal spokesman of the government before it, promoting the government bills which make up its legislative program, and defending the Cabinet's policies. The Prime Minister recommends the dissolution of Parliament and thus chooses the time for a general election.

The Privy Council, the Cabinet, and the Ministry. Before the eighteenth century, the principal advisory and administrative assistance to the king was provided by the Privy Council. This body in time became too large to offer advice effectively, and many of its members ceased to have any political responsibilities. Even so, it continues to have legal authority, though substantially altered functions. The Privy Council today is composed of some three hundred members. In addition to all present and past Cabinet members (for it is only through the Privy Counsellor's oath that a member is officially sworn to loyalty and secrecy as Her Majesty's Servant), the Council contains a number of persons accorded the distinction as a reward for important public service. As a body, it has only formal functions: the promulgation of Orders in Council and the giving of official effect to other executive acts.

The Cabinet originated as a gathering of the most important members of the Privy Council, and for most of its history was unknown to the law. Though its existence has finally been recognized in the Ministers of the Crown Act, 1937, it is a conventional organ, composed of those ministers whom the Prime Minister invites to serve as a deliberative council with him. Though in the earlier history of the Cabinet the Prime Minister played a role described as "first among equals," his position today is far stronger than that. While the selection of Cabinet members rests with him, the choice of his Cabinet colleagues involves a number of considerations. The ministers heading the principal departments must be included because of their importance—hence, the Chancellor of the Exchequer, the Foreign Secretary, and the Ministers of Defence, Home Affairs, Commonwealth Relations, Transport, and Labour are all bound to be included. For practical reasons, too, the Cabinet must contain some effective debaters, and several members from the House of Lords. Other choices will rest on such varied factors as political obligation, administrative needs, and personal convenience. As a result, the size of the Cabinet, though not fixed by law, can scarcely be much less than twenty.

Thus, the Prime Minister's selections are not entirely unrestricted, and the alternatives available to him are not nearly so many as those of an American President. Once organized, the Cabinet is collectively responsible for its acts and policies. In shaping and leading this team the Prime Minister must display a large measure of talent for leadership. He may go a considerable distance on his own discretion, but he must always carry his Cabinet with him. Whatever internal differences may arise, the Cabinet must present a united front to the outside. Now and then a dissident member may be dropped, or an ineffective minister replaced, but harmony and mutual trust are indispensable and the Prime Minister must lead in paths which all his colleagues will follow.

As the central institution between the executive and legislative branches, the functions of the Cabinet are most important. First, its members collectively decide broad matters of policy, involving foreign affairs, finance, and other matters of concern to the entire government. Second, the Cabinet formulates the legislative program which is annually placed before Parliament, and its individual members lead in introducing, defending, and overseeing the enactment of the legislation. Third, the Cabinet co-ordinates and delimits the authority of the various departments of government.

The Ministry is composed of the Cabinet members, other ministers, government whips, and all politically chosen officials of the executive branch, who together constitute Her Majesty's Government. All the seventy to eighty members of the Ministry are selected by the Prime Minister and may be removed at his discretion. Most of them are members of the House of Commons, for it is before this body that principal accounting must be made for the policies and acts of government, but there must be some also who are members of the House of Lords, because the upper chamber requires some spokesmen for the Ministry as well.

The Parliamentary Executive in France and Germany. Two interesting variations of the cabinet type of government are illustrated in the political systems of France and Germany. In contrast to the British system, both of these are provided for in documentary constitutions adopted since World War II, and both reflect previous unsuccessful parliamentary experiences, rather than centuries-old accumulations of custom. In the France of the Third Republic (1871–1940), the existence of a multiparty system, extreme ideological differences between the major political groups, weakness of party discipline, frequent political scandals and other crises, among other factors, all rendered the French Cabinet unstable and weak. Formed always by coalition of a number of parties, French governments could adopt programs that were only provisional compromises over a limited number of issues, and were frequently and easily pulled apart from within or overturned by one or the other of the two houses of Parliament. During this seventy-year period, the average life of a Cabinet was no more than nine months, producing a situation of instability barely mitigated by repeated reappointment of many ministers. Of course, many proposals were made for strengthening the executive, but the memory of two Napoleons, and the fear of an all-powerful ruler, always obstructed their acceptance.

The Constitution of the Fourth Republic (1946) contained several provisions intended to give a new stability to the Cabinet and greater scope for leadership by the Premier. These included a limited power of dissolution for the Premier, a cooling-off period before votes of no-confidence or censure were taken by the National Assembly, to which house alone he was now accountable, and the establishment of a broad basis of support for a Cabinet before it was installed in office. Even so, experience with the wartime Vichy dictatorship of Marshal Pétain restrained efforts—especially those of General Charles de Gaulle—to create an executive with effective powers. And again, the habits and atmosphere of the Third Republic continued to prevail in politics; French governments turned over even more rapidly—on the average every five months. Inevitably, the governments of the Fourth Republic proved increasingly less able to cope with France's serious domestic and foreign problems. In both the Third and Fourth Republics, this legislative superiority over the executive led to their description as systems of "assembly government" rather than "cabinet government." Mounting frustration with such executive instability—and with a National Assembly which could not govern but could prevent the Cabinet from doing so—led to widespread support for General de Gaulle's proposal of a new constitution, and its adoption in 1958.

The new Fifth Republic displays a governmental system with a curious blend of features from both the parliamentary and presidential types of executive, as well as a style reminiscent of Napoleonic plebiscitary government. The President was initially chosen by electoral college, but a constitutional amendment of 1962 provides for his election by popular vote for a seven-year term. He is intended, however, to be much more than a titular head of state, and is given power to permit him to act as arbiter between the government, the parties, and the Parliament. The Premier and members of the Cabinet are appointed by him, but on accepting office they must resign their seats in Parliament, if they are members of that body, and ministers may be appointed from outside it. The government may still be forced to resign by a vote of censure, passed by an absolute majority of the National Assembly. Thus, an attempt is made to apply both the principle of a limited separation of powers, which De Gaulle insisted is the essential basis for executive stability, and also the principle of ministerial responsibility, which French tradition views as essential to representative government. The President is further empowered to dissolve the National Assembly, though not more than once a year. Whether any or all of these institutional reforms can, in the long run, overcome France's long-standing political habits is still doubtful. The French distrust strong governments and disdain weak ones, so the present regime seems only another temporary solution to the vexing problem of reconciling liberty with authority in that country.

In French government, the executive has been weak and unstable; in

Germany, by contrast, the tradition has been to overconcentrate authority in the executive and make him formidably strong. Even after putting aside autocratic rulers and an authoritarian dictator, the German preference for a stable and highly concentrated center of authority is demonstrated in the Bonn Constitution, adopted in 1949, and in the politics of the German Federal Republic. The federal President is elected for a five-year term by a special federal assembly composed of the members of the *Bundestag* and an equal number of representatives of the *Länder* (state) Diets. He has the role of the usual republican head of state, with powers nominal rather than real. All his political acts are countersigned by the Federal Chancellor, who is the political executive, and is chosen by the President because he commands a majority in the *Bundestag*. Thus, the essential principle of parliamentary democracy—ministerial responsibility—is maintained.

Beyond this, however, virtually all arrangements operate to make the office of Chancellor considerably more stable and dominant than that of an ordinary prime minister. The Chancellor alone is specifically authorized to determine general policy. He chooses and dismisses the ministers, who need not be members of Parliament, but may be high-ranking civil servants or experienced in *Land* government. The Chancellor is under no obligation to consult his cabinet colleagues, and in practice does so far less than do British and French prime ministers. What is most unique in the German arrangements is the constitutional provision that the *Bundestag* may vote its lack of confidence in the Chancellor only by simultaneously electing his successor by a majority vote of its members—a so-called "constructive" vote of no-confidence. Thus, a Chancellor is virtually irremovable unless a majority opposing him is equally united behind another leader, or until a general election alters the political composition of the legislature. For this reason, Germany has had no problem of cabinet instability, and the first Chancellor of the Republic, Konrad Adenauer, held the office without interruption during four terms for fourteen years until his retirement in 1963 at the age of 87.

The Parliamentary Executive in the New Nonwestern States. The widespread political awakening in the colonial world since the two World Wars has produced a host of new independent communities in Africa, the Middle East, and Southeast Asia attempting to become "nation-states." These countries, after long periods of colonial government—

which is essentially a form of authoritarian rule—are attempting, generally after only short periods of transition, and in some cases almost overnight, to begin the conduct of self-government with the paraphernalia of western parliamentary institutions. As might be expected, it is proving to be a difficult undertaking, for parliamentary or any other type of popular representative and constitutional government is a matter not only of forms but of spirit. Yet neither their indigenous traditions nor their experience of colonial rule have, for the most part, fitted their peoples for such a task.

To mention only some of the serious obstacles—the mechanisms of popular elections are entirely novel to these new states. The difficulty of election administration and, indeed, the partly questionable significance of its results is due to the fact that the voters are mainly illiterate and often unable even to spell their own names. Political parties tend to be organized around personalities, are highly hierarchical, and may well have had as their principal experience not the conduct of government but nationalistic agitation or conspiracy for independence. In some instances, parties reflect ancient tribal or regional differences and act as divisive rather than unifying agencies. And the new national leaders who assume the prime ministership and other ministerial offices may have little experience with the idea of political co-operation and collective responsibility. They also tend to be hostile to the existence of a parliamentary opposition, seeing it as dangerously obstructionist or downright treasonable. The art of compromise is frequently unknown in such societies, as is acceptance of the principle that the arena of politics is a place for the necessary display not only of moral courage but also of moderation and restraint. In some societies, on the other hand, the idea of compromise is so ingrained traditionally that complete government inaction results if unanimity cannot be obtained. All such countries have seen the conduct of effective governmental administration complicated by the absence of any counterpart to the western middle class, and the lack of an adequate supply of trained administrators, civil servants, scientists, technicians, and teachers. When it is considered, further, that great strains are imposed on these still frail and inexperienced governmental systems by the attempts of their leaders to effect thoroughgoing economic and social revolutions, immediate or even long-run success seems uncertain.

Western observers must be not merely sympathetic, but realistic, in viewing these ambitious aspirations and efforts of newly self-governing peoples to get from where they are to where we are by our usual means. We can hope that these states move toward democracy; we cannot expect them to achieve it quickly. Inevitably, there will be lapses from virtue and failures (as there have also been in the West), and their achievement of even limited successes will undoubtedly require much sympathetic encouragement and assistance on our part. At best, considerable experimentation with and modification of western institutions will probably be necessary, as well as decades of political experience and education, to produce viable and stable governmental systems. At worst, we should not be surprised if military control and dictatorship, or intervals of such rule—which have already been instituted in some of them—are to be part of the making of such states, unpleasant though that prospect may be.

An Evaluation of the Parliamentary Executive. It might be expected that, given its widespread adoption, the parliamentary or cabinet type of executive has important advantages in its favor. It does produce, especially in its effective British form, a close union of effort between the executive and the legislature, because the former is in effect a governing board drawn from the latter. A positive executive leadership of the legislature is both provided and accepted, and not left to chance. When a breach occurs between the two, it can be resolved; indeed, either a new ministry must be appointed or a new legislature elected. Once more, then, the executive and legislature move off on the same foot. There is, as well, always a clear distinction between the government majority that leads and the opposition that criticizes.

The tenure of the executive is not fixed, but rests instead upon the continuation of majority support in the legislature. Thus the parliamentary system creates an executive which is an excellent vehicle through which to express a popular mandate. And its policies must stay closely attuned to public opinion, for it has no calendar lease on office. Because the cabinet's powers are dependent upon a minimum degree of legal definition, its authority may be adjusted to the demands of the times; when necessary in emergency, political authority can be quickly centralized. Finally, the cabinet in the parliamentary system represents a considerable accumulation of political experience; its members reach their positions only after long apprenticeship in a parliamentary career. When a government loses office, its members then enter the opposition, where they remain within direct observational range of the conduct of public affairs and can hope, at least, for an early return to office.

Of course, the parliamentary type of executive displays certain disadvantages. For one thing, the lack of a fixed tenure of office for the cabinet creates a degree of uncertainty—both for those within the government who must plan their program without knowing what time is available for carrying it out, and for those outside who must adjust their affairs to the new government's policies. Certainly, the advantage of some expectation of continuity in policy for a definite period is sometimes lost. In the absence of a separation of powers setting apart the legislative and executive branches, there is a lack of means to prevent one branch from overextending itself. The principal restraint upon the executive must be effected by its accountability to parliament; it is difficult to create others by law. Although some limitations may be imposed—the forces of custom and public opinion are most important in Great Britain—they cannot be counted upon to apply effectively everywhere. Thus, a common consequence has been failure to achieve an equilibrium between the two branches of government. In Great Britain and West Germany, the executive has enjoyed a dominance over the parliament to an extent that there are complaints of "cabinet dictatorship." In France of the Third and Fourth Republics, on the other hand, the executive was so dominated by the parliament, often acting arbitrarily and irresponsibly, that effective orderly government was impossible.

Clearly, the parliamentary type of executive is most effective when supported by a stable majority, and this is likely to be found only in countries having a strong biparty system. Most countries which have instituted the cabinet system have been hampered in its operation by the fact that they have instead multiparty systems, and cabinets have tended to be indecisive and unstable. Various efforts have been made to resolve this problem by the application of mechanistic devices, such as cooling-off periods and "constructive" votes of no-confidence, but these have not succeeded in providing an adequate substitute for political stability, traditions of moderation, and reasonableness. This failure of the parliamentary system to produce stable and recognizable leadership has led to popular support for dictators and authoritarian government as a means of providing it. Ironically many countries have chosen the parliamentary in preference to the presidential system, fearing the latter type of executive to be so powerful that it might become dictatorial;

yet their failure to operate the cabinet system effectively has in many instances led to its easy conversion into a dictatorship. As we have already noted, this may occur frequently in the new non-western countries experimenting with the parliamentary system.

THE PRESIDENTIAL EXECUTIVE

An American contribution to political invention is the presidential type of chief executive, originated in the United States Constitution of 1789. It has had nothing like the widespread adoption of the parliamentary type of executive, however, having been instituted in such Latin American states as Brazil, Mexico, Bolivia, Chile, and Colombia, and in a few other states immediately associated with American political experience, such as Liberia and the Philippine Republic. A form of the presidential type of executive may also be seen in many new African states, formerly French colonies, such as the Republics of Dahomey, Chad, Ivory Coast, and Niger; here the executive position more nearly resembles the American than the French. It seems unfortunate that the presidential features and advantages have not been more widely appreciated. Among others, as a means of providing a strong and stable center of power within a newly created state embarked upon the difficult task of self-government, it might well prove less difficult to operate effectively than the more delicately adjusted parliamentary system.

Essential Features of the Presidential Executive. Essentially, the presidential system of government provides a chief executive who is not a member of the legislature, is chosen for a definite term of office, who holds a wide, popular mandate resulting from his election, and is largely independent of the legislative branch for the conduct of his administration. The president's formal powers are defined in a documentary constitution. The fact that his office combines the roles of both chief of state and political leader of the government provides a dual enhancement of his prestige and authority; there is no dispersal of fundamental executive authority and the power to exercise it. These features are demonstrated in the American presidency.

The American Presidency. The framers of the American Constitution in 1787 were obliged to undertake a substantial task of pioneering when they came to the problem of providing an executive for the new system of government. Given the still-vivid memories of the controversies with their former king, George III, the institution of monarchy, even with a set of responsible ministers, was popularly discredited. The inadequacies of a leaderless central government, with executive functions undertaken by legislative committees, had been fully demonstrated by experience with the Articles of Confederation since 1781. Although a single executive was feared by some as a possible opening wedge for monarchy, the alternative of a plural executive was opposed as being inefficient, lacking unity, secrecy, and dispatch. Agreement ultimately prevailed on the necessity for a single executive, modeled somewhat on the well-known office of governor in the individual states, though with considerably more power. The method by which the President was to be selected offered further difficulties. His election by Congress, it was argued, would place him too deeply into the debt of the legislature, and impair the principle of separation of powers; election by the people, even in face of the limited suffrage allowed at the time, appeared to offer the still more dangerous possibility of "mob rule." A compromise was found, therefore, in a system of selection whereby "presidential electors," chosen in each state as its legislature should prescribe, would select the President. Thus, the Constitution provided for a President, relatively independent of both Congress and the people, indirectly elected for a fixed term, and vested with the full executive powers.

Nomination and Election of the President. The rise of the great national political parties was to short-circuit the indirect method of selecting the President intended by the Constitution. Within a few years after 1789, the parties began to offer specific candidates for the presidency and vice-presidency, and to place on the ballot a list of electors pledged in advance to cast their state's electoral vote, if chosen, for the nominees of their party. Well before the mid-nineteenth century, the major parties also began to hold national conventions in which to nominate their standard-bearers, and thus introduced a further extension of party control.

Briefly, the election of the President today still includes the constitutionally prescribed forms, if diverging from their spirit. Party control of the nominating process is complete, and election is virtually on a popular basis, as the electors are so chosen. In the summer of a presidential election year, delegates from the state party organizations meet in national convention and choose their presidential and vice-presidential candidates. On election day in November, the voters in each state cast their ballots for the list of electors of that party they wish to support.

Approximately a month later, the group of electors which has been chosen meets at their state capital, casts the state's electoral vote (equal to the number of the state's Senators and Representatives in Congress—or three in the case of the District of Columbia), and forwards the results to Congress. Of course, the outcome of the election has long since become well known, but certain formalities remain. In January, Congress canvasses the states' electoral votes and announces as elected the two candidates who have received the electoral majority. If no candidate has a majority, the Constitution provides, the House of Representatives chooses a President from the three names highest on the list; in the same circumstances, the Senate chooses a Vice-President from the two highest candidates. The President and Vice-President (elect) take office on January 20.

The election is thus not strictly by popular vote, because the majority of electoral votes, not popular ones, is decisive. The voters' choice is not usually, but may be, affected by this stipulation. In two cases a popularly preferred candidate failed to obtain the office; Presidents Hayes and Harrison (in 1888) received fewer popular votes than their respective opponents, Tilden and Cleveland, but won the necessary electoral majority. A candidate may also win with only a plurality of the popular vote. Lincoln (in 1860), Wilson (in 1912), and Truman all lacked a majority of the popular vote, but obtained electoral majorities. Though numerous changes in the electoral system have been proposed, none has achieved necessary acceptance in the form of a constitutional amendment.

The Office of President. The President's term of office is fixed at four years. The Constitution originally raised no obstacle to his re-election for further terms, but long-standing tradition and political practice prevented any President from obtaining a third term until 1940. Subsequent reaction to Franklin D. Roosevelt's election to a third and fourth term led to advocacy, at least in partisan quarters, of a formal two-term limitation upon the office. The Twenty-second Amendment, added to the Constitution in 1951, provides, therefore, that "no person shall be elected to the office of the President more than twice." As is the case with all civil officers of the national government, the President may be removed from office "on impeachment for and conviction of treason, bribery, or other high crimes and misdemeanors," and a President is allowed to resign. None has resigned or been removed, however, though several have died in office.

The formal qualifications for holding the office are few. The Constitution stipulates only that the President must be a "natural-born" citizen, at least thirty-five years of age, and for fourteen years a resident of the United States. In practice, however, the nominating conventions, the prevailing political atmosphere, and the voters themselves erect other prerequisites for achievement of the presidential office. These customary qualities, though varying in any particular election year, ordinarily require conformance to what is known as the principle of "availability." The common characteristics displayed by presidential candidates suggest that in order to be accepted as wholly "available" he had best be a "family man" in his early fifties, of Anglo-Saxon stock, Protestant, college-educated, a veteran of military service, and serving successfully in public office, usually as governor of a politically pivotal state. Candidates without these characteristics have been at a disadvantage, though recently, religion seems less important, and the candidates have been cutting their political teeth in Congress. If a President is removed from office, resigns, dies, or is unable to perform his duties, the Constitution provides that the Vice-President succeed him. A law governing succession to the presidency beyond this point, adopted by Congress in 1947, provides that if there is neither a President nor a Vice-President, the office passes in turn to the Speaker of the House of Representatives, then the President pro tempore of the Senate, and thereafter to cabinet officers in the order of their precedence.

The constitutional enumeration of the President's executive authority is set forth in brief and general terms. Article II states that "the executive power shall be vested in a President"; that he "shall take care that the laws be faithfully executed"; and that he shall take an oath to "preserve, protect and defend the Constitution." He is made commander-in-chief of the armed forces; he is authorized to make treaties with the concurrence of two-thirds of the Senate; he is given power to appoint, with the consent of the Senate, diplomatic and consular officers, justices of the Supreme Court, and all other officers whose appointments are not otherwise provided for; he may grant pardons and reprieves for offenses against the United States. Finally, he may "require the opinion, in writing, of the principal officer in each of the executive departments, upon any subject relating to the duties of their respective offices."

Even more modest provision is made in the Constitution concerning the President's relations with the other branches of the government. He is authorized to give Congress information from time to time on the state of the Union, and may recommend measures for their consideration. He may call special sessions of Congress; if the houses disagree as to a time for their adjournment, he may determine it; and all bills and concurrent resolutions passed by Congress must be submitted to him for approval. We can see that the bare constitutional provisions concerning presidential authority, important as they are, can give but limited insight into the nature of the office and its actual powers. A discussion of the office in its broader aspects must be reserved for a later part of this chapter.

The President's Cabinet. The Cabinet of the American President is similar to its English counterpart in that it is composed of the principal department heads of the executive branch, but there the resemblance practically ends. The members of the Cabinet are appointed individually as secretaries of the ten major departments; their principal functions are administrative; they may not be members of Congress, though they may be chosen from that body's membership. Collectively the Cabinet members have consultative and advisory functions, though their responsibilities here are what the President cares to make them. He may consult them much or little; some Presidents, indeed, have preferred to seek advice from lesser officials or other persons with no official status at all. Of course, the Cabinet is available as an instrument through which to determine executive policy and to achieve administrative co-ordination, but it is not always employed to do so. The promotional responsibilities of its members are commonly stressed; President Lyndon Johnson said of his Cabinet that it "consists of nine salesmen and one credit manager."

The Constitution does not provide for a Cabinet, nor do the statutes. Rather, it arose informally in response to President Washington's desire for a body of advisers when the Senate refused to lend itself to this purpose (in any event, it soon became too large for such a function), and subsequent Presidents continued the practice. The basis upon which its members are selected accounts for still other reasons why it differs from the British Cabinet. Some of its members may well be outstanding leaders within the President's party, but this is not a primary requirement. As often as not, such appointments are made to reward party service or pay election "debts"; to give representation to principal geographical sections of the country or highly organized interest groups; and to obtain some members, even of the opposition party, who enjoy influence in the houses of Congress. The President's selections must be approved by the Senate, but usually go unquestioned; he may remove his appointees at any time. The members of the presidential Cabinet are thus the subordinates of the President rather than his colleagues. He is free to accept or reject their advice; and, in case of any differences, he may always have the last word.

Other Presidential Executives. The most extensive experience with the presidential executive outside the United States has been in Latin America. These states, winning their independence from Spain, for the most part in the first half of the nineteenth century, adopted constitutions which reflected their aspirations as much as their own traditions. Hence they looked in most cases to their sister republic to the north as a source of models for their political institutions. There was not, of course, blind copying of American arrangements; many of their institutions and ideas of democratic government were influenced by those of France and other countries. All of the states undertook to establish in some degree the separation-of-powers principle, though after a century of political development and constitutional revision, government in Latin America now commonly reflects the trend of indigenous experience toward a dominant executive branch.

Some comparisons of the presidential office in North and Latin America may be briefly noted. All of the Latin-American constitutions provide for the popular election of a president (except Uruguay, where executive power is vested in a nine-member National Council); five- or six-year terms of office are allotted in many cases, and most countries prohibit re-election, though in practice the restriction is not always observed. A vice-president is commonly elected at the same time as the chief executive, and provision is frequently made for the removal from office of both officials by impeachment.

Presidential power is everywhere supreme, mainly as a consequence of constitutional authorization, but also because of political tradition and practice. In much of Latin America, the major task of government is simply to maintain order. Weak administrations are quickly overturned, and a *caudillo,* or military chief, commonly assumes the reins of power. Most of these presidents enjoy, therefore, substantial emergency powers, and authority to initiate legislation and even to govern by decree. They may declare a state of siege and suspend constitutional rights; they may collect and spend taxes; they may appoint local governors; and in many other ways they may exert relatively complete authority. In practice, too, if not by constitutional stipulation, both the congresses and the courts are politically subordinated to the president. Although many strictures may be raised at such violations of the ideals of limited government and constitutionalism, it must be pointed out that in an area characterized by chronic political and economic instability, the real choice is often between strong, if arbitrary, government and the chaos of no government at all.

An Evaluation of the Presidential Executive. On balance, the presidential type of executive has fewer advantages in principle than the cabinet type, but those it has are none the less persuasive. Certainly, the presidential executive has met the test of time in the country of its origin, demonstrating its capability of bringing forward national leadership within the framework of the constitutional system. Comparatively, it seems obvious—despite the fear expressed by such foreign observers as John Stuart Mill and James Bryce that great men were not likely to become presidents—that the occupants of the office are entirely the equal, in general ability and practical capacity to govern, of the heads of governments produced by the parliamentary systems of Great Britain, France, or Germany. The president's fixed term of office assures a position of executive stability, particularly advantageous during times of crisis. The executive is separated from and independent of the legislature so far as his selection, basic powers, and terms of office are concerned. Such a situation has considerable merit, of course, in the eyes of those who believe in the desirability of a separation of powers, and oppose an excessive concentration of governmental authority in any one place. The legislature is also independent of the executive in the same fashion, and thus each has important means of restraining the other against possible excesses. The presidential system offers greater opportunity in form, at least, for popular choice in the selection of the executive, and thus permits the voter to identify himself more closely with the national political leader. Generally, the system has the distinct merit of providing a stable executive even without the presence of stable legislative majorities.

The principal disadvantages of the presidential type of executive largely reflect the merits of the cabinet type. No direct executive leadership of the legislature is provided, since the latter is a co-ordinate, not a subordinate, body. As a consequence of this situation, the president is often obliged to make extraordinary efforts—summoning all his resources of patronage, prestige, and personal influence—to accomplish the enactment of his legislative program. Not uncommon, too, is the display of legislative jealousy of the president's prerogatives. Unlike the cabinet executive, who achieves that position as the result of a long and successful career as a party leader in the legislature, the presidential executive frequently has had no such experience; indeed, he may well not have extensive knowledge of any part of the national government's processes. Further, the executive and legislative branches may fall under the control of different political parties and thus produce the possibility of a deadlock between them over certain important issues. Such a situation, which may be avoided in the cabinet system, can make most difficult the accomplishment of positive government action. A sometimes unsatisfactory feature, because a fixed term of office for the executive is provided, is that elections and changes in the government take place only at fixed intervals, when there may be no crucial political issue to be resolved, or may even occur in the midst of war or crisis, when any change is for the time being undesirable. It is not possible in the presidential system, also, to produce a change of executive when circumstances might definitely require it, because a president, once chosen, is practically irremovable until the end of his term of office. It should be noted, finally, that the presidential system as such does not preclude the establishment of dictatorial government. The president not uncommonly exercises dictatorial authority in many Latin-American states where democracy has never flourished.

THE DICTATORIAL EXECUTIVE

The features of the dictatorial type of executive have been displayed in modern political regimes as divergent as those of Mussolini, Hitler, Franco, Stalin, Tito, Mao Tse-tung, Perón, Nasser, and Castro. Which are the most typical and representative it is not, for several reasons, easy to say. Each dictatorship, while demonstrating a number of characteristics in common with others, has unique features; some are motivated by the extremist doctrines of the political right, others of the left; and, the length of their regimes and the extent of their powers have varied. Not all dictators are totalitarian—some undertake to monopolize political power without dominating all aspects of society. Such restraint does not make them attractive, of course, but it may make them less overwhelming. Finally, because the establishment of dictatorship involves the imposition of a large degree of personal political force in place of conventional political institutions, and conflicting authoritarian ideologies have had varying national impacts, extensive generalization is difficult.

In effect, then, one is obliged to examine the status of individual dictators and their particular system of ruling, rather than executive offices of government with legally defined authority. And, for our purposes, an examination of totalitarian dictatorship in the Soviet Union seems most useful. The Russian Bolshevik revolution produced the first major modern dictatorship, and three men have largely monopolized political power there for nearly fifty years. This political system not only commands one of the world's superpowers, but serves as a prototype for many states in the Communist bloc. Not least important is the fact that dictatorship in Russia appears as firmly entrenched as ever. To be sure, there are some, both inside and outside of the country, who insist that the dictatorship there is temporary, and some who argue that it is not a dictatorship at all. But after a realistic examination of the governmental system, it is difficult to accept any other conclusion than that political authority in the U.S.S.R. rests upon a dictatorial basis, and that it affords a significant example of authoritarian rule under a leader closely holding the reins of power.

The Soviet Dictators. The Soviet dictatorship, like that in many other countries, was originally the product of political crisis in a state where representative government had never been successfully established; it was ushered into existence by force and violence, along with very skillful agitation and propaganda; and it is maintained by such means under the aegis of a revolutionary political party bent upon extirpating all other forms of political activity. This first Communist dictatorship was established by V. I. Lenin in November, 1917, when he succeeded in grasping power from the fumbling hands of a provisional government attempting to maintain order after the collapse of the Czarist regime. Lenin, a militant and professional revolutionary, and leader of the small but well-organized Bolshevik movement, stepped into what was a virtual political vacuum, created a government, and successfully maintained his authority through the four years of counterrevolution and war which followed. By 1921, organized opposition was largely liquidated, and though Lenin's rule was supported by personal prestige and a certain measure of popularity, he used forceful measures without hesitation to maintain himself. By the time of his death in January, 1924, the contest had already begun for succession to his power.

The grim struggle which resulted took place largely behind the scenes, of course, but its outcome was clear. Of the principal contenders, Trotsky, the commissar for war, had won a reputation as an organizer and political theoretician; Zinoviev, leader of the Communist International, had a large personal following; Stalin, the other leading contestant, had become general secretary of the Soviet Communist party in 1922, and had created a well-established position within the party bureaucracy. By combining effectively his control over the party organization with a series of astute and ruthless political maneuvers, Stalin was able to draw the reins of power into his hands. Trotsky was dismissed from the government, then exiled, and finally even written out of Russian history books. All other possible opponents of Stalin, both real and imagined, were similarly eliminated in the years following, a process which culminated in the wholesale "party purges" and executions from 1934 to 1939. By 1941, of the seven men who had constituted the membership of the Politburo, or top party organ in 1924, Stalin alone was alive. Trotsky had now been murdered; Tomsky was reported to have committed suicide; Zinoviev, Kamenev, Rykov, and Bukharin had been shot.

Stalin himself, characteristically of most of the modern dictators, was a man of obscure and humble origins. Born Joseph Djugashvili, in Russian-occupied Georgia in 1879, his life began in poverty. Failing to complete his training for the Orthodox priesthood, because of his expulsion from the seminary, he early adopted the life of a political revolutionary, and was arrested and imprisoned by the Czarist regime a number of times. He became one of Lenin's lieutenants after 1905, and served as a commissar in the first Bolshevik government, but attracted little public attention until the contest for power began shortly before Lenin's death. Stalin's position of primacy remained unshaken through the political and economic crises of the 1930's, World War II, and the years thereafter until his death in 1953.

Once again several aspiring successors began to vie for position: Malenkov, Chairman of the Council of Ministers, and apparently Stalin's intended heir; Beria, head of the security police; and Molotov, the senior "old Bolshevik" and foreign minister. However, a more effective competitor for power, Khrushchev, who became principal party secretary nine days after Stalin's death, again demonstrated the strategic utility of that office. Within the year, Beria was arrested and executed without public trial for a long list of crimes. In 1955, Malenkov was suddenly demoted and replaced by Bulganin as Chairman of the Council of Ministers; another two years saw Molotov also removed from the center of power. Bulganin in turn fell into disfavor in 1958, and was replaced by Khrushchev, who then became the one front-rank leader. Once more the Soviet system demonstrated how collective leadership tends to give way inexorably to one-man rule, and why the problem of succession in a dictatorship produces crises, rather than an orderly transfer of power.

Nikita Khrushchev was born of a miner's family, in 1894, in the southern part of what is now the Russian republic. Working as a sheepherder and miner when young, he joined the Red Army during the revolution, and later received some modest education in party schools. He then worked as a party organizer, rising rapidly to high posts in the Moscow organization. By 1938, he was the Ukraine's party boss, and the next year a full member of the Politburo. He had various political and military duties during World War II, including, after 1944, the direction of the brutal and bloody Ukrainian purges that continued during the next three years. In 1949, he returned to Moscow, where he was soon to demonstrate his superior skill at ruthless political in-fighting, and success in outmaneuvering all opponents who stood in his way.

Khrushchev's fall from power came late in 1964, when he was unceremoniously ousted in sudden disgrace from government and party offices, without tears or cheers from a bewildered populace. A *Pravda* editorial blamed the deposed leader for "harebrained schemes, immature conclusions and hasty decisions and actions divorced from reality, bragging and phrase-mongering, commandism, unwillingness to take into account the achievements of science . . . armchair methods, personal decisions, and disregard for the practical experience of the masses." New leaders again divided the top positions, as in 1953; Leonid I. Brezhnev became first secretary of the Communist party, and Aleksei N. Kosygin, the premier. Several of Khrushchev's closest associates were removed from top posts at the same time. The turmoil surrounding this upheaval not only damaged the prestige of Soviet leadership at home and abroad; it demonstrated the political dangers raised by a great power that has no orderly process for a change of government.

The Dictator: Status and Powers. Some of the significant common characteristics of the modern dictator can be illustrated by example from the top Soviet leadership. First, the dictator gains his political position through means of violence, conspiracy, and maneuver. As the brief background descriptions of Lenin, Stalin, and Khrushchev indicate, none was chosen by election, either party or popular, to hold power. None came to the top according to any previously determined rules or within the framework of established political institutions, which is the case with democratic leaders. Rather, the dictatorial accession to power is marked by the breakdown of the existing political order; the dictator's power thus rests upon his ability to assert it, rather than upon any claim to legitimacy.

Second, the dictator's exercise of power is primarily dependent upon his position within the dominant ruling party or oligarchy rather than in an office of government. In the Soviet Union, the reins of political power are held not by a president or prime minister, but by the man who controls the Communist party. Three men alone—Lenin, Stalin, and Khrushchev—have been able to do this. Through more than a quarter of a century of absolute rule, Stalin held a governmental post but part of the time. Until 1941, when he became Chairman of the Council of Ministers, Minister of War, and Commander-in-Chief of the Soviet armies, he had held only party office. Khrushchev, likewise, took office as Chairman of the Council of Ministers only after he was politically well-entrenched, and Bulganin had committed the error of intriguing against him. Fundamentally, then, executive authority, regardless of where it is formally located, stems from party leadership; even collective rule requires an arbiter.

Third, the modern dictator forcibly maintains a one-party system and eliminates all opposition to his rule, whether from within the party or without. Lenin began by using the Bolsheviks, a comparatively small but highly organized and disciplined political association, to seize control of government in Russia. Once established, he did not hesitate to unleash the "Red Terror" in applying the most extreme measures against his counterrevolutionary enemies. The monopoly of political activity was formally conferred in the 1936 Constitution, which defines the Communist party as "the leading core of all organizations of the working people, both public and state." Those within the party are given no immunity from violence. The savage purge trials ordered by Stalin in the 1930's to liquidate possible centers of political opposition reached well into the group that had surrounded him most closely. Before his death, there were indications that in his mounting pathological suspiciousness, an even greater purge was being prepared. Although Khrushchev showed less tendency toward bloodthirstiness, curbing the secret police and closing most of the forced labor camps, if only because the highly developed Soviet industrial state can no longer be ruled by despotic terror alone, he did not abandon terror as a political weapon. Frequent threats are delivered in the U.S.S.R. to warn "spies, bourgeois nationalists, fascist collaborators, deviationists, diversionists, hooligans, revisionists, and anti-social elements" that no opposition centers will be tolerated.

Fourth, the dictatorial executive employs a body of trusted (but carefully supervised) political lieutenants who serve as an advisory staff and occupy the most important and strategic positions in the party and government. No dictator ever rules alone in solitary splendor; he must surround himself with a group of able lieutenants who, functioning in some respects as an executive's cabinet in a democratic government, can individually assume directing and administrative functions, and collectively assist in determining policies. In the Soviet Union this agency is the Presidium of the Central Committee of the Communist party, formerly known as the Politburo. The latter organization, created in 1919, usually contained a dozen members and one or more candidate-members; in 1952 it was replaced by the Presidium, though this change is one of name rather than function. This self-chosen and self-perpetuating group constitutes the "leading summit" of the party at which are decided questions of the highest concern, both foreign and domestic, in governmental policy. Its members also hold some of the highest governmental posts in the Council of Ministers, thus keeping a close grip on the armed services, the labor unions, the security police, the information media, and the constituent republican governments, as well as their influential party jobs.

Fifth, as leader of the state, the dictator is endlessly publicized, and given an artificial popularity through the manipulation of all devices that create opinion. In the earlier years of his rule, Stalin made only infrequent public appearances and his speeches were rare, intended as documents to be studied by party functionaries. He never engaged in the oratorical flights and dramatic displays that were the stock in trade of Hitler and Mussolini. During the 1930's, however, he began to appear more and more at the forefront; by World War II, his name, his portrait, and his statue were on view everywhere in Russia. Thereafter the name of Stalin was employed in the Soviet press only with accompanying praise and adornment. Such phrases as "the beloved and wise leader," "the great leader and teacher," "the steel colossus," "the towering genius of all mankind," were invariably used in reference to him.

Sycophantic adulation can reach its limits, and Khrushchev's agility in outmaneuvering his rivals was well demonstrated in the skillful manner by which he set out to put a new face on the dictatorship. At the Twentieth Party Congress in 1956, the dead Stalin was subjected to scathing criticism; Khrushchev himself denounced his late master as a sadistic tyrant. The "cult of personality," now discredited, was to be replaced by the "cult of party." Nevertheless, the change was really one of style rather than practice. A Soviet dictator must dominate the Communist party and use the collegial bodies that surround him as a screen to conceal the personalized nature of his power. Through his control of the party press—some 150 newspapers—Khrushchev kept his name and face steadily before the people; he received the most front-page space and the greatest applause. Where Stalin was taciturn and aloof, Khrushchev was garrulous and gregarious. He visited with peasants, talked to workers in the street, and appeared as a typical "family man." His visits abroad, to China, India, Great Britain, the United States, France, and elsewhere, brought him immense additional publicity, outside the Soviet Union as well as within it. Although he was not obliged to submit to popular elections, he behaved at times very much like a candidate for office in a democratic state. The purpose of all such devices of flattery and adulation is not so much to appeal to the personal vanity of the dictator as to solidify popular support for the political regime of which he is the symbol—a part of the propaganda undertaken to convince the public of the dictator's benevolence, wisdom, and competence. Yet Khrushchev himself seemed to have fallen victim to it; eventually his own personal and erratic style of rule was in turn denounced as a new "cult of personality."

Finally, we should note that the dictator's powers are not to be defined in terms of legal authority as is the case of the democratic executive. On the contrary, they are subject to no institutional or constitutional checks but are determined at the will of the dictator himself. Practically, of course, there are limits. A dictator must exercise some self-restraint or his recklessness can destroy himself and his regime; he must be capable

ABOVE: "The essential features of the parliamentary executive include, first, a titular head of state who may be a 'constitutional' and hereditary monarch. . . ." (p. 311) Queen Elizabeth reads the Speech from the Throne in the House of Lords at a state opening of Parliament. (*British Information Services.*) BELOW: ". . . The presidential executive has met the test of time in the country of its origin, demonstrating its capability of bringing forward national leadership within the framework of the constitutional system." (p. 329) President Johnson and Canadian Prime Minister Pearson at the signing of final agreements for the development of the Columbia River Basin; joining them are Canadian and American officials. (*Wide World Photos.*)

ABOVE: "A nation expects someone acting in its name to express national sentiments by appropriate means and to give tangible recognition to nationally accepted values." (p. 340) A crowd greets Dr. Heinrich Lübke after his re-election to a second term as President of the German Federal Republic in 1964. (*German Information Center.*) BELOW: "The democratic executive's powers are not unlimited, but must be exercised in prescribed ways and through designated officials; they will be subjected to legislative, and perhaps judicial, review." (p. 355) Swedish Prime Minister Tage Erlander, left, with his Minister of Finance outside the Cabinet Conference Room in the Royal Chancellery. (*American-Swedish News Exchange.*)

of reckoning what the traffic will bear. In his exercise of authority and influence he must always carry some of his political lieutenants and most of the party organization along with him. Because he has the whole machinery of the state at his command, however, he is in a position to monopolize the agencies that mold and manufacture public opinion. Persuasion is preferred, but there is no reluctance to employ coercion. Nor are dictators, however ruthless and fanatic, hated by all. In 1961, a spontaneous outburst of sorrow in the Dominican Republic followed the assassination of Trujillo, often labeled a "despised tyrant." It also appears that, among the communist dictators, Tito is widely admired and respected by the Yugoslav people. To deal with any recalcitrant minority who may still remain unconvinced, there are elaborate systems of espionage, secret police, concentration camps, and military forces. Thus, the dictator's power is most difficult to challenge; his removal is accompanied by conspiracy and violence, leaving turmoil in its wake.

Executive Organs in a Dictatorship. The Communist dictatorship in the U.S.S.R. has established an elaborate complex of institutions and offices of government which give formality to the exercise of political authority, though they are not the actual centers of it. There is no concept here, in theory or practice, of a separation of powers. Governmental organs are the tools to be used by the Communist party, a façade to conceal the true source of power, and window dressing to emulate the representative institutions of the democratic systems. Thus, the 1936 Constitution provides for a Presidium of the Supreme Soviet, as one of the "highest organs of state power," composed of a Chairman and thirty-two members selected nominally by the Supreme Soviet. The duties of this organ include the convening and dissolution of the Supreme Soviet, issuance of decrees, interpretation of laws, exercise of the right of pardon, declaration of war, ratification of treaties, and an extensive appointing power. The Presidium has no prototype in western political institutions, functioning as a sort of collective presidency, and combining the exercise of legislative, judicial, and executive roles. It is the principal law-issuing body, and since its composition usually includes several members of the party Presidium, it operates close to the apex of authority.

The more immediate administration of affairs is assigned to a Council of Ministers. "The highest executive and administrative organ of state power," according to the Constitution, this agency co-ordinates and directs the work of the various ministries of the state. Theoretically subordinated to the Supreme Soviet, it nonetheless prepares most of the legislation to be approved by that body, and, more importantly perhaps, issues the wealth of decrees, regulations, and ordinances essential to the day-to-day conduct of the government. The Council of Ministers is composed of the heads of various ministries and state committees, several other high officials of comparable rank, and some members of the Central Committee, numbering altogether some sixty members. Thus we see here another example of the interlocking relationships between party and governmental organs, as well as the means by which the top party leadership can control and co-ordinate a vast bureaucracy.

An Evaluation of the Dictatorial Executive. When advantages are claimed for dictatorial government, they rest upon a frame of values so fundamentally distinct from those employed to assess democratic forms that few bases of comparison really exist. In the main, the principal claims run somewhat as follows: first, dictatorship is necessary to provide the kind of government required by modern crisis conditions. When the existing political and social institutions of a state fail to function with full effectiveness, it is argued, the only solution is vigorous rule imposed by force to provide swift and direct action, unimpeded by the cumbersome, slow-moving, and inefficient machinery of democracy. Dictatorship claims to have a monopoly of truth and the only correct blueprint for the future. Further, dictatorship makes possible the authoritarian control of the citizens' lives, forcefully eliminating the dissensions and conflicts of democratic politics and enforcing a reconciliation of class, economic, racial, religious, and other interests. In this way, the dictator copes with competing interests, but within limits, and without a legislative opposition. It is asserted as well that authority enforced from above by the dictatorship strengthens the state militarily, socially, and economically, so that the government may gain a totalitarian command of all the state's resources, human and material. Finally, such a system claims to recognize the real inequality of men to participate in the political process. The exercise of power by a dictatorship places it in the hands of a natural leader who has demonstrated his ability by successfully seizing it—thus achieving dramatically a survival of the politically fittest.

Against any such claimed advantages, however, must be balanced some real and important disadvantages. The exercise of political power in a dictatorship lacks any basis in freely given consent by those who are ruled; it has no basis in law, regardless of retroactive pseudolegalisms.

Dictatorship need make only the most limited responses to popular demand; it is not held to account for its exercise of authority; it may ruthlessly silence any criticisms. Obviously, too, the exercise of political power subject to no restraint is inevitably corrupting, both of the ruler and the ruled. Because the reconciliation of interests by the dictatorship is an enforced one, it is, therefore, much more apparent than real. The compromise and adjustment of interests are effected by the sacrifice of minority rights—in extreme cases, by the liquidation of the minority itself. A close look will show, further, that dictatorships do not in practice produce real administrative efficiency; they may appear to do so because of their ability to conceal waste and blundering, and to withhold the truth about their operations. But these can never be indefinitely hidden. Again, dictatorship subverts all individual liberties, since the only freedom, if it can be called that, is one of supporting the regime in the manner prescribed by the government. If its authority is to be maintained, the dictatorship can scarcely allow the exercise of those rights most fundamental to democracy. Finally, the tenure of a dictator is usually terminated in disorder; each instance of succession involves a struggle, often to the death, by the contenders for power. The system is thus incapable of developing constitutional government because it rejects the concept either of a supreme legality or of stable institutions with real authority.

In sum, the exponents of dictatorship argue that the end—that is to say, the necessity of creating effective political authority—justifies any means, however violent or immoral. The opponents of dictatorship, on the other hand, insist that the means employed inevitably condition the ends achieved—so that illegal and immoral means can only result in producing a corrupt and corrupting state.

III. EXECUTIVE FUNCTIONS

We have observed in our discussion of the executive's historical evolution that in early governments there was no conception of executive functions, as such, distinguished from legislative or judicial ones. All powers of government rested in the same hands. As the performance of governmental responsibilities became more complex, however, a division of labor and a specialization of function began to develop. Further, as a means of imposing some restraint on arbitrariness and of limiting governmental authority, responsibilities in the realm of policy determination and adjudication tended to be conferred on separate organs—legislatures and courts. Neither the legislative nor the judicial functions, however, can ever be mechanically distinguished or wholly divorced from that of the administration of policy; executive functions inevitably resist any precise compartmentalization, even in such systems of government as that of the United States where the constitutional framers intended to impose a sharp separation of powers. The lines of demarcation arising from this somewhat artificially conceived threeway division of government functions, therefore, are invariably blurred in modern democratic states, and intentionally obliterated in the dictatorships.

The functions and responsibilities of the executive branch of government thus continue to be varied, spectacular, and decisive. We shall demonstrate, indeed, how wide must be the field of competence for this branch which stems from the trunk of all original political authority.

Symbolic and Ceremonial Functions. The importance of symbolic and ceremonial functions is often underestimated, particularly in democratic societies, which emphasize the ideal of social and political equality for all citizens; yet experience indicates their indispensability in government, and their necessary performance by the executive. Human nature appears to call for some personification of the abstraction which is the state, if only because the civic loyalty of many persons attaches far more readily to an individual than to an impersonal institution. The highest governmental authority requires not only dignifying but also the keeping of some distance between ruler and ruled if overfamiliarity is to be avoided. As President de Gaulle observed, "There can be no prestige without mystery." A nation expects someone acting in its name to express national sentiments by appropriate means and to give tangible recognition to nationally accepted values. To be sure, many of the modern dictatorships have tended to surround the national leader with such circus-like spectacles of pomp and ceremony as to verge on the ludicrous. If some peoples prefer less emotionalism in the realm of government, none has proved to be so politically sophisticated as to dispense with symbolism and ceremony altogether.

The British offer here one of the principal justifications for their hereditary monarchy, even though its powers have ceased to be of great political importance. The titular head of state and others in the royal family can be usefully employed to spare the Prime Minister, the working executive, a considerable burden. Moreover, it is the general British view—and one which represents long experience—that their monarch performs these functions far more effectively than would a plain citizen temporarily elevated to high office. Queen Elizabeth symbolizes both the British state and the unity of Commonwealth and empire, acting as a tangible tie binding together Commonwealth citizens in all parts of the world. Her personal presence lends dignity to, and represents the national interest in, such occasions as the opening of Parliament, the patronage of charitable undertakings, the review of military formations, the visiting of disaster-stricken areas, leadership in religious and patriotic celebrations, and the initiation of a large variety of national enterprises.

In its earlier history, as a struggling young republic determined to reject monarchical trappings, the United States sought to de-emphasize such activities and expected a minimum of such performances from its presidents. But symbolic responsibilities have accumulated, and the President as the working executive now has all the usual ceremonial duties to perform as well. His personal appearance before Congress to deliver his message on the state of the Union, entertaining at diplomatic receptions, the inspection of military forces, attendance at Veterans' Day ceremonies, and his issuance of Thanksgiving proclamations, for example, all evidence popular demand for his presence or performance. The greeting and entertainment of foreign heads of state and other important official visitors have recently taken so much of his time that he must limit such visits.

In the totalitarian state, of course, the symbolic and ceremonial functions of the dictator take on a special significance. Here the appeal to unquestioning obedience and undeviating loyalty—and the formation of the people into unbroken and disciplined ranks—focuses all attention on the exalted position of the national leader. In Germany a few decades ago, Nazi doctrine asserted that Adolf Hitler not only spoke and acted for the German people but as the people. At the same time, the mass rites over which the dictator presides are considered important as a means for inculcating an individual sense of identification with the regime. Mass activity is in effect offered as a harmless substitute for democratic participation in the governing process, hence the continual marchings, wearing of uniforms, mass calisthenics, chanted slogans, and party rallies. The individual is thus encouraged to believe he is sharing in the glory and superhuman strength of the dictator.

Political Leadership. The histories of governments indicate that some of them may operate without effective leadership for a considerable period—particularly in times marked by the absence of stress or crisis—by drawing upon a momentum gained earlier, but such cases and conditions are exceptional. Indeed, numerous examples of weak and unsuccessful government—such as the United States under the Articles of Confederation, the Russia of Czar Nicholas II, the French Fourth Republic, and the German Weimar Republic—all show notorious deficiency in bringing forward or sustaining effective leadership. By contrast, periods of national greatness are often identified with an Emperor Napoleon, a Czar Peter, or a Chancellor Bismarck; even in democratic states where popular sentiment is inclined to be suspicious of truly positive leadership, the statesman's laurels are belatedly granted and to only a few—a Gladstone or a Churchill, a Jackson or a Lincoln. Yet however widely the control of political power may be distributed, the necessity for leadership remains. In fact, without it democracies tend to paralysis as quickly as other systems. Leaders must reflect national aspirations, organize them into practical programs, and show how they may be accomplished. "To make possible that which is necessary," has been described as the leader's ultimate test. It is he who assumes the initiative in the decision-making process. We have earlier noted that the historical origins of political authority are closely associated with the exercise of leadership; despite the elaboration of organs which has taken place in subsequent centuries, the executive continues to be the "mainspring of government."

One of the great merits of the cabinet type of executive as developed in Great Britain is its effectiveness in encouraging—indeed, requiring—positive leadership. The process by which the British Prime Minister reaches that office is arduous and selective. He must expect to undergo a decade or two of service in the House of Commons, learning to speak and to negotiate persuasively. He will serve an apprenticeship as minister in one or more cabinets, demonstrating sufficient qualities of administrative efficiency to bring his appointment to one of the major departments of government. To make the last step to the prime ministership, he must become the choice of his colleagues to lead his party, whether in office or in opposition. As Professor Harold Laski pointed out, "no simple man has ever been Prime Minister of England," and the Prime Minister who fails to continue to lead with the necessary energy, judgment, and efficiency does not remain in that office. The head of a British government must have both legislative and administrative policies; he must be able to sustain not only the loyalty of his cabinet colleagues and the backbenchers of his party but the confidence of the public as well. When the Prime Minister does not lead, the entire machinery of government begins to idle.

The situation of the American President in this respect is rather different. The method by which he is nominated and elected, and the popular interpretation of what qualities an acceptable presidential candidate must display, neither require nor assure that the President will necessarily have either natural or practiced ability as a political leader. Indeed, a long and successful career at the center of national politics in Congress has often been considered a handicap to an aspiring candidate. Although a presidential nominee must somehow have identified himself with his party, he cannot be said as a rule to have become its national leader until he wins the presidential office and is able to employ its patronage and influence. The fact that the major American parties are really loose associations of state party organizations means that they will, at any time, have a number of state leaders rather than necessarily a single national one. Of course, an incumbent President is in a position to assert national leadership of his organization in a way that the various party chiefs in the states and in Congress cannot. He reaches a wider audience, as Professor Max Beloff observes, if only because "he also has more interesting and important things to say." The President's party leadership provides him a major means of exerting a unifying influence over the government—primarily the executive branch—and encourages collaboration with the individual state administrations controlled by the same party. Nowhere does his dominance of the party organization become more apparent than at the national convention held toward the end of his term of office, when he is able, if not to dictate his own renomination, substantially to influence the choice of his successor. It is worth noting that the outstanding American presidents have been strong party men; the less successful have been those who have seen the party organization break from their control, or who never mastered it at all.

In the modern dictatorships it is through the party, we have noted, that the dictator asserts and exercises his political leadership. The dictator tends to place more emphasis upon his role as party leader than upon his official post in the government. Mussolini as *Il Duce* of the Fascist party, Hitler as *Der Führer* of the Nazi party, and Stalin, "the great leader and teacher" of the Communist party, were in each case stressing the prime basis for their popular appeal. The dictatorships, indeed, make a fetish of leadership, proclaiming always as their especial virtue that they direct the destinies of the incompetent masses by placing the state under the control of the "true aristocrat." Hitler argued in *Mein Kampf,* for example, that rule by the principle of parliamentary majorities leads to the destruction of the idea of leadership, and that the state should be so constructed that the authority of leadership runs downward and responsibility upward. Undoubtedly, a most significant factor in the success of the dictator as a popular leader is that he has first become the master of a party organization. The years he devotes to organizational work, to winning the loyalty of a dedicated band of adherents, and the struggles with factionalism, underground intrigue, or "cold" civil war, all give him an exceptional schooling.

Policy Formation and Legislative Leadership. It is a common American belief—arising from a misconception of the true functioning of government—that the power of policy formation properly and necessarily belongs only to the legislature. Legislatures, so this simplified version of the governmental process goes, make laws and policies; executives merely carry them out. This view is hardly realistic. In these times, the executive can adequately discharge his responsibilities only if he himself first formulates and initiates policies—many of which, to be sure, may subsequently be presented to the legislature for criticism, modification, acceptance, or rejection. There are several reasons why this must be the case. First, the executive head of the government often has the only adequate sources of information that permit policy proposals which envision the whole national interest. Second, rapid changes in the course of events are produced by economic fluctuations, international crises, and war, so that the executive is constantly required to act upon matters over which a legislative decision would come too slowly. Modern legislatures are thus obliged increasingly to enact their legislation in general terms, leaving to executive determination the immediate application of principles to individual times and circumstances. Third, several of the most important government functions—those related to foreign and military affairs, especially—require a large exercise of administrative discretion. A legislature is scarcely organized to negotiate international agreements or to command military forces. To sum up, legislatures enact laws, but they look increasingly to the executive to propose their terms and to supply the information upon which they are based. Again, a legislature can establish administrative agencies, but the executive must determine the policies under which they operate; a legislature may declare war, but the executive must wage it. In each case, the executive clearly determines policy of the highest importance.

The British parliamentary executive is most definitely organized to assume responsibility for policy formation. The Cabinet, under the leadership of the Prime Minister, has distinct and undivided responsibility for all matters of policy, both legislative and administrative. Not only does the Cabinet formulate plans for the conduct of the government's business, but it prepares and presents a legislative program to which most of the time of Parliament is devoted. The British tendency, indeed, is to look upon the parliamentary function as one primarily to promote or criticize the effecting of Cabinet policies. The Parliament thus enacts much of its legislation in general terms, leaving to executive discretion the establishment of the circumstances whereunder it is to apply and, in some cases, even what the specific terms shall be. This is not to say, however, that these considerable executive powers have no accompanying responsibilities. As we have observed, the Cabinet is politically responsible to the House of Commons for all administrative acts and policies.

Although some of the largest areas of the American President's discretion are in the fields of foreign and military affairs, which are discussed below, vastly important ones in the field of domestic affairs also belong to him. American experience, like British, has conferred upon the executive a considerable amount of policy-making authority—well beyond that associated with the performance of narrow administrative functions. Part of this authority derives by implication from the Constitution, but considerably more is conferred by act of Congress. Although Congress may not delegate its legislative power to the President, strictly speaking, it may still grant him extensive policy-making functions, provided always it establishes some defined limits within which the President is to act. Some presidents in the past have, of course, taken a modest view of their responsibility to provide legislative leadership. Construing their duties as essentially ministerial ones, they have been content to let Congress muster such leadership as it can from within its own ranks. Such an attitude has been possible because the presidental system, unlike the cabinet system, will at least allow it; indeed, the makers of the Constitution in some respects seem to have intended it. As a consequence, the quality of leadership provided by the American President has depended largely upon his individual personality and temperament. Some have given full play to the potentialities of the office and their own talents as well; others have minimized their role. Increasingly, however, demands of the times have obliged recent presidents to take steps to lead public opinion in many matters, to advocate policies on subjects of major public concern, and to press Congress to take action—in short, to provide a national governmental voice in public affairs.

The exercise of the policy-making function in a dictatorship is essentially confined to the dictator and the narrow group around him. By its very nature, dictatorship precludes any wide sharing of authority, and leaves to the executive complete freedom of action. To be sure, after the establishment of dictatorships in Fascist Italy and Nazi Germany, the national legislatures were not abolished, and in the Soviet Union one was created, but in no sense was policy formation turned over to them. Rather, composed of hand-picked members, they have been employed as a convenient stage fixture before which the dictator can appear, creating the illusion of popular representation without granting its substance. The actual process of policy making must take place beyond the public gaze, and for this reason we do not know a great deal about it. The dictator obviously makes some important decisions himself; for others, he may consult his principal lieutenants, in some cases individually, in others collectively. There is even evidence that in certain circumstances the dictator delegates a share of authority to each of several competing underlings, and lets policy emerge from the results of the clash for power. At all events, executive decrees provide the most important form of legislation, and the legislature need not be consulted at all.

Supervision of Administration. In the supervision of administration the executive releases the initial energy, which is conveyed to the machinery of government and makes its wheels turn. Although the functions of policy formation and administrative management are closely related, as we have suggested, it is one thing to decide what to do and another to do it. The latter responsibility is clearly that of the administrative branch of the government which, headed by the chief executive, looks to him as the ultimate source of inspiration and authority. Only in a very limited degree is the chief executive an administrator himself. Given the large demands on his time and energy, only a portion of them can be devoted to the problems of administrative management; actual performance rests with his subordinates. But the chief executive must make some important initial decisions as to what and what not to do; to decide which laws and policies are to be applied and enforced vigorously; to set the tone and direction of government action; to co-ordinate a multitude of actions so as to produce a reasonably harmonious result; and to judge finally whether a majority of the citizens as the ultimate consumers of government action are benefited by and satisfied with the results. These are tasks which no subordinate administrative official can perform. And no matter how brilliantly the chief executive may conceive political policies, if he cannot have them translated into appropriate action, he has failed.

The British Prime Minister has in the Cabinet an admirable instrument for the supervision of administration. Composed of the principal majority party leaders, it controls the executive branch and co-ordinates its various ministries. Given the Prime Minister's central position, he need not go far to make his influence felt. Within the Cabinet is decided what legislation is needed to effect particular policies, while individual cabinet members see that their departments carry them out in appropriate relation to the government's program as a whole. The Prime Minister commands the "patronage" of the government, appointing and removing the principal officers, and is generally consulted in the selection of the senior permanent officials as well. Through the intermediary of the Treasury, he further exerts his influence; government operations require finance, and no ministry spends money or hires personnel without Treasury consent. Parliament has no share in the performance of these administrative functions. Formally, it can examine administrative actions through parliamentary questions, inquiries, and debates, but the vast detail of administrative management passes unnoticed or unchallenged.

The American President, like the British Prime Minister, is concerned as a chief executive to oversee the performance of administrative functions. The Constitution stipulates that he shall "take care that the laws be faithfully executed," and vests in him "the executive power." This delegation of authority is made in such broad terms that the Supreme Court has concluded that the President is responsible not only for the enforcement of acts of Congress and treaties, but also for "the rights, duties and obligations growing out of the Constitution itself, our international relations, and all the protection implied by the nature of the government under the Constitution." The President appoints most important officers of the national government; except where Congress has provided otherwise in a few instances, he also removes them at his discretion. He issues rules and regulations for the civil, diplomatic, and armed services; and, in many areas of concern even to ordinary citizens, promulgates codes and orders.

The President's powers of administrative supervision are no less than those of the British Prime Minister, but he is subject to a greater degree of legislative check in the exercise of some of them. Thus, almost all important federal officers are appointed with "the advice and consent" of the Senate. While appointments to the higher national offices are subjected to varying degrees of scrutiny, those to federal offices in the states are controlled by the practice of "senatorial courtesy." This means that the Senate will not approve appointments of such officers as United States district attorneys, collectors of customs, and court officials, unless the Senators from the state concerned have been consulted, or have themselves proposed the selection.

For the dictatorships, the problem of administrative supervision is even greater than for democratic states. Obviously, if the aims of the dictatorship are to be realized, there must be the most complete conformity to the leader's policies throughout the administration from top to bottom. A less obvious reason, however, originates in the magnitude of government machinery, which must perform not only normal state functions but extends its control to the economic, cultural, social, and even personal life of the individual. It is noteworthy that aspiring dictators usually level their guns at "the bureaucracy," "the red tape," and "the inefficiency" of the democratic system; yet when they come to power themselves, they invariably bring into existence an even more monstrous apparatus for the performance of state functions. One need not look deeply into the operation of dictatorial regimes to discover all of the usual administrative shortcomings, such as lack of responsiveness and imagination, extreme devotion to precedent and routine, and fear of individual responsibility and initiative, but frequently as well, the more extreme vices of arrogance, extravagance, and corruption. The dictator uses the power of appointment, removal, direction, and ordinance-making to keep the machinery of government in order; to these routine techniques of supervision, he commonly adds such devices as co-ordination through the single-party monopoly, personnel purges and reshufflings, intensive propaganda, and internal espionage and terrorism.

Diplomatic and Military Powers. Diplomatic and military functions have always been among the most important of executive duties, in earlier history as exclusive prerogatives of the monarch, and still today as those responsibilities practically amenable only to a single authority. Both functions are vitally related to the security of the state; they require decisiveness, dispatch, consistency, and a measure of secrecy in their performance. To no small degree the exercise of the one function is complementary to the other. The principal diplomatic powers are those of sending and receiving diplomatic representatives, including the power to recognize new governments, determine foreign policy, and negotiate and ratify treaties and agreements. The major military powers include those of commanding the armed forces, declaring and waging war, and proclaiming a state of martial law. While these powers are usually considered in democratic states as too momentous to be turned over to a single individual, their monopolistic exercise by the executive is an unvarying characteristic of dictatorship.

The control of diplomatic and military affairs has always been among the prerogatives of the British Crown, but long exercised in the monarch's name by the Prime Minister and Cabinet. Although Parliament possesses some ultimate check upon policies in these areas through the general operation of the principle of ministerial responsibility, it has not gained anything like the direct share in their determination enjoyed by the American Congress. The broad lines of foreign policy are shaped by the Cabinet under the principal influence of the Prime Minister and the Foreign Secretary. While the latter official selects most nominees for diplomatic appointment, the most important are chosen in consultation with the Prime Minister. Treaties and other international agreements are negotiated and ratified solely by executive authority; strictly speaking, no parliamentary approval is required for ratification, but it is the practice to lay important ones before the House of Commons in advance of such action, so that any objections may be raised and aired. Of course, if an agreement requires legislative action to implement it—and many do—legislative approval must ultimately be obtained. In the same way, a declaration of war is strictly an executive act, but no British Cabinet would take such a step without the knowledge that Parliament would stand behind it; prosecution of the war would not long be possible without parliamentary provision of necessary funds and legislation. The armed forces are at the disposal of the Cabinet, though commanded in the name of the sovereign. A Prime Minister must give considerable attention to their organization and disposition in peacetime, and during war they become, of course, his principal concern. In this connection, the historic determination of the British to keep the military forces under a degree of popular control is represented in the still effective requirement of the Bill of Rights making it unlawful for the Crown to raise or maintain a standing army in peacetime without parliamentary consent. To maintain order in extreme cases of domestic emergency, the executive may declare a state of martial law and employ military forces to support governmental authority.

The American President has chief responsibility for the formulation and execution of foreign policy. By constitutional authorization he appoints diplomatic representatives, receives those from abroad, and negotiates and ratifies treaties. His role in the field of foreign policy is, to be sure, partly what he wants to make it: some presidents have preferred to be, in effect, their own Secretary of State, while others have left to that official wide latitude in managing such affairs. The attachment of the President's name to such policies as the Monroe Doctrine, the Truman Doctrine, or the Eisenhower Doctrine, suggests how close the President must be to this function. Yet the President's authority is not absolute. The Constitution provides that he can ratify a treaty only with the consent of two-thirds of the Senate, and that body has been inclined to be most assertive of its right to approve. His appointment of ambassadors, ministers, and consuls also requires consent of the Senate.

The President does enjoy exclusive command over the armed forces, however; the Constitution designates him commander-in-chief of the armed services, and of the National Guard when the latter is called into federal service. Under this cloak of authority, the President can appoint officers, issue and enforce regulations, and make almost any disposition of the armed services he sees fit, but the Constitution still reserves to Congress the formal power to declare war. In wartime, Congress confers additional authority on the President, so that he may effectively defend the country, to such an extent that he has it within his discretion to command practically all resources of the nation.

Dictatorships invariably emphasize alteration of the international status quo, and incline toward national aggrandizement and militarism, so the dictator's preoccupation with diplomatic and military affairs may be expected. Dictatorial action almost inevitably maximizes the strength of the state for war, whether or not hostilities are viewed as imminent. The dictator must be assured of the complete loyalty, in a very immediate sense, of the armed forces—not only so that he will have all necessary force to maintain his power and resist internal opposition to his regime, but so that he can enjoy the advantages of accomplished military mobilization when he is dealing with other, less well-prepared states. Under these circumstances the diplomatic service of a dictatorship functions largely as an intelligence agency, as well as a propaganda corps, for the regime. Both become completely co-ordinated for the dictator's purposes; interference from other sources cannot be permitted. The usual devices of supervision over the diplomatic service are adequate for his purposes, but the dictator's control of the armed services is a much more difficult problem. Mass armies in the modern state may well come to constitute centers of power in themselves—particularly in states where traditions of effective civilian control are lacking—and, in domestic controversies over influence and power, can obviously get out of hand. To win and hold the personal loyalty of the military forces, therefore, the dictatorships have resorted to devices ranging from generous bribes to ferocious purges of the high commands. The lower ranks in the forces dare not be neglected either, as the Soviet army's use of political commissars and the Nazi systems of youth indoctrination suggest. But whatever the precautions, the relations between the dictators and their armed services are frequently uneasy.

Judicial Functions. A few of the functions commonly conferred upon the executive have a judicial character. The executive is commonly authorized to appoint judges. More immediate to the administration of justice, however, the executive is usually authorized to exercise clemency in the application of legal punishment. This takes the form of power to grant reprieves and pardons, as a means both of mitigating possible severity of judicial sentence in the interests of justice or mercy, and of rectifying judicial error when the liberty of the individual is at stake. Of course, these considerations are largely disregarded in a dictatorship.

In Great Britain, the power of pardon is a prerogative of the Queen, but actually exercised by the Home Secretary. The latter may also reduce sentences, fines, and terms of imprisonment. Judges are appointed in the name of the Crown, and derive their authority from it. The higher judges may be removed from office by Crown authority, but only after a formal request from Parliament.

The American President is authorized by the Constitution to grant reprieves and pardons to offenders against federal law, except in cases of impeachment. He may also grant an amnesty, which is the pardon of a whole group. The President appoints all federal judges, but they may be removed from office only after conviction following impeachment by Congress.

Since dictatorships have no intention of maintaining an independent judiciary, the exercise there of any judicial functions by the executive has considerably less significance. In the Soviet Union, for example, judges are elected—those of the Supreme Court of the U.S.S.R. by the Supreme Soviet, those to the lower courts by the soviets of the republics and regions, and locally by the people. But in either case, judges are closely supervised by the administrative apparatus and the Communist party, both as to their political reliability and the performance of their duties. The Presidium of the Supreme Soviet is granted exercise of the right of pardon, according to the Constitution, and the further power, partaking somewhat of judicial review, to annul decisions and orders of the councils of ministers, both all-union and republican. Cases involving failures of party discipline, ideological heresy, or "treason," are subject to trial and punishment by special tribunals, with neither appeal nor pardon allowed.

IV. *The* GROWTH *of* MODERN EXECUTIVE POWER

One of the most striking aspects of modern government is the constant tendency toward aggrandizement of the executive. In the extreme, the process has been consummated in the creation of dictatorship, where governmental powers are concentrated entirely in the executive's hands. Yet in such countries, no sharp break with precedent can be marked. Dictatorships, as we have noted, have generally been instituted where there has been little previous experience with representative institutions, where the legislature has held little or no real share in the political process, and where executive supremacy has long been traditional.

The appearance of similar tendencies of executive expansion in states where democratic institutions have been firmly established, however, is more noteworthy and, from some points of view, more worrisome. Several centuries of British constitutional controversy were devoted to establishing the principle of parliamentary supremacy over the monarch as the embodiment of executive power. Yet the present century has seen executive authority again grow apace. Through the Defence of the Realm Acts of World War I and the Emergency Powers (Defence) Act of World War II, adopted to give the Cabinet full powers to prosecute the war effectively, Parliament surrendered a large segment of its legislative authority. Though most of these extraordinary powers were relinquished after the end of hostilities, the executive nevertheless gained on balance. Further, the nationalizing of large portions of the British economy under the control of public corporations, and the continuing tendency to allow the Cabinet to legislate by means of administrative rules and orders, have brought a renewal of complaints against a "new despotism."

In like manner, the political disputes between American colonists and the English king were most bitter over the pretensions of royal authority, and led the framers of the American Constitution to elaborate a variety of arrangements to prevent an excessive concentration of power in the executive. Yet there has been a substantial and continuing enlargement of the powers of the American presidency. The mobilization of the nation during two World Wars brought tremendous augmentation of the President's authority—powers to control transportation, communications, manpower, foodstuffs, and raw materials. Almost as important in enlarging the scope of this office were the authorizations of the New Deal years, when the President was given substantial new power to levy war upon the economic depression. And urgent as the need was for vigorous executive action, no President who used his full authority during these crises escaped frequent charges of "dictatorship."

In still another example, we see in France of the Fifth Republic an expansion of the President's powers to such a degree that it is questionable whether "parliamentary government" is truly continued. The power relationship between the executive and legislative branches is distinctly shifted to the advantage of the former. The President makes a personal choice of the Premier, and cabinets are far less subject to parliamentary control than was the case with previous regimes. The President's power to dissolve the National Assembly is increased, and at the same time that body's right to delay action on the budget or other major pieces of legislation is reduced. An unprecedented clause in the Constitution gives the French President power to assume virtually unlimited authority to govern in time of emergency. To be sure, there seems little alternative to these constitutional innovations in France, reflecting as they do a reaction to the inability of the executive, in the declining years of the Fourth Republic, to govern at all. Thus, we find at the present that the executive in Great Britain, the United States, and France—to take but three examples—is, historically considered, at the apex of its powers. What, then, is the significance of these developments?

The Demand for Positive Leadership. Essentially, the continuing extension of executive activity is an accompaniment of the extension of all governmental activity. Modern government has been obliged to discard its earlier negative role in the community, the modest "night-watchman's function," and is now held responsible for providing positive leadership; because the executive alone of the three branches can perform this function of leadership with any degree of effectiveness, the results seem inevitable. Much of the executive's increased power is the result of legislative conferment of discretion upon him. Wherever legislative action is inappropriate to determine policy dependent upon narrowly technical findings, or where a high degree of flexibility in policy is necessary, or where the situation to be regulated is subject to frequent change, legislative bodies are inevitably inclined to leave a large share of policy application, even policy determination, to executive discretion. Again, the accelerated frequency of war and international crisis in the present century has tremendously increased executive authority. There seems here also no alternative to placing in his hands responsibility for the security of the state when it is threatened or attacked, since total war requires nothing less than the mobilization of all the state's resources at the executive's command. We should not overlook, too, the fact that all attempts to cope with modern economic crises have also extended executive power. It has become commonplace to allow the executive a wide choice of means to resuscitate the national economy when it verges on collapse. Most new functions of government fall upon the executive, and the expansion of these, requiring as they now do the services of millions of government employees and the expenditure of colossal sums of money, also tends to enhance the power of the executive who commands them. Finally, the executive assumption of the role of representative and spokesman for the nation as a whole, standing above the obvious discords produced in the multimember legislative body, assures him a central position in, and unrivaled influence over, the governmental process.

The Danger of Dictatorship? It seems clear, therefore, that leadership in modern democratic government must come from the chief executive and, given modern conditions, he must be a powerful one. It should not be surprising, therefore, that opposition to such a development arises from those who see, or profess to see, a growing identity between the powers of dictatorial and democratic executives. Can the charge of "dictator," frequently leveled at democratic executives in recent years, be sustained?

A re-examination of the observations made earlier in this chapter ought now to make clear that there are some very important differences between executives in democratic and dictatorial states. One lies in the source of their powers: the democratic executive has great authority because it has been conferred upon the office he holds by constitutional and legislative authorization, and not because of a self-assumption of authority to make his rule more absolute. A democratic executive's authority may be reduced if public opinion wishes it; this is not so in the case of the dictator. The democratic executive's powers are not unlimited, but must be exercised in prescribed ways and through designated officials; they will be subjected to legislative, and perhaps judicial, review. The democratic executive has achieved his powers because government has become an active force in social and economic affairs, seeking to equalize opportunities for all citizens and to promote the general well-being. This is in sharp contrast to the dictator's essential objective of maximizing his state's power, or his own. Finally, the democratic executive is a responsible one, subject to removal from office by popular decision. Here the contrast is the greatest of all.

So long, therefore, as the democratic executive is responsible and responsive to popular control, achieving his position within the framework of established constitutional arrangements, and performing his duties in accordance with the law, the concentration of authority he represents is not in itself a threat to democratic institutions or processes. The dictator appears after, and not before, representative and responsible government fails. Indeed, the absence of adequate executive power and the failure of the executive to provide leadership are far greater dangers to the successful continuation of democracy. Abraham Lincoln succinctly expressed the common dilemma of executive power when he asked, in 1864, "whether any government, not too strong for the liberties of its people, can be strong enough to maintain its existence in great emergencies." Obviously, a careful balancing is required if we are to avoid both of these extremes.

CHAPTER 10

The LEGISLATURE

THE SECOND traditional branch of government in our consideration is the legislative. At the outset, three significant aspects must be observed: First, the term "legislature" has long been used to designate a body of persons who propose, alter, and make laws. Actually, however, various organs of government may perform or participate in this function, so the modern legislature does not monopolize the activity. Besides, it now undertakes a number of additional functions in the governmental process. Nonetheless, lawmaking—a very great power in itself—is the principal and primary preserve of the legislature, and all of its activities relate in some manner to that process. Thus it is much more limited in its scope of action and responsibility than the executive branch.

Second, a most important aspect of the legislature lies in its representative character: fundamentally the legislature represents the people. It is intended primarily to be a source of popular views respecting public policy, rather than expert ones. We expect that the legislature will represent a broad range of experience and knowledge, reflecting the extensive diversity of personality, interest, and judgment of the peoples themselves. All efforts at devising acceptable systems of democratic representation are therefore necessarily directed at securing a recognizable reflection of public opinion and assuring a wide popular support of public policy. At the same time, the structure of the legislature also reflects a certain distrust of popular opinion—the unpredictable passions of the people—and various devices invariably are applied in the attempt to limit possible excesses and abuses in the exercise of legislative authority, and to protect other values.

Third, the legislature has been the indispensable organ of democratic government. Here the reader may usefully recall discussion of the relation between representation and democracy in the second part of Chapter 3. The alternatives to representative assemblies have long seemed to be only two: a system of direct democracy, which is scarcely practicable in modern times, or a system of absolutism, which is the obvious negation of popular government. Hence, the growth of modern democracy has been indissolubly linked with the extension both of legislative authority in the governmental process and popular participation in the election of legislators. Yet indispensable as the representative assembly was to the eighteenth- and nineteenth-century development of democratic government, in the present century its competence, efficiency, integrity, and even its representativeness have been increasingly criticized. Of course, democracy did not invent the representative assembly; it merely adapted it to newer objectives. We thus have the paradox that, although the representative assembly is the most characteristic feature of democratic government, it was not invented as a democratic institution and is increasingly found wanting in the contemporary democratic process. All these aspects of the legislative institution will be further examined.

I. *The* DEVELOPMENT *of the* LEGISLATURE

The modern legislative assembly, dating only from the seventeenth century, is manifestly of more recent origin than the organs of the two other major branches of government. Unlike the executive, the history of the legislature does not present an essentially unbroken continuity of institutions with authority and governing power; and, its significant development has come much later than that of the judiciary. Legislatures in the modern sense could come into existence only after there was a relatively advanced differentiation of governmental functions and a considerable degree of popular political sophistication. Of course, from the time of the ancient empires, consultative bodies of some kind, created to advise and assist the ruler, were commonplace. Such bodies were not representative in the modern sense; they did not "stand for" all particular interests and individuals. However constituted, they were generally presumed to express the "consent"—often required—of the people to certain acts of the ruler. In addition, they broadened the base of influence and information that contributed to the determination of the ruler's will. They were the earliest forerunners of the legislature, and we may examine their development briefly.

Greece. Although the ancient Greeks did not develop what we today would consider to be representative government, they did have various legislative institutions and were not unfamiliar with the function of representation. The greatest advance in such institutions came during the classical age in Athens. The popular organ, the *Ekklesia* or Assembly, brought together all adult male citizens who would attend—six thousand or so from all classes of society. Most of these assembly discussions were dominated by a few leaders, it appears, but all members were entitled to be heard and to vote.

The Assembly heard all important discussions of policy: control of foreign relations; treaties, alliances, questions of peace and war; apportionment of funds for public enterprises, temples, statues, roads, ships; pronouncement of ostracism, whereby leaders suspected of tyrannical ambitions were sent into exile; and election and supervision of magistrates. Ten times a year, all state officials were obliged to appear before the Assembly to account for the performance of their duties. The discovery of any irregularities was an occasion for a judicial trial of the offender. Powerful though it was, the Assembly was subject to some restraint; few measures appeared before it which had not been prepared and previously discussed by the Council, and a speaker who moved an illegal action was subject to punishment. Further, its decrees were always subordinate, theoretically at least, to the customary law.

The senate, or Council of Five Hundred, was composed of citizens thirty years of age or over chosen by lot for one-year terms, fifty each from the ten Athenian tribes. This body, functioning somewhat as an executive committee of government, heard reports, received foreign envoys, prepared measures for the Assembly, and issued decrees effecting Assembly decisions. This is as close as the Greeks came to the representative principle; selection by lot was considered to provide a fair sample of the citizenry. Practically, of course, the Council's functions were more nearly administrative than legislative; it was a body significant more for its influence than for its authority.

Rome. Roman experience did not carry the representative process substantially farther. Well before historic times, the Romans must have accustomed themselves to convening popular assemblies composed of all men of military age. Through the period of Rome's development from monarchy to republic, an assembly, or *Comitia,* was constituted variously on the basis of civil, military, or tribal organizations. The functions of the *Comitia* were not too precisely determined, and changed with the times. During the monarchy, for example, it elected the king, considered such matters as he placed before it, and performed certain religious and judicial functions. Still later, the *Comitia* became the lawmaking organ of the republic, and elected the higher magistrates. All of the assemblies made their decisions by majority vote—the votes being given by acclamation—but of the component units represented, rather than as individuals. They had no regular schedule of meetings, but were summoned by the appropriate officials as the occasion demanded and as the *augurs* indicated the omens were favorable. The members themselves neither initiated proposals nor debated them.

Opposed to this democratic element in Roman government existed an aristocratic element, the Senate. Herein both the wealthy and supposedly politically wise elements of the community were given representation. Appointed originally by the king as an advisory council, the members were later chosen by the consuls or censors from among the ex-magistrates. Senators seem to have been appointed for life, enjoyed rank according to the importance of elective offices previously held, and were selected as men of independent means and experience in public affairs, who could devote full time to civic matters. The size of the Senate varied, ranging from some three hundred members in its earlier history to an eventual six hundred.

Like those of the *Comitia,* the powers of the Senate were not precisely determined. Strictly speaking, it did not have legislative powers; its decrees were addressed to the magistrates, and it was more of an administrative body than anything else. It gave preliminary approval to matters to be laid before the Assembly, devoted particular attention to military and foreign affairs, appropriated money, and appointed certain officials. As Rome extended its empire and engaged in long struggles with its enemies, the Senate came increasingly to occupy a central role in the political process, absorbing slowly more and more of the powers of government as the only body capable of administering the complex affairs of state. With the beginning of the Christian era, the power of the Senate began to recede, however, as the absolute authority of the emperors increased, though it continued as a consultative body long after the popular assemblies had lost any significant functions.

Thus, the institutions and practices of Greece and Rome bear some analogies to those of the modern legislative process, but cannot be considered as their ancient counterpart. Athenian government was democratic in the sense that it was in the hands of the majority of its citizens, but in a direct and not representative sense. The *Ekklesia* was viewed as the citizens functioning in their deliberative capacity and not as a sovereign legislative body. Under the Roman republic, the *Comitia* was considered the sole legislative authority, but the political exercise of the lawmaking function passed in time to the smaller, aristocratic Senate, which was not at all popularly representative. In neither case did these institutions have precisely defined powers; their members had only limited rights of initiative and debate. Neither political parties nor internal organization developed. Consequently, their experience seems to have had little influence upon or relevance to subsequent legislative development.

The Middle Ages. The parliaments and councils which developed in medieval Europe were slow to achieve influence. Whether they owe their origination to Teutonic tribal institutions, to the practices of religious orders and church councils, or otherwise, is a matter of scholarly dispute. The government of the Germanic tribes described by the Roman historian Tacitus did include an assembly of freemen, known as the folkmoot, which discussed and decided all important questions. As the tribes were combined into larger kingdoms, these popular assemblies were replaced by councils of chieftains advising the king. But the facts we have do not demonstrate the exertion of any real influence on later developments; other circumstances, in combinations not clear to us, may well have been of greater importance.

At all events, rudimentary parliaments did not emerge until the fabric of European feudal society was thoroughly woven, and only the later middle ages saw the development of representative—though certainly not popular—institutions. Among the earliest, an Icelandic folkmoot or *Althing* functioned in the tenth century; a representative *Cortes* was convened in Spanish Aragon in 1133; and, the French Estates General appeared in the thirteenth century. So also did the English Parliament. Much of the background concerning the origins of the English Parliament, which would be interesting and useful to us, is simply unknown. There developed in Anglo-Saxon times a court of wise men, the *Witenagemot,* which had a variety of duties. This assembly of the chief men of the state served as an advisory council to the king and participated in functions we would today describe as legislative and judicial. After the Norman conquest this assembly was shaped by the Norman rulers into the *Magnum Concilium,* or Great Council. Composed initially of the great nobles, lay and clerical, after the middle of the thirteenth century, Parliament included with increasing frequency knights from the counties and burgesses from the towns, summoned by the kings to "council and consent" with respect to the business of the kingdom. Thus were the basic elements of Parliament assembled; in the fourteenth century its organization took firm shape and its powers grew substantially. These medieval bodies, even so, possessed no true legislative powers, but were convoked irregularly by the kings to approve taxes and to consult on matters of high policy. They represented not the population as a whole but the recognized estates, or classes with established legal and economic status, such as the clergy, the nobility, or the burgesses. In Sweden, four estates sat in separate houses with rural freemen set apart; in France, three; and in Scotland, a single house sufficed. The English bicameral Parliament derived from the broad division of represented class interests into two, Lords and Commons, and thus set the pattern most widely adopted by modern legislatures. Though imperfectly, the concept of representation began to be established in this period.

National Legislatures. The emergence of monarchical absolutism in Europe inevitably produced the decline or virtual reduction to impotence of most of these incipient national assemblies. After 1614, the Estates General of France was not convened again until 1789, on the eve of the revolution. The Russian national assembly was not summoned after 1649; soon thereafter the German Diets were reduced to insignificance. Perhaps such an eclipse was a necessary step in the evolution toward modern legislatures, as the absolute monarchs devoted themselves to the struggle against the privileged estates and their institutions. National unification of the many feudal units was a prerequisite to the existence of truly national parliaments. The augmentation of monarchical power next brought the rulers into direct conflict with the middle classes; as the extent of governmental activity and expense increased, bourgeois demand for a share in its control, commensurate with their growing economic interests in the nation, became inevitable. National legislatures were thus to become the vehicle through which an increasing degree of popular participation in government and a counterbalancing of the ruler's power could be achieved.

In a history of uneven development, England led the way. The thirteenth-century summoning of knights and burgesses to Parliament opened the way for a representation of commoners that could later be substantially broadened, and the power of Parliament was augmented as well. In the sixteenth century, having forced the King to assent regularly to its petitions as a condition for the granting of taxes, Parliament was able to exercise an increasingly influential share in the lawmaking process. In 1689 it deposed one monarch and bestowed the crown upon another, asserting its ultimate supremacy as spokesman for the nation. In France a legislative assembly was created after the revolution, in 1791, though full parliamentary government was not to be securely established until—after a number of false starts—the Third Republic emerged in 1871.

The institution of republican government in the United States also constituted an important landmark in the development of modern legislatures. In an extreme reaction to monarchical rule, and encouraged by the experience with the colonial assemblies as balance-weights against the English kings and colonial governors, the Americans sought initially to make their legislative bodies the paramount organ of government. Indeed, under the ill-fated national government of the Articles of Confederation, Congress was made the sole organ of government, to the exclusion of either a separate executive or federal courts; even under the Constitution of 1789, Congress was still intended to be the popular and most conspicuous organ.

By the early part of the nineteenth century, then, modern parliamentary institutions had developed in Great Britain, and had been installed in France and the United States, as well as in some of the smaller European countries, the Netherlands, Switzerland, and Sweden. By the close of the century, they had also emerged in Italy, Germany, Austria-Hungary, and Japan, though they lacked in these countries sufficient power and influence to control the executive. And not until 1906 was an elected body with a small share in the governing process, the *Duma,* convened in Russia—soon to be swept away by the 1917 revolution. In non-European areas there were some gains; national legislatures emerged in Canada, South Africa, Australia, and New Zealand, as these portions of the British empire gained autonomy. In Latin America, by contrast, the development of effective legislative institutions proved less successful.

In the post-World War I period, the increase of the European republics from two to seventeen in number saw the national legislature still more widely installed as an essential organ of modern governmental machinery, and optimistic observers believed that the victory of representative government was now practically complete. Yet any universality for the popular representative legislature was to prove illusory; within the next decade a majority of European legislatures had at best seriously declined in prestige or at worst become the pliant tools of dictatorial regimes. Only in those states where the roots of representative institutions ran deep into national history were they to survive.

The years following World War II did not prove to be an era of new flowering for parliamentary institutions. In Great Britain and the United States, Parliament and Congress proved equal to the challenge of supporting an effective prosecution of the national war effort, and were able to supervise an orderly peacetime restoration of the normal balance between executive and legislative authority. Both bodies, however, undertook extensive internal reorganization at the end of the war. The newly liberated countries of western Europe, Belgium, the Netherlands, Norway, Denmark, and France, all resumed popular government according to their respective national traditions, though in France of the Fourth Republic the attempt to reverse some of the less desirable of these did not succeed. The result has been a substantial reduction in the governmental role of the Parliament of the Fifth Republic.

The postwar regimes of Germany, Italy, Austria, and Japan established parliamentary systems, which have generally functioned with reasonable effectiveness; since they are yet untried by either unusual stress or long experience, however, they cannot be counted as successfully established for the future. At the same time, World War II permitted the Soviet Union to extinguish the independence—and thus the self-government—of the three small Baltic republics, Estonia, Latvia, and Lithuania, and shortly thereafter Communist dictatorships—euphemistically labeled "people's republics" or "people's democracies"—were procured in Albania, Bulgaria, Czechoslovakia, East Germany, Hungary, Poland, Romania, and Yugoslavia, as well as in China. In each case such regimes have obviously precluded any possibility of representative parliamentary government.

Whether, among the dozens of newly independent states that have emerged from colonial status during this period, and those which follow in the future, many will develop effective parliamentary systems, it is not yet possible to answer. Even among those relatively best qualified to do so, such as Israel, India, and the Philippine Republic, the ascent to stability is proving to be steep and perilous.

II. MODERN LEGISLATURES

After a brief history of the development of the legislative institution, we can now usefully describe the general character of several national legislatures before turning to an analysis of legislative organization, functions, and problems. This will give us some specific bodies to comment upon when we reach the discussion of the latter topics.

The British Parliament. The Parliament at Westminster, Britain's national legislature, easily deserves first attention here, not only because of its great age and continuous development, but because of its influence the world over in shaping the character of modern legislative bodies. The Queen in Parliament, as the formal term describes it, possesses the supreme legislative authority in the United Kingdom. Since the British have no documentary constitution, there are legally no limits to parliamentary authority, though there are traditional and practical ones, to be sure. Parliament can pass, amend, or repeal any law for all of the countries of the United Kingdom—England, Scotland, Wales, and Northern Ireland, though there is also a separate Northern Ireland parliament which may legislate on certain matters.

The composition of the second chamber, the House of Lords, derives from the medieval principle of representing the great estates of the realm. Its membership may be divided into two principal groups: first, the Lords Temporal, which include a few Princes of royal blood; some nine hundred hereditary peers; the Lords of Appeal in Ordinary, that is, nine eminent judges who are appointed for life and who perform the judicial functions of the House of Lords; and, the life peers and peeresses, a small number of persons of "eminence and authority," also appointed to serve for life. Second, the Lords Spiritual, consisting of the Archbishops of Canterbury and York and twenty-four Bishops of the Church of England, serve for the length of their ecclesiastical office. Peers receive no salary for their service, though they may claim some modest expenses for attendance in the Lords.

By no stretch of the imagination can the House of Lords be considered a democratically constituted body; at best it represents a very narrow segment of the British population and its interests. Yet it is not merely the preserve of hereditary and aristocratic privilege. Its unrepresentative character is, indeed, largely mitigated by two factors: first, constitutional limitations prevent the Lords from exercising anything like equal power to that of the House of Commons; and second, by custom the actual work of the Lords is performed almost exclusively by "first-generation peers" and the life peers and peeresses—individuals who have been ennobled themselves rather than having inherited titles. These individuals have been honored in recognition of generally distinguished careers in the military, diplomatic, or civil service, or in the House of Commons, business, or the professions, thus bringing to the House of Lords a considerable knowledge and experience of public affairs. Peers with hereditary titles, and also without other qualifications, are neither obligated nor expected to attend. Most apply for "leave of absence," indicating they do not wish to participate in the work of the House.

Despite its large potential membership, then, the Lords as a working body is small. The requirement for a quorum is only three, and rarely are more than one hundred peers present at a sitting. Many of these will be so-called "government peers," individuals who are members of the ministry and are present in their official capacity. The Lord Chancellor, an important member of the government, presides, though unlike the Speaker of the Commons, he is partisan, speaking and voting on measures before the chamber. The daily sittings of the Lords last for only a few hours and debate is quite free; otherwise procedure is similar to that of the Commons.

The House of Commons is composed of 630 members, elected by universal suffrage from single-member constituencies with an average population of some seventy thousand people. Members of this house have a term of office for the life of a Parliament, a period not exceeding five years, since the law requires a general election at least that often; the members are paid for their services. As individual seats may become vacant in the interim they are filled at by-elections. With a few exceptions, and excluding of course members of the House of Lords, any British citizen who is of age may be elected to Commons. An interesting difference between the British and American qualifications for legislators is that there is no local residence requirement for a parliamentary candidate. The British view is that better candidates are obtained when they may be drawn from the nation at large, and that both voters and M.P.'s are encouraged to think more of national than of local interests.

The presiding officer of the Commons is the Speaker. Formally, his office is filled anew with each Parliament; actually the choice of a new Speaker is necessary only when the incumbent retires. The majority party will then put forward its candidate, but on his achieving the office, he will sever his party connections, and, unlike his American counterpart, thenceforward perform his functions with entire impartiality. Thereafter, he will be rechosen as long as he wishes to serve, and ordinarily has no difficulty in being re-elected to the House from his own constituency. His chief duty is to preside over Commons debates; he grants recognition to speak, makes rulings, announces votes, and keeps members in order and addressed to the subject under discussion. The importance and prestige of his office are considered very high, because he symbolizes the powers and dignity of the popular house of the Parliament.

The Commons has only a small number of standing committees, and except for the Scottish and Welsh Committees, they do not specialize as to subject matter, as do American ones. Their role in the legislative process is far more limited, since they receive bills only after they have been approved in principle by the House; they have no authority to undertake wholesale revision of bills, much less to throw them out entirely, and thus may concern themselves only with details of draftsmanship. Because the overwhelming proportion of bills is introduced by the Cabinet, these leaders are unwilling to permit other centers of legislative power to be organized.

The two houses of the British Parliament do not possess co-ordinate powers. It is to the House of Commons alone that the Cabinet answers for its political responsibility; the Lords cannot overturn a government. Further, the Lords' function in the legislative process is definitely restricted by the Parliament Acts of 1911 and 1949; accordingly, they have no power at all over money bills, that is, taxation and appropriation measures, and can interpose a delay of only one year to the adoption of other public bills, if the Commons should pass a desired bill twice. The Lords' principal contributions to the legislative process, therefore, are to serve as a revising body to improve, but not obstruct, legislation, and to provide a more leisurely forum in which to debate important issues for which Commons' time is lacking. Thus the Lords are relegated to a position of distinct inferiority, and the Commons is the real center of legislative power.

The United States Congress. The creation of a bicameral American Congress was obviously inspired by the two-house British Parliament, though the framers of the Constitution had further practical reasons. They wanted to prevent any organ of government from becoming all-powerful—hence the objective of having one house to serve as a "check" on the other; and they were obliged to resolve a controversy over whether Congress should represent the states equally or according to their population—a bicameral legislature could do both.

The Senate was intended as an "upper house," rather than as a "second chamber." The Constitution stipulated that it should be composed of two Senators from each state, and that no state should be deprived of equal representation in the Senate without that state's consent. Since large states and small alike have an equal vote in this body, its base of representation is undemocratic to that extent, though no longer is the Senate more representative of rural than of urban areas. Further, the Constitution originally provided that Senators were to be chosen, not by the people, but by state legislatures. The Seventeenth Amendment (1913) required the Senate to be popularly chosen, as was the House.

The one hundred Senators are elected at large from their states for six-year terms, approximately one-third at each biennial election. It is thus a continuous body whose composition will not likely change considerably as a result of any one election. The constitutional qualifications for being elected a Senator are not highly selective; one must have attained the age of thirty, been nine years a citizen of the United States, and be an inhabitant of the state from which he is chosen. Senators and Representatives receive equal salaries; liberal allowances for expenses are also provided them, somewhat more generously for Senators, in view of their larger number of constituents.

The presiding officer, the President of the Senate, is the Vice-President of the United States. Because of that body's tradition of full and free debate, and because he is not himself a Senator, the presiding officer has nothing like the powers of the Speaker of the House of Representatives. He thus has much less opportunity to assist his party in the legislative process. Because, too, the Senate is a comparatively small body, it does not require the elaborate organization and rules of the lower house. Its sixteen standing committees are centers of real power, and several of them can be included among the most influential bodies within the machinery of American government. Further, party discipline is considerably more relaxed than in the House. In all respects, the individual Senator counts for much more than the individual Representative.

The House of Representatives consists of 435 members elected from single-member districts into which the states are divided, containing an average of over 400,000 people. The House is intended to be directly representative of the people; seats are apportioned among the states according to their population as determined by each decennial census, with each state having at least one Representative, and election is by those persons who qualify in their states to vote for the "most numerous branch" of the state legislature.

To qualify for a seat in the House, the Constitution requires only that a member be at least twenty-five years of age, seven years a citizen of the United States, and an inhabitant of the state from which he is elected. There is no legal requirement that he must also be a resident of the congressional district, but custom has long insisted upon it. In this respect it is clear that the American party organizations and the voters are willing to support only a "local man," who must serve first the interests of the district. The fact that the term of office of the Representative is only two years further reinforces his obligation to be rather immediately responsive to the opinion of his constituents; otherwise, his congressional career will be brief.

In view of the size of the House—a body in which few individual members can expect to play a leading role—it has a more elaborate organization and more restrictive rules than does the Senate, both of which aim to ensure, as the House *Manual* says, that "a majority may work its will at all times in the face of the most determined and vigorous opposition of a minority." And, majority dominance begins at the top. The Speaker of the House enjoys extensive authority, not only from the rules of procedure, but because he is an influential leader of the majority party. As a frankly partisan officer, he has been elected to his office by

ABOVE: ". . . The legislature has the signal responsibility to review executive policies and actions; to publicize those which are inefficient, ineffectual or extravagant; to champion the cause of persons treated unjustly or arbitrarily; and to place the findings before the forum of public opinion." (p. 402) The Israeli Knesset in session. (*Israel Office of Information.*) BELOW: "In their constitutions these new states commonly have adopted the formal structure of western parliamentary bodies, but have discovered that something more is required to breathe life into them and to develop a parliamentary *esprit de corps.*" (p. 374) The Legislative Assembly of the Republic of Somalia. (*United Nations.*)

ABOVE: "Despite the fact that dictatorship constitutes the very negation of representative government, modern dictators have, paradoxically enough, managed to find at least a formal place in their system for the legislative institution." (p. 375) Deputies of the Yugoslav National Assembly hearing a report. (*Yugoslavian Information Service.*) BELOW: ". . . Public works and services, generally undertaken previously for quite limited purposes, have become both more numerous and of very broad impact in the life of the modern community." (p. 455) Government land reclamation projects in Japan are widely being undertaken in order to mitigate the land shortage problem of the country. (*Consulate-General of Japan, New York.*)

the majority party, and if party control of the House changes as the result of an election, he will be replaced. This is not to say that he uses the power of his position arbitrarily; in the performance of his function as presiding officer to grant recognition, put votes, make rulings, and keep order, he observes the House rules—which duly regard the right of the minority to be heard. To further the program of the majority, there are additional components of the party organization: the caucus, to make decisions on policy matters; the majority floor leader—field general and strategist of the majority forces; the whips, who function under the floor leader to marshal party members for crucial votes; the steering committee, which is headed by the floor leader and operates to supervise the majority party's legislative program; and the majority members of the House Rules Committee. The minority party, of course, organizes in similar fashion.

The House is also organized by an elaborate committee system, through which its work is primarily performed; indeed, the principal functions of the House as a whole are to take action upon its committees' recommendations. These are of several types: the select committee, created to consider some special question, of which type the committee of investigation is best known; the conference committee, appointed from members of both houses to reconcile differences between them when they disagree over a bill; the joint standing committee, to deal with matters of common concern to the two chambers, such as the printing of documents; and the standing committee. The last is the most important, organized on a permanent basis according to subjects of legislative action, for example, agriculture, armed services, foreign affairs, judiciary, and ways and means. The House has twenty of these committees, whose size ranges from nine to fifty members, constituted on a bipartisan basis roughly reflecting the strength of the two parties in the whole House. All bills introduced in the House must be referred to the relevant committee, which exercises powers of life and death over legislation. Memberships in the more influential committees, therefore, are eagerly sought.

A comparison of the functions of the two houses of Congress reveals a striking fact—that the upper house is manifestly the more powerful of the two. Among the second chambers of the world, only the American Senate enjoys this distinction of superiority. From the viewpoint of legislative authority, the houses stand virtually even; and although the Constitution specifies that "all bills for raising revenue shall originate in the

House," this has had little practical significance, since there is no limit upon the Senate's power to amend such bills. Shifting the balance in the other direction are the constitutional arrangements for several special Senate powers: it has the responsibility of trying impeachments, to consent to the President's ratification of treaties, and to consent to the appointment of thousands of officials of the federal government. Yet important as the latter two functions are in securing for the Senate a share in the executive control of patronage and foreign affairs, they do not alone account for the Senate's paramount position. Reasons are also to be found in the fact that the Senate is a smaller, hence more select, body and tends to attract abler and more experienced men; its members have longer terms, and may see both Presidents and House members come and go; and its members are in a position to speak for their entire state. These factors, then, combined with equality in legislative responsibility, make the Senate a national forum of unrivaled influence.

The French Parliament. The French have a long history of attempts to achieve a satisfactory equilibrium in government with a responsible and representative parliament as its base, demonstrating how difficult the problem may be for a nation torn by dissension over its fundamental goals, and how little the problem may be solved by alterations in the mechanics of government. The Parliament of the Third Republic (1875–1940), following the autocratic government of the Second Empire, was composed of two houses: the Chamber of Deputies, popularly elected, and the smaller Senate, indirectly elected. The houses enjoyed equal powers, practically speaking, with respect both to legislation and control of the executive. Though Parliament predominated among the organs of government, the two chambers functioned—undoubtedly more enthusiastically than intended—as a check upon each other, thus reflecting the dominant republican desire to avoid an overconcentration of political power. An ever-widening division among the French people, drawing them toward either the political left or right, however, made parliamentary operations increasingly ineffective. By the close of the 1930's, Parliament was widely held in low esteem within the country, and blamed for much of France's ills, especially the weakness of the executive.

At the end of World War II, the French electorate voted overwhelmingly to replace the governmental system of the Third Republic. Under the leadership of the parties of the left, a constituent assembly thereupon offered a first draft constitution providing for a unicameral parliament, but this was rejected in a popular referendum by a narrow margin. A second draft constitution, largely resembling the first, re-established a second chamber, though one with extremely restricted powers, and this draft was adopted in another close popular vote. The new Parliament of the Fourth Republic (1946–1958) was thus at least bicameral in form. The National Assembly, the successor to the old Chamber of Deputies, was composed ultimately of 626 members elected for five-year terms by a modified system of proportional representation. It alone now possessed the power to control the executive, and was expected therefore to display a sense of responsibility commensurate with its authority.

The new Council of the Republic, however, was scarcely more than the ghost of the former Senate; its powers were not only less than those of the British House of Lords, but so limited that its contribution to the legislative process was largely in advisory or brief delaying functions. Its 320 members were chosen by a system of indirect election for six-year terms, one-half every three years. Though its members soon reacted to their position of impotence, and sought to obtain a greater share in authority, they achieved only modest concessions. Even so, in the eyes of most Frenchmen, the National Assembly was soon behaving as disappointingly as its counterpart in the preceding regime. At the same time, the other significant constitutional feature of the Fourth Republic—the arrangements to give greater stability to the ministries—proved entirely unsuccessful, as we have noted in the previous chapter, and Parliament continued to make the life of French governments brief. As a result, in the face of an increasingly confused political situation, fiscal weakness, and insurrection in Algeria, the regime was abandoned and a still newer one created.

The Constitution of the Fifth Republic (1958) substantially changed the structure and function of Parliament. Once again it has bicameral form, but is removed at the same time from the center of political power. The size of the National Assembly is now related to population—one deputy for each 93,000 inhabitants—and elected from single-member districts for five-year terms, with a runoff election a week later if no candidate is chosen by a majority in the first. The present Assembly thus contains 482 deputies, including ten from overseas *départements,* and seven from overseas territories. The second chamber, now restyled the Senate, consists of 274 members elected indirectly by local electoral colleges for nine-year terms. The powers of the new Senate are placed somewhat between those of the Third Republic and the Council of the Republic of the Fourth. It still is denied any power to overturn a cabinet, and if the two houses disagree over bills submitted to them, and a government-requested joint committee cannot reconcile the differences, the National Assembly may decide the matter definitively. Other limitations in the process of government imposed upon the present Parliament restrict the length of yearly sessions, the power to legislate, and the opportunity to control the executive. The National Assembly may also be dissolved. It seems likely that this state of flux in French institutions may continue for some time.

Other National Legislatures. A brief examination of a few other representative bodies will indicate some of the various possible structures. The parliamentary functions in the German Federal Republic are performed by a Federal Diet, or *Bundestag* (sometimes itself designated as the Parliament), and a Federal Council, or *Bundesrat;* they may also be collectively described as a parliament. The *Bundestag* is popularly chosen by a combined system of direct election from single-member districts and proportional representation. Members of this body, which is subject to dissolution, are elected for four-year terms; it performs the usual parliamentary functions, but shares some of them with the second chamber. The *Bundesrat* represents the ten *Länder,* or states, composing the Republic; each *Land* has at least three members, and some of the larger have additional ones, to produce a total membership of forty-one. These members are appointed by and drawn from their state governments. They may introduce bills and exercise a suspensive veto over those passed by the *Bundestag*. As the delegates are bound by the instructions of their individual governments, and are essentially officials of their state administrations, rather than legislators, they must co-ordinate the administrative and legislative processes within the federal system. The *Bundesrat* has no control, however, over the executive, a situation which tends to minimize its partisanship.

A legislature influenced by the British Parliament, but reflecting its own national circumstances, is the Canadian Parliament. It is a bicameral body containing a House of Commons and a Senate. The House has 265 members, popularly elected like those of Great Britain at least every five years; the Senate has 102 members apportioned among the ten provinces. The second chamber had inevitably to take a form different from that in Britain. For one thing, Canada has a federal system of government, and the Senate was intended particularly to protect provincial interests. For another, Canada has no hereditary peerage with which to constitute a House of Lords. In consequence, its Senators are appointed for life by the Governor-General on the nomination of the Prime Minister; they must be property owners and at least thirty years of age. Although the Senate has formally the same powers as the House of Commons, in practice it is a much less active and influential body. Indeed, so unimportant has its contribution been to the governmental process that Canadians have frequently discussed reforming it substantially or abolishing it outright. In the Canadian Parliament, since about one-third of Canada's population is French-speaking, either the French or the English languages may be employed in the debates of its houses, though by no means are most of the members bilingual.

One of the more unusually constituted legislative bodies is the Parliament of Norway, the *Storting,* which might be described as a unicameral chamber with certain bicameral modifications. Containing 150 members, 50 from the towns and cities, and 100 from rural areas, the *Storting* is elected by a scheme of proportional representation which, among other things, supplies an alternate member available to replace each elected one, should the latter enter the cabinet or otherwise vacate his seat. Following each quadrennial election, the *Storting* selects 38 of its members to constitute the *Lagting,* or Upper Section, with the remaining 112 making up the *Odelsting,* or Lower Section. For certain purposes, including constitutional amendment and financial legislation, the members sit together as the *Storting*. For others, they sit in separate sections under their individual presiding officers. A bill intended to become formal law is introduced in the *Odelsting,* and if passed, is sent to the *Lagting,* which may approve or reject it. If, after passage again by the Lower Section, the Upper Section rejects the bill a second time, both bodies are convened in joint session, where the bill may then be passed by a two-thirds vote.

A last generalization—about Latin America—will conclude this section. Here, as we have observed in the preceding chapter, the national congress is definitely subordinated to the executive, even when dictatorship does not prevail, and regardless of constitutional stipulations. Legislators representing different parties may sit in the houses, and may well have been more or less the choice of the voters in a popular election. In the sessions of the legislature, personal and political differences between members, indeed, may lead to bitter debates and even violence. If these circumstances seem to offer refreshing contrast to the unquestioning unanimity displayed by legislatures in the fascist and communist dictatorships, they should not be taken as evidence of congressional ability to exercise any significant measure of power in the process of government. Most of the legislators are likely to be the president's men—and he uses them, or ignores them, largely as suits his purposes.

The Legislature in the Emergent States. The modern legislative assembly is one of the more recent western governmental institutions, and one most difficult to operate effectively under the best of circumstances. To no one's surprise, the legislative institution has been the least successful of the organs of government introduced by the states of the "third world." In their constitutions these new states commonly have adopted the formal structure of western parliamentary bodies, but have discovered that something more is required to breathe life into them and to develop a parliamentary *esprit de corps*. The result has been legislatures in the main weak, unrepresentative, executive-dominated, and redundant.

A principal reason is the absence of any parliamentary traditions, previous governments having usually been colonial or monarchical, bureaucratic and even quasi-dictatorial. And, without well-organized popular parties and associational interest groups, these parliamentary bodies represent only a small portion of the population. Also, in a legislature either dominated by a single-national party or divided and immobilized by a multiparty system, the opposition is ineffective and offers no alternative government. Thus, such legislatures tend to act as "rubber stamps" for the executive, rather than as deliberative bodies independently weighing the special interests against the general welfare.

In many respects, the new regimes tend to resemble those in central and eastern Europe following World War I. Here such states as Germany, Poland, Austria, Hungary, and Yugoslavia, lacking significant parliamentary traditions, were unable to develop legislative institutions capable of coping with the stresses of the times, and succumbed to dictatorship. It seems clear that tradition and training are vital. Where legislative bodies in the newer states have demonstrated some measure of success and ability, they are also drawing on earlier experience. For example, members were first elected to the Philippine Legislature in 1907; to the Indian Legislative Council in 1909; and, to the Nigerian

Legislative Council in 1922. These states were thus able to build on their own legislative traditions and experience when they achieved independence after World War II.

National Legislatures in the Dictatorships. Despite the fact that dictatorship constitutes the very negation of representative government, modern dictators have, paradoxically enough, managed to find at least a formal place in their system for the legislative institution. This is the best evidence, perhaps, that the legislature has come to be universally viewed as essential to popular government and the promotion of mass interests. Though the method of selecting its members and the practical limitation of its powers will assure that it exercises no real political authority, the dictator has some very good reasons for paying tribute to the outward forms of democracy.

First of all, the presence of the legislature, in form if not in substance, helps to conceal—both at home and abroad—the naked concentration of authority. Modern dictators, like medieval autocrats, find some reassurance in the appearance, albeit manufactured, of popular support and approval. The election of its members, even though they are carefully chosen by the single-party monopoly, provides an opportunity for placing the stamp of pseudo-legality on the ruler's acts—conducting propaganda, disseminating information, and arousing enthusiasm. The meetings of the legislature in a dictatorship also offer occasions for the party leaders to instruct the masses in official political doctrines. At the very least, finally, the legislature can be used to provide additional titles, jobs, and emoluments with which to reward the politically faithful. We may see these factors demonstrated in the case of Fascist Italy, Nazi Germany, and Soviet Russia.

Fascist Italy. During the period of the constitutional monarchy, the Italian Parliament had resembled the British in form—though never in effectiveness—being composed of a popularly elected Chamber of Deputies and a Senate appointed for life. The Fascist dictatorship in Italy (1922–1943), however, substantially altered the organization and role of Parliament. Indeed, it barely escaped abolition, for Mussolini and his supporters avowed their contempt for the doctrine of majority rule and their aim to end parliamentary corruption and inefficiency.

Though popular elections gave the Fascists only a small foothold in the Chamber of Deputies, Parliament was coerced into adopting a new electoral law in 1924. The result was the election of a Fascist-packed

Chamber; soon after, all opposition parties were abolished, and the Senate was brought into line. Mussolini also secured his government's complete independence of legislative control by insisting on authority from Parliament to rule by decree. In 1939, the lower house was reorganized as a Fascist and Corporative Chamber, composed of some six hundred appointed Councillors. Though acclaimed by Mussolini as something new in representative institutions, the body proved to be only a creature of the dictator, and had no further significance.

Nazi Germany. Hitler even more rapidly imposed a similar fate on the German Parliament established by the Weimar Republic (1919–1933). Under the Republic, the *Reichstag,* the main legislative organ, was chosen by popular election; the *Reichsrat,* which shared the legislative process, was a council of the seventeen German states, and its sixty-six members appointed by them. Following Hitler's designation as Chancellor in January, 1933, the existing *Reichstag* was dissolved and new elections called. Even in the face of Nazi pressure, propaganda, and violence, the German voters elected only 288 Nazi deputies out of the total *Reichstag* membership of 647—less than half. But by winning support from a small group of Nationalist members, Hitler was able to command a bare majority, and by excluding the Communists he then pressed through an enabling act authorizing legislation by executive decree. This attack on the *Reichstag* opened the way for Hitler to dissolve all non-Nazi parties and complete his absolute dictatorship. The *Reichsrat* was abolished outright in 1934 when the federal system was suppressed; meanwhile, the *Reichstag* was converted into an exclusively Nazi preserve. It degenerated rapidly as an organ of government; for the remainder of its existence it held only twenty sittings and approved seven laws. Though *Reichstag* elections continued to be held, the body performed no real function other than to provide an audience and cheers for an occasional speech by Hitler.

The Soviet Union. The Supreme Soviet of the U.S.S.R. is neither the vestigial remainder of a previous regime of representative government, as was the case of the Fascist and Nazi chambers, nor is it a real parliamentary body, comparable to the national legislatures of Great Britain and the United States. No parliamentary tradition ever developed in Russia. Following revolutionary uprisings in the country, the Czar was obliged in 1906 to set up a two-chamber body, composed of a *Duma,* or popular assembly chosen by a restricted system of election, and balanced by a Council of State, which could be controlled by the autocratic ruler. Four elections to the *Duma* were held between 1906 and 1917, and though this body made continuing attempts to break down the despotism of the Czar, it failed. Elected by an increasingly restricted suffrage, limited in power to legislate, unable to enforce any ministerial responsibility, and with its membership continually manipulated toward still more conservatism, it was largely ignored after the outbreak of World War I in 1914, and was finally swept away by the Bolshevik coup d'état in 1917. Consequently, after this most modest experience with parliamentary bodies, the Russian people would thereafter know only the soviets, or councils, managed by the Communist dictatorship.

The current Soviet Constitution of 1936 provides for a Supreme Soviet, composed of a Soviet of the Union, now containing nearly 800 members chosen on the basis of one deputy for each 300,000 people, and a Soviet of Nationalities of over 600 members chosen from the various constituent republics, regions, and other political subdivisions. If one were to examine the constitutional provisions relating to the Supreme Soviet, he might well conclude that the Soviet legislature differs little from those of the western democracies. The Constitution states that the Supreme Soviet is "the highest organ of state power in the U.S.S.R.," and that it exercises "exclusively" the legislative power. Elaborate provisions also govern the nomination and election of deputies, and describe immunities, procedures, functions, and powers of the two bodies. However, the difference between constitutional provision and actual practice is vast.

First, the nomination of candidates for membership is controlled entirely by the Communist party, which approves a single candidate for each electoral district (though not all those nominated are members of the Communist party); no other candidates are allowed to compete. After an elaborate electoral campaign, the expenses of which are borne by the state, the voters on election day must either vote for the official candidates, or deface the ballot. Negative votes are discouraged in a variety of ways, and as a consequence, somewhat more than 99 per cent of the voters cast affirmative ballots in this one-sided contest. In the second place, the Supreme Soviet is given very little to do. It meets once or twice a year, for a week or two at the most, listens to speeches from party and government leaders, and occasionally is invited to approve a law or a resolution. In these carefully staged proceedings there is a complete absence of any really critical debate, questioning, or examination of budget matters and, of course, no opposition. Indeed, these two likeminded houses have never in their history refused a request, nor have they adopted any measure other than unanimously. Clearly, though the Supreme Soviet superficially resembles a legislature, its legislative functions are purely fictitious.

As may be expected, the position of the legislative bodies in the "people's republics" is very much like that of the Supreme Soviet of the U.S.S.R., with some differences in terminology and detail. Here, however, the national assemblies are mostly unicameral, and political activity is conducted by Communist-dominated "united fronts of workers' parties" rather than by the Communist party exclusively. Though this practice is a distinction largely without difference—because no party may be outside the official coalition—it at least attempts to create the illusion of a variety of parties, and serves somewhat to conceal the extent of Communist, and for certain matters Soviet Russian, domination. Whether the subjects of these dictatorships really feel in any way represented by these pseudo-legislative institutions seems unlikely.

III. PROBLEMS *of* REPRESENTATION

Within democratic systems of government, legislatures have certain features broadly in common, though they vary in details of organization and procedure. What factors account principally for these features? First of all, England, the "Mother of Parliaments," from its long and successful parliamentary history has influenced the character and procedures of all legislative bodies to some extent, and those of the Commonwealth and the United States quite considerably. Further, because the institution of democratic government is closely associated with the idea of universal suffrage, its achievement requires that one parliamentary chamber be organized as a "popular" house. Also, during the century or more in which the modern legislature has prevailed, most countries have had one or more occasions to reorganize their legislative institution. In such event, within particular national traditions, there were usually efforts to make the legislature more representative, more responsible, or more efficient. In sum, all national legislatures have been influenced in part by their English prototype, by universal ideals of representative government, and by their own national experience.

The Number of Houses. Most parliamentary bodies are composed of two houses. There is, of course, nothing sacred about bicameralism, and medieval assemblies originally had from one to four houses. Nevertheless, the centuries-old English model of a two-house parliament has been most influential and most generally instituted for several major motives. First, it permits a dual basis of representation. A second chamber may represent different areas, various institutions, subordinate levels of government, or particular classes within a nation, in addition to the representation of the population on a direct basis by the lower house. A particularly important justification for bicameralism is found in federal states, as in the United States, Canada, Australia, India, Switzerland, and Germany, where previously independent areas are joined in a single political union and given special representation. Other bases for the second chamber may be provided by an hereditary aristocracy, as in the British House of Lords; by vocational groups and educational and cultural bodies, as in the Irish Senate; or by ethnic elements, as in the Burmese Chamber of Nationalities.

Second, bicameralism avoids concentrating the legislative power, and reduces the possibility of its despotic exercise. This was an argument that appealed strongly to the framers of the American Constitution, who were convinced of the desirability of incorporating checks and balances into the political system. In Great Britain, as well, there has been apprehension at the thought of the great parliamentary powers concentrated in a single body of men, subject to no documentary constitutional or judicial restraints. The members of a second chamber will not as a rule possess equality of powers with the first chamber, but they may commonly be given certain special functions.

Third, two houses can obtain fuller deliberation. In the nature of things, the action of a legislative chamber can be hasty, inadequately considered, ill-advised, or based on insufficient information. A second chamber therefore may act as an examining and revising body, drawing on the special knowledge and experience of its membership, to review the work of the popular house. Thus, the members of the German *Bundesrat* are state government officials; the French Senate is composed in large proportion of persons who are former members of the National Assembly or who are experienced as local government officials; the House of Lords contains many peers with a large experience of public and political life.

Finally, bicameralism may impose a conservative restraint upon a popular, directly elected body. At first glance this may seem undemocratic, but democracy is not merely a matter of effecting the will of the majority; it requires some protection of the interests of minorities as well. And, although it is not popular to speak of "the excesses of democracy," many examples may be found. An upper house need not be conservative in a partisan sense, but may be so constituted as to be resistant to extremist tendencies, from whatever direction, as well as to emphasize continuity and stability in policies. To be sure, a second chamber is commonly given only delaying influence and not power to impose an absolute veto; however, it may oblige the popular chamber to re-examine its action, thus allowing time for public opinion to form and assert itself, before a final decision is reached. Examples of bodies intended to perform this conservative function include the Canadian Senate, whose members are appointed for life; the Italian Senate, whose members are elected from regional areas (by voters twenty-five years of age, or older); and, the British House of Lords.

Yet the organization of the legislature into two houses does not automatically produce these results, nor is the arrangement necessarily relevant to every national situation. In some states there may be but one significant basis upon which to rest representation. And, bicameralism as such has not always been a bar to despotism and dictatorship, as the Italian, German, and Russian experiences attest. Also, it does not even guarantee greater deliberation. The chambers of bicameral bodies not uncommonly act in haste on occasion and assume that the other house will be more deliberate; when both houses make that assumption over the same measure, the result can be most unfortunate. Finally, the opportunity for conservative delay is no assurance of parliamentary wisdom; the British House of Lords was shorn of much of its power in this century as a result of its failure to keep up with changing times and political opinion.

Bicameralism is by no means a universal institution, however, in part undoubtedly because it does not always produce all of its claimed advantages. Approximately one out of four national legislatures is, indeed, a one-house assembly. The countries where unicameralism has been instituted tend to fall into one of several categories. These are principally: several small and homogeneous states which place a high emphasis on egalitarian democracy, such as Denmark, Finland, and

New Zealand; some of the small states of Latin America, which lack any significant bases for dual systems of representation, for example, Costa Rica, Guatemala, Haiti, Honduras, Panama, Paraguay, and El Salvador; several states of the Near East whose representative systems are of relatively recent creation, such as Greece, Israel, and Lebanon; many of the new states of Africa and Asia, as Guinea, Mali, Indonesia, and Thailand; and, most of the communist states. It may also be noted, incidentally, that the unicameral form is found in many subordinate legislative bodies, even in states which have bicameral national parliaments. Among these are the *Landtage* (Diets) of the German Federal Republic's *Länder* (except Bavaria), the legislatures of the Canadian provinces, and of Nebraska.

Unicameralism is supported by several arguments. Because authority is concentrated in a single house, the electorate knows where responsibility rests for any legislative action. A single house also avoids duplication of effort, additional expense, and the tendency of separate bodies to disagree for the sake of asserting their independence. Further, procedure through a single house may allow greater speed in the legislative process —a significant consideration in modern times when action rather than delay is a significant consideration. Finally, it is asserted that unicameralism is more democratic because it avoids the possible obstruction of the popular will by an unrepresentative upper house. Nevertheless, none of these propositions is easily demonstrable in practice, nor have they been largely persuasive, it would seem, in determining the incidence of unicameralism. Unicameralism is not a Scandinavian fixture, for Sweden has a bicameral parliament. Ireland and Austria, also with bicameral parliaments, are at the same time both small and homogeneous countries, and are scarcely likely to be more heedless of expense or legislative delay than New Zealand or Israel. Certainly the unicameral legislatures of the Central American states hardly reflect any significant democratic aspirations. Indeed, unicameral national assemblies are also found in the communist-dominated states of Bulgaria, Czechoslovakia, East Germany, Hungary, Poland, and Romania; in the Chinese People's Republic; and in Spain under the Franco dictatorship. In these countries, where the legislature has no authority, or where in others it has relatively little, it obviously makes no difference whether there is one house or two. It appears, then, that the presence of unicameralism must be explained by individual national circumstance. It seems likely, too, that the general preference will continue for bicameralism, given the useful functions a well-constructed second chamber can perform. There is rarely much opportunity left for it to obstruct democratic demands; such conflicts have largely been resolved by reducing its powers or making it as popularly elective as the lower chamber.

The Size and Terms of the Houses. Legislatures may be large or small. What factors, then, properly determine their dimensions? Ideally, a parliamentary body should be large enough to represent the varying interests of all sections and classes of a nation's population effectively, and small enough to be able to deliberate efficiently. The translation of these propositions into parliamentary arithmetic, however, is not a matter of any particular agreement, though a few generalizations may be drawn from an examination of existing bodies. Lower houses tend to fall into one of three categories: first, those with less than one hundred members, such as Luxembourg and most of the small states of Latin America; second, those which range between one and two hundred members, including such states as Austria, Ireland, the Netherlands, Switzerland, Australia, South Africa, and the larger states of Latin America, among them Argentina, Chile, and Mexico; third, the most populous countries, in the range from four hundred to upward of six hundred members, such as France, the German Federal Republic, Great Britain, India, Italy, Japan, and the United States.

The size of upper chambers tends to be more limited, with most of them between twenty-five and one hundred members. Several states exceed this, of course; the Italian Senate has 246 elected members, the French Senate, 274, and the British House of Lords more than 900, at least potentially. Generally speaking, unicameral legislatures compare more closely in size with upper rather than lower chambers; the New Zealand Parliament has 80 members, and the Israeli *Knesset,* 120. Yet the single house may be a large one even in small states: the Parliament of Finland numbers 200, and that of Greece, 300.

In determining parliamentary dimensions, pressure for wide representation weighs more heavily than the need for efficient deliberation. A body of a hundred or so can debate and deliberate with effectiveness, permit the presentation of a wide variety of views, and still achieve a degree of consensus upon relatively complex matters that may appropriately be described as "the sense of the house." When legislative chambers contain four or five hundred members or more, however, the process becomes increasingly difficult. Only a small proportion of members can be heard on any particular subject; their views are thus less likely to be representative of the whole, and any specific agreements they accept will probably have been reached by their parliamentary leaders and committees. The United States Senate of one hundred members, for example, takes pride in its tradition of allowing full and unlimited debate.

By the time the United States House of Representatives reached a membership exceeding four hundred, however, there was already feeling that it had grown too large; it inevitably has very restrictive rules governing debates and length of speeches, and the Speaker is authorized large discretion in directing proceedings. In the British House of Commons, a substantially larger body, similar circumstances prevail, and it is also assumed that extensive absenteeism will keep to manageable proportions those members participating in any one debate. Nevertheless, backbenchers express continual dissatisfaction over the monopolization of debate time by ministers and opposition front-bench speakers. The House of Lords, with an even greater membership, manages to operate because rarely are more than one hundred members present at any particular sitting. Yet there is little inclination toward a reduction in size of the large—and inevitably unwieldy—national legislatures of the major states. By their nature, their populations tend to great heterogeneity; they have social, economic, and external problems of great complexity; and their multitude of interests and urban localities each demands a special delegate. Indeed, such states also have invariably a huge governmental apparatus, and only through the intermediary of what they feel is their own local representative can the administered masses believe their voice will be heard at all.

There is also little in the way of principle governing the subject of legislative terms. Ideally, the office term of the member of a popular chamber ought to be sufficiently long to permit him to gain a useful familiarity with his duties, and short enough to keep him responsible to his constituency. The first of these propositions is reinforced by the fact that the continuity of membership in most such bodies is not high; a turnover in 25 to 50 per cent of the seats at each election is common. Also, too-frequent elections oblige the legislator to devote excessive time and attention to his re-election; they bore the voters and encourage apathy among them. Very short terms also detract from continuity in legislative policy, and reduce the opportunity for an assembly to complete a comprehensive legislative program. To be sure, at intervals the legislator needs to account to his constituency; the occasion for his constituents to grant or deny his return to office is the most accurate measure of public opinion on his representativeness.

It should be obvious, once more, that these considerations cannot be translated into mathematical formulas. Probably most voters, and certainly most legislative representatives, would consider a one-year term —and thus annual elections—a downright harassment. Further, many members of the United States House of Representatives, as well as a number of students of the problem, believe that their two-year term is too short for maximum effectiveness. On the other hand, a lower-house term as long as six years, which is to be found only in a few Latin-American states, certainly does little to enhance the representative character of government. And, given the rapid pace of events in modern public life, a popular chamber close to the end of even a five-year term not uncommonly appears tired, indecisive, and uncertain how to apply such mandate as it may have received at the time of its election. As a result, the most general practice is to give the popular house a four-year term. However, a five-year term applies in Canada, Great Britain, France, India, Ireland, Italy, and South Africa; Australia and New Zealand set the limit at three years. Even so, all such terms of office in parliamentary systems of government are maximum, and will be shorter if parliament is dissolved earlier. This is in contrast to systems where terms are rigidly fixed, as in Switzerland and the United States.

An upper chamber, as we have noted, is commonly constituted on a basis of representation separate from that of the popular house, and is intended to be a more independent body. There are three principal forms of organization, which may also be used in combination. In a few cases members may have life terms, as in the British House of Lords or the Canadian Senate. Or, the chamber may be a continuing body, with a portion of its members chosen at fixed intervals; for example, one-eighth of the Swedish upper chamber is chosen each year, one-third of the United States Senate is chosen every two years, and one-half of the Australian Senate is chosen every three years. Finally, members of the upper house may simply be given longer terms than the lower, as in Italy, Mexico, and South Africa. All of these devices give the second chamber, in varying degree, some independence of the electorate and some continuity in membership. Whether they produce a greater wisdom, a more mature opinion, and a keener awareness of the national interest is debatable.

Systems of Representation. We come now to the problems of selecting members of legislative chambers. Historically, the oldest form of parliamentary representation is by estates, that is, the representation of a political or social group or class sharing recognizable interests, rights, and status. In medieval Europe, the clergy constituted one estate, the nobility another, the commoners a third, and in some countries, the rural freemen a fourth. However, these were in time generally drawn into two houses, providing the basis for bicameralism. But representation by estates has long been abandoned; the British House of Lords represents a vestigial—and virtually the sole—survival of the system. At present there is little either in principle or practice to recommend it. In the complex societies of the modern world there simply are no longer a few clearly distinguishable groups with identical and identifiable interests into which people can be separated, and any attempts to do so would produce the most artificial results.

Modern representation has long been based, therefore, on territory or geography. The result is a simple and, at first glance at least, a logical system. Representatives are chosen from districts—either those already existent, or which can be created, large or small, many or few, as may be needed, by drawing on a map. They then undertake to represent all the people in the given territory. The system has the further advantage that the representative can easily recognize his constituents, and vice versa; he can visit with or live among them; identify their interests, general and special; and note improvement (or decline) in their situation. Obvious examples of such territorial units of representation are the American congressional district, the British parliamentary borough, or the Norwegian *fylke* (county).

Despite its simplicity and utility, territorial representation is not a system of perfection. Its validity rests substantially upon the proposition that all of the people living in a given area are much alike and as a result have common interests. Obviously, this is not and cannot be so in many respects: geographical propinquity does not automatically produce homogeneity. Hence, the organization of voters into geographical areas produces a certain amount of dissatisfaction. In an age, therefore, where universal suffrage in the selection of the popular legislative chamber is so general, the question is no longer who should choose the representatives, but how should they be chosen? In consequence, a system of "functional" representation of the electorate has sometimes been proposed. But advocates of such systems are few, and hardly in agreement over their specific arrangements. Presumably, representatives would be chosen by voters grouped according to their "function" in society—their occupation, economic activity, or vocational interests. But any such scheme confronts serious practical and theoretical obstacles. Any one person has a great diversity of interests; he may at the same time be manager and employee, property owner and debtor, producer and consumer, taxpayer and government pensioner, and so on. In which category each such person should be represented, and what sort of legislative institution would be the product of such representation, are difficult to imagine. Surely, the functional cure would appear to be worse than the territorial complaint.

Electoral Systems. We have observed that the territorial basis of representation is almost universally employed for the selection of representatives. Within it, however, considerable variations are possible in constituting the electoral system, though these generally reflect one of two forms. The first, the single-member district system, involves choosing each representative from a single electoral district. In its simplest form, this may be observed in an American congressional district, from which one Representative is chosen, or in a British parliamentary constituency, which selects one Member of Parliament. Election in each case is by plurality vote, that is, there may be any number of candidates, and the one with the largest number of votes wins. The deputies of the National Assembly in the French Fifth Republic are also elected one from each constituency, but here they must receive a number of votes equal to a majority of those cast and to at least a quarter of the total number of voters registered. If no candidate receives this many, in order to encourage a greater degree of electoral consensus, a second balloting or "runoff election" is held. This time a plurality suffices for election.

The single-member district system is best suited to countries with a stable biparty system. It is simple to count the votes, and the electorate easily understands the results. It emphasizes the direct relationship between the representative and his district, for his success in election depends in part on his association with it. The system also encourages the maintenance of the two-party system, and obliges candidates to make broad, rather than narrow, appeals to the electorate. This tends in turn, however artificially, to produce a majority for one party in the legislative assembly.

The system is criticized, however, upon two principal grounds. First, it may exaggerate or even distort popular majorities when translated into legislative seats. In 1945, for example, the British Labour party with 48 per cent of the popular votes gained 61.4 per cent of the seats in the House of Commons. In 1951, however, the Conservative party got 48.0 per cent of the votes compared to Labour's 48.8 per cent, but won 51.3 per cent of the seats in Commons. Second, it tends to discriminate against the representation of minor parties, especially those whose support is not concentrated in single constituencies. For example again, the Liberal party in the British election of 1959, with 5.9 per cent of the popular votes, won barely 1 per cent of the seats; in the 1964 election, despite doubling its popular vote to over three millions, 11.2 percent of the poll, it won less than 2 per cent of the seats. The exaggerations of the single-member district system may also be seen in an extreme form in the French election of 1962, where the second balloting permits candidates and voters to make political realignments to the disadvantage of small or extremist parties. On the first ballot, the Communist party won 21.8 per cent of the votes, and on the second, 21.3 per cent; the (De Gaullist) Union for the New Republic won 31.9 per cent and 40.5 per cent on the same ballots, respectively. As a result of the second ballot, however, the Communists received only 41 seats, less than 9 per cent of the total in the National Assembly; the U.N.R. took 233 seats, or 48 per cent of the total. Obviously, on the second ballot many voters concentrated on the moderate non-Communist candidates.

For more than a hundred years, therefore, there have been various proposals for a second type of electoral system, based on the principle of proportional representation. Of course, all systems may produce proportionate results to a degree, unless the voter must take all legislators from one single national list or another. The essence of proportional representation systems, however, is that the allotment of seats in the legislature is directly proportionate to the distribution of votes cast. Though a very considerable number of schemes to this end have been applied, at various times, in such countries as Belgium, France, Germany, Ireland, Israel, the Netherlands, and the Scandinavian countries, for example, the fundamental variations are two. The first, known as the single transferable vote system, was developed by Thomas Hare in mid-nineteenth-century England. Briefly, the voter is allowed to express a series of preferences for candidates whose names are arranged alphabetically on the ballot; on the basis of the total number of ballots cast, a quota for election is established to permit the choosing of as many candidates as will fill the prescribed number of seats; and, the ballots are so distributed that some candidate may receive usable support from each voter.

The other major form of proportional representation is known as the list system. Here, each party offers a list of candidates to the number of the legislative seats to be filled, arranged in an order it determines. The voter casts his vote for one of the party lists, and the seats are distributed from the top down in each party list according to its share of the total votes cast. In this manner, a party receiving, say, 25 per cent of the votes will secure the election of the top fourth of its list.

Several advantages are claimed for systems of proportional representation. There is less distortion of popular preferences in constituting the legislature, and a party with the fewer votes cannot obtain the most seats. Minor political parties of any significant dimensions secure representation which reflects the extent of their popular support. It is thus easier for new parties to win a place in the legislature, and for small ones to perpetuate themselves. It is also asserted that the mathematical consistency of proportional representation renders it more democratic. Despite the zeal with which proportional representation is supported by some of its advocates, its opponents insist that such systems have serious defects. The most obvious, of course, is that the average voter does not find it easy to comprehend the mechanics of such systems, particularly the Hare system. The voter also feels no particular sense of association with the candidates chosen, who in turn cannot easily recognize their supporters. Opponents also contend that such systems unnecessarily encourage small minor parties, and do nothing to discourage, at least, a multiparty system, which they fear may prove to be dangerous to stable democratic government.

To assert any distinct superiority between the single-member district system and proportional representation is scarcely possible, if only because one must weigh what are certain practical advantages against certain theoretical preferences. If one sees the prime purpose of the legislature as that of creating large stable majorities to sustain a government and enact its legislative program, the single-member district system is preferable. Minority groups are not thereby repressed or destroyed; rather, they generally must resort to other means than direct legislative representation for the expression of their interests and the influencing of governmental policy. If as well a people are habitually willing and able to make rough-and-ready compromises in the conduct of politics, and are devoted to a biparty system, they will undoubtedly have little enthusiasm for elaborately technical election arrangements. The experience of the English-speaking peoples has generally run along these lines, and they seem to be reasonably well satisfied with the single-member district system.

On the other hand, if the primary purpose of the legislature is seen as the provision of a wide and varied range of all possible political opinions, then a proportional representation system is preferable. This is likely when a multiparty system exists, and each organized political group has as its first concern the ability to exercise a veto over any legislative or administrative action—a feeling that may well reflect past experience of political repression or fear of it in the future. Thus, the choice of electoral system in a particular country seems to reflect, rather than primarily to determine, the kind of party system it has. The evidence really does not support the conclusion that the electoral arrangements create the party system. In Canada and Australia the single-member district system has not preserved a biparty system; in the Scandinavian countries proportional representation has not precluded the creation of stable government majorities. The German Federal Republic elects one-half of the members of the *Bundestag* by each method, and it appears that if either system were employed exclusively the results might not be substantially different. The best electoral system for a particular state will be one which will provide a legislative institution that, to the satisfaction of the electorate generally, is capable of performing the major legislative functions. To do so effectively, however, it is unnecessary either to make arbitrary exclusions of minor parties, or to insure that it offers a mirror-like reflection of every single political interest.

The Character of Legislative Membership. Legislative representatives, whose role is one of standing for, or in the place of, other persons, have the greatest influence on the character and quality of the legislature. And, probably no other official of government is regarded with so much cynicism, is so quickly criticized, and so often maligned. Why is this so? First of all, legislators of the present are commonly and invidiously compared with those of some "golden age" in the past. "There were giants in those days," it is asserted. Yet to the extent that such feeling is not the result of illusion, or downright bad memory, it constitutes an unfair comparison. A century ago, legislators were much more likely to be drawn from the then relatively smaller educated, propertied, and privileged classes—though to that extent they were far less popularly representative. Moreover, they were called upon to deal with public issues certainly fewer in number and of far less complexity than those of today, and about which the average voter might be able to have a relevant or interested opinion. He might then see his representative as a better informed and more fluent advocate of interests than the voter could be himself. Today, however, legislation calls for little oratory, and it is not primarily an intellectual occupation. Instead, the representative is likely to be a hard-working servant of his constituency, dividing his time between sessions of the legislature and numerous visits to his electoral district, where he must be available for meetings, conferences, and innumerable services to his constituents.

In the second place, the legislative representative is often unfavorably compared with the executive. The executive may well be a politician, but he can also be something of an expert; he draws on official sources of information; he may act, and be judged by his actions. The legislator is also a politician, but he must be essentially a generalist; he reflects the layman's opinion; he must talk and vote—functions less impressive than taking action; and if he is not a member of the majority, he must continually oppose—a practice which casts him into an apparently unconstructive and negative role. The executive is commonly obliged to take the large view; the legislator may be induced to take the small one. In a legislature where party discipline is strict, the legislator's vote may be controlled by his party; and where it is not, it is controllable largely by local considerations prevailing in his constituency. He may advocate a policy, but knows the frustration that by his own efforts he cannot put it into effect. He makes speeches, persuades, obstructs, maneuvers, trades votes, and compromises. To be most effective in his various roles as politician, broker, critic, investigator, and lawmaker he must often abandon the ideal dignity of the statesman. Rarely can he appear to be heroic.

The legislature's membership is obviously affected by the sources from which it is drawn. Significant legal qualifications are rare, and usually only those of a voter are essential, though in upper chambers, particularly, some additional maturity of age may be required. Women are almost everywhere equally eligible with men, yet their numbers in the legislature are always disproportionately small. Legislators tend to be drawn from much narrower occupational groups than those prevailing in the nation as a whole. Some approximation of this situation may be demonstrated in the accompanying table which compares four national legislatures of recent years. It should be noted, incidentally, that the percentages indicated suggest only tendencies; they were collected at different times under varying schemes of classification, and thus are not precisely comparable.

OCCUPATIONAL BACKGROUNDS OF LEGISLATORS

	A BRITISH HOUSE OF COMMONS	A FRENCH NATIONAL ASSEMBLY	A GERMAN FEDERAL BUNDESTAG	A UNITED STATES HOUSE OF REPRESENTATIVES
Business	23%	20%	16%	18%
Law	18	15	8	54
Agriculture	3	12	11	8
Workers	17	10	16	—
Public Employees	8	10	27	—
Miscellaneous (mainly professional)	31	33	22	20

A comparison of the proportions illustrates some features of public life in the several countries. The proportion of representatives with a business background is much the same in each country, and nowhere are they the dominant element. Lawyers in each case are present in much greater numbers than the proportion their profession bears to the total of occupations, and they compose more than half of the membership of the American Congress. Primarily this prominence of lawyers reflects their customary employment as agents of interest groups, it would seem, rather than an overrepresentation of the legal profession. Representatives with an agricultural background display the relative economic importance of this enterprise in each country, though it may be expected that most such representatives will be substantial landowners rather than "dirt farmers." Again, the representatives of workers' groups tend to be trade union officials, and indicate the presence of Socialist (and in the case of France, Communist) parties, which draw much of their leadership from these elements in European countries. Public employment is not incompatible with legislative membership in Europe as it is in the United States, and hence the varying distributions in the table. The elements of the miscellaneous category are widely assorted, but in the European parliamentary bodies constitute mainly journalists, teachers, doctors, clergymen, engineers, and those from the professions other than the law, none of which is found in comparable numbers, however, in the legislative bodies of the United States.

Finally, the quality of legislative representatives, though not always as distinguished as might be hoped, is much higher than popular esteem ordinarily accords it. Whether compared in terms of age, amount of formal education, professional position, performance of military service, political and public office experience, or economic status, all studies suggest the legislator achieves a considerably higher average than that of the constituents whom he represents.

IV. LEGISLATIVE FUNCTIONS

At the outset of this chapter, we indicated that though the legislature is primarily concerned with lawmaking, it does not monopolize that activity. Further, we noted that the legislature has some other functions in the governmental process, though these are all inescapably related. Unlike the executive, the legislature was not the original possessor of the broad authority to govern. Instead, it grew out of the elaboration of the governmental process and the emergence of democratic government. Inevitably, then, the modern legislature's functions reflect the essential purposes for which it was called into existence, or which it was subsequently obliged to assume during its evolution to its present form. Thus the original representation of interests, the counseling of the ruler, the supply of revenue, the supervision of the administration, and the presenting of grievances—all are clearly reflected in the functions of contemporary legislative institutions. We may now examine the five major functions these bodies perform today.

The Representation of Opinion and Interests. In the most general sense, the legislature is a great national forum in which representatives, through their debates and votes (and, not unimportantly, through private discussions in the lobbies and other gatherings), inform those exercising political authority of what the people think, want, and need, and also inform the people of what their government is doing. The provision of this informing function, of course, is the justification for making assemblies multimember bodies, often constituted into two houses and, for one of them at least, popularly elected at frequent intervals. The legislature is that organ of government intended most immediately to be the voice of the people. Yet we cannot discuss this function without confronting an ineluctable problem: whom does the legislator represent? Does he speak for all the people of the nation, or all of those in his constituency, or only some of them, or merely for himself? Is he, indeed, a *representative,* present in the place of his constituents and acting as a free agent on their behalf, or is he a *delegate,* pressing demands and carrying out instructions furnished him? These questions have never been satisfactorily answered. The classic response was provided—and deserves quotation—by Edmund Burke in his address to the electors of Bristol in 1774. Speaking of the relationship between a representative and his constituents, he said in part:

Certainly, gentlemen, it ought to be the happiness and glory of a representative to live in the strictest union, the closest correspondence, and the most unreserved communication with his constituents. Their wishes ought to have great weight with him; their opinion high respect; their business unremitted attention. It is his duty to sacrifice his repose, his pleasure, his satisfactions, to theirs—and above all, ever, and in all cases, to prefer their interest to his own.

But his unbiased opinion, his mature judgment, his enlightened conscience, he ought not to sacrifice to you, to any man, or to any set of men living. These he does not derive from your pleasure—no, nor from the law and the constitution. They are a trust from Providence, for the abuse of which he is deeply answerable. Your representative owes you, not his industry only, but his judgment; and he betrays, instead of serving you, if he sacrifices it to your opinion.

My worthy colleague says his will ought to be subservient to yours. If that be all the thing is innocent. If government were a matter of will upon any side, yours, without question, ought to be superior. But government and legislation are matters of reason and judgment, and not of inclination; and what sort of reason is that, in which the determination precedes the discussion; in which one set of men deliberate, and another decide; and where those who form the conclusion are perhaps three hundred miles distant from those who hear the arguments?

To deliver an opinion is the right of all men; that of constituents is a weighty and respectable opinion, which a representative ought always to rejoice to hear; and which he ought always most seriously to consider. But *authoritative* instructions, *mandates* issued, which the member is bound blindly and implicitly to obey, to vote and to argue for, though contrary to the clearest conviction of his judgment and conscience—these are things utterly unknown to the laws of this land, and which arise from a fundamental mistake of the whole order and tenor of our constitution.

Parliament is not a *congress* of ambassadors from different and hostile interests which interests each must maintain, as an agent, and advocate, against other agents and advocates; but Parliament is a *deliberative* assembly of *one* nation, with *one* interest, that of the whole—where not local purposes, not local prejudices, ought to guide, but the general good, resulting from the general reason of the whole. You choose a member indeed; but when you have chosen him, he is not a member of Bristol, but he is a Member of *Parliament*. If the local constituent should have an interest or should form a hasty opinion, evidently opposite to the real good of the rest of the community, the member for that place ought to be as far as any other from any endeavour to give it effect.

Although Burke provided a counsel of excellence, and an ideal to which many legislators do perhaps aspire, it is not simple to apply in practice. Most persons may not find it difficult to assert that "what is good for my nation is good for my community and me, and vice versa." But the determination of what truly are the national and local interests, and whether they are identical or opposed, is the very essence of politics. This is not a matter that constitutions can solve. The British Parliament recognizes a right of petition, but also draws a line, not always easy to determine, between legitimate political activity and illegitimate pressures on members, so that any attempt by improper means to influence parliamentary conduct is a punishable "breach of privilege." The United States Constitution guarantees the right of the people "to petition the government for a redress of grievances"; it provides also that "for any speech or debate in either house [the members of Congress] shall not be questioned in any other place." The Basic Law of the German Federal Republic (1949) stipulates that members of the *Bundestag* "are representatives of the whole people, not bound by orders and instructions, and subject only to their conscience." The French Constitution of 1958 states that "All binding instructions [upon members of Parliament] shall be null and void. The right to vote of the members of Parliament shall be personal."

Still and all, legislators have to answer to more than their conscience. They are party members; they owe their party organization some debt for their election and hope for its assistance in re-election. They must in the nature of things share a point of view with their party leaders and fellow members and see certain matters in the light of partisan policy. Legislators are also influenced in varying degree by the pleas, and sometimes pressures, of interest groups. They hear constantly from their constituents, both individual and organized, and many of their demands are not lightly disregarded. From what we have said about the occupational background of legislators it should not prove surprising, finally, to find that some, at least, have their own axes to grind. Thus, the voice of the people may sound from many directions, and the best of legislators must either largely relinquish any unshakable convictions of his own, or cultivate a rather extreme adroitness, if he is to continue to be returned to office.

The Formulation of Policy. As a result of these varied influences, the individual legislator determines his position and takes his stand on the issues. In the chamber of which he is a member, it is necessary that the total of these be reconciled, at least into some kind of majority compromise, so that broad national policies can be achieved. National policies, in the simplest terms, relate to what the government will do and how it will go about it. Their formulation is an incredibly complex and frequently difficult task, and legislators are by no means left to their own resources in the process. Other influences of significance will likely be brought to bear directly on the legislature in the making of policy: the proposals of the chief executive and his cabinet, the needs of administive officials, the programs of political parties, the force of national traditions, the influence of various interest groups and perhaps foreign governments, views expressed in the press and other communication media, the testimony of scholars and experts, and public opinion generally.

General lawmaking and financial legislation are, of course, an aspect of policy determination, but the latter function is considerably more extensive, for laws and appropriations are normally the consequence of major policy decisions. Thus, a legislature may choose a national policy in the face of depression conditions to revive the economy by large infusions of government spending, the construction of extensive public works, and substantial public support of unemployed persons. Or, it may approach the problem by adopting a policy to nationalize under state ownership substantial proportions of the factors in economic production. Again, national policy in foreign affairs may be, in the face of threatening aggression by other states, to maintain a well-armed defensive position, to wage a vigorous propagandist and economic offensive, or to embark directly upon large-scale hostilities. In addition to the adoption of legislation and the appropriation of funds, then, legislative policy may be expressed by resolutions, the authorization of treaties and other international agreements, the elaboration of administrative agencies, and the approval of appointments to office.

In this process of formulating policy the legislature must be provided leadership, though we should note the differing means employed to accomplish this in parliamentary and presidential systems of government. In the parliamentary system, as illustrated by Great Britain, legislative leadership is provided by the Prime Minister and his Cabinet, who are members of Parliament. The standing-committee system is not highly elaborated in the House of Commons; the committees control neither the content nor the destiny of legislative measures. The Speaker of the House of Commons is an impartial moderator, and has no part in expressing partisan views or applying party discipline. As we have noted in the preceding chapter, the British Cabinet is well situated to exert a very positive leadership of Parliament. It monopolizes the framing and introduction of all important legislation, controls the allocation of parliamentary time, decides on adjournments and dissolutions, and has an assured majority to back its decisions.

In the presidential system, as it prevails in the United States, the provision of legislative leadership is more complicated. The President and his Cabinet are not present in Congress; to exercise leadership of that body the President must be unusually ingenious. The Constitution gives him only indirect powers: messages to Congress and a reversible veto of bills it may pass. Beyond these, he must depend largely upon the exertion of personal or party influence, the judicious distribution of such patronage as is available, and appeals directly to the people. Not surprisingly, in the absence of any executive leadership inside Congress, both the House of Representatives and the Senate organize their own. The House, therefore, has a set of powerful standing committees, each controlled by the members of the majority party. The Speaker functions as the parliamentary moderator, a responsibility which he administers with impartiality, but he also acts as majority party leader, and is expected to assist, in any appropriate manner, the enactment of his party's legislative program. He is aided by the floor leader and the chairman of the Rules Committee, who are also majority party members. The situation in the Senate is similar. Thus, both houses have leadership provided partly on an external and partly on an internal basis.

In both systems, the complexity of the governmental process renders the legislature increasingly dependent upon the executive for the initiation of major policy proposals. The nature of the parliamentary system obliges the legislature to assume what is essentially a reviewing role: to examine such proposals, criticize them, and modify, adopt, or in extreme cases reject, them. The American Congress has found itself increasingly cast in a similar role, but here the tradition of the separation of powers, along with the capacity of the houses to provide something of an internal leadership of their own, makes this passive position more difficult for congressmen to accept.

The Control of Finance. The power to control the purse strings is one of the oldest functions of the legislature. The levy of taxes and the appropriation of funds are not only an aspect of policy formulation, for all significant policy decisions have financial consequences, but are also important devices for the control of the executive and the supervision of the administration. In addition, the control of the purse has come to be a central activity in the operation of government for the reason that public finance exerts a major influence on the state of the national economy. Through the use of the tax power, the legislature can influence the general standard of living, as well, by directing, limiting, or even virtually prohibiting, various kinds of consumption. The initial obligation for the preparation and presentation of a comprehensive government budget, proposing the monetary needs of the various departments and services balanced with the expected or required revenues, is generally regarded as an executive responsibility. But it is also the hallmark of representative government that the legislature retains the final right to authorize taxes and grant appropriations. The principal ways in which legislatures exercise this control, whether as an immediate or as an ultimate power, may be demonstrated in the contrasting American and British arrangements.

Under the Constitution of the United States, Congress is given the power "to lay and collect taxes, duties, imposts, and excises, to pay the debts and provide for the common defense and general welfare. . . ." Bills for raising revenue must originate in the House of Representatives, though the Senate may amend them. The Constitution further stipulates that "no money shall be drawn from the treasury, but in consequence of appropriations made by law. . . ." The Budget and Accounting Act

(1921) established a budget bureau—headed by a director now immediately under the authority of the President—which prepares the annual financial program to be presented to Congress. Once this has been done, Congress is free to do what it wishes with the President's proposals, and the procedures it employs in enacting the budget display a distressing lack of integration. The supply portion of the budget is considered by the separate Appropriations Committees in House and Senate; revenue measures are considered first by the House Committee on Ways and Means, and subsequently by the Senate Finance Committee. Further, individual members of Congress are entirely free to introduce bills involving the expenditure of funds for individual projects, and to trade votes with other congressmen to effect their mutual adoption, without any responsibility to secure compensating revenue. As a result, the President's budget is only a starting point for financial legislation; Congress independently exercises its power to reduce or increase the proposals made. The President may veto whole financial bills, of course, but not individual items in them, so that this authority is only a rough instrument for effecting economy, and Congress has thus a very immediate control over finance. In truth, then, the budget's enactment requires a long series of involved skirmishes, and some outright battles, between the President and Congress.

In Great Britain, the principle that the Crown may tax only with the consent of Parliament goes back to Magna Carta (1215), and the right of the Crown to spend only with the same consent is prescribed in the Bill of Rights (1689). Since 1911, this parliamentary authority has rested entirely with the House of Commons. It is also a constitutional rule that only ministers may propose a tax or an expenditure. The House could vote to refuse or reduce an appropriation, legally speaking, but any such action would constitute the withdrawal of its confidence in the government. The preparation of the budget is a responsibility of the Treasury, headed by the Chancellor of the Exchequer, who also presents it annually to the Commons. Supply and ways and means are considered separately by the House while sitting as a committee of the whole; standing committees have no power over financial measures. At no time, therefore, do the ministers relinquish control of the budget proposals; they may agree to accept certain amendments, but for the most part they do not, and need only crack the whip of party discipline to produce the required majority support for their demands. Consequently, since members of the House may not by their own orders increase the financial estimates, and cannot for political reasons expect to reduce them, the several weeks of debates allotted to the budget are devoted to a discussion not of public expenditure at all but of public policy. Thus the House of Commons has only an ultimate control over finance; it can alter the budget contrary to the government's wishes only by the extreme step of driving the latter from office.

The highly integrated system of budgeting is widely admired, and in its general features is the one most usually employed, though it is somewhat less ideal than many of its advocates claim. For one thing, it does not produce the same results in all parliamentary systems. In France, for example, in the absence of a biparty system, ministers have been frequently overthrown by legislative rebellion against their budgetary proposals; in Great Britain none ever is. The British arrangements do have the great merit of centering responsibility for the budget in the executive, who prepares it with the assurance that it will be enacted, and with the obligation to see that expenditures and revenues are brought into balance. Members of Parliament are relieved of any pressure by interest groups seeking to "raid the Treasury" and denied any opportunity to refuse to support government programs or to organize "pork barrel" schemes of their own. But there are disadvantages. The Cabinet is not necessarily more "economy minded" than Parliament; indeed, the pressures of interest groups seeking government expenditures are not eliminated, but are merely transferred to the executive. In any event, British expenditure has risen every bit as steadily as that in other comparable countries. Members of Parliament, having no opportunity to participate actively in the preparation of or hearings upon financial measures, acquire little expertness on the subject; in practical effect, then, the power of the purse is in the hands of the Treasury.

The criticisms of the American system center on its diffusion of responsibility, and on the opportunity it affords for legislative extravagance. The first is probably an inevitable result of the separation of powers and the essentially equal authority conferred on the houses of a bicameral Congress. It is not likely that either of these fixtures of the American system would be relinquished for replacement by the parliamentary system. Instead, the solution for these deficiencies seems to lie in the direction of integrating the congressional financial committees, consolidating appropriation measures, and authorizing a single-item veto power to the President. One might also conclude, on reflection, that a legislative judgment respecting the national fiscal interests is not always and inevitably inferior to one made by the executive, and, unmitigated "cabinet dictatorship" in the field of finance comes close to turning legislative control of finance into a fiction.

It may be noted in concluding this section that control of allocation is, to be sure, always prospective. For that reason, legislative bodies take a large interest in seeing how funds provided have actually been spent, and new appropriations are inevitably made with an eye to how effectively money has already been applied in public programs; hence, the various national systems of post-auditing executive accounts by the legislature. At their best, however, such systems have only a limited utility, illustrating a proverbial locking the barn door after the horse has been stolen.

The Supervision of the Executive. The function of the representative legislature which steadily grows in importance is the supervision and control of the executive. It receives the greatest emphasis in parliamentary systems, whose principal feature is the enforcement of executive or ministerial responsibility to the parliament, and it has also gained continually in importance in the presidential system, where the control of the great and ever-enlarging powers of the president is a major problem. The operation of parliamentary controls follows various patterns, reflecting the relationships between ministers of a government and their parliamentary bodies. There are, first, those states where ministers may not be members of either house, as in France, the Netherlands, Norway, and the United States; second, those where ministers must be members, as in Australia and Ireland (this is also the usual practice in Great Britain and Canada); and, third, those where ministers may but need not be members, as in Belgium, Denmark, Finland, Italy, Luxembourg, and Sweden. We noted in the preceding chapter the apparently inevitable tendency toward the expansion of executive authority; yet if the principle of limited and responsible government is to be maintained, the executive must be held to a continuous accountability for the exercise of his powers.

There are several methods whereby the legislature supervises the executive. The first is the legislative control of executive appointments and certain official acts. In the parliamentary system this power amounts to full legislative control only of the selection of the prime minister and his ministry. Where a biparty system is in operation, as in Great Britain for example, the majority party naturally will accept only the leader of their party for appointment as prime minister, who makes his own choice of ministers. However, the ministry as a whole must have the support of a majority or it will not be able to govern. Where a parliament is in the hands of a number of parties, its control over the personnel of the ministry is even greater; each party joining to form the majority coalition will bargain for ministerial posts. In the United States, though Congress does not choose the President, the Senate must approve all of his appointments to the higher offices of the national government. These include the members of his cabinet, other heads of establishments, ambassadors, consuls, federal judges, and others—to a total of some 25,000 appointments. Certain other executive acts are, in various countries, made subject to legislative approval; these include ratification of treaties, issuance of decrees having the force of law, and declarations of emergency.

A second, and extremely important means of controlling executive officers in all systems is the requirement that they furnish information to the legislature. Essentially, if the legislature is to hold the executive accountable, it must know what he is doing. In consequence, all departments and agencies of government are obliged to issue a great volume of reports, regular and special, accounting for their activities. A most efficacious device for day-to-day surveillance of the executive is the parliamentary question period, employed in Great Britain and the Commonwealth countries, in which members require ministers to answer specific questions relating to matters within their jurisdiction. Another device, the interpellation, is employed in Belgium, Switzerland, Italy, the Netherlands, formerly in France, and in other parliamentary systems, and involves an even more thorough inquiry into a minister's actions and policies, followed by a formal vote reflecting favorably or unfavorably upon him. These techniques are not available in the United States, for cabinet members may not appear on the floors of Congress, though something of a counterpart may be found in the occasions congressional committees take during hearings on legislative and financial proposals to question thoroughly cabinet members and other administrative officers. Ministers and other officials may also be "invited" to give statements to and discuss policies with committees or informal groups of congressmen; their desire to stand in well with the legislators is ordinarily sufficient inducement to accept such invitations.

Parliamentary bodies also have power to establish select or special committees to conduct investigations of executive actions or the results of administering certain legislation. Exercising its authority to obtain essential information upon which legislation may be based, the United States Congress has through its history investigated subjects ranging from American Indians to "un-American activities." These have commonly proved a useful device through which to supervise administration in some respects. Certain efforts of recent years, however, where some congressional committees have turned essentially from examining the administrative process to inquire into the beliefs of private citizens have produced widespread feeling that individual congressmen in these circumstances have abused their authority. In the case of *Watkins* v. *United States* (1957), Chief Justice Warren agreed that congressional investigatory power is "inherent in the legislative process," but cautioned that "there is no congressional power to expose for the sake of exposure."

A third legislative control is found in the practice of discussing and criticizing executive action, formally by debates on motions of confidence and censure, or indirectly on other subjects. Arising from information obtained in ways just described, the legislature has the signal responsibility to review executive policies and actions; to publicize those which are inefficient, ineffectual, or extravagant; to champion the cause of persons treated unjustly or arbitrarily; and to place the findings before the forum of public opinion. Here, then, the legislature acts as the "grand inquest of the nation." As Sir William Anson, in his *Law and Custom of the Constitution,* described the attributes of members of Parliament, they may "discuss all matters of national or imperial concern, and criticize the conduct of ministers; either House collectively may address the Crown on matters of general policy, may institute inquiries, in the public interest, into the conduct of persons or public bodies; while in the last resort, Parliament may bring to justice a great political offender." And for the result, Woodrow Wilson, in his *Congressional Government,* concluded that: "The informing function of Congress should be preferred even to its legislative function. The argument is not only that discussed and interrogated administration is the only pure and efficient administration, but, more than that, that the only really self-governing people is that people which discusses and interrogates its administration."

Finally, as a fourth device, there is the legislative power to drive the executive from office. In terms this narrow, this is a function of the legislature only in the parliamentary system, where ministers are collectively and individually responsible to the popular chamber, though it is not entirely without counterpart in the presidential type of government. Even among the former types of government this authority is not identically employed, but it is in all of them "the shotgun behind the door" as a weapon against an entirely impossible executive. As we noted in the previous chapter, a British ministry is virtually irremovable unless an election alters the party balance in the Commons. Restraint is also imposed in this function upon the German *Bundestag,* which can vote a ministry out of office only by agreeing on its successor. In the Third and Fourth French Republics, however, Parliament exercised its power to drive ministries from office so zealously and frequently as to destroy all governmental stability. In the American presidential system, Congress does have the power to remove the President, the Vice-President, and all civil officers of the United States from office "on impeachment for, and conviction of, treason, bribery, or other high crimes and misdemeanors." Such procedure is not intended, of course, to resolve merely political differences between the two. However, excepting the President, all offices and agencies of the national government are created by act of Congress, as well as being equipped with authority, staff, and funds. Not surprisingly, if Congress does not obtain a considerable measure of co-operation from the President, it may choose to restrict the resources with which he acts.

The Enactment of Law. We are discussing this function of the legislature last, not because it is the least important, but because it is the most obvious and the one to which parliamentary bodies devote the largest amount of their time. We may note at the outset that it is customary to distinguish legislative proposals as either public bills, those of general application, or private bills, which apply only to individual persons or localities, and to subject them to somewhat different procedures. Bills originate from different sources; the largest proportion in most assemblies come from the executive, are known as "government" bills or "administration" measures, and are initiated or introduced by a minister. All others are private members' bills (to use the British phrase that sharply distinguishes them), which may be of either public or private application. In the United States, it may be noted, where Congress is rather uniquely organized to originate legislation on its own, private bills constitute a very large proportion of legislative measures.

To carry out its duties, a legislative assembly undertakes its formal organization at the beginning of each session. It chooses a presiding officer, variously titled Speaker, President, or Chairman, one or more deputy officers to serve in his absence, a clerk, and certain other officials as are necessary. The function of the presiding officer is, of course, to maintain order, to recognize members wishing to speak, to ensure that they do so more or less relevantly, to rule on matters of procedure, to put questions, to announce the result of votes, and to sign bills and resolutions. The moderator usually also has power to repress disorder, if necessary, by suspending proceedings. He is everywhere an official of authority and dignity, though none exceeds in impressiveness the Speaker of the British House of Commons, splendid in wig and gown.

The legislative process in all chambers divides consideration of measures between the house as a whole and its committees. Every assembly organizes a set of standing or permanent committees, each provided as a rule with competence over a specific area of governmental activity, and which receives all bills upon that subject. Parties are represented on these committees in proportion to their strength in the house. Committee consideration may come either before or after first consideration of a bill by the whole assembly, depending upon the particular parliamentary procedure; in either case, its function is to act as the "house in miniature" and to subject the bill to such revision and amendment as will commend it to the membership generally. A bill is normally considered by the entire house at least twice, so that both its general principles and its details may be examined. The United States, Great Britain, and the Commonwealth countries also make use of a committee of the whole house, which is essentially a means of proceedings under less formal rules which will permit wide participation in debate. Parliamentary bodies create other kinds of committees, of course, for special purposes.

The parliamentary procedure of a legislative chamber is ordinarily governed in part by constitutional provisions and statutes. In addition, an assembly adopts a set of standing rules, around which grows up a body of precedents derived from rulings of the moderator, and supplemented by orders of the day and special rules. The elaborate and formal rules of a parliamentary body have several purposes. They ensure that party leadership can make itself felt, and that the more important measures will receive priority of consideration; to let members know at any one time precisely what action may be taken respecting a measure;

to allow the minority to be heard, to oppose, and to offer alternative measures; and to expedite procedure so that the majority may work its will.

Debate proceeds either from specific motions, as in English-speaking countries, or on more general subjects, as is the European practice. The presiding officer usually has some discretion in recognizing members, though in his selection of those who may speak, he is sometimes assisted with lists provided by the party leaders; where ministers may be present in a house, they ordinarily enjoy preferment, as do also committee chairmen. It is common to set advance limits to the length of a given debate, and nearly everywhere the majority can adopt a closure motion so that action may be taken. Voting practices vary, of course, though several methods are widely used. These include the viva voce vote, in which members call out in turn the ayes and noes; voting by sitting and standing, which has much the same effect; by division, which involves a physical separation of the ayes and noes, and their count by tellers; balloting, either open or secret; and roll call, by which members' votes are recorded as their names are read. Only a few parliaments, among them those of France, Sweden, and Finland, have adopted electric voting machines.

Where the legislature is bicameral, there must be some procedure to deal with the important matter of reconciling differences between the two houses over the terms of a bill. As we have previously noted, upper chambers in most instances do not enjoy an equality of power with the lower; consequently, in such countries as Australia, France, the German Federal Republic, Great Britain, and Ireland, there are procedures permitting the popular chamber to override the second house. In others, such as Belgium and Italy, a bill is passed back and forth between the chambers until agreement is reached, or it is obvious that none can be. A third arrangement, applying in Denmark, Sweden, and the United States, is to draw a joint conference committee from the two houses to reconcile their disagreements. The final step in the process of legislative enactment involves executive approval of the bill. In parliamentary systems, the titular head of state normally must approve or promulgate a bill for it to become effective as a legislative act. Since he is guided by the advice of ministers, the exercise of the veto if there is one actually rests with them, and only under rather unusual circumstances are they likely to wish to reject bills they have themselves originated and guided to passage. In the United States, the step has some real importance, however; the President may veto a bill passed by Congress, which can in turn repass it against his objections by a vote of two-thirds of each house. To be sure, this power fails to provide the President with legislation he may want, but it is commonly effective in dealing with legislation he does not.

V. *The* DECLINE *of the* LEGISLATURE

The legislature, we have already noted, in modern times has always been considered the indispensable organ of democratic government. The emergence of legislative authority was directly related to the extension of modern democracy, reflecting the principle of government by the consent of the governed. Yet the ideal conception of the legislature as a central institution conducting all affairs of state, formulating policies and laws, and overseeing their administration, is no longer valid. Parliamentary bodies have lost much of the power they held in the eighteenth and nineteenth centuries; unlike the executive, they have made few adjustments to the changed circumstances of the twentieth century. Several decades ago, the distinguished authority on legislatures, Robert Luce, warned that "the old methods of representative government are nowhere equal to the problems springing from the complexities of modern life."

That the legislature has substantially lost place to the executive is by now a well-confirmed phenomenon. British "parliamentary government" has evolved into "cabinet government"; American "congressional government" has become "presidential government." The German Federal Republic has been facetiously described as the German "Chancellor" Republic, while the traditional "assembly government" of France has been replaced, under the Fifth Republic, by the "presidential government" of General de Gaulle, and reduced, in one view, to being little more than "a technocracy managed by bureaucrats." But parliamentary bodies have suffered subordination to more than just the executive. As Professor Peter Campbell has observed: "National policy is made by the governing party's leaders, subject to the influence of their backbenchers and their supporters outside parliament, the civil service, and the various sectional interests and opinion groups; the fate of governments is decided mainly by the voters at general elections. The government, the majority party, the civil service, the pressure groups and the electorate at large—it is from their discussions that decisions emerge; only a small part of these discussions take place in the two chambers and their lobbies." Inevitably, then, the legislature's role becomes somewhat subsidiary. We may now briefly examine the twofold basis upon which much of the disparagement of the contemporary legislature rests.

The Problem of Legislative Power. First of all, the subordination of legislative power is an inevitable reflection of the aggrandizement of the executive. The idea of parliamentary supremacy was originally concomitant with the object of replacing absolutist by popular authority. But, as we have seen, the expansion of governmental activity has produced an inevitable extension of executive powers; and the need for strong leadership and vigorous action respecting the problems of defense, foreign relations, and domestic economy of the modern nation has obliged the executive to accept the central role in the political process. Even states with the strongest parliamentary traditions, emphatically committed to the maintenance of executive responsibility, have witnessed this phenomenon.

Second, the role of the legislature is reduced by the difficulty within the modern state of effecting consensus upon national goals and policies. More and more nations are finding it almost impossible to resolve satisfactorily various constitutional, political, economic, or diplomatic crises confronting their society. For all states, whether among the most or the least powerful, circumstance and not choice dictates their degree of involvement and position in the international community and their relative success in reconciling the various domestic conflicts of interest. As parliamentary bodies frequently mirror society's opposing and hostile interests, and find themselves unable to resolve the controversies raised by them, they further accentuate irreconcilable conflicts within the fabric of the nation itself, and cease themselves to be functioning, coherent institutions.

Third, the weakness of parliamentary traditions and spirit frequently renders the legislative institution impotent. As we have pointed out earlier in this chapter, the periods following both World Wars I and II witnessed the difficulties of a number of new states suddenly confronted with the problem of self-government, either because their heretofore autocratic system was overthrown or their colonial status of dependency was terminated. Obliged for the first time to undertake the responsibility of operating complex parliamentary institutions, they have faced formidably difficult tasks. In these new governmental systems, the distractions of personal jealousies, partisan rivalries, nationalistic sensitivity, and economic complications do not make the going easier. Such states as Burma, Ceylon, Indonesia, the Korean Republic, Pakistan, and Thailand, to name only a few, all have had experience with these problems.

The Problem of Legislative Efficiency. Legislatures, even in states with long traditions of effective representative government, display various institutional shortcomings. One of these inevitably arises from the problem of leadership. Though leadership cannot dispense with the personal element, if it is to be truly effective and continuous it must be institutionalized through the mechanism of party. Where party leaders are able to apply a strict parliamentary discipline, however, as in Great Britain and the German Federal Republic, a common complaint is that members of parliament are the servants of the party machines—frustrated, denied the exercise of initiative or discretion, and dragooned through divisions. Where parliamentary party discipline is weak, on the other hand, as in France and the United States, the criticism is made that the party is unable to carry out its election promises or accomplish its mandate, and that the individual legislator is inordinately sensitive to and preoccupied with the demands of local or special interests. Thus, few legislatures have satisfactorily achieved an ideal middle ground where party leadership is neither too strong nor too weak.

Critics of the legislature today also remark upon the inability of such bodies to cope with the volume and complexity of legislation before them. Legislative procedures are commonly described as slow, cumbersome, and anachronistic, and under them legislators are called upon to make decisions involving matters of the utmost technicality and complexity. There is always pressure upon parliamentary time; yet legislators commonly appear not to make effective use of what they have, often occupying themselves at length with trivial affairs, then rushing through with indecent haste legislation of the highest importance. In the United States Congress, for example, far too much time is devoted to private bills dealing with matters that might more properly be delegated to administrative authority. In an age when few subjects of legislation can be simple, the legislature appears most inadequately equipped with expert staff and advisory assistance.

Still further, parliamentary bodies are widely criticized as having inadequate means of supervising executive authority. The traditional methods for holding the executive accountable appear definitely insufficient in the face of the expanding powers and activities of modern government. Assemblies continually struggle unsuccessfully to obtain sufficient information about what the executive is doing, and yet without it effective criticism of the administration is impossible. An inattentive and ineffective opposition may prefer to air spectacular but petty grievances rather than perform the hard work of systematically surveying a government's policies and proposing reasonable alternatives to them. Where party discipline is strong, governments are virtually irremovable, except by the electorate; where party discipline is weak, and responsibility is diffused among many small parties, the power to overturn governments can be easily abused. Even in Great Britain, despite the finesse with which legislative-executive relationships were shaped, it is frequently asserted that the executive has long since upset the balance, and that "cabinet dictatorship" of Parliament is the result. Such entirely legitimate devices of control as the investigating committee can be abused when conducted in a hostile, partisan manner; the American tableau of congressional bloodhounds scurrying in all directions and baying loudly at every suspicious scent is certainly not a reassuring spectacle.

Finally, it is clear enough that legislatures have suffered a serious decline in prestige, reflecting an adverse popular view not only of the legislature's membership but also of its organization and operation. It is a commonplace in Great Britain today that truly independent-minded men no longer will offer themselves as candidates for House of Commons seats. The German *Bundestag* is contemptuously spoken of as *Die Schwatzbude* (the gossip shack); and during serious political crises, Frenchmen have been known to post signs on their automobiles stating: *"Je ne suis pas député"* (I am not a Deputy). As Walter Lippmann observed a few years ago, "it is one of the great facts of our public life that the Congress of the United States is today short of men of ability and high purpose and much too long on blatherskites." These views, though not universally held, do not, even so, reflect mere momentary irritations. They are, rather, commentaries on a variety of unsatisfactory aspects of the legislative institution: its frequently unrepresentative character, its dilatory procedures, its solicitude for narrow and selfish interests, and its unseemly propensity for maneuvering and bickering over trifles of partisan advantage. It is unnecessary to elaborate, for we have already suggested a number of other grounds for criticism, and the list quickly grows long.

The Improvement of the Legislative Institution. After examining such a list of criticisms, one might be led to conclude that the legislature ought to be abolished. Yet the democratic state cannot dispense with the legislature; its essential functions cannot be performed by any other agency of government. The task of democracy, then, is to find ways to restore the legislature to a position in which it can effect its fundamental purposes. To examine the welter of proposed solutions for such a restoration, in even modest detail, would take us far beyond the allowable dimensions of our present discussion. Yet the student should ponder the problem, which can probably be resolved as much by changes in public opinion and parliamentary spirit as by alterations in laws and forms. Certainly there is room for improvement in several principal directions: among them, raising the representative character of parliamentary bodies, streamlining and modernizing their procedures, forging more effective devices for their supervision of the executive, and improving the quality of the legislators. In this latter regard, though a minimum age for legislators is sometimes constitutionally required to assure appropriate maturity, nowhere have retirement ages been established. Yet the matter deserves attention; given the need of these bodies for members with stamina and mental vigor, it seems highly desirable that they not become refuges for the senile and superannuated.

These are matters of the highest concern today, not simply in order to dispel popular disillusionment with legislative bodies, but because the fate of representative government is everywhere at stake. It may be true that we expect more of parliamentary bodies than they are able to give, and that we set our expectations at unattainable levels of perfection. Nonetheless, the enhancement of the reliability and efficacy of our representative legislatures must be a continuing process if we are to avoid the collapse of the popular foundation upon which our entire democratic edifice rests. Parliamentary bodies are everywhere today confronted with weighty and vital tasks, and the wisdom needed to resolve them is not theirs for the asking. "To govern is to choose, no matter how difficult the choices become," Pierre Mendès-France has observed. To choose rightly, and to support political authority that can, is the challenge facing the legislature in this perilous world.

CHAPTER 11

The JUDICIARY

THE cry for "equal justice under law" rings through the centuries; it has been one of the most potent political demands in western civilization. Although justice may be separated from law, and even from equality, the linking of these three terms has supported the development of the third great institution of government, the judiciary, as an independent system of courts and judges. But sometimes, as we shall see, the pursuit of justice—or some more mundane objective—can lead to a judiciary more like an arm of government than an independent branch of it. Such differences in the organization and activity of the judicial power make it extremely difficult even for judges to say precisely what the judicial process is. Nonetheless we can indicate its general distinguishing characteristics.

Government presupposes a social order, some parts of which at least are defined in law. We have seen that the legislative process, basically, elaborates such laws through representation, deliberation, and decision. The executive process, basically, maintains this legal order through the employment of the power of the community. These are, of course, responsibilities which may be performed in diverse ways, and also variously distributed among persons and groups. But what, then, is the judicial process?

In any society disputes are likely to arise among private parties, and between public officials and private persons, concerning their respective rights, powers, and responsibilities within the framework of law. The judicial process resolves such disputes: it hears and decides causes. In doing this the judicial power completes and co-ordinates the other two processes of government; naturally, its own organization and procedures, its degree of independence or lack of it, will depend to some extent on how and to what end the executive and legislative functions are exercised. Once we have clarified as best we can the essential nature of the judicial power, therefore, we must observe the various forms that it has taken in practice.

Like the legislative, the judicial organ marks a branching off from an original concentration of authority in a single ruler. It derives from a refinement in distinguishing governmental functions and a division of labor among those who exercise public power. The legislature is a relatively modern development in its present form, however; the judicial institution is much older. Indeed, in very ancient times, rulers appointed judges to administer justice in their behalf. Courts have, therefore, a very long history and, of all the parts of government, they have changed the least in form and function. The reason for this is probably inherent in the nature of their work and their role in society.

Characteristics of the Judicial Process. Three characteristics have always marked the judicial process. The first has to do with the object of judicial proceedings: this is, simply, to administer justice. The search for the meaning of the powerful abstraction "justice" has continued for centuries in legal and philosophical thinking, and many different conclusions have resulted. We will not pretend, then, that we can simply define it here. Doing justice, in a primarily legal sense, was defined by Ulpian as rendering to every man his due. Others have defined it differently. Even so, some essential qualities of justice are well known; we associate what is just with what is rightful, equitable, virtuous, reasonable, and lawful. To assure justice to individuals in their various affairs is clearly one of the oldest service functions of government. As Augustine observed: "Set justice aside, then, and what are kingdoms but great robberies?"

A second characteristic relates to method: the provision by the state of an impartial judge to decide a cause. A man is not justly to be condemned or his rights prejudiced without being heard. In the process, impartiality is the judge's first duty, and to ensure this he must be entirely without personal interest in the proceedings before him, and free from all interference in his performance. We insist on judicial integrity of a very high order; irregularities in character or behavior displayed in the executive or the legislative branches are considered intolerable in a judge. As Lord Hewart observed: "Justice should not only be done, it should also be seen to be done." Thus the judiciary plays a unique role; the legislature must enact general rules and cannot apply them to individual cases; and, for the executive to have final authority to settle disputed cases would often make it judge in its own cause.

The third characteristic of the judicial process is its conduct by determinate standards: that causes be resolved according to law. This feature gives the qualities of order and predictability to the disposition of individual interests. Despite the difficulties in attaining it, judicial administration clings to the ideal of certainty. There must be a sense of substantial continuity in the character of prevailing rules or the judicial process will not serve its essential social purpose. Let us now examine briefly these rules and the legal systems they constitute.

I. LAW *and* LEGAL SYSTEMS

The term "law" is another great abstraction used in a number of senses, and defined in many different ways. Men speak of *divine* law, as composed of commandments and precepts they believe have been ordained by God, and contained in such works as the Bible, the Koran, or the Torah; of *moral* law, as rules of ideal human conduct based upon personal conscience and community opinion; and of *natural* law, which has been considered to be rules inherent in nature or the universe. The term *scientific* law is used to describe the sequence of cause and effect in natural phenomena, which operates entirely without reference to man's will. Obviously, these various laws differ greatly as to their source and their sanction, that is, the means which induce obedience to their rules. None of them, however, constitutes the kind of law we are primarily concerned with in the conduct of government.

THE NATURE OF LAW

Positive Law. Ordinarily, we speak of *jural* or *positive* law, which is man-made law; it may be broadly defined as the rules of conduct that will be enforced by public officials. The purpose of law is to order and stabilize human relations in society; yet it is not the only means which is employed to this end or which determines how men behave. Society prescribes conduct in several different ways. As Professor Munroe Smith has observed: "To knock a man down, for example, or to wrest from him portable valuables is, in most instances, at once unmannerly, immoral and illegal." The observance of manners is enforced by the desire to avoid ridicule and to achieve social ease; and of morals, by the desire to avoid shame and social ostracism and to achieve honor and good conscience. The rules of law, however, are distinguishable from other social controls in that they are expressed through the organs of government, and will be enforced by them, if necessary, with physical force. Moral and legal rules are further distinguishable in that the latter can be formulated in terms of rights, and hence are capable of judicial application. In sum, then, positive law is laid down through the machinery of the state and is discernible particularly as those rules that the courts will enforce.

In primitive societies, men tended to make little distinction between morals, customs, religious beliefs, natural phenomena, and positive law. They saw all rules of behavior, for things animate and inanimate, as prescribed by their environment, immutable, and implicitly to be obeyed. They assumed, in other words, that the same controlling forces determined all rules, whether prescribing the movement of the tides, the forms of politeness to one's mother-in-law, or the exercise of rights over personal property. Thus what we call positive law was originally considered to be something fixed and static; laws were not deliberately made but discovered. Through most of the history of law the attitude prevailed: law was what had ever been, it was found, and declared. Not until well toward the end of the middle ages was the idea fully accepted that laws might be made.

The Sources of Law. Rules of law are drawn and developed from several starting points. Moral and ethical principles have always, of course, provided important guides to human action; it is obvious that these will be given jural sanctions in many instance—murder is a crime as well as a sin. To be sure, some positive law rules are based upon little more than convenience or expediency, but the larger body of law may be seen as reflecting man's fundamental moral sense. The idea of natural law, for example, a concept known to men from the ancient Greeks to the American founding fathers as an ideal law to which positive law should approximate, exerted an influence throughout the entire formative period of western institutions. Men have disagreed, of course, over what constitutes the law of nature. To some it has been an emanation from God; to others, it is dictated by and discoverable in reason, or in man's ability to distinguish right from wrong; but in any case its rules are considered by many to have a reality and force apart from any positive action or consent by individual men or states. As Alexander Hamilton wrote: "The sacred rights of mankind are not to be rummaged for among old parchments or musty records. They are written, as with a sunbeam, in the whole volume of human nature, by the hand of the divinity itself, and can never be erased or obscured by mortal power."

A second source of positive law has been custom. In the life of a community certain practices acquire the support of tradition and common usage. When such practices come to be enforced through government we may say that they have become part of the positive law. Such provisions, often called customary law, are an important part of all bodies of law, and even in modern times customary practices continue to be turned into customary law through the process of public, or judicial, recognition. The assertion that custom is a source of law, however, is ambiguous. Adherents of the "historical" school of jurisprudence hold that custom —representing a long and uniform development of a rule together with a conviction of its "rightness"—is an instance of society, not government, creating law. More usually today, however, it is held that only public officials can create law as such, although it is admitted that customary practices may in fact dictate the content of the legal norms they create. But in either case, it is difficult to determine just when and to what extent a custom becomes a legal rule, for customary law is necessarily unwritten law. The advantage of customary law is that it may be expected to enjoy popular support and to reflect common sense and experience; but it tends to be slow-developing and conservative. For this reason it is not so significant in contemporary judicial processes as it was in those of less revolutionary periods.

A third source of law is found in adjudication. Presumably, the rules of law are developed in this manner by a judge called upon to decide controversies between individuals. The local customs or customary laws are declared, the judge chooses among these and other available rules, and judicial rulings assimilate them to the total body of law. The classic example of judge-made law is found in the English system. In its development the judges were not, technically speaking, considered to be the source of the law; rather, they were the means by which its existence was declared. The fiction was that the royal justices merely applied "the custom of the realm." Actually, however, this development of a body of precedents, by professional lawyers and judges, constituted the making of law. English law thus became a "case law" rather than a "customary law" system; once the rolls of the courts began to be kept, the law was unwritten only in the sense of being uncodified.

Finally, a source of law is legislation. In the broadest sense, legislation is enacted law, whether comprising constitutions, constitutional laws, treaties, statutes, or decrees. As we have seen, the legislative power may be exercised by the people in constitution-making, by the legislature in adopting a statute, or by the executive in issuing a decree. Only the judiciary may not "enact" law, though as we have suggested, they may well "make" it. Legislation is considered superior in rank to judge-made rules; it is a more democratic form of lawmaking, and provides the means whereby old rules may be modernized, and new rules given immediate effect. A significant aspect of legislation is that it clearly displays the element of command by the sovereign. This is most important in the view of the "analytical" school of jurisprudence; its adherents consider law as the command of a superior to an inferior, supported by a monopoly of force, and these elements as essential to its validity.

The views of the historical and the analytical schools of jurists undoubtedly cannot be reconciled, but their conflicting perspectives do help to emphasize important characteristics of law. Law must be enforced by the machinery of state, or we have not distinguished it from other means of social control; but no state, however despotic, can successfully command obedience to that which is utterly repugnant to the community. An effective body of law, enjoying stability and continuity, must reflect a general conviction as to its rightness and appropriateness; it is a part of human culture and civilization.

LEGAL SYSTEMS

Historically speaking, the law of the western world has been drawn from numerous elements. The oldest of the ancient systems known to us is found in the Code of Hammurabi, published by the king of Babylon about 2000 B.C., which drew mainly upon old Sumerian law. The Code reflects a society well advanced from barbarism, and it probably had considerable influence in other areas of the Mediterranean. Relatively little is known of other ancient systems. Despite its great achievements in intellectual speculation elsewhere, Greece made no significant contributions to jurisprudence. It was left to Rome and Norman England to originate the two great legal systems of the world.

The Civil Law System. The civil law system developed in continental Europe, taking its name as well as its contents from the *jus civile* of Rome. Rome's first great law code, drawing together the early customary law and dating from about 450 B.C., was the famous Twelve Tables; it constituted the foundation upon which Rome's monumental legal edifice was constructed. The Romans thereafter developed two bodies of law, a *jus civile* for Roman citizens, and a *jus gentium* for the subjects of their empire, which in time largely superseded the former. After Rome's civilization and empire were well in decline, however, it produced a crowning effort to the work of ten centuries of jurists: the celebrated Code of Justinian, dating from approximately A.D. 533. This restatement of the Roman law constituted a legacy which enriched the legal systems of Europe and much of the world.

The Justinian Code was soon superseded, as the collapse of Rome opened the way for other bodies of law to prevail in Europe. A German system of law, originating in tribal rules extensively intermingled with those from Roman law, provided the rude society of the times with a limited scheme of tort and criminal proceedings. It was much more primitive than the Roman system, but became of increasing importance as the royal authority of the Teuton kings was consolidated. Later, compilations of feudal law were made; an important example, the *Libri Feudorum* from Lombardy, reflected the way in which the similar conditions of land tenure of the times produced substantially uniform rules. In addition, a body of canon law, the law of the Church, based extensively on Roman legal ideas, evolved as the Church itself became a great estate in medieval Europe. From its concern with morality in general and jurisdiction over the clergy in particular, the Church developed rules of law and a court system to govern such varied matters as marriage, wills, usury, oaths, contracts, and a considerable list of crimes. The canon law became particularly influential as it was compiled and codified after the twelfth century. Finally, the growth of cities, their development as mercantile communities, and the extension of foreign commerce gave rise to bodies of commercial and maritime law, the law merchant.

During the twelfth century, interest in Roman law revived and study was renewed in the universities of southern France and northern Italy. The rediscovered Roman law now proved particularly valuable: to the doctors of law, for offering solutions to the new social and economic problems confronting Europe; to the kings, for suggesting means to strengthen royal absolutism; and generally, for supplementing and refining local customary law. Roman law naturally exerted its greatest immediate influence within those areas which had been most intensely subjected to Latin civilization. But it ultimately exerted influence well beyond these, in England, Scotland, Scandinavia, and the Slavic countries.

Through the next several centuries, the various legal rules commingled, but Roman law, at first secondary to local customary law, increased in influence through the writings of jurists and the teachers of law in the universities. Obviously, the extent to which the several bodies of rules—Roman, feudal, customary, canon, and commercial—would prevail in a particular country varied considerably; the inclinations of the ruler, the depth of the roots of the local law, the effectiveness of the court system, and the complexity of the contemporary society were all factors. Yet the tendency everywhere was to reduce the rules to writing. Though this restricted an extensive development of the law by judicial decision, it gave impetus to its codification.

France produced the first great contribution to the modern civil law system in 1804 with the French Civil Code, prepared for the Emperor Napoleon, and four other major codes followed. The French Civil Code was widely imitated or adopted; those of Belgium, Italy, the Netherlands, Portugal, Spain, and the Latin American countries were all based upon it. French influence also carried to the German-speaking countries. After the unification of the German Empire, a German Civil Code was completed in 1896. As non-European states, such as Japan and Turkey, sought to modernize and Europeanize their institutions, they too drew from the civil law system. Indeed, all civil law countries owe something to the French, German, or Swiss codes.

The Common Law System. The common law system prevails in most English-speaking countries, and takes its name from the medieval English practice of describing the rules administered by the king's courts as that law common to the whole realm. It, too, can be explained only in terms of its historical development. For more than three centuries, England was a province of the Roman empire and governed by Roman law. In the fifth century the Roman soldiery were withdrawn, and thereafter England was invaded by the Anglo-Saxon tribes. Making England their homeland, they seem to have obliterated all but some physical traces of Roman civilization, replacing it with Germanic customs, institutions, and law. In the ninth century the invading Danes, and in the eleventh century the conquering Normans, further reinforced the Teutonic influences. Although William of Normandy created no new legal system, he and his successors established a system of government and judicial administration that did.

In the two centuries following the conquest, Anglo-Saxon law, a multiplicity of local rules and customs, was largely reduced to a single body of rules, as the Norman rulers began an unprecedented centralization of power, which their successors extended. Though continuing the old communal courts of the hundred and the shire, they established powerful and superior royal courts at Westminster. The king's judges were also sent on circuit to administer justice in his name among the localities. The new doctrine of the king's peace broadened royal authority to punish offenses; the king's inquest as a method of finding facts became the basis for the jury system; and, the king's writs were used to enlarge the scope of judicial remedies. If Germanic custom and doctrine provided the raw material for the earliest common law rules, still other influences made their mark upon English law. These were, indeed, essentially the same elements that went into the making of the civil law system. As on the continent, the revived Code of Justinian was studied at the English universities, and attracted the interest of men of learning. English feudalism also developed its rules, among them the most advanced system of land tenure in Europe. In this formative period most of the king's judges were also clergymen, trained in the canon law; inevitably its principles were absorbed, especially after the jurisdiction of the ecclesiastical courts was restricted. England also knew the commercial and maritime law of Europe. Important, too, in shaping the common law system were the contributions of legal scholars, such as Glanvil and Bracton in the thirteenth century, and the guilds of lawyers, gathered in the Inns of Court, which were organized soon thereafter. Though the works of jurists did not have an importance here comparable to those of the civil law countries, Coke's *Institutes* and Blackstone's *Commentaries* on the English law of the seventeenth and eighteenth centuries, respectively, and Kent's *Commentaries on American Law* (1826–1830), are outstanding contributions to its literature.

Especially significant in the formulation of English law from the beginning was the practice of following precedent. Over a number of centuries, this convenient practice hardened into binding principle; hence the singular technique of the common law system: *Stare decisis et non quieta movere* (To adhere to precedents, and not unsettle things established). When deciding a case, judges normally referred to prior decisions rendered in similar circumstances. Case by case, then, over many years the judges selected, reinforced, and shaped their legal principles, weaving together the great fabric of judge-made law. Thus, although the common law is described from its origins in customary or conventional law, it was the custom of precedent in judicial decision—and not of popular usage—that determined its specific quality.

Even so, the common law system does not comprise judge-made rules alone. Almost alongside of it grew the rules of equity. Originally, these were special dispensations made by the king as "the fountain of justice." Then this function was handed over to the king's chancellor, acting as "keeper of the king's conscience," to supplement the common law rules where they failed to be equitable, and to insure substance as well as form in the administration of justice. In time a separate court of chancery, or equity, was provided; it developed a further body of rules to be merged into the English system. Finally, in the thirteenth century, legislation by Parliament began to acquire significance, though for some time to come, Parliament's role was more nearly that of declaring or clarifying the law than of enacting it. Not until the nineteenth century did Parliament undertake an extensive recasting of the common law, modifying and modernizing its rules to meet the needs of an industrial and urbanized society. Thus the modern English common law system was integrated from the three strands of law, equity, and statute.

The common law system was also brought to prevail in Ireland, and, among the Commonwealth states, in Canada (except Quebec), Australia, and New Zealand; it has further influenced the legal systems of India, Israel, and to some degree the Scandinavian states. It was early carried to the American colonies by British settlers, though the colonists at first had no need of such an advanced system of law. Its reception later came to be extensive. In 1774 the Continental Congress claimed that the "colonies are entitled to the common law of England," and some states subsequently stipulated its adoption formally, either by constitutional or statutory provision. Its spirit and doctrines do provide, of course, the basis for American jurisprudence, and most of the rules applicable to American situations have been absorbed either by judicial decision or statute. American law has been extensively developed and codified by statute, and each state has its own system, but all, excepting that of Louisiana, derive from the common law.

The Common and Civil Law Systems Compared. It should be emphasized at the outset that in distinguishing these two major systems we are speaking actually of two broad patterns of legal origin and development. All states now have much that is indigenous in their particular national system of law. The American system, for example, not only differs in many respects from the English, reflecting its own local circumstances, but actually includes a number of different state systems. Again, though France, Germany, and Switzerland are all civil law jurisdictions, their respective national systems are not at all the same as the classical Roman type, and differ much from each other as well. We have observed that the civil and the common law have, indeed, drawn from much the same historic sources; they are distinguished, then, primarily in the way in which these elements have been proportioned and developed. In sum, the civil law is a complete code of rules promulgated by a central authority; the common law is a system of reported precedents developed by judicial reasoning.

Developed by precedent through the continuing process of judicial resolution of actual legal controversies, the rules of common law must be searched out of decided cases. Hence they are capable of endless extension by judicial reasoning and improvisation; as Coke said, "the common law is nothing else but reason." Yet rules developed by argument over precedents and adherence to *stare decisis* may produce some conflicting results; the common law may be reasonable, but it is not always logical. "The life of the law," said Justice Holmes, "has not been logic; it has been experience." Statutes and codes are only a part of the system, no matter how completely they may be developed, for even when they replace common law rules, the latter still serve to provide definition and interpretation. We may note, lastly, that in part because of its origin in custom, and in part because of the role played by courts in the Anglo-American countries, the common law has been particularly solicitous of the individual's rights as against the government. Its doctrine of "the rule of law," that all public officials as well as private persons are equally subject to the same law in the ordinary courts of justice, is one of its proudest features.

The civil law system is characterized by its adherence to code, which is the sole authoritative exposition of the law. It has always been amenable to restatement by codification; as Sir Henry Maine observed of the Roman system, it "begins, as it ends, with a code." The preparation of the great national codes has been the work of jurists and scholars; it is scarcely an exaggeration to say that law here has been developed, not by courts, but by universities. It is the legislator, then, and not the judge who may give approval to new rules. The civil law also has given high place to reason and logic; hence, it displays in great measure symmetry, consistency, balance, and polish. A general grasp of the rules of civil law can more readily be obtained by the individual citizen; he is less indebted for explanation by a lawyer than is his counterpart in common law countries.

In the administration of the civil law, reference is always to the letter of the code and not to judicial decision or precedent. The civilian does not know the principle of *stare decisis.* Nonetheless, it should not be thought that in civil law systems there are no judicial precedents or that judges can apply the codes mechanically. Lower courts follow the decisions of higher courts, important commentaries supplement the codes, and "interpretations" of the codes do accumulate. Although judicial decisions are delivered in such brief form in France, for example, that the development of anything like "case law" is virtually impossible, in German-speaking countries rather full decisions are delivered and reported, especially by appellate courts. Also, the Swiss Civil Code goes so far as to authorize the judge, when the Code furnishes no applicable provision, to decide according to customary law, or lacking that, according to the rule he would establish as a legislator. Finally, it may be observed that, reflecting its origin, the civil law as the conscious creation of a central authority tends to assert the interests of the state before those of the individual. Perhaps this is inevitable. The civil law reflects more rapidly the collectivist and centralizing tendencies of the modern state. Moreover, its judges, as we shall see, do not occupy a position that permits them to act primarily as the defenders of individualism, as has been their role in English-speaking nations.

Islamic Law. Of course, systems other than the civil and the common law widely prevail. The Islamic system applies today, in part at least, to the some four hundred million Moslems in Africa and Asia. Undertaking to regulate the entire area of human conduct, it is both legal and moral law. As a religious law, it is considered immutable and divine, resting upon the will of Allah, the Supreme Being. Though based upon the principles of the Koran, it is not, contrary to general impression, drawn from that source. Its actual derivation is from the *Sunna,* or practices of Mohammed, as elaborated in the several centuries after his time by the *imams* (priests), and it rests on the elements of Arabic customary law. The Islamic system thus covers subjects ranging from fasting and pilgrimage, contracts and inheritance, to dietary and criminal laws.

As the various Moslem areas extended their contacts with the western world, and developed their commerce, the monolithic law of Islam proved inadequate to achieve the social progress and modernization desired in many of these countries. During the nineteenth century, therefore, civil codes from Europe were adopted to supplement Islamic law in Egypt and Turkey, among others; Turkey later officially adopted civil law entirely. Most of the other states have retained, in combination with the civil law, part of their traditional law, especially in such matters as personal status and family relations; these states include Iraq, Lebanon, Morocco, and Tunisia. A few, such as Pakistan and Saudi Arabia, however, have attempted to retain their Islamic inheritance unimpaired.

Soviet Law. In distinct contrast to a system based upon long tradition is Soviet law. In one respect only, in the view of Soviet jurists, is their system like others. Marxists see the state as an exploitive organization which promotes and defends the interests of the dominant class, and the law merely as the will of that class. Soviet law, therefore, acknowledgedly gives expression to the will and interests of the Soviet state, and thus by definition affords class justice to the proletariat. Its uniqueness, in the official view, stems from the fact that, unlike western systems, it is the first law which does not exploit; it promotes only the interests of the classless (workers') society; it is based on the existence of socialist public property; and it is guided by "the dictatorship of the proletariat."

To develop an exclusive philosophy of communist law, however, has been a difficult problem for Soviet theoreticians. In the first place, Marxist doctrine regarded law as only another capitalistic institution for the promotion of "bourgeois" interests. With the establishment of a classless society, the state would ultimately "wither away" and, so Marx and his adherents believed, most of its compulsory machinery would no longer be necessary. However, the Russian communist leaders have not found it possible to dispense with an elaborate set of laws. Secondly, though claiming that they have adopted a wholly new socialist form of law, the Soviet leaders have not been able to detach their legal organization completely from the past. Because so much property is state property, and so many aspects of individual activity are subjected to state regulation, there is an enormous preoccupation with offenses against the state, which are viewed as considerably more serious and punished with greater severity than those against an individual. By the same token, a distinct category of private law is not recognized; there can be no private rights exercisable against the state. Nevertheless, Soviet law codes cover much the same ground as do those of other continental systems, drawing partly upon Russian traditions and partly from the European civil codes, as well as upon communist ideology.

In the third place, Soviet law is viewed officially, in its essence, as an instrument of the class struggle, that is, as comprising whatever rules will perpetuate and promote the Soviet regime. It can have no objectivity; it cannot serve to limit the exercise of government authority, either by substantive or procedural restrictions. Its rules are frequently vague, often purposely so, and sometimes not even published! The difficulty here, of course, is that by its very nature law embodies the ideas of stability, continuity, and certainty. None of these are qualities Soviet law may acquire so long as it is purely an instrument of policy in the hands of the Soviet rulers. One can only conclude that in such totalitarian systems of government there cannot exist a system of law in the usual sense of the term; there can be only administrative orders and ordinances.

THE DIVISIONS OF LAW

Legal Classification. The rules of law have been developed to regulate a considerable variety of relationships between individuals and institutions. As a result, there are a number of ways in which legal rules may be classified to distinguish the category of persons to which they apply, the kind of activities they control, or the functions which they perform. The description of these major divisions is a useful, though admittedly not a very exciting, exercise. A first broad division distinguishes *international* law, or the rules observed by states in the international community as legally binding in their relationships (discussed in Chapter 13); and *municipal* law, or the rules regulating all internal or domestic affairs of the state. Municipal law, in turn, may be divided into the categories of *public* law, which governs the organization of the state and its relations to the individual; and *private* law (or *civil* law), which regulates the relations of individuals with each other.

Public Law. Public law, as we have seen, is subdivided into three broad divisions: constitutional, administrative, and criminal. *Constitutional* law (discussed in Chapter 5) was defined as the rules relating to the scope and nature of the powers exercised by government. It may be studied in historic charters and constitutional documents, fundamental statutes of constitutional importance, and in the decisions of the highest national courts. *Administrative* law (discussed in Chapter 12) consists of the rules specifying the competence and procedures of government agencies. Its rules are to be found in statutes, executive orders, and in the rulings of administrative agencies and courts. *Criminal* law is concerned, of course, with crimes and their punishment. Crimes may be offenses against the state or public authority, in the oldest historic sense, as treason, rebellion, or regicide, or offenses injurious to the public, as arson, burglary, murder, rape, or robbery. In either case, they are acts injurious to the peace and security of the community which the state will take cognizance of and punish. Although originally recognized by customary and common law, crimes are everywhere today also meticulously defined in statutory codes. It may be noted, too, that the law of both civil and criminal procedure is a part of public law.

Private Law. Private law is concerned with the rights and duties of individuals to each other. In general, the state does not intervene in the face of many invasions of the individual's rights in private law. It merely provides judicial machinery and rules with which the wronged individual may undertake the enforcement of his rights. Private law has a number of subject subdivisions. These include, employing common law terminology, contracts: agreements creating an obligation and enforceable at law; domestic relations: marriage, divorce, parent and child, guardian and ward; personal property: movable things, goods and chattels; real property: lands, tenements, and hereditaments (in the classic phrase); and, torts: civil wrongs which are not breaches of contract, such as assault and battery, deceit, defamation, negligence, and trespass. A particular act may constitute a tort and, under certain circumstances, a crime as well.

The common and civil law systems do not classify laws in identical fashion. In France, for example, as in other civil law countries, there are a number of subject matter codes: the Civil Code, Code of Civil Procedure, Commercial Code, Code of Criminal Procedure, Penal Code, and others. It may be properly emphasized, too, that there are not only variations in the rules of the two systems, but that many identical legal terms, as used in the various national systems, vary in meaning.

Other Classifications. From the standpoint of function, law may be distinguished as *substantive* and *procedural.* Substantive law defines primary rights; procedural or adjective law defines the remedies by which infringements of substantive rights may be redressed. There are also some special divisions of municipal law. *Military* law is the body of rules governing the members of the armed services and is enforced by courts-martial. *Martial* law (or "state of siege" to use the comparable civil law term) may be proclaimed for the civilian inhabitants of an area in emergencies when civil administration is replaced by military authority; it is a state of affairs—a martial rule—rather than a body of rules. Military government is further distinguished from the preceding terms as a system of military administration for a hostilely occupied or conquered enemy territory. We may note, lastly, the existence of the body of *maritime* law, the rules relating to navigation, ships and crews, marine contracts, cargoes, and marine commerce generally.

II. JUDICIAL ORGANIZATION

The law's history is accompanied by a history of judicial development. The administration of justice is also a means of creating and developing law; hence, the judicial function must be as old as the law as our knowledge of ancient history confirms. Precisely how the earliest judges began to function, whether they were arbitrators or adjudicators primarily, is debatable. It seems clear, however, that the judicial function was only one of a number of prerogatives exercised by the ruler; and the earliest judges probably had a variety of duties of general administrative or supervisory character.

The Development of the Judicial Institution. The office of judge, authorized in the ruler's name to resolve disputes and apply the law, was known in Babylonia, Egypt, Assyria, and elsewhere in the ancient world. Again, the Greeks took the next step forward: to distinguish judicial institutions from other governing agencies in the community. As Athens evolved through monarchy, aristocracy, and democracy, the judicial power was transferred from the old council, the *Areopagus,* to the *archons* (magistrates), and then to the *Heliaea,* the judicial assembly. The latter became too large a body to operate as a court; during the classic period, the *archons'* function came to be the preliminary examination of civil and criminal suits, after which they were turned over to the dicasteries, or jury courts, of several hundred citizens drawn by lot from the *Heliaea.* Though this practice introduced a substantially popular element into the administration of justice, it also prevented the development of a professional class of lawyers and judges, as well as a significant body of law.

The Roman courts evolved from primitive forms to a most highly elaborated system, and ultimately produced what had not existed before —a body of professional jurists. Judicial power passed from king to consul when Rome became a republic. Then, in the fourth century B.C. judicial administration was entrusted to the *praetor,* an elected magistrate. Typically, he conducted the preliminary hearing of a case, depending upon the jurists for expert advice as to the law, after which he turned it over to the *judex,* a kind of referee or jury of one, for decision, supplying the juror with the applicable legal formula. Under the empire, the magistrates were appointed by the emperor and required to be learned in the law. They dispensed with the *judex,* heard cases in their entirety, and rendered decisions. A supreme court was also established, to which appeals could be taken. In addition to professional judges, a class of practicing lawyers emerged. The Roman practices were further strengthened by the fact that the ecclesiastical courts, organized by the Church during the early medieval period, were modeled on the late Roman system.

The Germanic peoples in western Europe originally administered justice through a tribal assembly, or *Thing.* When all warriors of the tribe convened, the king presided; a lesser assembly of the hundred was held under a prince or count. Proceedings were crude, but formal, conducted largely by the recitation of precise formulas; the contenders made their pleas, the wisemen proposed the judgment or the "word," and the assembly pronounced the "full-word," or assent. Courts such as these, for the shire and the hundred, prevailed in England until after the Norman conquest.

Throughout the medieval period, European feudal lords maintained the hundred courts to deal locally with crimes and controversies, the latter mainly over land tenure. The emergence of more powerful monarchs was accompanied, of course, by the creation of royal courts. One aspect of the centralization of royal authority in the later middle ages was an extensive competition and controversy among the various feudal, ecclesiastical, and royal tribunals. Significant innovations during this period were the royal employment of *missi,* judges sent on circuit to administer the king's justice, and the development of the inquest. In the Germanic courts, the methods of proof had been limited to oath and ordeal; the inquest, used initially as a royal measure to obtain evidence from reputable persons in a locality, gave rise to the jury system. Full success in supplementing local judicial power by royal judicial authority came first in England, as we have seen; the process was slower and more difficult on the continent.

By the same measure, the personal authority of the king in the governmental process was also first greatly restricted in England. It may be recalled, from our discussion in Chapter 9, that the defeat of the Stuart claims to absolutism in the seventeenth century resulted in enhancing the power of both Parliament and the English courts. Their enforcement of the supremacy of law against the king's will gave them an unrivaled and assured position of independence. On the continent, however, the royal courts continued to be employed to reinforce the position of the monarch. Both practice and civil law doctrine, as well, combined to retain the courts as a part of the general system of royal administrative machinery. Inevitably then, even after the popular revolutions of the nineteenth and twentieth centuries, national court systems continued as auxiliary to the executive, or as essential elements in the bureaucratic system, rather than achieving the status of independent branches of the government.

The Hierarchy of Courts. The organization of a judicial system is hierarchical, that is, the courts are ranked in a graded order, with a base of ordinary courts at the foundation, an intermediate level ranged above, and still higher, a final supreme court. Broadly speaking, then, judicial tribunals fall into one of two categories: courts of original jurisdiction and courts of appeal. Courts are thus always accorded a specific "jurisdiction": the precise authority to hear and determine particular causes.

The standard court of first instance is a trial court with general jurisdiction to hear original actions and prosecutions in civil and criminal proceedings, respectively. Usually with a single judge on the bench, it must consider the facts and apply the law; it proceeds by the taking of evidence and the argument of attorneys. If a jury is employed, which is usual in criminal prosecutions and available in some civil actions, it will be at this level. The jury reaches a verdict, or formal finding; the judge delivers the official decision of the court in the form of a judgment. In civil proceedings the judgment is enforced by a writ of execution or similar measure; in criminal cases, if the jury finds a verdict of guilty, the judge imposes a sentence. Among courts of first instance, or ranged below them to hear minor cases under limited or special jurisdiction, are the justice of the peace, police, traffic, juvenile, and probate courts.

A smaller number of courts are appellate; they review the work of those below them to correct judicial errors and to ensure the uniform interpretation of the law. In certain instances an appeal from the decision of a lower court is available as a matter of right; generally, however, permission to appeal must be granted either by the trial court or the appellate court. Only a small proportion of all cases is appealed. As the function of the appellate court differs from that of the original court, it employs a different procedure. It reviews questions of substantive law and the procedures by which the facts were determined; but it does not collect additional evidence, and has no need of a jury. Instead, procedure is by submission of a certified record of the lower court's proceedings, a statement of the points in controversy, and printed briefs or arguments of the attorneys, which may be supplemented by their oral arguments if the court wishes them. Depending upon its findings, the court of appeal may reaffirm or reverse the judgment of the lower court, or return the case for retrial because of errors in procedure. An appellate court is composed of a collegial or multimember bench; it reaches its decision by majority vote, and if a common law court, delivers a majority opinion; however, individual judges may write dissenting opinions. English judges, it may be noted parenthetically, deliver their opinions seriatim; in civil law courts dissenting opinions as such are not feasible, though individual judges may show their disagreement with a majority decision. The highest court in any jurisdiction, usually designated the supreme court, is the tribunal of last resort, beyond which there is no further appeal. We may now undertake a brief examination of several national court systems to observe specifically how judicial institutions may be organized.

The United States Court System. One significant feature of American judicial organization, the dual system of federal and state courts, is a product of the federal division of powers; another, establishing the judiciary as a separate branch of government, results from the application of the separation-of-powers principle. The jurisdiction of the state courts extends broadly over the general body of civil and criminal law as defined by the state constitutions and statutes. The fifty American state systems do not provide a carefully unified body of courts. Each state has courts of first instance, including those with general civil and criminal jurisdiction over cases of importance, variously styled county, circuit, district, or superior courts. About a third of the most populous states have one or more intermediate courts of appeal, whose decision in many cases is final. All of the states have a supreme court—though it goes under a different title in some of them—which is final on those legal questions solely within the state's jurisdiction. Where rights under the federal Constitution, federal law, or treaties are involved, however, there may be further appeal to the Supreme Court of the United States. The minor courts of the states exist in considerable variety, with numerous municipal and other limited-jurisdiction courts dealing with petty cases and special subjects.

The federal judicial system has a much more limited jurisdiction. Without entering into technicalities, we may say that its jurisdiction is determined by the Constitution upon a twofold basis: according to the character of the controversy—principally those involving the Constitution, the laws, and treaties of the United States, and cases of admiralty and maritime jurisdiction; and according to the character of the parties to the case—including those to which the United States is a party, between two or more states, between citizens of different states, cases to which foreign ambassadors and consuls are a party, and certain others. Federal jurisdiction, where applicable, is usually but not always exclusive. The United States district courts, approximately ninety of them, are the courts of original jurisdiction, hearing both civil and criminal cases. The eleven circuit courts of appeals have from three to nine judges each, with two constituting a quorum; they hear only appeals from the district courts and from some of the federal regulatory agencies. The United

States Supreme Court is composed of the Chief Justice of the United States and eight associate justices. This highest federal court has original jurisdiction in two types of controversies: those affecting foreign diplomatic and consular representatives, and those to which a state is a party. Otherwise, it hears cases only on appeal. Congress has also provided courts for the District of Columbia, and some others to hear special controversies over patents, customs, and claims.

The English Court System. The English court system (it applies also in Wales, but not in Scotland, and with modifications in Northern Ireland), though reflecting its long historical evolution, is integrated and entirely independent. While all courts derive their authority from the Crown, they are not subject to control by the Queen or the Prime Minister, and are equally free of interference by Parliament. The English courts are broadly distinguishable as civil and criminal, but not precisely so in every case. Ordinary civil cases are heard in the county courts, of which there are over four hundred, presided over by single judges. At London is the Supreme Court of Judicature, composed of the High Court of Justice and the Court of Appeal. The High Court sits in three divisions: Queen's Bench, which hears the most important civil cases; Chancery, which hears proceedings derived from the equity system and certain other cases; and Probate, Divorce, and Admiralty, covering an assortment of cases as its name would imply. Appeals are taken to a Court of Appeal, and by leave may even go finally to the House of Lords, which is the highest court in the United Kingdom, as well as the second house of Parliament. Its judicial function is not performed by the peers generally, of course, but by the Lord Chancellor and the law lords.

There are several courts with criminal jurisdiction. The courts of summary jurisdiction, which try minor offenses without a jury, are known as magistrates' courts. In London and some of the largest cities these are maintained on a full-time basis by a stipendiary (paid) magistrate; elsewhere the magistrates are justices of the peace, who are unpaid, and need not be lawyers, but are persons of some distinction in the community. More serious criminal offenses are tried with a jury in the courts of quarter sessions; these are presided over by a chairman sitting with a number of magistrates—except in some cities where the recorder, a barrister, presides and serves as sole judge. The most serious offenses are tried before the courts of assize, held throughout the country three times a year, and conducted by a Queen's Bench judge, or appointed commissioner, traveling on circuit. Assize courts use juries in criminal proceedings, and they may also hear some civil cases. London, Liverpool, and Manchester have their own permanent courts of assize; that of London is known as the Central Criminal Court. Appeals from the magistrates' courts go to quarter sessions, and on points of law to the High Court; those involving serious offenses go to the Court of Criminal Appeal and, in rare instances, beyond that to the House of Lords.

The French Court System. The most striking feature of French judicial organization is the array of two separate systems of ordinary and administrative courts. Like the English, civil and criminal courts are also distinguished. At the lowest level some 450 courts of first instance hear minor civil cases. Above them are the courts of grand instance, with unlimited civil jurisdiction, and the courts of appeals. Lesser criminal cases are heard by police and correctional courts; appeals go to assize courts, which also have jurisdiction over the most serious criminal offenses, when they will employ a jury. The highest of the ordinary courts, the Court of Cassation, hears appeals in its civil and criminal sections; if it overrules the decision of a lower court, the case must be retried by another tribunal at the same lower level. There are certain other courts with special jurisdiction, such as labor, commercial, and juvenile courts. It may be noted that most French courts have a collegial bench of three, five, or more judges, depending on their rank.

France provides the classic example of a system of administrative courts applying a distinct body of law. Its structure comprises the twenty-four administrative tribunals at the regional level, and the Council of State at Paris. The regional tribunals hear the lesser cases; the Council of State, which has administrative as well as judicial duties, exercises jurisdiction at the highest levels. In either case, they hear complaints against government officials and employees for wrongful, negligent, or illegal administrative acts; they may annul them by re-establishing any rights denied, and even assess damages to be paid by the government to the complainant. There are also other bodies with special administrative jurisdiction over matters of military service, public instruction, and pensions. To resolve any controversy over whether a case belongs to the ordinary or the administrative courts, there is a Court of Conflicts.

Because Anglo-American legal doctrine has always emphasized the amenability of all public officials, high and low, to the ordinary courts, the idea of a special system of administrative tribunals has tended to be viewed by common law lawyers as providing public authorities an undue privilege. According to the French doctrine of the separation of powers, however, the ordinary judiciary should not be allowed to interfere with the executive or the legislature. Hence, administrative courts are provided to control the administrative machinery of the government. They are designed, then, not to defend the executive generally, but rather to hold public officials to their legal authority and thus protect individuals and the public interest against the excesses of bureaucracy. To the extent that administrative courts provide the citizen with speedy and inexpensive redress for such wrongs, there is much to be said for them.

The Soviet System of Courts. It should be emphasized at the outset that the judiciary of the Soviet Union is an instrument of state power. Like Soviet law, it functions to promote the interests of the regime; it is not, therefore, in any way independent, but a part of the administrative apparatus. Because the Soviet Union nominally has a federal system, there are technically separate union and constituent republic courts; actually, however, they are ranged in a single system.

At the lowest level is the people's court, composed of one judge and two people's assessors (lay judges), which has minor civil and criminal jurisdiction. Next are the regional courts, which may operate at several levels in the larger republics; these have civil jurisdiction over litigation between public enterprises and the state, criminal jurisdiction over offenses against the state and socialist property, and appellate jurisdiction over the courts below. The highest judicial organ of a republic, the supreme court, has primarily appellate jurisdiction, though it may hear cases of the greatest importance in original jurisdiction. Finally, there is the Supreme Court of the U.S.S.R., composed of a chairman, two vice-chairmen, nine judges, and a number of people's assessors, all chosen by the Supreme Soviet. Organized into three divisions, civil, criminal, and military, it hears appeals in these classes respectively, with the latter type coming from the high military tribunals. The Supreme Court may also have original jurisdiction.

The people's assessors, sitting at each judicial level with the regular judge when cases are heard in original jurisdiction, are presumably a means of introducing popular participation in the judicial process, for there are no juries in the Soviet Union. The assessors are elected, along with the judges, in groups attached to each court and serve a few days a year. They are allowed a vote to decide questions of law and fact equally with the judge; however, they are not just average citizens, but are chosen from among leading Communist party members, and rarely disagree with the judge.

One aspect of Soviet judicial organization is most important: the role of the procuracy. The procurator-general has supreme supervisory power to ensure observance of the law. Chosen by the Supreme Soviet for a seven-year term, he appoints all procurators at each court level below. The procuracy has broad authority on behalf of the Communist leadership to intervene in all phases of judicial and state administration. It not only prosecutes criminal cases, but determines that "socialist legality" is maintained; it may remove cases from any court, challenge decisions, or appeal them. The procuracy has equally broad authority over administrative agencies. Thus it guides, supervises, and centralizes the enforcement and administration of Soviet law.

Court Systems in Other States. The court systems of other states display one or more of the characteristic features of the national systems we have just briefly described. A few federal countries, such as Brazil and Mexico, follow the American practice of organizing a dual system of courts, state and national. Most federal states, however, including Australia, Canada, the German Federal Republic, India, and Switzerland, have no separate federal courts except for a supreme national tribunal to review the work of the courts below. Some states observe the British practice of maintaining a system of ordinary courts only; these include Denmark, Norway, Israel, and the Commonwealth countries generally, where common law ideas have affected judicial arrangements. Most of the continental European countries, such as the German Federal Republic, Italy, Spain, and Sweden, have systems of administrative courts in addition to the ordinary institutions, though they are not all of equal importance to those in France. Also, as might be expected, the "people's republics" of eastern Europe have judicial systems resembling that of the Soviet Union in function and organization, including the "people's courts," assessors, a supreme court chosen by the national assembly, and a powerful procuracy. Lastly, among the developing states, the organization and administration of the courts have frequently tended to be among the most westernized of their institutions where traditionalist or tribal procedures are being replaced. This not only reflects a widespread ambition to modernize, but the fact that judges and lawyers are commonly European-trained and thus have well-established professional standards to observe as well as a stake in maintaining them.

The Judicial Office: Selection and Tenure. The method of recruiting and appointing judges has an influence on the character of the judiciary. Broadly speaking, judges are drawn to office in one of two ways. In the civil law countries, generally, judicial service rests as a rule upon a career basis. All judges are members of the magistracy, which they enter by obtaining an appropriate law diploma and passing competitive government examinations on the completion of their formal legal education. They begin service as court attachés or judges at the lowest level; vacancies in the various ranks are filled by promotion. In the common law countries, judges are drawn from the membership of the bar, after some years of experience in practice before the courts and the attainment of some distinction in the profession. There is as a rule little in the way of promotion of such judges from court to court.

Which method of recruitment is to be preferred is certainly debatable. The career system insures a high degree of professionalism, for the examinations are rigorous and the magistracy is especially trained for its function. Nonetheless, such judges early identify themselves as government functionaries, acquire certain bureaucratic tendencies, and become immediately dependent upon the preferment of government superiors for advancement. Judges chosen from the bar, on the other hand, while not specially trained to preside, have had a more practical experience of affairs, and are more likely to have independent inclinations. The quality of their professional attainment is measured in their maturity, and this permits evaluation of their suitability for the highest judicial office. Of course, such a method of selection may afford somewhat greater opportunity for the exercise of partisan influence, though this is not automatically eliminated in the career system.

There are essentially four different ways in which judicial appointment is made. The first, popular election, is not widely used, and in the view of most observers not to be recommended. Its principal employment is in the state courts of the United States, where it was stipulated by the democratic zeal prevailing during the middle of the nineteenth century. For rather different reasons, the judges of the people's courts in the Soviet Union are also popularly elected, though the party leadership here always offers only one official candidate in such election. The principal objections to popular election are that the voters simply are not qualified to make an informed and intelligent choice of a judge, considering that his qualifications are professional and not representative; that to oblige a judge to seek votes in an election is incompatible with the dignity and obligation of the office; and that an elected judge may be made intolerably dependent upon popularity, publicity, or partisan support. To be sure, the practice is mitigated to an extent in some of the American states by electing on a nonpartisan basis, by allowing large influence to informal nominations or endorsement of candidates by the bar association, and by re-electing incumbent judges without opposition. Obviously, some good judges are obtained by election, but this must be largely despite the system rather than because of it.

A second method is election by the legislature. This is not much of an improvement on popular election if judges are selected for fixed terms, because it opens the way to immediate partisan interference with the courts. In the Soviet Union, judges above the lowest courts are elected by the Soviets for five-year terms; obviously their political reliability will be frequently re-examined. In addition to the Communist states, some of the Central American states also employ the legislature to elect judges, mainly as a means to free them from executive control. The members of the Swiss Federal (Supreme) Court are elected by the Federal Assembly for six-year terms. These judges are usually re-elected, and here, perhaps, legislative election can be justified as a means of assuring an appropriate distribution of German-, French-, and Italian-speaking members of that bench. In a few countries, as a third means, provision is made for judicial selection of judges. In some of the Latin-American countries, among them Bolivia, Honduras, Nicaragua, El Salvador, and Uruguay, the Supreme Court appoints the members of the inferior courts. The Supreme Court of Finland also chooses the lower court judges. Judicial selection has the merit of ensuring that those appointed to judicial office are likely to be professionally qualified; it tends to make the judiciary a self-perpetuating body, however, and somewhat limits the independence, not of the judiciary, but of the individual judge.

A fourth method, appointment by the executive, with or without exclusive discretion, is the most widely employed. In the United States all federal judges are appointed by the President with the consent of the Senate. The British judiciary is entirely appointed by the Crown; the choice of judges for the House of Lords and the Supreme Court of

Judicature is made by the Prime Minister, usually in consultation with the Lord Chancellor, who selects the lesser judges. Executive appointment is also the practice in such countries as Canada, New Zealand, Denmark, Norway, and Sweden. In the German Federal Republic, federal and state judges are chosen by the ministers of justice in consultation with committees of their respective legislatures. A modified system of executive appointment is found in France and Italy, where judges are chosen by a superior council of the judiciary, composed of the President of the Republic, and representatives of the Parliament and the judiciary. The weight of practice and opinion in the preferment of executive selection of judges is substantial; it concentrates responsibility, permits flexibility, and affords opportunity, at least, for well-informed choices to be made.

Judicial tenure may range from a fixed period of years, during good behavior, until a fixed retirement age, or for life. Fixed terms generally accompany popular or legislative election, and may extend from two or three years to as many as twenty. In the career systems judges usually hold office until a determined retirement age is reached. British judges originally served at the pleasure of the Crown, but they now, like American federal judges, and those in some of the states, serve "during good behavior"; in any case this amounts to life tenure if they choose not to retire. Provision is usually made for the removal from office of judges who misbehave or become incompetent or incapacitated. The judges of the Soviet people's courts and those in some of the American states may be removed by recall through popular vote. Federal judges of the United States may be removed only by impeachment and conviction; this method is available in the fifty states as well. Great Britain and the Commonwealth states generally, as well as a number of others, authorize the removal of judges on an address presented by the parliament to the executive. A considerable number of countries allow removal only by a superior court. In still a few others, such as France and Italy, judges may be disciplined, but are irremovable from office.

Judicial Independence. We have emphasized previously the great importance of judicial impartiality. If a judge is to be impartial he must be independent, that is to say, free from control or interference by anyone wishing to influence the administration of justice. Here we can see again the objection to the popular election of judges, for one who must answer to the electorate at relatively short intervals may need partisan political support. Even elections which are officially non-partisan do not always exclude party influence; and where judges must be party men, and the party is machine-controlled, the result has been in some states to corrupt the administration of justice. In the career system, though judges may be secure in their tenure, they can still be made dependent for promotion upon the favor of a political minister of justice, which introduces another kind of partisan influence; and though immune from popular pressure, such judges may be overly susceptible at least to an "official" point of view.

Judicial compensation can also affect judicial independence. If tenure is to mean anything, compensation must be not only adequate but secure. Judicial salaries must compete with the rewards available to practicing attorneys and, though they cannot equal those of the most successful, they ought to be sufficient to attract men of superior talent. Where salaries are abnormally low, they have inevitably reflected on the prestige of the judiciary and, in some countries, even opened the way to bribery. Where it is the intention to secure judges against financial reprisals, it is the usual practice, as in the American Constitution, and those of most of the states, to stipulate that judges' compensation "shall not be diminished during their continuance in office."

The Legal Profession. The legal profession is closely associated with the system of judicial administration, for any but the most primitive requires a body of trained professional lawyers. Their professional status is therefore recognized in their acceptance as officers of the courts, authorized to receive fees for giving legal advice and prosecuting or defending causes. In Great Britain the legal profession is divided into two categories. The larger is composed of solicitors, who provide legal advice, draft legal instruments, and conduct litigation. They may appear only before the lowest courts; if a client requires higher court counsel, the solicitor retains on his behalf the services of a barrister. Barristers are limited to appearing in the higher courts; being much more specialized in their function, they are a small group numbering barely two thousand. Professional judges are drawn solely from their ranks.

The legal profession in the United States and in most of the Commonwealth countries has not retained this division. Attorneys-at-law perform as both adviser and counselor. This is also the case in the German-speaking countries, where the *Rechtsanwalt* performs a dual function. In France, on the other hand, there is a still larger professional division of labor than in Great Britain. Here the *avocat* corresponds roughly to the barrister, and the *avoué* to the solicitor, while the *notaire* prepares deeds and acts as their custodian. Soviet lawyers, though not officials of the government, are organized under governing bodies regulated by the ministries of justice. Like Soviet judges, they may not disinterestedly pursue the ends of justice, nor even the interests of their client, for the interests of the state take precedence over all. The position of the Soviet attorney is thus ambiguous, and may become rather awkward when he undertakes to defend a client accused of a serious political offense.

III. JUDICIAL FUNCTIONS

The nature of the judicial process inevitably limits the extent of judicial functions, as compared with those of the executive and the legislature, though in no sense reduces their importance. We have already seen that in many countries, the judiciary does not constitute a separate branch of government. And even where it does, we may note, it is definitely the weakest branch. The courts are, after all, dependent upon the executive to provide the ultimate enforcement of their orders, and upon the legislature for their organization and financial support. Their very role is essentially a passive one; courts are said "to sit," which means that, like legislatures, they conduct their transactions in a particular place. But unlike legislatures, they do not initiate; judicial institutions examine only such controversies as are brought to them, whether in civil or criminal cases, by private persons or public officials. Though judicial affairs have as a rule neither the spectacular quality of the executive process, nor the popular aspect of the legislative process, the judicial process involves functions that are nevertheless wider and more varied, perhaps, than is commonly appreciated. To hear and decide causes actually requires the performance of several different functions, which we may now examine.

The Establishment of Facts. Most legal controversies involve a dispute as to facts, and their precise determination is commonly more difficult than establishing what is the law. Courts are particularly qualified to perform this function both because of the impartiality of the judges and because of the elaborate procedural rules employed in receiving evidence, that is, the means by which any matter or fact is proved. Evidence may consist, among other things, of public records, documents, articles, or the oral testimony of witnesses. In many proceedings the judge alone may determine the facts. Where the case is of substantial importance, however, or the establishment of a particular fact has most critical consequences, as in a criminal trial, a jury may be used to decide what facts the evidence tends to prove.

The procedures employed by common law and civil law system courts diverge in certain ways. The common law courts generally treat hearsay evidence as inadmissible; and, the determination of matters in dispute in a civil controversy is effected mainly by the pleadings of the opposing attorneys. The civil law courts take a much wider view respecting the admission of relevant evidence; their judges, too, have an influential role in selecting the issue in a case upon which a decision will be based. There are also procedural distinctions in criminal trials. The common law courts follow a procedure characterized as "accusatorial." A person may be tried for an offense only after a preliminary determination that there appears to be sufficient evidence to warrant a charge being made. The trial begins, nevertheless, with a presumption of innocence of the accused, who may choose not to testify with respect to the charge and cannot be obliged to incriminate himself. The prosecutor must make out the case against him by evidence he has collected, or obtained in conjunction with police authorities, and introduced according to strict rules which give the benefit of the doubt to the accused. The judge presides as an umpire between the prosecution and defense, and instructs the jury as to the significance of the facts and the law; on the charges brought, the prosecution must prove the defendant's guilt to be "beyond reasonable doubt." Civil law system courts, by contrast, employ what is described as an "inquisitorial" procedure. A professional judge makes a thorough pretrial investigation of a crime, examining both witnesses and suspects and, if he believes one justified, delivers an official accusation. The accused then stands trial. Though it would be going too far to say that in the civil law system one is considered guilty unless he proves himself innocent, there is a substantial presumption against him at this stage. The judges, as well as the prosecution, interrogate the defendant in order to get at the truth of things, and it remains only to prove or disprove the pretrial findings. Of course, the differences between the two systems can be exaggerated, and both have their respective merits.

The Finding and Interpretation of Law. Essential to the judicial process is the function of deciding what rules of law are applicable to a given set of facts. Sometimes this is immediately apparent, and with the facts resolved, the appropriate rules of law fall into place. But often it is not at all clear what law is relevant. In common law countries, it may be necessary to choose from among Constitution, statute, and common law rule; in the latter instance, the parties to a controversy may offer conflicting citations of precedent and a choice must be made between them. There may be contradictory clauses in a single statute, or ones enacted at different times may be in conflict. While this is less of a problem under the civil law systems, it is not unknown, and even there the judge must decide, perhaps, by which part of a code a controversy is to be governed, or whether by ordinary or administrative law.

But in any case, bodies of law are not self-interpreting. By their very nature they are general commands and prohibitions; their rules must be applied to an endless variety of acts and circumstances. As Justice Cardozo has observed, "No doubt the ideal system, if it were attainable, would be a code at once so flexible and so minute, as to supply in advance for every conceivable situation the just and fitting rule." Yet there is no such system. Statutes are ambiguous, if only because they are composed of words. The judge must take cognizance of many things: the intent of the legislator, the reasonable meaning of words, judicial precedents, and the practical consequences which will follow various constructions of a particular legal principle. Penal statutes are generally construed strictly, those conferring substantive rights liberally, and so on. Hence, the judge always has a sifting and elaborating function in deciding what the law is and what its rules require. As Justice Holmes said in a classic remark, "General propositions do not decide concrete cases."

Judicial Lawmaking. We have observed that there is a judicial function of lawmaking. To find and interpret the law is to participate in its creation. The English common law system was indeed developed by generations of judges. In the national common law systems today the contributions of the judiciary to this process continue, even though somewhat diminished, and are more extensive than is commonly realized. To be sure, judges are always reluctant to acknowledge that they make law, if only because this would suggest that its rules lack predictability and constancy; nor do they wish to be accused of usurping the province of the legislator. Hence, adherence to the principle of *stare decisis* helps to maintain a general consistency between the decision in one like case and another. Yet every decision leaves its residue, and as each judge contributes his own small embellishments, the law is "broadened down from precedent to precedent." Of course, such judicial contributions are more modest in the civil law systems, but they do not thus avoid accumulating "interpretations" and a judicial shaping of the law.

Probably the most obvious demonstration of judicial lawmaking occurs in connection with the exercise of judicial review, that is, the power of a court to determine the constitutionality of a legislative act and to decline to enforce it if found in conflict with the superior law of the constitution. The exercise of this power has been raised to its highest degree in the United States, where any court may examine the constitutionality of an act when it is immediately necessary to dispose of a case before it. Because the United States Supreme Court is the court of last resort for the judicial interpretation of constitutional questions, its decisions in this respect are of great importance. It may not only determine what the clauses of the Constitution mean, but may set aside acts of Congress and of the states, or parts of them, as contrary to the supreme law.

When, as a significant example, the Supreme Court ruled (in *Brown* v. *Board of Education of Topeka,* 1954) that "in the field of public education the doctrine of separate but equal has no place. . . . Segregation is a denial of the equal protection of the laws," it was clearly deciding what the law is. The Constitution did not specifically confer the power of judicial review upon the courts, but they have considered it a necessary incident to the judicial power under the American system of government. "It is emphatically the province and duty of the judicial department to say what the law is," said Chief Justice Marshall for the Supreme Court in *Marbury* v. *Madison* (1803). "Those who apply the rule to particular cases, must of necessity expound and interpret that rule. . . ."

The power of judicial review exists in more limited form elsewhere. The High Court of Australia and the Supreme Court of Canada may review the constitutionality of the acts of their respective states and provinces. The postwar Constitutions of Austria, the German Federal Republic, and Italy all provide for special Constitutional Courts with review power over the legislation of the national governments and their subdivisions. France of the Fifth Republic has also undertaken the creation of a Constitutional Council to review the constitutionality of laws. In Great Britain, by contrast, acts of Parliament are not subject to judicial review, though of course the courts are obliged to construe them. Judicial review may have political significance, as well—an important one that political disputes may be argued in legal rather than political terms; we have discussed it in that context as an aspect of constitutionalism, in Chapter 5.

The Enforcement of Authority and Remedies. Judicial institutions are considered to possess a right of self-preservation, with inherent powers to maintain their dignity and to enforce order in their proceedings. They may punish persons for contempt in consequence of disturbing their proceedings or for disobeying or resisting their orders. Contempts committed in the presence of the court may be punished summarily by the presiding judge.

To oblige compulsory attendance at court proceedings the common law system developed a variety of writs. A writ is an order issued by a court, directed to an officer, and authorizing him to execute it. A *warrant* authorizes the arrest of a person charged with an offense and his detention in court custody, or permits the search of a house or other place for stolen goods, unlawful articles, and such things. A *summons* is a notice to a person calling for his appearance in court to answer a civil complaint. A *subpoena* commands a person to appear in court to testify as a witness, or to produce there papers or other items relevant to a proceeding.

The common law system also provides numerous other writs which permit the courts to enforce their judgments, such as a writ of *execution,* or which provide remedies for the infringement of individual rights. The writ of *mandamus* commands a public officer, an inferior court, or a public corporation to perform some duty imposed upon it by law. Another important procedure, arising out of the old writ of *quo warranto,* requires a public officer or corporation to make an appearance to show by what authority it is exercising certain functions. A writ of *prohibition* is an order from a superior to an inferior court commanding it to cease proceeding in a case because the matter is beyond the jurisdiction of the inferior court. Most famous of all is the writ of *habeas corpus,* which directs a person detaining another to produce him in court and thus permit the judge to determine if he is being legally confined. If the detention is unlawful, the judge sets the person free. This writ has long been cherished in the common law countries as a means of removing arbitrary or illegal restraint of personal liberty.

There are, finally, certain preventive actions which courts employ to avoid injury to an individual's rights or the performance otherwise of certain unlawful acts. Among these equitable remedies, two are best known. The writ of *injunction* is an order of a court commanding a person to do, or not to do, some particular act. The injunction is used in a great variety of circumstances, with its essential purpose being to prevent irreparable injuries, for which the payment of damages would not be sufficient or recoverable. A decree of *specific performance* is a court order directing a party to a contract to the performance of his obligations. It may thus also provide a remedy preferable to recovery of damages for breach of contract. Although there are counterparts to many of the common law writs in the civil law systems, in some important instances there are not. In a civil law country, most such interferences with executive actions will be undertaken only by administrative courts. The civil law system does not provide the great writ of habeas corpus; however, certain civil law countries, such as Greece and Japan, provide somewhat similar means for safeguarding personal liberty by constitutional guarantee.

Administrative Responsibilities. Finally, we may observe that it has become common practice to assign various administrative responsibilities to the courts. These miscellaneous functions do not involve controversial matters in every instance; judicial performance is desired because of its impartiality and independence. In other instances, elements of controversy are present, and here the courts are preferred, of course, because of their experience as arbiter of differences. There has been a particular inclination in the United States to devolve various administrative duties upon individual courts. Here they may have such tasks as probating wills and the management of estates of persons deceased, granting and revoking licenses, granting admission to the bar and disbarment, administering bankruptcy proceedings, performing marriages and granting divorces, and administering the naturalization of aliens. British courts have somewhat similar duties, though with the important exception of naturalization; and disputed parliamentary elections, if involving corrupt and illegal practices, are decided by two judges of the Queen's Bench. Here, however, as in most states the conferment of citizenship by naturalization is an administrative act. In the civil law countries, the courts have fewer duties of an administrative character, though they commonly exercise jurisdiction over probate, divorce, bankruptcy and, in some instances, elections.

IV. *An* EVALUATION *of* JUDICIAL ADMINISTRATION

We have surveyed the development and characteristics of legal systems, and the organization and functions of courts. We may now undertake some evaluation of the judicial process related to the ends it serves. We shall not give further consideration here to such administration in the totalitarian states; as we have already observed, both their law and their courts are the instruments of their rulers, devoted to enforcing the policy of the regime as their major purpose, and being denied impartiality or objectivity. The judicial process is characterized essentially as the just resolution of causes by an impartial judge according to determinate standards. We are concerned here with judicial administration only where the ideal, at least, is a government of "laws, not men." Of course, this is nowhere perfectly achieved, because laws are man-made, and judges, lawyers, and those who appear in court are human. But courts are expected to rectify human fallibility, not to perpetuate it; this is why the legal and judicial ideas of the totalitarian states constitute little more than a literature of injustice.

Criticisms of Judicial Administration. In what ways, where the traditional ideals of justice prevail, does the judicial institution fall short? Complaints over the administration of justice reveal several dissatisfactions. A basic one arises from the inability of any legal system to assure the certainty of law. The state does not dispense justice automatically; civil disputes arise under the body of private law, and invasions of one's rights in property generally require him to take the initiative and seek redress by litigation. Though both litigants in a controversy presumably appeal to the same law, one must ordinarily be disappointed. To many a layman, the intricacy of legal rules, the complexity of legal terms, and the processes of the courts themselves are mysterious, if not suspect; they appear to threaten means of taking from him as much as ways of giving him his due. It is this feeling, probably, which gives rise to a popular belief that lawyers would not consider it in their interest to simplify these mysteries, even if they could. There are, in addition, some very real concerns.

In the next place, the costs of litigation are high. Though justice may not be bought, to contest for it can be an expensive enterprise when court costs, fees, travel to the place of the court, and attorney's retainers are considered. Persons without means to afford these may thus be deprived of the opportunity to enforce or defend their rights. There may also be differences in the administration of criminal justice for the rich and the poor. Although it is the usual practice to furnish legal counsel to an accused person who cannot provide it for himself, such assistance is not likely to be the equal of expensive legal talent others may be able to command. The price of taking an appeal is also great; in addition to further costs and fees, the appellate briefs and other materials must usually be printed, and this can be a substantial expense. Thus, a litigant or defendant who can afford the costs of appeals and their delay is distinctly at an advantage. Even after a litigant secures judgment in his favor he may have won a hollow victory if its execution goes unsatisfied. As Voltaire said, "I was never ruined but twice—once when I won a law suit, and once when I lost one." There appear to be no easy solutions to these problems. It would scarcely be practicable for the state to assume all the costs of resort to the courts; public provision of legal-aid bureaus and voluntary help by members of the bar seem to be all that is obtainable under the circumstances.

There is a further problem of congestion in the courts. The dockets of the courts are usually long, and those seeking a judicial resolution of their legal differences may be obliged to await many months their day in court. The "law's delay" is a centuries-old complaint, yet the delay of justice can well be a denial of justice. Through various maneuvers and appeals, one litigant can avoid a final judgment sometimes for years, while to remain in the contest, the other litigant may be required to exhaust not merely his patience but his funds. Moreover, defects in legal procedure attract much criticism. In the attempt to enhance certainty and restrict judicial discretion in the matter of procedure, simple rules are turned into complex ones, and over the years become encrusted with a myriad of technicalities. The rules of evidence alone have become so complicated that today few judges or lawyers can hope to master them. No more here are there simple solutions to the problem. Courts are, after all, obliged in reality to construe and apply rules; they have no Olympian license freely and easily to distribute justice as a kind of largess. Implicit in the judicial process is a much greater inflexibility than in other ways of transacting man's affairs.

We should know that there are substantial strictures raised everywhere against the administration of criminal justice, in some cases because of its harsh treatment of the accused, and in others because of its leniency. The efficiency of criminal proceedings in British courts is often much admired, and those charged with crimes rarely seem to escape their just deserts. Yet most persons sentenced there have been convicted in summary jurisdiction by professionally untrained justices sitting without a jury. The speed with which those accused of the most serious crimes in Great Britain are charged, tried, convicted, given an appeal, and hanged is also considered impressive. But again, it might further be remarked that a principal argument employed by those Britons who oppose capital punishment is that their higher courts do, in fact, occasionally and irretrievably hang the wrong man!

By contrast, American criminal procedure frequently appears overly generous to the accused, most of whom, after all, are likely to be guilty. Leaving aside the many criminals who are not apprehended, and all of those who are, but avoid prosecution, the courts of many states seem barely equal to the task of convicting any but the most stupid and impoverished—or confessed—criminals. In many American jurisdictions judges are simply not allowed to be the masters of their courtroom. Trials become battles of wits and wrangles between opposing attorneys, judges' rulings are subjected to inordinate exceptions and appeals, witnesses are intimidated, and juries are allowed to reach verdicts irrelevantly in matters beyond their competence. It scarcely need be added that when, in addition, newspapers are permitted to exploit cases *sub judice* and turn sensational trials into public orgies, the dignity and impartiality of the courts are gravely impaired. We need not discuss this matter further as it applies in civil law systems; suffice it to say that most of them produce at intervals their own *cause célèbre*.

The Search for Justice. We end as we began with the search for justice under law. The administration of justice has nowhere been perfected in this age, but where it has not been perverted to the service of totalitarian government, it widely produces practical results in general accord with the public ideal of it. To ask for complete judicial "efficiency" is to propose a different sort of judicial procedure than is now generally acceptable. A completely efficient procedure in civil suits would require the discarding of many social and humanitarian considerations which we now apply to the exercise of property rights; likewise, a completely efficient criminal procedure could be had by the ruthless prosecution of all accused or even suspected of crime and the abandonment of traditional safeguards established to protect the innocent. Examples of these kinds of "efficiency" are well displayed in dictatorships.

To allow access to the courts too cheaply and conveniently would probably swell the volume of litigation to extravagant levels. Even the "law's delay" often works in favor of one party to a dispute, just as it penalizes the other. Both sets of obstacles, then, may well encourage the settlement of differences out of court. Most persons get through life, indeed, without recourse to the courts. Perhaps their greatest significance in a state based upon the rule of law is that appropriate courts are open to the public; that they can provide a juristic, as opposed to a personal or an administrative, resolution of disputes; and, that peaceable means to bring conflicts and disputes to an end are available. For what it is worth, the judicial institution attracts less criticism than the executive or the legislature, and apparently comes closer than these to fulfilling popular expectations in performance. To executive and legislative participation in the pursuit of justice through democratic government, the judiciary adds the sense that justice is being done in each individual case—an element essential to confidence in the legitimacy and reasonableness of political power. Nevertheless, it is not the judiciary which maintains democratic government; rather, it is the other way around, for courts can provide "justice under law" only when the society in which they operate entrusts them with this high purpose. Law is not inherently democratic, or even just, in its objectives; in a dictatorship, indeed, it may after all express merely the will of a tyrant. The democratic objective of freedom, however, realizable only by limiting political power to avoid arbitrariness, requires a free judiciary that alone can administer law with justice. And justice is, as Madison wrote in *The Federalist,* "the end of government. . . . It ever has been and ever will be pursued until it be obtained, or until liberty be lost in the pursuit."

CHAPTER 12

The ADMINISTRATION

"FOR FORMS of government let fools contest; whate'er is best administer'd is best." These lines from Alexander Pope's *Essay on Man* (1733) are perhaps too often quoted; they draw a very naive distinction and represent the thought of an age that made limited demands on political leadership and imagination. The efficient conduct of what Pope assumed to be obvious governmental business was his dominant concern and, in the corrupt English conditions of that time, this was in fact a worthy aspiration. Even though political controversy, channeled through "forms of government," cannot be so easily disposed of, however, controversy is not normally an end in itself, nor are good intentions worth much if they cannot be implemented. Public policy expresses the objectives a political community sets for itself in various ways; the public administration is one of the principal means through which such objectives are clarified and promoted.

The extent, organization, and procedures of public administration itself are closely influenced by the objectives being pursued and the social conditions prevailing. Since these are not constant, neither are the forms of administration. In the ancient Greek democracies, for example, ordinary citizens took their turns in administrative as well as deliberative and judicial offices; this was desirable, given the political ideals they held, as well as practicable, because of the small size of their communities. The Roman empire, however, developed expert administrators and an organized service, which continued into the Byzantine and Turkish empires. In feudal Europe of the middle ages, however, only minor and occasional exceptions are to be found to the disappearance of a specialized administration. Apart from the Roman Catholic Church, which built up an impressive and influential administrative system, all political responsibilities were undifferentiated and highly decentralized functions of land ownership.

With the collapse of the medieval order systematic administration flourished for some time as an offspring of mercantilism, in which absolute monarchies endeavored to organize their realms effectively to expand their power. Such regimes were most developed in England, Prussia, Austria, and France. As the middle classes came to power and democracy emerged, however, interest in administration flagged. Representation of the people became the central political demand, and the political process was seen most often as one of deliberation, issuing in legislation defining the rights and duties of citizens. Law so created was expected to require little more than judicial processes to enforce it. Except for an occasional criminal prosecution, private citizens would initiate the legal actions necessary to protect their rights. Few public officials—as distinct from judges and political representatives—were required for such a government, nor was it assumed that their responsibilities were particularly exacting. Loyalty to their political superiors was generally taken to be the principal desideratum in public officials. The consequence, frequently, was inefficiency and corruption.

Against this development a reaction set in during the last half of the nineteenth century, resulting in both a renewed study of public administration and significant changes in the organization and procedures of administration in government. The aim was to secure integrity, political accountability, and efficiency in the public service. At the same time, it became increasingly apparent that legislative enactments and constitutional provisions were not self-sufficient vehicles for public policy, and that policemen and judges were not the only instruments of government needed in the modern community. The reaction was in part a protest against corruption, but even more a response to the expansion of public functions in modern life. We must discuss, therefore, the development of governmental activities in order to lay the foundation for an analysis of the nature of contemporary public administration.

I. PUBLIC POLICY *in the* MODERN STATE

History clearly teaches that the range of governmental activities and their importance to the community is not static, but varies with the aspirations of men and the conditions within which they live. Public policy—to use the current phrase denoting the purposes and programs governments pursue—has not always been democratic, but it always reflects the values of those most influential politically, together with their judgments of how in prevailing conditions those values may be promoted. The last few centuries—and particularly the last few decades—have witnessed most remarkable changes in the distribution of political influence, in the nature of the values most highly held, and in the character of the conditions within which men must act. Public policy has been radically affected.

Traditional Public Policy. Governments have always engaged in what we today call "public works" or "public services." Ancient empires of the Middle East constructed and maintained irrigation systems necessary for their agriculture, and public buildings and highways have been the mark of every advanced civilization. Most, too, have been closely identified with a religion, which they sought to preserve or promote. Nonetheless, the basic and indispensable end served by all governments has been the maintenance of order. Government must preserve the peace among its own people and protect them against attack from abroad. Failure to do this precludes success in any other endeavor. The nature of the order governments have attempted to maintain at home, and the sort of foreign policy necessary to preserve security, are not subjects for easy generalizations, however. In both the studies of philosophers and the council rooms of active officials, interpretations of these needs have varied widely, according to circumstance and attitude.

Throughout much of the world until very recently governments have been primarily engaged in the preservation of an existing and quite stable order, and particularly with maintaining the customary privileges of a traditional aristocracy. Among the more progressive communities of western Europe in the eighteenth century, however, arose the idea of a dynamic society based on equal rights and freedom, in which the role of government was important but limited. The watchword was *laissez faire, laissez aller* (literally, let things alone, let them go of themselves), in the phrase of the French physiocrats, which Adam Smith's influential *The Wealth of Nations* (1776) generally supported in England. Government was not to interfere with citizens taking care of their own legitimate business, on the assumption that they could do so best, to their own advantage and to that of the whole community, guided by an "invisible hand" through free competition. Laissez faire was an idea appropriate to the needs and attitudes of an optimistic, self-confident middle class, and in their opinion was opposed only to the decadent interests of traditional aristocracies which the economic and social regulations of mercantilism had protected. To the middle-class liberals, proper public policy was restricted to the preservation of peace, the enforcement of criminal law and of contractual obligations, and the provision of a relatively few broad services—such as sound monetary systems, standards of weights and measures, postal operations, and public education—necessary to society, but not profitable to private entrepreneurs.

The Expansion of Public Functions. Laissez faire, with its bias against positive government action in any realm which could possibly be managed privately, was generally dominant in more advanced countries in the nineteenth century. Yet the "negative state" had a brief and imperfect reign, even in the United States, where commitment to it was greatest. Ideas of desirable economic and social development, coupled with private desires for special favors which government could bestow, led inevitably to public support of particular interests through protective tariffs, land grants, and other assistance. Furthermore, critics soon denounced the "negative state," accompanied in fact by many special privileges inadequately controlled in the public interest, as neither efficient nor humane in its consequences. When such countries as Germany and Japan began to develop modern economies at the end of the last century, laissez faire was ignored; and in Britain, France, and the United States, its dominance gradually declined. By the mid-twentieth century, following the impact of depressions, great international conflicts and tensions, and the "necessity" of economic and social transformation in formerly colonial and backward areas, the "negative state" has almost completely been replaced by the "positive state." Co-operation through government to improve the lot of men everywhere, despite its obvious dangers, is the theme of twentieth-century politics, even more than laissez faire was that of the nineteenth.

It is impossible to treat fully here the extensive activities of contemporary governments; even a survey of the economic policies of such a regime as the United States would require a substantial volume in itself. The advent of highly organized industrial society, with its complex patterns of interdependence and its great promise, has produced a tremendous expansion of public policy aimed at remedying its evils, co-ordinating the fantastically diverse activities of its members, and promoting progressive development according to some idea of a general welfare. At the same time, however, given the nature of the contemporary community and its international environment, even the traditional functions of government have become enormously more demanding of imagination, skill, energy, and organization than in days gone by.

Social control and community life, of course, are inseparable. Throughout most earlier history people have been closely and narrowly controlled by informal social influences exercised through family, church, and neighborhood, and the role of government has been generally minimal. Such informal controls, however, are based largely upon customary values, ways of thinking, and authority, which are undermined in a period of rapid and great change. Their effectiveness has recently declined, therefore, and more formal political machinery has had to take up at least some of the slack. Consequently, never before have so many people been so involved in government—both because they are directly affected by what it does, and because they are participants in its activity. Also, far more than any previous community—except for otherwise incomparable religious organizations and the Greek city-state—is the modern nation-state a self-conscious community, highly organized through government for the exchange of goods and services and for cooperation in pursuit of recognized common ends.

The Regulatory State. The rise of industrial economies and the weakening of earlier ethical limitations on economic activity and social relationships led very quickly to miserable and dangerous working conditions, long working hours, low incomes, and great insecurity for large numbers of people. The result, first appearing in Britain in 1819, was legislation to control these evils, regulating working conditions and hours, requiring compensation to employees injured at work, and providing assistance to the unemployed. At the same time, it was observed that the collection of industrial workers within towns created problems of public health and of care for the aged and incapacitated which had been largely unknown to agricultural communities. Governments were early compelled to undertake "welfare" services in these fields, and they have grown into far-reaching responsibilities. To meet these needs, furthermore, governments had to increase greatly their financial resources and broaden their powers of inspection, regulation, and condemnation of dangerous conditions.

In the new economic order, also, people received their supplies of food and drugs through increasingly impersonal channels, from sources of which they knew little, and in forms which made it quite difficult for them to judge the quality. To protect the consumer against unscrupulous exploiters of these conditions the labeling and advertising of such products came to be controlled. Meanwhile, the extraordinary dependence of cities, with their industries, upon adequate power, water, communications, and transportation, led to new legislation concerning public utilities, which if not directly owned and operated by governmental units were subjected to public controls. In the United States, as an effort to maintain a competitive economy in the face of increasing concentration of industrial control, antitrust legislation was also enacted, if only with limited effect. Somewhat more effective has been the attempt to control the use of power by industrial and financial giants. To implement the Clayton Act of 1914, Congress created for the United States a Federal Trade Commission, with the task of preventing "unfair methods of competition." Neither in the United States nor abroad have such devices been strikingly successful, but the policy of ensuring honesty and fairness in business remains an important one of all governments today.

The Promotional State. Such regulatory activities were the dominant aspects of the "positive state" until the 1930's, although the small Scandinavian countries undertook extensive welfare activities much earlier. Since that time, however, among the highly industrialized states public policy has extended increasingly beyond attempting to prevent this evil or that, to actively pursuing the welfare and expansion of the economy. The Soviet Union's program of total social and economic reconstruction, begun in the 1920's, is an extreme example—doctrinaire and undemocratic in its means if not its ends—but it has been highly influential nonetheless. In ways more pragmatic and more compatible with liberal values, the Rooseveltian "New Deal" in the United States experimented with a new and more positive political economy, and after World War II Britain and France followed suit, and even undertook substantial economic operations by the state. As new states were formed in the postwar period, those with sufficient unity and drive—such as India and Israel, for example—joined those employing an extensive array of governmental powers for social and economic development.

These powers are quite diverse. In the first place, public expenditures for traditional as well as new purposes have become immense; government has become the largest single employer and purchaser of supplies in all countries. Variations in how, when, and where public funds will be spent have great effect upon economic activity. Second, many of the public regulatory functions, although initially aspects of the "police power"—to provide for the health, safety, and morals of the population—may equally be used to control the character of and to encourage economic development. Government action in the realm of flood control, slum clearance, payments to the unemployed and disabled, and minimum wage levels may or may not be designed primarily for their effect upon the economy in general, but an effect they do have. Third, all governments may affect substantially the extent and nature of investment and purchasing power through adjustments in the amount and incidence of taxation, and through the control they now possess over their central banking systems.

Fourth, most governments protect some industries through tariffs, minimum price controls, and other forms of aid—agriculture in the United States and France is a prime example—and thus influence the production of those industries directly, and of others indirectly. In times of shortages and when production cannot immediately expand to meet demand, governments have also established maximum price levels and introduced rationing. Fifth, and finally, public works and services, generally undertaken previously for quite limited purposes, have become both more numerous and of very broad impact in the life of the modern community. In many respects they amount to a clear subsidization of some private entrepreneurs who use their services, while at the same time competing with others; at their best, however, such public enterprises also make possible improvements in both quality and efficiency of production. Typical of such activities are agricultural and other scientific research, together with programs to encourage use of its results; construction and operation of public transportation and communication facilities; great programs of river development, such as that of the Tennessee Valley Authority, and of rural electrification; and, less frequently, operation of coal mines in Britain and automobile factories and coal mines in France. Public housing developments have also become quite general, usually for low income groups, with special credit facilities available to assist others.

Planning and Public Policy. This brief sketch can give but the most rudimentary idea of the tremendous range of contemporary governmental activities and their impact on the whole of social life. Yet it should indicate clearly the desirability of their co-ordination if coherent purposes are to be achieved. Thus, the crowning public policy should be—logically—a social and economic plan. Planning is no more than an integrated choice of programs realistically appropriate to the ends sought and the conditions prevailing. It is an activity whose value no rational person can deny; however, it is also an ideal very difficult to implement in a complex and economically advanced community. In such circumstances, very often, agreement upon an integrated set of goals is unobtainable, and clear knowledge of alternatives and consequences is likewise not sufficiently available. To some, any proposed plan seems unacceptable and foolish and its implementation likely to involve excessive coercion. Consequently, the problem of planning, or co-ordinated policy, has been met—or not met—in very different ways.

In communist economies, such as those of Russia and China—industrially primitive at their inception—public policy has been integrated by the dogmatic objectives of rapid industrialization and political unity under communist leadership. Most of the new states of the last few decades have much in common with the needs these objectives reflect, and even if noncommunist in ideological conviction, they are often drawn to the Soviet Union as a model rather than to the western democracies. On the other hand, immediately after World War II the West Germans, the Dutch, the British, and the French adopted quite extensive planning, but still far short of the total economic controls of the communists. Public officials, labor and business leaders, and experts and politicians elaborated programs for economic rehabilitation and growth, and the diversified powers of government were employed to facilitate the realization of those programs. Yet their considerable success should not lead one to overlook that in these cases the problem was one of reconstruction after decades of economic stagnation and war. Important priorities were fairly obvious: essentially, increased production of basic resources, improved efficiency and quality, and direction of production so as to reduce foreign trade deficits. As their immediate objectives were realized and priorities became more disputable, the early dominance of integrated economic plans declined.

Apart from extraordinary circumstances, in other words, public planning is a much more flexible activity than the term seems to imply. While no government today can abdicate responsibility for the general well-being and strength of its community, and thus for the effects of its far-flung activities at home and abroad, planning tends more to be manifested in pragmatic co-ordination of diversified programs than in the imposition of a unified policy. Innumerable technical and political advisers to government leaders play an important role in this. They collect and evaluate information concerning existing conditions and likely developments, and suggest limited plans in such realms as resource conservation, defense needs, financial stability, or employment levels. Yet over-all planning agencies are rare, and those with any significant authority are nonexistent, in democratic countries with developed economies. The co-ordination of public policies in most countries remains essentially *ad hoc,* a matter of continuing political and administrative decisions as practical problems arise. The emerging international organizations—such as the European Common Market, the European Free Trade Association, the United Nations Economic Commission for Africa, and the Organization for Economic Co-operation and Development—manifest a similarly limited tendency even in the realm of broader and more extensive action. This characteristic of public policy in economic and other matters makes the relationship between politics and administration a special problem.

II. POLITICS, LAW, *and* ADMINISTRATION

The great expansion of governmental activities in recent years has entailed a concomitant expansion of the civil administrative staff of government. Civil employees of government have increased in number far more rapidly than the population at large in all modern communities, and even in noncommunist regimes comprise from 10 to 20 per cent of the total working force. Various problems are raised by this development. One concerns how large numbers of people may be organized, recruited, disciplined, and motivated for the effective performance of their tasks, and also what means of action their tasks today require—topics to be given attention in the later sections of this chapter. Another, which will be treated briefly here, concerns the political and legal context of administrative action. Administration can hardly be a self-contained process, yet its relations with political and legal aspects of government are far from clear. Since successful government depends not only upon the efficiency but also upon the responsibility of public officials, the problem is obviously an important one.

Responsibility is a rather ambiguous word. When we say that a person is responsible we may mean that he is trustworthy or that he is technically competent. We may also mean that he is answerable to someone else. All these senses of the term are important in securing responsible government, although it is evident that conflicts may develop between them—the conscience or technical knowledge of an official may compel him to reject the instructions of those to whom he is accountable, for example. The difficulties are ultimately very subtle and efforts to overcome them have not been entirely satisfactory. As a practical matter, however, in the development of political and administrative institutions and procedures, a considerable range of methods has emerged through which the responsibility of public officials can be maintained. The relation between these diverse techniques remains uncertain, of course, but through continuing pragmatic adjustments they have, in most instances, been kept in reasonable balance.

Legal Responsibility. Once government and its activities had expanded to the point where personal loyalty to a king was no longer a sufficient guarantee of responsible service—and especially after representative assemblies had come to share the basic political responsibility—an accountability of public officials in courts of law for the legality of their acts became quite firmly established. A continuing ideal of constitutional government in the western tradition has been that public officials must have legal authority for all their acts. The ultimate determination of whether such an authority was present in any particular case has generally been held to be properly judicial, for the function of judges is to define rights according to the provisions of existing law. Distinct and highly refined procedures governing justiciable cases, forms of trial, interpretation of legal rules, admissibility of evidence, and impartiality of judges were gradually evolved in modern governments, tending to ensure objective determination of official authority according to established law.

Two quite different interpretations of the legal responsibility of officials emerged in the western world, however. The Anglo-American approach has been to hold officials accountable in the ordinary courts of law, and according to the same standards which apply to private citizens in their controversies with one another. The approach of continental European countries, with French practice particularly outstanding, has been to insist that public officials are not ordinary citizens, but that in the execution of public purposes they must have both exceptional powers and be subject to exceptional restrictions. Consequently, these countries developed a special administrative law and, usually, special administrative courts to develop and apply it.

Both patterns, of course, were designed to ensure the responsible performance of administrative functions, but the Anglo-American approach reflects especially the ideal of carefully limited government, while the French system reflects a greater concern with the effectiveness of the public service. The relative merits of the two systems were hotly debated a few decades ago. More recently, however, the Anglo-American world has accepted an increasing amount of special administrative law, developed through legislation, decisions of ordinary courts, and administrative practices. On the other hand, experience has shown that administrative law and special courts are not necessarily destructive of the rights of private citizens who claim to be injured by administrative action. Actually, the problem today is not a choice between defense of private rights and effective administration, but the reconciliation of these. In this, France has done at least as well as Britain and the United States.

A rather different approach to the control of continually enlarging administrative authority is manifested in the Swedish *Ombudsman,* or parliamentary commissioner, originating by royal appointment in 1713, but with the present system established in the constitutional settlement of 1809. More recently, Denmark, Norway, and New Zealand created comparable offices, and several other countries have been considering doing so. The growing interest in the Ombudsman reflects increased concern for fair treatment of the citizens in administrative decisions and actions, and an awareness that this may not adequately be ensured by traditional judicial protection. The Ombudsman is elected by, but is not a member of, parliament. Acting on its behalf, he has sweeping powers to investigate citizens' (and civil servants') complaints of administrative arbitrariness, negligence, or discrimination. Through inspection, recommendation, mediation, publicity, and even occasional prosecutions—the procedures and scope of authority varying among the countries—the parliamentary commissioner acts to keep administrative officials functioning according to their legal responsibilities and in the public interest.

Political Responsibility. The ideal of the "rule of law" suffers important limitations. On the one hand, we now recognize that men make and interpret the law; on the other, that the laws directing administrative action these days inevitably leave room for considerable discretion. To prevent administrative irresponsibility, administrators must be accountable to political leadership, and in democracy this means primarily to elected officials. Such political responsibility, however, is not automatic; plentiful experience indicates that civil servants, long in office and secure, are likely to reflect particularly the ideas of those who originally appointed them, or the dominant opinions among their fellow officials, or narrow professional interests and ideas, and that these may be quite at odds with the programs and ideas of their political superiors.

Two extreme reactions to the resulting problem may be noted here. The radical democracy of Jacksonian America inaugurated a "spoils system," in which the victorious party in an election appointed its "friends" to as many posts, high and low, as it wished and for whatever reason. Unfortunately this led in practice even more to corruption than to political responsibility; and the method, never adopted by any other stable government, was soon progressively limited in the United States. On the other hand, the totalitarian regimes of this century have attempted to ensure political responsibility—to the dictator, of course—by placing highly disciplined party members in crucial positions and by organizing party "cells" throughout the administrative structure. Conformity to party policies is enforced through direct hierarchical control, through intensive indoctrination, and through punishment for deviations from the party line or failure to fulfill expectations. Fortunately, no democracy has such techniques available.

The methods used to promote political responsibility in modern regimes other than totalitarian dictatorships are more limited, but are also quite varied, for they unavoidably reflect the general constitutional character of the regimes. Well-established governments depend heavily upon a tradition of "administrative neutrality," according to which administrative officials take their lead from duly constituted political officials, and within the law faithfully serve whatever leadership electoral or other fortunes place above them. In Britain, such "neutral" permanent civil servants comprise the entire staff of all executive departments except for the political minister and a very few aides. In Sweden they comprise the totality of administrative departments, which are independent of the political ministries although subject to rules they set forth. In all stable governments, permanent civil servants—politically neutral in presumption if not always in fact—constitute the bulk of the administrative staff.

Given the size and complexity of contemporary government, however, and the fact that many politically important decisions must be made below the level of the minister or department head, a limited version of the "patronage" system is often employed. Especially in the United States, persons sympathetic to the policies of the chief executive and the department head are placed in numerous "policy-making" positions in each agency, presumably ensuring that political responsibility is more effectively maintained throughout the entire administrative structure, but without interfering with the efficient performance of technical and routine operations. Still, the political life of a modern nation is not neatly summed up in the policies of its chief executive, or even in the laws passed by a parliamentary majority. Political responsibility is also maintained through channels other than the normal executive hierarchy, although it becomes rather diffuse in the process. Individual representatives and legislative committees, especially concerned with the activity of one or another administrative agency because of their own interests or those of their particular constituents, are able in many states to investigate and influence the work of administrative officials at all levels of government, especially where discretion is being exercised. Private interest groups—as often legitimately as otherwise—are similarly active in all free countries. Additionally, much administrative activity is appropriately conducted primarily through co-operative arrangements between private parties and administrative officials, although always ultimately subject to executive or legislative review and sanction. The complexities these additional practices introduce into the preservation of political responsibility are somewhat baffling, to be sure; but as modern government is no simple thing, neither can be the political responsibility of its administrative organization.

Professional Responsibility. The public administration of today is a professional bureaucracy. The term "bureaucracy" is often used derogatorily, but properly means only a large-scale organization of appointed officials, systematically interrelated in the realization of complex purposes. It is unavoidable in modern life, and is found not only in government but also in business, labor, and religious organizations. It does, of course, have its disadvantages, tending toward impersonality, conservatism, inflexibility, and slowness in action. These are in good part, however, merely the obverse of its virtues, which include deliberateness, predictability, specialization of function, and a formal and open organization of co-operation. Any machinery has its costs of operation; only idealistic utopias promise benefits without them.

The characteristics of contemporary public bureaucracy will be indicated at some length hereafter; only a few words concerning the relationship of professional bureaucratic administration to responsibility in government are possible here. To begin with, administrative personnel is drawn in large measure from the politically dominant classes of the population, and is therefore at least indirectly representative of them. In democracies, that personnel is drawn widely from the people, and is to a degree a cross section of them. Over the last century, civil service recruitment has slowly become increasingly democratic as popular government has become established. Popular representativeness of the bureaucracy is far from perfect, of course, and an important reason for this is that the modern bureaucracy is also a professional one. That is to say, it must comprise persons of special abilities, intelligence, and training in its more crucial positions. That it neglected this in its enthusiasm for a democratic service was the error of the Jacksonian patronage system. Only with widespread educational opportunities can these two needs of democratic administration be brought even reasonably close together.

However, professional skills—whether of surveyors, educators, or those expert in organizing the work of men—do in themselves provide their own particular responsibility and representativeness. Communities do not manifest themselves only in the momentary whims and fancies which so often elect politicians, but also in the way those politicians sometimes transcend popularity contests to deliberate on public issues.

Similarly, communities express themselves significantly in the science and technology in which administrative officials have been educated, creating professional standards to which those officials at their best hold themselves responsible. The informed criteria for judging what to do and how to do it, with which a professional bureaucracy is imbued, are particularly important when public policy thrusts upon them heavy responsibilities but limited guidance from either judges or political leaders. Because this is precisely the case in most nations today, professional responsibility in the public service must be granted its place alongside the traditional legal and political forms of responsibility in government.

III. ADMINISTRATIVE ORGANIZATION

To organize administration is to give some ordered structure to the means of enforcing public policy. The subject has been given significant attention only in the last hundred years. Prior to this time there was little need to do so. As we have seen, the number of government functions was limited and the level of government services low. The articulation of government offices, too, was relatively simple; law enforcement was a matter largely for police and courts, and fiscal management and record-keeping were the principal tasks of administration.

The emergence of the modern regulatory and promotional state, however, produced big government in the past half-century, and along with it large new problems in contemporary public management. It is easy enough to say that the ideal of administrative organization is to arrange government structures to be responsible and responsive, efficient and economical, integrated and flexible. Yet there are no simple answers to how to do it. We shall only suggest, for the present, some of the principal features of administrative organization as it has developed.

General Aspects of Administrative Organization. While there are no universal rules of administration, there are certain fairly standard arrangements which account for the principal features of any particular administrative system. First of all, we find everywhere means of exercising control throughout the structure by a series of superior-subordinate relationships. A long line stretches from the head of a government to the postmen, customs officers, tax clerks, and others carrying out their duties in direct contact with the public; there must be many intermediate units of administration between them. In order to enable a large organization to act as a single, cohesive body it is commonly given a hierarchical structure. Thus administrative organization, like that in all military, many industrial, and certain ecclesiastical systems, follows some kind of pyramidal pattern, with lines of authority running down and lines of responsibility running up, linking together the lower, intermediate, and higher units of administration.

There are numerous variations in the ways a pyramiding hierarchy may be constructed. A highly "integrated" hierarchy with a direct "chain of command" is clearly displayed by military organization in the relations of the squad, platoon, company, battalion, regiment, and so on upward. In civil administration rarely is authority of each higher level so complete and hierarchy so tightly knit; however, well-integrated administrative structures approximate such a pattern. In contrast, some administrative systems are decentralized to the point that agencies or departments may have areas of independence from control by the chief executive. In American state government, commonly, the several administrative departments are headed by independently elected officials. There may be some benefit, of course, in having a nonhierarchical chain of command to handle functions that do not readily fit into the existing organization. For example, in the United States the Central Intelligence Agency, rather than being embedded within the hierarchy of the Department of Defense, reports through the National Security Council directly to the President. A high degree of integration may be ideally preferred in terms of administrative considerations; authority and responsibility reconcentrated at each succeeding level produces a distinct unity of command. But practical political considerations often call for a measure of disintegration and a dispersion of authority to permit various kinds of legislative or popular control.

In the second place, organizational structure must reflect some form of division of labor. Traditionally, the criteria for administrative organization are considered to be four: purpose, process, clientele, and area. The term "area" refers, of course, to geographic territory; the term "process," to specialized forms of action and skills involved; while "clientele" refers to persons being served. The distinctions are ultimately arbitrary, since such a purpose as public health clearly involves a "process" appropriate to it, deals with some portions of the population

ABOVE: "Urbanism, particularly metropolitanism, produces a distinct way of life. . . . Important political consequences ensue from all this: the need for new forms of social control . . . and for substantial physical, protective, and welfare services." (p. 487) The Information Room, Scotland Yard, headquarters of London's Metropolitan Police. (*British Information Services.*) BELOW: "In many countries, local government historically antedates that of the central authorities. It performs a number of functions that touch very closely the everyday life cf the people." (p. 483) The Mayor of West Berlin, Willy Brandt, addressing a session of the City's Chamber of Deputies. (*German Information Center.*)

ABOVE: ". . . We have local provision or administration of schools, libraries, hospitals and clinics, swimming pools and public baths, and various kinds of assistance for the aged, infirm, dependent children, and even the construction of housing." (p. 484) Newly completed low-cost housing for workers in Livorno, Italy. (*Italian Cultural Institute, New York.*) BELOW: "The postwar Nürnberg and Tokyo war crime trials, as well as others conducted by national tribunals of the allied powers, set precedents which must still be reckoned with today." (p. 524) The opening of the Eichmann trial at Beit Ha'am in Jerusalem, April 11, 1961. (*Israel Office of Information.*)

more than others, and even determines its own appropriate area—an epidemic is not likely to respect boundaries drawn for political and administrative purposes. Thus, patterns of organization vary so far as these criteria are concerned according to convenience and historical accident more than from the objective validity of one criterion or another. Yet, to be manageable, administrative organization must be broken down into interrelated parts, and these terms indicate roughly how this usually has been done.

These divisions of labor may be simply illustrated. It is clearly a purpose of government to protect life and property; to do so it organizes police, safety inspection, fire, and coastguard services. The police themselves may be employed for considerably different services, however, dealing with separate kinds of persons or problems, such as juveniles and narcotics, or using different skills or techniques, as in traffic or detective work; hence, administrative structure within a police force may appropriately be based on separate services meeting these particular needs. Finally, police may also be separately required for different areas and their respective law enforcement programs: national, state, district, or local.

Another kind of division of labor within administrative organization is the distinction between line, staff, and auxiliary services. The line departments and agencies conduct the major substantive programs of government and directly serve the public. A department of agriculture, a ministry of pensions, a post office, and a highway department are all line agencies. A staff advises officials or agencies; it has no operational responsibilities and is not formally in the line of command. It plans, studies, conducts research, and advises the executive. The American Bureau of the Budget and the French Council of State, with respect at least to part of their functions, are staff agencies. An auxiliary service provides technical, secondary, or "housekeeping" assistance of various kinds to the line agencies; these may be devoted to personnel recruitment, supply and purchasing, legislative drafting, and so on. Both staff and auxiliary services exist to aid the effectiveness of the line agencies and have no justification apart from the needs of the latter, neither planning, nor economy, nor purchasing being ends in themselves.

A third important feature of administrative organization is displayed in the extent and character of its centralization. From one perspective this is a political question: a decision by constitution or statute at what levels below the central one there are to be vertical subdivisions for administration—regional, provincial, local, and the like, and how many there should be. The other perspective is administrative: how to divide responsibility between central and field offices. A highly centralized system maximizes the concentration of authority and discretion at the higher levels and heavily circumscribes it at the lower; a highly decentralized system does, of course, the contrary.

As the problems of government become increasingly complex and of greater national concern, and as communication and travel have become so rapid, there has been a distinct tendency toward centralization in administration. This is usually desirable to produce integrated policy and uniform administrative procedures. But, central authority is often remote and unresponsive, and excessive centralization weakens initiative and flexibility in the field. Among the three major aspects of administrative organization we have mentioned, this is probably the most crucial; failure to achieve some appropriate balance between centralization and decentralization produces "bureaucratic" administration in its most negative sense.

National Systems of Administration. Every country has its own particular administrative structures, arrangements, and techniques. Nevertheless, within the western world two main patterns may be observed: a continental European type, developed largely by France and influential within the Roman law countries; and, an Anglo-American type, the product of British and American experience, and extended also to the Commonwealth countries. They are in the main the result of three differences: in attitudes over the centralization of state power; between the two legal systems; and in their nineteenth-century experiences.

The continental type generally has continued the traditions of concentrated monarchical ruling power and the control of government from its center. Though the French revolution destroyed the authoritarian *ancien régime,* Napoleon restored central control of the administrative hierarchy, and created the office of prefect to give him direct authority in local areas. The growth of government in the nineteenth century thereafter tended to be an elaboration of this well-entrenched central authority. Here, therefore, local levels of government are viewed primarily as administrative conveniences, to be dominated by the center, rather than as autonomous units for self-government. The public service is professionalized, and relies particularly on the expert. As an accompaniment of the civil law system, there is commonly a separate body of administrative law and courts.

The Anglo-American pattern of administrative arrangement is the product of a greater dispersion of authority traditional in these countries. Their earlier development of and experience with representative government encouraged more popular—and certainly, more legislative—control of administrative authorities and administration. The tradition of local self-government has also been strong. In both countries, too, the large growth of government in the nineteenth century was mainly at the local level; only in the twentieth has higher authority loomed large in local affairs. Finally, under the common law system, officials are responsible to the ordinary courts, which have also applied more in the way of "ordinary" legal controls to integrate the administrative process.

We have been speaking, of course, of highly generalized patterns. Important variations are introduced from state to state both by national traditions and, for example, where a federal as opposed to a unitary form of government exists. In France's unitary system, the central government's ministries apply to subordinate levels a *tutelle administrative* (tutelage), through their own inspectors, the prefects in the *départements,* and the mayors of the communes, that directly reaches local government. The result, as a President of France once observed, "is a republic at the top but an empire at the base." In Germany on the other hand, there has been some tradition of local self-government, but it has been considerably stifled by tendencies to authoritarianism at the top. The present German Federal Republic, though reflecting much of the continental pattern of administration, continues the German tradition of leaving to the *Länder* (states) the bulk of administrative organization, including the enforcement of much federal law and the administering of many federal services. The federal ministries are thus relatively small, since they administer directly only the postal service, customs, finance, and railroads, as well as defense and foreign affairs. Local government is created and regulated by *Land* law and, in turn, performs many functions for the *Länder.*

Within the Anglo-American pattern, there are also obvious differences. Great Britain, with a unitary system of government operating within a relatively small area, has only two main governmental levels, central and local. There are no intermediate levels of state or provincial government as in the United States and Germany; neither are there prefects, as in France, representing central authority at the local level. Only a few of the British ministries maintain sizable regional or local services of their own; much of their administration is effected through local governments, over which they exercise a variety of controls; though these are not centralized in a single ministry, they nonetheless achieve a very close supervision of local authorities. The American administrative system reflects its English origins in many ways, but owing to the American federal system and an even greater commitment to "home rule," it is much less centralized. The federal government has maintained its own administrative field service, relying on direct state and local conduct of its programs only in limited instances. And under the federal system, of course, control of local government is a function of the states.

Administrative Agencies. The principal administrative agency is the department or ministry. There is no standard terminology. British usage speaks of "the governmental departments," but all are actually designated "office" or "ministry"; France also uses the term *ministère;* a *département,* it should be noted, in French usage describes an administrative area. These primary administrative entities are devoted to some broad and substantive purpose, such as domestic order, foreign affairs, government finance, commerce, or health. The number varies from country to country. The United States has thirteen, Norway, fourteen; France, India, and Australia, often two dozen; in many states the number changes from time to time as political or administrative convenience requires. The principal subdivisions of departments or ministries have more narrowly defined functions, and again no uniformity in their terminology—which makes their comparative discussion difficult. The Hoover Commission in 1949 proposed that the American usage, in descending order, be department or agency, bureau, division, branch, section, and unit. In Britain, however, the principal subdivisions of ministries are called departments or divisions; they are *directions* (directorates) in France, and services in Canada.

By no means are all administrative agencies contained within and under the control of the departmental hierarchy. Indeed, it is a phenomenon of modern government that an increasing number of "independent" entities have everywhere been established and set apart, to some degree, from superior administrative authority. There are various motives for doing so, but they result primarily from the desire to achieve a measure of regulation, adjudication, or management independently of the chain of command in the regular administrative hierarchy. Some of these agencies are headed by one man; others are controlled by multimember boards or commissions. A number of important independent agencies have been created by Congress; these include the independent regulatory commissions, of five or more members, appointed by the President for fixed terms, but not removable by him or subject to his direction. Among the important ones are the Interstate Commerce Commission, regulating the railroads and other carriers; the Federal Communications Commission, regulating telephone, telegraph, radio, and television; the Securities and Exchange Commission; and, the Civil Aeronautics Board. Other forms of this device may be seen in such bodies as the British Independent Television Authority, the Danish Monopoly Inspection Board, and the Japanese Board of Audit.

As the business of government has expanded, increasing the number and variety of private claims and official decisions affecting private persons, the conduct of public affairs has come to require greater speed, simpler procedures, and more specialized knowledge than the ordinary courts can usually provide. Special administrative tribunals, as a second kind of agency, have consequently been established in most modern states to consider claims and review on appeal many official decisions protested by those affected. Such are, for example, the Unemployment Compensation Boards in the states, and the Court of Claims in the federal government in America. The independent regulatory commissions just mentioned also have authority to conduct administrative adjudication, thus joining quasi-judicial functions to their quasi-legislative powers of making, within the limits of their enabling legislation, rules and regulations having the force of law. In Great Britain a vast number of administrative tribunals are arrayed throughout the government's structure, reviewing cases and controversies in such matters as pensions, claims, transport, town planning, public housing, and so on. Their decisions can usually be appealed to the ordinary courts; appeal is to administrative courts, where they exist, as in France.

A third kind of independent agency commonly employed is the public corporation. To be sure, examples abound of direct ministerial operation of governmental commercial undertakings: the postal system in the United States, the railroads in the Scandinavian countries, public forests in New Zealand, and the like. A frequently preferred device for operating a nationalized industry, however, is its separate control through an independent public corporation, which is created analogously to a private corporation and provided with somewhat similar powers. This may be done where highly specialized management is required, to allow appli cation of commercial techniques and profit-making, or to give an enterprise freedom from normal budgetary or other "political" influences or controls. The use of the corporate form of organization is displayed in the Tennessee Valley Authority and St. Lawrence Seaway Development Corporation; British Overseas Airways Corporation and National Coal Board; in Électricité de France and Gaz de France; and in the Norwegian State Liquor Monopoly.

IV. *The* CIVIL SERVICE

As important as the form of administrative institutions and their relationships are the people who comprise them. Every government today, and its citizenry generally, must be concerned with what has come to be called "public personnel administration"—the recruitment, training, organization, and management of civil servants. This acquired its special significance as government reached its modern dimensions.

The Development of the Modern Civil Service. The civil service had its beginnings with the emergence of the modern nation-state, as monarchs organized royal services to centralize and extend their power and employed bureaucracies as instruments of government. Appointments to the service were largely a matter of monarchical patronage; prevailing qualifications were those that met their internal requirements of effectiveness. On the European continent, these were essentially centralization, discipline, and efficiency. In their higher reaches, the services became the preserve of the aristocracy; state service was thus an exclusive occupation, and royal prestige enhanced the civil servant's status at all levels. After absolute monarchy was generally ended in the nineteenth century, the traditions of a professionalized service, aristocratic in tone, still prevailed and largely continued with the qualities which have characterized the continental pattern of administration.

In England, however, the establishment of parliamentary supremacy over the monarchy in the seventeenth century prevented the creation of a comparably centralized royal service. Under parliamentary control, the English civil service became instead a source of patronage for parliamentary politicians, filled with their relatives and partisans to an extent that, during the eighteenth and much of the nineteenth centuries, it was looked upon as a system of "outdoor relief" for the aristocracy. The result was administration sometimes corrupt and often inefficient; its ineffectiveness was shockingly revealed in the Crimean War. The sweep of the nineteenth-century reform movement touched this, as it did other realms; some tests for "merit" were first applied for appointments to the service in India, and subsequently to the home service. By 1870, appointment by competitive examination was made obligatory throughout the service, and recruitment through a merit system continued thereafter. Similar systems have been carried to the Commonwealth countries, though Canada's reflects more typically American characteristics.

The United States inherited the eighteenth-century English tradition of a patronage-based system. Yet in the post-revolutionary period some attempts were made to displace it by providing extensively for elected and rotated offices in state and local government. In the earlier decades of federal administration, too, a reaction to excessive democracy prevailed; President Washington's precedent was for some time continued in requiring a recognizable competence for appointment to the limited number of federal offices. But in the 1830's the spirit of frontier equalitarianism and "Jacksonian democracy," bolstered by the emergence of popular political parties, ushered into government service a "spoils system"—soon to be deeply entrenched at every level. All too easily, the democratic dogmas of the day, insisting on the equal ability of all citizens to discharge the functions of public office or employment, and the need of a multiplicity of elected officials to have rewards for loyal supporters, succeeded in placing the public service of the United States in the hands of party politicians. This array of officeholders—or would-be officeholders—joined the ranks of "political machines" and made "political bosses" of those with access to substantial patronage and privilege. Once introduced, they were self-perpetuating, and nearly impossible to dislodge. Ultimately, demands for reform followed those in Britain—if approximately a generation behind—and in 1883 the Pendleton Act introduced the merit system in the federal service. State and local governments much more belatedly began to institute the practice. With increments over the years, the merit system extends almost throughout the federal service; at the lesser levels of government, however, it has made slow and limited progress.

The Levels of Public Administration. From top to bottom in the administrative structure three principal levels operate in the executive branch: top leadership, middle management, and rank-and-file. The top leadership embraces those persons close to the chief executive, involved in policy making—the department heads or ministers, their undersecretaries, in some cases bureau, service, or division chiefs, and others at this level—who are concerned with the department and its program as a whole. Because of their primary concern with policy, these officials are usually appointed directly by the chief executive or the department head out of political considerations, though in some cases, as in Britain, the three or four highest permanent civil servants—the permanent secretary and his deputies—are included in this group. This is obviously a small and narrow category. As a rule these officials are politically answerable to the legislative institution; they are spokesmen for their department before the public as well; and they ordinarily lose office with changes of government. They function in a "civil" capacity, of course, and yet they are not, except in the instance mentioned, a part of the civil service.

The rank-and-file, on the other hand, make up the largest category of civil servants. The "production personnel," as they have been called, includes the army of clerks, draftsmen, inspectors, accountants, postal workers, guards, foresters, and so on, who perform the routine and unsung—but indispensable—tasks in public service. A major part of the employees of government, it should be noted parenthetically, are to be found in arsenals, docks, nationalized industries, public corporations, and in the schools and utility services of local government. Though technically within the civil service, most such employees are recruited as are their counterparts in private business and industry and have similar status. The popular imagination commonly overlooks this fact, and often prefers to conjure up, from the total number of government employees, the image of a monstrous empire of superfluous clerks and petty bureaucrats "feeding at the public trough." Yet most of these people are not engaged in "government," "politics," or even "administration," in the ordinary sense of those terms; rather, they do work that would need to be done regardless of the form of government or whatever the division between the public and private sectors of enterprise.

It is the middle-management group in the public service that is most concerned with administration in the strict sense. In this category are some of the bureau and division chiefs, other primary supervisors, officers of the departmental auxiliary agencies, and directors of field offices and institutions. Their duties are those of management, direction, and supervision; they constitute the repository of departmental knowledge of accumulated experience. Transmitting orders and decisions downward and information upward, they are at the center of the organizational communications system. They create and conduct programs appropriate to departmental policy, and they see, in short, that the work is done. Upon the professional skill, energy, and efficiency of the middle managers rests to a very large degree the success of administrative operations.

The Service Classes and Their Recruitment. The ways in which governments classify and recruit the career members of their civil service vary considerably, and reflect differing national traditions. The British system follows broadly the distinctions in service levels we have outlined above, and is tied as well to its educational and social class system. There are three major classes: first, a small administrative class of a few thousand, recruited by highly competitive examinations from among recent university graduates with arts or science degrees, whose members plan and direct policy and advise the ministers; second, an executive class, drawn from those having an academic secondary education, which acts as the managerial force in directing and supervising work programs; and third, a clerical class, the largest, to perform the routine tasks of clerking, accounting, and recording, and recruited at the age of sixteen or seventeen from those with some secondary education. Other classes, such as professional and scientific workers, or post office workers, are appropriately recruited for specific jobs.

The American federal service has no counterpart to the administrative class of the British service, with its exclusive and aristocratic traditions. Many appointments at the highest administrative levels are filled, as we observed, by political appointees who are not civil servants. Instead, the federal service has a General Schedule, with eighteen grades, ranging over clerical and office positions at the bottom to professional and scientific positions at the top. A separate Crafts, Protective, and Custodial Schedule of ten grades covers nonclerical workers. College graduates are recruited ordinarily at Grade GS-5, through competitive examinations based on a variety of college "majors," and can aim, at least, at achieving by promotion the higher ranks that range up to GS-18. Appointments at the higher grades are based not on competitive examinations but upon the evaluation of evidences of academic training and professional experience.

In France, West Germany, and European countries generally, the service classes are organized and recruited much like the British and follow the principal levels of educational attainment. The highest category in France, that of *administrateur civil,* is chosen by extremely rigorous examinations open to university graduates in political science, history, or law and to civil servants already members of the executive class. These are then given several years of additional training in the École Nationale d'Administration, combining academic and "on the job" work, which must be successfully completed. In Germany, the higher service (*der höhere Dienst*) comparably seeks those of distinctive academic attainment. It is accessible only to university graduates, generally in law; candidates must pass a very difficult competitive examination, following which they serve three years of preparatory training in various offices, and then must pass a second examination.

An Evaluation of the Civil Service. In evaluating the problems of obtaining an effective civil service, it will be useful again to distinguish between the upper and lower ranks of personnel. To acquire an effective rank-and-file, all services require a wide variety of persons with particular skills, most of which have similar or fairly close counterparts in private enterprise. The need here is to recruit persons by essentially practical tests who already have such skills or who are sufficiently educable that they can become qualified in them by a reasonable period of in-service training. A merit appointment system, then, is properly based not on some negative idea of "keeping the rascals out" but on positive assurance of competence at entry. If appointments are not to be partisan spoils, civil servants must also be given some kind of tenure system, which protects them against political dismissals, though by no means making them irremovable under any circumstances.

A job classification system is essential to ensure equal pay for equal work, compensation appropriate to duties, and some avenue for advancement by promotion or increased pay. In the public interest, too, some decision must be made as to which categories of employees cannot be allowed to strike, and how to provide alternative methods for them to present grievances and have them settled. There must be a determination of "sensitive" areas in government employment, what characteristics should disqualify particular employees from serving in them, and sensible means of ensuring loyalty and security. To make continued careers in the service attractive to the able, frequently at lower pay than in comparable nongovernmental work, requires a retirement and pension system, and attention to other similar morale-building factors.

At this level of specific job performance in public administration, the undesirable features of bureaucracy are likely to be felt most immediately by the general public. There is no sovereign remedy for them, but a recruitment system that sets standards of competence for appointment and advancement is probably the best. Most of the vices of bureaucracy reflect shortcomings in organization and management of service at this level. Officiousness is not infrequently the product of incompetence; apathy, of poor morale; delay, of understaffing; red tape, of excessively enforced routine; unimaginativeness, of rigid supervision; graft and corruption, of a spoils system of appointment and inadequate pay. And all are remediable if the public so demands and refuses to pay what are the real, if hidden, costs in incompetent and irresponsible administration.

The problems of staffing the higher service, while including many of these points, are much more complex. The European approach has been to create a separate administrative class to head the bureaucracy. This is truly an elite corps, recruited from young university graduates. Whether stressing traditional general education as in Britain, intellectual sophistication as in France, or legal training as in Germany, in each case emphasis is placed on securing persons who give early promise of a high order of attainment. The result is to offer attractive careers in state service to the most talented and to produce a politically impartial class of experts devoted to the interests of the state and possessed of high morale and prestige. These are not inconsiderable accomplishments, yet they have certain drawbacks. Men who go from university to service career leave one rarefied atmosphere for another; often they have little experience with the practical side of the world and its affairs. The products of a relatively exclusive higher education (as is the case in Europe) tend to be drawn from the upper classes, and in the superior grade of service perpetuate a sense of caste status. Such administrative classes—expert, professional, and entrenched at the highest levels—are also a powerful influence in policy making, and sometimes resist complete political control.

As we have observed, the United States has no such administrative class. The American tradition has been that the public business is the public's business and not service in the glory of "the state." Although the federal government has placed substantial emphasis in recent years on attracting young college graduates to administrative positions, they enter them at the considerably less exalted levels of lower middle management. The recruitment system also continues to emphasize the selection of professional technicians rather than the best broadly educated students the universities produce. Admission to the service commonly stresses equality of opportunity, without low age limits for entry, with the result that persons may find haven in it after being sifted out of other employment. The highest administrative positions are also frequently filled by political selection, intermingling partisan and career appointees. The resulting interchange between the worlds of government, business, politics, and education has some advantage, but it produces a service uneven in quality and experience, and a turnover rate that is unsettling. Anything in the nature of caste spirit—even of the intellect—is also avoided, satisfying popular American prejudices, if not necessarily needs. Thus, the higher American service tends to be political-minded, practical, and democratic in its outlook, and technically proficient for the most part. Its principal shortcomings, as distinguished from national differences—when compared with its European counterparts—are perhaps its failure to incorporate a sufficient number of persons with breadth of outlook, and with capacity for effective communication across departmental and functional lines, necessary to meet the demanding responsibilities of administering mid-twentieth-century public policy.

In the underdeveloped states, European influence and example have shaped efforts to organize effective civil services. A major obstacle to such accomplishment has been the insufficient supply of trained administrators for the middle-management level. A relatively small top leadership can be commonly drawn from among the western-educated; a widespread ambition to be on a government payroll brings many applicants—frequently an overstaffing—for jobs with the rank-and-file, who can be minimally qualified by brief on-the-job training. But all such countries lack professionally trained and practically experienced technical personnel, who are the heart and brains of an effective bureaucracy. As most of these regimes seek advancement to their ambitious goals through highly centralized systems of administration, they impose severe burdens on its upper levels. Not uncommonly, the functioning of these new services is impaired by the presence of buck-passing and inertia, nepotism and corruption, the grip of custom and excessive legalism—as well as by the absence of traditions of personal initiative, sufficient resources, popular habits of co-operation, and above all, competent personnel. Egypt's President Nasser summed up this great need of the emergent states: "I can import machinery," he said. "I cannot import Egyptians."

V. *The* METHODS *of* ADMINISTRATION

To treat in full scope, or in any detail, the methods of administration would take us well beyond the space available. But it will be useful if we make a brief excursion into the procedures of handling the public business. Public administration, though it may often resemble its counterpart in private enterprise in certain ways, differs significantly. The public business is essential, not optional; it has an urgent and frequently monopolistic character unlike private pursuits. Legal rules alone govern and direct its conduct and determine the funds available to it, and its continuance is dependent upon neither "success" nor "profit." It serves equally all persons with claims to service, and does so under public scrutiny. We shall examine it from two principal perspectives: first from that of administrative management, which concerns its internal operations; and second, from that of administrative action, which involves its external procedures.

ADMINISTRATIVE MANAGEMENT

Organizing the Work of Administration. A fundamental step in the organization of administrative activity is "program-planning"—the formulation of plans and policies to reach a chosen objective. A program may have the most ambitious aims or purposes, but it still must be conducted by limited means. An administrative agency is assigned any particular program by the legislature, through statute, or by superior executive authority, through administrative order. In either case the agency head necessarily must decide what shall be done and how to go about it in terms of the finances and manpower available to him. From his general instructions he evolves more particular ones, and issues them in the form of policy directives; these in turn produce additional specific orders as they move down the line. In today's complex administrative system, the administrator can no longer rely on simple "common sense" as the basis for planning and policy making. He depends upon his staff and auxiliary services to provide advice and information, to conduct research, make surveys, and consult with other agencies.

Program-planning is followed by "management-planning"—the formulation of schemes for the conduct of a particular activity. Perhaps the existing administrative structure can absorb the new program, or it may be necessary to design additional administrative entities. Personnel required by the program must then be recruited, assigned, and organized into the chosen number of operating units, and these must be related to staff and auxiliary services. A system of office management must also be established, equipment installed, and secretarial, filing, communications, custodial, and other services provided. Finally, a method of work distribution must be instituted so that production or operations may get under way.

Controlling the Work of Administration. The work of an administrative agency is internally controlled in a number of ways, of which budgeting is highly important. We have seen that the preparation and proposal of the government budget is an executive function, and its adoption, a prerogative of the legislature. The annual executive budget is organized from the requests made by each department and agency head, based upon their estimates of needs and responsibilities. These are examined by the central budget office, along with the justifications accompanying them, forecasting programs to be performed, staff additions and salary increases, capital equipment and expendable supply needs, and so on. Under the direction of the head of the government, the central budget office determines the actual figures to be presented to the legislature; after the budget's adoption—and quite possibly revision—by that body, an allocation of funds is made to the operating agencies. So that an agency will live within its means, it must divide its funds into allotments to cover the budget period, relating them to commitments already assumed and contingencies which may arise.

Effective management of funds further requires that expenditures be made only for purposes legally authorized. This is accomplished by a system of accounting, recording, and review both to control funds available for disbursement and to account for expenditures already made. Attention must also be given to supply and purchasing. Procurement of supplies is commonly performed by a central auxiliary agency, which sets standards and specifications for matériel, contracts for the supplies on the basis of competitive bidding, and inspects, stores, and issues the goods it receives. Finally, it may be noted, an administrative agency must give attention to reporting and public relations. Government agencies are avid record-keepers, not only because this may be one of their substantive functions, as in the case of a census bureau or a pensions office, but because they must account for their transactions and funds through reports to and audits by superior executive authority and the legislature. But official accounting alone never entirely suffices in democratic societies, where public opinion is important; an administrative agency must also look to its public relations to inform the citizenry of its performance and progress.

Organizing a New Administrative Program: The Peace Corps. Most administrative agencies in government are well-established and long attuned to their basic responsibilities; they conduct programs sustained by inner momentum and steady routines. When a new agency with new responsibilities is created, however, we see the problems of organizing and controlling administration all raised simultaneously; the founding of the United States Peace Corps in 1961 illustrates such a situation. President Kennedy established the Peace Corps originally by executive order on a "temporary pilot basis"; he then obtained legislation by Congress to make the corps permanent.

The mission assigned the corps was to organize and send abroad a body of volunteers to help as trained manpower in underdeveloped countries inviting them. Teachers, farm specialists, nurses, engineers, and construction and development workers of many kinds were most in demand by the host countries. It was initially decided that the Peace Corps should be a semiautonomous agency under the Department of State. Organizing began with the appointment of a director, who gathered a staff of some forty persons, many with relevant experience in overseas aid programs, "borrowed" from existing agencies. Financing the program was essential; to the end of June for the first year funds already appropriated to the Mutual Security program were drawn upon; thereafter, specific congressional appropriations were necessary. Initial budget estimates could be made only roughly. To send 2,000 workers overseas, it appeared—at a cost per year of $10,000 to $12,000 each for training, transportation, living allowances, medical care, and administrative overhead—required annual funds between $20 and $24 millions.

At its inception the agency was obliged to determine certain basic policies. How was the program to be related to American foreign policy and other international operations abroad? (The corps would co-operate with United Nations organizations such as the World Health Organization and the American International Co-operation Administration; it would in no way be related to the Central Intelligence Agency or any political or religious agencies.) What kind of people would be sent abroad? (They would be mature persons, chosen for their emotional stability, work skills, language facility, and intelligence.) How should they be recruited? (They would be selected after passing written examinations, personal interviews, and security checks.) How should they be trained? (Training would be at centers established at a number of universities, and later at additional overseas training stations.)

Once such basic policies as these were established, their implementation became necessary. This involved such matters, for example, as the design of application forms, announcements, and descriptive literature, and the organization of a work program to process applications. Negotiations with universities for training programs were initiated; instructional manuals were prepared; liaison was established with other agencies operating abroad, and so on. After the program got under way the headquarters staff increased and supervisory officers were sent overseas to direct the corpsmen. Within a few years, the Peace Corps established itself as a going concern; it had over 12,000 volunteers abroad, where a rising demand for them exceeded the supply. Many of those returning from tours of overseas duty were applying their experience in the administration of the corps, as well as in other government and business services. From its very nature, Peace Corps successes have been of the solid rather than spectacular kind, but this unusual experiment has added "a new dimension to America's foreign policy."

ADMINISTRATIVE ACTION

We turn now to the process of administration in its external aspects—administrative action affecting the public. The procedures available here are considerable in number, and constitute those activities most peculiar to public administration. Without attempting to examine them all, we may give attention to four principal categories of action.

Publicity and Education. We have emphasized before that governments do not rely exclusively upon coercion to achieve their objectives. The devices of publicity and education are important means, therefore, to persuade people to act in particular ways consonant with the aims of some public program. Publicity is quite likely to be used where a government desires, but has no authority to require, a particular action—as when the head of a government may make public appeal in time of rapid inflation for people to buy less and save more, or in the face of business recession, to buy more and save less! Educational programs are also commonly employed to support and supplement coercion in realms where the public generally is concerned or involved. Programs of education in traffic safety, fire prevention, the conservation of natural resources, the protection of public forests and wildlife, are continuous. We are also all familiar with government efforts to educate regarding such matters as public health, infant care, income tax returns, and social security benefits.

Inspection and Licensing. Inspection involves official examination to insure that certain standards are met. It is a coercive device, yet it emphasizes preventive rather than punitive action and seeks to avoid harm or loss before they occur. By inspection, government oversees such things as the purity of water, drugs and cosmetics, the wholesomeness of foods, the safety of aircraft and factory machines, and the seaworthiness of ships and life preservers. Licensing consists in granting an official permit to perform a particular service or to exercise a certain privilege. It may be employed as a regulatory device to control the practice of highly skilled professions, such as medicine, law, engineering, or teaching; or to limit and supervise in the public interest the conduct of particular enterprises, such as theaters, bars, dance halls, private detective agencies, small loan offices, and the like. In all such instances, administrative authority to suspend or revoke such licenses, or institute judicial proceedings to such ends, carries highly important supervisory power. In many cases, however, the issuance of licenses is not intended as a restrictive or selective process, but rather for the purpose of collecting revenue, as for automobiles, hunting, and fishing.

Regulation. The essence of regulation is rule-making, which is one form of the lawmaking process. We have seen that authority to make laws is one of the oldest functions of government. Originally it was a generalized power of the monarch, but in time specialized legislative and judicial institutions came to exercise a measure of it; constitutional doctrine of the eighteenth century, indeed, established the representative legislature as the primary lawmaking body. Yet the executive function of administering the law never excluded it from a share in lawmaking, if only to provide by the issuance of subordinate rules for more effective application of statutes. With the growth in complexity of modern societies and in the technical nature of matters requiring regulation, administrative rule-making has become commonplace in the twentieth century. Legislatures simply cannot anticipate every possible situation or provide for every circumstance. Statutory legislation is now commonly adopted, therefore, in general terms, and administrative agencies are authorized in many cases to supplement it with necessary rules and regulations. As we have seen, too, it is now common practice to create special regulatory agencies in certain realms and endow them with power to issue orders of individual as well as of general application and to conduct adjudication respecting their enforcement. Nevertheless, administrative rule-making is always viewed with some degree of misgiving. It is often seen as a partial surrender of power by the legislature, allowing anonymous administrators to create legal rules inadequately criticized or publicized in their formulation and application, and encouraging executive arbitrariness. Yet rule-making has clear advantages in introducing flexibility to administration, capitalizing on the administrator's expert knowledge, and avoiding undesirable delay. It is a practice that requires proper safeguards, but it has become unavoidably an essential form of administrative action today.

Enforcement and Prosecution. At some stage in the administrative process it may become necessary to enforce authority by distinctly coercive action. Common among these procedures are withdrawal of benefits, such as exclusion from farm benefit payments for failure to restrict production; revocation of license, in refusing to allow a radio or television station to continue broadcasting; the destruction of unlawful goods, as narcotics or gambling machines; the deportation of aliens, for illegal entry or habitual criminality; the attachment and sale of property, for nonpayment of taxes; and so on. Prosecution, of course, normally is available as a final coercive device to deal with those who wilfully resist authority or violate the law. Criminal prosecution requires resort to the courts and involves, on conviction, punishment by fine, imprisonment, or both. But as we suggested earlier, coercive measures in the administration of government are the exception rather than the rule. This is partly because they are always present in the background; but it is also because the citizenry generally accept the moral and social advantages of co-operation with administrative authority.

VI. LOCAL GOVERNMENT *and* ADMINISTRATION

We have given attention largely to central governments throughout our discussions, and we shall shortly turn to their affairs at the international level. Inevitably, the authority and functions of national and international bodies tend to attract our principal concern and attention. But these by no means constitute the only important parts of government, and should not be allowed to obscure the importance of local forms. In many countries, local government historically antedates that of the central authorities. It performs a number of functions that touch very closely the everyday life of the people. Most significant is the fact that city government is local government—and today's cities are the centers of our civilization. We shall not be able to do justice to the subject of local government and its administration, but we may at least draw attention to its importance.

The Functions of Local Government. The functions of local government, most obviously, consist to a large degree in providing a great array of services, with the extent and nature of these varying as a rule in fairly close proportion to the concentration of people within the particular area. Thus, rural local governments, with sparse populations, may be confined to a few limited services such as police protection, road-building, and elementary education. The government of a large metropolitan community, by contrast, may well undertake more distinctive activities than we could possibly enumerate on this page. Other factors also control the matter. There may be local choice; activities are mandatory in some cases, and discretionary in others. While some functions involve purely local concerns, others constitute the carrying out of duties for superior levels of administration. There are differences in local financial resources, too; some functions depend upon locally collected revenues, while others are supported, in whole or part, by senior levels of government.

Although there is no precise way in which to classify local government functions, they fall generally into six principal categories. First are the physical services: these include provision of streets and sidewalks, parks, public buildings, and sewerage. Second, local governments may conduct proprietary services; many operate one or more public utilities, furnishing water, electric power, gas and transportation—tramways, bus lines, subways, and ferries. Third, there are the protective services: these include police, fire, and public health services, waste and refuse collection, and street-cleaning. In a fourth category are various welfare services. Here we have local provision or administration of schools, libraries, hospitals and clinics, swimming pools and public baths, and various kinds of assistance for the aged, infirm, dependent children, and even the construction of housing. Fifth, there are the regulatory services: planning and zoning, many kinds of licensing and inspection, the regulation of building construction, of markets, restaurants, and other places of public resort, and the abatement of nuisances. Finally, there are the many administrative services which local government units may perform on behalf of higher authority. These may involve such matters as general law enforcement, the conducting of elections, the registration of vital statistics, judicial administration, military recruitment, and road, bridge and highway construction.

Local Government Systems. It is impossible to fit the variety of local government systems into any significant scheme of classification. Particular national systems are a product of their own philosophy of government, their historic needs and experiences, and their style of administration. To some degree, local government by its nature must always be subordinate government under the control of a higher level. Yet there is considerable variation in the extent to which local inhabitants influence the conduct of their government; there may be substantial or little self-government. Another significant feature of the pattern of local government results from the number of tiers into which the local body politic is organized. There may be a single local level of government—an "all-purpose" local authority which performs all functions; or, more commonly, there may exist several different levels, ranged one above another to form successive layers of authority. In some countries local authorities are treated permissively and exercise broad grants of power and discretion, but in others their operations are narrowly defined in detail.

Further, there are major differences in the extent to which local government is supervised; the matter may be left largely to the legislature and courts, and thus to general legal controls, or the central government may apply a close administrative tutelage. There is also considerable disparity in the extent of uniformity among local government entities and their structure. In some countries all are poured from the same mold; in others, particularly if their organization rests with the individual provinces or states of a federal system, they are likely to take a number of different forms. Finally, there are many different ways of constructing the governing body of a local authority. There may be a council or committee, or several of them, producing a type of government in which responsibility is highly diffuse; there may be local counterparts to the three main branches of central government—executive, legislative, and judicial; or the governing authority may be primarily executive.

A brief examination of some national systems of local government will suggest how these several features may be combined in practice. In the American federal system, the organization and control of local government is left to the fifty states. The traditions of self-government and "home rule" are strong, and administrative supervision by the state has been limited, but is increasing because of local dependence on state financial aid. There is, therefore, uniformity neither of unit, structure, nor function. Local government is basically two-tiered, with the states divided into some three thousand counties altogether, and the counties subdivided in turn—though with very little regulatory power over the subordinate units—into cities for urban government or towns, townships, and the like, for village and rural government. A feature of American local government is the extensive use of special single-purpose districts created to maintain schools, build roads, or provide parks, and the like; these exist in considerable number separate from the basic units of local government, often overlapping them and each other.

Canada, also a federal state leaving local government control in the hands of the provinces, has a system uniform in neither structure nor terminology. Generally, local government is one-tiered, with rural municipalities established for rural areas and urban municipalities—village, town, or city, depending on size—governing in the more populated areas. There are exceptions to this pattern: Ontario and Quebec, for example, have two-tiered government with county municipalities superior to, and containing, the local municipalities. Also, the sparsely settled areas of the north are largely administered directly by provincial departments of municipal affairs. Provincial supervision of local government has increased considerably in recent decades, particularly in the realm of finance and accounting; there has also been a tendency toward provincial assumption of the administration of some services in health, education, and welfare.

British local government displays a still higher degree of subordination and supervision. Britain, too, shares the tradition of local self-government, but the integrating tendencies of its unitary form and the density of its population have come to produce an ever-increasing supervision of the work of local authorities by central government departments—though still short, to be sure, of the degree of control customary on the European continent. British local government is one-tiered in the largest population centers, which are organized into county boroughs; there are over eighty of these, resembling what would be called "county-city" consolidations in the United States. Otherwise, local government is essentially two-tiered, with the rest of the country divided into administrative counties, and these subdivided into either municipal boroughs, urban districts, or rural districts according to the degree of population concentration.

Our fourth example of local government systems is the French. It has been said that France has no local government but only local administration—an exaggeration, of course, but it emphasizes the high degree of subordination, supervision, financial control, and uniformity of structure imposed by central authority. Local government is formally four-tiered: the country is divided into ninety *départements;* these are subdivided into *arrondissements;* these, in turn, into cantons; and the latter, into communes. Only the *départements,* as the principal area for central government administration, and the communes, which are units of local administration, both urban and rural, are of real importance. Both have elected councils, though of distinctly limited powers. The departmental prefects, appointed by and answerable to the Ministry of the Interior, are the key figures in local administration. The communal mayors are locally selected, but act as agents of the central authorities and are removable by the prefect. With individual variations, the commune or *Gemeinde* (in the German term) is the common unit of local government on the continent.

Urban Government. The subject of urban government deserves some special attention; though cities are legally subordinate as units of local government, they are not at all politically unimportant. Some great cities of Europe—London, Paris, Madrid, Rome, and Vienna—had their beginnings as centers of government and trade. With the development of the industrial revolution still other urban centers came into existence, such as Birmingham, Liverpool, Hamburg, Marseilles, New York, and Chicago, as centers of industry, commerce, and transportation. Urbanization, the concentration of large populations within a limited land area, has become one of the most important features of contemporary life. In Great Britain, France, Germany, Sweden, Belgium, Denmark, New Zealand, Canada, and the United States, among others, more than half of the population lives in urban areas, and in some cases even in metropolitan areas. For the western world, wealth, power, education, and culture have concentrated with the masses of people in the large cities.

Urbanism, particularly metropolitanism, produces a distinct way of life, in which the individual becomes relatively mobile and largely anonymous. City life requires a high division of labor and a wage economy; it produces splendor and slums; it concentrates yet segregates; it spreads culture but also disease; it increases crime and decreases the birth rate. It tends to alter familial, religious, and other traditional attitudes and to disorganize personal and social behavior. The result is an atmosphere of impersonality, tension, and strain. Important political consequences ensue from all this: the need for new forms of social control replacing those which have broken down, and for substantial physical, protective, and welfare services. The supply of these requires more government, and one vastly more elaborate, complex, and expensive than for simpler communities.

Though facing quite similar problems, city governments vary considerably from country to country. The great cities of Britain are organized into county boroughs, as we noted, and are governed by a council, composed of popularly elected councillors and a small number of aldermen co-opted by them. Annually, the council selects one of its number to serve as mayor. There is no single municipal government for the great urban complex of London, there being really several Londons. The mile-square City of London at its heart has its own Lord Mayor and Council. Greater London, containing the Counties of London and Middlesex, and parts of other adjoining counties, is governed by the Greater London Council and organized into thirty-two metropolitan boroughs for administrative purposes. London's Metropolitan Police District provides a single force under the direct control of the Home Office for a wide area extending beyond Greater London.

In France, municipal government, whether small or large, is conducted by the commune, but the standard pattern is altered for Paris. National governments traditionally have been reluctant to allow Paris any real measure of political independence, and have kept it under the close control of central authority. The reorganization of government for this great urban area is being undertaken over a period of years; when completed, it will extend a common Paris government, nationally supervised, to an enlarged metropolitan area. German cities are not so uniformly constituted as the French; however, they are generally organized as *Gemeinden,* with an elected council and a *Bürgermeister,* in some cases chosen by the council, and in others by the voters.

The forms of city government in the United States are anything but standardized; nevertheless, they involve variations upon three principal patterns. The mayor-council type operates in about half of the American cities, and particularly in the largest. It reflects adherence to the separation-of-powers principle, with legislative authority exercised by the council and executive power by the mayor. In some cities, however, executive authority is so divided between the mayor and other elected officials that the arrangement is characterized as the "weak-mayor" system. The commission type of municipal government places authority in an elected commission, usually a nonpartisan body of five members, who collectively exercise legislative authority and individually head one of the city's administrative departments. One commissioner serves as mayor. The council-manager type is composed of an elected nonpartisan council which forms policy; it appoints for an indefinite term a professional city manager who is responsible to it for the administration of the municipality's affairs. He is expected to recruit and manage the personnel of the municipal departments on a merit basis. The commission form has declined steadily in incidence since World War I, while the council-manager type has spread widely, especially among medium-sized cities. Mayor-council government may be seen in New York and Chicago; commission government, in Memphis and Omaha; and, council-manager government, in Kansas City and Oakland.

An Appraisal of Urban Government. The great cities have their individual problems, of course, but they share several in common. The city is the child of the state, it has been said, but it is often treated as the legendary "stepchild." Professor Luther H. Gulick has observed, "The major institutions of our free society were not evolved by or for metropolitan communities." As a result city government is far too commonly a ramshackle affair, burdened with a collection of unsatisfactory compromises and belated afterthoughts. A general disinclination to make the city into a strong and effective unit of government has widely prevailed, with unfortunate consequences often for the majority of the population. There are, for example, more people in London than in both Scotland and Wales; there are five American cities each more populous than any one of sixteen American states. Yet cities are commonly equipped with inferior governing power and facilities. Not surprisingly, then, a recent report of the World Health Organization declared: "After the question of keeping world peace, metropolitan planning is probably the most serious single problem faced by man in the second half of the 20th century."

The reasons for civic inadequacies are not hard to find. During the past century, cities have simply outgrown the forms of government provided them; yet there is still reluctance to afford them adequate modernization and sufficient jurisdiction. Their difficulties accumulate because they "just grew," inadequately planned or arranged for the tasks confronting them. Today it is a rare city that does not have substantial "blight" areas; excessive noise, air pollution, and overcrowding; strangling traffic and insufficient open space; and inadequate housing and transportation. The remedy for such ills calls, among other things, for larger, one-tiered, all-purpose units of urban government, a better balance between central control and self-government, a sounder basis for municipal financing, and far-sighted programs of planning and modernization. It ought to be clear that city government of the future is going to have an increasing variety of functions and will become substantially more expensive.

The problems of city government in the United States have been intensified by several circumstances. The growth of cities has been more than ordinarily haphazard, rapidly assembling, but not always assimilating, their populations from rural and immigrant elements. They have been regulated most commonly by rural-minded and even urban-hostile state legislatures with results—to take only the inadequacy of their tax and spending powers, for instance—that are often grotesque. They have been obliged to contend with dispersed and overlapping multitiered units of local government dating from another age, and staffed by amateur and partisan-selected personnel. And, not least important, they have been afflicted with graft and corruption, in part because there have been both popular attempts to make illegal such things as liquor, gambling, prostitution, and narcotics—and at the same time popular demands for them.

Fortunately, there is some evidence that a new day in urban government is to dawn; many cities have begun to bestir themselves with efforts at confronting the significant problems of urban and metropolitan life of the sort we have mentioned. Most such efforts aim at eliminating the jurisdictional conflicts, overlapping of territory, and duplication of functions, as well as their attendant excessive cost and inefficiency, by the consolidation or federation of county, city, suburban, and special district units into a single local government for the entire metropolitan area. The creation of the Municipality of Metropolitan Toronto offers a progressive model of what may be done by federation. Here Toronto and a dozen suburban areas were merged; a metropolitan council and mayor administer water supply, highways, parks, sewerage, housing, and planning for the entire area; local municipalities provide police, fire, most public health services, and building regulation. Complete city-county consolidation has been attempted in some instances, though it has usually failed for constitutional, political, or practical reasons; Baton Rouge and Nashville are among the few exceptions. Separation of a city from the county, and consolidation of city-county functions in the one remaining level of government, may be seen in Baltimore, Denver, St. Louis, and San Francisco with generally beneficial results. Other cities, Boston, Miami, Los Angeles, and Seattle have also attracted attention to their efforts at achieving integration of their metropolitan areas for special functions. The city has been expected to serve as the school of the citizen; if we allow it to break down from the unbearable weight of its burdens, we have undermined all our democratic foundations. Far too long we have been inclined to dismiss municipal matters as of little importance, forgetting perhaps that "God fulfills Himself in many ways," as G. K. Chesterton wrote, "even by local government."

PART SIX:

WORLD *in* TRANSITION

WILLIAM GRAHAM SUMNER

If you want war, nourish a doctrine. Doctrines are the most frightful tyrants to which men ever are subject, because doctrines get inside of a man's reason and betray him against himself. Civilized men have done their fiercest fighting for doctrines.

SPINOZA

Men will find that they can prepare with mutual aid far more easily what they need, and avoid far more easily the perils which beset them on all sides, by united forces.

CHAPTER 13

The MODERN STATE *in* INTERNATIONAL LAW

THERE WILL not be one law for Rome and another law for Athens, nor one law today and another tomorrow, but among all peoples and for all time one and the same law will apply." When Cicero delivered these lines he was looking to a future unity of law—an ideal, of course, still unattained. But though there is no "world law," there is a body of international law and, in part, the relations of states in the international community do take place according to certain rules. Even where no rules exist, the actions of states are influenced both by the qualities inherent in their statehood and by the dictates of community life. To understand the character of interstate relations, then, we must see how the community originated, the nature of its members, and of their legal relations.

I. *The* DEVELOPMENT *of* INTERNATIONAL RELATIONS

The modern western or nation-state system has a long history. Though it is very largely a product of the last five centuries, it has its roots in antiquity. Our knowledge of the ancient world begins from written history sometime in the fifth millennium B.C.; by this time man had already evolved relatively elaborate forms of political organization.

Contributions of Antiquity. The earliest state system of principal significance to the west originated in the Middle East. For the ancient empires of Egypt, Assyria, Babylonia, and Persia, however, there was little in the way of regularized international relations. War was their normal form of intercourse; yet some treaties of peace, alliance, and arbitration date from as early as 3100 B.C. Diplomatic emissaries were also occasionally employed, though negotiation was as likely to be undertaken to aid the promotion of war as to substitute for it. In all, the influence of the ancient empires on subsequent international relations was slight.

The development of the great Greek civilization after the second millennium B.C. produced the characteristic city-community. The existence of numerous independent, relatively equal, and small entities encouraged the establishment of relations among them, and ancient Greece became a world community in miniature. In their mutual relations, at least, the Greeks considered peace to be the normal condition. They exchanged diplomatic representatives and entered into treaties, coalitions, and alliances. A rudimentary body of practices, "the customs of the Hellenes," regulated the exchange of envoys, the right of asylum, truces, and the status of aliens. The conduct of war was considered subject to some rules, except in the case of hostilities with barbarians, who were viewed as natural enemies having no rights. The Greeks also employed arbitration to resolve disputes involving territorial boundaries and commerce.

Rome made further contributions to the development of international relations. In its earlier history it entered into treaties with its neighbors, though it was unwilling at later periods to deal with non-Roman countries on a basis of equality. Rome nonetheless continued to emphasize the observance of formalities in interstate relations—the sanctity of ambassadors, the practice of extradition, and the special status of aliens. It also acknowledged certain rules for the conduct of hostilities as binding on all belligerents, and distinguished between "just" and "unjust" wars.

Two branches of Roman jurisprudence distinctly influenced subsequent international law. One body of rules, the *jus fetiale,* governed the declaration of war and the ratification of peace treaties. Another, the *jus gentium,* was concerned with judicial principles common to all the nations under the administration of Roman magistrates. Although the latter body of rules dealt primarily with commercial matters, it was most influential in the law of the middle ages. Rome made other practical contributions; its rules on the subject of jurisdiction were later drawn upon when the European states began to concern themselves with precise boundary demarcation.

The Middle Ages. Following the collapse of the Roman empire, the creation of the Frankish kingdom in the sixth century permitted a line of Merovingian and Carolingian kings to bring under their rule a large portion of western Europe. This accomplishment was celebrated in A.D. 800, when the Pope crowned Charlemagne, the accomplished ruler of this kingdom, emperor at Rome. But despite this proclamation of universal authority for the Holy Roman Empire, European society was actually splintered into many small units, both joined and separated by the arrangements of the feudal system. War was common and was waged often for casual reasons. Fortunately, the Church was able to mitigate some of the barbarism of the times. Through the "peace of God" and the "truce of God" the Church placed an interdiction on warfare levied against noncombatants and during specified periods of the year. Popes and bishops extended the range of canon law, and often undertook to arbitrate political disputes.

Definitely more influential upon later international relations were other practices instituted during the middle ages. The growth of commerce brought about the development of a body of maritime law and, beginning in Italy, the institution of the first consulates and embassies. By the year 1200, the office of consul, exercising jurisdiction over foreign merchants in major trading cities, was well established. The system of foreign representation and the development of diplomacy as an art were particularly advanced by Venetian practice during the thirteenth century, and thereafter were widely imitated in Europe. Also significant was the establishment of the principle, arising out of the feudal system of land tenure, that the exercise of political authority is coincident with the possession of territory. Feudalism had at least the further merit of ultimately reversing the disintegrative tendencies of the time, and out of it emerged the modern nation-state.

The Age of the Nation-States. The process by which the nation-state emerged in western Europe was gradual and uneven. Prior to 1500,

England, France, Spain, and Portugal were clearly recognizable as national entities. Thereafter Sweden, Poland, Prussia, Switzerland, and the Netherlands, among others, appeared, and the Italian city-states won a precarious independence of papal and imperial control. All that was lacking was some formal act of recognition of the new European state system, and this came out of the Thirty Years' War.

If any one landmark will serve to mark the establishment of the new order, it is the several treaties comprising the Peace of Westphalia, 1648. This was Europe's first international conference of states, and the constitutional foundations for the modern community of independent nation-states were laid. Although the Holy Roman Empire nominally continued, it was now confined to the Germanies, and the sovereign power of each German prince was acknowledged. All other states of western Europe, moreover, were entirely released from any further political allegiance to the Emperor or to the Roman Church. Thus, states could now exist independently in "an exact and reciprocal equality," whether Catholic or Protestant, monarchical or republican, and without acknowledging any legal superior.

Given the recognition of individual state equality within the international community, the multi-state system could now develop with all its appurtenances—international wars, alliance and balance of power arrangements, treaties and international law, diplomacy and statecraft. National rulers were now largely free, unhampered by any superior control, to exercise full jurisdiction over all persons and things within their domain to the extent of their power. By the sixteenth century, the practice of exchanging resident diplomatic emissaries, personally representing the monarch, became general. The conduct of diplomacy developed increasingly into a profession—albeit one of dubious honesty. In Sir Henry Wotton's often quoted double-entendre of the seventeenth century, "An ambassador is an honest man sent to lie abroad for the commonwealth." Large impetus was given to the formalization of diplomatic practice after 1648, with the formal categories of diplomatic agents as they exist today being laid down by the Congress of Vienna in 1815.

The international community was originally composed exclusively of European Christian states, associated by many common bonds and a similarity of interest. In time, however, this western state system began to accept additions to the community and to extend itself to non-

ABOVE: ". . . The arsenals of modern military establishments are so complex in their equipment that it is impossible to be dogmatic today about the results to be achieved by any particular national system of armaments." (p. 538) A United States Air Force Minuteman intercontinental ballistic missile is shown as it leaps skyward from an underground silo. (*The Boeing Company.*) BELOW: "If the Security Council has recovered somewhat from its near paralysis during the height of the cold war, the veto power still causes a decline in reliance on that organ. . . ." (p. 593) A general view of the Council Chamber as representatives vote on a resolution. (*United Nations.*)

ABOVE: ". . . A vast network of bonds of association is steadily being drawn around various groups of states. . . . Thus do they create new bases for the existence of larger communities than those of the nation-states." (p. 609) The European Court of Justice meets at the Villa Vauban in Luxembourg; on the bench with seven judges are two advocates-general and the clerk. (*The European Community.*) BELOW: ". . . That there can be a 'UN presence' as a force to be reckoned with at international danger points is now a fact of international life." (p. 593) A member of the Canadian contingent of the UN Peace-Keeping Force in Cyprus maintains wireless communication with his base camp. (*National Film Board of Canada.*)

European and non-Christian areas. Successful colonial revolutions in the Americas created a number of new republics. The opening of the east to contacts with the western world brought the admission of such states as Turkey, Persia, China, and Japan. Concessions to the nationalistic aspirations of eastern European peoples brought the establishment of still other states. Finally, the political turmoil surrounding World Wars I and II, the decline or collapse of the great colonial powers, and the even freer application of the principle of national self-determination, have greatly increased the number of states composing the international community.

II. *The* CONCEPT *of* STATE *in* INTERNATIONAL LAW

The world today, we have seen, has come to be organized into distinctive units known as states. It may be recalled from the discussion in Chapter 2 that the concept of "state" is a complicated one, and may be approached from a variety of standpoints. Our concern here, however, is with the state as the international person, an entity having a status in international law.

THE STATE

The Definition of State in International Law. As a subject of international law, the term "state" cannot be defined with precision; yet it has commonly accepted essentials. The first article of the Montevideo Convention (1933), for example, among the American republics provides that the state as a person of international law should possess the following qualifications: a permanent population, a defined territory, a government, and a capacity to enter into relations with other states.

It is impossible, of course, to conceive of a state without people, though international law does not require any minimum size for its population. The people who compose a state commonly constitute a nation. The terms "nation" and "state" are often used interchangeably in designating the members of international society, but strictly speaking they are not synonymous. A nation is a body of people who feel they are united by several factors such as common ethnic origin, historical association, culture, language, religion, and customs. Most nations are so united, though the people of some display considerable diversity in their religions, as in the United States and Great Britain; they may speak more than one language, as in Switzerland and Canada; and they may contain a number of ethnically distinguishable groups, as in India and Brazil. The ties of nationhood are essentially social and cultural, and such a group inevitably aspires to statehood as the means to preserve the unity and advance the objectives of the nation. Thus, most nations comprise a state; but there are also multinational states, as Yugoslavia and the Soviet Union.

A state must have a defined territory, both to provide an area where its population may exist and over which its jurisdiction may be exercised. A people who were scattered about the world, however united otherwise, or nomadic tribes, could not constitute a state. Also essential is an organized government. The state must contain some constituted authority which commands reasonably habitual obedience from its inhabitants, maintains order, and assumes responsibility for the discharge of its obligations to other states. International law is not concerned with the form or character of the government. A violent or revolutionary change of government does not affect the state's existence; indeed, during wartime a government may even be driven "into exile" without the state's ceasing to exist.

These three elements may, of course, also be components of other organizations—such as universities, colonial settlements, and municipalities—that are not states. A state must also have a degree of independence providing a capacity to enter into relations with other states. This is not so easily understood, and we shall offer a brief explanation.

Independence and Sovereignty. The term "independence" is employed to describe the capacity of a state to be free of the legal authority of other states. Independence is not absolute, of course, and no state has unlimited freedom of action. The fact that a state is a member of the international community is taken to mean that it has implicity assented to the rules of international law, which place some limits on the state's freedom of conduct. States further find it necessary to enter into a considerable number of treaties and other international agreements. Also, states are limited by fear of the power of other states. Finally, states are obligated to undertake many kinds of international co-operation if they are adequately to protect their national interests. We shall discuss this matter further in the next section.

The singular attribute which has been historically claimed for the state to justify this independence, and which sets it apart from all other social organizations is its "sovereignty." The United Nations Charter, for example, speaks of the "sovereign equality" of all its members as one of the basic principles of the organization. What is the meaning of this term? The word "sovereignty," we should warn, is a highly abstruse one to which are given many confused, and sometimes intentionally confusing, meanings. Because it is so commonly used in the terminology of international affairs to distinguish those organizations recognized as states, we must understand its significance.

The term "sovereignty" was introduced into political terminology in 1576 by a Frenchman, Jean Bodin, who defined it as the "supreme power of the state over citizens and subjects, unrestrained by law." Bodin was concerned with formulating a legal justification for the exercise by the monarch of supreme and undivided power as a means of consolidating the authority of the central government within the state. It served, then, as a legal rationalization of the authority of the monarchical sovereign or the powers of the crown to oppose the disruptive and decentralizing tendencies of feudalism, and to justify centering in the monarch the responsibility for the conduct of foreign affairs.

Although absolute monarchs no longer reign, the concept of the sovereign state endures. And today, the state may claim itself sovereign in the sense that it alone, through the agencies provided by its fundamental law, has exclusive power to legislate for its citizens. As one authority put it in a famous arbitral award, "Sovereignty in the relations between states signifies independence. Independence in regard to a portion of the globe is the right to exercise therein, to the exclusion of any other state, the functions of a state." This legal conception of sovereignty, carried no further, creates no international problems.

But some philosophers have sought to interpret the doctrine in an external sense to mean that there can be no earthly authority above or beyond the state that may impose law or restraint upon it. The maintenance of this view, it will be apparent, places great difficulties in the way of organizing international law; treaties have no legal effect, but become mere promises; member states of international organizations cannot be obligated to any commitment or responsibility whatever. To view sovereignty as conferring upon the state the exercise of unrestrained political power is to allow the concept to become a justification for the conduct of international relations on the basis of power alone. This can only produce—as indeed it often has in the past—international anarchy and chaos.

The conclusion is, consequently, that it is acceptable to designate the state as sovereign, when the term is intended to connote no more than the state's power to make law within its own territory, its position of independence and of separateness from other states, and its capacity to enjoy full membership in the international community. It is not surprising, however, that in view of its exaggerated use, many scholars have insisted that the term "sovereignty" should be discarded from the terminology of international relations as both practically and theoretically meaningless. The simpler term, "independence," they assert, could be more aptly and usefully employed.

OTHER PERSONS IN INTERNATIONAL LAW

There are a number of political entities encountered in the international community which, because their exercise of independence and full state powers is impaired, or because they are not states at all but do exercise some kinds of governmental powers, have some status in and are recognized by international law. The number of such entities and the variations in their legal character are so considerable that they are easier to describe individually than to classify generally. However, a few main types may be noted.

States under Special Limitations. One type of state lacking full legal freedom of action in international relations, though enjoying free control over its internal affairs, is the perpetually neutral or *neutralized state,* which has accepted a guarantee of its territorial integrity by other states and in return has renounced an intention to participate in war. This position was arranged for Switzerland by a treaty of 1815; for Belgium from 1831 to 1919; for Luxembourg from 1867 to 1944; and for Austria in 1955. Such states may have normal diplomatic relations with other states, and may be armed, but agree to abstain from alliances, and to take up arms only to defend themselves.

Another instance of restricted status was the case of Cuba, between 1901 and 1934, when it was obligated to the United States not to alienate any of its territory, under certain circumstances to permit American intervention therein, and to accept other restrictions on its freedom of action. After World War I, the succession states of eastern Europe were obliged to afford by treaty certain guarantees to the minority populations within their territories. After World War II for some years, both Germany and Japan were forbidden by the Allies to possess armaments.

Dependent States. Another group of political entities includes those whose international personality is obscure or quite seriously limited. A protected state, or *protectorate,* is placed under the protection of another state, in return for which it relinquishes control over its foreign affairs. Monaco was placed under the protection of Sardinia in 1815, and subsequently under that of France in 1918; San Marino agreed to a treaty of protection with Italy in 1862; Japan obtained a protectorate over Korea by treaty in 1905, and then annexed it outright in 1910; Tonga, the Sheikhdom of Bahrain, and South Arabia are protectorates of Great Britain. Sikkim stands in this relationship to India. Protectorates are denied the right to engage in any relations with third states except through the intermediary protecting state, though they normally retain control of the powers of internal government.

A *vassal state,* or a state under suzerainty, was a type well known as recently as the nineteenth century. It was one ordinarily in the process of becoming independent, so that it enjoyed the grant of a considerable measure of autonomy from the parent state; however, the latter still retained control of its foreign affairs. Russia and China recognized Outer Mongolia as under Chinese suzerainty by declaration in 1913; its independence was recognized in 1946. As other examples, Egypt was considered a vassal of Turkey until 1914; the tiny republic of Andorra has been under the co-suzerainty of France and the Spanish Bishop of Urgel since 1278. Andorra appears to be the last remainder of this feudal status.

In the turbulent years prior to and following World War II, still another type of dependent state appeared, the *satellite.* To be sure, this is a political, rather than a legal term, applied to states allowed to keep many of the outward manifestations of control of their domestic affairs and external relations, yet dominated through ideological, political, economic, and military means of various kinds by the paramount state. Japan's creation and control of Manchukuo and Germany's of Croatia and Slavonia are examples. Contemporary satellite relationships are demonstrated in Communist China's influence over North Korea and North Vietnam, and the Soviet Union's paramountcy in Outer Mongolia, East Germany, and other east European states. Given the ideological ferment at work within the communist bloc, however, these relationships seem "subject to change without notice."

Members of Unions and Federal States. Certain political associations possess common organization or ties of various sorts which condition their international personality. The members thereof may enjoy essentially unimpaired international status or may be denied it entirely. The members of the then British Commonwealth of Nations, for example, defined their status at the Imperial Conference of 1926 as "autonomous communities within the British Empire, equal in status, in no way subordinate one to another in any aspect of their domestic or external affairs, though united by a common allegiance to the Crown. . . ." Today, even Crown allegiance is not essential, since several of the members are republics, and recognize the Queen as Head of the Commonwealth. Consequently, the *Commonwealth countries,* the United Kingdom, Canada, Australia, New Zealand, India, Pakistan, Ceylon, Ghana, Nigeria, and roughly a dozen other former portions of the British Empire exercise all of the rights of fully independent states. The association is neither an alliance nor a federation; as a British Commonwealth Secretary, Duncan Sandys, observed: "To us, the Commonwealth is, above all, a collective relationship in which we consult together, think together and, as far as possible, work together for the advancement of broad, common objectives."

The Constitution of the U.S.S.R., as amended in 1944, authorizes its sixteen Union Republics "the right to enter into direct relations with foreign states, to conclude agreements with them, and exchange diplomatic and consular representatives with them," and to maintain their "own military formations." It is not clear what, if any, international status the Soviet Constitution intended to confer upon the constituent Republics by this authorization. Two of them, the Byelorussian and Ukrainian Republics, have been given separate memberships in the United Nations, but this action was taken in recognition of the Soviet Union's political importance and not of the constitutional provisions mentioned.

Confederations usually have been composed of a number of independent states bound together by a compact and with certain common organs of government. The confederation is not recognized as a state in international law because its members retain their international personality. A *federal state,* on the other hand, is a single entity, and the members of its federal union, as in the case of the United States, are denied any international status. According to the United States Constitution, the individual states may not "enter into any treaty, alliance, or confederation," nor, without the consent of Congress, "enter into any agreement or compact with another state, or with a foreign power, or engage in war. . . ." The states of the American Union are thus not states at all in the sense we have been using the term, and they are clearly not sovereign.

Dependencies, Mandates, and Trust Territories. A *dependency* is a territory distinct from the metropolitan area of the state that holds title to it and exercises legal control over it. The term *colony* is sometimes used synonymously—through strictly speaking a colony has been settled by the citizens of its controlling state, who remain subject to it. At the end of World War I Germany and Turkey were obliged by the peace treaties to relinquish their dependent and colonial possessions. By Article 22 of the League of Nations Covenant, these were placed as *mandated territories* under the control of various mandatory powers who were given their administration in behalf of the League of Nations. Most of the fifteen mandated territories have now become independent states. The mandate system was replaced at the end of World War II by an international trusteeship system of the United Nations, whereunder, by agreement, remaining mandated territories and certain others have been constituted as *trust territories*. Dependencies and colonies have no international personality recognized by third states, but mandated and trust territories do have some limited international status, because the arrangements for their control are the product of international agreement.

International Entities. Increasingly in recent years various bodies and organizations, which are not states but associations of them, have acquired such important governmental functions as to give them some degree of international personality. These *international entities,* created by treaty or convention, include the general international organizations, as we may describe the League of Nations and the United Nations; the regional organizations, such as the Council of Europe and the European Coal and Steel Community; and various specialized and functional organizations, such as the International Labor Organization and the Universal Postal Union.

In a decision handed down in 1949, the International Court of Justice stated that the United Nations "was intended to exercise and enjoy, and is in fact exercising and enjoying, functions and rights which can only be explained on the basis of the possession of a large measure of international personality. . . . It is a subject of international law and capable of possessing international rights and duties. . . ." The United Nations Charter (Article 105) stipulates that "The organization shall enjoy in the territory of each of its Members such privileges and immunities as are necessary for the fulfillment of its purposes. Representatives of the Members of the United Nations and officials of the Organization shall similarly enjoy such privileges and immunities. . . ."

As another example, we have the European Economic Community (Common Market) formed by the Treaty of Rome (1958), joining France, West Germany, Italy, and the Benelux countries. Its purpose is to create a customs union for these states, between which tariff barriers are ultimately to be eliminated, and to establish uniform tariffs against other states. Its executive is a nine-man Commission, with headquarters and staff at Brussels. Here again is a body, along with now more than a hundred other such organizations, that must be recognized as clearly possessing a degree of international personality.

Manifestly, such entities as these are not sovereign states, but they have a capacity to enter into relations with states. They may administer territory and property, confer a degree of diplomatic immunity on their officials, be parties to suits before courts, impose fines, and so on. To the present, their status rests largely on treaty; before a clearer definition of their international status can be made, the present rules of international law will have to be considerably extended.

III. *The* INTERNATIONAL COMMUNITY

The aggregation of states in the world was described as recently as the nineteenth century as the "family of nations." Obviously, this has ceased to be an appropriate term, when association is no longer limited primarily to the sovereign princes of Europe; and as we have seen, it is not "nations," strictly speaking, which enter into association, but "states." Let us examine, then, what is better described as the community of states.

The Community of States. The term "community" is variously employed to describe a body politic, or a body of persons having common interests; it indicates the presence of a group who share, or have an identity or likeness of, interests. There can be no doubt that the some three billions of people who live in the world today, and are divided among well over one hundred independent political entities, constitute a community in some sense. These states do share at least existence on the same globe, and therefore must "coexist" to some degree.

Yet it is a community which is certainly not made up of uniform or homogeneous units. Some of the states existed with a high degree of integration before the concept of statehood even originated; others are creations of the last few years. They display the most extreme differences in area, population, geographic character, military power, wealth, degree of civilization, and form of government. Some are at the center of every international activity; others exist almost unnoticed at the remoter byways of the world. Their ambitions, objectives, and policies are often in conflict; they engage in frequent disputes and periodic wars. These are some of the reasons why it is so difficult to organize and maintain a real sense of community.

Nevertheless, there is present something of a legal basis of association for the states of the world. By general acceptance and definition, the international community is composed of all states which accept the rules of international law. Limited in character in so many ways as this legal system is—a subject we shall discuss later in this chapter—the community has achieved something more than the anarchy of the jungle, or the vigilante-maintained order of the frontier. But many vestiges of these conditions still remain.

The Creation and Recognition of New States. A few states were original members of the international community; most, however, have achieved membership by admission, granted by the other members through the process of recognition. Recognition is the act by which one or more states indicate that they are willing to have full diplomatic relations with the new state, and that they acknowledge this state as independent and capable of acting responsibly for the people and territory it controls. It is tacitly assumed that their relationships will be governed by the accepted rules of international law. Usually, the major powers take the lead, and when they have granted recognition the smaller states follow. Though recognition is occasionally granted collectively, it is ordinarily an individual action. An occasion for recognition also arises when the government of a state is overthrown and replaced by violent means. Then all other states must decide whether they are willing to acknowledge the legitimacy of the new political regime and to undertake normal diplomatic relations with it.

In each case, a state is free to grant or withhold recognition to a new state or government, and there is no right to demand it. Because the granting of recognition is often based upon political rather than legal considerations, states may withhold it as a matter of national policy, as when most states refused to concede the existence of an independent state of Manchukuo in territory wrested from China by Japan in 1931. Further, they may even use the act of recognition on occasion to help ensure the achievement of the independence supposedly being recognized, as in the case of the precipitous American recognition of Panama in 1903. The occasion for the recognition of new governments arises even more frequently, and in granting it, states are especially prone to pass a self-interested judgment on the new regime. Most states, for example, were in no haste to recognize the Bolshevik government of Soviet Russia after 1917, and many have been even more reluctant to do so in the case of the Communist government of China.

The creation of new states may take place under several circumstances. The most common is when a dependent territory capable of undertaking its own government and maintaining its independence is separated from the state which has been in control of it. This may come after a successful colonial revolution, as in the case of the American colonies, or by peaceful agreement, as in the case of the Philippine Republic, India, Pakistan, and Ceylon. Occasionally, an existing state has been dissolved, as when in 1905 Sweden and Norway voluntarily separated as independent states, or when the Austro-Hungarian Empire was divided into a number of new states by the peace treaties in 1919. A new state may also be created by joining together several existing ones, as was the case with Italy in 1860, and with Germany in 1871. The contemporary era has been prodigious in the birth of new states; their number has more than doubled since World War II.

The Diversity of States in the Community. The members of the international community display the widest kind of diversity. They range in number of people from China with an estimated 710,000,000 population and India with over 460,000,000 to Iceland with 180,000 and the Sheikhdom of Bahrain with 150,000. There are equally great variations in area. The Soviet Union covers a territory some 8,600,000 square miles in extent, and Canada, 3,800,000; on the other hand, Israel possesses less than 8,000 square miles, and Lebanon, barely 4,000. The populations of the United States and the United Kingdom are more than 95 per cent literate, while those of Haiti and Saudi Arabia are more than 90 per cent illiterate. States may be composed of island chains, as are Japan, the Philippine Republic, and Indonesia, or they may be entirely landlocked, as are Austria, Switzerland, and Bolivia. The United States and western Europe account for nearly two-thirds of the world's total production; national per capita income ranges from over $2,500 annually in the United States to $60 in some underdeveloped countries. Particularly significant for the character of the international community is the great variation in the power position of its members, which ranges from super, major, and secondary, down to minor power status. But whatever the formal acknowledgment of their equality, we shall see, some are bound to be much "more equal than others."

Consequences of Membership in the International Community. The legal position of the state in the international community can be generally described, but not very accurately defined. The classic treatises on international law discuss in some detail the "rights" of members of the community, though they give much less attention to the "duties." As a means of assuring some minimal order in the community and recognizing the personality of the state, attempts are still being made to get agreement upon what these should be.

Two recent efforts in this direction are the Inter-American Convention on the Rights and Duties of States, signed by the twenty-one American republics in 1933, and later included in the Charter of the Organization of American States; and the Draft Declaration on Rights and Duties of States, prepared by the United Nations International Law Commission, and submitted to United Nations members for consideration. The two documents stipulate that the rights of states include independence, self-defense, choice of governmental form, legal equality, and the exercise of jurisdiction over their own territory. Duties involve such obligations as not to intervene in the affairs of other states, not to recognize territorial acquisitions obtained by force, and to settle disputes by peaceful means.

That the terms "rights" and "duties" in this context are not entirely satisfactory must be acknowledged. It is a very old legal axiom that for every right there must be a remedy; yet the international community has as yet created no court before which a state may be assured even the fundamental right to exist. The establishment of such a system is still an aspiration, and the "rights" and "duties" described are in the final analysis only principles of desirable and responsible conduct for states. This is not to say that such propositions as these have no significance; they are statements of what states do expect in their relations with each other. The widely adverse reactions to interventions of recent years in Suez, Hungary, Cuba, and New Guinea, for example, lend testimony to the general resentment of states to such acts of intervention.

Indeed, we should observe that international relations are conducted practically as if such rights and duties do exist. Each state does expect equally, for example, to be entitled to grant or withhold assent to any new rule of international law, to be capable of becoming a party to a treaty, and to have one vote—in the absence of agreeing otherwise—in any international conference or organization. Certainly no state will concede that it may not be its own judge of what measures it may take in the interests of its self-defense and security. It expects to send and receive diplomatic representatives, and much diplomatic protocol is devoted to the preservation of the illusion, at least, of state equality. Each state determines the laws which will apply to the persons and things within its territory, as well as the conditions under which those who are alien may enter it. It undertakes to assume the protection of its citizens abroad, and holds accountable any government which fails to exercise due diligence in protecting the safety of its nationals. The history of diplomatic practice is replete with instances wherein one government has paid substantial damages to another for its negligence in such matters.

Independence and Interdependence. It is ironic that, as more and more states achieve independence in the international community, they also become more and more interdependent. One can begin to see why this is the case if one reflects that half a century ago, when Europe was mainly composed of large states such as France, Germany, Austria-Hungary, and Russia, the states of Europe could be much more independent of each other than they can today, when the continent is divided among more than two dozen. A state's real independence, in the sense of its freedom of action, is considerably dependent upon the amount of power and influence it can exercise, and that which other, stronger states are willing to concede to it. The many newly created small states, therefore, do not necessarily enjoy a large measure of assertable independence.

No one can observe the history of international relations since World

War II without seeing plainly how great is the fiction of state independence, and how extensively most states are dependent upon others. At the end of the war, the United Nations Relief and Rehabilitation Administration (UNRRA) expended some four billions of dollars—three-fourths of which were contributed by the United States—to provide food, clothing, housing, and the restoration of public utilities in the war-torn areas of the world. Afterward, the United States Marshall Plan poured an additional four times as many dollars into a program for restoring the economies of the west European countries. In recent years, the United States has been providing financial aid by grants or loans and technical or military assistance to at least a hundred countries. And several dozen other states, on both sides of the Iron Curtain, have also undertaken foreign assistance programs of some sort. Also, the postwar tendency of states to organize for economic purposes, as in the European Economic Community and the European Coal and Steel Community (ECSC), and to associate as international "pressure groups," as in the case of the Arab League, the communist bloc, the Latin American bloc, and so on, constitute further evidence of the inability of single states to promote their interests successfully by reliance solely upon their own efforts.

The increasing tendency of states as well to organize international alliances for their collective self-defense offers additional evidence of the lack of ability to ensure their security solely with their own resources. Soon after the end of World War II, the American republics organized an alliance by the Rio Treaty. In 1948, Great Britain, France, and the Benelux countries joined in the Brussels Pact. The next year, these and other states, including the United States, formed the North Atlantic Treaty Organization (NATO). The Australia, New Zealand, and United States (ANZUS) defense treaty, and the Southeast Asia Treaty Organization (SEATO) offer other examples of states committing their defense to collective responsibility, and demonstrate that a country even as powerful as the United States feels the inadvisability of "going it alone" in today's uneasy world. Indeed, in the exigencies of war, as demonstrated during World War II, when states are making the supreme effort to defend themselves and to maintain their independence, they are most obliged to subordinate their freedom of action and to co-operate with their allies. The necessity to make common cause in the war effort against Nazi Germany, for example, obliged the United States, Great

Britain, and even the Soviet Union to a far greater degree of mutual co-operation than has been achieved among them since the war ended.

We should also keep in mind that though states are the persons of the international community, it is their people who have international relationships. Official relationships are conducted by government officers and diplomatic representatives; otherwise, the people who cross international boundaries are tourists, businessmen, students, soldiers and sailors, and so on. Millions of people would not live well, nor some perhaps live at all, if goods and funds could not exchange internationally: the position of the populations of Great Britain, Switzerland, and Israel, for example, obviously bears testimony to this fact. As self-sufficient a country as the United States depends heavily, or exclusively in some cases, on foreign supplies of oil, rubber, nickel, chromium, newsprint, coffee, bananas, and many other items. Many of the world's leading corporations, such as British Petroleum, Royal Dutch Shell, Standard Oil of New Jersey, International Harvester, Union Carbide, and International Telephone and Telegraph, are examples of business enterprises international in character and operations. Most persons engaged in the scholarly and scientific professions, in art, music, and religion, inevitably have interests, and frequently associations, which transcend their national community.

We have indicated some of the paradoxical and anachronistic features of the modern international community. As M. Joseph Avenol, the Secretary-General of the League of Nations remarked some years ago, "The community of nations exists already; it is merely a question of defining and regulating it. Only one condition is necessary; it is a condition indispensable to all human communities, and it is this: a respect for undertakings once given; a respect which is sanctioned by public opinion and informs the education of the public mind." A discussion of the problems and possibilities of providing it with international organization requires first some examination of the legal basis of the international community, to which we now turn, and of the dynamic forces at work in the community of states, which will be undertaken in the next chapter.

IV. INTERNATIONAL LAW

Definition. International law is the body of rules and principles commonly observed by states as legally binding in their relationships. It undertakes to perform for the international community—though far more imperfectly—functions somewhat similar to those performed by the body of municipal law within the domestic community; that is, it is used as a regularizing force upon the actions of its subjects, independent states. It originated mainly because necessity and convenience induced states to conduct their relations with some degree of uniformity and order. While it assumes the basic independence of states, it arose as a product of community life as states realized that complete international anarchy is impossible. Its concepts have sometimes been criticized as unreal and utopian, and some writers have sought to argue that there really is no such thing as "international" law; at the other extreme, its most ambitious exponents have claimed far more for it than at present seems at all realizable. Before we examine some of the features of international law, we should be clear as to what it is not.

International Law Distinguished from International Practices. Some of the misunderstandings about the nature of international law may be avoided if we make certain distinctions at the outset. First, international law should be distinguished from international ethics. There is, of course, no lack of views as to how states ought to act in their relations with others. To the extent that there is some consensus upon the principles of justice to which state conduct should ideally conform, and of the moral duty for states to observe them, we have a body of international ethics, inadequately developed as it may be. But these are not rules of law which states are obliged to observe.

We should not confuse international law with international comity. The latter consists of practices which are observed as a matter of courtesy and convenience between states, but which, again, involve no obligation. Canada and the United States, for example, allow each other's citizens to enter their territory for short visits without passports, but they need not do so, and do not extend this privilege to other foreign travelers. Still further, international law is not the same thing as foreign policy. A state's foreign policy lies in the more or less consistent attitudes and courses of action it adopts in its relations with other states and areas. The Monroe Doctrine, a basic principle of American foreign policy, bars the intervention of non-American states in the affairs of the western hemisphere. Yet our policy cannot legally forbid other states to undertake such intervention, and the Doctrine is effective not as a rule of law, but because of the power of the United States.

We are concerned here only with public international law. The body of rules known as "private international law" deals primarily with the position of individuals who, because of diversity of nationality or national jurisdictions, are subjected to two or more sets of national law, and thus require some reconciliation of their status. This body of law is also known as the "conflict of laws"—which more aptly indicates its nature. Similar to this in certain ways are the rules of admiralty and maritime law, which comprise the usages and principles accepted by commercial nations in regulating maritime commerce. Both of these branches of law are applied in the main by national courts.

International law is to be distinguished, finally, from those obligations imposed by treaties, which are written agreements between two or more states. Generally speaking, treaties are not international law, but are analogous in the relations between states to contracts between persons of municipal law. Although their obligations are expected to be observed in good faith, as indicated by the ancient doctrine of *pacta sunt servanda* (agreements must be observed), their terms are subject to change at the agreement of the parties. The great many simple bipartite treaties cover matters that are of concern only to the immediate parties, dealing with such subjects as commercial relations, immigration, boundaries, and extradition. On the other hand, treaties may be employed specifically to create rules of international law. Such "lawmaking" treaties are multipartite in character, and to be effective generally they must be ratified throughout the international community. The terms "treaty" and "convention" are commonly used synonymously, though strictly speaking, a convention is an international agreement of a technical character, and one of less permanent importance.

THE DEVELOPMENT OF INTERNATIONAL LAW

The Origins of International Law. The Peace of Westphalia (1648), to which we frequently recur, constitutes the first formal recognition of the modern nation-state system; it also marks the origin of the modern system of international law. As we have already noted, states began to regularize some of their relations in earlier times; the ancient maritime law, the customs of the Hellenes, the *jus gentium* of Rome, the laws of the Hanseatic League and other medieval trading cities, all evidence this. The substantial development of a "law of nations," however, was dependent upon the existence of an international community of states, which emerged in the seventeenth century.

The existence of a new state system inevitably stimulated the interests of jurists and scholars in its resulting legal problems. Although several writers of the sixteenth century, notably Vitoria, Ayala, and Gentilis, produced commentaries on the international practices of the times, the title of "father of international law" is generally conceded to Hugo Grotius, a Dutch scholar and diplomat. Appalled by the international lawlessness of his day, Grotius searched for the existence of some law higher than that of individual monarchs which could restrain the anarchical character of interstate relations. His major work, *De jure belli ac pacis* (On the Law of War and Peace), published in 1625, exerted an immediate influence in Europe. If his treatise was concerned more with the laws of war than of peace, it was still the first systematic treatment of the whole subject. Grotius ransacked written history to find precedents for his conclusions, but largely formulated his doctrines upon the basis of "right reason." He dealt much more with what he thought the law of nations ought to be than with what he could demonstrate it really was. Nevertheless, Grotius' treatise was mainly responsible for the introduction of the study of international law in the universities of seventeenth-century Europe; it served as an inspiration for numerous other studies in the subject to follow; and its authority is still appealed to by writers and publicists today.

The international law which thereafter developed did not become a tidy and easily ascertained body of rules. During its formative period in the seventeenth century, states drew first on fundamental precepts of justice and right which were considered to be provided in the principles of natural law—that law inherent in the universe and existing independently of any promulgation by man. Grotius employed its tenets to provide a rational basis for his system of international law and, in this practice, he was subsequently supported by other writers of the seventeenth and eighteenth centuries. Thus, in the earlier stages, the principles of natural justice, reason, and equity provided a source of international law; and its rules gained much in ethical content thereby.

Once the concept of an existing body of international law became widespread, it was substantially expanded by a second source, that of rules based upon consent and actually observed, or positive law. Positive law as distinguished from natural law is established by some human authority. Positive international law, then, rested upon state consent to its rules, which might be expressed either in custom or agreement. Custom is, of course, the oldest source of law generally, and inevitably made a large contribution to the original rules of international law. Expressed in practice, usage, habit, and sentiment, customary law enjoys a most powerful sanction; states are led to observe its rules because they are accustomed to do so. Agreement, on the other hand, involves explicit consent, most commonly obtained by adopting treaties or conventions in which states consciously acknowledge their acceptance of a particular rule.

For some time, there was considerable argument over whether the foundations of the system should be theoretical or practical. The disputes of schools of jurists were overtaken by facts, however; the eighteenth century saw international law expanded increasingly on the exclusive basis of consent, and its progress since has rested much more on development by general agreement to specific rules of conduct, than upon appeals to abstract principles of justice. As a source of international law, then, positive law has emphasized practicality; rules are only accepted as binding when states acknowledge them as law, and fail when they do not. While such an attitude has retarded the growth of international law in some directions, it has effected its easier acceptance in others.

THE NATURE OF INTERNATIONAL LAW

The Evidences of International Law. The term "evidences" of international law is used to designate the various documents and acts that are adduced to prove the existence of a rule of international law. In some cases it is possible to find adequate evidence from a single international act. More often, however, the proof of a specific rule is very difficult, particularly because a large portion of international law rests upon customary development. At what point, therefore, does a particular international practice acquire the necessary general acceptance to be regarded as a binding legal rule? To answer this question is often as puzzling as to determine at what precise moment, say, a set of wagon tracks becomes a road. Generally speaking, when evidence exists that all or nearly all states have given express or tacit recognition to the obligatory character of a principle, it becomes an effective rule of international law. It is not enough to show that states commonly act in a certain way, for such usage may be indicative of no more than international comity, state policy, or convenience; what is required is that the evidence demonstrates that states do believe the rule to be a binding one. There are fewer absolute rules than is commonly imagined, for such general agreement among states is extremely difficult to attain.

The Statute of the International Court of Justice (1945) provides that in the general order of their obligation, the principal evidences of international law are the following: (1) Treaties, conventions, and other international agreements by which states avowedly declare their acceptance of international rules. By no means do all treaties have this purpose; most, indeed, as we have pointed out, look only to the establishment of contractual agreements between states relative to matters of immediate and mutual interest. The number of treaties that are intentionally "lawmaking" ones, however, has tremendously increased in recent years, and it seems likely that international law will continue to have its greatest development through this means. (2) Customary rules, which have originated in the practice of states and have come to be so widely accepted as to create obligation, represent definite state consent. The evidences of customary law may be found in many places: historical documents recording international practice, state papers, the records of foreign offices, the practices of international organizations, and even state laws. (3) General principles of law recognized by civilized states. Here many rules derive authority, not because they are a part of the legal system of particular states, but because they reflect substantial principles of justice to which virtually universal adherence can be found. Particularly influential in developing rules on this basis have been arbitral tribunals, prize and admiralty courts, the international courts, and the highest national courts, such as the United States Supreme Court. (4) Decisions and writings of jurists, publicists, and other authorities on international law who are qualified to express opinions on the basis of their learning and experience. Such works, a justice of the United States Supreme Court stated on one occasion, "are resorted to by judicial tribunals, not for the speculation of their authors concerning what the law ought to be, but for trustworthy evidence of what the law really is."

The student wishing to acquaint himself with the extent of the cosmopolitan resources available to demonstrate the rules of international law should examine one of the standard casebooks on the subject.

The Enforcement of International Law. Another unusual characteristic of international law is found in the arrangements—and lack of them—for its enforcement. The doctrines respecting the character of international law were developed concurrently with those of state sovereignty, with a resulting international legal system in which the enforcement of rules against states was left to the states themselves. This has not meant that international law has gone unenforced, but that compliance with it must be essentially voluntary.

The fact that the rules are based upon consent and agreement makes it a matter of simple convenience for states commonly to observe them. The very nature of international law produces a close coincidence between its rules and the standards of conduct which states are ordinarily willing to observe; they have never accepted rules which substantially limited their freedom of action in matters of vital importance. There is also a distinct advantage to states in their reciprocal relations to observe rules with which they expect others to comply. Further, states may obey the rules out of long-standing habit, because of the power of world opinion, and in a desire to be of good conscience and reputation. These forces are not insignificant; habit, convenience, and self-interest foster the usual observance of international law as they do, ultimately, of all law.

But observance is not the same thing as enforcement. When a state commits an intentional and flagrant violation of the law, who is to assume responsibility to see that the breach of law is redressed and justice done? According to international law, only the state or states injured as a result are normally expected to take notice of the matter, and bring the offending state to terms. The devices available for this purpose have included retaliation and reprisals, blockades and economic pressures, forceful intervention, and war. In effect, enforcement rests upon the offended state's ability to use its national power, or self-help. And if the injured state is the weaker of the two, unwilling or unable to apply measures of force, fearful of risking a war, unable to obtain any assistance, or for any other reason takes no action, the violation will likely go unpunished. On the other hand, if the injured state is the more powerful, it may be quick in retaliating on the slightest provocation, or may apply force far beyond what is required to redress the injury, or depending on the international balance of power, may even find its superior power disadvantageous.

Under these circumstances, each state acts as its own attorney, judge, and executioner; there is no compulsory machinery for enforcement by and in the interests of the entire international community. And though the frequency of clear violations of international law is not great, the inadequacy of the system of enforcement is a substantial obstacle to the development of rules that regulate much more than the procedural aspect of international relations. Recently, through the League of Nations and the United Nations, the international community has organized procedures for the application of international sanctions. These will be discussed in a later chapter. It must be noted, however, that they were intended mainly to deal with breaches of the peace, and not so much with the ordinary rules of international law.

The Scope and Content of International Law. The rules of public international law apply almost entirely to states, who are thus the persons or subjects of its rules. Ordinarily, individuals are subjected to regulation by it only indirectly through their own governments. Thus, the Constitution of the United States, for example, gives Congress the power to "define and punish . . . offenses against the law of nations," and a decision of the Supreme Court has stated that "international law is a part of our law and must be ascertained and administered by the courts of justice of appropriate jurisdiction, as often as questions of right depending upon it are duly presented for their determination." The rules of international law do operate, however, to give a partial status to some entities which do not qualify as states. Thus, international organizations and juridical entities, belligerents, insurgents, prisoners of war, pirates, and individuals in certain circumstances and certain areas may be subject to some of its rules.

Traditionally, the subject matter of international law has been grouped under three headings: the laws of peace, war, and neutrality. The laws of war have been developed primarily on a conventional basis, and are concerned with such matters as the rights and duties of combatants, rules for the conduct of hostilities, treatment of enemy property and nationals, prisoners of war, and occupation of conquered territory. There is no question but that this portion of the rules has tended to shrink in the present century, if only because the character of World Wars I and II, and the Korean War, has produced weapons and techniques of warfare that scarcely lend themselves to the humanization of hostilities. It is important to note that, contrary to popular belief, the rules of international law do not prohibit war in every circumstance; they not only acknowledge its existence but recognize the results of conquest arising out of it. To be sure, its rules do seek to regularize hostilities, holding them to some civilized standards. But war itself has not thereby been made illegal; rather, it has only been regularized as a necessary, if unpleasant, evil.

The laws of neutrality, largely developed in the nineteenth century, govern the position of states and their nationals who are not parties to a war, their rights and duties as regards the belligerents, and such subjects as blockade and prize law. The total wars fought in the twentieth century have made many of the traditional rules respecting neutral status anachronistic. It is even possible to argue that, with the emergence of schemes of collective security, neutrality is an untenable position in the face of world-wide total war, and that, if hostilities are to occur primarily when force is being applied by the majority of states in the community to an international malefactor, no such status can be allowed.

The laws of peace, so-called, cover the principal topics of international law—among them, persons of international law, rights and duties of states, state succession, jurisdiction, boundaries and territorial waters, nationality, aliens, asylum, treaties, and diplomatic and consular status and immunities. Space does not permit a detailed discussion of these rules. We can do little more than to suggest that, under such a rubric as jurisdiction, for example, exist rules which determine to what extent and over what persons and things a state may enforce its law. These include laws governing the acquisition of territory, fixing of national boundaries, status of vessels and persons on the high seas, control of airspace, exemptions from jurisdiction, questions of national conflicts of jurisdiction, and such matters.

The Legal Character of International Law. The student following the discussion so far must have asked: Is international law true law? The answer to this question turns essentially, of course, on how the term "law" is defined—and there are few terms more diversely employed. The "positive" school of jurisprudence accepts the definition of law enunciated by the English jurist, John Austin, as "a rule laid down for the guidance of an intelligent being by an intelligent being having power over him." This definition emphasizes law as an emanation from superior state authority enforced against political inferiors, violations of which can be penalized by the superior. Necessarily, this definition will not include international law within its specifications. Arguing from this point of view, then, a negative answer to the question might be: Since the sovereign state recognizes no political superior, the rules of international law cannot be the commands of such a superior; a state may thus reject the obligation of any particular rule; there are no sanctions or external forces to compel obedience; the very idea of rules binding a state is incompatible with state sovereignty, or unlimited power; and, therefore, the rules may be violated with impunity. Thus international law is relegated to being essentially a body of moral obligations, but of no compelling legal effect.

However, another definition, accepted by the "historical" jurists, identifies law with custom; that is to say, law is what has been sanctioned by immemorial usage, and the test of law is in its observance and not in its source of authority. This definition rejects the Austinian view as more nearly explaining "legislation" than "law," and as being narrowly restrictive. By the test of the historical school of jurists, then, international law may qualify as true law. On the basis of this view—that law may be derived from sources other than the command of the sovereign—an affirmative case is presented. It is argued that historically law arose out of custom and was not originally considered to be man-made; that consent is as important as authority in obtaining obedience, and states do consent to be bound by the rules of international law; that sanctions are available for its enforcement, ranging from the influence of public opinion to outright war; that the sovereignty of the state must necessarily be subject to limitation externally; and that all laws are violated on occasion, but consent largely determines whether particular rules are or are not regularly observed.

How is a choice to be made between these opposing arguments? What is evident, of course, is that neither the sources nor the sanctions of international law are identical with those of domestic law. But regardless of the theoretical line of reasoning pursued to define the concept of "true" law, any resulting conclusions which exclude international law still face a barrier of hard facts. As we have observed, abundant evidence is available to show that states consider themselves and other states legally bound by its rules; they enter into solemn engagements defining these rules; their national legislatures, courts, and sometimes their constitutions, acknowledge the rules; and they join in the creation of international tribunals empowered to decide disputes according to international law. All over the world, litigants win and lose cases in national courts on the basis of rules of international law. The rules of international law do, perhaps, lie at the extreme frontier of law, and are in a less advanced and more imperfect state than those of municipal law; but no great harm is done to the concept of law by including them.

AN EVALUATION OF INTERNATIONAL LAW

The Contributions of International Law. In formulating a balance sheet upon the effectiveness of international law, we can show that as a force in the international community it has made important and useful contributions. Too much should not be claimed for it, assuredly, and we must not deny its imperfections; however, we need not be disdainful of its accomplishments. International law is of some significance if only for the fact that it has been brought into existence at all. Its very concept posits the existence of some sort of community of states—if indeed a rather primitive one—and a body of rules defining it. Lacking this concept of a community, we could make no progress toward its ordering at all. It provides evidence of the willingness of states to make some concessions in their freedom of action to the need for organizing an international community. International law also has had the effect of regularizing to some extent the conduct of warfare, particularly to the end of mitigating its more barbaric features and minimizing, where possible, its consequences for combatants and noncombatants. As defined by the Geneva Convention for the Amelioration of the Condition of the Wounded and Sick in Armed Forces in the Field (1949), for example, "wilful killing, torture or inhuman treatment, including biological experiments, wilfully causing great suffering or serious injury to body or health, and extensive destruction and appropriation of property, not justified by military necessity and carried out unlawfully and wantonly" are "grave breaches" of the agreement. Even so, shocking lapses from these standards are still encountered today.

The body of international law further provides an extensive collection of rules regulating the conduct of international relations on a peaceful basis. The broad scope of its subject matter has already been indicated, but attention might be drawn here to the single topic of state jurisdiction, which has been defined in considerable detail and has largely eliminated the endless misunderstandings that might result between states if there were no accepted rules on the topic. International law has been in a constant, if not always even, process of growth, and one cannot turn to any half-century period since 1648 without remarking important additions to its rules and its obligations. In spite of admitted setbacks within periods of international conflict, and recurring attacks on international order made by totalitarian dictatorships, the obligations of international law have reduced some areas of state irresponsibility.

International law has led, finally to the elaboration of the machinery of international government. Increasingly, the need for the extension and refinement of its rules has brought the adoption of new multipartite lawmaking treaties and conventions, the calling of international conferences upon legal subjects, and the creation of an increasing number of international administrative and judicial bodies. The broad experience of mankind suggests that the development of law has been, historically, antecedent to the organization of elaborate governmental machinery, and for the international community, this principle is probably not an exception. Much of the present international organization could, indeed, come into existence only after some sort of body of international law existed. Certainly, the task of organizing the United Nations would have been immeasurably more difficult in the absence of any such rules. If international law has not played the fully effective role in the international community which might be hoped for it, its contributions are not at all negligible.

The Deficiencies of International Law. The contributions of international law to the problem of world order cannot obscure its deficiencies, however. Its shortcomings are easy to discover and, to one not acquainted with the slow and painful process by which its rules have been brought to their present development, might be considered so serious as to damage its whole structure. At best, international law stands as a "motley and haphazard" collection of rules, having grown slowly within a limited range. It fails to provide any rules at many of the points where international friction is most intense. In those areas where states have been unwilling to see their freedom of action limited, as in the practice of imperialism or the promotion of military security, the community of states has failed to agree upon any rules. International law also places excessive emphasis on state sovereignty, requiring the individual consent of every state to each new rule. Thus each state is encouraged to oppose any rule which might prove to be especially inconvenient to it. The result is that *inter*national law is a law *between* states, but not a *supra*national law *above* states.

International law is seriously deficient in legislative bodies which might actively participate in the process of developing new rules and reinterpreting older ones, as well as inadequately equipped with international tribunals to administer these rules. So long as the development of new rules is left to the slow-moving process of custom, or the calling of infrequent international conferences for the adoption of lawmaking treaties, the rules will continue to lag behind the needs. International law further lacks adequate agencies for its enforcement. To the present, enforcement of its rules falls essentially to the individual state or states immediately concerned when an infraction of rights occurs. In our domestic communities, we have long abandoned the idea that rules will enforce themselves, or that an individual may "take the law into his own hands," and yet that is essentially the case internationally. Finally, international law has not prohibited resort to war or the use of force as an ultimate means of settling disputes between states. Indeed, the existence of the rules of war as part of international law has had the effect of legalizing the employment of war and force, so long as they are confined to certain prescribed practices. Whatever else a community may hope for from the existence of law, the most important expectations include at least a demand for the maintenance of peace and order, and the exercise of force only by constituted and controlled authority. By this test, international law is woefully inadequate.

The Future of International Law. The more serious deficiencies of international law have brought a number of proposals concerning what remedial steps the international community could take if such law were to be brought to its full effectiveness in contributing to international order and peace. Some of the more important proposals are the following: (1) To formulate rules to extend to those areas of state action as yet unregulated, and to codify existing rules which now rest largely on a customary basis. (2) To establish appropriate machinery of a lawmaking and law-interpreting character to keep pace with the needs of a dynamic international community. (3) To create adequate agencies for the enforcement of international law to control the powerful forces that are unleashed in the community, and to prevent the irresponsible use of force by its individual members. (4) To bring states to recognize a legal duty to settle their disputes by pacific means conformable to previously established principles. (5) To extend the rules, finally, to apply directly to individual human beings as its subjects, both in order to hold to legal accountability persons guilty of waging aggressive warfare and committing crimes against international society, but also to provide a measure of protection to the inhabitants of each state against inhumane treatment by their own governments.

These suggested essentials for an adequate body of international law, it ought to be clear, will not soon be achieved in the present world atmosphere. We have undoubtedly lost ground in these directions during the present century. The waging of two long, total world wars, and their consequent periods of prolonged international instability and tension, have strained many of the well-established rules of international law to the breaking point. New weapons, such as submarines, airplanes, rockets, and atomic bombs, had led to the complete disregard by the end of World War II of traditional rules seeking to distinguish combatants and noncombatants, and to prevent the conduct of hostilities against the latter. Neutral rights counted for less and less, and became increasingly incapable of winning respect when virtually all of the world's military power was drawn into the struggle.

Another fragmenting effect on international law results from the attitudes of the communist states, which tend to pick and choose among rules and their interpretation according to their usefulness to the communist cause, and from the attitudes of the vast number of newly independent nonwestern states, which incline to see some traditional rules as framed only to the advantage of the advanced western states, and therefore no longer appropriate and binding upon them. With the world thus divided into three mutually suspicious and dissentient camps, the prospect dims for a rapid development of universal law.

Even where opportunity is offered, states appear to be reluctant to move forward vigorously. The preamble of the United Nations Charter announces a determination "to establish conditions under which justice and respect for the obligations arising from treaties and other sources of international law can be maintained." Article 13 charges the General Assembly to "initiate studies and make recommendations for the purpose of . . . encouraging the progressive development of international law and its codification." In pursuance of this Charter provision, the General Assembly created an International Law Commission, which has been at work since 1947. It has produced, in addition to the Declaration on the Rights and Duties of States, a restatement of the Nürnberg principles respecting "crimes against peace," "war crimes," and "crimes against humanity," and codes of existing law on several other subjects. But states have generally been unwilling to assent to them. The General Assembly has also approved a Convention on the Prevention of Genocide, as well as two Covenants on Human Rights, but these have also failed to achieve general support.

Nevertheless, something like an international criminal law appears to be developing. The postwar Nürnberg and Tokyo war crime trials, as well as others conducted by national tribunals of the allied powers, set precedents which must still be reckoned with today. Since 1945, at least seventeen states have passed laws embodying the Nürnberg principles and establishing retroactive liability for crimes against humanity. The sensational trial in 1961 of Adolf Eichmann, under Israel's Nazis and Nazi Collaborators (Punishment) Law of 1950, was based on charges that Eichmann had caused the killing of "millions of Jews" while head of a Gestapo department. He was convicted on several counts, and executed, for crimes against the Jewish people, crimes against humanity, membership in a hostile organization, and for a "war crime." Although jurists over the world are not in accord upon the validity of the law on which the trial was based, the court's claim to jurisdiction, or the impartiality of the Israeli tribunal, many have agreed, as the prosecutor argued, that "the conscience of the world" demanded it.

What of the future of international law? Clearly, the body of international law developed to the present is weak law—a system of customary rules which have been refined and augmented to a considerable extent by treaty-made law. Such a customary system of law can serve the needs of only the most primitive sort of community. Further, it cannot bring order to an international society which has as yet only partially, and for limited periods of time, restrained its anarchistic impulses. The solution to the problem of international order, we believe, is not to be found through adopting more or new rules of international law, but through the effective organization of the international community. In the last analysis, the system of law for the international community can be no stronger than the community itself.

CHAPTER 14

The ELEMENTS *of* INTERNATIONAL POLITICS

TO PORTRAY objectively the realm of international politics is difficult, for, as Shakespeare asks, "Who can be wise, amazed, temperate and furious, loyal and neutral, in a moment?" Here we examine the political relationships of nation-states in their contest for power and influence. This process is often described as the conduct of "power politics," though that term is essentially redundant, for the conduct of any politics always involves some element of power. Its application to international affairs, however, results from the fact that here the role of power is commonly displayed most nakedly. Certainly one need not look far to find examples.

The present century has been marked by a succession of wars, hot and cold, and no end is in sight. In a world seething with unrest, new international tensions are constantly engendered; the contraction of one state's power only invites the aggrandizement of another's; the resolution of one crisis may well set the scene for a graver one; the overwhelming of one aggressor can bring into the field another even more powerful. We live thus in an age of drama, excitement, and danger. It is all too easy, therefore, to treat the subject of international politics in terms of "blood and thunder." But, however titillating, such an approach scarcely adds clarity.

International politics is much more than the study of the dramatic global happenings of our time, and goes beyond the topical reorganization of the materials of current international events. It involves, rather, a searching examination of the forces that direct the relations of nation-states in the international community. As we undertake an introduction to the subject in this chapter we wish to enter two cautions. First, our treatment must be brief, and an examination of the confusing array of facts and theories of international life within limited dimensions will not provide any mastery of the subject. Second, we must simplify, even though Professor Alfred Zimmern has pointed out, ". . . the greatest danger which confronts our subject is to regard it as a subject for beginners. . . . Our subject is not easy; it is difficult. International relations are not simple; they are complex. To simplify them is to destroy their essence, to eliminate the whole substance of their problem." What follows therefore is, in modest compass, a survey of the principal elements of national power, of the nature of foreign policy, and of the means employed by states to promote their interests internationally.

I. NATIONAL POWER

We have observed that a feature of the international community is the great variation in the power possessed by the many countries it comprises. So important is power status, indeed, that states are commonly referred to, in diplomatic terminology, as "powers"—great, middle, or minor, as the case may be; thus, even the very smallest think, and are thought of, in power terms. The purpose of this part of our discussion, then, is to examine the nature of power, its instruments, and manifestations.

Power. In international politics, "power" describes the capacity of the state to exert strength, authority, or influence. Possession of power allows a state to exercise command, control, or coercion in international affairs; it makes possible the achievement of certain ends against the will of others. There is sometimes argument over whether states contest for power or for ends that power can produce. Both reasons are true; power is prized for itself as well as for what it can achieve. States like to enjoy reputation for power, which confers prestige, enhancing national status and influence. Of course, national prestige is acquired by means other than the possession of sheer power alone. A reputation for dignity, restraint, responsibility, acceptance of and faithfulness to obligations may accord a state prestige. Canada and Switzerland, for example, enjoy such a cachet. And, one may ponder the fact that the United States formerly enjoyed a greater international prestige in certain respects when it possessed much less power than it does today.

The state's search for a minimum of power, at least, is as much a matter of need as choice; a powerless state cannot protect its rights, redress offenses, or defend its existence. We have previously noted that the international community does not guarantee the existence of its members; though the language of international law has sometimes spoken of the state's "right of existence," this is no more than a right to self-defense. States which cannot defend themselves in the long run, or find others to do so, cease to exist. A state's will to live thus requires a willingness to utilize the instruments of power.

Power is always a relative and changing quality; it does not exist in a vacuum. A state's power cannot be measured in any circumstances with great precision. It must always be weighed with reference to other states and their position. The power of a state is affected by a considerable number of factors; for any state these may alter in the course of time, the power position of other states may change, and new instruments of power may come into existence.

Power in itself is neither good nor evil. It has been glorified in some states, not infrequently with disastrous results, and deprecated in others, usually from a misunderstanding of its nature. It has been an American tendency to consider power as immoral—as we say, to prefer right to might—largely because of the United States' long isolation from the centers of power in Europe, where its use has produced recurring warfare. Only recently have the American people become conscious of their own power and of their responsibility to employ it—sometimes thanklessly—for the defense of the free world. Actually, the central problem of power in international affairs lies in its control, for it may be directed to good ends as well as bad. Unfortunately, much human experience of power internationally has been with its application for selfish national ends beyond the control of the international community. For most of the world, the obvious lesson has been the conclusion reached by

Thucydides: "The powerful exact what they can, and the weak grant what they must." We may now examine the major factors in state power.

The Factor of Nationalism. Any analysis of state power must place nationalism as easily the most powerful and dynamic force in world politics. We introduced the concept of "nation" in earlier chapters as representing a body of people who feel they are united by such characteristics as ethnic origin, historical association, culture, language, religion, and customs. Yet it is by no means necessary that all such characteristics be identical, for the same nation may well include persons of differing race, religion, or language, for example, and their sense of historical association may be as old as England's or as new as Nigeria's. "What constitutes a nation," said Ernest Renan in his classic essay, "is not speaking the same tongue or belonging to the same ethnic group, but having accomplished great things in common in the past and the wish to accomplish them in the future."

Nationalism, the sense of loyalty and attachment to the nation, began to emerge as a most significant sentiment in the eighteenth century following the creation of the important modern nation-states in Europe. It became the dominant political emotion of the masses in nineteenth-century Europe, and has spread to all corners of the world in the twentieth. As the feeling of separate national identity is aroused within a people, they seek its full gratification in the possession of separate statehood. This claim to "national self-determination"—to organize the nation as an independent state—came to be spoken of as a basic political right in the nineteenth century, and has helped to unleash wars and upheavals continually since that time.

Nationhood inevitably has statehood in prospect, and in the case of a dismembered nation, in retrospect as well. Thus nationalism may operate within a state both as a centrifugal and as a centripetal force. Nationalism tends to pull a multinational state apart, as each nation seeks to go its own way. Where a portion of one nation is contained within the state territory of another, such a "national minority" will also tend to seek political association with those of the same nationality on the other side of the frontier. The demands for such concessions to national self-determination have added greatly to the international tensions and frictions of the past century, and many European frontiers especially have smoldered as a result. The Soviet Union is the only important multinational state existing today, and it is held together largely by force;

indeed, at least part of the repressive character of its government can be attributed to efforts at holding political control of national groups against their will.

As a unifying force, nationalism acts to induce men to give their highest loyalty to the nation-state, to submerge their personal interests into those of the nation, and to make the ultimate sacrifice of their lives in its behalf. As a state of mind, nationalism evokes emotional ties to the group of a strength and depth that could not be engendered through mere appeals to a legal duty owed the state. "Put only Americans on guard tonight!" "England expects every man to do his duty." "France—and France alone!" All such rallying cries reflect the same theme. In modern times men have generally proved likely to respond to the cause of nationalism as superior to any other appeal, whether to personal conscience, religious conviction, Marxist-Leninist or communist class loyalty, or to the brotherhood of mankind. In an extreme form, it has been characterized as "integral nationalism"—the exclusive and absolute devotion to national power.

Not surprisingly, the means employed extensively by society in every nation-state to promote devotion to national loyalty rarely encounter substantial resistance. National symbols, slogans, myths, heroes, holidays, and competitive victories weld the people of a nation together, and reinforce a sense of national superiority, from which the individual receives a heightened consciousness of his own status and importance. Thus, national solidarity becomes an important source of power in itself. This circumstance permits evaluation of power in terms of national character, energy, and morale: the ways in which a people—especially as a "nation in arms"—will behave, work, persevere, and fight in behalf of its perpetuation and defense. To develop these qualities, and to achieve the strength which they supply, the peoples of Asia and Africa during recent decades have enthusiastically embraced the cult of nationalism at the very time when many peoples of the older western states have begun to react against its excesses. It seems likely, then, that the dynamics of nationalism will continue to exert a profound influence on world affairs, disrupting political associations which repress national interests, and promoting or supporting widespread international quarrels and clashes.

The Geographic Factor. It is fairly obvious that the geography of a state affects its power, but what precise conclusions follow from that proposition are debatable. Geographic factors determine the physical dimensions of a state, its setting, and its immediate material supply. But size, shape, topography, climate, location, and resources are in no case conclusive determinants of strength; they produce in conjunction and interaction with each other a fairly unique human ecology for the population of every state. Though some writers see the geographic factor as the most permanent element of power, it is actually largely contingent. That is to say, geographic features generally remain constant, but their significance may well vary in time and place.

For example, great area may permit the presence of large populations, as in China and India, but does not assure them—most of the comparably extensive territories of the Soviet Union, Australia, and Canada, for example, are uninhabited. The relative immensity of the United States and the U.S.S.R. adds to their great power status by giving them military advantage; both are difficult to invade, destroy by aerial attack, or occupy. On the other hand, small island states such as Great Britain and Japan have been great powers in modern times; today, however, their vulnerability to air attack makes them difficult if not impossible to defend. Some states are the rather obvious creation of their topography, such as Spain, Switzerland, or Turkey, with natural features historically improving their defensibility; others, like Belgium and Poland, have seen their territory used again and again as highway and battlefield by more powerful neighbors. A state's terrain may either promote or hamper its national unity. Natural frontiers, however, such as mountains, forests, and oceans have in recent times steadily declined in strategic value.

Climate is influenced both by topography and location; it has much to do with the support of human life and the expenditure of human energy. The great industrial centers of the world are all located within the temperate zone; however, industrialization is not inherently excluded from other areas by climatic circumstances alone. Location determines such matters, for instance, as whether a state may possess a navy and achieve sea power, or whether it is to be landlocked, and practically excluded from using the maritime highways of the world. The advantage to states of access to the north Atlantic or to the center of Europe, and their important trade routes, has long been obvious. Location may constantly embroil a state deeply in the military struggles of its neighbors, as in the case of Korea, or largely remove it from the scene of any significant controversies, as in the case of Liberia.

Attempts have been made to derive a system of geographic determinism from the study of the relationship between space and politics and its influence upon national aspirations. Those of Ratzel, Kjellén, Mackinder, and Spykman, among the more notable, led to the formulation of a body of theories to which Kjellén gave the name "geopolitics." After the establishment of the Nazi regime in Germany, Adolf Hitler encouraged the development of geopolitical doctrine both to assist and to justify his plans for aggression. Although the chief Nazi geopolitician, Karl Haushofer, claimed the achievement of a new "science," the resulting mixture of political geography with Nazi doctrine and German expansionist ambition produced only a pseudoscientific cover for Hitlerian conquests. The subject's popular attraction has declined considerably since the Nazi disasters at the end of World War II, though it has heightened an awareness of the basic determinants of national power.

A concomitant of the geographical factor of power is the availability of natural resources and raw materials. A state must possess or have access to these, in substantial measure, to be powerful. First in importance, of course, is food. Most major powers are essentially self-sufficient in basic foodstuffs, though Great Britain has been a well-known exception, obliged to import half or more of its supply, and obviously dependent upon a continuing ability to do so for national survival. Next come standard fuels, such as coal and petroleum products (for which hydroelectric power or atomic energy can be a partial substitute), and the basic raw materials of the industrial process, such as iron, bauxite, timber, lead, tin, copper, and nickel. Of ever-growing importance are certain "critical" materials, essential to the complex technology of modern industrial and military production, such as chromium, cobalt, manganese, tungsten, uranium, and vanadium. Finally, states with aspiration to power require substantial supplies of such agricultural commodities as cotton, wool, and rubber—or appropriate substitutes; it is also rather obvious that the maintenance of national morale in many western states requires ample quantities of beef, cacao, coffee, tea, sugar, and tobacco.

Clearly, only a highly industrialized state can be powerful, but no industrialized state can any longer be self-sufficient in raw materials. Inevitably, states have been led to seek ample supplies of the commodities their industry requires, preferably by immediate expansion of their own territory, as both the United States and the U.S.S.R. have done extensively; or by the development of overseas colonial empires, as did Great Britain, France, and Italy. States, or their private enterprisers, may also develop the resources of others outside their territories, or buy needed commodities as they are offered on the world market. Ideally, the latter practice should serve as the best means to give the people of all states access to the world's resources, but states much prefer to control them, if at all possible, at their source. Otherwise, supplies may be insufficient, overpriced, or withheld as a result of war or for various political reasons, and at a time when need can be most critical. Hence, states are driven to acquire controllable sources of supply for the materials they require—a situation bound to provoke rivalry and conflict in international relations.

The Factor of Population. The very term "manpower" suggests that population size constitutes a measure of national strength. Yet once again we must emphasize the relativity of population as a power factor. If a state is to command substantial power, it must have a large population, not only to equal the numbers of those great powers which do, but to supply the masses of soldiers and workers essential to military strength. To be sure, mere millions of people do not automatically make for power in an era when technology has provided some means of equalizing Voltaire's maxim that "God is always on the side of the heaviest battalions." The most modern weapons for air, sea, and land use can, of course, vastly augment the firepower and destructiveness of the individual soldier, but to the extent that they permit any reduction in the number of men needed at the front, they substantially increase those required for service and supply in the rear echelons. It is not at all likely that the day of mass armies has passed or that the infantryman (even though motorized or airborne) is obsolete. World War II saw all belligerents pressed for manpower before its conclusion and, even then, large forces were required to occupy the defeated states.

A huge population may, nonetheless, be a liability where the national economy is unable even in peacetime to support it at or above a subsistence level. During war, such a population continues to consume and can thus be an even greater burden. Overpopulation is not a new phenomenon historically, but its growing accentuation in certain areas of the world is creating serious problems. For centuries, the world's population grew slowly, kept in check by famine, disease, and war. From an estimated one-half billion in the seventeenth century it is now approaching six times that figure. In the western world generally, though the average life span has been substantially extended, population growth has been moderate; birth limitation, urbanization, and industrialization have, indeed, permitted a general rise in living standards where the population increase has been orderly. Certain areas of the western world have also achieved a very high but manageable population density—Great Britain, Belgium, the Netherlands, and the eastern portion of the United States. Yet it was the leaders of Nazi Germany, Fascist Italy, and Japan who a few decades ago were insisting that "population pressure" required them to undertake aggressive wars of expansion. Nevertheless, this "pressure" was rationalization rather than cause; these governments were at the same time attempting to encourage the increase of their nations and diverting to military production wealth which might have raised living standards.

Asia is having a real population "explosion." In five Asian countries alone, China, India, Indonesia, Japan, and Pakistan, live approximately one-half of the world's population, and on less than 10 per cent of the world's land area. Only Japan, among these states, has been able, through its industrialization and by recently halving its birth rate, to support its growing population. For the others, their slow and modest increases in industrial production and food supplies barely keep alive their increasing numbers. It is not at all clear, however, how long they can keep ahead of starvation for many; in recent years, the increase in world food production has ominously lagged behind that in population. If existing trends continue, the present world population will more than double, demographic analysis suggests, to reach six billions in the course of the present century. Whether we call this "overpopulation" or "under-development" makes little difference; it is bound to provide a serious cause for international tensions in the decades to come.

The Economic Factor. The economic measure of power is determined by the interaction of the basic elements of production: land (with its resources), man's efforts, and capital. A territory that is rich in resources and contains a population able to provide a large labor force is not enough. There must be a generous supply of highly skilled managers, scientists, technologists, and workers, supported by abundant capital (that is, accumulated wealth capable of producing more wealth) for the state to have a high degree of industrialization—and economic power. Thus stated, it may seem simple, but it is not. Today's high level of industrialization in western countries is the result of the commercial, industrial, and technological revolutions of the past four centuries; even so, it has been reached in only limited portions of the world. Let us examine its requisites.

Only a small portion of the state's population must be devoted to food and agricultural production. By the mechanization of agricultural methods, including the use of fertilizers, insecticides, and selected seeds, and by controlled methods of breeding, maintaining, and feeding of livestock, abundant food supplies can be produced for a population while leaving the largest part of its labor force available for industrial work. The industrial plant, in turn, must be large enough to permit mass production of all significant goods under the direction of managers and technologists, and by workers possessing the knowledge and skills to operate at highly efficient levels of productivity. To permit the population to consume the foodstuffs and goods so produced, there is required further an effective system for their distribution and marketing, and this in turn depends on well-developed systems of transportation and communication, and substantial provision of service trades. Not least essential to a high level of industrialization is surplus capital, which must be saved or accumulated—whether by private or public means, whether voluntarily or under duress—to provide the wealth to build and expand industry, replace obsolete facilities, support research, provide the machines which build machines, hazard the risks of economic venture, and so on.

Advanced industrialization not only affects a state's power, among other things, but supports the forward impetus of further industrialization. The resulting increments to the gross national product of a state (unless drawn off by a totalitarian government for the direct increase of its power) permit a steadily rising standard of living for the population. Better quality or greater variety in consumers' goods; higher standards of education, nutrition, and medical care; adequate housing and other amenities; and improved opportunity for recreation and entertainment are among the earmarks of the national condition. Important, too, is the ability of an industrialized society to defer the entrance of a large portion of the younger population into the labor market, and to support it through a longer period of formal education, thus extending the scientific and technical knowledge essential to military and technological efficiency. More and more educated people and educational facilities are needed to keep complex modern societies running. National power is further enhanced by the fact that the industrialized state is a substantial consumer of goods produced abroad, as well as a supplier of them and of surplus capital. Finally, such a state is able to afford and to produce the military establishments and armaments which are themselves a further measure of power.

It is in the economic context that the contrast between the highly industrialized and the "underdeveloped" countries is sharpest. The characteristics of the underdeveloped state are, indeed, the very opposite of those we have been discussing and—to make matters worse—they tend to perpetuate its reduced circumstances in a vicious circle. Most of its population is devoted to subsistence farming, with resulting substandard living conditions, inadequate nutrition, enervating disease, and illiteracy. Its economic resources available for sale abroad are limited to one or a few primary products for which world demand is not elastic; it is thus vulnerable to world competition in its exports, and lacks sufficient foreign exchange to purchase goods abroad. It has an inadequate educational system and is unable to train the administrative, scientific, and technical personnel and skilled workers essential to efficient industry; generally, modern industrial and business practices are not known. Thus large-scale industry is lacking; this is also because the demand for capital exceeds the supply. Capital must be saved, either at home or abroad, but the absence of industrialization makes this difficult on any large scale at home. The efficiency of government in an underdeveloped country is not likely to be high; the many grievances and dissatisfactions of the population offer fertile ground for exploitation by political extremists. In the face of resulting political instability, even small domestic accumulations of capital may well be sent to safer repositories in Great Britain, Switzerland, or the United States. Foreign suppliers of capital are not attracted to a situation unpromising for the protection either of their investment or the income from it. The frustrations of such underdeveloped states have become a particularly disturbing factor in international relations in recent years, since they seek to lay blame for their lot at the door of a powerful neighboring state, of the "colonial powers," or of the rich "capitalist states."

The Ideological Factor. Ideas have always been powerful; men and nations are not only what they know, but also what they feel or believe. Politics at the international level then, as at all others, is significantly influenced by the patterns of ideas we call ideologies. By "ideology," we mean generally a body of doctrines, beliefs, and symbols. Ideologies may undertake to interpret reality or to conceal it in elaborate disguise—to explain the world or remake it. They may rest upon generally accepted truths, but are as likely to contain substantial myth. Because ideologies are accepted primarily on faith, they may indeed be compounded of completely synthetic dogma.

One should not underestimate the importance of the role that ideologies serve, for they fulfill some very basic human yearnings. Men not only live by them but die for them. To the great questions and problems about the ends and aims of human existence, for example, they may offer answers which are not found by ordinary methods of ascertaining the truth. They give men a sense of certainty and security, of purpose and self-justification; they supply the reassurance of absolutes that otherwise tend to be lacking. Ideological doctrines may well be too complicated to be fully understood by the masses of people, but their slogans and symbols can be widely grasped and disseminated. Considering that such doctrines are often embraced by relatively sophisticated people, their impact upon masses of illiterates or semi-illiterates can be enormous.

Historically speaking, the first ideologies with important political significance were religious. Such controversy inspired in part the Christian-Moslem and Catholic-Protestant wars of the later middle ages. Substantial secular ideologies produced the English, American, and French revolutions in the seventeenth and eighteenth centuries; thereafter they emerged in considerable profusion, and are seen in a wide range from the racialist creeds of Pan Slavism in imperial Russia and the *apartheid* of South Africa to the politico-religious doctrines of Shintoist-emperor worship of Japan and the *Satyagraha* of Gandhi's India, among many examples. Ideologies commonly interact with national character and culture. Indeed, the most ubiquitous ideology in the contemporary world is nationalism and, in combination with liberalism, socialism, militarism, imperialism, or tribalism in different countries, it may provide a variety of particular and most exclusive ideological systems. Liberalism, it is worth noting, is still one of the major competing ideologies today, and has certainly been a revolutionary force far longer than communism, even though non-western peoples are now much attracted toward authoritarian systems of belief.

Ideologies are a source of national strength, and may become a cause of international conflict. Most are exclusively national, and thus unsuited for export, even assuming there were some demand for them abroad; they are also mostly limited and competitive in their appeals. The present century, however, has seen the emergence of totalitarian political ideologies, such as communism and fascism, claiming from their followers allegiance in all things, and setting exclusive value standards. German Nazism was too peculiarly Teutonic to have more than minor appeal beyond Germany. In communism, however, the communist leaders have fashioned the theories of a nineteenth-century German, Karl Marx, into a dynamic, expansionist, and militant creed, which serves not only to maintain the oligarchic control of their own countries, but also to subvert other systems of government and augment the international power of the communist states. Intensive conspiratorial efforts to introduce and impose such militant ideologies throughout the world by creating or exploiting political and social disruption in other states inevitably provoke international friction and controversy. This is bound to continue as long as totalitarian ideologies are promoted with fanaticism and violence.

The Military Factor. Military strength is such an obvious element of state power that it tends to be viewed as its prime indicator. It also appears sufficiently tangible to measure, for some of its components, such as infantry divisions, bombers, aircraft carriers, and missiles can be counted. But such evaluations rest largely on weighing the nature and quantity of a state's military "hardware," and the number of its men in military service, and measuring these against the general results produced in a previous war when men used similar weapons. Actually, however, military strength can never be gauged with any accuracy until it is applied in war in conjunction with all other elements of national power, with which it is inextricably involved, and the final verdict of victory or defeat is pronounced. Although states may intentionally undertake to deceive others respecting their military strength, they will do so unintentionally in any event. Certainly, no two states in the past hundred years were ever more preoccupied with estimating each other's military strength than France and Germany; the events of 1870, 1914, and 1940, nonetheless, show what grievous errors were made on both sides. The measure of military power is so complicated for many reasons.

First of all, for centuries military strength consisted essentially in formations of armed men, afoot or mounted, equipped with weapons that were only variants of the spear, the sling, and the sword. Even the invention of gunpowder, and the development of a variety of small arms, did not alter the relatively equal effectiveness of individual soldiers similarly equipped. In like manner, navies were long merely sea transport for soldiers, though they ultimately provided floating gun platforms as well. Approximately a century ago, however, a revolution began in the character of weapons. The result has been the development of armored ships, long-range heavy artillery, machine guns, submarines, tanks, poison gases, flying fortresses, and nuclear weapons, among others, reflecting the technological advances of the contemporary era, and permitting new destructiveness in the conduct of warfare. In consequence, the arsenals of modern military establishments are so complex in their equipment that it is impossible to be dogmatic today about the results to be achieved by any particular national system of armaments.

Second, military strength depends upon men, and the human element inevitably adds another unknown quantity. All else being equal, military units commanded by professional soldiers trained in the science of strategy and tactics should enjoy an advantage over those which are not. Men of intelligence, with high morale, sound physique, and mechanical aptitude should prevail over those without. The volunteer ought to be superior to the conscript, the offensive-minded to the defensive-minded, the better equipped to the poorer, and so on. But things never are equal, as the outcome of battles and wars has often so surprisingly demonstrated. Leadership and valor, as the long history of warfare attests, are qualities required for martial achievement from the commander-in-chief to the last man in the ranks, and displayed at the right time, they may well be the determinant in victory. Yet how and why they are produced is something that cannot be predetermined, nor are they unchanging and unchangeable qualities of any one people and any one military force. Hence, the unpredictable nature of human performance further adds to the uncertainty of military power.

Finally, we may observe that military strength depends upon the other factors of power. Modern land, sea, and air forces require large space for training and deployment. They are voracious consumers of raw materials and resources—foodstuffs, wool, nitrates, steel, copper, lead, and oil. They need communications systems, transport, docks, and arsenals. Manpower is necessary not only to fill their ranks but to provide the work force essential to their support. Scientific laboratories, universities, factories, and industrial plants must develop and produce their war matériel. They must be inspired with a sense of mission and a will to fight. The extent to which these and other elements of power are possessed by a state affects not only the degree of military preparedness which it can achieve at any time but, equally important, its military potential for the long run. Thus, the factor of military strength is also a relative and continually changing element of national power.

As we enter the age of astronautics the defensive posture of the most heavily armed state becomes even more uncertain. Several infantry divisions, a few ships of the line, a scattering of forts and coast artillery placements which, even a few decades ago, could be counted upon by most states as adequate defense against any surprise attack no longer suffice. In an age of chemical and bacteriological weapons, of intercontinental ballistic missiles and electronic computers, of death-rays and brainwashing, of moon shots and space stations, the efforts of states merely to ensure their security and defense—not to mention the attempts of those ambitious for overwhelming military superiority—seem often as much to increase, rather than reduce, the danger of the disturbing international crises of these times.

II. NATIONAL POLICY

A substantial proportion of the study of international politics is devoted to the subject of foreign policy. Concern with the policies of one's own country and its resulting international position is inevitable, and given the dimensions of international relations today, concern with the policies of other states is scarcely less important. We cannot undertake an analysis of various national policies, but we may offer a brief account of the principles underlying some of them, how and why certain ones are chosen, and by what agencies they are administered. The interests of any state ought ideally, it might reasonably seem, to be those of all men. Hence, it might appear that there would be common national goals, and that international collaboration would best enhance each nation's interests. Unfortunately, international behavior is at sharp variance with such an ideal.

FOREIGN POLICY: NATURE AND OBJECTIVES

The Nature of Foreign Policy. The term "foreign policy" describes the attitudes, courses of action, and objectives that a state's government adopts in its relations toward other states and areas abroad. It may be consciously and carefully chosen, or it may reflect only a fairly consistent behavior, influencing situations abroad without any precisely selected aims. Foreign policy reflects what a state does as well as what it seeks to do. Foreign policy is not something applied only abroad, existing in a compartment distinct from domestic policy; they are inevitably both aspects of a state's total national policy. Thus, national policies are foreign policies to any extent that they affect or influence other states. The character of state policies varies considerably. Toward certain countries a state may have very specific objectives and may seek to apply carefully delineated courses of action; toward others it may have no more than indefinite aims, perhaps of maintaining "peace" or "commerce." The foreign policy of a state can hardly be thought of as a blueprint, exact in its measures and specifications. Relations with other states are too unpredictable for that to be possible. Like any national policies, those which are foreign are a mixture of elements—reactions to the past and present and plans for the future.

The Determinants of Foreign Policy. The basic determinant of a state's foreign policy is commonly found in the objective "to promote the national interest." National interest, however, is a vague concept; it is generally considered to embrace the state's security and welfare. But what specific goals will best achieve the safety and well-being of a state are rarely matters of agreement and often subjects of serious disagreement. Security may be sought in terms of a superiority of armaments to repel or deter attack from any other state; yet this very superiority may appear menacing to other states, constituting aggressive behavior in their eyes, and may induce them to take reciprocal action. The nation's welfare is after all bound to be differently interpreted by various economic groups within the state—by farmers and manufacturers, exporters and importers, workers and employers. It has been suggested that national interest is equivalent to national security, which in turn is essentially equivalent to national power. But even if they are close to being identical, the circular character of such an equation is not very helpful in defining the national interest. Thus we shall, shortly, examine further how interests are interpreted in the formulation of policy.

A second determinant of foreign policy objectives is the state's capabilities. In the preceding section of this chapter we examined the major factors which allow the state to act and exert power and influence in the international community. These characteristics, both tangible and intangible, clearly condition—though without necessarily determining directly—what a state may undertake in its relations with others. Its capabilities may well deny it particular courses of action, but beyond that a variety of choices can ordinarily be made. To take a hypothetical example, Mexico would lack the capability to force the United States to cede it California; it might, however, be able to induce Great Britain to undertake a boundary rectification at the expense of British Honduras; it undoubtedly could oblige Guatemala to relinquish territory in its behalf.

A third determinant of foreign policy is provided by prevailing international circumstances. No matter how carefully a state chooses its policies, and however accurately they reflect its capabilities, its courses of action must be accommodated to the existence of other states, the policies they are pursuing, and the climate of international relations which results. It is probably not sufficiently appreciated how much the making of any one government's foreign policy is frequently little more than a reaction to those of other states. State policies inevitably interact, and the extent to which other states co-operate or compete is of large consequence. For example, in the early post-World War I period Poland behaved as the *enfant terrible* of eastern Europe, effecting many of its objectives by force; in the 1930's, caught between a rearmed Germany and Russia, its freedom to act became much more circumscribed; in 1939, when the latter two powers joined in its dismemberment, Poland as a state ceased to exist. Again, Italy was able to take advantage of the prevailing international situation—the mutual preoccupation of the principal major powers—to seize Tripoli in 1911, conquer Ethiopia in 1936, and annex Albania in 1939. But as an Axis partner in World War II, it was quickly knocked out of the lists in 1943 when confronted with the military power of Great Britain and the United States.

The Objectives of Foreign Policy. We have seen that the foreign policy of a state is determined by its interpretation of its national interest, its capabilities, and the international atmosphere. It may then attempt to achieve various goals; broadly speaking, however, these aim at producing certain external and internal effects. From an external point of view, a state may seek to increase its power; this requires, of course, a change in the over-all distribution of power, and it distinctly affects other states. Such a policy may incline the state toward imperialism, gaining dominance of strategic areas or critical resources, or aggressive warfare and the conquest of territory. This is a policy of expanding state power. Or, a state may seek a more modest goal, with its external objectives aimed at preserving the "status quo," that is, the existing situation, especially so far as its own power position is concerned. Although this is a more conservative response to one or more states seeking a change in the power distribution, it can also be intentionally chosen by a state satisfied in its power aspirations. Though such a policy may lead the state to various kinds of passive reactions, such as undertaking defensive alliances, appeasement, or offering to bargain and make concessions, it may also lead to the employment of the same devices as those used by an aggressive state, on the theory that the best defense is a good offense. This is a policy of maintaining power. A third alternative is a policy of neutralism, whereby a state withdraws entirely from the power contest, and refrains from involvement in power controversies or with states which do enter them. This is no less a self-interested policy than the others, of course, chosen as a rule by states unable to exercise significant power in international politics, and based on the assumption that such abnegation will be respected by all other states. However, very few countries have been able successfully to follow this policy—the renunciation of power—for any length of time.

Innumerable examples of these various policies may be found. Germany and Russia, for instance, pursued expansionist goals before both World Wars I and II. Great Britain and France were expansionist in the nineteenth century, but adopted status quo policies after World War I. Switzerland and Sweden have traditionally pursued a neutralist course effectively through more than a century; Austria and Finland have attempted to do the same since World War II. A state may at the same time follow different policies in different areas. It may be said—though without absolute consistency—that the United States in the latter part of the nineteenth century observed a policy of neutralism toward Europe, one of the status quo toward Latin America, and one of expansion toward the Pacific area.

From an internal point of view, the objectives of foreign policy are to preserve or attain certain conditions within the state. Obviously a state hopes to achieve security, for contained under this rubric are its self-preservation, protection against attack, and freedom from foreign intervention and interference. As we have also noted, the maintenance of national welfare leads the state to seek wealth and goods, to enrich the national life, extend production, improve living standards, support a larger population, and generally to enhance its power. Beyond these basic goals, a state's foreign policy may seek a variety of internal consequences. It may pursue an expansionist policy partly from fear of an aggressive rival, as did Japan toward Russia at the turn of this century. Or quite perversely, a state may press an expansionist policy partly to engender counterpressure and tension, which it can then capitalize upon in promoting harsh domestic policies, as do contemporary Communist China and Soviet Russia. The nursery has not been the only place where bogymen, since they did not exist, had to be invented. A state following a status quo policy may be seeking to enhance its role as an international middleman, broker, and trader; it avoids pronouncing moral judgments, giving offense, and is generally willing to do business with anyone—as in the case of contemporary Britain. Even so, its attempt to restore the Middle East's status quo in 1956, after General Nasser nationalized the Suez Canal, led it to join with France and Israel in a military campaign against Egypt. Where states pursue an external policy of neutralism, they may be attempting to effect a kind of national isolation, as in the case of the United States through much of its history. Such a choice of policy is based on the conclusion that the national security and welfare can best be promoted by "contracting out" of the power struggle.

FOREIGN POLICY: FORMULATION

It is difficult to imagine a much more complex process than that by which the foreign policy of a major power is determined. In the space available here we can do no more than sketch the main outlines. Certainly, for example, vastly more has gone into the making of United States policy toward Latin America than the insertion of a few paragraphs into President Monroe's annual message to Congress in 1823, and much more into India's policy of neutralism than some quiet meditation by Prime Minister Nehru. Contributions to the formulation of foreign policy are made by a number of agencies of government and in this task they are subjected to influences by a great variety of groups and institutions.

Government Organs. The central role in the formulation of foreign policy is assigned everywhere, as we have noted earlier, to the executive.

This is, indeed, one of the major executive functions, and the president, prime minister, or premier holds his office in part because of certain expectations concerning his approach to foreign affairs held by those who voted for or supported him. He must, in short, have made some fundamental interpretations of his country's national interest, and chosen certain means to achieve them. In the last analysis, it is the executive who has the authority to commit the nation to a course of action and to speak for it within the community of states, and who must accept ultimate responsibility for declarations made and actions taken. Depending upon his personal inclinations and the international political climate, the chief executive may or may not have a primary interest in foreign policy, though in recent decades it has become virtually impossible for him to avoid a deep concern with such matters. In performing his responsibilities the executive is assisted by a minister of foreign affairs, who is often chosen because of his special knowledge and experience in this realm, and who has the function of conveying the views of the head of the government to the foreign ministry, and of providing his chief and his fellow cabinet members the results of the studies and staff work undertaken in the foreign ministry, as well as the information and views furnished by foreign service officials abroad.

Concern with and advice upon foreign policy is not a monopoly of the foreign affairs department, however. One of the difficult problems such ministries face these days is that foreign-policy making cannot be confined to this ministry alone. The nature, cost, and complexity of modern weaponry and warfare require that the military establishments be included in the policy-making process. Yet how and at what point is a matter of considerable controversy. Any particular national policy requires certain military postures and may well involve certain military risks; such a policy can scarcely be chosen if military leaders are unwilling to answer for its consequences. A serious difficulty arises here, however, because it is not a great step further to allow purely military considerations to determine policy; but if there is military dictation of foreign policy, the result is a military-civil authority relationship incompatible with constitutional government. To have learned this one lesson alone might well have saved Germany disaster twice in the first half of this century.

The treasury secretary is bound to reflect concern with the taxing and spending consequences of foreign policy. Intelligence agencies, information services, and government departments involved with trade, commerce, labor, law enforcement, agriculture, and fisheries, for example, will inevitably contribute. It is the task of the chief executive, of course, to weigh these various considerations affecting policy and to unify them into some degree of consistency.

Though the executive is given the exclusive right to speak, listen, and act for the state in foreign relations, this does not exclude the legislature from a share in foreign-policy formulation. Legislative influence may be exerted directly by such means as the grant or withholding of consent to make certain appointments, to ratify a treaty, to annex or relinquish territory, to join an international organization, to contract an alliance, or to declare war. Even where such actions are discretionary with the executive, a parliamentary body may withdraw support from a government whose policies it does not approve. The legislature may apply further influence indirectly through its control of financial and lawmaking power generally, through interrogations and investigations of executive officials, by participation of legislators in international conferences and as diplomatic negotiators, through debates, and generally by all the usual means available for supervising the executive.

Some measure of legislative supervision of foreign policy is, of course, intended to reflect popular sentiments and attitudes over matters which deeply affect, even if they do not actively concern, the mass of the people, and to provide some control over the exercise of authority to commit the state. To the extent that parliamentary bodies effectively perform this representative role, and ameliorate certain bureaucratic propensities which the professional formulation of foreign policy may produce, their value can be recognized. Nonetheless, legislative participation in this area has not been without unfortunate consequences on some occasions, and does not always prevent unwise executive action. Legislators may be inadequately informed, narrow in their interests and outlook, and inordinately influenced by partisan or local demands. As we have suggested before, a parliamentary body is not capable itself of formulating and administering foreign policy, but it can, by a sufficient degree of irresponsibility, make it extremely difficult for the executive to do so.

Public Influences. Foreign policy in a democratic system of government, then, to a large degree must be made in public. That is to say, major policy proposals must be placed before parliamentary bodies, and thus the general public; they will be discussed and debated, and they must meet to a considerable extent whatever popular demands are imposed upon them. At the same time the proposed policies, their motives and objectives, necessarily become equally known to all foreign governments, friendly and unfriendly, concerned and unconcerned alike. Yet policy makers find such procedures and their attendant revelations, given the necessary characteristics of effective policy—which may well require secrecy, decisiveness, and flexibility—always difficult and sometimes nearly impossible. Theoretically, the foreign policy of a state rests upon a base of prevailing public opinion, and is guided and sustained by it. But public opinion is a nebulous concept, which by no means always provides the kind of solid and stable footing that adequate policies require. There are a number of reasons why this is the case.

The number of people who have an interest in foreign affairs is limited, partly because of a general lack of concern, and partly because most persons lack information, experience, and understanding of the nature or problems of countries outside their own. Several studies have demonstrated that perhaps no more than a quarter of the electorate in countries of the western world is reasonably well-informed about international affairs, while a third or more is entirely ignorant or unaware of such matters. The remainder of the electorate, often the majority, falling in between these positions, is only occasionally qualified to offer considered views. To be sure, a great many who could without much difficulty inform themselves are simply unwilling to make the effort. Despite the opportunities offered by the guarantees of press freedom generally in democratic states, most newspapers provide, and their readers demand, little in the way of serious consideration of international affairs. Most of the daily press little resembles America's *New York Times,* Britain's *Guardian,* France's *Le Monde,* or Switzerland's *Neue Zürcher Zeitung.* Rather, much of the press is insular if not xenophobic, devoted to sensationalism and diversion, to commercial ends, or to partisan polemics. Radio and television give even less attention to foreign affairs, and tend to confine themselves to simplified versions of current events, or to the presentation of their government's official views.

Additional influences on policy making are exerted by political parties, both to the extent that they shape public opinion and that their leaders hold executive or legislative office. As a rule, political parties represent their differences on foreign policy to be greater than they actually are, for the basic determinants in national policy are likely to offer far narrower alternatives than the parties are willing to admit. In a biparty system, indeed, a considerable consensus may well exist, so that controversy inclines to the question of means rather than ends. Where a multiparty system exists, especially when reflecting conflicts of ideological preference, differences may well be greater, if only because no one of the several parties is likely to have an opportunity to put its advocacy into full effect. Interest groups and minorities of various kinds may also have an effect on policy making, whether their influence is exerted through the legislature, or directly on the executive. Differing economic interests inevitably lead business, agricultural, and labor groups to take different stands respecting foreign trade, tariffs, immigration, public expenditure, and related subjects. Veterans' associations usually express strong views about foreign policy; religious organizations may exert influence in behalf of their coreligionists abroad; minority ethnic and nationality groups may have particular attachments to or interests in various areas abroad.

Obviously, then, the formulation of foreign policy in a democracy is a difficult task. The general public is slow to accept new policies; much of it does not want to be obliged to ponder the subject; and often most of it is not sufficiently informed to have truly relevant opinions. Also, the average person tends to view foreign nations in terms of "stereotypes," and thus does not appreciate the complex and dynamic nature of international politics. Popular communications media largely ignore foreign affairs, or distort the information they do provide. Political parties often avoid discussion of the real problems or alternatives of foreign policy for fear of losing popular support. Organized groups frequently promote narrow or self-interested objectives. In consequence, only leadership of a very high order can hold the democratic state to the sustained pursuit of a successful and practicable foreign policy.

Foreign Policy in the Dictatorships. The formulation of foreign policy in the totalitarian dictatorships contrasts with democratic procedures. Obviously, policy making occurs at a highly elevated and centralized level in a dictatorship; it can thus be made with greater speed and less controversy than by democratic methods. This is not to say that there may be no high-level differences over policy; often great controversy, not always entirely concealed, may take place among the top leadership until a course of action is selected. Foreign policy can be closely co-ordinated with other national objectives and programs, however, heightening the over-all appearance of consistency and unity. Within a dictatorship, policy is made secretly and may then be applied with considerable surprise to seize the initiative. The dictator is not obliged to consult or reckon with legislative, popular, or interest group influences or interferences. Instead, the dictatorial party machine, the press, and all other media of communication are employed to shape popular opinion—while censorship helps blind it to any conflicting views—for the support of the centrally chosen policies. Finally, the dictatorship is free to reverse its foreign policies.

These circumstances give certain considerable advantages to the dictatorial regime. Yet one should not fail to observe that the means condition the ends—that they have important consequences upon policies, not all to the interest of the dictatorship in the long run. Foreign policies generally reflect the regime's striving for power, its aggressiveness, and its need continually to stimulate international tension, even if by artificial measures. The opportunism present in dictatorial policy is rarely successfully disguised, at least abroad, and works to reduce the dictatorship's dignity and to deny its disinterest. Though generally well repressed, popular dissatisfaction may nevertheless be present, weakening the apparent monolithic unity of the totalitarian state and people. Moreover, with the elimination of any adequate correctives, such as popular debates and criticism, policy may well reflect the worst features of bureaucratic formulation, as well as possible psychopathic tendencies of the dictator. Still worse, the ideological prepossessions of the dictatorial leaders often limit their ability to interpret objectively the affairs of the external world, and thus may color their decisions and constrict their choice of policy alternatives. In sum, although the dictatorship may at times produce a strikingly successful turn of policy, it is inevitably prone to catastrophic errors of judgment, as the histories of many such regimes, now defunct, will readily attest.

FOREIGN POLICY: ADMINISTRATION

The Executive. The administration of foreign policy, especially at its higher levels, is only partially separable from its formulation. Nevertheless the two processes are sufficiently distinct in important ways to justify separate consideration. Foreign-policy administration begins, of course, with the executive, who everywhere possesses the authority to direct the conduct of foreign relations and their related activities. The role of the formal chief of state in such matters is normally limited to ceremonial and social occasions. The functions of the head of a government, however, as a political executive, are considerable. He has certain regular responsibilities of appointing diplomatic envoys, receiving those from other states, ordering negotiations with and representations to be made to foreign governments, and so on, and he enjoys considerable discretion over the extent to which he will devote his immediate personal attention to such activities.

The executive may choose to send special agents to represent him on particular missions abroad, as did President Eisenhower with Richard Nixon and President Johnson with Robert Kennedy. He may also undertake personal diplomacy by means of direct correspondence, telephone conversations, good-will visits abroad, and meetings with the heads of other governments. The employment of high-level personal diplomacy acquired in the years before World War II a special vogue which lasted through the next two decades. Such practice can undoubtedly be useful and expeditious when employed by two or more heads of friendly governments for the purpose of exchanging views, consultations, and the alignment of policies to be pursued jointly. The use of such procedures, however, in an attempt to negotiate a settlement of serious international disputes and differences between states has much less to recommend it. There were widespread criticisms of the results of the Munich Conference (1938), the Yalta Conference (1945), and the Geneva Conference (1955), among others. But the pronounced setback to American diplomacy resulting from the collapse of the much-publicized Paris "summit conference" in 1960, followed by the cancellation of President Eisenhower's good-will visit to Japan, led to the announcement by his Secretary of State that the administration would return to "traditional channels and procedures of international contact." Extensive summit diplomacy has not been employed by subsequent administrations.

The advantages claimed for this sort of personal diplomacy are that heads of government, who are the chief policy makers, can speak with the highest authority; that they may gain a direct appreciation of the views of their opposite numbers; that top-level meetings focus public attention on the issues being discussed; and that national leaders are able to break through the complex bureaucratic process of policy making and other possible impasses to achieve needed agreements. The procedure carries with it nonetheless some serious disadvantages. In the first place, such meetings must be hurried. Government heads are ordinarily not professional diplomats and may well lack skill in conducting negotiations; since they are themselves the source of authority, their maneuvers may lack flexibility and range; they may dangerously overcommit themselves through ill-considered compromises; and such conferences may degenerate into contests of propaganda. And the attention attracted to such meetings may unreasonably raise popular expectations; if no substantial agreements are reached their failure is glaringly emphasized and magnified. Not surprisingly, many experienced diplomats view such occasions with strong misgivings.

The Ministry of Foreign Affairs. Governments have one ministry or department principally responsible for the administration of foreign policy. Its head—with such various titles as Secretary of State for Foreign Affairs in Great Britain, Secretary of State in the United States, Minister of Foreign Affairs in France, Secretary of State for External Affairs in Canada—is the regular intermediary between his goverment and those of foreign states, sending and receiving communications, overseeing the negotiation and execution of treaties, and many other similar functions. He is responsible for supervising the foreign ministry and directing the work of the foreign service. His importance is marked by enjoyment of first place in precedence among government ministers; in the parliamentary type of executive, the prime minister on occasion even assumes the office of foreign minister himself, thus lending it further prestige. In addition to his policy-making and advisory functions earlier mentioned, and administrative duties respecting his ministry, the foreign minister has the further important task of assisting the chief executive in explaining the government's foreign policy to the legislature and to the electorate. Finally, the foreign minister has come to be the principal diplomatic negotiator for his government; to an even greater degree than the chief executive in recent years, he has tended to engage in personal diplomacy with other foreign ministers, by-passing the conventional channels. Both advantages and disadvantages result from this kind of summitry—generally similar to those arising from negotiations by heads of governments.

In the performance of his many duties the minister is aided by several deputy and assistant ministers, who may have special responsibilities, and a number of undersecretaries, who administer the various divisions of the foreign office. Obviously each foreign ministry follows its own practices and needs in organization, but they are all similar. Some of the divisions will be organized to deal with staff functions such as legal affairs, press and information, archives, personnel, finance, passports and visas, security, research and intelligence, and protocol. Additional divisions may be geographic in character, supervising the work of embassies, legations, and consulates by particular areas, such as western Europe, eastern Europe, the Middle East, Latin America, and Africa. Still others, finally, may be devoted to particular subjects, such as economic affairs, international conferences, the United Nations, and like matters. The foreign ministry is thus the administrative center at which, on various levels, decisions over policy application are made, information collected, research conducted, messages received, instructions distributed, and programs reviewed.

The Diplomatic Service. The diplomatic service is distributed abroad in the form of missions established at the seat of government of each state with which diplomatic relations are maintained. The head of a mission holds one of three ranks: ambassador, which is the highest; minister, usually exchanged with small states; or chargé d'affaires, a member of the mission temporarily substituting for the regular envoy. The diplomatic agent has several functions; as Bagehot contended, "an ambassador is not simply an agent; he is also a spectacle." He formally represents his government both as a symbol and spokesman in residence and as a participant in ceremonial and social occasions. He observes and reports home upon all significant developments of a political, economic, and international character. He conducts negotiations, ranging from formal conferences producing treaties and other international instruments, to informal conversations and exchanges of views leading to mutual understandings. Finally, he is responsible for protecting and promoting the interests of his government and his fellow countrymen in the state to which he is accredited.

A considerable staff assists the envoy in the performance of his duties. These other members of the mission are designated counselors, secretaries, attachés, and officers of various grades. The foreign service usually is constituted on a career basis—though the United States uniquely uses some political appointees as heads of missions—with a highly selective system of entry; its members ordinarily may be interchanged in either diplomatic or consular posts, or assigned to work within the foreign office. In order that they may perform their duties effectively and without interference, and to avoid affronts to national dignity that might otherwise occur, members of the diplomatic corps are granted certain privileges and immunities. These include their full immunity from criminal or civil action, from the local law, and the inviolability of their official premises and residence, when on duty abroad.

The Consular Service. The foreign service also includes consular officials stationed abroad in important cities to promote various interests of their government and to provide assistance to their fellow nationals. It is important to note that consular officers do not act as official spokesmen to the government of the state in which they are authorized to perform their duties—a function limited to the head of the diplomatic mission. Their relations are with local officials instead. Consular duties embrace a wide range of activities, which include the collecting of information, particularly on commercial matters; ensuring observance of their immigration, navigation, and tariff laws; and performing general administrative tasks related to the visa of passports, attesting of legal documents, registering marriages, births, and deaths of their own nationals, and jurisdiction over merchant ships and seamen of their country when in local ports. On behalf of their fellow nationals they perform certain services, including provision of information about local economic and trade conditions, aid to those in legal difficulties, and assistance in international emergencies. Consular officers enjoy a partial immunity from local jurisdiction in the performance of their official duties, and some exemptions may be granted to them by treaty or as a matter of local courtesy.

Other Agencies. In the broadest sense, the administration of foreign policy is no longer limited to members of the foreign service alone. The increasing complexity of foreign relations and the broadening of its dimensions throughout the world have vastly extended the instrumentalities through which the international objectives of states, particularly the major powers, may be effected. Governments now commonly employ information services and short-wave radio stations to explain their views. Trade, scientific, technical, and agricultural missions are sent abroad to assist and advise other governments. The military establishments have become increasingly important; several of the major powers station large bodies of troops abroad, and commonly send military missions to the aid of lesser states in which they have a particular interest. Cultural and educational programs, involving orchestral tours, ballets, art exhibits, teacher and student exchanges, supplies of books and periodicals, are also devices for exerting influence abroad. Even private citizens, entirely outside of any official direction or program, are considered to play a part in international relations. Every student, soldier, businessman, professor, or tourist makes some kind of an impact on foreign public opinion when he goes abroad, and to some degree—not always a limited one—helps to create in foreign eyes an image of his country, its character, and its objectives.

III. *The* PROMOTION *of* NATIONAL INTERESTS

States have several means available for the promotion of their national interests abroad: diplomacy, imperialism, war, political warfare, and international organization. What choice they make is dependent, first, on the measures of national power they possess, and second, on the foreign-policy objectives they adopt. The first three means are the traditional devices for achieving national goals in the international realm; the last two are, to an important extent, much more recent in their development. A third factor also conditions the choice of means. The reduced effectiveness of diplomacy, the retreat from western imperialism, and the now most obvious hazards accompanying resort to war have drawn states to other measures for promoting their national interests. The totalitarian states have elected political warfare for the most direct achievement of their strategic objectives short of actual war—a choice unquestionably influenced by the distinct advantage they derive from the employment of such weapons. The democracies, unfortunately, have responded with the comparably less effective counterweapons available to them, and have failed to become committed to a degree of international co-operation and organization among themselves which would be immediately to their advantage against totalitarianism, and could substantially improve their defensive capabilities. We may now examine the nature of these means.

Diplomacy. The term "diplomacy" has been used in several confusingly different ways; it is employed by some as a synonym for foreign policy—much too general a sense—and by others as signifying the professional skill of the diplomat—an overly limited usage. Essentially, diplomacy means the conduct of negotiations between governments. As we have seen, these are undertaken by heads of government on occasion, nowadays frequently by foreign ministers, but most commonly by diplomatic agents. The key to the concept of diplomacy is negotiation; forensic duels, the exchange of vituperation, public haggling, and the threat or use of force, whatever other place they may have in international relations, are not negotiation. The process of diplomacy has several essential characteristics. It requires a modicum of shared confidence between governments intending to treat with each other, a recognition of their mutual needs, and a reciprocal belief that each is acting in good faith; it proceeds by persuasion, the pressing of advantage, and the offering of concessions; it produces compromise and agreement in which there is mutual benefit.

Diplomacy has a twofold utility: first, it has been the normal and traditional method of states to promote their interests, and it is certainly the most inexpensive. States use diplomacy to promote co-operation with other governments and to effect collaboration to some purpose; to obtain political or economic concessions or the recognition of other special interests; and to contract alliances or create international associations of various kinds. Second, diplomacy is a method for the peaceful settlement of disputes. As Cicero characterized the matter, "There are two methods of settling a difference, the one by argument, the other by force, . . . the former is characteristic of men, the latter of beasts. . . ." Negotiation is thus the simplest procedure for resolving a controversy and terminating a dispute. It is an alternative to the use of forceful means and war. To be sure, diplomats may here press any advantage their state possesses, including a superiority of power, but an ultimatum accepted in the face of *force majeure* is not truly within the transactions of diplomacy.

In view of what we have already said about the administration of foreign policy, we can be brief in our conclusions. It should be noted, however, that there is definite disagreement about the importance of diplomacy as an instrument for the alteration of relations between states. On the one hand, some assert that the promotion of national interests is best entrusted to professional diplomats; men of similar training, background, experience, and ideals, given reasonably generous room in which to maneuver, are then able patiently and quietly to conduct continuous and confidential negotiations, employing their special skills, knowledge, and finesse. Such procedures achieve bargains of mutual advantage and the maintenance of peace. On the other hand, some deflate the importance of traditional diplomacy. They insist that it was only truly effective in the once-narrow circle of European states, when societies were largely united in values even if rivals in aspirations, and that the emergence of communist governments, rejecting any standards, have put an end to this situation. Diplomatic agents as individuals are said to count for very much less today; diplomatic success is not dependent upon the personal charm, the social grace, or professional skill of the envoy, but upon the policies of his government, backed by will, resourcefulness, and power. It is argued finally that traditional diplomacy has been considerably supplanted by modern means of communication, the availability of other sources for foreign information, and the personal diplomacy of national leaders.

The actual utility of diplomacy seems to lie between these two extreme positions. It has its greatest effectiveness, particularly in the representational and reporting functions, between states which are basically friendly and share some common interests and objectives. As a continuous process it can usefully strengthen the co-operation of states in association or alliance, and it offers a technique for the solution of minor disputes between them. Its ineffectiveness—and here is the nexus of the problem with the world today—lies in the fundamental fact that all differences between states cannot be solved by negotiation. States do not invariably misunderstand each other's motives and policies; sometimes they understand them only too well. When, as in the present century, the major powers include totalitarian dictatorships, dedicated by rigid ideologies and political structures to the overthrow of the prevailing international order, the conflicts of national interest become too great to be adjusted by accommodation. With differences so extreme, between states unable to relinquish their objectives without accepting disastrous defeat, there is little about which to bargain. Diplomacy, then, cannot resolve the irreconcilable, for the basic decision to negotiate always precedes, rather than follows, the practice of diplomacy. In this situation, diplomacy will undoubtedly continue to decline.

Imperialism. To provide an effective definition of the term "imperialism" is no easy task. At the very least it is almost always used as an "attitude-word" carrying some subjective coloration, and it is often used for propaganda purposes as an emotion-laden epithet to cover sins real and imagined. Many Britons have believed, with Lord Rosebery, that imperialism meant "a greater pride in Empire, a larger patriotism," while communists accept Lenin's arbitrary definition of imperialism to mean "decaying capitalism." Scholars are no more in agreement. Some define imperialism in terms of national policy, as any expansion of a state's powers beyond its frontiers; others view it in terms of national goals, often stressing the economic ones. There is no possibility of reconciling such indiscriminate usage. The term has significance, therefore, only in some precise and limited meaning; we shall use it here to describe the forceful exercise by a state of continued political control over an alien people.

Empire-building at the expense of foreigners is a very old institution. Ancient and medieval periods of history witnessed the imperialism, among others, of the Persians, Saracens, Romans, Mongols, Turks, and Muscovites, who sought land, loot, and slave labor. From the early sixteenth to near the end of the eighteenth century, the more powerful states of western Europe pursued overseas imperialist ventures, combining colonization and mercantilism, mainly in the western hemisphere, while those of eastern Europe conquered vast contiguous land domains. The empire of the Russians was ultimately to extend from the Baltic across Asia to the Bering Sea. In the latter part of the nineteenth century a new imperialistic surge resumed, led by Britain and France and directed mainly at Africa and Asia, in which the non-European powers, the United States and Japan, were partly joined. Finally, as a result of the alteration in major-power status after World War II, when most of the imperial powers moved into retreat, the Soviet Union and Communist China pressed new imperialist courses.

The essence of imperialism is the adverse political domination of a foreign people. It involves an exercise of state power for the purpose of extending power and prestige by establishing control over a people, their territory and resources. Imperialism constitutes a superior-inferior relationship, the action of the strong against the weak, of course, and the imposition or perpetuation of some sort of authoritarian rule, whether including or excluding part of the local inhabitants, on behalf of the imperialist power. There are several methods for exercising authority over an alien people. These include annexation and full or partial absorption; colonization; the establishment of various kinds of dependencies, such as protectorates, leaseholds, and mandates; and the creation of puppet regimes and satellite states. Some of these arrangements are, indeed, intentional disguises for imperialism, though they vary rather more in name than in substance, when the intent to imperialize is present.

Thus, British domination in British Honduras, of Communist China in Tibet, of the United States in Okinawa, of the Soviet Union in Hungary, and of France in New Caledonia—despite the great variety in the means by which they established themselves and the motives for which they remain—are all acts of imperialism. After completing its continental expansion, the United States undertook a limited program of overseas imperialism at the turn of the present century with the acquisition of the Philippines, some other Pacific islands, and Puerto Rico, and the retention of certain controls over a Cuba liberated from Spain. But these actions were not generally popular for any length of time, seeming false to the American tradition of anticolonialism, and the imperial associations subsequently were terminated. Great Britain has also steadily abandoned, partly by necessity and partly by design, its important imperialist positions in recent decades. The Soviet Union, which after 1939 forced within its domain some twenty-four millions of people and under communist domination another ninety millions, is today the leading imperialist power.

We should be clear about what imperialism is not. It is not a product of "capitalism," for empire-building was practiced centuries before the system of economic arrangements bearing that label came into existence; it is actively being practiced by states that are avowedly anti- and non-capitalistic; and, indeed, only a relatively few states have empires, colonies, or satellites, whatever their economic arrangements. Further, every form of political or military interference within a foreign territory does not constitute imperialism; interventions for a particular occasion, such as for the protection of nationals or property, the contraction of alliances and the stationing of military forces abroad in a common defense program, or the military occupation of territory at the end of war—all have other purposes. Such acts are intended to effect a particular result, and ordinarily are not continued, unless they are a prelude to, or concomitant of, actual political domination. Finally, the exercise of every kind of economic role or cultural influence abroad is not imperialism, though these might accompany political domination. The investment of American capital in Canada, the teaching of English literature in India, or the performance of Russian ballet companies in the United States may variously redound to the profit and prestige of the countries in which they originate, but they are not imperialism.

Just as the means of expanding national power by imperialism are extensive, so are its motives, as a review of the various factors in national power will suggest. Nationalism has stimulated imperialism, for example, to promote the prestige of the nation, providing it a "place in the sun," and supplying it with attributes of adventure and glory. Geographically speaking, imperialism can be a method of extending the national domain, establishing buffer belts or strategic frontiers, and winning resources. From the standpoint of population, imperialism may increase manpower or provide outlets for emigration. Among economic motives, imperialism may seek raw material resources, markets, and investment opportunities. The ideological motive is present when states seek the propagation of religion, to win converts to communism, or to liberate a people from totalitarian rule. Lastly, military interest may motivate imperialism as a device for securing military bases or resisting an opponent's military expansion.

Needless to say, imperialist policies do not produce all these ends, many of which may be only rationalizations, nor is empire-building invariably profitable. And even when benefits are produced, they tend to be most unevenly and disproportionately distributed. Certain groups within an imperialist state may well enjoy returns, ranging from monetary profit to emotional satisfaction, though these are often at the expense of the entire nation as taxpayers as well as of the dominated people. To be sure, in certain cases of colonialism those subjected to domination may have been benefited to some extent by the imperial power's introduction, say, of order, transportation, sanitation, education, industrialization, and so on. If imperialism is everywhere resented today, and resisted where possible, the reasons are not hard to find. Those under domination have in this age been introduced to a knowledge of higher standards of living than those prevailing among them, and ferment is widespread to achieve them. They are aware that, whatever the improvements received from imperialism, they are essentially the by-product of exploitation, rather than the consequence of co-operative development, and many such areas have been selfishly used indeed. They also not unreasonably resent the inferiority of their dominated status, often made doubly offensive when accompanied by racial, religious, or cultural discrimination. Finally, imperialism has scattered the seeds of nationalism—if they were not already present—and no matter how poorly prepared for independence they may be, the dependent peoples are convinced that "good government is no substitute for self-government." Even though newer techniques of enforcing political domination by the powerful over the weak may be expected—and some of the peoples most recently released from imperialist domination have already set about applying it to others—imperialism is in decline. The large colonial empires of the West are rapidly dissolving, and future conquests by the communist powers will not be attained with the ease of some of their earlier expansion.

War. Within the community of states, war is international conflict waged by armed force. We may distinguish a "state of war," which is a legal condition in the relationship between states who are formal belligerents, from the conduct of hostilities themselves. In modern times, civilized states have normally declared war before commencing military operations—though the 1941 attacks of Nazi Germany on the Soviet Union and of Japan upon the United States are notorious exceptions—and a state of war may continue until a peace treaty is signed, often some time after a truce or an armistice has suspended hostilities. War has always had an important part in the advancement of national interest—in the classic dictum of Clausewitz, it "is nothing else than the continuation of state policy by other means." It is also the most universally condemned method of promoting national goals, attracting such adjectives as hateful, wasteful, inhuman, destructive, wanton, and barbaric, sentiments epitomized by General Sherman—"War is hell."

It would be easy with a subject so great and the literature upon it so vast to become lost in its reaches; we are concerned here only in dealing with it briefly as another instrument of national policy. War involves the direct application of the state's military power to some end, supported by other forms of national strength. Differences in the extent of such commitment are among the distinctions between two basic types of war. Through most of the history of the nation-state system, wars could be characterized as limited. A limited war is one waged for specific objectives, involving and affecting only a small portion of a nation's population, and terminated when its restricted objectives are achieved or become demonstrably unachievable. A classic example of such a conflict is the Franco-Prussian War (1870–1871); more recently, except in the eyes of the Korean people, of course, the Korean War held to these essentials—despite the efforts of some to convert it into a total one. In total war essentially all of the resources of the nation, human and material, are put behind the war effort; weapons of mass destruction are employed against combatant and noncombatant alike; and it aims at nothing less than forcing the enemy to unconditional surrender—hence, the attainment of total victory. These features characterized World Wars I and II, prolonging their length and enlarging their cost and destructiveness, and leaving totalitarianism and international instability in their wake.

War has inevitably come to be seen as the major political problem of our time; no other kind of activity conducted by government comes near to being so costly as wars—past, present, and future. Endless studies have searched for the causes of war. They have produced a great complex of answers, in terms of causes underlying and immediate, primary and secondary, just and unjust, psychological and material, and with many of them conflicting. Explanations have ranged over many disparate factors, from trade restrictions to a decline in religion. Yet the matter need not be overly complicated. It is clear that states may go to war over any question of national interest; given the existing international community, war always presents itself as an alternative means of state action. The fundamental question, of course, is why states choose war at some point in preference to other means of promoting national interest. Recalling our earlier observation that there may be substantial disagreement, in affairs great and small, over what is in the national interest, we can only say that somehow a calculation is reached that war is advantageous—that it is, under given circumstances, preferable to other alternatives—for any purpose from national enrichment to national survival. The solution to the problem of war, however, will not be found by categorizing its causes, but through fundamental alterations in the character of the international community—and this is a topic we shall treat in the next chapter.

Yet something needs be said here about the current re-evaluation of the role of war. Traditionally, war involved a partial employment of national power to a particular end—an end which might be bad or good —and manifestly much good resulted from some wars. It was, it has been said, the paramount method of "changing the other fellow's mind." But the two great total wars of this century involved costs entirely out of proportion to any objectives sought by the belligerents at their outset.

And as hostilities continued, they grew in bitterness, and the warring nations' aims were translated into moralistic and ideological principles —rather than specific ends—which were by their nature entirely unattainable. Not least important, their total quality and the total defeats suffered by the vanquished produced international chaos and convulsion following their end. Such total wars obviously carry a price which no state can afford to pay. They therefore cease to be a controllable instrument of national policy.

In the second place, the world is now obliged to confront military weapons having a capacity for total destruction. The advent of thermonuclear weapons, revolutionizing warfare, has produced a situation unprecedented in human history: a national power able to destroy humanity and all human values. A state in possession of these—and the number is growing—can utterly destroy an enemy, and with not insignificant side-effects upon many, perhaps all, other states as well. Of course, such extreme weapons need be aimed only at enemies who possess them, and who are by that fact capable of retaliating in kind. Because such weapons offer an enormous advantage to the aggressor, states who are members of the nuclear club must also be prepared to respond instantaneously. Thus atomic war has become a potential instrument of mutual suicide; as General Douglas MacArthur declared in his address to Congress in 1951: "The utter destructiveness of war now blocks out this alternative. We have had our last chance." If a decline in war will be effected only when there is a clear decline in its utility, one might think that would end the matter. But the grim tragedy of our time is, regrettably, that it does not. For one thing, not all states are equally reluctant to use force. And, there is a basic streak of irrationality as well as intelligence in the makeup of *Homo sapiens*. Those who are reassured by the thought that only a madman would start World War III can only have forgotten that it was a madman who started World War II.

Political Warfare. The term "political warfare" can be used to describe generally the promotion of national interest by belligerent means short of declared or full-scale hostilities. It is a condition neither of war nor peace between states. It involves relations virtually the obverse of the Clausewitz formula—the continuation of war by other means. Though often reflecting very old ideas and practices, the fundamental weapons of political warfare were developed by the major totalitarian dictatorships after 1917. They have thus been significantly shaped by communist, fascist, and Nazi ideologies, and reflect techniques developed by revolutionary political groups to gain power within a state, and then applied in the international community with the full power of a heavily armed police state behind them. The totalitarian states find a number of advantages in political warfare, beginning with the fact that they are themselves less vulnerable to it. It is less expensive than actual hostilities, and offers greater room for maneuver and the practice of opportunism. It further gives an advantage to the aggressor in that it can be broken off largely at will, and occasions relatively low risks.

It must be emphasized again that political warfare is warfare, not peaceful relations, and that those engaged in it really seek to win victory over their chosen enemy. The citizens of a democratic state at whom it is aimed may properly find it distasteful, like all war, and may be disinclined to use it themselves, because they are not accustomed to similar political techniques at home. But moral indignation is no defense, and a rather pointless response to it; as in all war, the ends chosen are thought to justify the extremity of means, and telling lies to people, confusing or frightening them, is, if anything, less reprehensible than killing them. So long as political warfare, like any kind of war, offers an alternative means of self-interested state action within the international community that prevails, we cannot entirely pretend surprise or dismay that some states will choose to wage it.

We have an instructive contemporary example of the formidable and effective weapons of political warfare in the "cold war" (or policy of "competitive coexistence" as the communists prefer to call it) conducted from the bastions of world communism against the United States. It has in most respects come to dominate all international developments related to the world power struggle, and even many that are not. The objectives of political warfare, as we have indicated, are those of war—essentially, to allow one state to force its will upon others. More immediately, the objectives of the communist offensives are to win an acknowledgment of their superiority of power and a surrender to their terms in all international relationships. To this end they seek to create fear and to provoke hysteria. They attempt to induce cautiousness in western policy, a withdrawal from forward positions, and a general weakening of democratic government and its procedures. It is also aimed at attacking the United States' reputation and prestige abroad, to unsettle and divide American allies, and to win over uncommitted states to "positive neutralism" or outright alliance with communism. Finally, it seeks to undermine all traditional institutions that contribute to order and stability in the international community: the practice of diplomacy, the observance of international law, and the utilization of international organization.

The arsenal of weapons employed in the political warfare offensive—and which we can only partially list here—testifies to the ingenuity and relentlessness of its practitioners. From the communist base of operations, propaganda is conducted through an array of channels, interspersed with insults and name-calling. Falsehoods are routine, issues are regularly confused, and siren calls alternate with fearsome threats. Censorship restricts outgoing and incoming news and information, increasing uncertainty and confusion. The perversion of diplomacy turns negotiations into endurance contests of bazaar haggling. The harassment of foreign diplomats and nationals, the forgery of documents, the use of *agents provocateurs,* and the show trials of "spies" manifest contempt and arrogance toward rivals. Border incidents make displays of combat readiness, and are supposed to demonstrate the aggressiveness of the "enemy."

Still other measures are used or applied abroad. Subversion, by infiltration, sabotage, and conspiracy, and the disaffection of police and military forces, seek to weaken or overthrow government authority, and "wars of liberation" are encouraged. Communist political parties and their adherents organize "peace demonstrations," political strikes, prolonged riots, and stimulate guerrilla and civil warfare. The nuisance value of small or underdeveloped states is exploited; in return for promises of economic aid and military support they are induced to confiscate foreign property, harass aliens, crusade against "imperialism," and emulate communist policies generally. Intervention is threatened in order to force expensive military mobilizations, engender repression, enfeeble authority, and thus foment political and economic crisis. Economic pressures are applied wherever opportunities are exposed. These various techniques are alternated, and often regularly intermixed, with apparently peaceful and friendly overtures, to put the victims off guard and render them increasingly vulnerable to shock tactics.

There are no certain defenses in political warfare, and countermeasures are often awkward and difficult. A high degree of military preparedness, forward bases, counterespionage, and general deterrence all help to maintain security, provide a position of strength from which to resist, and to contain intervention or expansion, though these are extremely expensive, and are of limited use against nonmilitary attacks. Information programs, especially where they publicize the truth, are of some help in combating propaganda; yet some slander always sticks, perhaps, and its honest refutation never fully restores reputation. The "big lie" technique in the hands of any government, it has been demonstrated many times, can be extraordinarily difficult to controvert. Alliances are a means of strengthening the will of other states to resist political warfare, especially when helping to repair military or economic deficiencies. Economic aid and technical assistance, though particularly helpful to underdeveloped countries, are no sovereign remedy against their subversion.

It should be observed that programs of economic aid to foreign states, whether through UNRRA, direct loans, the European Recovery Program, or subscriptions to the International Bank and other such agencies, are not necessarily related to political warfare. They may variously serve as an aid to effective diplomacy, reflect humanitarian considerations, be viewed as good business, or help to advance stability and peace. But where one government promotes the interests of another, even so, its action is an interpretation of some aspect of its own national interest. It might be noted, too, that many states cannot afford to contribute much aid, and none can give unlimited amounts of it. Like alliances, aid programs may also oblige association with and support of governments that are not always politically respectable.

"Brinkmanship" has also been employed as a counterweapon, a practice which John Foster Dulles was quoted defining as "The ability to get to the verge without getting into the war. . . ." Perhaps necessary on occasion, it is obviously a risky weapon if its practice becomes mutual and "hot war" is unleashed. Finally, of course, counterweapons include the identical political warfare weapons of the aggressor.

We must point out that to reply in kind—to fight fire with fire in this situation—is the least attractive solution. To employ the totalitarian arsenal of lies, deceit, ruthlessness, and treachery is to embrace all that democracy opposes. The question is often asked, in anxiety or anger, "Why should the devil have all the best tunes?"—why, indeed, cannot the democratic states launch a fierce counterpropaganda and a relentless subversion campaign? The answer inescapably is that democracy by its very nature is not a militant creed, to be preached by zealots, nor is it a kind of consumers' goods, to be merchandised like soap. Nor is it a packaged and exportable system of political and economic arrangements which a government can impose. There are also dangers in conducting foreign policy by slogan: a substantial one is coming to believe one's own propaganda! Unlike communist governments, democracies cannot give away what does not belong to them. There are no means of subverting a political system to democracy; the values of freedom and individualism must be chosen and practiced by a people.

Communism is attractive to some in the backward countries because it appears to offer means for rapid industrialization and the maximization of national power, if with little regard for life or humane values. Nevertheless, communism has been extended more by military coercion than by persuasion; and even among those impoverished, discriminated against, and disaffected, it does not generally sell well. To counter the totalitarian offerings the democracies must display better ones of their own that will assist the widespread aspirations of other peoples to freedom, dignity, and a higher standard of living. This is not primarily a matter of conducting the right propaganda, nor largely one of spending money. Friends and allies for democracy cannot be purchased—governments that sell themselves do not "stay bought." This is not the place, of course, to offer a blueprint for democratic strategy and policy. It should be enough to say that, while the control of events is not entirely in their hands, the democratic states of the West have by no means capitalized sufficiently upon their superiority of wealth, energy, technical knowledge, and moral purpose.

The democracies may be properly concerned that they do not lose the vital contests of political warfare, but they should also not deceive themselves about the fact that many of their policies and countermeasures in the eyes of others are also as provocative, suspect in motive, and lacking in virtue as those of the communists. Propaganda has undoubtedly already been overdone in the contemporary world. In the long run, people are most impressed by what governments do, and not by what they say. As Adlai Stevenson once observed, "We are not going to beat the Godless materialism of the Russians with a Godly materialism of our own." The democracies do continue, indeed, to allow nationalist emotions to obstruct the kind of effective collaboration among themselves by which they could, if truly united, contribute both to world order and their own preservation and prosperity.

International Organization. This heading is entered at the end of this chapter, then, to help remind the reader that international organization is also a means of promoting national interest—perhaps the one with the most significant potentialities. Thus the topic relates distinctly to the pattern of the discussion we have been pursuing. But it is also a subject which requires discussion at some length—the nature, possibilities, and problems of international co-operation and peace through international organization—and to which we shall devote the next chapter.

CHAPTER 15

INTERNATIONAL ORGANIZATION *and the* PROBLEM *of* PEACE

THE MINIMAL objectives of government whether local, national, or international, do not differ fundamentally: to maintain peace and order and advance common human interests. The larger the area, the wider the peace, security, and interests that the same government is able to protect. Small wonder, therefore, that the concentration of political authority produced by the Roman empire, which extended to most of Europe, and its resulting Pax Romana, were long considered in the western world as one of mankind's greatest achievements. By contrast, the disorganization and fragmentation of political authority during the middle ages seemed scarcely effective in performing some of the most elementary responsibilities of government. And, for those who sought peace instead of unremitting war, the emergence of the nation-state system was only a little less frustrating. Indeed, it has become increasingly clear that under such a system no state is capable of accomplishing—except partially and sporadically—the principal objectives of government. Not only is it incapable, in many instances, of promoting its national interests without effective co-operation by other states, but also of ensuring unilaterally its own security. Thus, the aspiration to create machinery for international organization by which states could be associated for co-operation, their interests promoted by common instrumentalities, and some limitations imposed collectively upon national power—so that disorder and warfare might be reduced—was supported both by the popular desire for peace, and the practical necessity for co-operation.

I. *The* DEVELOPMENT *of* INTERNATIONAL ORGANIZATION

The Desire for Peace. As is so often the case with major political innovation, some centuries of the sort of thought usually labeled "utopian" preceded practical attempts to deal with the problem of international organization. One of the earliest of these pleas to organize against disorder, reflecting as well a medieval nostalgia for the Roman empire, was made by Dante Alighieri. In his *De monarchia,* written in the fourteenth century, Dante argued that "the human race is at its best state when it is ruled by a single prince and one law. So it is evidently necessary for the welfare of the world that there should be a single monarchy or princedom, which men call the Empire."

A contemporary of Dante's, the French lawyer Pierre Dubois, with considerable realism for the times, proposed creation of a league of the independent European princes, with a consultative council, an arbitration court, and collective action when necessary to restore peace. The seventeenth and eighteenth centuries saw further such schemes brought forward. The "Grand Design" of Henry IV, possibly originated by the Duc de Sully, proposed the organization of Europe into a federation of fifteen units, governed by a general council which would pacify quarrels and command an international army to enforce its decisions. Other projects, most of them virtually unnoticed by the people or their rulers in this period, were propounded by the monk Emeric Crucé, the Quaker colonizer William Penn, and the French diplomat the Abbé de Saint-Pierre. When the latter sent copies of his *Project to Bring Perpetual Peace in Europe* to contemporary monarchs, Frederick the Great is supposed to have remarked, "The thing is exceedingly practical, nor is anything wanting for its accomplishment—except the consent of all Europe and some other such trifles." Nevertheless, neither the rebuffs of rulers nor the continuation of wars of ever-increasing extent and destructiveness deterred other political thinkers from searching for ways of uniting the independent nation-states. Later in the century, Rousseau, Bentham, and Kant all elaborated similar themes on ways to perpetual peace.

Plans for international organization multiplied after 1800, and the peace movement was extended as numerous private national and international peace societies generally attempted to promote pacifism, convened peace conferences, and otherwise sought to eliminate war. The wealth of philanthropists provided the Nobel peace prize, the Carnegie Endowment for International Peace, the World Peace Foundation, and similar institutions. The popular strength of the peace movement was nowhere better demonstrated, indeed, than in the espousal of pacifism by nearly all of the European political parties characterized as socialist or proletarian, which received the support of large sections of the working-class population.

By the beginning of the twentieth century, when it was recognized that large-scale war would be of unprecedented cost and destructiveness, many began to insist that international organization for peace was no longer merely desirable, but had become imperative. And far from being antagonistic to the interests of individual states, it was asserted, effective forms of international organization were the only means for preventing the self-destruction of the nation-states, and the ultimate undermining of civilization itself. The great Hague Peace Conferences of 1899 and 1907—unlike most "peace conferences" in that they were convened not for the termination of a war but to mitigate or avoid warfare between states—were, therefore, the outgrowth of a century's efforts and almost universally expressed desires. But even at this relatively late date, the accomplishments of these two conferences were extremely modest, and the prospects for promoting peace in the twentieth century little more likely of realization than six centuries earlier. When the second Hague Conference convened, there had already occurred the first of the major diplomatic crises which would lead to world war in 1914. An English writer, Norman Angell, who warned in his book *Great Illusion* that war would bring disaster to victor and vanquished alike, was only one among many who recoiled before the international tendencies of his day. His book was a "best seller" of 1910, but made little impression at the centers of European political and military decision.

The Necessity for Co-operation. Not only did the peace movement grow steadily throughout the nineteenth century, but this same period marked an important turning point in western civilization, and produced profound changes in the character of international relations. The "age of discovery" of the fifteenth and sixteenth centuries enormously increased Europe's contacts with the rest of the world and, as we have seen earlier, opened an era of great expansion in the number of units composing the international community.

Such an enlargement of the geographically known and accessible world further expanded the range of international intercourse and set in motion powerful forces of economic change that produced the tremendous expansion of world trade known as the "commercial revolution." As the number of national boundaries increased, improvements in the standard of living permitted huge expansions of the populations behind them. As their wants increased, some could be satisfied only from outside their national domain. Such innovations as the manufacture of goods by power-driven machinery, development of the factory system, and techniques for standardized mass production, which characterized the "industrial revolution," brought forth an even greater need for international markets as sources of raw materials and outlets for manufactures. Thus did raw materials, foodstuffs, and goods begin to move across national frontiers in ever-increasing volume. Under the impact of modern capitalism, nations and peoples were inevitably pushed into closer contacts and relations. These developments in turn gave rise to a world-wide network of transportation and communication facilities. Modern technology produced a host of new instrumentalities—the telegraph, telephone, and radio, and the railroad, steamship, and automobile—whose efficient use was partly dependent on some degree of co-operation and regulation by the international community.

At the very time, then, when the world was being rapidly divided into a larger number of politically independent units, it was also slowly being drawn together by their cultural and economic interdependence. By the nineteenth century, money, ideas, and people also began to cross national frontiers with ease. Tariffs were low and trade restrictions few; the gold standard prevailed for the major currencies, and these could be quickly converted for exchange purposes. Efforts at political censorship were declining except in a few despotic areas. Passports were likewise unknown—except in Russia, for movement abroad—and people were free to go about the world for travel or emigration.

Throughout most of the western world, modern scholarship, science, art, and music continued to reflect the development of universal cultural standards. Epidemics, illiteracy, slavery, and the narcotic drug traffic were recognized as problems calling for international attention. The economic welfare of every state was recognized as being increasingly dependent on world trade, world markets, world prices—and world depressions. We had, in fact, reached such a stage of world interdependence that most important national problems now had their global counterparts. As no state could live in self-sufficient isolation, states would somehow have to live together. So, without conceding any diminution of their formal independence, states were inexorably led, all during the nineteenth century, to make considerable concessions to expediency, and to employ increasingly measures of international co-operation. In a brief survey, let us examine the nature of this experience.

The Growth of International Organization. The evolution of the body of *international law,* as we have seen, brought about the legal definition and organization of the community of states. On the foundation of this law—and in the absence of any central political authority within the world—the European powers, with the increasing participation of the non-European states, began to create a number of instrumentalities of international organization, based upon co-operative effort and interstate agreement. Even today, these still provide the principal institutional framework of international government.

Following the Napoleonic Wars, the European powers had frequent resort to *international conferences,* which were assemblies of governmental representatives—heads of states, diplomats, or technical experts—for the purpose of simultaneously exchanging views and reaching agreement on some given subject. Earlier international conferences, such as those of Westphalia (1648), Utrecht (1713), and Vienna (1814–1815), had been employed to achieve peace settlements ending major wars. But now representatives of states began to meet frequently in international conferences to secure common action on all sorts of international problems as the normal means of advancing state interests generally. Between 1826 and 1907, more than three hundred were held, dealing with such matters as Belgium's neutralization, independence for Greece, establishment of the International Red Cross, conditions for the acquisition of African colonial territory, treatment of social questions, and so on.

Another device employed to achieve uniformity of action on a particular matter was the multilateral *international convention,* whereby a number of states registered their formal agreement on a matter of international policy, and defined their reciprocal obligations thereunder. The multilateral convention was, of course, an extremely simple form of international collaboration, since the responsibility for carrying out the agreement was left entirely to the governments that were parties to it. Usually framed at an international conference, the convention became an important instrumentality of nineteenth-century state relations. Major conventions were adopted on such subjects as the navigation of the Elbe river (1821), creation of the Cape Spartel international lighthouse (1865), protection of North Sea fisheries (1881), protection of submarine cables (1884), suppression of the African slave traffic (1890), and control of pelagic sealing in the north Pacific (1911).

This same period marked the creation of a rudimentary international administration, dictated by the increasing complexity of economic interests, the growth of communications, and the recognition of social problems. This kind of international agency, known as a *public international union,* was organized to deal with the common interests of a number of states by the establishment of a permanent administrative office or bureau. The international union was created by an international convention framed at an international conference, which could be reconvened from time to time for revising or supervisory functions; the bureau acted as a permanent secretariat to collect and distribute information, enforce rights and duties, supervise the regulated subject, and to perform other similar administrative activities. Some twenty such organizations were created prior to World War I, including the Universal Postal Union, Rhine and Danube River Commissions, International Telegraphic Union, Pan-American Union, International Office of Public Health, and International Opium Commission.

Still further, the international community had available by 1914 a variety of procedures for the pacific settlement of international disputes. The most commonly employed method of settlement was *diplomatic negotiation.* Ordinary disagreements could usually be settled through the adjustments of diplomacy if states acted in good faith to reach an understanding over their differences. If states did not reach settlements by negotiation, a third state might intervene to the extent of bringing the parties at issue to a renewal of negotiation, which constituted the exercise of *good offices;* or a third state might go a step further, offering a solution to the dispute, which constituted *mediation.* Where international differences resulted from disagreements on points of fact, the parties could agree to the creation of a *commission of inquiry,* which, undertaking an impartial investigation to elucidate the facts, might provide a virtually automatic solution of the difference. Where parties to a dispute referred it to a commission or third state to conduct a hearing and recommend a basis for settlement, they employed the procedure of *conciliation.* Finally, the device of *arbitration,* which was as close as states had come by 1914 to anything resembling an international judicial procedure, involved the settlement of a controversy between states by its submission to a tribunal whose award after a hearing, it was agreed, would be recognized as binding upon them. Arbitration was long conducted by arbitrators especially selected by the disputants, but the Hague Conference of 1899 was able to create a Permanent Court of Arbitration with national panels of judges designated as available to act as arbitrators, though still to be selected for each occasion.

Summing up the nature of the system of international organization developed by 1914, then, we find within the international community: first, a body of international law which only moderately restricted a very broad freedom for state policy, and was not concerned, in the main, with issues of peace and war. Indeed, the existence of war was taken for granted, and international law attempted little more than to mitigate its effects. Second, a system of international conferences, convened primarily on an *ad hoc* basis, that is, formed only for a particular occasion, initiated and organized by an interested state, and providing no continuity or regularity in approach. Third, a collection of multilateral international conventions, whereby states effected a degree of uniformity in some of their national policies, and were able to develop some new regulatory standards or rules of international law. Fourth, a group of public international unions, confined largely to the administration of the technical aspects of international relations, but easing the way for international co-operation where power considerations were not present. And, fifth, a variety of methods for the settlement of international disputes on a peaceful basis as an alternative to settlement by force or war. Yet states were under no compulsion to employ peaceful methods, or having employed them, to accept any solutions thus proposed, and governments were unable to agree upon the creation of a permanent international judicial body with compulsory jurisdiction over states involved in justiciable disputes.

Thus, the world organization developed to this point was haphazard, piecemeal, and unco-ordinated; it could often deal effectively with practical and unspectacular matters; but it had little to do with the great political issues that divided the major powers and perpetuated the insecurity of all states. Governments did co-operate for the solution of specific and routine problems on a basis of consent and where their self-interest was rather immediately served. But they had not agreed to the creation of any general or universal international organization. In 1914, there was still no conviction that such organization was necessary to the international community.

II. EXPERIMENTS *with* INTERNATIONAL ORGANIZATION

The nineteenth century is usually thought of as "a century of peace." Though it began with the Napoleonic Wars—which raged over the continent from Spain to Russia and were the greatest military conflict Europe had theretofore known, and no decade afterward escaped additional hostilities between two or more European states—it was nevertheless an age of relatively small-scale wars, short in duration, and fought by professional soldiers for limited objectives. At least, for a hundred years, no general war upset the substantial order and equilibrium established by the Congress of Vienna or seriously alarmed civilians by its destructiveness.

The Concert of Europe. Throughout this period, the intermittent consultations and conferences of the major European powers, known as the Concert of Europe, were a leading factor in maintaining the general peace. None of its members—Great Britain, France, Prussia, Austria, or Russia—enjoyed anything like enough power alone to flout successfully the wishes of the others for any length of time. Then, too, with large areas of southeast Europe, the Middle East, Africa, and Asia yet available for division into spheres of interest, there was quite as much to be gained by the powers in concert as in conflict. It was still an era of little popular interest in or control over the conduct of foreign relations—it was the golden age of the professional diplomat, who could devote himself to the achievement of skillful and secret compromises. When the powers acted in unison, therefore, they were able to arrange and enforce agreements for their own benefit, and if necessary coerce the smaller states.

It must be emphasized that the Concert of Europe rested on nothing more than an informal consensus; it had no treaty basis, no organization, no regular meetings. It functioned rather effectively in the earlier part of the century when the powers were disposed to meet, consult, and act together. It faltered after 1879, when the alliance system began the division of Europe into two heavily armed camps whose every difference produced a diplomatic crisis and a new test of strength. It failed entirely when the conflicting forces of European nationalism, imperialism, and militarism produced the final crisis of 1914, and "peace hung upon the mercy of an accident." Though many invitations were issued to have the Austro-Serbian controversy submitted to an international conference, the leading antagonists on each side, Germany and Russia, both feared that their acceptance would be interpreted as signs of weakness and irresolution. They rejected further negotiation, and instead ordered military mobilization; and their people cheered as military steps were taken that political action could not recall. Thus, the European powers were rapidly propelled into World War I. "The lamps are going out all over Europe," said Sir Edward Grey, the British Foreign Secretary, "we shall not see them lit again in our lifetime."

World War I. Although both sides had chosen to submit their differences to the arbitrament of force, neither governments nor their peoples were prepared for the holocaust that was to follow. Military leaders on both sides had planned short campaigns to produce early and decisive victories, but the conflict degenerated into one of attrition and virtual stalemate until the United States joined the Allies in 1917 and finally tipped the scales in their favor. In a war lasting over four years, involving much of the world, and nearly total in character, the costs in human life and wealth were staggering. Some sixty-five million troops were mobilized for military service; nine million were killed, and another twenty-two million were wounded. The conduct of hostilities produced even more civilian deaths, and some ten million refugees. The material costs of munitions, supplies, property losses, and diverted production were estimated for all belligerents to reach over $300,000,000,000—

some ten times the total national income of the United States in 1914. Still further, lasting wounds—psychological as well as physical—that could not be counted nor valued monetarily were left on the European continent.

Long before the war came to a conclusion, therefore, demands were widespread in the Allied countries for the creation of some kind of permanent international organization that could make a recurrence of such a conflict impossible. Indeed, it seemed to many that only such an achievement could possibly justify the four years' drain on blood and treasure; thus the Allied governments called forth the final efforts of their citizens with an appeal that they could now win "the war to end war."

The League of Nations Covenant. The Paris Peace Conference of 1919 had the twofold task of arranging peace terms for the defeated Central Powers, and preparing the Covenant, or constitution, of the League of Nations. Though many diplomatic figures participated in the conference, the creation of the League was mainly the work of Anglo-American political leaders, and of these Woodrow Wilson exerted the greatest influence. He had advocated the idea of a league in his Fourteen Points in 1918, and insisted on making the Covenant a part of the peace treaties ending the war. The drafting of the Covenant was accomplished early in 1919, and the signing of the Versailles treaty in June of that year joined together in permanent association the thirty-odd countries—excepting the United States, which failed to ratify it—that had been at war with Germany. Since the League aimed at universal membership, additional states were invited to accede to the Covenant, and forty-two nations were represented at its first meeting in 1920. Later, the defeated states were admitted (Germany in 1926), and by 1935 the League reached a membership of sixty-three, though still without an isolationist-minded United States. But quite as important as the effort to make the League a universal organization was the attempt to create, within a single framework, a piece of machinery sufficient to deal with virtually every aspect of public international affairs. This comprehensiveness of the League's scope and organization established it as the first real experiment with international government.

The League was to carry out three principal purposes: first, to promote international co-operation generally, through such functions as the registration of treaties, encouragement of economic and social advancement, protection of national minorities and nonself-governing peoples, and co-ordination of the work of international bureaus and technical commissions; second, to be responsible for carrying out some of the provisions of the peace treaties, such as the supervision of the Saar and of Danzig; and third, to achieve "international peace and security." Because the greatest motivating force behind the creation of the League was the desire to prevent war, this last objective was considered by all odds the most important, and the League's success would be measured largely by its effectiveness in maintaining peace.

The League was intended to undertake both indirect and direct approaches to the problem of war. Generally, occasions for war were to be minimized by the more extensive promotion of international co-operation, the practice of "open diplomacy," the review and revision of treaties that might endanger the peace, the achievement of a scheme of armaments limitation, and the employment of peaceful means for the settlement of international disputes. Article 10 of the Covenant obligated members of the League "to respect and preserve as against external aggression the territorial integrity and existing political independence of all members of the League." The most novel feature of the Covenant's approach to the problem of war was found in Article 16, which provided for the collective coercion of a Covenant-breaking state. The League's security system did not go so far as to declare war illegal, but provided that if a state resorted to war in disregard of certain Covenant obligations to attempt a peaceful settlement, members of the League would subject it to economic sanctions by breaking off all commercial and financial relations with the offending state. The language of the Covenant suggested that application of such an economic boycott would be automatic, though this was not to be the case in practice. Finally, Article 16 also anticipated the possibility of collective military sanctions, to be recommended by the Council, though it made no specific provision for them, and none was ever attempted.

The League Organs. The machinery of the League to carry out its purposes was truly something "new under the sun," though its antecedents are clearly recognizable in the forms of international organization developed during the nineteenth century. The Assembly, very much like an annual international conference, was constituted as a representative body in which each member had one vote. It was given power to deal with any matter "within the sphere of action of the League or affecting the peace of the world," and specifically, to admit new members, control the League's budget, and advise upon the reconsideration of treaties. This body was obliged to adopt its decisions by unanimous vote, except for procedural questions, which required only a two-thirds majority. Generally, the Assembly was intended to serve as a sounding board for world opinion, a center for international co-operation, and a forum for the discussion of international problems where smaller states might be heard.

The Council resembled the earlier Concert of Europe, as well as the various inter-Allied councils of World War I. It was a small body in which the major powers enjoyed predominance and possessed permanent seats; during the League's existence it varied in size from eight to fourteen members, with nonpermanent seats rotated among the smaller states elected by the Assembly. The Council met at least four times a year and had the same general scope of authority as the Assembly, as well as such special functions as supervising mandated territories, formulating plans for disarmament, convening in case of war or threat of war, conciliating disputes, and recommending enforcement actions. The rule of unanimity applied to all Council decisions so that, in effect, each member had a "veto." Although the Council was in no sense an international executive, it was the organ within which major power authority was concentrated, and in practice provided the center wherein the principal world statesmen could exert leadership.

The League's third principal organ—and its only truly international one—the Secretariat, was a more elaborate version of the international bureau, and constituted a permanent international civil service. Headed by a Secretary-General, the Secretariat's staff was responsible for providing secretarial services for the Assembly and Council, registering treaties, preparing for conferences, and maintaining the archives, library, public relations, and translation services. The Secretariat was located at League headquarters in Geneva; its six hundred officials and employees were recruited from over forty different countries. It served as a clearinghouse of information on world problems, the center for the co-ordination of League activities, and, as the one permanently organized institution of the League, became the repository of accumulated experience and continuity in international administration.

The League system was rounded out by several related agencies. These included the Permanent Court of International Justice, with fifteen judges, the first truly international court for formal adjudication of legal disputes between states; the International Labor Organization, to improve working conditions and promote social welfare legislation; and a variety of agencies to perform specialized functions, such as the Economic and Financial Organization, Health Organization, Institute of Intellectual Co-operation, and so forth.

The League Evaluated. Any evaluation of the League presents difficulties, if only because conclusions about its effectiveness and accomplishment tend to vary with the expectations of the evaluator. Since the League did not prevent World War II, and is no longer in existence, the conclusion that it was a failure might seem inescapable. We do better, however, to take a closer look at what the League was, what it was expected to do, and the conditions under which it was obliged to seek its objectives.

The League was the first experiment with a general international organization, it must be emphasized, brought into operation without precedent to guide it, without the whole-hearted determination of the major powers to support it, and without any general realization that only a new sense of international community-mindedness could maintain it. It was not remotely a world-state, not a supranational authority, nor even an alliance; rather, it was a loose association of states, all continuing to possess undiminished sovereign powers and virtually unlimited freedom of action, so far as their obligations to the League were concerned. It is unreasonable, therefore, as well as unrealistic, to expect the League to have worked some kind of revolution in the nature and conduct of international relations, much less to have reversed all of the tendencies of the nation-state system, within the short period of only twenty years.

League Achievements. In examining the League's record in terms of the purposes set for it, we find first of all that it enjoyed a mixed but promising success in promoting international co-operation. Membership in the League was voluntary, and though every important state but the United States found it advantageous to be a member of the League at some time, a number of states were members only part of the time. But the League always lacked the membership of some of the major powers. Aside from the United States, the Soviet Union did not become a member until after Germany withdrew; subsequently Japan and Italy withdrew also. By the outbreak of World War II, even so, there were still forty-eight members. This failure to achieve universality of membership always obstructed the development of a sense of corporate responsibility for international problems. Indeed, truly close co-operation of the wartime Allies, which had initially sustained the League movement, was largely dissipated even before the League began to function in 1920. But beyond question the League did achieve considerable successes in the technical, health, financial, social, and humanitarian fields. Operating on an annual budget that never exceeded seven million dollars, it proved to be a generally efficient and economical means for attacking such international problems. The achievements in this category were rarely spectacular, but they should not be overlooked.

The League's record in the administration of certain peace treaty terms was generally unexceptionable. It arranged for effective conduct of the specified plebiscites, administration of the Saar and Danzig, and achieved some gains for the inhabitants of the mandated areas. Although the League had no responsibility for the terms of the peace treaties of 1919–1920, it was inevitably identified with these settlements to some degree, particularly in the defeated countries. It increasingly lost prestige, therefore, as respect for the treaty settlements declined. Its authorization to re-examine treaties and effect a measure of "peaceful change" proved to be entirely a dead letter. Thus, the partial revision of some treaties was obtained outside the League in ways that clearly lessened esteem for it.

League Failures. In its ability to restrain aggression and prevent war, however, the League was least effective. It never succeeded in organizing a system of collective security that all, or even most, of its members would support. Some states insisted that no security system could be effective unless there were a general reduction of armaments; but other states were equally insistent that they could not discuss disarmament until they felt reasonably secure! No other problem occupied so much League time and produced such meager results. Though it dealt with over sixty international disputes, and resolved or saw resolved some thirty-five of them peaceably, these successes were mostly with the smaller states. When the major powers were concerned, success was much more problematical. The kinds of difficulties the League was to encounter were displayed as early as 1923, when both Poland and Italy flouted League authority; other instances of great power intransigence were soon to follow. But most disastrous to the whole League system was the widespread mushrooming of dictatorship throughout postwar Europe, and the accompanying deterioration of peaceful relations among European states.

Thus, the League was not faced merely with the problem of resolving honest differences or misunderstandings between states; rather, it was confronted with a series of coldly calculated acts of aggression by states bent upon revenge, expansion, and the ruthless destruction of their chosen victims. After its depredations in Manchuria, Japan refused to accept League condemnation as an aggressor, and withdrew its membership in 1933. The crisis for the League came when Italy invaded Ethiopia in 1935, and defied both attempts to conciliate the dispute and the application of economic sanctions imposed upon it for going to war in disregard of the Covenant. Sterner and longer-continued measures might ultimately have been effective against a state as vulnerable as Italy, but the League's leadership remained cautious. With an isolationist United States, an unco-operative Soviet Union, and a hostile Germany all on the sidelines, neither Great Britain nor France was willing to risk further steps that might draw the retaliatory military action Italy threatened. So, the first major attempt to apply economic sanctions to enforce a League decision and maintain collective security against an aggressor ended in failure. League machinery was not employed to obstruct later Italian and German intervention in the Spanish civil war, nor German aggressions upon Austria, Czechoslovakia, and Poland, the last launching World War II in 1939. The expulsion from the League of the Soviet Union in December of that year for its attack on Finland was only an anticlimactic gesture of disapproval.

These situations recall the words of Hobbes, from several centuries earlier, that "Covenants without the sword are but words." It has indeed been frequently asserted that, since the League was unable to exercise compulsory jurisdiction over disputes and lacked means to enforce its decisions, its ineffectiveness was inevitable. The solution to the League's weakness, it was often suggested, was to put "teeth" in the Covenant; then it could compel states to keep the peace, and coerce any that did not. A great deal of criticism has also been visited upon France and Great Britain which, after the defection of the United States, were left to organize and lead the League, and sometimes have been charged with greater responsibility for the League's collapse than the Axis states which unleashed the hostilities that destroyed it. Was the League's debacle the result of defective machinery or inadequate leadership?

To be sure, both of these left something to be desired. The machinery of the League was slow, formal, and cumbersome; but the states that organized the League had not intended for it to be otherwise. Likewise, League members had no intention of giving it compulsory means to settle disputes and effect its decisions. If these states let themselves be bluffed by Italy in 1935, when they might have brought Mussolini's armies to a halt, they faced an actual superiority of power in the cases of Germany and Japan, as the military developments of 1939–1941 clearly demonstrated. What must be emphasized is that the League of Nations was not a source or center of power itself; its Covenant provided only the machinery through which collective action could be organized—but machinery is not operative in and of itself. Most fundamentally, what was lacking was a general inclination to employ the League as the common means by which all aggression would be resisted. The failure of the League, then, was really the failure of the major powers: of Germany, Italy, and Japan, which chose to achieve their national aims by force and violence; of Britain, France, and the United States, which preferred taking individual views of what acts of aggression directly threatened their security and failed to co-operate to defend it soon enough; and of the Soviet Union, which sought to exploit the failures on both sides. Thus it was that in 1939, the world was confronted with its second global war of the century—a war that could scarcely be put down this time to inadvertence, or to lack of an organization available to settle international disputes. Rather, the moral and material concern to prevent war was not equally shared throughout the international community; this atmosphere was fatal to the League.

World War II. World War II was an even greater disaster than World War I. It lasted for nearly six years; it involved virtually all of the important states of the world; in life and property it was the most destructive conflict in history. Some fourteen million combatants were killed, another thirty-one million were wounded, and twenty-seven million were listed as prisoners of war or missing. Over thirty million civilians lost their lives, and seventy-five million were uprooted from their homes to become "displaced persons." It will probably never be known what the total material losses were; one estimate has put the costs at well beyond $1,000,000,000,000! The United States has listed its share alone at over 330 billion dollars—or more than the total for all belligerents in World War I, and the Soviet Union has claimed even greater costs. Alongside such figures as these must be placed incalculable but very real costs in human anguish and despair; vast destruction of mutual confidence, good will, and creativeness; and tensions and maladjustments from which the world will not soon recover.

III. *The* UNITED NATIONS

The outbreak of war in 1939 meant the effective end of the League of Nations, but so great was the popular impact of the "League idea" that the Allied powers made re-creation of a general international organization one of their principal war aims. The matter was given attention as early as the Atlantic Conference in mid-1941, and the principles of the Atlantic Charter, which spoke of "the establishment of a wider and permanent system of general security," were affirmed by the Declaration of the United Nations, January 1, 1942, signed by twenty-six states resisting the Axis powers. Altogether, forty-seven states had acceded to the Declaration by 1945, when this wartime alliance could turn to the constructive problems of creating a new international association.

The United Nations Charter. The international conference to draft the Charter of the United Nations, convening at San Francisco, April 25, 1945, met in a different atmosphere from that of Paris in 1919 when the League Covenant was framed. Although an end to the war now seemed in sight, neither Germany nor Japan had yet surrendered; it was widely hoped, therefore, that the United Nations alliance co-operating for a military victory would help to ensure similar co-operation in the creation of a new general international organization, and that the states associated against a common enemy would be much more inclined to recognize the necessity of making such an organization a strong and effective one. Further, the conference was not obliged to undertake the pioneering efforts that the creators of the League faced in 1919. It was now possible to draw on some twenty years' experience with the League, advice of officials who had served with it, and consultations of those who had carefully studied its operations. Certainly, there was no lack of suggestions, official and unofficial, as to what inadequacies of the League ought to be overcome. The conference had, in addition, the extensive Dumbarton Oaks proposals—a blueprint for the new organization which the major powers had agreed would be the basis for discussion—as well as decisions reached by international agreement on several fundamental aspects of the new organization. Against this background, then, representatives of fifty nations were able to complete their work in two months, and the approved Charter was signed on June 26, 1945.

Despite the attitude of many governments that the new organization would have to improve upon, as well as replace, the League of Nations, the United Nations organization as established proved to be modeled closely upon its predecessor. Its announced purposes also followed those of the League: to maintain international peace and security; to develop friendly relations among nations; to co-operate in solving international problems of an economic, cultural, or humanitarian character; and to be a center for harmonizing the actions of nations in attaining these ends. The Charter indicated further that the organization was based on the principle of the "sovereign equality" of its members, and was not to intervene in "matters essentially within the domestic jurisdiction of any state"; that members would settle their international disputes by peaceful means, refraining from the threat or use of force; and that members would fulfill their Charter obligations in good faith, giving "every assistance" in any action taken in acordance with the Charter.

To augment the original United Nations membership, the Charter provides that other "peace-loving" states may be admitted if in the judgment of the organization they are able and willing to carry out membership obligations. New members are admitted by a two-thirds vote of the General Assembly, upon the recommendation of the Security Council—so that membership nominations are subject to major power "veto." The Charter does not mention any right to withdraw from the organization, though in the same manner as states are admitted, the Charter provides, they may be suspended or expelled.

The General Assembly. One already familiar with the structure of the League will not find that of the United Nations strikingly different. The General Assembly is composed of all members, with each state possessing one vote. It is authorized broadly to discuss and make "recommendations" on any matters within the scope of the Charter, general principles of co-operation, and the maintenance of international peace and security. It receives reports from and supervises other UN organs, initiates studies, approves the budget, apportions expenses, admits new members, and has duties in connection with constituting the membership of the several councils, as well as other miscellaneous functions. The General Assembly decides "important questions" by a two-thirds vote, others by a majority, and meets at least once annually.

The Security Council. In the belief that the League Council had more responsibilities than it was able to perform effectively, the framers of the Charter provided for three councils in the United Nations organization. The most important is, of course, the Security Council, composed of five permanent members (the United States, the United Kingdom, the Soviet Union, France, and China), and six nonpermanent members, elected by the General Assembly for two-year terms. Organized to function continuously, the Security Council is given primary responsibility for the problem of peace and security. Its principal functions are to investigate any situation or dispute likely to endanger peace, intervene to recommend means of settling it, and, in the event of aggression, decide on measures to restore peace and security. In recognition of their special responsibilities and interests, the five major powers not only enjoy permanent seats in the Security Council, but also a privileged vote, or "veto." This results from the requirement that Security Council decisions on procedural questions may be made by the affirmative vote of any seven members; an affirmative vote on substantive questions, however, must also include the concurring votes of all five permanent members. This means that any one of the major powers casting a negative vote on a substantive question may prevent action.

The Economic and Social Council. As the organization to be especially concerned with human welfare, the Charter provides for the Economic and Social Council. It is composed of eighteen members, elected for three-year overlapping terms by the General Assembly. Each member has one vote, and decisions are taken by a majority. The Council holds two meetings a year, lasting about one month. The Charter gives it responsibility for promoting higher standards of living, full employment, cultural co-operation, and human rights. The Council undertakes its functions by recommendations to the United Nations members, preparing reports, drafting conventions, calling conferences, and through liaison with the "specialized agencies."

The Trusteeship Council. Another organ of the United Nations system is the Trusteeship Council, created to replace the League's Mandate Commission for the supervision of the trust territories. The trusteeship system applies to three types of territories: those that are former League mandates; those taken from the Axis states at the end of World War II; and, those voluntarily placed under the system by states responsible for their administration. The Council does not have a fixed number of members. The Charter stipulates that its membership shall be composed of those members administering trust territories, the powers having permanent seats on the Security Council which are not trustees, and other states elected by the General Assembly to give an equal balance of representation between administering and nonadministering states.

The Trusteeship Council meets at least once a year; each member has one vote, and there are no "vetoes," with decisions taken by a simple majority. Acting under the authority of the General Assembly, the Council collects information, receives reports, examines petitions with respect to the trust territories, and may send visiting missions to them. It may also make recommendations, not only to the General Assembly, but directly to the administering authorities. Originally, eleven areas were put under trusteeship; most of these have now achieved independent statehood.

The Secretariat. The organ, above all others, which gives continuity and cohesion to the United Nations is the Secretariat. As in the League system, provision is made for an international civil service to perform the secretarial functions for the whole system of international government. The Secretariat is composed of the Secretary-General, appointed by the General Assembly on the nomination of the Security Council, and the staff appointed by him under regulations determined by the General Assembly. The several thousand officials and employees are recruited internationally on as wide a geographic basis as possible. Protection of the international character of the Secretary-General and his staff is provided by the stipulations that they may not seek or receive instructions from any government or any other authority outside the organization, and member states agree to respect their status.

The Secretary-General is the chief administrative officer of the United Nations, and is responsible for directing the performance of all Secretariat functions, such as providing research, editorial, interpreting, legal, budgeting, and liaison services. Although the Secretary-General assists at meetings of the General Assembly and the three Councils, he is intended to be more than an administrative officer, and to provide much more positive leadership than was permitted to this office under the League system. The Charter authorizes him to exercise certain political functions in the operation and co-ordination of the various organs, including that of bringing to the attention of the Security Council any matter threatening international peace and security. The first Secretary-General, Trygve Lie, of Norway, was given a five-year term of office, later extended for three more years; in 1953, Dag Hammarskjöld, of Sweden, was appointed as his successor, and received a further five-year term in 1958. Hammarskjöld's untimely death in 1961, while on a UN mission, led to the appointment of U Thant of Burma; he was elected to a full four-year term in 1962.

The International Court of Justice. The principal judicial organ of the United Nations is the International Court of Justice. Modeled closely upon the earlier Permanent Court of International Justice, it is composed of fifteen judges, elected for nine-year terms by the General Assembly and the Security Council. The Court may render judgments in legal disputes between states where the parties agree to adjudication, either in advance or in a particular case, and may deliver advisory opinions to organs of the United Nations and the specialized agencies. The Court is located at the Hague, and is permanently in session. It decides cases submitted to it in accordance with the rules of international law, and reaches its conclusions by majority vote. The members of the UN accept the principle that the decisions of the court are binding upon the parties.

The Specialized Agencies. A number of independent technical and expert bodies, though they are not United Nations organs, are recognized as related agencies rounding out the whole system. Known as the "specialized agencies," these fourteen bodies have their own treaty statute, staff, budget, and authority, and perform functions in the economic, cultural, educational, and health fields. They are not created by the Charter, but are "brought into relationship" with the UN, and help to effect its objectives. The specialized agencies include the International Labor Organization (ILO), Universal Postal Union (UPU), Educational, Scientific, and Cultural Organization (UNESCO), World Health Organization (WHO), International Bank for Reconstruction and Development (IBRD), Food and Agriculture Organization (FAO), International Civil Aviation Organization (ICAO), and International Atomic Energy Agency (IAEA), among others.

The United Nations Security System. Inevitably, one of the most significant aspects of the United Nations Charter is its arrangement for the maintenance of international peace and security. Fundamentally, the framers of the United Nations sought to create a tighter and more elaborate system of "collective security" than was provided by the League Covenant. The Charter establishes the general obligation, therefore, that all members shall settle their disputes by peaceful means, and that they shall refrain from the threat or use of force against the territorial integrity or political independence of any state.

The Charter also assumes that the world is imperfect, however, and that the foregoing obligations will not always be self-enforced. So the Security Council is given primary responsibility and special powers, as we have seen, for maintaining international peace and security, and the members agree to accept and carry out Security Council decisions. Under the terms of Chapter VI of the Charter, which deals with the pacific settlement of disputes, parties to a dispute are obligated, first of all, to seek a noncoercive solution to it by means of their own choice. The Security Council is further empowered to investigate any dispute or situation to determine if it is likely to endanger international peace and security; it may then call on the parties to settle their dispute peacefully, and it may recommend methods for its adjustment. If the parties still fail to settle their dispute, they are obligated to refer it to the Security Council, which may again recommend procedures or terms of settlement.

If these procedures fail, the Charter then provides, in Chapter VII, for enforcement actions. Here the Security Council is authorized to determine the existence of any threat to peace, breach of the peace, or act of aggression, and decide what measures shall be taken to maintain or restore peace. These may be measures short of force, such as the "complete or partial interruption of economic relations, and of rail, sea, air, postal, telegraphic, radio, and other means of communication, and the severance of diplomatic relations"; or the Security Council may decide on action by means of air, sea, or land forces. United Nations members, according to the Charter, undertake to make armed forces available to the Security Council by special agreement. The Charter also provides, finally, for the establishment of a Military Staff Committee to advise and assist the Security Council, and to command the international forces placed at the Council's disposal.

Comparing, now, the League Covenant and the United Nations Charter systems for the maintenance of peace, we can see some marked differences. The Charter more broadly forbids the "use of force" against the territorial integrity or political independence of another state to prevent possible recourse to undeclared war. It provides that the Security Council, and not each individual state, shall determine threats to the peace and enforcement measures, and all members are obligated by such a decision. The Charter also obliges members to supply armed forces to the United Nations, and in other ways to improve upon the weaker League machinery for collective action. But though it is clear that the framers of the Charter sought to avoid some of the shortcomings of the Covenant, they left many arrangements unaltered in principle, indicating that most states were still unwilling to accept radically new limitations upon their freedom of action.

The whole system of the Charter does assume, however, that the major powers will settle their own disputes. It does not give the Security Council any power to enforce a settlement upon disputing states under Chapter VI, though the Council may take enforcement action under Chapter VII in the event of a threat to the peace. But here the power of the Security Council is subject to the veto, which has proved to be a large obstacle to effective action, for each of the major powers may not only avoid taking action itself, but prevent the others from acting. Further, the agreements to make available standing armed forces for the United Nations, which the Charter anticipated, have never been made. War is still not declared unequivocally illegal, for a state is recognized as retaining "the inherent right of individual or collective self-defense" if an armed attack is made upon it. Finally, the United Nations is forbidden "to intervene in matters which are essentially within the domestic jurisdiction of any state." It should be obvious, therefore, from the barest outline of its arrangements, that the Charter provides no complete solution to the problem of putting "teeth" into a security system, and ensuring a certain collective defense of all states.

The United Nations Evaluated. A full and fair evaluation of the United Nations would require, of course, the detailed consideration of all its operations for a number of years, to an extent not possible here. Further, we cannot close the books on the United Nations, as we have for the League of Nations; the former is still in operation, an evolving and developing concern, and no observer can know what its future will be. Only some tentative conclusions, therefore, can be made.

Certainly, the United Nations organization got under way with some advantages not enjoyed by the League: it began with the membership of all the major powers, including the United States and the Soviet Union; it could take advantage of some twenty years of League experience, precedents, and trained officials, and thus did not have to blaze an entirely new trail in international organization; and it possessed a much greater degree of popular support, arising out of the widespread belief that international co-operation was now vitally necessary if mankind were not to be led to even greater acts of self-destruction than those of World War II. But it could scarcely be maintained that the United Nations was bound to be more successful than the League, immediately or eventually.

Once again, only a loose international association of states, based upon the recognition of their "sovereign independence," had been brought into existence. The United Nations could not begin its operations where the League left off, because many serious new problems had to be faced and procedures established; the world-wide dislocations produced by World War II raised appalling difficulties. The tendency, indeed, to thrust upon the United Nations a much greater variety of functions, and so burden the organization with such extensive responsibilities, brought many warnings against overenthusiasm about its potentialities. As the Australian delegate to the San Francisco Conference, Mr. Herbert Evatt, warned, the United Nations must beware of acquiring "more harness than horse." Still worse, no major peace settlements, constituting a viable status quo, accompanied the creation of the United Nations. The situation prevailing when the Charter was adopted was a military one, and was not thereafter regularized diplomatically by agreement of all states concerned. Thus the new peace organization was really provided with no peace to maintain! Perhaps worst of all, the expected mutuality of trust and fundamental agreement between the major powers, which was to be the foundation of the new system, never materialized. With the end of hostilities in World War II, differences between the United States and the Soviet Union pyramided so rapidly to the open breach between them that no machinery seemed capable of resolving the East-West schism. The United Nations became itself one of the battlegrounds of the cold war.

Some United Nations Accomplishments. To be sure, a large part of the work of the United Nations has been in the area of economic, cultural, and social work, arising not only out of postwar reconstruction needs, and motives of simple humanitarianism as well as of national self-interest, but in the effort to create the kind of world conditions that many thought would provide a substantial foundation for world stability and peace. The various United Nations organs and the specialized agencies have, therefore, sought to undertake such activities as relocation of displaced persons, increase of food production, control of disease, reduction of illiteracy, provision of capital and technical knowledge for backward and undeveloped areas, aid to children, international definition of human rights, and so on. This realm of activity has been called "the UN that nobody knows," for these constructive if undramatic programs generally attract little popular attention. Yet the Expanded Technical Assistance Program and the Special Fund for Economic Development, to take two examples, already show how much can be done with modest resources, and how the UN and its related agencies may further develop a creative and positive thrust. Of course, international programs are not automatically conceived in wisdom, free of duplication of effort, and always certain to maximize each state's own effort and responsibility. But in the main, the UN's work has been devoted to matters of general concern, amenable to solution only by co-operative international action. Clearly, the UN has already done much that, if unspectacular, is worthwhile and even necessary to the mitigation of world tensions and the advancement of human progress.

Beyond the areas of general co-operation and technical assistance, the United Nations has provided a world forum where contact between East and West continues to be possible, and where states unattached to the groups of contending powers can exert some ameliorating influence. Large and small states alike find advantages in the opportunity for simultaneous negotiation with many governments. This international assemblage of states is, of course, sometimes used for the dissemination of propaganda, but this practice is not confined to one country or one side alone. That membership in the UN is valued, and as something more than a "status symbol," is evidenced by the eagerness with which new states seek entrance to it. Even the Soviet Union, so often negative in its attitude to the organization, has not been inclined to withdraw and leave the field to its adversaries. On balance, then, the UN does provide a center where world diplomacy may be conducted, and under more favorable circumstances which could yet arise, might come to have a very great significance.

Of high importance are the developments surrounding the great crises in which the United Nations has intervened. At a time when it seemed the UN system might be falling into the kind of desuetude that characterized the League after its failure to halt the Italian aggression against Ethiopia, it gained new esteem from its action following the attack of the North Korean Communist forces on the Republic of Korea, in June, 1950. Here the United Nations took the strongest action in its history, and with a speed that was scarcely anticipated. This dramatic display of how effective an enforcement action could be was undoubtedly the consequence of a number of factors, some of which would not necessarily always be present, such as the self-chosen absence of the Soviet delegate to the Security Council, the presence of large American armed forces in Japan, and a resolute President Truman determined to respond with military power to this act of aggression. Whether the ultimate stalemate and armistice achieved in Korea, after bitter fighting and prolonged negotiations, was the kind of a solution the UN should have finally accepted is a question that has been much debated. But the UN enforcement action met its minimum objectives of containing and throwing back the attack on the Korean Republic, avoided an unlimited war over the issue, and demonstrated that, through international resistance, aggressors can be forced to pay a higher price than the possible benefits are worth. As a test of UN effectiveness, this experience can scarcely be conclusive, of course, but the organization did respond to the most serious overt challenge that has confronted it.

If the United Nations has not been equally resolute or effective in all controversies, it has at least helped to prevent a number of disputes from becoming a serious threat to international peace. An important precedent was set when it won a "cease fire" at Suez in 1956 and established the UN Emergency Force (UNEF) to act as a buffer between Israel and Egypt. Still another was added in 1960 when the UN Congo Force (ONUC) separated warring local elements, forestalled possible major power intervention, and salvaged the disintegrating governmental machinery and services in that troubled African state. It was followed in 1964 when the Security Council authorized the stationing of a UN Peace-Keeping Force in Cyprus (UNFICYP). The effectiveness of UN intervention in any particular situation still depends on a number of contingencies, including the mood of its membership, but that there can be a "UN presence" as a force to be reckoned with at international danger points is now a fact of international life.

Finally, the United Nations has shown itself capable of growth, and adaptation to changing international conditions. It seems clear that any successful system of political institutions must possess sufficient flexibility to adjust to unforeseen circumstances and meet newly arising needs. Naturally, not all of the changes in the UN system—as it was envisaged by the Charter—have clearly worked to its strengthening and improvement. If the Security Council has recovered somewhat from its near paralysis during the height of the cold war, the veto power still causes a decline in reliance on that organ, in the number of its meetings, and the significance of its agenda. This development has tended to increase the importance of the General Assembly which, as its membership has swelled far beyond a hundred states, is a much more "democratized" body. Even if the many small new states in it are not saints, their behavior and judgment do not appear notably inferior to those of the major powers. Other organs have had indifferent success: the International Court of Justice averages only one case a year, largely because states seek other methods of settling disputes. The Economic and Social Council has produced little in the way of quick results, mainly because states have shown such small interest in the near-utopian objectives set for it. The Trusteeship Council is in decline, but obviously because the transfer of most of the territories to independent statehood properly puts it out of business. At the same time, the specialized agencies, dividing responsibilities on a functional basis, have definitely flourished and expanded because they have met real international needs. Equally noteworthy, the Secretariat has gained in stature, and the Secretary-General has come closer to becoming an international executive, in an international organization with a life of its own, than might have been expected two decades ago.

Some United Nations Shortcomings. On the other hand, the United Nations organization displays some obvious shortcomings and weaknesses, and nothing is gained by refusing to acknowledge them. These arise, mainly, in attempts to achieve its objectives of maintaining international peace and security. We have already mentioned the Charter's assumption of fundamental unity of purpose among the major powers. Not only has such unity not existed, but some insist that this assumption was so unwise and unfounded as to constitute a fatal defect in the system. The Security Council veto has been employed by the Soviet Union to an extent that has frequently paralyzed that organ, and despite extensive discussion of the "veto problem," it is probable that no change in the voting machinery would be capable of covering the breach between the communist and anti-communist powers. Even in the absence of East-West conflict, the veto will be a frequent problem as long as there are great powers in competition, and great powers always tend to compete. In 1960, the Soviet Union even sought to extend a veto power to the Secretariat by pressing for replacement of the independent Secretary-General by a "troika" or three-man directorate equally representing the western, communist, and neutralist blocs.

For a while it was possible to be optimistic about some arrangements called forth for the most part to tighten security measures and circumvent Soviet intransigence, such as the 1947 creation of the Interim Committee, or "Little Assembly," and the 1950 "Uniting for Peace" resolution, which were expected to permit the General Assembly to deal with peace problems and possible aggression when the Security Council was deadlocked. But the growth in size of the General Assembly has made it more and more difficult to construct effective majorities in that body, and it may find itself increasingly seized with the paralysis affecting the Security Council. "Recommendations" by the General Assembly in an enforcement action, as authorized by the "Uniting for Peace" resolution, are not a really satisfactory substitute for determined actions by the Security Council, with the power to move quickly and enforce its decisions. The General Assembly simply does not have the authority to oblige states to act, and its recommendations, often reduced to innocuous compromise in order to win broad support, may represent only a preponderance of votes, and not of power.

Further, states continue to evade stated Charter obligations, despite the solemn promises made when accepting their terms. The history of international events since 1945 makes it evident enough not to require description how widely the members of the United Nations have failed to meet their undertakings to observe the principles of international conduct laid down by the Charter—whether generally to settle all their disputes by peaceful means, refrain from the use of force, and co-operate for social and economical advancement, or more immediately, to implement the Charter by agreements for disarmament, place armed forces at the disposal of the Security Council, or even to meet their financial obligations to the organization, modest as these are. Some states have refused to pay specific assessments to support activities of which they disapprove; still others, including some original members, are badly in arrears. National interests as they are nationally interpreted continue to take precedence over international obligations. Thus, the blunt fact is that states continue to ignore rules and resolutions that do not please them, secure in the knowledge—if not in conscience—that they are not likely to be obliged to do otherwise.

Still further, it is once again clear that the creation of a general international organization, such as the United Nations, does not change the actual distribution of power internationally. Despite the attempts to improve upon the League system, the UN has not solved the problem of how to apply force effectively against a state engaged in aggression. In the absence of American military power, the Korean enforcement action could not have succeeded, and would not likely even have been undertaken. In other instances of aggression, the Soviet Union in Hungary, India in Goa, Communist China in India, and Indonesia in Dutch New Guinea, for example, no UN action was forthcoming. States are so far from feeling any real sense of security from the existence of the UN that they continue to multiply military alliances, a practice which, though authorized by the Charter, a really successful international organization would make unnecessary. Thus, the real core of power in the world today is provided not by the UN, but is found in the military alliances of various groups of states.

Finally, it is impossible to avoid the conclusion that once again, as with the League, the greatest difficulty is that the United Nations is not used as the principal means by which states seek to solve their international conflicts and problems. The criticism has become common that the UN may be weakened more from the neglect of its friends than the opposition of its enemies. In this respect, then, the western world, as well as the East, has a share of responsibility for its ineffectiveness. The UN has been used as a place to talk, and properly so, but it must also be a place in which to act, and here states draw away. Indeed, it sometimes seems as if the UN may end by drowning in its own sea of words. It must be obvious again that the structural features of the organization are not really the source of difficulty; no machinery can be effective if national political leaders lack the will and the skill to use it. On the closest inspection, therefore, the defects of the UN are those already inherent in our entire system of international relations. Small wonder that some have concluded that the kind of world conditions which would make the UN truly successful would also make it unnecessary!

We can only briefly summarize the situation for the present. The United Nations is neither success nor failure, but is a political institution, imperfect, and as such, developing under stress and strain in the only way it can become a viable and functioning organization. If it has not figured as importantly as was anticipated in the affairs of the major powers, it has won an even greater role in those of the new and smaller states, who see it as their international "town meeting," the most likely agency for their protection, and as a source of reasonably disinterested aid and assistance. Whereas, paradoxically, the original premise was that the major powers should intervene in all international disputes and disorders, world peace seems increasingly better secured if the major powers, especially the United States and the Soviet Union, are kept out of as many controversies as possible. Whether the UN may yet become a significant "third force" in world diplomacy will much depend on whether the cold war is eased or intensified, and whether members of this organization, following the precedent of several major powers, pursue a "rule-or-ruin" policy to impede UN actions wherever they cannot control them.

IV. *The* SEARCH *for* INTERNATIONAL ORDER

Our discussion so far should make it clear that the major international problem in the world today is how we may prevent war and maintain international order. Since we are now able to destroy much—perhaps, indeed, all—of human life in a new world war fought with thermonuclear weapons, the need for a solution to the problem could scarcely be more urgent. Not since the dawn of history has the survival of man and his civilization been made so uncertain, or of such widespread concern.

How then can international order be attained and conflict avoided? What kinds of solutions are proposed? Where can we look for fundamental principles of international organization to aid us? At the very least, it may be asked, what sort of policies in this respect should the United States promote as its contribution to this most perplexing question of our times? There is no end of answers, of course. Statesmen and scholars have advocated panaceas in a wide variety: national armaments, alliances, compulsory arbitration, general disarmament, pacifism, the "outlawry" of war, even unilateral disarmament, and so on, at one time or another. But none of these has proved to be fundamentally effective —except in quite limited circumstances—and none attracts much general support today. Most contemporary discussion, rather, tends to center on the relative merits of two other devices, "collective security" and "balance of power," both of which have long ceased to be new ideas, but still enjoy advocacy of their basic principles. We may examine these in turn.

COLLECTIVE SECURITY—THE "IDEALIST'S" SOLUTION

"Let it be said again," writes Andrew Martin, a distinguished authority on international law, in his *Collective Security: A Progress Report,* ". . . peace in our time depends upon the acceptance and the application of the principle of collective security. . . ." Many students of international affairs share this conclusion, and support it with extensive argument. In view of the unsatisfactory experience with the League and the United Nations, they propose that states simply must go forward to the adoption of further obligations which would create the universal collective security system they have shied from so far.

Collective Security Defined. Collective security is a political, rather than a legal, term and is used broadly to describe a system by which states, through an agency of international organization, jointly agree to use coercive means against any other state breaking the law, committing violence, or levying war upon them. The collective sanctions, or means employed to resist and coerce such an aggressor, may include reprisals, economic pressures, and even war itself. Because the advocates of such a system assume the possibility of a rational and moral international order, it has been labeled by some critics as a praiseworthy "ideal," but impossible of practical achievement, and hence an "idealist's" solution.

Assumptions. The idea of collective security rests upon the proposition that the totality of international power is superior to any national power. Since domestic governments enforce the peace and maintain order against violators of their domestic law, it is asserted, why should not states do the same thing through the framework of international government in the international sphere? States cannot assure their own security by unilateral efforts, but acting in concert the members of the international community can create a force so great that no one state could stand against it. The very existence of such an organization, furthermore, would substantially decrease the occasions when it would have to act, it is maintained, because international order would be strengthened by the fact that aggressive states would face the certainty of being met and resisted by overwhelming force. Hence, international violence would tend to disappear, because people and governments everywhere would be brought to realize its hopelessness.

What would be the concomitant principles of such a system? Clearly, an effective scheme of collective security assumes that war is a matter of moral concern and, indeed, of vital interest to the entire international community. There must, then, be a level of disarmament by individual states that will minimize their ability to undertake aggression or resist collective coercion. Also required is a method to define aggression and determine who is the aggressor in the event of conflict. Such a system will depend upon the availability of some sort of international police force, preferably of components already organized and designated, to apply military sanctions when the necessity arises. It will further exclude the right of a state to adopt a position of neutrality toward the belligerents in such a situation, for no state could be permitted to take an impartial stand against aggression. Finally, within the framework of international government, there must be substituted for resort to violence and war adequate means for making adjustments in the status quo when political, social, or economic inequalities and controversies appear. In a word, methods of "peaceful change" and "peaceful settlement of disputes" must be available. Thus, although the effecting of a scheme of collective security does not require a world government, it does necessitate an assured system of international organization.

Experience with Collective Security. We may now recall our discussion of the League of Nations and the United Nations, and our description of their arrangements and efforts to maintain the peace. These associations provide our only experience with collective security, since nothing of this sort was attempted before 1919. Both provide the machinery for the application of collective sanctions. That of the League was only partly developed, however, despite many proposals to extend it, and in the Italo-Ethiopian war the economic sanctions applied against Italy were not effective, as we have noted. The international tensions then prevailing did not favor co-operation of the major powers through the League; the member states were unwilling to embargo oil shipments to Italy in the face of Italian threats that such action would mean war; and the League could not assure their protection if an Italian attack were provoked. Finally, the League simply did not have the authority to use, or oblige its members to use, armed force against an aggressor. And, as acts of aggression spread, the League states backed away steadily from all proposals to create any such authority.

The United Nations Charter provides a more elaborate scheme to achieve collective security, as we have seen, but this has only been partly implemented, and suggests once again the unwillingness of states to accept in advance irrevocable commitments to act collectively in the employment of force. At the time of the Korean enforcement action, indeed, which was effected only by an unusual combination of circumstances, forty-four of the then sixty UN members declined to send combat troops or failed even to reply to the Secretary-General's request to come to the aid of the Korean Republic. And of the sixteen nations responding, only the United States, Great Britain, and Canada provided more than token forces. Whatever else may be said of this experience, then, it was scarcely *collective* action to the extent that the terms of the Charter anticipated, and it is perhaps even arguable whether it was a true instance of collective security, as it was achieved almost entirely by American military effort. Certainly no state can yet depend solely on the UN for its protection.

Criticisms of Collective Security. Under the circumstances, some students of international affairs insist that advocates of collective security are vainly seeking a system which logic brands unworkable, and experience demonstrates to be impossible. States have not achieved it, they say, because states would not—and still will not—accept its obligations. Essentially, they assert, such a system obliges states to renounce war in behalf of their own national interest, but expects them to fight in wars that do not concern, or are even contrary to, such national interest. Such disinterestedness in international affairs is most unlikely. Drawing on the experience we have mentioned above, they then insist that all states simply will not act in concert in such a crisis because all do not feel equally threatened at the same time.

They argue, further, that states are not persons, and that coercive measures in collective security enforcement do not consist of action by a group against one—in the analogy of domestic society—but of war against a whole nation of people. The nation in its very nature is bound to resist to the utmost. Thus, the people of the law-enforcing states who must wage the war are punished as much as those of the law-breaking state, at least until they achieve victory. The critics of the idea also maintain that no satisfactory method has been devised to determine in every controversy which is the state aggressed upon, and which is the aggressor, deserving of coercion and punishment; that collective security substitutes universal war for local war, because all states are obliged to participate in every controversy; and that states cannot reasonably be expected to disarm substantially until they can feel greater assurance of their security—hence, even a prerequisite of the system is almost impossible to achieve.

Finally, it is argued that the disparity between the military strength of the large and small states is so considerable that there is no practicable possibility any longer of an association of small states successfully coercing a major power. Obviously, no combination of states was powerful enough to deter Nazi German aggression in 1939, and only after a long and costly world war, drawing on the efforts of Great Britain, France, the Soviet Union, and the United States, among others, was Germany finally defeated. What combination of states, it may be asked, would challenge the United States, the Soviet Union, or other states armed with nuclear weapons? Further, aggression is not always committed by one state alone, so that the problem can become one of coercing a number of states. In view of all these considerations, the critics of the idea believe it cannot be successfully defended or seriously advocated.

BALANCE OF POWER—THE "REALIST'S" SOLUTION

". . . The balance of power and policies aiming at its preservation are not only inevitable but are an essential stabilizing factor in a society of sovereign nations," writes Professor Hans J. Morgenthau in his well-known and stimulating study, *Politics Among Nations*. Many of similar persuasion thus believe that the alternative to the inadequacies of collective security is a balance-of-power system to prevent violence and promote order.

Balance of Power Defined. The balance of power, in the international community, describes an equilibrium of forces sufficient to keep the peace among states by preventing one member from gaining a dangerous domination over the others. It may constitute a simple balance, as when there is an equilibrium between two states or groups of states; or the balance may be complex, with power distributed widely and fairly equally among a number of states. The advocates of balance of power, whether as a device or a policy to maintain international order, have sought to style it the "realist's" solution to the problem on the grounds that it makes proper allowance for the role of power in international affairs and, indeed, draws on the dynamics of power to accomplish its effect.

Assumptions. Advocates of the balance-of-power system begin with the same constructive goal as the supporters of collective security: the protection of national independence and maintenance of international peace. But they claim to avoid expectations of idealized state conduct and unreal disinterestedness. Their solution depends upon neither moral nor legal standards of action, and requires no formalized machinery of organization. It takes the form, rather, of a *modus vivendi,* with only a general understanding as its basis. The individual security of states can best be maintained, supporters assert, by giving full play to the inclination to combine in resistance to any state seeking to overthrow the international equilibrium. Thus, the balance of power can operate automatically, if not artificially restricted, because states that are threatened have a natural tendency to join together against a common enemy or aggressor.

It is further argued that, in the attempt to achieve and maintain the "condition" of balance of power, states will be led to adopt its goal as a leading principle of their "policy" in international affairs. If one state should undertake the dangerous aggrandizement of its power, it will be restrained peaceably if possible, but forcibly if necessary, by other states, and the balance will be restored by the defeat of the aggressor. War is therefore discouraged and likely to be prevented because attempts to disturb the status quo or to employ policies of aggression are made difficult and perilous. Further, states are encouraged to undertake a diplomacy of adjustment, and maintain peace by consultation, concessions, compensations, and bargaining. Finally, states are left free to be the judges of their own national interest.

Experience with the Balance of Power. Despite its recent fashionableness, the principle of the balance of power is quite old, and its practice even older. It was recognized in Europe as early as the fifteenth century in the relations of the Italian states. It led to the creation of coalitions which fought in the Thirty Years' War, and its principle was incorporated in the Peace of Westphalia which followed in 1648. The seventeenth century saw the idea further established in European politics. It was recognized in the Peace of Utrecht, in 1713, and revived again by the powers arrayed against Napoleon. The basis of the peace settlements ending the Napoleonic Wars, in 1815, was the establishment of a European equilibrium, which was increasingly extended on a worldwide basis in the decades following.

The work of the Congress of Vienna seemed to have vindicated the doctrine for the nineteenth century, yet at no time did the defeat of an aggressor actually discourage the next one. Far from providing a permanent solution to the problem of international order, the balance of power did not prevent a series of wars throughout the so-called "century of peace." And World War I came in 1914 as the culmination of attempts by Germany to overthrow the balance and establish a hegemony over the European continent. The Peace of Paris (1919–1920), based upon the principles of national self-determination, disarming the aggressors, and collective security, clearly constituted a discarding of the idea. But the failure of collective security after both World Wars I and II has led to revival of the idea of the balance, and new advocacy of its utility.

What conclusions, in short, may be drawn from historical experience with the balance of power? It does seem to have been most effective in demonstrating the merits claimed for it when power is widely and somewhat evenly divided among a number of fairly equal political units, so that a considerable variety of alignments and combinations of states is possible. A true fluidity of the international situation thus seems almost indispensable for its effective operation. The balance-of-power system has also been able notably to maintain international stability for short periods, thus perpetuating the multistate system and preserving the existence of small states which would otherwise be unable to defend themselves. But the existence of the balance has never completely discouraged the ambition of one or more states to overthrow it, or the anxiety of others to maintain it. Both sides are thus led to secure their ends by military alliance systems, rivalry between heavily armed camps, displays of force, successive crises beween the coalitions and, finally, general war in which few important states are able to avoid involvement.

Criticisms of the Balance of Power. After examining the extensive history of the balance of power—only briefly surveyed here—many students of international affairs insist that dependence upon it as a device to preserve world order can only be blindness in the face of facts. The advocates of such a principle, they say, far from having discovered how power can be controlled, are only pseudo-realists guilty of an incomplete analysis of international life. They point out that the balance-of-power system affords no fair representation or protection of the interests of all states—that it permits only the great powers to maneuver for their advantage, while the smaller states are used as pawns and buffers.

They assert, further, that the balance of power is at best a crude and tentative arrangement. It is always uncertain whether it has been truly established and how effectively the states comprising it will continue to sustain their existing positions. The dangerous risk is ever present that someone will miscalculate the situation and precipitate conflict. It is argued, as well, that it is even questionable whether states ever really seek the equilibrium so neatly assumed in theory; rather, they are more likely to strive for what inevitably seems more congenial to their national interest—a superiority of power in their own favor. And this step creates the very condition which balance of power is supposed to prevent: tampering with the balance, and a trial of strength producing war.

Finally, it is asserted that developments in the post-World War II era may have rendered the whole balance-of-power concept obsolete. The effects of World War II and the development of nuclear weapons by the United States and the Soviet Union reduced the number of major contenders in the power contest to two. This produced for some years a simple balance of power, but also an extremely dangerous and unstable international situation, reaching a crisis in the "eyeball to eyeball" confrontation over Cuban missile sites in 1962. If this event demonstrated the primary power of the United States, it showed clearly as well what little else stands between some world order and chaos. More recently the two great ideological blocs have begun to split apart. The world is thus no longer polarized about the two superpowers, and some new centers of power are emerging. But the result is scarcely balance or stability. Communist ambitions for expansion and aggrandizement have not been extinguished, and wars continue whether by means "hot" or "cold," conventional or unconventional. Further, full-scale nuclear war is still entirely within the realm of possibility. Of its probability, we shall have something to say at the end of this chapter.

V. *The* PROBLEM *of* WORLD AUTHORITY

Looking at the limited development and modest accomplishments of international organization, one recalls the remark of Victor Hugo, who was once asked what he thought of civilization. "Civilization?" he said, "It's a good idea. Someone ought to start it." Certainly it is clear that we have so far achieved only the most limited forms of anything that could be called international *government,* and nothing resembling a real world authority that might provide for the population of the globe the kind of peace and security that men claim, at all events, to be seeking. Ought we to try to start it?

It is a commonplace to observe that the League of Nations has failed, and that the United Nations has not yet, at least, succeeded. They have not produced effective systems of collective security, nor demonstrated that such systems are really practicable in the present world. No more, however, does it seem possible to rely on the operation of a balance of power. The coalitions of the "Triple Entente" versus the "Triple Alliance" in 1914, and of the "democracies" versus the "dictatorships" in 1939 were unable to prevent unleashing two total wars in the first half of the twentieth century; coalitions of the "West" against the "East" today seem hardly more promising for peace-keeping. Let us examine, then, some of the proposals that have been made to suggest possible ways of breaking with the past, and starting in new directions.

It is quite possible, of course, that no new directions exist; that the states of the world will continue directly upon their present course; that we shall move forward to World War III. On the other hand, there has been inevitable speculation upon the opportunities of some new departures in our world political arrangements that would carry us beyond the present level of international relations and achieve the establishment of some kind of world political authority. Several of these merit our consideration.

World Empire. One of the most obvious means by which a central world authority could be brought into existence is through the establishment by one state of a political hegemony over all others, and the creation of a world empire dominated by that state. Such an entity would constitute a kind of "superstate," with a single sovereignty, government, law, and citizenship, presumptively, and might achieve the complete merging of the present multistate system into a single whole. History offers some precedent for this possibility. The Roman empire, though not world-wide, extended partial control over the western world of its time—the Mediterranean rim and Europe. The Pax Romana which it made possible was as great a force for universal peace as man had then known. Even the Pax Britannica of the nineteenth century was acknowledged to be a force for law and order to a larger extent than any previously seen in the modern world. Still other efforts at wide imperial hegemony have been made by Alexander the Great, Genghis Khan, Napoleon, and Hitler, though all ultimately failed.

Could such an attempt succeed in the world today? It seems beyond argument that a single global state could not be brought into existence voluntarily by the acquiescence of existing states; it would have to be created by conquest and force. Yet it can scarcely be denied that the technological means for the establishment of world empire are within the reach of modern man. The whole apparatus of the modern police state—weapons of overwhelming power and destructiveness, rapid air transportation, radio communication, ubiquitous propaganda and censorship, and so on—have already demonstrated their effectiveness in the hands of authoritarian rulers to hold hundreds of millions of people in complete submission. Thus, there is no technological obstacle to the extension of such a system of control to the entire world. There are even those who would argue that a world rule is desirable, even if it must be achieved by the use of force. All that is needed is a state willing and able to create such an empire. Are there any so willing?

Those who advocate a world empire almost always envision its creation and control by their own state. Since virtually all states would forcibly resist domination by another, however—and some could put up a fairly effective resistance—it seems likely that such a world dominion could not be achieved except after long and bitter world-wide war, and what could be won in this way would not only create a most unpromising basis for political organization, but for its cost, might not even be worth having. It is difficult, further, to imagine that today any but the two great superpowers could marshal the necessary overwhelming strength for such an effort. Clearly, the United States is not a likely candidate to undertake such a war of conquest for world domination, a venture which would be wholly foreign to its historic national policies and objectives.

The Soviet Union and Communist China are another matter. We have ample testimony of expressed communist aims, at least, for world revolution and domination, and the communist technique of subversion and satellite control is well known. For the time being, however, the communist leaders seem not inclined to undertake a frontal assault on the rest of the world. Whether this is because other means for extending their hegemony—such as infiltration, subversion, economic competition, and civil war—seem more profitable, or whether, for the present, they judge their armed strength insufficient to insure success, or that differences among themselves are too serious, we can only guess. At all events, a communist attempt at world conquest would undoubtedly meet fierce resistance, in any future period now foreseen. If this, then, is the only avenue to world empire, we may conclude that it is a most unlikely solution to the problem of world order.

World Federation. A second approach proposes the creation of world authority through the union of existing states by federation. Federalism is a form of government wherein, essentially, a constitution divides political power between the central government and the governments of component units of the federation; the sphere of authority of each level of government is defined, and may not be altered by either alone; and both levels may exercise authority directly upon individuals. It permits the central government to deal with matters of general interest to the federation which require common action, and permits the governments of the component units to manage local matters. The federal system is well known, of course, exemplified in the political systems of Switzerland, the United States, Mexico, Canada, Australia, Germany, and, in form at least, in the Soviet Union. How would the principle apply in the establishment of world government?

Most proposals for world federation tend to follow many features of the American Constitution. They assume a central world government would be representative and democratic, composed of the usual three branches. Thus, there would be an executive agency to enforce world law and maintain order, a legislature to frame law and policy, and a world court with compulsory jurisdiction for the settlement of disputes. Advocates of world federalism all agree, as a minimum, on the necessity for sufficient coercive authority and monopoly of armaments to maintain peace; others, however, would go further, to provide such features as a common world citizenship, currency, free trade, a bill of rights, and so on, thus tilting the balance of political power in favor of the central government.

A number of organizations, some with eminent supporters, have at various times undertaken the promotion of this cause, particularly since World War II. Some would proceed to their chosen goal by revamping the United Nations Charter; others by making a completely fresh start and drafting a world constitution. Some believe that a modest degree of federal union would be at least a halfway house on the road to world government, while others plump for nothing short of a full-blown world state immediately. Several of the groups believe that a start could be made by the federation of even a few states, which would serve as a nucleus for the gradual extension of membership to all. Most advocates of the idea feel that however extreme their proposals may appear at first glance—and even if they are impractical for the present—they have at least the value of bringing the problem forward for discussion, and familiarizing people with the issues at stake.

Nevertheless, the project scarcely seems realizable in the political atmosphere pervading the world at present. No government has sought to promote it. There is even no private advocacy of the idea on the other side of the Iron Curtain, and communists oppose it as a "capitalist plot." Nationalists and superpatriots have as readily denounced it for its infringements on national independence and sovereignty, labeling it as the dream of "rootless cosmopolitans." Even among those willing to take a reasonably objective view of world federation, there are serious practical obstacles which cannot easily be dismissed. The ineluctable fact remains that few, if any, states are today prepared to enter such a political system, conceding, as they would have to, so much of their freedom of action—whether real or imaginary—to others. Democratic states do not relish the idea of joining in a world government well over half of whose people have had no experience of democracy. Those with relatively high standards of living are concerned that they would be reduced to the level of those much lower. It is even argued that the states of the world are by now far too disparate in power to make their federation practicable. The formal abolition of national sovereignty, for instance, would not necessarily abolish the power centers that exist in the world today. The superiority of manpower, natural resources, and industrial potential of the two great superpowers would still remain, in fact, and constitute factors of reality to be reckoned with, even if the United States and the Soviet Union voluntarily relinquished their legal expression in theory. Under all circumstances, then, the belief in the desirability or necessity of world federation is not widely enough shared to provide soon a basis for world political organization.

World Functional and Regional Integration. Despite the unpromising prospects for developing world authority by the creation of a world empire—which would be actively resisted—or by the creation of a world federation—which is simply being ignored—there is possible a third path, which already has advocates. It involves neither a predetermined scheme of action by one state, nor a blueprint of organization agreed upon by all. It is, indeed, little more than a method: the achievement of authority through the integration of lesser authorities, by gradual growth and development, along lines already discernible.

The supporters of this approach to world order reject extreme and sweeping solutions. They point out that stable and truly effective political structures are more like trees than houses; they are grown, rather than built. Thus, the sense of community among people fosters the creation of common institutions, and these in turn help to solidify and maintain the community. The central weakness of all proposals for the immediate creation of world government, in consequence, is simply that there is no world community upon which it could be constructed. There is, instead, an international community composed of many independent nation-states. And it is to the nation-state that men still give their highest loyalties, and within which there exists the commonality of cultural interests, moral standards, and patterns of political behavior that provide the strongest sense of identity among a group of people.

But these considerations, it is asserted, while they may explain the virtual impossibility of creating world government by an immediate and positive act, do not exclude the possibility for its development by the gradual integration of states along "functional" and "regional" lines. The process, in fact, is already underway; it may well be continued to much greater degrees. We have seen that during the nineteenth century states began to deal with common international problems through the creation of various sorts of international organization. Most of these were established not to deal with the larger issues of international politics but with specific problems in specific areas.

The practice has continued at an accelerated rate in the twentieth century, accompanying the development of the League of Nations and United Nations systems, so that the number of separate international agencies with particular responsibilities—known as *specialized* or *functional* international organizations—has grown greatly. The International Labor Organization, Food and Agriculture Organization, International Civil Aviation Organization, and Universal Postal Union are only a few of the better known agencies of this sort devoted to dealing with a variety of technical international problems. Still others, known as *regional* international organizations, whether of general purpose or specialized in their approach to international affairs, are constituted on a geographic basis. Examples of these include the Organization of American States, European Coal and Steel Community, European Economic Community, Organization of African Unity, and North Atlantic Treaty Organization.

In effect, then, a vast network of bonds of association is steadily being drawn around various groups of states. And as these new unions develop in importance and effectiveness, their members find themselves increasingly led to employ them to resolve "political" as well as "technical" problems. Thus do they create new bases for the existence of larger communities than those of the nation-states. To be sure, the functional and regional association of states does not automatically or invariably feed into a general trend toward world integration; in some cases, for a time at least, it may well obstruct a higher level of world association. But the advocates of "functional integration" believe that from the continuation and gradual extension of communication, accommodation, and co-operation among the nation-states, in many ways and for many purposes, a wider peace, a larger community, and a higher level of political authority may be brought into existence. Although we may not yet discern its ultimate form, we may imagine its results.

Conclusions. Obviously, we cannot foresee how or if the problem of creating an adequate world authority is to be resolved. Whether it can be done by one of the alternatives we have briefly discussed, or by still some other method, it is probably idle to guess. In the second half of the twentieth century, many men have come to believe that the division of world society into the historic nation-state is a source of much international trouble, and have intensified the search for newer political configurations to meet traditional political needs in more effective ways.

It does seem quite possible that the individual nation-states, in the long run, will be obliged to abandon their conventional claim to "sovereignty"—that is, to absolute independence of decision and control over their own population, as well as freedom of action in regard to other states—and thus make way for the organization of world society into newer forms and levels. So urgent is this necessity, indeed, that the state as we have known it may even be on the road to extinction. What sort of political associations are likely to emerge? We are inclined to expect they will be federal structures of various types, so that the future political life of man may have something in common with the middle ages, and develop a great variety of relatively independent, functional, and territorial groupings. The world can probably be organized but loosely in the short run, and such a system seems most appropriate to its needs and possibilities. Associations such as the United Nations, North Atlantic Treaty Organization, European Economic Community, then, while they may well give way in time to newer organizations, may also be seen as the forerunners of this trend.

"Had we but world enough, and time. . . ." The achievement of a more effective political integration of the world will certainly take much time—no more than Rome can it be built in a day—and it is not at all clear that the basic conflict between democratic and communist powers, which can conceivably escalate into full-scale nuclear war, assures us a sufficient margin of time for it. Yet it is also possible that the equal ability of both the United States and the Soviet Union to destroy all significant military targets in the world has created an atomic weapons stalemate, neutralizing their use by either. For the balance of power, we may have substituted what Sir Winston Churchill called the "balance of terror." Each side may thus be deterred from the "suicide pact" which employment of the ultimate weapon would involve, if only because each must stop and draw back before a step that could destroy civilization itself. Man has, after all, come a long way from barbarism; perhaps he can outdistance it entirely.

We prefer to think, finally, that mankind will not destroy itself, though in this frequently disordered world, we can scarcely be sure. If future generations are able to look back on our "race between education and catastrophe," they may well be inclined to apply to it the Duke of Wellington's blunt summing up of the Battle of Waterloo—"It was a close-run thing, the damned closest-run thing you ever saw in your life!"

PART SEVEN:
CONCLUSION

DICKENS

It was the best of times, it was the worst of times, it was the age of wisdom, it was the age of foolishness, it was the epoch of belief, it was the epoch of incredulity, it was the season of Light, it was the season of Darkness, it was the spring of hope, it was the winter of despair.

MONTESQUIEU

I will here exhort all men to reflect on their condition and to form thereof sound ideas. It is not impossible that they live under a happy government without realizing it: for it is the nature of political happiness that one does not know it until it has been lost.

CHAPTER 16

EPILOGUE

POLITICS AND the political order are certainly no longer identical with "the good life," as the ancient Greeks thought, but neither are they alien to it, as men have often held in the centuries since. In the kind of life many of us in the twentieth century have come to take for granted, and toward which other millions aspire, the order and activity we call political is so essential that we cannot avoid being the most political people in history since the days of Plato and Aristotle. If our political regime is faulty, few aspects of our lives will not suffer the consequences. But while any thoughtful person can recognize this if he directs his attention from narrow and immediate interests to their context and implications, no agreement with others on standards to judge the adequacy of political regimes necessarily follows. Not even political science has been able to create or discover universally acceptable criteria. When students of politics observe the world about them, they find not only differences but even contradictions; when along with other citizens they endeavor to make reasonable choices, they encounter dilemmas. Understanding seems at best partial, and what to one man is dispensable is essential to another. However, we must recognize that human freedom, when present at all, is particularly manifested in political life, and that our inability to comprehend politics completely springs from the fact that freedom breeds diversity and conflict, and obliges us to make choices that are not usually easy.

Most political scientists have seen democracy as the form of government most closely related to the condition of freedom, a perspective generally maintained throughout our discussion. In ideal, this is undeniably true. In practice, however, the conclusion is less certain, for if democracy does not work it cannot serve freedom or any other end. The theoretical analysis of democracy presented in our early chapters was supplemented by considerable subsequent discussion of how both democracies and dictatorships operate and the domestic and international issues they confront today. Our conclusion will therefore be most useful if it helps the reader evaluate the various forms of institution, process, and policy in the light of the urgent political needs of today and tomorrow. Only thus can we understand requirements and possibilities in contemporary politics and discern the place of democracy.

Early in American history, Fisher Ames gave a grudging tribute to the democracy he was not particularly fond of. He observed that monarchy is like a great ship, which sails majestically, but should it strike a rock it sinks forever. Democracy, on the other hand, is like a raft; though it never sinks, your feet are always in the water. Now, some men of idealistic temper might at any time prefer to sail majestically, even at the risk of catastrophe, rejecting with contempt those who would settle for less. Not only the criticism but even the defense of democracy has often been couched in these terms, as friends of democracy claimed for it not only unsinkability but also the majesty of truth and justice. The reader of our earlier chapters should be aware that we consider such claims to be of dubious merit, if not dangerous. The virtues of democracy are more modest, although far from inconsequential.

The distinction Ames made, then, appears basically sound, though somewhat disconcerting. Men imbued with a strong sense of righteousness and determined to make right prevail through government find it difficult—if not impossible—to accept a regime which promises such limited achievement—keeping us only afloat. Popular government has consequently been subjected to the unflagging criticism of idealists; the only variable aspect of the criticism has been the nature of the ideals and the degree of disillusionment of the idealists with "the people."

The problem of democracy today, however, is somewhat different, and it bothers realists no less than idealists. Ames took it for granted that, while democracy did not embody the highest of virtues, it was at least durable. It did not occur to him, apparently, that an unsinkable raft might still shake to pieces—that the qualities of democracy might be inadequate not only from the best ethical insights but even from the standpoint of its survival. In his day, of course, it mattered not greatly what government did or did not do. Today, however, there are few things central to our concerns for which effective governmental support is not essential, even if the support is indirect and unnoticed. We are committed at home to broad humanitarian purposes requiring intense and skillful co-operation for their realization. Abroad, we are engaged in remarkably hazardous enterprises in a world full of dangerous conflicts. Miscalculation and ineffective action are likely to be more than merely disappointing; they may be fatal. To be sure, our rather haphazard and pragmatic methods, usually involving much trial and error, probably would produce acceptable results ultimately if sufficient time were at our disposal. But time is of the essence, and it may be running short.

We may wonder, though, whether this criticism of democracy is really any more significant than those of old. Indeed, it is much the same, except that survival rather than virtue is set forth as the end democracy allegedly cannot attain. Both the idealists of old and the realists of today insist that men are not equal—or always and equally rational—and that the bulk of mankind is not capable of imaginative genius and creativity. This is quite likely true; most men commonly desire nothing more than the preservation of the status quo once its benefits are generalized. But that argument does not in itself invalidate democratic government. Those who reject democracy must do more than deny the omnicompetence of the "average man." If they pretend to a rational demonstration, they must show that those whose rule they would prefer actually possess all the qualities required in modern government—not only knowledge and virtue, but also the capacity to exercise them in effective statecraft. This they have never been able to do. As Plato discovered ages ago, the search for perfect governors is doomed to failure. The complexities of political action and values are too great; politics is inevitably cut of rather coarse cloth. While it is not hard to find this and that wrong with democracy, there is—unfortunately or not—no alternative form of political regime which will effectively remedy all of democracy's failings, or even a substantial number of them.

These statements are not offered to deny that democratic governments confront critical problems and difficulties today, but only to suggest the context in which they must be evaluated and met. The possible alternative to democracy is not another form of government, whether better or worse, but a succession of various types of governments, each temporarily serving particular purposes and meeting particular problems, and each in turn being overthrown, as conditions change, with all the confusion accompanying revolutions. Revolutionary zeal is most pronounced precisely among those who do not understand the nature of democracy or its benefits—or are active where democracy does not exist and may be impossible. For democracy in practice is unique; inherently experimental, it is the only form of government in history which specifically tends to promote a reasonably automatic adaptation to changing conditions and objectives. Where democracy has been established—unfortunately in relatively few places—its performance has earned description as institutionalized peaceful revolution. Of course, there is no proof one way or another as to democracy's capacity to continue in this vein, for its experience has been short and our data modest. We may well conclude, therefore, with a brief discussion of what appears particularly crucial to the survival of democracy—and of western civilization.

Traditionally, political thought—and to a considerable degree practice as well—seem to have fluctuated between two poles: one of responsibility and one of leadership. The distinction is a matter of emphasis, in part at least, for effective leadership is bound to be responsible to something, and a responsible official becomes a focal point of authority and a symbol of the values which, in his being responsible, he accepts. Yet the distinction remains an important one. The two contending political theories of the contemporary world differ largely because democracy is rooted in the ideal and the processes of responsibility in government, while totalitarian dictatorship rests its case entirely on the necessity of uncontrolled leadership. Until recently, democrats have paid a quite inadequate attention to the subject of leadership and its provision. Responsibility was seen as the key to good government, to be achieved by subordinating officials to the rule of law and to an electoral accountability. Their most debated question, consequently, has been what to do if these two forms of control conflict in their demands on officials. Leadership, according to the dominant view, was primarily a matter of private initiative among the people at large. And since they assumed it would arise there spontaneously, no special provision for it was necessary—except to limit and regulate it.

This intense concern of constitutionalists and democrats with the various forms of preserving responsibility in political life is most worthy of respect; tyranny is the consequence of rejecting it. History is full of instances, however, in which its inadequacy as a sufficient political perspective has been evident, and at no time more than in recent decades. We have discovered that in some circumstances this exclusive interest in responsible government is a luxury, at the least, and perhaps not even a very meaningful preoccupation. Such circumstances are those in which people are no longer sure what a government should be responsible to or for—all their values and standards relevant to political judgment having been upset by change. In the event, their need for leadership is overwhelming, and talk of responsibility—except in a broad sense, such as providing for this need—suggests a nostalgic or utopian romanticism.

The rise of totalitarian dictatorships in this century reflects this fact; they were not the product only of the ruthlessness and demagogic skill of a few men. Although conditions are fortunately not always so extreme, we do now see that leadership is an essential need of human life, and most obviously and powerfully in periods of great change and confusion, of which the twentieth century is a prime example. Dictatorship can be prevented, therefore, only if some other effective forms of leadership can be provided. Furthermore, some traditional liberal ideas to the contrary notwithstanding, it is inevitable these days that leadership come in good part from government, distinctly the central and crucial institution of modern social life.

Yet, an exclusive predilection for leadership is characteristic of dictatorial, not of democratic politics, and it in no way serves our purposes if in adapting democracy to new conditions and insights it is so transformed as to be abolished. As the discussion in previous chapters dealing with democracy and its challenge indicated, plebiscitary dictatorship, despite superficial resemblances to democracy, is still dictatorship and suffers all its disadvantages. And though the insights of democratic thought of the past must now be modified, they have not been rendered invalid. We believe it may be asserted with confidence that the future rests with those communities that can so manage the modification as to work out patterns of effective leadership while maintaining the standards of responsibility which earlier democratic thought elaborated. Because leadership intrinsically seeks to escape such limits, and because controls necessary to ensure responsibility are frequently hostile to innovating leadership, this demand will not be easily met. Our ability to promote responsible leadership is the great test of our political genius today.

The more successful democracies of the present—goaded by their own many and serious problems and stimulated by the occasionally spectacular, if narrow, achievements of dictatorial regimes—have already come a long way in meeting this test. One can hardly compare the institutions and policies of British, French, and American governments of the turn of the century with those of today, for example, without being struck by the considerable increase in government participation within the affairs of the community, serving the general welfare, and by the gradual elaboration of new institutions and procedures to render that participation more effective. Comparably impressive has been the great increase in the power and prestige of chief executives, who today far outshine in many respects the absolute monarchs of the past. Indeed, in generally recognized emergencies their actual powers are not substantially less than those of the dictators. The transformation is most spectacular in the United States, where the idea of government extremely limited both in power and functions was formerly most pronounced, and the supremacy of the representative assembly over the executive was accepted dogma. Not so long ago, as Woodrow Wilson pointed out in *Congressional Government* (1885), the most powerful men in the country were likely to be in Congress—if they were in government at all; now it is fairly clear that they surround the President.

Many are troubled by this trend; some because they feel no need for executive leadership, and others because they are aware of the increasing difficulty of enforcing responsibility against an official of such overwhelming power and prestige. It was precisely a sense of this which created many republicans in days of monarchies. Nevertheless, such complaints are often exaggerated, since the checks on presidents and prime ministers in modern democracies remain numerous and effective. Executive leadership still requires that these men "sell" their proposals to many and diverse groups of people, in and out of government, who if not persuaded are quite able to thwart that leadership. Nevertheless, it is a problem to which democracies must remain alert—preventing the concentration of leadership from undermining the independent power of others which alone can enable them actually to call the executive to account and hold him responsible. Effective power is a matter of legal authority only in part; it is at least as much one of social conditions, economic organization, and so on. Each country has to meet this problem in its own way.

One aspect of any possible solution to this problem, however, seems of universal validity. Responsibility in government is impossible in totalitarian, and possible only in pluralistic, communities. One can be responsible only to something other than himself, after all. This means, at the very least, that the operations of officialdom should not completely replace private initiative and decision making, and that the public realm should not become so comprehensive as to leave no room for independent private realms. "Laissez faire" was simply too extreme an application of an otherwise significant principle; the proper function of government, as Lincoln observed, is to do those things for the people which they cannot do, or do as well, for themselves. There is little room here for a priori ideas; what needs to be done and how best to do it are not constant but variable in time and place in a world greatly diverse in its development. But in the best democratic practice of recent generations the role of government has been seen as filling in gaps, repairing deficiencies, stimulating and supplementing private activities.

This bias against too much government reflects an essential standard of responsible government, because a government which has acquired too many functions and the overwhelming powers necessary to fulfill them probably cannot be controlled by its citizens, and therefore cannot be responsible in the democratic sense of the term. Throughout many parts of the world today the problems of social and economic reconstruction are so fundamental—not only material resources must be developed but ways of thinking and social structures must be transformed if aspirations to modern life are to be realized—that the inevitably revolutionary leadership resulting may make adherence to this standard impossible. Indeed, everywhere, even in long-established communities, some such difficulties are present, rendering no one immune to irresponsible leadership. Responsible democratic governments are not everywhere feasible, thus, at least today. But that where they exist they may be preserved, and where they do not yet exist they may be promoted, depends upon whether those who have any discretion in the matter are guided by democratic standards in their actions. If all communities require leadership, the only leadership democracies can tolerate is that which arises in a pluralistic social life, with many centers of informed initiative kept accountable through mutual checks and balances. Wise leaders will promote that condition.

Would democracies then be able to meet the challenges of life in the world today? Would they then be able to meet the threat of communist expansion, fulfill their chosen responsibilities toward the underdeveloped countries, and overcome their own tendency to live from hand to mouth rather than planning for their long-range needs? There is no guarantee. Continuing development of an effective political science will help, as would even more the spread of its insights and information among the people, if they are willing to undertake the discipline of politics and try to make democracy work. Yet politics is more than a science or philosophy; it is also an art, demanding more than knowledge. Thus, the future of democracy cannot be taken for granted. In the end, people cannot be protected from their own perversities, stupidities, and lack of imagination; there is no way of ensuring their happiness and survival. Thucydides long ago discerned the only answer: "The secret of happiness is freedom, and the secret of freedom, courage."

A STUDY GUIDE *to* POLITICAL SCIENCE

A STUDY GUIDE *to* POLITICAL SCIENCE

REFERENCE MATERIALS

GUIDES TO BIBLIOGRAPHIC INFORMATION

Paul Wasserman, *Information for Administrators; A Guide to Publications and Services for Management in Business and Government* (Cornell University Press, 1956) is an extremely useful volume describing the character and utility of various information sources, including government agencies, periodicals and newspapers dealing with public affairs, handbooks, encyclopedias, and general reference works. The appendix contains, among other things, a list of information services of foreign governments.

Bert F. Hoselitz (ed.), *A Reader's Guide to the Social Sciences* (Free Press, 1959) contains a chapter on political science by Heinz Eulau in the form of a critical essay which discusses many of the classics of political science, recent writings on methodology, and important works on politics, public administration, and international relations.

Peter R. Lewis, *The Literature of the Social Sciences; An Introductory Survey and Guide* (The Library Association, London, 1960). While covering the general area of the social sciences, the larger portion of this volume is devoted to political science, public administration, law, and international affairs. Emphasis is on British publications, but others are not excluded.

Carl M. White (ed.), *Sources of Information in the Social Sciences; An Annotated Bibliography* (Columbia University School of Library Service, 1959) ranges over the various social sciences listing books and other resources by various categories, and is partly annotated.

A. S. Beardsley and O. C. Orman, *Legal Bibliography and the Use of Law Books,* 2nd ed. (Foundation Press, 1947), undertakes full treatment of the subject for the Anglo-American legal system and covers the law report series.

Frederick C. Hicks, *Materials and Methods of Legal Research,* 3rd ed. (Lawyers Cooperative Publishing Co., 1942), is also a full treatment of legal research, law books, legal periodicals, and law reports.

Everett S. Brown, *Manual of Government Publications: United States and Foreign* (Appleton-Century-Crofts, 1950) is an excellent introduction to governmental documentation and publications, especially American and British, but with attention to other governments and international bodies.

L. F. Schmeckebier and Roy B. Eastin, *Government Publications and Their Use* (Brookings, 1961) is a substantial and comprehensive guide to government documents in the United States.

Monthly Catalog of United States Government Publications is a useful listing of current publications. *Monthly Checklist of State Publications* records those state documents received by the Library of Congress.

DICTIONARIES

Edwin V. Mitchell, *An Encyclopedia of American Politics* (Doubleday, 1946) constitutes a useful guide to the principal terms and personalities which have figured in American politics.

Jack C. Plano and M. Greenberg, *The American Political Dictionary* (Holt, 1962) is organized into broad subject areas.

Edward C. Smith and Arnold J. Zurcher, *New Dictionary of American Politics* (Barnes & Noble, 1949) treats both political and legal terms in a wide array of entries.

Hans Sperber and Travis Trittschuh, *American Political Terms: An Historical Dictionary* (Wayne State University Press, 1962) is a substantial work revealing something of the flavor of American politics.

Walter Theimer, *An Encyclopedia of Modern World Politics* (Rinehart, 1950) is a broadly based treatment of concepts, terms, problems, and national political systems.

Wilbur W. White, *White's Political Dictionary* (World Publishing, 1947) ranges over the entire area of political terminology from politics to international affairs.

F. Elliott and M. Summerskill, *A Dictionary of Politics* (Penguin, 1961) is a general guide whose entries deal with leading statesmen, political institutions, political parties, and related matters.

Bouvier's Law Dictionary; Baldwin's Student Edition (Banks-Baldwin, 1948) is probably the standard, treating all legal terms and concepts in a one-volume reference work.

Henry C. Black, *Black's Law Dictionary; Definitions of the Terms and Phrases of American and English Jurisprudence, Ancient and Modern,* 4th ed. (West, 1951), also covers the field of legal terminology in concise entries.

The major college dictionaries in their recent editions are helpful to the student. Well known in this category are *American College Dictionary* (Random House), *Standard College Dictionary* (Funk & Wagnalls), *Webster's New World Dictionary* (World), and *Webster's New Collegiate Dictionary* (Merriam).

ENCYCLOPEDIAS

Encyclopedia of the Social Sciences, 15 volumes (reprinted in 1948 in 8 volumes), is an extensive compendium. Published originally between 1930 and 1935, and thus out of date at many points, it is still a valuable reference work, international in scope. Articles were contributed by outstanding scholars and authorities and are signed, with accompanying bibliographies. A new *International Encyclopedia of the Social Sciences,* with publication projected for 1965, should be informative and reflect current scholarship.

Worldmark Encyclopedia of the Nations (1963) devotes Volume I to the United Nations and related agencies; the remaining four contain geographic, historical, political and other data of 135 countries. There is also much of value for the student in the major general encyclopedias: *Encyclopedia Americana,* 30 vols. and supplementary *Annual; Encyclopedia Britannica,* 24 vols. and supplementary *Book of the Year; Collier's Encyclopedia,* 20 vols., providing briefer accounts; and *Columbia Encyclopedia,* 3rd ed., a single volume useful for ready reference.

YEARBOOKS AND HANDBOOKS

World Almanac and Book of Facts. Annual. A very comprehensive collection of factual information, including political data.

Whitaker's Almanack. Annual. A British publication, emphasizing data respecting the United Kingdom and the Commonwealth.

Annual Register of World Events. A historical and factual summary of world affairs, with British emphasis.

Survey of International Affairs. Irregularly produced but aimed at systematic coverage of the years, emphasizing recent political developments, national and international. A publication of the Royal Institute of International Affairs.

United States in World Affairs. Annual. An important and objective treatment of American foreign relations and international events of concern to the United States. Published by the Council on Foreign Relations, Inc.

Documents on American Foreign Relations. Annual. Contains a substantial selection of representative documents on the subject, also published by the Council on Foreign Relations.

Statesman's Year-Book. Annual. Treats each country, briefly describes its governmental system and other features. Statistical, historical, and diplomatic information for ready reference.

Political Handbook of the World. Annual. Contains data on the parliamentary bodies, political parties, the press, and the principal government officials of most national governments.

Europa; The Encyclopedia of Europe. Looseleaf. A directory of international organizations, international agreements, and general political and statistical information about the European countries.

Everyman's United Nations. This compact and comprehensive reference guide, published at intervals by the United Nations, gives details of the organization, functions, and achievements of the UN and its specialized agencies.

Yearbook of the United Nations. Annual. Also published by the UN, it provides a review of its activities and functions.

Official Congressional Directory for the Use of the Congress. Issued frequently, it contains official biographies of the members of Congress, as well as considerable other information about the United States government and its principal officials.

United States Government Organization Manual. Annual. A major and official compilation of information about United States government organization, its departments, agencies, offices, their statutes, and publications.

Book of the States. Biennial. Issued by the Council of State Governments, it provides extensive and authoritative information about American state governments and their activities.

Municipal Yearbook. Annual. Articles and data on American city government, particularly to meet the needs of municipal officials.

MISCELLANEOUS REFERENCE AIDS

Facts on File. Weekly, looseleaf. This American-produced digest of world news includes such categories as world affairs, national affairs, and foreign affairs. Cumulative indexes from fortnightly to annually.

Keesing's Contemporary Archives. Weekly, looseleaf. A British diary of world events containing selections and summarizations of news, reports, statistics, and data drawn from an array of sources. Cumulative indexes.

A. J. Peaslee, *Constitutions of Nations,* 3 vols., 2nd ed. (Nijhoff, 1956), provides an English-language version of the constitutions of 89 states of the world.

A. J. Peaslee, *International Governmental Organization: Constitutional Documents,* 2 vols. (Nijhoff, 1956), is a compilation devoted to international organizations created by states and having governmental functions.

Encyclopedia Britannica World Atlas. Unabridged. In addition to its collection of maps, this atlas contains much useful political data and a comprehensive statistical treatment of more than 200 states and political units of the world.

Advanced Atlas of Modern Geography and *Columbus Atlas* (both McGraw-Hill) and *Cosmopolitan Atlas* and *Goode's School Atlas* (both Rand McNally) are also useful reference aids.

V. O. Key, Jr., *A Primer of Statistics for Political Scientists* (Crowell, 1954) provides an explanation of basic statistical concepts and assumptions.

Harold T. David, *Political Statistics* (Principia, 1954) introduces the subject for the beginner.

POLITICAL CLASSICS

The study of politics is an old and variegated discipline, and is very closely related to the history of political life itself. The writings of contemporary political scientists are concerned primarily with the political life of today and the interests dominant in that life. But though it is not always clearly recognized by the writers themselves, those writings are also rooted in a tradition of political practice and thought. Therefore, study of this tradition helps to understand the political science of the present, and it may best be approached through numerous works of such genius and perceptivity that they have been generally recognized as comprising the classic literature of the discipline. These works are extremely diverse in their conceptions of the scope, methods, and objectives of political science, and one discovers in them progenitors of all the contemporary "schools" of the discipline as well as learns from them much about the nature of western civilization in which political science arose.

In the brief and inevitably inadequate characterization of the classic works of political science and thought which follows many minor figures must be ignored. Some of these are of great importance to a specialist in a field or historical period, but for general and introductory purposes we may limit our attention to works that are the milestones in the development of the subject. General surveys of the history of western political thought are numerous, and may be of aid to the student who desires further discussion and analysis. For many years the standard text has been George H. Sabine, *A History of Political Theory*, 3rd edition (Holt, 1961), which covers the entire period thoroughly and intelligently. Other texts by Thomas I. Cook, *History of Political Philosophy from Plato to Burke* (Prentice-Hall, 1936) and G. E. G. Catlin, *The Story of the Political Philosophers* (McGraw-Hill, 1939), are very useful and interpretive works by well-known scholars. Andrew Hacker, in *Political Theory: Philosophy, Ideology, Science* (Macmillan, 1961), presents a series of excellent essays on the major writers. Lee C. McDonald, *Western Political Theory: The Modern Age* (Harcourt, Brace, 1963) covers the period from the seventeenth century. Available also are extensive excerpts from the more important works, accompanied by commentary. A valuable series in this vein is *Masters of Political Thought*, in three volumes: M. B. Foster, *Plato to Machiavelli* (Houghton Mifflin, 1941); W. T. Jones, *Machiavelli to Bentham* (1947); and L. W. Lancaster, *Hegel to Dewey* (1959). W. Y. Elliott and N. MacDonald, *Western Political Heritage* (Prentice-Hall, 1949) is also a good survey of this type, and William

Ebenstein's *Great Political Thinkers* (Rinehart, 1951) contains a particularly helpful bibliography.

Among the classical writers themselves, Plato is a fountainhead for much that comes after. His *Republic,* dating from the early fourth century B.C., in ancient Greece, has intensely stimulated both followers and critics throughout the ages. In it a highly ethical and rationalist conception of politics is set forth, culminating in an ideal of rule by philosophers. Toward the end of the same century, Aristotle subjected political life to a somewhat different sort of analysis in his *Nichomachean Ethics* and *Politics.* While ethical elements remain preponderant, Aristotle was particularly aware of the gap between theoretical absolutes and practical relativities. He stressed the importance of law, and with considerable empiricism recognized the significance of social classes and of custom. Despite its historical importance, later antiquity produced no comparably great political writings, and the political thought of the medieval period is inseparable from its theology and from its somewhat nonpolitical social order. However, the *City of God* of St. Augustine in the early fifth century and the *Summa Theologica* of St. Thomas Aquinas in the mid-thirteenth include penetrating analyses of history, law, and political life from a Christian perspective which have been extremely influential.

Modern political science is often said to spring from the writings of Niccolò Machiavelli in early sixteenth-century Italy, largely because he carefully separated politics from ethics and theology, and insisted that he dealt with men as they are rather than as they ought to be. Actually, both the *Prince* and the *Discourses on the First Ten Books of Titus Livius* were intended to be practical handbooks to those concerned with the creation and preservation of states, and his realism was that of the man of affairs and not that of the scientist. Because in the anarchy of renaissance Italy no existing order could be taken for granted, Machiavelli was compelled to emphasize power and expediency, and won an enduring notoriety when in the *Prince* he argued—with appropriate illustrations—that political leaders must sometimes be immoral.

Early modern developments in northern Europe culminated in two great works of seventeenth-century England, which were also concerned with the creation and preservation of states but emphasized less the power and craft of princes than the consent of the people expressed through a social compact. Most radically displaying the impact of the new scientific outlook and the individualism of the age was the *Leviathan* of Thomas Hobbes. Hobbes saw men as driven by vanity and fear into an endless war with one another unless, stimulated into a more profound rationality by their fear, they accepted a common sovereign, who through law would maintain the peace. Hobbes' idea of government was thoroughly absolutist—radically so—but it was nonetheless rooted in radical ideas of individual consent and justifiable only as it served the needs of the individual.

Toward the end of the century John Locke, in his *Second Treatise of Gov-*

ernment, moderated the extremes of Hobbes' views and founded modern liberalism. He assumed individual natural rights to life, liberty, and property, and also a natural law which men can rationally recognize and generally will follow. Social harmony is more natural to men, then, than the Hobbesian war. Social institutions, including governments, are created by men to perfect this harmony by maintaining the law and preserving individual rights. If they violate this "trust," revolution is justified. To Locke the majority in a community, which created and judged governments, was the ultimate political power and source of law. The perspective of the American Declaration of Independence is overwhelmingly that of Locke.

The desire for freedom under law gave rise to two particularly influential works in eighteenth-century France. *The Spirit of the Laws,* by Montesquieu, is famous as the first reasoned discussion of the separation of powers as a means of promoting freedom under law, although it is interesting also as an early attempt at "sociological" study of law and politics. Jean-Jacques Rousseau, however, argued in his *Social Contract* that law is the "general will" of a community—a genuinely shared will regarding a common good. Rousseau was the first unqualifiedly democratic theorist, who assumed that individuals find their true meaning and freedom in a shared community and denied any separate private rights. He rejected the actual social life of his time as corrupt, and his reasons for doing so foreshadow much recent sociological and psychological thinking.

Edmund Burke's *Reflections on the Revolution in France* represents one of the leading conservative works of all time. Rejecting the ideas of Rousseau, and even the more radical aspects of those of Locke, Burke glorified tradition and aristocratic leadership. He abhorred metaphysical speculation, including that asserting natural rights, and insisted that rights, freedom, and all other values be considered in context rather than as isolated abstractions. Likewise opposed to metaphysics, but equally to an a priori traditionalism, was the utilitarianism of Jeremy Bentham, whose writings spanned the end of the eighteenth and the early nineteenth centuries. In *Fragment On Government* and *Principles of Morals and Legislation* Bentham presented a case for analyzing laws and institutions according to whether they produced the greatest happiness of the greatest number, and invented a "felicific calculus" to aid therein. More accessible than Bentham's writings are those of James Mill and his son, John Stuart Mill. James Mill's *Essay on Government* was, for the time, a radically democratic and liberal tract. In three essays—*Utilitarianism, On Liberty,* and *Representative Government*—John Stuart Mill in mid-century very largely defined the views of modern liberalism. His utilitarianism—judging things by their consequences and particularly their tendency to produce pleasure—was merged with a sensitivity to progressive change and "higher values," which made possible a strong—almost unconditioned—commitment to freedom as a good in itself, and also to democracy as a means of popular education as well as self-expression. John Stuart Mill has regularly been accused of inconsistency, but these writings have been a major influence nonetheless over the last hundred years.

The highly individualistic and matter-of-fact utilitarianism was challenged, however, by an "idealism" which sprang in good part from Rousseau via a German philosopher of the late eighteenth century, Immanuel Kant. Except for his *Perpetual Peace* Kant's philosophy is highly academic and technical and not easily understood. More immediately pertinent—although not more easily comprehensible—are two works of G. W. F. Hegel, from the early nineteenth century. In *Philosophy of History* and *Philosophy of Right* Hegel developed the ideas of the dialectical evolution of history, of this evolution as one toward greater freedom, and of the modern state as the embodiment of that freedom. Probably the most accessible statement of the Hegelian political perspective is *The Philosophical Theory of the State,* by the Englishman, Bernard Bosanquet. Finally, contrasting both with pragmatic utilitarianism and with idealism in the development of nineteenth-century liberalism was a movement often called Social Darwinism. Although manifested also in nationalistic versions, Social Darwinism's principal expression was in terms of individualistic competition for survival and a rejection of welfare policies as interference with the elimination of the "unfit." A classic in this perspective is Herbert Spencer's *Man versus the State,* written late in the century. It is the capstone to Spencer's evolutionary sociology, which saw humanity as tending toward ever greater individuality.

In the nineteenth century, also, socialism arose in challenge to liberalism's individualism and its faith in private undertakings. Socialist writers were legion, but predominantly important and influential among them was Karl Marx. As political literature, the principal Marxist text is the *Communist Manifesto,* together with Marx's analyses of the more radical revolutionary experiences of his day as given in *The Class Struggles in France* and *The Civil War in France*. More explicit philosophical discussion of such basic ideas as dialectical materialism and economic classes appear in *The German Ideology* and *Critique of Political Economy*. A brief and helpful discussion of Marxism—and of other socialist ideas from a Marxist bias—is to be found in Friedrich Engels' *Socialism: Utopian and Scientific*. These writings are largely of the mid-century; later developments in socialist thinking are reflected well in three works: V. I. Lenin's *State and Revolution* emphasized the revolutionary in Marxism, while Eduard Bernstein's *Evolutionary Socialism* questioned doctrines of class struggle and historical inevitability and laid the groundwork for democratic socialism in Europe. *Fabian Essays in Socialism,* edited by George Bernard Shaw, indicates the pragmatic gradualist idealism of British socialism at the turn of the century. Henry George's *Progress and Poverty* and Edward Bellamy's *Looking Backward,* finally, are good representatives of American radicalism in the face of the new problems of industrial civilization as they burst upon a nation not congenial to doctrinaire socialism, Marxist or otherwise. The scope of these and many other recent works is somewhat limited, however, and their inclusion in a list of political classics may be questioned. References to other pertinent writings of the last half century or so will be made in relevant part and chapter bibliographies, which follow.

SUPPLEMENTARY READINGS

This portion of the Study Guide introduces the student to an annotated selection of literature in English which relates to the principal parts and chapters of the present work. It is not intended as a bibliography of political science, but rather as a sampling of major studies, textbooks, and monographs on various topics which will encourage further reading, with some variety of viewpoint.

Of necessity, many important and useful works are omitted. Emphasis is placed on the more recent books and ones likely to be useful to the beginning student. However, the lists are not limited to elementary studies, and some of the items are appropriate for the more advanced student who brings considerable background to his reading and wishes to undertake independent study.

In most of the works indicated there will be found extensive specialized bibliographies which will provide additional aid for further study.

PART ONE: INTRODUCTION

CHAPTER 1: THE NATURE OF POLITICAL SCIENCE

Stephen K. Bailey *et al., Research Frontiers in Politics and Government: Brookings Lectures 1955* (Brookings, 1955) provides a symposium of articles appraising the range of political science investigation.

Arnold Brecht, *Political Theory* (Princeton University Press, 1959) presents a broad argument in favor of "science" in the study of political life, with some imaginative applications to traditional problems.

David E. Butler, *The Study of Political Behaviour* (Hutchinson, 1958) treats the various methods employed to study political behavior.

J. H. Chamberlin, *Careers for Social Scientists* (Walck, 1961) discusses vocational opportunities.

Committee for Advancement of Teaching, American Political Science Association, *Goals for Political Science* (William Sloane, 1951). Though by no means accepted in its main conclusions by all political scientists, it offers an inventory of thinking on the subject.

Contemporary Political Science: A Survey of Methods, Research and Teaching (UNESCO, 1950) is a substantial report by an international conference of political scientists describing national variations in the study of the subject.

Bernard Crick, *The American Science of Politics* (Routledge and Kegan

Paul, 1959) is a critical evaluation of American political science and its tendencies.

David Easton, *The Political System: An Inquiry into the State of Political Science* (Knopf, 1953) offers a critique of political science and advances an "equilibrium" theory of politics.

Heinz Eulau, *The Behavioral Persuasion in Politics* (Random House, 1963) presents some essays about "what man does politically and the meanings he attaches to his behavior" to exemplify the "behavioral persuasion."

Heinz Eulau, Samuel J. Eldersveld, and Morris Janowitz (eds.), *Political Behavior: A Reader in Theory and Research* (Free Press, 1956) is a useful collection of materials on the subject.

Carl J. Friedrich, *Man and His Government* (McGraw-Hill, 1963) begins a comprehensive treatment of political life with a discussion of the nature of politics and its study.

Lyman J. Gould and E. W. Steele, *People, Power, and Politics: An Introductory Reader* (Random House, 1961) collects a wide array of materials, stressing a comparative approach.

Howard D. Hamilton (ed.), *Political Institutions* (Houghton Mifflin, 1962) is an excellent collection of general readings.

Charles Hyneman, *The Study of Politics: The Present State of American Political Science* (University of Illinois Press, 1959) is addressed to students, and discusses various views of the scope and methods of political science.

Harold D. Lasswell and Abraham Kaplan, *Power and Society: A Framework for Political Inquiry* (Yale University Press, 1950) constitutes a formulation of basic concepts and hypotheses, emphasizing concern with power.

Harold D. Lasswell, *The Future of Political Science* (Atherton, 1963) is a discussion of the state of the discipline by a leading practitioner, with research recommendations.

Leslie Lipson, *The Great Issues of Politics,* 2nd ed. (Prentice-Hall, 1960) is a general treatment of political society and its organization, with some methodological discussion.

Charles E. Merriam, *Systematic Politics* (University of Chicago Press, 1945) offers a work of breadth synthesizing sociological and historical points of view.

Dorothy M. Pickles, *Introduction to Politics* (Sylvan, 1951) is an introductory discussion of the basic problems with which political speculation is concerned.

Austin Ranney (ed.), *Essays on the Behavioral Study of Politics* (University of Illinois Press, 1962) illustrates well the diverse aspects of this approach in political science.

Arnold A. Rogow (ed.), *Government and Politics: A Reader* (Crowell, 1961) provides an introductory collection of varied readings.

W. G. Runciman, *Social Science and Political Theory* (Cambridge University Press, 1963) is a thoughtful study, stressing the relationships between philosophy and science.

Leo Strauss, *What is Political Philosophy?* (Free Press, 1959) is a collection of essays, arguing that political science must have a practical and philosophic basis.

Vernon Van Dyke, *Political Science: A Philosophical Analysis* (Stanford University Press, 1960) examines the discipline, its methods, approaches, and possibilities.

Dwight Waldo, *Political Science in the United States of America: A Trend Report* (UNESCO, 1956) is a discussion of the general direction of research and writing in the 1950's.

T. D. Weldon, *The Vocabulary of Politics* (Penguin, 1953) is a theoretical discussion of political semantics and their relation to the basis of obligation.

Roland Young (ed.), *Approaches to the Study of Politics: Twenty-two Essays Exploring the Nature of Politics and the Methods by Which It Can Be Studied* (Northwestern University Press, 1958) suggests the variety of methods of political inquiry.

PART TWO: POLITICAL COMMUNITY

Ernest Barker, *Principles of Social and Political Theory* (Oxford University Press, 1951) is a scholarly and illuminating analysis of the history and character of the political community in the western tradition.

Waldo Browne (ed.), *Leviathan in Crisis* (Viking, 1946) collects interesting and useful essays by twentieth-century writers, displaying many diverse perspectives on the modern state and its future.

William Ebenstein, *Today's Isms,* 4th ed. (Prentice-Hall, 1964), interprets and contrasts the totalitarian and democratic ways of life and thought.

Erich Fromm, *The Sane Society* (Rinehart, 1955) builds, upon the psychological view displayed earlier in *Escape from Freedom* (Rinehart, 1941) and *Man for Himself* (Rinehart, 1947), a social critique rich with political implications.

Sebastian de Grazia, *The Political Community* (University of Chicago Press, 1948) extensively discusses the psychological foundations of authority.

Jean Gottmann, *Megapolis: The Urbanized Northeastern Seaboard of the United States* (Twentieth Century Fund, 1961) gives a good picture of the developing modern community for which appropriate political forms must be found.

Bertrand de Jouvenel, in *On Power* (Viking, 1949) and *Sovereignty* (University of Chicago Press, 1957), undertakes in two complementary books an analysis of modern state power in its democratic and aristocratic aspects.

Harold J. Laski, *A Grammar of Politics,* 4th ed. (Allen and Unwin, 1938), is a broad appraisal of modern political life from a pluralist and libertarian perspective.

Walter Lippmann, *The Good Society* (Little, Brown, 1937) is a critique of liberalism, fascism, and communism, and an appeal for a reconstruction of liberalism to secure freedom under law.

Robert M. MacIver, *The Web of Government* (Macmillan, 1947) is an original and penetrating study of the rise and nature of political communities and of the place of myth and authority in them.

CHAPTER 2: SOCIETY AND THE STATE

William C. MacLeod, *The Origin and History of Politics* (Wiley, 1931) provides an anthropological inquiry into the beginnings of government.

R. H. Lowie, *The Origin of the State* (Harcourt, Brace, 1927) is a classic anthropological study.

E. M. Sait, *Political Institutions: A Preface* (Appleton-Century, 1938) is a concentrated discussion of the rise of western political systems and their various patterns of government.

N. D. Fustel de Coulanges, *The Ancient City* (Doubleday, 1956) although written almost a century ago remains an informative and imaginative treatment of the roots of our political culture.

Alfred Zimmern, *The Greek Commonwealth,* 2nd ed. (Oxford University Press, 1915), remains the standard over-all study in English of the nature of the classical Greek community.

Leon Homo, *Roman Political Institutions,* 2nd ed. (Barnes & Noble, 1962) is a classic study, with recently enlarged bibliography.

Marc Bloch, *Feudal Society* (Routledge and Kegan Paul, 1961) is an outstanding piece of historical analysis, emphasizing the structure of the feudal order.

J. H. Morall, *Political Thought in Medieval Times,* 2nd ed. (Hutchinson, 1960), gives a good brief account of medieval contributions to western political thinking and practice.

Carl Stephenson, *Medieval Feudalism* (Cornell University Press, 1956) is an excellent introduction to the subject.

William Kornhauser, *The Politics of Mass Society* (Free Press, 1959) considers thoughtfully and systematically contemporary tendencies toward "mass" rather than "pluralistic" politics.

R. M. MacIver, *Community,* 3rd ed. (Macmillan, 1931), is a classic attempt at broad social analysis, based essentially on western liberal developments.

David Riesman *et al., The Lonely Crowd,* abridged edition with a new preface (Yale University Press, 1961) gives an interesting social analysis in terms of "inner" and "other-directed" personalities.

G. E. G. Catlin, *The Science and Method of Politics* (Knopf, 1927) presents an analysis of politics in terms of "political acts," which are basically individual assertions of power over others within an institutional framework.

Bernard Crick, *In Defense of Politics* (University of Chicago Press, 1962) attempts to distinguish politics from other forms of government and control, as a process through which free men make public decisions.

John Dewey, *The Public and Its Problems* (Gateway Books, 1946) gives a stimulating analysis of politics and governments in terms of attempts to control the consequences of innovating activity.

Harold J. Laski, *The State in Theory and Practice* (Viking, 1935) contrasts the adulation of "the State" of philosophical idealism with the pragmatic liberal perspective.

H. D. Lasswell, *Politics: Who Gets What, When, How* (Meridian Books, 1958) is an important work in which an early advocate of the use of psychological insights in political science discusses politics in terms of influence and the influential.

Karl Loewenstein, *Political Power and the Governmental Process* (University of Chicago Press, 1957) is an outstanding work of comparative political analysis, founded upon a clearly developed conception of politics as the organization of power.

Charles E. Merriam, *Political Power* (McGraw-Hill, 1934) is a pathbreaking analysis of political life in terms of power and the context in which it is exercised.

Frederick M. Watkins, *The State as a Concept in Political Science* (Harper, 1934) gives a good brief account of the rise of the state, but insists that politics more properly concerns the exercise of power by and within associations pursuing autonomy.

R. M. MacIver, *The Modern State* (Oxford University Press, 1926) is a substantial survey of the state in its history, forms, and authority.

Daniel J. Boorstin, *The Genius of American Politics* (University of Chicago Press, 1953) considers America an example of the superiority of politics as pragmatic accommodation rather than acting on principle.

Ernst Cassirer, *The Myth of the State* (Yale University Press, 1946) offers an analysis of the ideas and beliefs which have shaped our political life in modern times.

Karl W. Deutsch, *Nationalism and Social Communication* (Wiley, 1953) is an innovating work, treating nationalism empirically in terms of communications theory.

K. W. Deutsch and W. J. Folz (eds.), *Nation-Building* (Atherton, 1963) is a collection of diverse essays treating the development of nations and includes a good bibliography.

Carlton J. H. Hayes, *Nationalism: A Religion* (Macmillan, 1960) sums up nicely the data and conclusions of one of the leading historians of nationalist movements.

Frederick Herz, *Nationality in History and Politics* (Kegan Paul, 1944) is a thorough study of nationalism as historical fact and as ideology.

Boyd C. Shafer, *Nationalism; Myth and Reality* (Harcourt, Brace, 1955) is a sensitive historical study.

Louis L. Snyder, *The Meaning of Nationalism* (Rutgers University Press, 1954) combining historical, political, sociological, and psychological insights in an effort to understand nationalism, concludes that it is an essentially arbitrary distinction among men.

CHAPTER 3: DEMOCRACY IN THE MODERN WORLD

A. F. Hattersley, *A Short History of Democracy* (Cambridge University Press, 1930) is a useful survey.

Leslie Lipson, *The Democratic Civilization* (Oxford University Press, 1964) is a wide-ranging historical and analytical treatment of the subject.

A. H. M. Jones, *Athenian Democracy* (Blackwell, 1957) is an excellent study of the scope and character of Greek democracy.

G. P. Gooch, *English Democratic Ideas in the Seventeenth Century* (Harper Torchbooks, 1959) is a classic study of the revolutionary period which greatly influenced the development of modern democracy.

Edwin Mims, Jr., *The Majority of the People* (Modern Age Books, 1941) presents a well-argued case for something approaching populistic democracy.

J. L. Talmon, *The Rise of Totalitarian Democracy* (Beacon, 1952) analyzes the eighteenth-century mass, or nonliberal, democratic ideas. *Political Messianism* (Praeger, 1960) continues with those of the nineteenth century.

Leonard T. Hobhouse, *Liberalism* (Holt, 1911) is the best introduction to the perspectives of twentieth-century liberalism.

Ernest Barker, *Reflections on Government* (Oxford University Press, 1942) is a thoughtful study of liberty, democracy, and the contemporary problems of democratic government.

Carl L. Becker, *Modern Democracy* (Yale University Press, 1941) discusses briefly the democratic ideal in history, contrasts it with reality, and considers whether the dilemma can be overcome.

C. W. Cassinelli, *The Politics of Freedom: An Analysis of the Modern Democratic State* (University of Washington Press, 1961) is a cogent study of democracy and the relation between procedures and values.

Robert A. Dahl, *A Preface to Democratic Theory* (University of Chicago Press, 1956) is a rigorously logical discussion of several democratic perspectives, utilizing carefully developed models. The same author's *Who Governs? Democracy and Power in an American City* (Yale University Press, 1961) gives a sophisticated empirical picture of democratic political community in a modern urban environment.

Anthony Downs, *An Economic Theory of Democracy* (Harper, 1957) utilizes the concepts of utility analysis in economics to attempt a coherent and realistic theory of democracy.

Carl J. Friedrich, *The New Image of the Common Man* (Beacon, 1950) is a broadly ranging discussion, including careful and insightful consideration of the contemporary inadequacies of many traditional democratic ideas.

John H. Hallowell, *The Moral Foundations of Democracy* (University of Chicago Press, 1954) argues that democracy is possible only for men sharing moral principles.

F. A. Hermens, *The Representative Republic* (University of Notre Dame Press, 1958) is a broad comparative and historical study, developing a theory of democracy emphasizing unifying institutions and leadership.

A. D. Lindsay, *The Modern Democratic State* (Oxford University Press, 1943) is a particularly valuable study, viewing democracy as the product of "operative ideals" arising in all aspects of western life throughout history.

Henry B. Mayo, *An Introduction to Democratic Theory* (Oxford University Press, 1960) is an excellent over-all study of democratic practices, values, and accomplishments.

Reinhold Niebuhr, *The Children of Light and the Children of Darkness* (Scribner, 1944) is an effort of an eminent theologian and social critic to distinguish the transitory from the permanently valuable elements in democracy.

Joseph A. Schumpeter, *Capitalism, Socialism, and Democracy,* 3rd ed. (Harper, 1950), develops a theory of democracy and endeavors to show its relation to, as well as distinction from, particular economic orders.

Yves R. Simon, *Philosophy of Democratic Government* (University of Chicago Press, 1951) is a searching analysis of democratic concepts, critical of the most commonly accepted interpretations of them.

T. V. Smith, *The Ethics of Compromise and the Art of Containment* (Starr King, 1956) is a thoughtful essay, illustrating well the delicate balance that democracy requires between principle and expediency.

M. T. Swabey, *Theory of the Democratic State* (Harvard University Press, 1937) is a carefully reasoned, pragmatic argument for democracy as both humane and scientific.

Rupert Emerson, *From Nation to Empire* (Harvard University Press, 1960) is a careful appraisal of the political future and the possibilities of democracy in the nonwestern world.

Edmond Cahn, *The Predicament of Democratic Man* (Macmillan, 1961) analyzes the moral involvement of citizens in the unjust acts of democratic governments.

George A. Graham, *America's Capacity to Govern* (University of Alabama Press, 1960) is a stimulating discussion of the values and problems of contemporary democracy.

Suzanne Labin, *The Secret of Democracy* (Vanguard, 1955) is a vigorous defense of the faith of democracy.

Seymour M. Lipset, *Political Man* (Doubleday, 1960) is a sociological analysis of politics and the conditions of democracy.

Thomas L. Thorson, *The Logic of Democracy* (Holt, 1962) is an original, if not entirely satisfactory, justification of democracy.

Joseph Tussman, *Obligation and the Body Politic* (Oxford University Press, 1960) is an original analysis of democratic citizenship and its responsibilities.

CHAPTER 4: THE CHALLENGE TO DEMOCRACY

Guy Stanton Ford (ed.), *Dictatorship in the Modern World* (University of Minnesota Press, 1939) treats in a collection of articles the dictatorships following World War I.

R. N. Carew Hunt, *The Theory and Practice of Communism,* 5th ed. (Macmillan, 1957), is a very able survey of communism from 1848. His *Marxism: Past and Present* (Macmillan, 1954) is a short and clear discussion of the philosophical basis of communism.

Sidney Hook, *Marx and the Marxists: The Ambiguous Legacy* (Van Nostrand, 1955) is a useful analysis and also contains excerpts from writings of Marx to Stalin.

Alfred G. Meyer, *Marxism: The Unity of Theory and Practice* (Harvard University Press, 1954) is a perceptive discussion of the subject, giving especial attention to the internal contradictions of Marxism leading to schism. His *Leninism* (Harvard University Press, 1957) is a careful study of one issue of the breakdown in Marxian unity, and develops Lenin's contributions to modern communism.

Joseph A. Schumpeter, *Capitalism, Socialism, and Democracy,* 3rd ed. (Harper, 1950), gives a valuable treatment of the diverse facets of Marx and his ideas.

Gustav A. Wetter, *Dialectical Materialism: A Historical and Systematic Survey of Philosophy in the Soviet Union,* rev. ed. (Praeger, 1963) is a critique of the Soviet effort to impose a unity upon all science, philosophy, and politics.

Adam B. Ulam, *The Unfinished Revolution: An Essay on the Sources of Influence of Marxism and Communism* (Random House, 1960) treats the appeal of Marxism in the underdeveloped countries.

Z. K. Brzezinski, *Ideology and Power in Soviet Politics* (Praeger, 1962) analyzes the institutionalized revolution in Soviet government at home and abroad.

R. T. Holt and J. E. Turner (eds.), *Soviet Union: Paradox and Change* (Holt, 1962) treats developments in the Soviet system since Stalin's death.

David Footman (ed.), *International Communism* (Southern Illinois University Press, 1960) presents scholarly research on a variety of aspects of its subject.

Elliot R. Goodman, *The Soviet Design for a World State* (Columbia University Press, 1960) discusses Soviet aims at political aggrandizement through the absorption of other states.

Milovan Djilas, *The New Class* (Praeger, 1957) offers unsparing criticism of the gap between ideals and realities in communist regimes.

Allan Bullock, *Hitler: A Study in Tyranny,* 2nd ed. (Harper, 1964), offers one of the best studies of German National Socialism in terms of its leader.

William Ebenstein, *The Nazi State* (Farrar and Rinehart, 1943) studies the regime in its theory and its institutions.

Herman Rauschning, *The Revolution of Nihilism* (Alliance, 1939) is a graphic contemporary account of the development of the Nazi regime in Germany.

William Ebenstein, *Fascist Italy* (American Book, 1939) provides a careful study of the Italian dictatorship.

Hannah Arendt, *The Origins of Totalitarianism,* 2nd ed. (Meridian, 1958), presents a striking interpretation of totalitarianism, imperialism, and antisemitism.

C. J. Friedrich (ed.), *Totalitarianism* (Harvard University Press, 1954) contains diverse essays analyzing many aspects of totalitarianism in theory and practice.

C. J. Friedrich and Z. K. Brzezinski, *Totalitarian Dictatorship and Autocracy,* rev. ed. (Praeger, 1961), provides a comparative analysis of totalitarian systems and their principal features.

Erich Fromm, *Escape from Freedom* (Rinehart, 1941) analyzes the rise of Nazi Germany in terms of the failure of liberal democracy to meet basic psychological needs.

John K. Galbraith, *The Affluent Society* (Houghton Mifflin, 1958) is a cogent analysis of some important social consequences following the American emphasis on a high production economy.

Friedrich von Hayek, *The Road to Serfdom* (University of Chicago Press, 1944) is a bitter attack on socialism and planning as leading from liberal democracy to totalitarian dictatorship.

Barbara Wooton, *Freedom Under Planning* (University of North Carolina Press, 1945) in rebuttal of Hayek, defends the compatibility of planning and democracy.

T. B. Bottomore, *Elites and Society* (Watts, 1964) is a short discussion of elitist theories, their applicability in the world today, and their relevance for democracy.

Charles Frankel, *The Democratic Prospect* (Harper, 1962) gives a perceptive, yet optimistic, discussion of the difficulties of liberal democracy in contemporary life.

Robert J. Harris, *The Quest for Equality* (Louisiana State University Press, 1960) considers the history of equality in regard to civil liberties in the United States.

Emil Lederer, *The State of the Masses* (Norton, 1940) is an eloquent analysis of the totalitarian tendencies inherent in twentieth-century democratic communities.

Walter Lippmann, *Essays in the Public Philosophy* (Mentor, 1956) discusses the standards of responsibility which the author insists democracies are falling away from today.

Gunnar Myrdal, *Beyond the Welfare State* (Yale University Press, 1960) is a provocative analysis of how the future of democracies depends upon their ability to transcend their old ways.

J. Ortega y Gasset, *The Revolt of the Masses* (Norton, 1932) is a classic work, arguing that modern democracy means the dominance of those who recognize no challenge or responsibility.

R. S. Rankin and W. R. Dallmayr, *Freedom and Emergency Powers in the Cold War* (Appleton-Century-Crofts, 1964) deals with the threat to civil liberties in the expansion of executive powers, in terms of specific cases.

Clinton Rossiter, *Conservatism in America,* rev. ed. (Vintage Books, 1962) analyzes the conflict between liberal and conservative perspectives in American democracy.

Francis E. Rourke, *Secrecy and Publicity: Dilemmas of Democracy* (Johns Hopkins University Press, 1961) discusses thoughtfully one of the serious problems of contemporary democracy in its American setting.

Renzo Sereno, *The Rulers* (Praeger, 1962) is a good analysis of elitist theories of government and their inadequacies.

David Spitz, *Patterns of Anti-Democratic Thought* (Macmillan, 1949) analyzes the various nontotalitarian indictments of democracy, mainly in modern American criticisms. The same author's *Democracy and the Challenge of Power* (Columbia University Press, 1958) suggests that democratic government is no guarantee against the abuse of power and denial of freedom.

C. O. Porter and R. J. Alexander, *The Struggle for Democracy in Latin America* (Macmillan, 1961) are optimistic, but indicate some of the difficulties in developing democracy where it has not existed.

Immanuel Wallerstein, *Africa: The Politics of Independence* (Vintage Books, 1961) gives a good survey of political developments and democratic possibilities in post-colonial Africa.

PART THREE: ORDER AND FREEDOM

Carl Becker, *Freedom and Responsibility in the American Way of Life* (Knopf, 1947) analyzes with historical erudition the important liberties of the modern world, the responsibilities which are their counterpart, and the constitutional order which supports both.

Morroe Berger *et al.* (eds.), *Freedom and Control in Modern Society* (Van Nostrand, 1954) is a collection of excellent studies, generally of a sociological nature, illuminating freedom and order by showing how they are interrelated.

Harold Laski, *Liberty in the Modern State,* new ed. (Allen and Unwin, 1948), identifies liberty with the existence of social conditions furthering individual happiness, and thus sees liberty and order closely related.

Peter Laslett *et al., Philosophy, Politics and Society* (Macmillan, 1956) contains ten essays on various central aspects of political order, manifesting the technique and utility of analytic philosophy.

H. Mark Roelofs, *The Tension of Citizenship* (Rinehart, 1957) explores the relations between "private man and public duty" and nicely illustrates order and freedom in political life.

F. Lyman Windolph, *Leviathan and Natural Law* (Princeton University Press, 1951) is an interesting essay, showing that liberty, justice, and democratic constitutional order can only survive together.

CHAPTER 5: CONSTITUTIONS AND CONSTITUTIONALISM

Carl J. Friedrich, *Constitutional Government and Democracy,* rev. ed. (Ginn, 1950), is a basic and original work, developing a theory of constitutional government and examining its manifestations in governments of the past and present.

C. H. McIlwain, *Constitutionalism, Ancient and Modern,* rev. ed. (Cornell University Press, 1947), surveys the development of constitutionalism in terms of the restraints of law in western history, and criticizes modern constitutionalism for its attempt to divide power.

Franz Neuman, *The Democratic and the Authoritarian State* (Free Press, 1957) contains valuable essays on basic constitutional concepts, such as power, law, and political freedom.

E. M. Sait, *Political Institutions: A Preface* (Appleton-Century, 1938) discusses the rise of basic western political institutions and patterns which form our constitutional heritage.

F. M. Watkins, *The Political Tradition of the West* (Harvard University Press, 1948) analyzes the western constitutional tradition in terms of its principal ideas and poses its main contemporary problems.

Francis D. Wormuth, *The Origins of Modern Constitutionalism* (Harper, 1949) emphasizes the English contribution to the basic ideas of constitutionalism.

Herbert J. Spiro, *Government by Constitution* (Random House, 1959) is a comparative study of constitutional governments, utilizing an unusual and fruitful analytic scheme.

Michael Stewart, *Modern Forms of Government* (Allen and Unwin, 1959) is a comparative survey of forms of government.

C. F. Strong, *A History of Modern Political Constitutions* (Capricorn, 1963), surveys constitutionalism and constitutional arrangements through a variety of political systems.

K. C. Wheare, *Modern Constitutions* (Oxford University Press, 1951) is a brief introductory survey.

L. S. Amery, *Thoughts on the Constitution,* 2nd ed. (Oxford University Press, 1953), presents penetrating analysis of the British constitution, based upon both study and long experience in political life.

Walter Bagehot, *The English Constitution* (Oxford University Press, 1936) is a classic study of the mid-Victorian constitution.

A. B. Keith, *The Constitution of England from Queen Victoria to George VI* (Macmillan, 1940) constitutes a major work surveying English constitutional law and custom.

Geoffrey Marshall and Graeme C. Moodie, *Some Problems of the Constitution* (Hutchinson, 1959) is an analysis of Britain's "unwritten" constitution.

O. Hood Phillips, *The Constitutional Law of Great Britain and the Commonwealth,* 2nd ed. (Sweet and Maxwell, 1957) is a substantial survey of the subject.

E. S. Corwin and J. W. Peltason, *Understanding the Constitution,* 3rd ed. (Holt, 1964) is a historical and analytical consideration of the American Constitution and related documents.

Herbert W. Horwill, *The Usages of the American Constitution* (Oxford University Press, 1925) shows the effect of practice and custom on constitutional interpretation.

Howard L. McBain, *The Living Constitution* (Macmillan, 1927) is a short classic interpretation of the American Constitution.

Robert G. McCloskey (ed.), *Essays in Constitutional Law* (Knopf, 1957) is a stimulating collection of essays on the American Constitution.

Conyers Read (ed.), *The Constitution Reconsidered* (Columbia University Press, 1938) is a collection of essays by distinguished scholars, treating the American Constitution from many perspectives.

Roy C. Macridis and Bernard E. Brown, *The De Gaulle Republic: Quest for Unity* (Dorsey, 1960) discusses the development of constitutional debate in France from the Liberation.

E. Drexel Godfrey, Jr., *The Government of France,* 2nd ed. (Crowell, 1963) is a concise account of the constitutional arrangements.

E. Litchfield *et al., Governing Postwar Germany* (Cornell University Press, 1953) includes studies of the Constitution of the German Federal Republic and of particular aspects of its government and politics.

Elmer Plischke, *Contemporary Government of Germany* (Houghton Mifflin, 1961) is a thorough treatment of the constitutional structure of the German Federal Republic, with a contrasting chapter on the government of East Germany.

Charles H. Alexandrowicz, *Constitutional Developments in India* (Oxford University Press, 1957) discusses selected basic constitutional issues.

Merle Fainsod, *How Russia is Ruled,* rev. ed. (Harvard University Press, 1963) is a major work on Soviet government which includes a chapter on "constitutional myths and political realities."

John N. Hazard, *The Soviet System of Government,* 3rd ed. (University of Chicago Press, 1964) is another useful and stimulating general study.

Herbert J. Spiro, *Politics in Africa: Prospects South of the Sahara* (Prentice-Hall, 1962) attempts to assess the possibility of distinctive patterns of constitutional government in Africa.

H. E. Cohen, *Recent Theories of Sovereignty* (University of Chicago Press, 1937) is a good brief survey of twentieth-century conceptions of sovereignty, and a pluralist criticism.

A. T. Vanderbilt, *The Doctrine of Separation of Powers and Its Present Day Significance* (University of Nebraska Press, 1953) discusses the history of the doctrine and criticizes deviations from it today as a danger to free government.

Robert R. Bowie and C. J. Friedrich, *Studies in Federalism* (Little, Brown, 1954) is a thorough study of various functional and organizational aspects of federalism.

Jane P. Clark, *The Rise of a New Federalism* (Columbia University Press, 1938) analyzes American federalism in terms of functional cooperation rather than mutually exclusive jurisdictions.

Robert A. Goldwin (ed.), *A Nation of States* (Rand McNally, 1963) presents a collection of diverse, generally conservative essays on the history, nature, and principles of American federalism.

William S. Livingston, *Federalism and Constitutional Change* (Clarendon Press, 1956) studies the major federal constitutions through the nature of their amending processes.

Arthur W. Macmahon (ed.), *Federalism: Mature and Emergent* (Doubleday, 1955) is a symposium on the subject, gathering a variety of approaches and views.

K. C. Wheare, *Federal Government,* 4th ed. (Oxford University Press, 1964), is a substantial comparative study of the principal federal systems.

Clinton L. Rossiter, *Constitutional Dictatorship: Crisis Government in the Modern Democracies* (Princeton University Press, 1948) treats the problem of preserving constitutional government in times of crisis.

Charles L. Black, Jr., *The People and the Court* (Macmillan, 1960) is a careful reappraisal of the place of judicial review in American democracy.

Robert G. McCloskey, *The American Supreme Court* (University of Chicago Press, 1960) is an excellent introduction to the nature of judicial review and its rise in American history.

Arnold J. Zurcher (ed.), *Constitutions and Constitutional Trends Since World War II,* 2nd ed. (New York University Press, 1955), is a collection of essays on problems of constitution-making in postwar Europe.

CHAPTER 6: LIBERTY AND THE STATE

Christian Bay, *The Structure of Freedom* (Stanford University Press, 1958) attempts to analyze freedom according to the concepts of psychology and other behavioral sciences, yielding a valuable if confusing work.

Maurice Cranston, *Freedom: A New Analysis* (Longmans, Green, 1953) offers a useful linguistic analysis of the term and a brief history of liberalism to illustrate the diverse meanings "liberty" has been given.

Dorothy Fosdick, *What Is Liberty?* (Harper, 1939) does much to clarify the meaning and show the possibility of freedom for men.

R. L. Hale, *Freedom Through Law* (Columbia University Press, 1952) discusses, with American illustrations, how law in controlling private coercive economic power furthers liberty.

F. von Hayek, *The Constitution of Liberty* (University of Chicago Press, 1960) is a considered and extensive treatment of liberty as the absence of coercion, and argues that increasing governmental activity is the greatest threat to it.

Milton R. Konvitz and Clinton Rossiter, *Aspects of Liberty: Essays Presented to Robert E. Cushman* (Cornell University Press, 1958) furnishes a collection of essays, ranging from broad discussions of freedom to specific treatments of the condition of civil liberties in recent years.

Felix E. Oppenheim, *Dimensions of Freedom* (St. Martin's, 1961) is a good example of the use of logical analysis in an effort to clarify a complex concept.

Patrick G. Walker, *Restatement of Liberty* (Hutchinson, 1951) is a broad analysis of liberty in history and the problems it confronts, ultimately resolvable only by acceptance of moral responsibility.

H. S. Commager, *Freedom, Loyalty, and Dissent* (Oxford University Press, 1954) is a vigorous defense of the importance of freedom, founded largely upon a pragmatic and experimental outlook.

S. E. Morison, *Freedom in Contemporary Society* (Little, Brown, 1956) discusses political, economic, and academic freedom.

Walter Berns, *Freedom, Virtue, and the First Amendment* (Louisiana University Press, 1957) is a thoughtful criticism of the libertarian perspective.

A. S. P. Woodhouse, *Puritanism and Liberty,* 2nd ed. (University of Chicago Press, 1951), is a valuable collection of materials and an introductory essay, dealing with Puritan contributions to English freedom, constitutionalism, and democracy.

Freda Casteberg, *Freedom of Speech in the West* (Oceana, 1960) is a study of the law regarding free speech in the United States, France, and Germany.

Z. Chafee (ed.), *Documents on Fundamental Human Rights* (Harvard University Press, 1951–1952) is an extensive collection of legal materials defining civil liberties, mostly in the Anglo-American tradition. His *Free Speech in the United States* (Harvard University Press, 1942) is a classic history and analysis, which may be supplemented by his *Government and Mass Communications,* 2 vols. (University of Chicago Press, 1947).

Robert E. Cushman, *Civil Liberties in the United States* (Cornell University Press, 1956) is a broad survey.

W. L. Chenery, *Freedom of the Press* (Harcourt, 1955) is a useful treatment of the history as well as the contemporary situation of press freedom.

John Eaves, Jr., *Emergency Powers and the Parliamentary Watchdog: Parliament and the Executive in Great Britain, 1939–1951* (Hansard Society, 1957) deals with the problem of constitutional rights through parliamentary protection.

David Fellman, *The Defendant's Rights* (Rinehart, 1958) and *The Constitutional Right of Association* (University of Chicago Press, 1963) present and comment on the law and constitutional rights on these topics.

Peter J. Fliess, *Freedom of the Press in the German Republic, 1918–1933* (Louisiana State University Press, 1955) shows how in some circumstances political order may not survive unlimited liberty.

Walter Gellhorn, *American Rights* (Macmillan, 1960) is perhaps the best brief study of American procedural and substantive liberties.

Terrence J. Murphy, *Censorship: Government and Obscenity* (Helicon, 1963) analyzes the situation and problems on the subject in the United States, and questions libertarian assumptions.

John F. Golay, *The Founding of the Federal Republic of Germany* (University of Chicago Press, 1958) discusses the defining of civil rights in the German Constitution.

Arthur N. Holcombe, *Human Rights in the Modern World* (New York University Press, 1947) is a short discussion of efforts in the United Nations at drafting an international bill of rights.

Harold M. Hyman, *To Try Men's Souls* (University of California Press, 1959) offers a history of the use of loyalty tests in the United States.

M. R. Konvitz, *Fundamental Liberties of a Free People: Religion, Speech, Press, Assembly* (Cornell University Press, 1957) analyzes the basic rights guaranteed by the First Amendment to the American Constitution.

Alexander Meiklejohn, *Political Freedom* (Harper, 1960) is one of the strongest defenses of freedom of speech in the public interest.

D. A. Schmeiser, *Civil Liberties in Canada* (Oxford University Press, 1964) describes Canadian practice and law and compares it with that in Britain and the United States.

David H. Bayley, *Public Liberties in the New States* (Rand McNally, 1964) is the first comprehensive survey of the subject.

PART FOUR: PEOPLE AND POLITICS

V. O. Key, Jr., *Politics, Parties, and Pressure Groups,* 5th ed. (Crowell, 1964), is an authoritative study treating the subjects of American political parties and interest groups.

Hugh A. Bone and Austin Ranney, *Politics and Voters* (McGraw-Hill, 1963), is a short treatment of American parties, with attention to interest groups and opinion measurement.

Avery Leiserson, *Parties and Politics* (Knopf, 1958) introduces the behavioral as well as the institutional approach to the subject and treats it in realms outside the American context.

William Goodman, *The Two-Party System in the United States,* 3rd ed. (Van Nostrand, 1964), is a carefully organized volume emphasizing the American scene.

E. E. Schattschneider, *The Semisovereign People* (Holt, Rinehart and Winston, 1960) is a provocative analysis of the conditions and character of political participation.

D. W. Brogan, *Citizenship Today: England—France—The United States* (University of North Carolina Press, 1960) presents a short but perceptive discussion of the role of the modern citizen.

Alfred DeGrazia, *Public and Republic* (Knopf, 1951) is an analysis of the problem of political representation in American life.

G. A. Almond and S. Verba, *The Civic Culture; Political Attitudes and Democracy in Five Nations* (Princeton University Press, 1963) analyzes civic loyalty and political participation.

Lucian W. Pye, *Politics, Personality, and Nation-Building* (Yale University Press, 1962) attempts to account for the difficulties of transitional societies with a psychological approach.

C. P. Snow, *Science and Government* (Harvard University Press, 1961) shows that when scientists participate in government they remain human beings.

Fred R. von der Mehden, *Politics of the Developing Nations* (Prentice-Hall, 1964) analyzes the forces at work among the new states and obstacles to their stability.

CHAPTER 7: INTERESTS AND OPINION

David B. Truman, *The Governmental Process* (Knopf, 1951) is the most comprehensive and analytic treatment of interest groups and offers an important theoretical basis for their consideration.

Henry W. Ehrmann (ed.), *Interest Groups on Four Continents* (Pittsburgh University Press, 1958) provides an extremely valuable collection of papers devoted to interest groups in nine different states, emphasizing comparisons and contrasts.

Donald C. Blaisdell (ed.), "Unofficial Government: Pressure Groups and Lobbies," *Annals of the American Academy of Political and Social Science* (September, 1958), Vol. 319, contains a group of short articles treating interest groups from many different perspectives.

Harmon Zeigler, *Interest Groups in American Society* (Prentice-Hall, 1964) is a useful treatment of interest group functions in the American setting.

Karl Schriftgiesser, *The Lobbyists* (Little, Brown, 1951) is an interesting account of the extent and consequences of lobbying in the United States.

Allen Potter, *Organized Groups in British National Politics* (Faber, 1961) is the most extensive treatment of the subject.

J. D. Stewart, *British Pressure Groups* (Oxford University Press, 1958) is a careful study of group activity directed at the House of Commons.

Joseph La Palombara, *Interest Groups in Italian Politics* (Princeton University Press, 1964) is a substantial study of the subject based on field research.

Philip Williams, *Politics in Post-War France* (Longmans, Green, 1954) includes a chapter on French interest groups and their influence.

John N. Hazard, *The Soviet System of Government,* 3rd ed. (Chicago University Press, 1964), is a very informative study that gives attention to interests and their control in the communist dictatorship.

V. O. Key, Jr., *Public Opinion and American Democracy* (Knopf, 1961) is a major work reflecting the substantial research on the subject.

R. E. Lane and D. O. Sears, *Public Opinion* (McGraw-Hill, 1964) is a short introduction emphasizing opinion formation.

R. M. Christenson and R. O. McWilliams (eds.), *Voice of the People: Readings in Public Opinion and Propaganda* (McGraw-Hill, 1962) provides an anthology of materials, ranging broadly.

Francis G. Wilson, *A Theory of Public Opinion* (Regnery, 1962) attempts a philosophical and critical analysis of public opinion.

Bernard R. Berelson and Morris Janowitz (eds.), *Reader in Public Opinion and Communications*, 2nd ed. (Free Press, 1953), contains an excellent collection of articles drawn from a variety of sources.

Charles S. Steinberg, *The Mass Communicators: Public Relations, Public Opinion, and Mass Media* (Harper, 1958) emphasizes the relation between public opinion and public relations.

Clarence Schettler, *Public Opinion in American Society* (Harper, 1960) is a well-written and thoughtful approach to the subject.

Wilbur Schramm, *Mass Communications*, 2nd ed. (University of Illinois Press, 1960), is a collection of readings reflecting the varying views of the social sciences upon the subject.

Walter Lippmann, *Public Opinion* (Macmillan, 1922) is an early work of analysis considered one of the classics on the subject.

Lindsay Rogers, *The Pollsters* (Knopf, 1949) is a sharp attack on the assumptions and methods of public opinion polling.

Wilbur Schramm, *Mass Media and National Development; The Role of Information in the Developing Countries* (Stanford University Press, 1964) discusses the role of communications in the underdeveloped states.

CHAPTER 8: VOTERS AND PARTIES

Neil A. MacDonald, *The Study of Political Parties* (Doubleday, 1955) is an excellent short introduction to the subject.

Maurice Duverger, *Political Parties; Their Organization and Activity in the Modern State* (Wiley, 1954) is the only important comparative study of modern parties; its emphasis is on structure and function.

Sigmund Neumann (ed.), *Modern Political Parties* (Chicago University Press, 1956) contains a wide-ranging collection of studies of party systems in various countries.

James W. Garner, *Political Science and Government* (American Book, 1928) contains a chapter on the electorate with much reference to earlier views.

William H. Riker, *Democracy in the United States* (Macmillan, 1953) devotes discussion to the relationship of American suffrage and democracy.

W. J. M. MacKenzie, *Free Elections* (Allen and Unwin, 1958) discusses electoral systems in general, with attention to voters, candidates, voting methods, and elections.

E. Lakeman and J. D. Lambert, *Voting in Democracies,* 2nd ed. (Faber, 1959), is a study of election systems and voting, with extensive treatment of proportional representation.

Clinton L. Rossiter, *Parties and Politics in America* (Cornell University Press, 1960) offers a succinct and analytical account of American politics.

R. T. McKenzie, *British Political Parties,* 2nd ed. (St. Martin's Press, 1963), constitutes an important study emphasizing internal structure and operations of the major parties.

Ivor Bulmer-Thomas, *The Party System in Great Britain* (Phoenix, 1953) is an extensive treatment of the party system with useful material on party organization and the minor parties.

J. A. Laponce, *The Government of the Fifth Republic* (University of California Press, 1961) devotes the larger portion of his discussion to French parties and their organization.

Louise Overacker, *The Australian Party System* (Yale University Press, 1952) is the fullest treatment of the subject.

Dankwart A. Rustow, *The Politics of Compromise* (Princeton University Press, 1955) is an important study of Sweden's political parties and their organization.

R. A. Gomez, *Government and Politics in Latin America* (Random House, 1960) is a useful short treatment of the electoral process and politics in Latin America.

Myron Weiner, *Party Politics in India* (Princeton University Press, 1957) provides an intensive study of the subject in one of the newer states led by a "national" party.

Thomas Hodgkin, *African Political Parties: An Introductory Guide* (Penguin, 1961) is an instructive essay on the subject.

Stanley G. Payne, *Falange: A History of Spanish Fascism* (Stanford University Press, 1961) characterizes the fascism of the Franco regime and its divergence from Italian and German forms.

Robert R. Alford, *Party and Society: The Anglo-American Democracies* (Rand McNally, 1963) shows how the factors of class, age, and religion produce differing voting behavior in different countries.

Henry J. Abraham, *Compulsory Voting* (Public Affairs, 1955) is a useful brief treatment of the topic.

William Kornhauser, *The Politics of Mass Society* (Free Press, 1959) provides an extensive treatment of marginal and extremist political movements.

E. E. Schattschneider, *Party Government* (Rinehart, 1942) is an informed and significant work on the American party system.

J. F. S. Ross, *Elections and Electors* (Eyre and Spottiswoode, 1955) treats the subject mainly with reference to British elections.

Alexander Heard, *The Costs of Democracy* (University of North Carolina Press, 1960) is an important study of financing politics.

The Institute of Electoral Research, *A Review of Elections 1954–58* (Scorpion, 1960) contains a useful compilation of election figures and notes on party systems in various countries.

Angus Campbell, P. E. Converse, *et al., The American Voter* (Wiley, 1960) is an excellent demonstration of survey research applied to the subject of electoral behavior.

H. Daudt, *Floating Voters and the Floating Vote* (Stenfert Kroese, 1961) is a Dutch scholar's critical review of electoral behavior research.

Carl J. Friedrich and Z. K. Brzezinski, *Totalitarian Dictatorship and Autocracy,* rev. ed. (Praeger, 1961), treats the theory of dictatorship, with discussion of the totalitarian party.

John S. Reshetar, *A Concise History of the Communist Party of the Soviet Union,* 2nd ed. (Praeger, 1964), is the best succinct history of the party's development.

PART FIVE: INSTITUTIONS OF GOVERNMENT

Harry Eckstein and D. E. Apter (eds.), *Comparative Politics: A Reader* (Free Press, 1963) discusses present trends in comparative politics and major institutions of both developed and underdeveloped countries.

R. C. Macridis and B. E. Brown, *Comparative Politics; Notes and Readings,* rev. ed. (Dorsey, 1964), treats problems of comparative analysis and both western and nonwestern political systems.

Gwendolen M. Carter and John H. Herz, *Major Foreign Powers,* 4th ed. (Harcourt, Brace, 1962), treats individually, but in parallel fashion, the four major European governments, and furnishes a good bibliography.

Robert G. Neumann, *European and Comparative Government,* 3rd ed. (McGraw-Hill, 1960), offers a well-written survey of the four major European systems, and a fifth section devoted to comparative treatment of institutions.

Samuel H. Beer and Adam B. Ulam, *Patterns of Government: the Major Political Systems of Europe,* 2nd ed. (Random House, 1962), compares the four European governments in terms of political culture, power, interests, and policy.

Taylor Cole (ed.), *European Political Systems,* 2nd ed. (Knopf, 1959), includes attention to Italy and the east European countries, with each section written by a specialist.

G. Lowell Field, *Governments in Modern Society* (McGraw-Hill, 1951) is a basic analysis of the governmental process, valuable for its comparative treatment of the principal institutions.

R. McGregor Dawson, *The Government of Canada,* 4th ed. (University of Toronto Press, 1963), is a good treatment of the subject.

James M. Burns and Jack W. Peltason, *Government by the People,* 5th ed. (Prentice-Hall, 1963), is a readable study of American government.

Thomas H. Eliot, *Governing America: The Politics of a Free People,*

2nd ed. (Dodd, Mead, 1964), constitutes an authoritative introduction to American political problems and processes.

J. C. Livingston and R. G. Thompson, *The Consent of the Governed: An Introduction to American Government* (Macmillan, 1963) is a fresh approach emphasizing the theory of American democratic government.

J. Harvey and L. Bather, *The British Constitution* (St. Martin's, 1963) is a good survey and critical analysis.

Graeme C. Moodie, *The Government of Great Britain,* 2nd ed. (Crowell, 1964), is a thoughtful treatment.

Merle Fainsod, *How Russia Is Ruled,* rev. ed. (Harvard University Press, 1963), is the standard study of the subject.

Richard C. Gripp, *Patterns of Soviet Politics* (Dorsey Press, 1963) is a good introduction.

Herbert McClosky and J. E. Turner, *The Soviet Dictatorship* (McGraw-Hill, 1960) offers a scholarly treatment of Soviet institutions.

Z. K. Brzezinski, *The Soviet Bloc; Unity and Conflict,* rev. ed. (Praeger, 1961), gives detailed treatment of these states and their relationships.

Hugh Seton-Watson, *The East European Revolution,* 3rd ed. (Praeger, 1956), treats the background and development of the Soviet satellite system.

H. E. Davis, *Government and Politics in Latin America* (Ronald, 1958) offers a stimulating discussion of Latin American political affairs.

Don Peretz, *The Middle East Today* (Holt, 1963) is a good survey of its contemporary history and government.

George McT. Kahin (ed.), *Major Governments of Asia,* 2nd ed. (Cornell University Press, 1963), is an excellent survey of China, Japan, India, Pakistan, and Indonesia. He has also edited an equally valuable volume, *Governments and Politics of Southeast Asia,* 2nd ed. (Cornell, 1964).

G. M. Carter (ed.), *African One-Party States* (Cornell University Press, 1962) examines the political patterns developing in six of these countries.

Gabriel Almond and James L. Coleman (eds.), *The Politics of the Developing Areas* (Princeton University Press, 1960) constitutes the first significant study comparing nonwestern political systems.

John H. Kautsky (ed.), *Political Change in Underdeveloped Countries; Nationalism and Communism* (Wiley, 1962) collects a number of articles on the subject.

CHAPTER 9: THE EXECUTIVE

Ivar Lissner, *The Living Past: The Great Civilizations of Mankind* (Jonathan Cape, 1957) is a survey of early civilizations which includes discussion of ancient governments.

Ewart Lewis, *Medieval Political Ideas,* 2 vols. (Knopf, 1954), contains useful materials on political authority in the middle ages.

O. Jászi and John D. Lewis, *Against the Tyrant: The Tradition and Theory of Tyrannicide* (Free Press, 1957) discusses the problem of resistance to authoritarian rule.

Douglas Verney, *The Analysis of Political Systems* (Routledge and Kegan Paul, 1959) is an introductory treatment comparing presidential and parliamentary executives.

Charles Petrie, *Monarchy in the Twentieth Century* (Andrew Dakers, 1952) explains the office of monarch in Britain and several European countries.

Dermot Morrah, *The Work of the Queen* (William Kimber, 1958) is an interesting account of the Queen's role in British government.

Charles Petrie, *The Modern British Monarchy* (Eyre and Spottiswoode, 1961) emphasizes both continuity and change in the institution and its representative quality.

Ivor Jennings, *Cabinet Government,* 3rd ed. (Cambridge University Press, 1959), is a classic work on the British executive.

John P. Macintosh, *The British Cabinet* (Stevens, 1962) is a substantial recent study by a British scholar.

Byrum E. Carter, *The Office of Prime Minister* (Princeton University Press, 1956) provides a useful treatment of the British executive.

Edward S. Corwin, *The President: Office and Powers,* 3rd ed. (New York University Press, 1948), is an important work on the subject.

Edward S. Corwin and Louis W. Koenig, *The Presidency Today* (New York University Press, 1956), is a judicious discussion of the American executive and calls for his closer collaboration with Congress.

Sidney Hyman, *The American President* (Harper, 1954) discusses the president as a political leader, treating men who have held the office.

Clinton Rossiter, *The American Presidency,* rev. ed. (Harcourt, 1960), is a very readable account of the subject with attention to the expanding powers of the presidency.

Richard E. Neustadt, *Presidential Power: The Politics of Leadership* (Wiley, 1960) offers large insight into American presidential politics.

Richard F. Fenno, Jr., *The President's Cabinet* (Harvard University Press, 1959) examines the cabinet's role in administrations from Wilson to Eisenhower.

William W. Pierson and F. G. Gil, *Governments of Latin America* (McGraw-Hill, 1957) is a topical treatment of government in this area.

Martin C. Needler, *Political Systems of Latin America* (Van Nostrand, 1964) gives attention to the executive.

Sigmund Neumann, *Permanent Revolution* (Harper, 1942) offers a useful analysis of modern dictatorship, its means and methods.

A. Cobban, *Dictatorship: Its History and Theory* (Scribner's, 1939) is a thoughtful analysis of dictatorial government and its social and ideological foundations.

G. W. F. Hallgarten, *Why Dictators?* (Macmillan, 1954) presents an interesting analysis of dictatorial regimes, distinguishing various types.

John A. Armstrong, *Ideology, Politics and Government in the Soviet*

Union: An Introduction (Praeger, 1962) is a short treatment giving attention to the executive.

H. V. Wiseman, *The Cabinet in the Commonwealth: Postwar Developments in Africa, the West Indies and South-East Asia* (Stevens, 1958) treats the extension of cabinet government to the postwar Commonwealth states.

W. M. MacMillan, *The Road to Self-Rule: A Study in Colonial Evolution* (Faber, 1959) discusses the problems of self-government among peoples emerging from British colonial rule.

CHAPTER 10: THE LEGISLATURE

J. A. O. Larsen, *Representative Government in Greek and Roman History* (University of California Press, 1955) is a scholarly treatment of representation in the ancient world.

K. C. Wheare, *Legislatures* (Oxford University Press, 1963) is one of the few comparative studies of the legislative institution; short, but thoughtful and informative.

Inter-Parliamentary Union, *Parliaments* (Cassell, 1962) is a comparative study of 41 parliamentary bodies, but descriptive and uncritical, rather than evaluative.

Ivor Jennings, *Parliament,* 2nd ed. (Cambridge University Press, 1957), is the standard work on the British institution.

Strathearn Gordon, *Our Parliament,* 6th ed. (Hansard Society, 1964), is a very useful examination of the British Parliament, including its origin and development.

K. R. MacKenzie, *The English Parliament* (Penguin, 1950) is a short account of how Parliament developed to its present form.

Alexander Brady, *Democracy in the Dominions,* 2nd ed. (University of Toronto Press, 1952), gives a comparative treatment of the older Commonwealth governments.

Sydney D. Bailey (ed.), *Parliamentary Government in the Commonwealth* (Philosophical Library, 1952) collects a brief and readable set of essays.

Herbert Morrison (now *Lord*), *Government and Parliament,* 3rd ed. (Oxford University Press, 1964), writes as an experienced politician on parliamentary, ministerial, and party procedures in Britain.

Roland Young, *The American Congress* (Harper, 1958) is a readable and informed survey of the subject, including attention to improvement of the institution.

George B. Galloway, *The Legislative Process in Congress* (Crowell, 1953) presents a comprehensive treatment of Congress, its organization and procedures.

D. W. S. Lidderdale, *The Parliament of France* (Hansard Society, 1951) is a thorough treatment of the subject into the Fourth Republic.

Stephen King-Hall and Richard K. Ullmann, *German Parliaments: A Study of the Development of Representative Institutions in Germany* (Hansard Society, 1954) is a useful short treatment.

Elis Håstad, *The Parliament of Sweden* (Hansard Society, 1957) is a contribution to the literature upon parliamentary institutions.

E. van Raalte, *The Parliament of the Kingdom of the Netherlands* (Hansard Society, 1959) treats one of the less known institutions.

C. J. Hughes, *The Parliament of Switzerland* (Cassell, 1962) gives a picture of this body in some depth.

John C. Wahlke *et al., The Legislative System: Explorations in Legislative Behavior* (Wiley, 1962) is a comparative study of four American state legislatures.

F. A. Hermens, *Democracy or Anarchy? A Study of Proportional Representation* (University of Notre Dame, 1941) is a substantial and critical study of the practice of proportional representation.

H. E. Read, J. W. MacDonald, and J. B. Fordham, *Cases and Other Materials on Legislation,* 2nd ed. (Foundation Press, 1959), is a collection of legal materials relating to American practice and interpretation.

John C. Wahlke and Heinz Eulau (eds.), *Legislative Behavior: A Reader in Theory and Research* (Free Press, 1959) is a collection of materials dealing with the subject from a variety of points of view.

Lord Campion and D. W. S. Lidderdale, *European Parliamentary Procedure: A Comparative Handbook* (Allen and Unwin, 1953) gathers useful comparative data on a number of European parliamentary bodies.

Harvey Walker, *The Legislative Process; Lawmaking in the United States* (Ronald, 1948) is a general discussion of American legislative institutions, their functions and procedures.

CHAPTER 11: THE JUDICIARY

Arthur T. Vanderbilt (ed.), *Studying Law,* 2nd ed. (New York University Press, 1955), is an excellent introduction to the subject, aimed primarily at prospective law students.

C. Gordon Post, *An Introduction to the Law* (Prentice-Hall, 1963) is a useful discussion of the American system.

William S. Carpenter, *Foundations of Modern Jurisprudence* (Appleton-Century-Crofts, 1958) is a short historical survey of the subject.

Jerome Frank, *Law and the Modern Mind* (Brentano's, 1930) offers psychological and sociological analysis of legal thought.

William Seagle, *The Quest for Law* (Knopf, 1941) is a very readable discussion of the nature and development of western legal systems.

Carleton K. Allen, Law in the Making, 7th ed. (Clarendon, 1964), is a massive treatise on the subject of legal development and jurisprudence.

Rudolf B. Schlesinger, *Comparative Law: Cases and Materials,* 2nd ed. (Foundation Press, 1960), includes useful materials comparing the common and civil law systems.

Munroe Smith, *The Development of European Law* (Columbia University Press, 1928) examines the subject from the fall of Rome to recent times.

F. H. Lawson *et al.*, *Amos and Walton's Introduction to French Law*, 2nd ed. (Clarendon, 1963), treats the subject in detail.

W. F. Murphy and C. H. Pritchett (eds.), *Courts, Judges, and Politics: An Introduction to the Judicial Process* (Random House, 1961) is a useful collection of materials on the subject in the American context.

K. Grzybowski, *Soviet Legal Institutions* (University of Michigan Press, 1962) is a brief but scholarly discussion.

Rudolf B. Schlesinger, *Soviet Legal Theory* (Kegan Paul, 1946) treats the Soviet conception of law and its sociological character.

John N. Hazard, *Settling Disputes in Soviet Society* (Columbia University Press, 1960) examines the early Soviet effort to establish a new system of legal administration.

Harold J. Berman, *Justice in Russia* (Harvard University Press, 1950) discusses and interprets the Soviet system of law.

J. N. D. Anderson, *Islamic Law in the Modern World* (New York University Press, 1959) is a short authoritative account of the legal system of Islam.

Edward M. Sait, *Political Institutions: A Preface* (Appleton-Century, 1938) contains useful chapters on Roman and English law.

Bernard Schwartz (ed.), *The Code Napoléon and the Common-Law World* (New York University Press, 1956) is a general collection of essays on the French code and its influence.

G. R. Y. Radcliffe and G. Cross, *The English Legal System*, 3rd ed. (Butterworth, 1954), is an historical account from the Anglo-Saxon period to the present.

R. M. Jackson, *The Machinery of Justice in England*, 3rd ed. (Cambridge University Press, 1960), discusses the principles and organization of the judicial system.

Harold G. Hanbury, *English Courts of Law*, 3rd ed. (Oxford University Press, 1960), treats the organization and functions of judicial institutions.

Robert H. Jackson, *The Supreme Court in the American System of Government* (Cambridge University Press, 1955) is an account of this body by an associate justice of the court.

A. T. Mason, *The Supreme Court from Taft to Warren* (Louisiana State University Press, 1958) discusses the court in contemporary times as an interpreter of the Constitution.

Jack W. Peltason, *Federal Courts in the Political Process* (Doubleday, 1955) examines the role of the courts in constitutional and legal interpretation.

Arthur T. Vanderbilt, *Judges and Jurors: Their Functions, Qualifications and Selection* (Boston University Press, 1956) is a short but useful discussion of judicial office and juries.

Benjamin Cardozo, *The Nature of the Judicial Process* (Yale University Press, 1921) is a small classic by a distinguished jurist.

Robert McCloskey, *The American Supreme Court* (University of Chicago Press, 1960) is a readable historical survey of the court as a policy-making body.

Sybille Bedford, *The Faces of Justice* (Collins, 1961) through an impressionistic approach, provides an unusually interesting comparison of judicial administration in European countries.

CHAPTER 12: THE ADMINISTRATION

William J. Siffin (ed.), *Toward the Comparative Study of Public Administration* (Indiana University Department of Government, 1957) discusses the topic with a collection of essays.

Poul Meyer, *Administrative Organization; A Comparative Study of the Organization of Public Administration* (Stevens, 1957) is the work of a Danish scholar and constitutes the only comparative study of the subject.

Dwight Waldo, *The Administrative State: A Study of the Political Theory of American Public Administration* (Ronald, 1948) is a critical examination of the public administration movement.

Public Policy; A Yearbook of the Graduate School of Public Administration, Harvard University (Harvard University Press, annually) contains essays of value on the subject of administration and public policy.

Solomon Fabricant, *The Trend of Government Activity in the United States Since 1900* (National Bureau of Economic Research, 1952) is an informative statistical review of the development and changing distribution of public activities among levels of government.

M. Fainsod, L. Gordon, and J. C. Palamountain, *Government and the American Economy*, 3rd ed. (Norton, 1959), is a classic work, recently revised, thoroughly discussing public policy in regard to the full range of economic and welfare matters in American experience.

Gilbert Walker, *Economic Planning by Programme and Control in Britain* (Macmillan, 1957) gives a good picture of the development of British economic policy in recent years.

Warren Baum, *The French Economy and the State* (Princeton University Press, 1958) is a useful over-all view of contemporary French public economic policies.

Mario Einaudi *et al., Nationalization in France and Italy* (Cornell University Press, 1955) presents a good comparative analysis of nationalization of industry, as well as special studies.

Oliver Franks, *Central Planning and Control in War and Peace* (Harvard University Press, 1947) offers many valuable insights into the formulation and implementation of economic plans.

Harry Schwartz, *Russia's Soviet Economy*, 2nd ed. (Prentice-Hall, 1954), is the best general study of the organization and operation of the Soviet economy, giving geographical, historical, and ideological background, as well as governmental policies.

Charles Hyneman, *Bureaucracy in a Democracy* (Harper, 1950) is a broad study of administration centered on advocacy of political responsibility.

John Whyatt, *The Citizen and the Administration: The Redress of Grievances* (Stevens, 1961) provides the results of a British investigation into the Ombudsman as a device for administrative control.

John Gaus *et al., The Frontiers of Public Administration* (University of Chicago Press, 1936) contains among several stimulating essays, one discussing professional responsibility.

J. R. Pennock, *Administration and the Rule of Law* (Farrar and Rinehart, 1941) is a classic treatment of legal responsibility in administration, not rendered substantially obsolete by recent developments.

James L. McCamy, *Science and Public Administration* (University of Alabama Press, 1960) suggests that scientists, citizens, and public officials must come to understand one another and work together.

Inter-University Case Program (University of Alabama Press) provides over the years numerous valuable studies by diverse authors of American administrative problems and incidents in specific policy contexts. See also for many of these studies, Harold Stein (ed.), *Public Administration and Policy Development* (Harcourt, Brace, 1952).

Joseph La Palombara (ed.), *Bureaucracy and Political Development* (Princeton University Press, 1963) gives useful attention to the needs of the developing states.

Fred W. Riggs, *Administration in Developing Countries* (Houghton Mifflin, 1964) deals with theory and method in transitional societies.

F. Morstein Marx (ed.), *Elements of Public Administration* (Prentice-Hall, 1959) provides a collection of essays on the theory and practice of administration within the American context.

Marshall E. Dimock and G. O. Dimock, *Public Administration,* 3rd ed. (Holt, 1964) is a general survey treating administration in its relationship to public policy.

John M. Pfiffner and Robert V. Presthus, *Public Administration,* 4th ed. (Ronald, 1960), seeks to combine traditional and recent experimental approaches to the subject.

E. N. Gladden, *The Essentials of Public Administration,* 2nd ed. (Staples, 1958), provides a broad and useful treatment of the subject by a British scholar.

W. J. M. MacKenzie and J. W. Grove, *Central Administration in Britain* (Longmans, Green, 1957) systematically discusses the British civil service and departmental operations.

F. M. G. Willson, *Administrators in Action; British Case Studies* (Allen and Unwin, 1961) presents a collection of cases demonstrating internal handling of administrative problems.

Georges Langrod, *Some Current Problems of Administration in France Today* (University of Puerto Rico, 1961) is a broad treatment of the subject.

Brian Chapman, *The Profession of Government: The Public Service in Europe* (Macmillan, 1959) treats comparatively the organization and administration of the principal public services in thirteen European countries.

O. Glenn Stahl, *Public Personnel Administration,* 5th ed. (Harper, 1963), is a thorough treatment of the subject within the American setting.

Norman J. Powell, *Personnel Administration in Government* (Prentice-Hall, 1956) similarly covers the various specialized aspects of personnel programs in public service.

William A. Robson (ed.), *The Civil Service in Britain and France* (Hogarth, 1956) contains a number of informative and critical essays.

J. E. Hodgetts and D. C. Corbett (eds.), *Canadian Public Administration* (Macmillan, 1960) offers a view of the administrative process in Canada.

F. Morstein Marx, *The Administrative State: An Introduction to Bureaucracy* (University of Chicago Press, 1957) discusses the role of bureaucracy in modern government.

R. K. Merton *et al.* (eds.), *Reader in Bureaucracy* (Free Press, 1952) is a collection of readings touching the subject in the United States and western Europe.

Austin F. MacDonald, *American State Government and Administration,* 5th ed. (Crowell, 1955), is a well-known text giving attention to administration at the American state level.

William Anderson *et al., Government in the Fifty States* (Holt, 1960) gives attention to the process of state administration.

Charles R. Adrian, *State and Local Government: A Study in the Political Process* (McGraw-Hill, 1960) is an informed discussion of intergovernmental relations in the United States.

Samuel Humes and E. M. Martin, *The Structure of Local Governments Throughout the World* (Nijhoff, 1961) is a comparative study and describes many local systems.

Charles R. Adrian, *Governing Urban America,* 2nd ed. (McGraw-Hill, 1961), emphasizes the importance of the city in American government and politics.

George S. Blair, *American Local Government* (Harper, 1964) ranges widely over the subject, and includes attention to metropolitan problems.

Oliver P. Williams and Charles Press, *Democracy in Urban America* (Rand McNally, 1961) is an interesting collection of readings relating to American urbanism.

Webb S. Fiser, *Mastery of the Metropolis* (Prentice-Hall, 1962) synthesizes the approaches to urban problems.

Werner Z. Hirsch (ed.), *Urban Life and Form* (Holt, 1963) discusses urban affairs from varied perspectives.

S. D. Clark (ed.), *Urbanism and the Changing Canadian Society* (University of Toronto Press, 1961) shows the influence of city development on Canadian life.

R. A. A. Chaput De Saintonge, *Public Administration in Germany* (Weidenfeld and Nicolson, 1961) provides a detailed picture of regional and local administration in one of the West German *Länder.*

Brian Chapman, *Introduction to French Local Government* (Allen and Unwin, 1953) discusses all aspects of the subject.

W. Eric Jackson, *The Structure of Local Government in England and Wales,* 4th ed. (Longmans, 1960), is a short, informative, and recent account.

Donald C. Rowat, *Your Local Government; A Sketch of the Municipal System in Canada* (Macmillan, 1955) provides a short discussion covering the variety of Canadian provincial systems.

W. A. Robson (ed.), *Great Cities of the World: Their Governments, Politics, and Planning* (Allen and Unwin, 1954) is an unusually interesting collection of essays on the world's major cities.

PART SIX: WORLD IN TRANSITION

Quincy Wright, *The Study of International Relations* (Appleton-Century-Crofts, 1955) examines various approaches in seeking a theoretical view.

H. V. Harrison (ed.), *The Role of Theory in International Relations* (Van Nostrand, 1964) contains several essays on general international relations theory.

Norman D. Palmer and H. C. Perkins, *International Relations,* 2nd ed. (Houghton Mifflin, 1959), is a solid and well-written survey covering the topics of international relations.

Charles P. Schleicher, *International Relations: Cooperation and Conflict* (Prentice-Hall, 1962) examines the broad range of international relations and includes chapters on various areas by specialists.

Fred Greene, *Dynamics of International Relations* (Holt, 1964) is a comprehensive treatment including a useful survey of international affairs since 1871.

John J. Herz, *International Politics in the Atomic Age* (Columbia University Press, 1959) offers insight into the dilemmas posed by the advent of the nuclear age.

W. W. Kulski, *International Politics in a Revolutionary Age* (Lippincott, 1964) provides an especially good treatment of the underdeveloped countries in this context.

Georg Schwarzenberger, *Power Politics; A Study of World Society,* 3rd ed. (Stevens, 1964) is a broad treatment of international affairs by a British scholar.

Kurt London (ed.), *New Nations in a Divided World: The International Relations of the Afro-Asian States* (Praeger, 1964) is an interesting symposium on problems of the newly independent states.

CHAPTER 13: THE MODERN STATE IN INTERNATIONAL LAW

J. L. Brierly, *The Law of Nations,* 6th ed. (Oxford University Press, 1963), is the best brief introduction to the subjects discussed in this chapter.

Green H. Hackworth, *Digest of International Law,* 8 vols. (U.S. Government Printing Office, 1940–44), is a major reference work emphasizing American interpretation and application of the law.

Marjorie M. Whiteman, *Digest of International Law* (U.S. Government Printing Office, 1963–) began with Volume I in that year as a successor to Hackworth's work; it contains entirely new materials.

H. W. Briggs, *The Law of Nations: Cases, Documents, and Notes,* 2nd ed. (Appleton-Century-Crofts, 1952), and W. W. Bishop, Jr., *International Law, Cases and Materials,* 2nd ed. (Prentice-Hall, 1962) are two convenient collections of cases and other materials on the nature and rules of international law.

Arthur Nussbaum, *A Concise History of the Law of Nations,* 2nd ed. (Macmillan, 1954), offers a readable survey from ancient times to the present.

C. W. Jenks, *The Common Law of Mankind* (Praeger, 1958) proposes the creation of a new system of international law to meet the present needs of the international community.

J. G. Starke, *An Introduction to International Law,* 5th ed. (Butterworth, 1963), is a well-organized and fresh treatment by a British author; it includes attention to the status of international institutions.

Philip C. Jessup, *A Modern Law of Nations* (Macmillan, 1948) calls for a systematic re-examination of the traditional body of international law.

Quincy Wright, *Contemporary International Law: A Balance Sheet* (Doubleday, 1955) is a brief but cogent discussion of strengths and weaknesses.

Morton M. Kaplan and N. Katzenbach, *Political Foundations of International Law* (Wiley, 1961) draws on a systems theory of international relations and includes treatment of new areas of international law.

Percy E. Corbett, *Law and Society in the Relations of States* (Harcourt, Brace, 1951) is a realistic analysis of the development and character of international law.

Georg Schwarzenberger, *A Manual of International Law,* 2 vols., 4th ed. (Stevens, 1960), is useful as a brief treatment, but especially valuable in volume two with its study outlines citing relevant cases and extensive reference materials.

Urban G. Whitaker, Jr., *Politics and Power; A Text in International Law* (Harper, 1964) is a good introduction intended for the political science student.

Rosalyn Higgins, *The Development of International Law through the Political Organs of the United Nations* (Oxford University Press, 1963) is a pioneering piece of research on the subject.

H. Duncan Hall, *Mandates, Dependencies, and Trusteeship* (Carnegie Endowment, 1948) is a substantial treatment of the League mandate system and the beginnings of the trusteeship system.

James N. Murray, Jr., *The United Nations Trusteeship System* (University of Illinois Press, 1957) discusses the system as an institution of international organization.

J. D. B. Miller, *The Commonwealth in the World* (Duckworth, 1958) is an excellent treatment of the evolution and contemporary problems of the Commonwealth association.

J. E. S. Fawcett, *The British Commonwealth in International Law* (Stevens, 1963) covers the subject thoroughly.

Arthur P. Whitaker, *The Western Hemisphere Idea* (Cornell University Press, 1954) provides a stimulating discussion of regional association and its problems among the American states.

A. H. Robertson, *The Council of Europe* (Praeger, 1957) is a full discussion of one of the newer international entities.

H. Lauterpacht, *Recognition in International Law* (Cambridge University Press, 1947) provides a scholarly study of a major topic of international law.

Julius Stone, *Legal Controls of International Conflict* (Rinehart, 1954) is a substantial monograph dealing with the legal aspects of international disputes and war.

Walter Schiffer, *The Legal Community of Mankind* (Columbia University Press, 1954) discusses the legal requirements of a world state and its theoretical aspects.

Robert K. Woetzel, *The Nuremberg Trials in International Law* (Praeger, 1960) finds them to be a significant precedent in international law.

Hannah Arendt, *Eichmann in Jerusalem; A Report on the Banality of Evil* (Viking, 1963) offers a detailed, though controversial, treatment of the Eichmann trial and the issues it raised.

Wolfgang Friedmann, *The Changing Structure of International Law* (Stevens, 1964) shows how the present era of international relations is shaping a new structure and scope for international law.

CHAPTER 14: THE ELEMENTS OF INTERNATIONAL POLITICS

Hans J. Morgenthau, *Politics Among Nations,* 3rd ed. (Knopf, 1960). A revolutionary work on its first appearance, it presents a "realistic" view of international relations, and important contributions to its theory.

A. F. K. Organski, *World Politics* (Knopf, 1958) offers not only an excellent critique of "realistic" theories, but an unusually thoughtful and penetrating analysis of international politics.

Frederick L. Schuman, *International Politics,* 6th ed. (McGraw-Hill, 1958), is a pioneering work in international politics, known for its vivid, if sometimes extravagant, style.

I. D. Duchacek, *Conflict and Cooperation Among Nations* (Holt, Rinehart and Winston, 1960) and David S. McLellan, *et al., The Theory and Practice of International Relations* (Prentice-Hall, 1960) are two excellent collections of readings and commentaries on the subject.

Stanley H. Hoffman (ed.), *Contemporary Theory in International Relations* (Prentice-Hall, 1960) is an important work of theory and doctrine, for the advanced student.

Harold and Margaret Sprout (eds.), *Foundations of International Politics* (Van Nostrand, 1962), is a collection of readings and text emphasizing the factors of national power.

Hans Kohn, *The Idea of Nationalism* (Macmillan, 1944) is a basic work on the subject discussing its nature and history.

C. J. H. Hayes, *Nationalism: A Religion* (Macmillan, 1960) is a useful concentrated discussion by a leading authority.

Nationalism: A Report by a Study Group of Members of the Royal Institute of International Affairs (Oxford University Press, 1939) is a survey of the complexities of the subject from a variety of viewpoints.

Hans Weigert *et al., Principles of Political Geography* (Appleton-Century-Crofts, 1957) treats the general geographic factors and their political implications.

Norman J. G. Pounds, *Political Geography* (McGraw-Hill, 1963) emphasizes a functional approach to geographic variation.

Roy C. Macridis (ed.), *Foreign Policy in World Politics,* 2nd ed. (Prentice-Hall, 1962), provides an introductory study of the foreign policy-making process in a number of states.

Richard Snyder *et al., Foreign Policy Decision Making* (Free Press, 1962) contains essays and case studies.

Joseph Frankel, *The Making of Foreign Policy* (Oxford, 1963) offers a discussion of the internal and external factors governing the process.

J. E. Black and K. W. Thompson, *Foreign Policies in a World of Change* (Harper & Row, 1963) surveys the foreign policies of 24 nations in essays by indigenous authors.

James L. McCamy, *Conduct of the New Diplomacy* (Harper & Row, 1964) is an excellent discussion of the problem for the United States.

J. Eayrs, *The Art of the Possible; Government and Foreign Policy in Canada* (University of Toronto Press, 1961) is a vivid treatment of foreign policy making.

Donald G. Bishop, *The Administration of British Foreign Relations* (Syracuse University Press, 1961) is an informative analysis, examining problems of foreign policy operations.

Charles O. Lerche, Jr., *Foreign Policy of the American People,* 2nd ed. (Prentice-Hall, 1961), and Cecil V. Crabb, Jr., *American Foreign Policy in the Nuclear Age* (Row, Peterson, 1960) are both excellent treatments of the foreign policy process emphasizing American experience and problems.

Ernest Satow, *A Guide to Diplomatic Practice,* 4th ed. (Longmans, Green, 1957), is the standard work on the subject, British in tone and viewpoint.

Harold Nicholson, *Diplomacy,* 2nd ed. (Oxford University Press, 1950), is an exposition of the methods and uses of traditional diplomacy by a British diplomat.

Charles W. Thayer, *Diplomat* (Harper, 1959) is a description of diplomatic duties and procedures written by an experienced member of the American foreign service.

Alan Burns, *In Defence of Colonies* (Allen and Unwin, 1957) adds balance to the picture of colonialism, presenting a British point of view.

Stewart C. Easton, *The Twilight of European Colonialism* (Holt, 1960) discusses in one of the few books on the subject the decline and present status of west European colonialism.

Julius W. Pratt, *America's Colonial Experiment* (Prentice-Hall, 1950) is an account of how the United States acquired and largely relinquished its colonial system.

Thomas R. Adam, *Modern Colonialism: Institutions and Policies* (Doubleday, 1955) is a brief exposition of modern colonialism as a political phenomenon.

Louis L. Snyder (ed.), *The Imperialism Reader; Documents and Readings on Modern Expansionism* (Van Nostrand, 1962) includes attention to communist imperialism.

Max F. Millikan and D. L. M. Blackmer (eds.), *The Emerging Nations; Their Growth and United States Policy* (Little, Brown, 1961) explores the development of these states and implications for American policy.

Brian Crozier, *The Morning After; A Study of Independence* (Oxford University Press, 1963) is an excellent survey of the results of independence on the leadership, politics, and economies of the emergent states.

Peter Lyon, *Neutralism* (Leicester University Press, 1963) treats the phenomenon in the context of contemporary international politics.

Melvin G. Schimm, *Population Control—The Imminent World Crisis* (Oceana, 1961) discusses the problem and possible solutions.

J. K. Zawodny (ed.), "Unconventional Warfare," *Annals of the American Academy of Political and Social Science* (May, 1962), Vol. 341, treats a form of warfare which is growing in significance and incidence.

Quincy Wright, *A Study of War,* 2 vols. (Chicago University Press, 1942), is a major treatise on the subject, ranging from history to the problem of control.

Alfred Vagts, *A History of Militarism* (Meridian, 1959) offers an interesting account of the evolution of armies and military attitudes.

Bernard Brodie, *Strategy in the Missile Age* (Princeton University Press, 1959) is a scholarly treatise on military policy with an eye to the future.

John Scott, *Political Warfare* (Day, 1955) offers a readable essay by an able journalist, examining political warfare on both sides of the Iron Curtain.

Charles Wolfe, Jr., *Foreign Aid: Theory and Practice in Southern Asia* (Princeton University Press, 1960) makes a substantial contribution to the problem of allocating economic and military aid.

George Liska, *The New Statecraft* (University of Chicago Press, 1960) provides an analysis of the structure of foreign aid and its employment as a weapon in political warfare.

CHAPTER 15: INTERNATIONAL ORGANIZATION AND THE PROBLEM OF PEACE

Clyde Eagleton, *International Government,* 3rd ed. (Ronald, 1957), is a rounded and objective treatment of the entire subject, with attention to historical background.

Inis L. Claude, Jr., *Swords Into Plowshares: The Problems and Progress of International Organization,* 2nd ed. (Random House, 1959), provides a penetrating analysis of the problems of and approaches to international organization.

Gerard J. Mangone, *A Short History of International Organization* (McGraw-Hill, 1954) treats the development along constitutional lines, with relevant documentary appendices.

Harriet E. Davis (ed.), *Pioneers in World Order: An American Appraisal of the League of Nations* (Columbia University Press, 1944) is an excellent weighing-up of the work of the League.

Felix Morley, *The Society of Nations* (Brookings, 1932) is a major study of the League from a contemporary perspective.

Francis P. Walters, *A History of the League of Nations* (Oxford University Press, 1952) is a standard history, covering the League from Covenant-making to World War II.

Stephen S. Goodspeed, *The Nature and Function of International Organization* (Oxford University Press, 1959) focuses attention on international relations as they center about the United Nations.

H. G. Nicholas, *The United Nations as a Political Institution,* 2nd ed. (Oxford University Press, 1962) is an informative brief description of how the United Nations works.

Leland M. Goodrich, *The United Nations* (Crowell, 1959) offers a solid, balanced, and readable account of the United Nations and developments surrounding it.

Andrew Boyd, *United Nations: Piety, Myth, and Truth* (Penguin, 1962) offers a brief but penetrating account of how the UN has developed.

Lewis B. Sohn, *Cases on United Nations Law* (Foundation Press, 1956) is a casebook treatment of the law of the United Nations.

C. Grove Haines (ed.), *European Integration* (Johns Hopkins University Press, 1957) constitutes a useful short treatment of the subject, with contributions by a variety of scholars and statesmen.

Ernst B. Haas, *The Uniting of Europe* (Stanford University Press, 1958) is a major work delineating the principal organizations and their functions involved in European union.

F. O. Wilcox and H. F. Haviland, Jr. (eds.), *The Atlantic Community: Progress and Prospects* (Praeger, 1963) extensively canvasses the subject.

J. Warren Nystrom and Peter Malof, *The Common Market; the European Community in Action* (Van Nostrand, 1962) is a brief survey of the subject.

Richard Mayne, *The Community of Europe* (Norton, 1962) is a general discussion of the development of the west European association from a British perspective.

Inis L. Claude, Jr., *Power and International Relations* (Random House, 1962) considers the contribution to international order of balance of power, collective security, and world government.

Gerard J. Mangone, *The Idea and Practice of World Government* (Columbia University Press, 1951) undertakes a theoretical analysis of the problem.

A. L. Burns and N. Heathcote, *Peace Keeping by U.N. Forces* (Praeger, 1963) treats the subject from Suez to the Congo, including attention to limitations and possibilities.

Lincoln P. Bloomfield *et al., International Military Forces* (Little, Brown, 1964) is a thorough discussion of this significant problem.

Charles A. Baker (ed.), *Problems of World Disarmament* (Houghton Mifflin, 1963) gives a variety of perspectives on the subject.

Elmer Plischke, *Systems of Integrating the International Community* (Van Nostrand, 1964) discusses the progress of the international integration movement from several viewpoints.

J. M. Mackintosh, *Strategy and Tactics of Soviet Foreign Policy* (Oxford University Press, 1962) examines the aims and weapons of Soviet expansionist policy.

Donald S. Zagoria, *The Sino-Soviet Conflict 1956–1961* (Princeton University Press, 1962) discusses the deep-seated causes of the great communist bloc schism.

Dale J. Hekhuis *et al.* (eds.), *International Stability: Military, Economic and Political Dimensions* (Wiley, 1964) considers the variables that affect the stability of the international system.

PART SEVEN: CONCLUSION

CHAPTER 16: EPILOGUE

Karl Jaspers, *The Future of Mankind* (University of Chicago Press, 1961) is an important work by a distinguished philosopher examining the problems posed by nuclear weapons.

The Rockefeller Panel, *Prospect for America* (Doubleday, 1961) presents discussions by more than a hundred contributors of foreign, military, economic, social, and educational policies.

The President's Commission on National Goals, *Goals for America* (Prentice-Hall, 1960) is a discussion by various authors from academic and public life of programs for action in the 1960's.

Hans J. Morgenthau, *The Purpose of American Politics* (Knopf, 1960) takes a penetrating look at the nature of American national purpose and its inadequacies.

Alexander P. De Seversky, *America: Too Young to Die* (McGraw-Hill, 1961) is a military analyst's discussion of the military program required for American survival as a democratic nation.

Sheldon Wolin, *Politics and Vision* (Little, Brown, 1960) is a very selective and analytic history of western political thought, the final chapters of which in particular illuminate the critical political issues of the present.

Edmund Stillman and William Pfaff, *The Politics of Hysteria; The Sources of Twentieth-Century Conflict* (Harper & Row, 1964) presents the gloomy view that western man is losing control of his society and heading for disaster.

Harry H. Ransom, *Can American Democracy Survive Cold War?* (Doubleday, 1963) covers the relevant issues and reaches a favorable conclusion.

I. R. Sinai, *The Challenge of Modernisation: The West's Impact on the Non-Western World* (Chatto & Windus, 1964) presents a penetrating if somewhat discouraging picture of the limited modernization of thinking and social structures in the nonwestern world.

PERIODICALS AND NEWSPAPERS

PERIODICAL INDEXES

Public Affairs Information Service Bulletin. A weekly guide, cumulating in annual volumes, indexing some thousand periodicals as well as books and documents, relating to political science, government, public administration, and other aspects of public affairs. A most valuable index.

International Index to Periodicals. Quarterly, annual, and triennial cumulative volumes index the content of nearly two hundred scholarly periodicals, with emphasis on the social sciences and the humanities.

Readers' Guide to Periodical Literature. A general periodical index, devoted to the more popular magazines, and therefore of somewhat limited use for scholarly purposes.

Index to Legal Periodicals. A general periodical index for the field of law, providing a guide to the principal American and British law reviews and certain related publications.

International Bibliography of Political Science. An annual world list of books, articles, reports, and government publications, in all languages, prepared by the International Committee for Social Sciences Documentation and published by UNESCO.

International Political Science Abstracts. A quarterly abstracting articles bearing upon political science from an international selection of periodicals; also published by UNESCO.

Information concerning periodicals generally in the area of the social sciences may be found in *World List of Social Science Periodicals,* 2nd ed., revised and enlarged, prepared by the International Committee for Social Sciences Documentation (UNESCO, 1957).

The selection of English language periodicals listed here as particularly useful to the political science student is divided into three categories: scholarly journals, which largely publish research and writings of an academic character; periodicals containing political information, which may be general or specialized, but whose content may be of use in political studies; and, journals of opinion, which are of interest because of their varying perspectives in interpreting political developments.

SCHOLARLY JOURNALS

Administrative Science Quarterly. Offers academic discussion of public administration, but broadly viewed, giving it utility to political scientists generally.

American Behavioral Scientist. Monthly, except July and August. Devoted to short articles on political theory, research, and interdisciplinary studies in the social and behavioral sciences.

American Journal of International Law. Quarterly. The major journal dealing with this subject, valuable for articles, notes, reviews, and documents, published by the American Society of International Law.

American Political Science Review. Quarterly. Published by the American Political Science Association, it contains articles on the discipline generally, often reflecting new research developments, and is invaluable for its book reviews, bibliographical articles, notes, and lists.

Annals of the American Academy of Political and Social Science. Bimonthly. Each number is devoted to a major topic within the social sciences and contains a number of articles by different authors, as well as a book review section.

Australian Journal of Politics and History. Semiannual. Carries articles mainly, though not exclusively, by Australian political scientists.

Behavioral Science. Quarterly. An interdisciplinary journal publishing articles on general theories of behavior and empirical research, especially in the realm of mental health.

Canadian Journal of Economics and Political Science. Quarterly. Publishes articles and reviews in economics, political science, sociology, and related fields.

Ethics: An International Journal of Social, Political and Legal Philosophy. Quarterly. Contains articles on the ideas and principles organizing and motivating human societies.

Foreign Affairs. Quarterly. Its authoritative writings cover the international scene and are contributed by leading statesmen, journalists, and scholars. Notes all important books in the realm of international affairs.

International Affairs. Quarterly. Published by the Royal Institute of International Affairs, this British journal treats general international relations.

International and Comparative Law Quarterly. A British journal dealing with comparative, private, and public international law.

International Conciliation. Five times a year. Published by the Carnegie Foundation for International Peace, each issue is devoted to a particular problem of international organization.

International Journal. Quarterly. Published by the Canadian Institute of International Affairs, it treats international relations generally as well as those with Canadian interest.

International Organization. Quarterly. Contains articles devoted to the subject generally, as well as a useful summary of activities of international organizations.

Journal of Commonwealth Studies. Semiannual. Carries articles and reviews on the Commonwealth association and its members.

Journal of Conflict Resolution. Quarterly. Reports research devoted to the subject of war and peace and other international processes.

Journal of International Affairs. Semiannual. Contains general articles on the subject, with each issue devoted to a particular topic.

Journal of the International Commission of Jurists. Semiannual. Devoted to scholarly articles on the rule of law, judicial administration, civil rights, and public law generally.

Journal of Modern African Studies. Quarterly. Surveys politics, economics, and related topics.

Journal of Politics. Quarterly. Published by the Southern Political Science Association, it carries articles and book reviews on political science generally.

Law and Contemporary Problems. Quarterly. Published by the Duke University School of Law, each issue is organized as a symposium devoted to the legal, administrative, or other social science aspect of current issues.

Middle East Journal. Quarterly. Treats the area by means of articles, book reviews, documents, and chronology of events.

Midwest Journal of Political Science. Quarterly. Carries articles and book reviews ranging over the discipline of political science, published by the Midwest Conference of Political Scientists.

Orbis. Quarterly. Contains scholarly articles and reviews on world affairs, published by the Foreign Policy Research Institute, University of Pennsylvania.

Pacific Affairs. Quarterly. Presents articles and reviews on political and other subjects relating to Asia and the Pacific, published by the Institute of Pacific Relations.

Parliamentary Affairs. Quarterly. Offers articles on the institution of parliamentary democracy and the comparative study of parliamentary bodies, published by the Hansard Society for Parliamentary Government, London.

Political Science. Semiannual. A New Zealand journal, carrying general articles and book reviews.

Political Science Quarterly. A journal publishing scholarly essays, research articles, and book reviews, edited by the Faculty of Political Science of Columbia University.

Political Studies. Three times a year. The journal of the Political Studies Association of the United Kingdom carries articles on political science generally and reviews.

Public Administration. Quarterly. A British journal, published by the Royal Institute of Public Administration, treats the subject largely, but not solely, in relation to British government.

Public Administration Review. Quarterly. Published by the American Society for Public Administration, it features general articles, reviews of books and documents, and notes on current developments.

Public Law. Quarterly. Devoted primarily to the constitutional and administrative law of the Commonwealth countries.

Public Opinion Quarterly. Contains research articles on all phases of the subject, with various disciplinary approaches, and book reviews.

Review of Politics. Quarterly. Published by the University of Notre Dame, it emphasizes a philosophical and historical approach to politics.

Russian Review. Quarterly. Devoted to Russia of the past as well as the present, it contains short articles and reviews; it is critical of Soviet communism.

Slavic Review. Quarterly. Formerly *American Slavic and East European Review,* it deals broadly, in scholarly articles, with various disciplinary approaches to the Slavic countries.

Social Research. Quarterly. Contains articles ranging over the several social sciences and emphasizes interdisciplinary discussion.

Southwestern Social Science Quarterly. Published by the Southwestern Social Science Association, it offers research articles and reviews in the various social science disciplines.

Soviet Studies. Quarterly. A British journal reviewing social and economic institutions of the Soviet Union.

Western Political Quarterly. Published by the Institute of Government, University of Utah, this quarterly contains scholarly articles and book reviews of general character and occasionally gives particular attention to affairs of the American western states.

World Politics. Quarterly. Published by the Center of International Studies, Princeton University, it presents articles on international affairs generally and book reviews.

Attention should be given to the many law reviews; they contain a great deal of political science scholarship. Among the outstanding are *Columbia Law Review, Harvard Law Review, Michigan Law Review, University of Chicago Law Review,* and *Yale Law Journal.*

PERIODICALS CONTAINING POLITICAL INFORMATION

Africa Digest. Quarterly. Covers and summarizes current political events in that continent.

Africa Today. Monthly, except July and August. Published by the American Committee on Africa; contains short articles and reviews.

American City. Monthly. Devoted to local government, it gives particular attention to administrative developments.

Atlantic Community Quarterly. Discusses the need for and problems of developing unity among the Atlantic states.

Atlas. Monthly. A selection of the world's press in English translation.

Bulletin of the Atomic Scientists. Monthly, except July and August. A magazine devoted to the area of science and public affairs.

Bulletin of the Institute for the Study of the USSR. Monthly. Carries articles on the current Soviet scene and contemporary events written by persons who have left that country and bring to their writing additional insight.

Congressional Digest. Monthly. An independent magazine discussing the legislative programs of Congress, and the major controversial issues before it.

Congressional Quarterly Weekly Report. Detailed news and reference data on Congress, elections, and American government generally.

Current. Monthly. Contains selections from a wide range of periodicals, newspapers, books, and addresses relative to contemporary problems of democratic society.

Current Digest of the Soviet Press. Weekly. Published by the Joint Committee on Slavic Studies, it presents in English translation a selection of the contents of the Soviet press and a weekly index to *Pravda* and *Izvestia*.

Current History. Monthly. A magazine written primarily for students, dealing with current affairs and contemporary political subjects.

Department of State Bulletin. Weekly. An official publication containing information relating to United States foreign relations and the Department of State.

European Review. Quarterly. A magazine whose articles discuss various aspects of the Atlantic community and European co-operation.

National Civic Review. Monthly. Current American municipal affairs are discussed, including political developments.

Newsweek. Weekly. A general news magazine treating government, politics, and international affairs among other things, written in a straightforward journalistic style; some of its articles are signed.

Round Table. Quarterly. A review of Commonwealth affairs and the politics of its members.

State Government. Quarterly. Published by the Council of State Governments, it features articles discussing government problems in this area.

Table. Annual. The journal of the Society of Clerks-at-the-Table in Commonwealth Parliaments, dealing with various aspects of parliamentary procedure.

Time. Weekly. A popular news magazine covering the political scene and public affairs among other topics; written in its own peculiar style, its articles are unsigned and often rather opinionated.

Time and Tide. Weekly. A British newsmagazine, conservative in outlook.

United Nations Monthly Chronicle. Published by the UN Office of Public Information, this is a comprehensive and documented account of UN affairs.

United States News and World Report. Weekly. A magazine discussing government, business, and public affairs, supplemented with documents, hearings, interviews, and addresses.

World Today. Monthly. A British periodical discussing current world problems and their background for the general reader.

JOURNALS OF OPINION

Atlantic Monthly. A magazine of high literary quality, emphasizing discussion of the contemporary scene, and carrying signed articles on public affairs and politics.

Commentary. Monthly. A journal of thought and opinion on Jewish affairs and contemporary issues.

Commonweal. Weekly. A review of public affairs, literature, and the arts published by Catholic laymen.

Economist. Weekly. A nonpartisan British journal reporting current political, international, and economic affairs, with an especially valuable "American Survey"; considered by many one of the best informed periodicals in the world.

Encounter. Monthly. A distinguished British journal of political opinion and literary criticism.

Harpers. Monthly. This well-written magazine contains signed articles on public and political affairs among various subjects of contemporary interest.

Manchester Guardian Weekly. Carries a selection of articles and reviews from the world-famous British newspaper; liberal in outlook, its editorial views are widely influential.

Modern Age: A Conservative Review. Quarterly. Contains articles, essays, and reviews from the perspective of political conservatism.

Nation. Weekly. Devoted to discussion of current public issues from a distinctly liberal perspective; generally pro-labor and anti-business, it aims at an intellectual audience.

National Observer. Weekly. A newspaper devoted to the domestic and foreign scene, by the publishers of the *Wall Street Journal*.

National Review. Weekly. A journal of opinion surveying the contemporary scene from an avowedly conservative point of view.

New Republic. Weekly. Militantly liberal and frequently dissenting in its discussion of the current political scene.

New Statesman. Weekly. A British review of contemporary affairs, presenting generally the views of the Labourite intellectuals.

Political Quarterly. A British journal, with articles and reviews reflecting a Labourite point of view.

Progressive. Monthly. From the political perspective suggested by its name, the journal offers signed articles, comment, and reviews.

Reporter. Fortnightly. A magazine of political news analysis and interpretation presented in signed articles; liberal and critical in its outlook.

Saturday Review. Weekly. A journal of ideas and criticism treating public affairs, literature, education, and the arts.

Spectator. Weekly. A British journal of opinion and criticism devoted to contemporary affairs, moderately conservative in viewpoint.

Swiss Review of World Affairs. Monthly. Articles in English translation, prepared by the staff of the famous Swiss newspaper, *Neue Zürcher Zeitung*, presenting a cosmopolitan view of world political and economic affairs.

NEWSPAPERS

New York Times. Daily. This independent newspaper is without peer in the world in terms of dimensions, thoroughness, and objectivity and presents the fullest treatment of political news, national and international. Its "News of the Week in Review" section, contained in the Sunday edition, is a news magazine in itself. Also of value is the *New York Times Index,* issued twice a month, and in annual volumes, useful both as a source of summarized news facts and as an aid in establishing dates of events.

Wall Street Journal. Daily, Monday through Friday, published in several regional editions. Although devoted primarily to news of business and finance, this newspaper provides well-written and informed news stories and features on national, foreign, and international affairs.

Christian Science Monitor. An international daily published in Boston, Los Angeles, and London, this newspaper gives substantial coverage to national, foreign, and international affairs in carefully written and thoughtful news stories and news analysis.

Toronto's *Globe and Mail* is the "national" paper of Canada, providing national and international coverage.

See the valuable compendium of J. C. Merrill, C. R. Bryan, and M. Alisky, *The Foreign Press* (Louisiana State University Press, 1964) for detailed information on newspapers published abroad.

POLITICAL NOVELS

The reader may obtain both entertainment and information from political novels. It is unnecessary here to define narrowly what works may fall within this category. We are concerned only to point out a literary form which can offer up slices of political life, social and political comment, establish national or historic atmosphere, or represent human behavior, problems, and aspirations as they may have some political consequences.

Whether as politicized fiction or fictionalized politics, political novels may have much literary merit or little, be interesting or dull; they may distill wisdom or disseminate propaganda, may represent the realities of life or distort them. It is well to keep in mind that few novelists are expert in political matters; in their effort to tell a good story they may exaggerate considerably and over-dramatize the situations they treat. As Balzac said, "Novels paint feelings and things in far brighter colors than those of nature."

For discussions of the political novel, see Morris E. Speare, *The Political Novel: Its Development in England and in America* (Oxford University Press, 1924); Irving Howe, *Politics and the Novel* (Horizon, 1957); and, Joseph L. Blotner, *The Political Novel* (Doubleday, 1955). The list of works in this genre which follows is not intended as more than a representative selection and their literary quality varies considerably. Many of them have been reprinted in paperbacks.

Abele, Rudolph von. *The Party*. 1963. A portrait of the Nazi leader, Hermann Göring.

Abramov, Fyodor. *One Day in the "New Life."* 1963. A Soviet writer's story of the frustrations in managing a collective farm.

Amis, Kingsley. *Lucky Jim*. 1954. A social comedy of a young instructor's life in an English provincial university.

Baker, Carlos H. *A Friend in Power*. 1958. The politics of selecting a new university president.

Boulle, Pierre. *A Noble Profession*. 1960. An intriguing story of espionage in France during World War II.

Bradbury, Ray. *Fahrenheit 451*. 1953. The satirical portrayal of a dismal future in the complex atomic age.

Brammer, William. *The Gay Place*. 1961. This award-winning novel offers a bold and unconventional treatment of politics in an American state.

Breit, Harvey. *A Narrow Action*. 1964. The story of a communist dictatorship in a Caribbean setting.

Breitbach, Joseph. *Report on Bruno*. 1964. A provocative story of contemporary European politics.

Burdick, Eugene. *The Ninth Wave*. 1956. A contemporary novel centering on California politics, by a political scientist.

Cecil, Henry. *Brothers in Law*. 1955; *Friends at Court*. 1956; *The Long Arm*. 1957; *Daughters in Law*. 1961. Authentic and highly amusing accounts of an English barrister before the courts.

Chevallier, Gabriel. *The Scandals of Clochemerle*. 1937; *The Wicked Village*. 1955. Droll stories of politics and life in a small French village.

Clark, Walter Van Tilburg. *The Ox-Bow Incident*. 1940. A Western, depicting mob action and frontier justice.

Condon, Richard. *The Manchurian Candidate*. 1959. An American spy thriller, with political, satirical, and psychoanalytic overtones.

Cozzens, James. *Guard of Honor*. 1948. A novel of Army politics and a young general.

Crane, Stephen, *The Red Badge of Courage,* 1895. A story of the American Civil War as seen by a young Union soldier.

Dickens, Charles. *A Tale of Two Cities.* 1859. A vivid portrayal of life set against the French revolution.

Dostoevski, Feodor. *The Possessed.* 1872. One of the great political novels, a portrait of revolutionary politics in nineteenth-century Russia.

Drury, Allen. *Advise and Consent.* 1959. A dramatic contemporary novel with the United States Senate as its setting. *A Shade of Difference,* 1962. Intrigue, suspense, and deft characterization with a setting in American and United Nations politics.

Fielding, Gabriel (pseud. of Alan Gabriel Barnsley). *The Birthday King.* 1963. An upper-middle class German family survives the Nazi regime and World War II.

FitzGibbon, Constantine. *When the Kissing Had to Stop.* 1960. A fantasy of British politics in the near future, with the country succumbing to Soviet occupation.

Gary, Romain. *A European Education.* 1960. The poignant life of young people with Polish partisan forces in World War II.

Golding, William C. *Lord of the Flies.* 1955. A fantasy on the conflict between civilization and barbarism.

Greene, Graham. *The Quiet American.* 1955. Satirical comment on American "innocence" in Indo-Chinese politics. *Our Man in Havana.* 1958. An entertaining thriller, burlesquing espionage.

Hailey, Arthur. *In High Places.* 1962. Personal intrigue among high government officials; Canada is the setting.

Hawthorne, Nathaniel. *The Blithedale Romance.* 1852. A disguised account of Brook Farm, an American utopian experiment.

Hemingway, Ernest. *For Whom the Bell Tolls.* 1940. A romantic episode of an American loyalist volunteer in the Spanish civil war.

Hersey, John. *A Bell for Adano.* 1944. American military government and its problems in the Italian occupation.

Hlasko, Marek. *Next Stop—Paradise.* 1960. A novel of disenchanted workers in communist Poland.

Hugo, Victor. *Les Misérables.* 1862. A classic work portraying life of the poor in post-Napoleonic France.

Huxley, Aldous. *Brave New World.* 1932. Satirical projection of life in a future world where freedom has been destroyed.

Karp, David. *All Honorable Men.* 1956. A story of foundation politics and loyalty investigations.

Keon, Michael. *The Durian Tree.* 1960. An adventure story of communist guerrillas against British authority in postwar Malaya.

Koestler, Arthur. *Darkness at Noon.* 1941. The drama of a communist purge trial.

Lampedusa, Giuseppi di. *The Leopard.* 1960. A highly praised Italian novel of society and social conditions in Sicily during the Risorgimento.

Lederer, William J. and Eugene Burdick. *The Ugly American.* 1958. A provocative criticism of American overseas operations in Southeast Asia.

Mailer, Norman. *The Naked and the Dead.* 1948. A G.I. view of the invasion of a Pacific island in World War II.

Malraux, André. *Man's Fate.* 1933. A prize novel; the setting is Shanghai in the 1920's.

Marquand, John P. *The Late George Apley.* 1937; *So Little Time.* 1943. Apt characterizations and deft satire of American life are offered in these works by a famous modern novelist.

Michener, James A. *Hawaii.* 1959. A panoramic historical novel of empire building in the 50th state.

Mirvish, Robert F. *The Last Capitalist.* 1963. A vivid picture of Soviet life during World War II.

Monsarrat, Nicholas. *The Tribe That Lost Its Head.* 1956. A satirical account of British colonial government in Africa.

O'Connor, Edwin. *The Last Hurrah.* 1956. Boston politics thinly disguised and an Irish-American politician.

O'Flaherty, Liam. *The Informer.* 1926. Dublin during the time of the insurrection against British rule.

Orwell, George (pseud. of Eric Arthur Blair). *The Animal Farm.* 1946. An allegorical satire on modern dictatorship; *1984.* 1949. The projection of a future police state, ruled by an omniscient "Big Brother."

Pasternak, Boris. *Dr. Zhivago.* 1958. A story of life in the Soviet Union and the struggle with regimentation.

Paton, Alan. *Cry, the Beloved Country.* 1948. A depiction of the problem of race relations in South Africa.

Pearson, William. *A Fever in the Blood.* 1959. A novel of American state politics at the grass roots.

Remarque, Erich Maria. *All Quiet on the Western Front.* 1929. The famous German novel of trench warfare in World War I; *The Arch of Triumph.* 1945. A refugee from Nazi Germany goes underground in Paris.

Romains, Jules (pseud. of Louis Farigoule). *Men of Good Will.* 14 vols., 1933–46. This great series of novels covers French life, war, and politics from the turn of the century into the 1930's.

Ruark, Robert. *Something of Value.* 1955. A brutally realistic account of the Mau Mau movement and British colonial life in Kenya.

Shaw, Irwin. *The Young Lions.* 1948. A novel of World War II and its impact on American and German soldiers.

Shute, Nevil (pseud. of Nevil S. Norway). *On the Beach.* 1957. A cautionary tale in an Australian setting; life in the world is coming to an end after a nuclear war.

Silone, Ignazio. *Bread and Wine.* 1936. A portrait of Italian life under the Fascist regime; *The Fox and the Camellias.* 1961. A man finds greater value in charity and love than in doctrinaire politics.

Sinclair, Upton. *Presidential Agent.* 1944. One in the ten-volume "Lanny Budd" series, treating the eve of World War II.

Skinner, B. F. *Walden Two.* 1948. In novel form, an imaginative debate on the character and possibilities of a contemporary American utopia.

Snow, C. P. *The Masters.* 1951. A realistic account of English university politics in choosing a new Master for a Cambridge college. *Corridors of Power.* 1964. A crucial period in the life of an ambitious British politician.

Solzhenitsyn, Alexander. *One Day in the Life of Ivan Denisovich.* 1963. An eloquent account of life in a Stalinist concentration camp.

Spring, Howard. *Fame Is the Spur.* 1940. English politics and the career of an ambitious Labourite politician, presumably Ramsay MacDonald.

Steinbeck, John. *The Grapes of Wrath.* 1939. The exodus of small farmers from the American "dustbowl" of the 1930's.

Stendhal (pseud. of Marie-Henri Beyle). *Lucien Leuwen.* 1894. France after the 1830 revolution, and conflict between monarchists and republicans.

Stowe, Harriet Beecher. *Uncle Tom's Cabin.* 1852. A period piece with profound effect upon antislavery opinion in the United States.

Uris, Leon M. *Exodus.* 1958. A popular novel dealing with the achievement of Israel's independence.

Warren, Robert Penn. *All the King's Men.* 1946. The career of a dictatorial Southern politician, presumably modeled after that of Huey Long.

Waugh, Alec. *Island in the Sun.* 1955. A West Indian setting for a story of British colonial life.

Zilahy, Lajos. *The Dukays.* 1949. The effects of two world wars on the old aristocratic order in Hungary.

THE PREPARATION OF INVESTIGATIVE PAPERS IN POLITICAL SCIENCE

Papers appear most presentable when typed double-spaced on one side of standard theme paper. Pages should be serially numbered and have margins on all four sides. The first page should contain the student's name, title of paper, name or number of course, and date. When a paper is fairly long, subtitles may be interspersed at appropriate intervals to improve readability.

A bibliography, listing all books, articles, documents, and other materials referred to in the paper, should be included at the end. Items are listed alphabetically by author, followed with title, edition and volume number where relevant, place of publication, publisher, and date of publication. Example:

Eliot, Thomas H., *Governing America: The Politics of a Free People,* 2nd ed. (New York, Dodd, Mead, 1964).

Plagiarism is the use of other persons' words without proper acknowledgment; courtesy demands also that research utilizing information or ideas taken from another's writings be credited to their source, either in the body of the text or in a footnote. This obligation applies equally to information taken from books, articles, public documents, encyclopedias, statistical data, newspapers, etc., whether signed with an author's name or not. Direct quotations should be reproduced accurately and enclosed in quotation marks. Within such marks, any additional words supplied by the writer are enclosed in brackets; the omission of any words is indicated by ellipsis marks.

The footnote acknowledgment is indicated by a small superior number (thus [5]) after the significant word, phrase, sentence, or paragraph which has been borrowed. Direct quotations exceeding five lines in length are usually single-spaced and indented. The citation is placed at the bottom of the appropriate page, or all may be gathered at the end of the paper, preceded by a small superior number matching the acknowledgment above. The purpose of the footnote is to give sufficiently complete information about the book, article, or document so that anyone else can easily find the same item and the page from which it was taken. Footnote numbers usually run in a single series throughout the paper.

Citation of a *book* should contain the name of the author, title, edition and volume number when relevant, place of publication, publisher (this may be omitted if contained in the bibliography), date of publication, and page number referred to. Example:

> [1] A. V. Dicey, *Introduction to the Study of the Law of the Constitution,* 9th ed. by E. C. S. Wade (London, 1939), p. 39.

Citation of a *periodical article* should contain name of author, title of article, name of publication, volume number, date, and page number. Example:

> [2] David Fellman, "Constitutional Law in 1959–1960," *American Political Science Review,* Vol. 55 (March, 1961), pp. 112–135.

Citation of a *government document* should contain author's name (if indicated), exact title of publication, source (i.e., government branch or agency), number if any, place of publication, publisher, date, and page. Examples:

> [3] *Conscription. Lowering Draft Age to 18 Years, Hearings,* 77th Cong., 2d sess., on S. 2748 (Washington, Government Printing Office, 1942), p. 70.
>
> [4] Department of Health, Education, and Welfare. *Teaching about the United Nations in the United States: 1956–59 Report* (Wash., Govt. Ptg. Off., 1960), pp. 1–3.

Variations in the style and arrangement of footnotes as here suggested are, of course, permissible, but it is important that whatever style is adopted be used uniformly throughout the paper. Note that the title of a book or document and the name of a magazine are printed in *italics* and should thus be underlined when typewritten. The title of a periodical article is enclosed in *quotation marks,* but is not underlined. A footnote always ends with a period. For other examples of acceptable footnote styles, consult the *American Political Science Review* or other such journals.

When a citation is repeated the reference need not be given again in full, and the Latin abbreviation, *ibid.* (*ibidem,* in the same place), may be employed subsequently. Example:

> [5] W. I. Jennings, *Cabinet Government,* 3rd ed. (Cambridge, 1959), p. 174.
> [6] *Ibid.,* p. 188.

If one or more citations to different sources intervene between the first full reference and successive references to the same item, the author's name alone, followed by the Latin abbreviation, *op. cit.* (*opere citato,* in the work cited), and the page number are sufficient. Example:

> [7] James Bryce, *The American Commonwealth,* ed. by Louis M. Hacker, Vol. II (New York, 1959), part 5, ch. 4.
> [8] Jennings, *op. cit.,* p. 197 *et seq.*

If footnote citations and bibliography are to be complete and accurate in the final draft of the paper, the necessary information for this purpose should be taken carefully and completely when the original materials are being collected. Care in note-taking avoids time-consuming rechecking later.

In recent years, English words have tended to replace Latin terms in scholarly usage (for example, see, note, compare, page, etc.). However, some of the classic abbreviations commonly encountered in formal research writings are:

cf.—(*confer*) compare.
e.g.—(*exempli gratia*) for example.
et al.—(*et alii*) and others.
ff.—following (pages).
i.e.—(*id est*) that is.
infra—below.
n.—note (referring to a footnote).
n.d.—no date.
p.—page; pp.—pages.
passim—here and there (discussed several places in a book).
q.v.—(*quod vide*) which see (used for cross referencing).
seq.—(*sequentes*) following.

supra—above.

v. or *vs.*—(*versus*) against (used in law to denote a legal action of one party against another).

. . . —(ellipsis marks) indicate a word or words are omitted.

. . . . —a fourth mark indicates a period.

INDEX